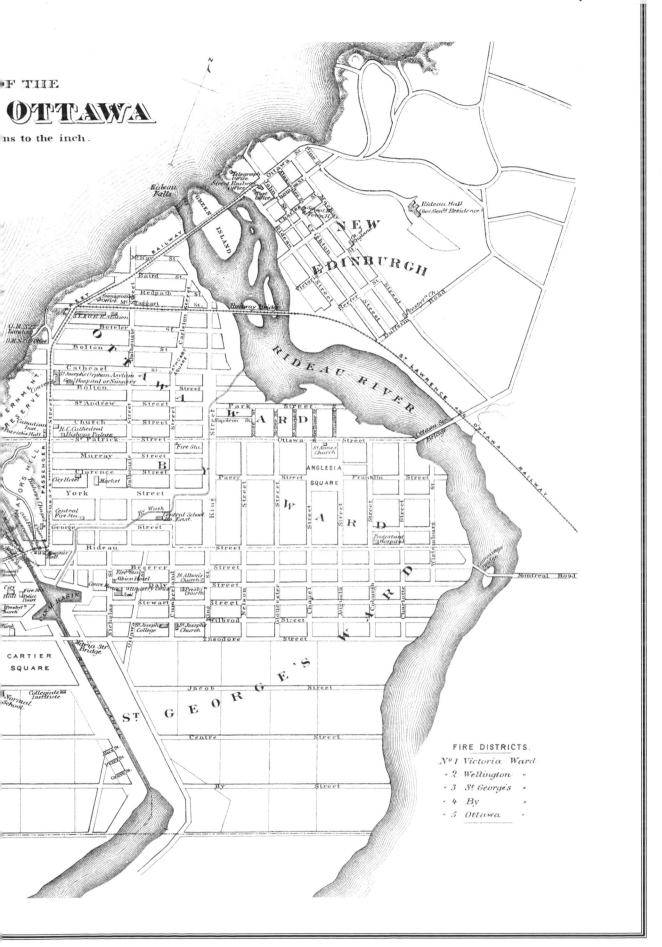

FIRE DISTRICTS.

Nº 1 Victoria Ward
" 2 Wellington "
" 3 St George's "
" 4 By "
" 5 Ottawa "

Each
Morning
Bright

Each Morning Bright

160 Years of Selected Readings

from the

OTTAWA CITIZEN

1845-2005

Doug Fischer, editor

Ralph Willsey, editor/designer

Each Morning Bright: 160 years of Selected Readings

Copyright, Ottawa Citizen Group Inc.

ISBN 0-9698908-8-5

Library and Archives Canada Cataloguing in Publication

Each Morning Bright : 160 Years of Selected Readings
Doug Fischer, editor ; Ralph Willsey, editor and designer.

Contains selected texts from the Ottawa Citizen, 1845-2005.
Includes bibliographical references and index.
ISBN 0-9698908-8-5

1. Ottawa (Ont.)—History—Sources. 2. Ottawa citizen.
I. Fischer, Doug II. Willsey, Ralph

FC3096.4.E22 2005   971.3'84   C2005-904831-X

DEDICATION

Each Morning Bright is dedicated, quite naturally, to the newspaper professionals of 16 decades who have put on the record this portrait of their lives and times, their city, their nation, and world; and to the readers and advertisers who made it all possible. But it is also dedicated to the nameless librarians whose skill and effort have allowed the pages to survive this long. The fact that some issues did not survive underlines how difficult that task has been.

from SONG OF THE NEW TYPE
February 21, 1860

Ho! ho! ha! ha! good luck! hurra!
Our destiny we bless!
As we stamp each sheet that flashes fleet
From the crashing printing press!
Our daily job 'twill be to tell
What this big world's about,
When the nations are bland, or take a hand
In the bloody battle rout;
Of rumours here and 'larums there,
Of kings, and cotton and corn,
Of things that were and of things that are,
And of things that are yet unborn!
Ho! ho! ha! ha! good luck! hurra!
And shout with double stress!
As we leap to light each morning bright
From the mighty printing press!

An anonymous poet—perhaps a printer—was moved to compose 72 lines like these in the voice of the
Ottawa Citizen's *new cases of sharp, clean type. As the jacket of this book shows, type grows old.*

Today's Citizen *is grateful to Linda Brown of Upper Canada Village for hand-setting our title in
24-point Century Nova Condensed, cast in traditional type metal, a mixture of lead, tin, and antimony.
The type on the jacket has been laterally reversed for readability; printers worked with letterforms that
were upside-down and backwards.*

Contents

Contents (continued)

'Literature of the People'

OH WATCH YOU WELL BY DAYLIGHT.

BY SAMUEL LOVER.

Oh, watch you well by daylight,
By daylight may you fear.
But keep no watch in darkness—
The angels then are near:
For Heaven the sense bestoweth,
Our waking life to keep,
But tender mercy showeth,
To guard us in our sleep.
Then watch you well by daylight,
By daylight you may fear,
But keep no watch in darkness—
The angels then are near.

Oh watch you well in pleasure—
For pleasure oft betrays,
But keep not watch in sorrow,
When joy withdraws its rays;
For in the hour of sorrow,
As in the darkness drear,
O Heaven entrust the morrow,
For the angels then are near.
Oh, watch you well by daylight,
By daylight may you fear,
But keep no watch in darkness—
The angels then are near.

April 6, 1850

NEWSPAPERS AREN'T SUPPOSED to be like this. They are ephemeral things, the common logic goes, transient histories that are literally here today and gone tomorrow. Rapidly compiled, edited at lightning speed, printed on cheap paper and unceremoniously hurled at subscribers' doors at an ungodly hour each and every day, newspapers are the antithesis of books. This book, for example, took two skilled *Ottawa Citizen* journalists—Doug Fischer and Ralph Willsey—and a slew of researchers the better part of a year to produce. Yet, this, too is a newspaper; the stories, as you will see, from the 1840s or the 1930s retain their immediacy and their sense of urgency. And whether it's politics or bad driving (see page 129 for an illustration of how to handle the reins), the stories have the strength of literature.

Neil Reynolds, my mentor and immediate predecessor as editor of the *Citizen*, understood better than any journalist that what we do here at this paper every day has lasting value. "Some journalists understand the importance of the written word and the stories they write; many don't," Reynolds wrote in 1996, "Readers, I think, always do. The written word remains the primary influence on human action in the modern world. And newspapers remain—beyond all dispute—the primary forum for the written word. Newspapers remain the literature of the people."

Reynolds' paper was also a vehicle for moral instruction. He believes that "almost every headline, in almost every newspaper, makes a public statement of some kind on moral conduct." This is a statement that makes politically correct hackles rise in anger (who are we to preach?) but would seem a simple truth to the vast majority of editors who preceded Reynolds, as many of the stories in this book illustrate. Contem-

ix

porary editors are embarrassed by their connection to morals like "children who don't want to be seen walking in public with their parents."

The *Citizen* began as a crusading paper and it is a tradition that remained more or less intact over the succession of nameplates, owners, publishers and editors. This paper pushed hard to have Ottawa declared the capital of the united Canadas, it maintained a vigorous 19th-century campaign against "slatternly women" and it was the first newspaper, at great cost to the bottom line, to drop tobacco advertising. It has been an outspoken proponent of animal welfare and such an opponent of corrupt government that its denunciation of Mackenzie King's war-time government earned it a sedition charge.

When Conrad Black bought the *Citizen* in 1996, he dismissed the paper's journalism as "soft, left, envious pap," and said he wanted it to become a paper worthy of the capital of a G7 nation. The *Citizen* had had some lean years for sure, but Black didn't have the whole picture. What he would have been better to say—and, in fact, what he accomplished—was that he wanted to give the *Citizen* what it needed to restore its mission as a great newspaper, an obsessed servant of journalism at its best. This collection of stories embodies that mission.

Scott Anderson,
Editor in chief, *Ottawa Citizen*
August 2005

October 7, 1854

An Instrument of Revenge

BY DOUG FISCHER

WILLIAM HARRIS HAD HARDLY settled into the muddy lumber town of 4,500 in March 1845 when the rumours started. At first it was just the Tories who were buzzing. Harris, it was said, was a supporter of the Reform movement, forerunner of the Liberal party, and he had come to Bytown to start a newspaper. Didn't he know this was Tory territory?

True enough, Bytown had been sending Conservatives to the legislature and to town hall for years. Its only newspaper, the weekly *Bytown Gazette and Rideau Advertiser*, was as Tory as the pretty lakes across the river in the Gatineau hills were blue.

But even his one scouting trip to Bytown earlier that year told Harris there was more to the place than its aristocracy. He knew only landowners could vote, and they tended to be Tory. That explained the town's political representation. What about the hundreds of Irish and French labourers who lived in the clusters of rowhouses in Lowertown and the flats along the river to the west? Surely, Harris thought, they had an appetite for a community free of sectarian strife and a country where everyone—Catholic and Protestant, English and French, landowner and tenant—enjoyed the same chance for success. His newspaper could feed their hunger for a better life, Harris believed.

And so it was that on March 29, 1845, a balmy early spring Saturday 22 years before Canada became a country and a decade before Ottawa became a city, a 29-year-old Irish immigrant gave Bytown *The Packet*, its first liberal newspaper. Under the banner on Page 1, Harris printed the words "Fair Play and Daylight," the paper's motto. One hundred and sixty years later, those words still appear in the *Ottawa Citizen*, the

THE PACKET.
"Our Country."
BY-TOWN· SATURDAY, OCT'R. 7, 1848.

☞ *SEE FIRST AND FOURTH PAGES.*

"THE PACKET UNMASKED."

THERE appeared in the *Gazette* of last week a letter signed " A Lumberman," to which our attention has been directed by a Correspondent. Although the statements put forth by the writer of the letter in question are decidedly ill-founded, and the indecent tone assumed is indicative of a mind degraded, yet we deem it necessary to say a few words in a very mild way to this very intemperate traducer, believing that his insiduous attempt to vilify us may be attributed to a desire to create a diversion in favor of Mr. STEWART and other Tory hacks who have discovered in the question at issue an opportunity to wreak their vengeance on the true friends of the people, and of Lumbermen in particular. We do not believe that any Lumberman who is merely interested in the Lumber Trade or the welfare of the comunity generally would so commit himself as to pen or dictate the letter alluded to—a letter which bears upon its face the imprint of an immagination brutalized and soured by disappointment, and upon whom richly deserved scorn and contempt has been heaped by a discerning public. This writer has accused us of turning traitor to the interests of the Lumber Trade. May we ask how this assertion is founded, and upon facts can be adduced in support of such a charge? This self-styled Lumberman has not dared to impugn our conduct previous to the Meeting at Bedard's, for our character as a zealous defender of the rights of Lumberers was too well established—too frankly owned by all concerned, to give the slightest ground for such an imputation ; but the breach is attempted in this wise—that our desertion of the Lumbermen has taken

newspaper that emerged from that unlikely four-page journal.

•

There's little question Harris thought his newspaper could make a difference in Bytown. Living in Kemptville a year earlier, he had thrown himself into the rough and tumble of Ottawa Valley politics. He organized meetings and wrote speeches for Reform candidates; briefly, he even considered running for office. He believed in the possibility of change.

But Harris also had a darker, more personal reason for starting a newspaper. He wanted revenge.

In early April 1844, almost a year to the day before he launched *The Packet* in Bytown, Harris was jailed for 20 days and given a year's probation after a sensational—and humiliating—libel trial instigated by Ogle Robert Gowan. The case excited newspapers from Toronto to Halifax, and not only because Gowan, an influential journalist, Tory politician and the powerful Grand Master of the Orange Lodge, was a man who naturally attracted controversy. For years, he had also acted as political mentor to the younger Harris, who printed Gowan's stridently Tory newspaper, *The Statesman*, based first in Brockville and later in Kingston.

Their public clash was big news, especially for newspapers sympathetic to the anti-Tory, anti-Orange Reform movement. They were only too pleased to comment that "these Orangeists are deserving of the anguish they bring upon each other," as the Montreal *Pilot* put it.

But Harris was no Orangeman. Although he had fallen under the persuasive sway of Gowan for several years after the two began their newspaper partnership in 1836, Harris later pleaded the innocence of youth. When he first met Gowan, Harris said, he was the impressionable 19-year-old son of a farmer who had arrived in Kemptville three years before from County Carlow, Ireland.

"It is true, that at an early age, I, like a great many other inconsiderate young persons, out of mere curiosity, became a member of that superlatively silly society," Harris wrote in an 1844 letter designed to set the record straight. In reality, Harris said, he'd quietly disavowed the Orange Lodge's fierce dedication to the defence of Protestantism and the preservation of Canada's colonial subservience to Britain after reading Lord Durham's 1839 report on Canada's political structure. Durham proposed more powers for elected officials—and fewer for the governor general—and the union of the provinces of Canada West and Canada East.

Despite his misgivings about Gowan's politics, Harris kept up his newspaper partnership. It's possible that the outside printing work he got through Gowan paid well, and Harris needed money to buy land and settle down with Harriet (Hessy) Crawford, a young woman he was engaged to marry in 1844. But early in the fall of 1843, Harris's tolerance was pushed to the limit. Gowan's *Statesman*, now in Kingston,

January 15, 1848

xii

published a series of scathing criticisms of Reform politicians, French Canadians and Catholics. Driving Gowan's passion were two simmering issues: the power struggle between governor general Charles Metcalfe and the elected Reform government over political appointments (Gowan favoured Metcalfe); and the government's plan for a Secret Societies Act prohibiting Orangemen and Masons, among others, from holding public office.

Within a month, Gowan and Harris had split—by "mutual consent," according to a back page announcement—with Harris's printing work going to Gowan's nephew, Harcourt. Elsewhere in the paper, Gowan assured his readers that his break with Harris would not affect his "unbowed" determination to fight the "papists" and other "enemies of the Empire."

Harris returned to Kemptville to begin the search for land. Looking back in an 1851 letter, he said his experience with *The Statesman* had soured his outlook on newspapers and he intended to use his time in Kemptville to consider his future.

•

Harris hadn't lost interest in politics, though. He began to write speeches for Reform candidates and organize town hall meetings to stir interest in the Reform cause. Using the pseudonym Cobbett—an homage to the crusading 18th-century British journalist William Cobbett—Harris also began writing columns on Leeds and Grenville County politics for the *British Whig*, a pro-Reform newspaper at war with *The Statesman* in Kingston. In a dispatch published Feb. 2, 1844, three days before his marriage to Hessy, Harris issued a withering attack on Gowan, calling him "cowardly, treacherous, slanderous, selfish, intriguing and dishonest." He accused Gowan of accepting "secret service money" from the governor general and intimidating voters with his mobs.

Two weeks later, a pair of police constables visited Harris, taking him to Brockville where he was brought before a panel of magistrates, charged with several counts of libel and forced to post bail in order to remain free until his trial in April. In court, Harris never stood a chance. In his opening statement, Gowan, assisted by a lawyer, said he would produce witnesses who could identify Harris as the writer "Cobbett." Harris, representing himself, limply told the jury that because he had no legal training he couldn't be expected to understand libel.

Sensing victory, Gowan jumped to his feet, promising to drop every charge if Harris could prove just one of the accusations made in his column. Harris responded to the challenge by telling Justice Malloch, a noted Tory, he would call six witnesses to support his claims. But after Gowan finished presenting his side of the case, Harris changed his mind and threw himself on the mercy of the court. In addressing the jury, Judge Malloch said he'd never witnessed "a more flagrant, or

REMARKABLE SURGICAL OPERATION. —We had the pleasure the other day of seeing a most remarkable Surgical operation performed on a Club Foot by Dr. Van Cortlandt of Upper Town. The subject was a Child only a few months old.— Some of the tendons of the left foot were so much contracted that the sole of the Foot was actually turned upwards. Dr. Van Cortlandt performed the very delicate operation of cutting the tendons on the front of the foot at the ancle until the foot came to its natural position. It was then bound up, and the Child is now doing well. The operation is one that requires extraordinary skill, and although this case was a most aggravated one, the operation and treatment have been attended with complete success. In a very short time the deformed foot will be as well as the other.

January 12, 1850

xiii

more aggravated case" of libel. The jurors agreed, and within minutes announced Harris's guilt.

Again, Gowan rose and told the court that all he wanted was "vindication of my own character" and to show "the prisoner he should not slander with impunity." Now that the jury had cleared his name, and because he pitied and forgave the prisoner, Gowan asked the judge to "please pass upon this poor man a nominal punishment." Malloch agreed, sending Harris to the county jail for 20 days and requiring him to "post security against his good behaviour for a year." As a final humiliation, the judge told Harris to thank Gowan for his "merciful interference on behalf of a punishment so slight for the offence involved."

Little is known of Harris's time in jail. Court records show he served his complete sentence. A report on prison conditions prepared for the Johnstown District in the mid-1840s described the jail, then only a few years old, as "dank" but wholly acceptable for criminals. What we do know is that soon after his release in early May, Harris bought space in *The Eastern, Johnstown and Bathurst Districts Advertiser*, forerunner of the *Brockville Recorder*, to publish what might be considered the birth announcement of the *Ottawa Citizen*.

In a lengthy prospectus, Harris outlined his plan to start a weekly newspaper in Prescott called *The Packet*. Although it is carefully worded to avoid violating Harris's promise of good behaviour, the prospectus made it clear Harris intended *The Packet* to settle his score with Gowan. Everything his former partner stood for, Harris promised his paper would oppose. He would never publish "sectarian or clannish" articles. He would encourage partnerships between French and English and Catholics and Protestants. He would advocate government run by elected representatives and oppose the interference of the governor general, which he characterized as "imperial bureaucracy." He would oppose "mysterious patronage" and battle the heavy hand of the Family Compact.

At first, his plans were met with skepticism, even by Reformers who wondered about his sincerity. Over the next few months, as Harris published his plans for *The Packet* in other papers, he was mocked by Tories for being a turncoat to Orangeism and by Reformers for his convenient conversion to their movement. To convince the skeptics, Harris sent an impassioned letter to several papers confessing his careless youthful dalliance with the Orange Lodge, but making it clear he now considered its followers to be dangerous bigots.

Harris also wrote that if Gowan would only show "the goodness to manufacture a declaration to the world that one William Harris is an ex-Orangeman . . . I shall take it as a special favour at his august hands; and for the first time in my life acknowledge myself indebted to him." When Gowan didn't respond, Harris took a more daring step to prove his Reform bona fides. Through a Reform MP, he leaked a letter he'd received from Gowan the previous summer when they were still part-

THE PACKET.

"Our Country."

BY-TOWN: SATURDAY, APRIL 27, 1850.

VOTE BY BALLOT.

The elective franchise is justly regarded as the basis of civil liberty. Through it the people declare who shall be their rulers, and what shall be their policy; and interference by coercion, bribery, or other means, has always been severely denounced. But however much it has been denounced, interference has been unscrupulously practiced, and will be practiced so long as a system is retained which affords opportunities for practising both corruption and coercion. The great object avowedly is to obtain the voice of the country honestly and fairly,—and in whatever degree the means employed may be defective in not being capable of preventing dishonesty and unfairness, in that degree the object is defeated,—and when the mode admits of any considerable exercise of any such improper means, then, such election is nothing but a farce, and the people are wronged of their rights. Voting by the method now in use in Canada, is always more or less liable to these evils; and not that alone, but it tends greatly to cause disturbance and difficulties at the polling places. Whether the votes shall be taken in the usual way openly, or by Ballot secretly, cannot involve a political principle —it is merely the mode by which a principle is carried into effect. The end aimed at in either case is the same, and the question is limited to the mere mode of receiving the vote.

In too many cases the result of an Election is very far from being a *true* expression of public opinion. The Ledger is employed in place of logic, and men are *ordered* to vote for this or that Candidate rather than left to exercise their own choic. Both modes have their advocates and opponents, and the arguments for and against

ners. In the letter, Gowan boasted of a secret meeting with the governor general to plan the ouster of the Reform government and replace it with Tories.

When parts of the letter were published in the Reform-minded Toronto *Globe* and Montreal *Pilot*, an enraged and embarrassed Gowan called Harris a scoundrel for releasing private correspondence and demanded the letter's return. Harris refused. And while the leaked letter had the desired effect of humiliating Gowan and providing the Reform press with a field day for mockery, it backfired on Harris personally. Many Reformers seriously disliked the Grand Master of the Orange Lodge, but they were even less impressed with "the great impropriety," to quote the *Pilot*, of breaking a confidence, even with an enemy.

•

But Harris pressed on. He'd chosen Prescott for his new enterprise in the belief that the tiny riverside settlement, population 1,500 and without a newspaper, would soon become a major centre of water-borne commerce. Canals allowing deep-water ships to steer around the rapids at Lachine, Beauharnois and Cornwall had just been completed using an Imperial loan of 1.5 million pounds. There was talk of a ship-building industry.

With Harris as owner, editor and sole writer, the first edition of *The Packet* was published on Oct. 26, 1844, arguably the *Citizen*'s true birth date. Nothing, not even scraps of that paper, survive. Nor have any of the subsequent six editions Harris published until Dec. 7 before he abandoned Prescott for Bytown.

There's also nothing to suggest why Harris moved. Without a final edition of the Prescott *Packet* to consult, nor any early editions of the Bytown *Packet*, only speculation remains. Did Harris overestimate his opportunities in Prescott? Had he heard Bytown was among the country's fastest growing centres? Did he believe the crazy rumours, published as early as 1841, that the rugged logging town was being considered as a compromise seat of government? Harris must have known Bytown's only existing newspaper, the *Gazette*, was sympathetic to the Tories and the Orange Lodge, leaving an attractive gap for a Reform-minded journal.

Whatever his reasons, Harris re-launched *The Packet* in Bytown on March 29, 1845, an unusually warm Saturday for early spring. It's clear Harris considered the paper an extension of his earlier enterprise— the front page referred to it as Volume 1, Number 8, according to the *Gazette*, which tersely acknowledged the arrival of its new rival the following Thursday.

In his *History of Lower Town Ottawa, 1826-1854*, Michael Newton says Harris set up an office at William and George streets in a building constructed from timber salvaged from the original market building on George Street. "It was painted blue and in large white letters 'Packet

SONG.

The dream of existence is blissful and bright
In the radiant morning of youth,
When Hope has no cloud to o'ershadow her light,
And friendship is hallowed by truth;
When Love is all pure as a calm summer stream,
That slumbering 'mid flowers doth lie,
Reflecting the brightness of Heaven's own beam,
And wearing the tinge of the sky.

How chang'd is the vision when time hurries on,
And bring's the decline of life's day;
Then the sunbeams from Hope's fairy landscape
are gone,
Then friendship has failed away.
And then like a stream which the wind-spirit
wakes,
Is the once holy fountain of Love;
Then its troubled and wandering wave only takes
The hue of the storm-cloud above.

'Tis well, since we're speeding away to the tomb,
That youth's fairy pleasures should flee,
For could they return all their earlier bloom,
Too dear to our heart they would be.
And 'tis well, since the soul's lasting home is not
here,
That the love of its spring-time should die;
For could it still cherish an Eden so dear,
'Twould forget for its heaven to sigh!

February 15, 1851

February 15, 1851

Office' was spelled out," Mr. Newton writes. The paper was printed a few doors east along George Street by John George Bell, whose mechanical skills on a hand press and "sureness under pressure" were described in a 1927 study by newspaper historian Alexander Ross as "superior to any operating in the province at that time."

At first, it's likely no more than 200 copies of the four-page journal were printed and delivered by a half-dozen boys throughout the raw, mud-clogged lumbertown. Although only a few dozen editions of the Harris-edited *Packet* are still around today, it's possible to see why his populist mix of politics, town news, social notes, letters, items on science, moral behaviour and the law soon pushed sales of *The Packet* ahead of the *Gazette*.

Of course, Harris also found room among the text-heavy columns of nearly every edition of his *Packet* to attack Ogle Gowan. In early 1846, for instance, stories on a "mob" of Gowan supporters travelling to Grenville to bribe voters were reprinted gleefully from other Reform newspapers, and spiced with Harris's own editorial commentary.

Despite the paper's quick success in Bytown, Harris stayed at the helm barely a year and a half before selling out for $2,000 to Henry J. Friel, a future mayor with similar political ideals, but no newspaper experience. In an eloquent, self-congratulatory farewell letter to readers on Oct. 24, 1846, Harris declared that his "experiment"—bringing liberal ideas to the banks of the Ottawa River—had succeeded and his goal of drawing French and English, Catholic and Protestant, closer together had been achieved.

He also couldn't resist one final crack at Gowan, "the instrument of a bigoted and brutal hostility towards Catholics and the dirty satanic and public scourge of all Irishmen, Protestant as well as Catholic." Sounding an almost Messianic note, Harris boasted that he "came amongst" the people of Bytown, people of all stripes, and, "They saw me—heard me, and believed me. And all the questions asked were, 'Is he liberal?'—'Is he honest?'—'Is he competent?' Satisfied on these points, there were no further questions asked, and the most enthusiastic confidence given."

•

The column ended Harris's career in newspapers. He remained in Ottawa for another five years—an 1850 baptismal record for his fourth child lists him as a "student at law"—generally keeping a low profile. In 1849, Harris turned up at the centre of the infamous Stony Monday riots, an ugly clash between Tories and Reformers over an upcoming visit of the governor general. According to one account, Harris was about to take the stage to read an anti-Tory declaration when the fighting broke out. In another story, Harris and Friel are described holding wooden clubs to keep Tories from crossing the Sappers' Bridge into Lowertown.

Law society records suggest Harris never became a lawyer, but he did find a lucrative way to cash in on his political loyalty. In 1851, the Reform government named him to the patronage post of Crown Lands Agent for Renfrew County. The position put Harris in charge of selling Crown land, including the vast clergy reserves, to private owners. News that an "entire stranger" was getting the job was greeted with dismay by five of Renfrew's Tory reeves who thought the appointment should have gone to George Ross, a loyal Conservative. In response, Renfrew's Reform supporters held a rally to "hail with pleasure" the arrival of Harris. The Tories, getting wind of the meeting, descended on Coumbs Inn and soon the two sides—armed with clubs and fortified with drink—were brawling inside and along the streets outside.

When the dust cleared, Harris found himself in jail again, this time charged with assault. But there was not to be a repeat of his libel trial. Harris was acquitted in a lively trial after several witnesses said the new lands agent hit two Tories while coming to the aid of a defenceless old man they had thrown to the ground. The case seemed to signal the start of a new phase in Harris's life. In a letter written to county residents, Harris vowed to stay clear of politics and carry out his work with honesty and dedication.

He appeared to have kept his word. For the next 18 years, Harris and his family—records indicate he and Hessy had 10 children, two of whom died young—lived without incident in a log home he built on a spectacular site along the banks of the Bonnechere River outside Renfrew. Apart from his work as lands agent, which appears to have been routine, Harris rarely shows up on the public record during this period. Newspaper stories report that he helped form the Renfrew Agricultural Society, attended some St. Patrick's Society meetings and judged a grammar school writing competition.

On July 3, 1869, after a lengthy undisclosed illness, Harris died at home at age 55. His old newspaper, renamed the *Citizen* in 1851, made no mention of his death—he'd been gone from Ottawa nearly two decades—and a short obituary in the *Perth Courier* made no reference to his newspaper days, describing him only as a lands agent.

But Harris's legacy as a newspaperman had been forgotten long before he died. One 1859 account of the *Citizen*'s origins—then a mere 15 years in the past—omitted his name altogether, crediting Robert Bell with founding *The Packet*. Over the years, parts of Harris's story were restored (though no photograph, sketch or even physical description of him has been found). But even articles written to mark the *Citizen*'s 150th anniversary in 1995 continued to paint Harris as an Orangeman, and were uncertain about his age, birthplace, family and his life before and after he founded the newspaper that would outlast 22 rivals and survive into the 21st century.

March, 1853

About This Book

WHEN THE *Ottawa Citizen* decided to mark its 160th anniversary with a book, our first thought was to produce a history of the newspaper. To be sure, it's a fascinating story. When you're two decades older than the country and when you've been around longer than any other business in the city, your story is bound to be compelling.

But then we thought, a newspaper doesn't survive 16 decades—and outlast nearly two dozen rivals—simply because its owners made smart business decisions along the way. It lasts because it's been a good newspaper. And not just because some of the country's finest writers have graced its pages, although they have, or because it reported the big stories, which it did.

Like all venerable newspapers, the *Citizen* survived because it paid attention to the small things as well as the big—because its reporters and editors sat through tedious city council meetings, made sure to collect society news and attend concerts and inquests and speeches, tried to understand mill rates and the appeal of shopping malls, examined the quality of drinking water and the state of playgrounds, cheered sports victories and mourned sports defeats, celebrated good citizens and scorned the bad.

We don't expect a pat on the back for that. It's a newspaper's job to pay attention to the everyday as well as the exceptional. Both are the stuff of a community—and what value is a newspaper, to quote Robert Shannon, a 19th century *Citizen* editor, if it's not holding "a reflecting glass" to the community it serves?

So after some reflecting of our own, we decided to mark the anniversary in the only way that made sense: with a collection gathered from our own pages, 160 years of writing that tells both the story of a community and the newspaper that was there to record it.

But when you're drawing material from almost 44,000 editions—that's more than three million pages—and roughly 2,000 writers whose careers touch three centuries, how do you choose what to include? The quick answer: you look for stories that somehow transcend time. You search for good writing, for lively topics, for items that show how much we've changed—or how little we've changed. You keep an eye out for events of consequence, but because they have often been well chronicled elsewhere you try to find stories that give them a new twist. You watch for notable writers—Charles Dickens and Mordecai Richler made the cut—and stories that reflect long-gone norms (it was once routine to refer to blacks as darkies, or worse, and aboriginals as Injuns). You scour every part of the paper so the selections reflect its scope—editorials, columns, politics, sports, fashion, city news, world news, business and entertainment.

The final product—nearly 400 stories, presented chronologically over 16 chapters, one for each decade—should not be viewed as a comprehensive history. That was never the intention. Countless important local, national and world events are not represented here. Nor are many of the *Citizen's* finest journalists, from the past and the present, some of whose best work still lies in the future.

Nor can we claim to have examined every edition of the *Citizen;* there might never have been a book if we had. On microfilm at Library and Archives Canada—which possesses the largest collection—we did read every surviving edition of the *Citizen* (and *Packet)* from its 20-year period (1845-1865) as a weekly or twice-weekly publication. And we looked through a majority of editions from the rest of the 19th century. But by necessity, our examination of the larger newspapers after 1900 was random—usually one edition a week, often more during exciting news periods.

In an effort to include as many articles as possible, many items appear as excerpts. These are clearly marked with ellipses. We have tried wherever possible to retain the style—spelling, grammar, punctuation—of the originals, but have occasionally made changes in the interest of clarity or consistency. Information in rounded parentheses is original; information in square brackets was inserted to provide context for modern readers. Where lengthier explanations are required, we have used italics when setting up or concluding an article.

The illustrations in the margins are photographs of whole pages or parts, arranged in roughly chronological order. Only occasionally are they related to the adjacent text—they comprise a parallel journey through time, but a separate one.

In the end, it is our hope that we have compiled not only a lively portrait of our past, but a record that will inform the future and prove the adage that a newspaper is the raw material—the first draft—of history.

"If all sources of history had to be destroyed save one, that which would be chosen with the greatest certainty of its value to posterity would be a newspaper," the respected American librarian Clarence Brigham once wrote. "The fact that newspapers are put together by people who are not consciously recording for posterity—but providing a bird's-eye view of life as it happens—makes them even more valuable."

Doug Fischer and Ralph Willsey
August 2005

THE PACKET.

VOLUME VI.]   BY-TOWN (CANADA WEST): SATURDAY, APRIL 6, 1850.   [NUMBER VII.

THE PACKET.

A WEEKLY NEWSPAPER,

Devoted to Politics, Trade, Agriculture, and the dissemination of Moral Instruction and Useful Information amongst the People.

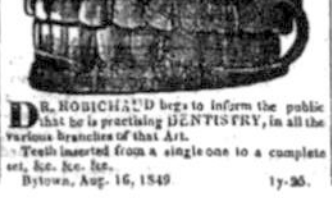

Is published every SATURDAY, in the building formerly known as the Old Market House, on Lowell Street, immediately adjoining the British Hotel, Lower Bytown, by R. BELL.

TERMS.—For three months, 3s.; for six months, 10s.; and for twelve months, 15s. No subscriber received, and no subscriber charged for any fractional part of these periods. Payments are expected to be made in advance.

2

Our Country

The First Decade, 1845-1854

LOOKING BACK from our perch 160 years in the future, we can only speculate about what prompted William Harris to sell his weekly newspaper after less than two years at the helm. We know it wasn't lack of success.

Within months of his arrival in Bytown in March 1845, Harris had already pushed sales of *The Packet* ahead of the town's establishment paper, the *Gazette and Rideau Advertiser. The Packet* was not only brimming with advertising, it was being printed by John George Bell, reputedly the best hand press operator in the province. Most of all, *The Packet*—by 1846 carrying the patriotic banner "Our Country"—fulfilled the young Irish-born democrat's dream of promoting liberal ideas in a town run by Tories.

He'd certainly gone to a lot of trouble to find success, relocating his paper from Prescott to Bytown after only seven editions, and then rushing to set up an office in the heart of the business district in the Byward Market. So why sell after just 75 issues of hard-won progress?

In a 1927 study of early Ontario newspapers, historian Alexander Ross speculated that Harris faced heavy debts and needed the money to support his growing family. That's certainly possible. Harris and Hessy, his wife of two years, had their second child in as many years in April 1846, five months before the sale of *The Packet*.

Ross also noted the paper would have placed large demands on Harris's time. He probably produced *The Packet*, a text-heavy, four-page journal, with the help of one junior reporter–errand boy. The bulk of the writing and all of the editing and proofreading would have fallen to Harris. And to save a clerk's salary, Harris likely sold the advertising, ordered supplies and paid the bills.

There's also some suggestion Harris had his eye on a law career. He

THE PACKET.

OUR COUNTRY.

BY-TOWN: SATURDAY, SEPT'R. 5, 1846.

IRELAND.

Never at any time did we feel more proud of our beloved native land than at the present moment—this we candidly confess. Never was there a period when Irish intellect shone greater—higher and higher does it burn, and more sweet and holy is the incense offered at the altar of Irish liberty. Day after day intellectual giants are raising their noble heads in

William Harris was Irish, which explains in part his antipathy to rabid supporters of the British Crown—Tories, as they were then known. He saw them as exploiters of the Irish people at home and in Canada.

ST. PARTICK'S SOCIETY.

THE THIRD ANNUAL QUARTERLY MEETING of the St. Patrick's Society will be held at Doran's Hotel on Tuesday next, the 5th instant, at 7 o'clock, P. M.; of which all Office-Bearers and Members of the Society are hereby requested to take notice. and give their attendance accordingly.

WM. HARRIS,
Secretary.

Bytown, 1st Decr., 1848.

Two years after he sold The Packet, William Harris reappeared in a new capacity.

3

was clearly fascinated by the law—his paper carried a regular feature on the workings of the courts—and an 1850 baptismal certificate for his fourth child listed Harris as a "student at law" (although Law Society records suggest he never became a lawyer).

Whatever his reasons, Harris sold *The Packet* in October 1846 for $2,000 to minority partner Henry J. Friel, a businessman with the same Reform party sympathies and no journalism experience. Although Friel lacked Harris's eloquence with a pen, he possessed a sharper business acumen. He soon turned the front page over entirely to ads— common practice in the 1840s—raising rates by 20 per cent and renaming the paper *The Bytown Packet and Weekly Commercial Gazette*.

What didn't change was the paper's commitment to the Reform movement, forerunner of the Liberal party. If anything, *The Packet*'s anti-Tory sentiments became even more zealous under Friel, whose fiery temperament matched his flaming red beard, and whose blunt writing style lacked the subtler touch of his predecessor. However, Friel's journalism soon took a back seat to his personal political ambitions. He was elected to town council in 1848, and set his sights on the mayoralty, which he won three times over the next two decades.

In late 1849, Friel sold the paper to Robert Bell, a man obsessed with bringing the railroad to Bytown and, more significantly for the newspaper, a Conservative. Bell moved *The Packet*'s political sympathies into the Tory camp with caution, hoping that by steering a middle course he could hang on to existing subscribers while adding new ones. It was

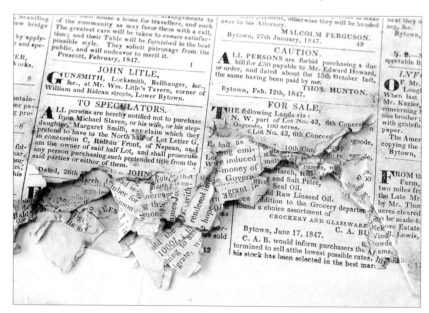

In 1845, no one knew that of the newspapers competing along the Ottawa, The Packet alone would survive. No copies of the first year's editions can be found and many later issues are also missing. Those that survive are not always fully legible, but still reveal vivid glimpses of old Bytown.

An ambitious engraving appeared at the top of the renamed Packet,
separating the words "Ottawa" and "Citizen."

an approach the paper would retain, through numerous owners, for
the next eight decades.

In February 1851, four years before Bytown itself became Ottawa, Bell
renamed his paper the *Ottawa Citizen*. He never really explained why,
although it's possible he hoped to expand his circulation area by
adopting the name—"the Ottawa"—commonly used to describe the
valley to the east and west of Bytown. In an editorial marking the paper's sixth anniversary, Bell said he hoped the new name and a magnificent new front page nameplate would make the *Citizen* the equal of
any "in Canada in respectability of appearance" and "increase its value
and usefulness."

It appears he succeeded. As the paper's first decade drew to an end
in 1854, the *Citizen* remained the largest and most influential newspaper in Bytown—which, by then, was home to three other publications—and was vying to raise its stature to the top ranks of Canada's
press.

THE PACKET, a weekly Newspaper, devoted
to Politics, Trade, Agriculture, and the dissemination of Moral Instruction and Useful Information amongst the people, is published every Saturday,
corner of Rideau and William streets, Bytown, Canada West, by WM. HARRIS.

J. G. BELL, PRINTER.

TERMS.—For three months, 5s.; for six months,
10s., and for twelve months, 15s. No subscriber
received, and no subscriber charged for any fractional part of these periods. Payments are expected
to be made in advance.

RATES OF ADVERTISING.—Six lines or under,
2s. 6d. first insertion, and 7½d for each subsequent
insertion; ten lines or under, 3s. 4d. for the first insertion, and 10d. for each subsequent insertion; a-
bove ten lines, 4d. per line for the first insertion, and
1d. per line for every subsequent insertion.

Advertisements without written directions will be
inserted until forbid, and charged accordingly.

A handsome discount will be made to those who
advertise by the year.

Advertisements must be handed in the evening before publication.

All letters to the editor must be post-paid.

November 21, 1846

•.• The *Packet* has attained an extensive and respectable circulation in the Dalhousie, Johnstown, Bathurst, and Sydenham Districts; and is, perhaps, the best medium for advertising on the Ottawa.

THE PACKET.
OUR COUNTRY.
BY-TOWN: SATURDAY, OCT'R. 24, 1846.

PATRONS OF THE PACKET!
KIND FRIENDS,—
        It becomes my duty to inform you that with this day's publication my connection with this Journal wholly ceases; a du-

September 5, 1846
WARM BATHING
Advice on clean, healthy living was a newspaper staple in the 19th century, and The Packet *was no exception, especially on matters of morality, drinking, dress and decorum. This item on the advantages of a warm bath, reprinted from a well-known 1841 book of household tips, was typical, as were the two June 12, 1847 articles found later in this chapter.*

Many erroneous notions prevail respecting the use and properties of the warm bath. To many persons, the idea of submersion in warm water on a summer's day would appear preposterous; but if it be rationally considered, it will be found that the warm bath may be taken with equal, or perhaps greater benefit in the summer than in the winter. During hot weather the secretions of the skin are much increased in quantity; and consequently, a greater necessity exists that it should be kept perfectly free from obstructions. Another prevailing error respecting the warm bath is that it tends to relax and enervate the body, for experience has sufficiently proved the fallacy of the opinion and many physicians have prescribed its use to patients laboring under debility. Not only have they suffered no ill effects, but have all felt invigorated, & mostly returned to health and strength. Many persons are deterred from using the warm bath, especially in winter, from the fear of catching cold; but this fear is groundless, for it has been found that the warm bath, by increasing the circulation on the surface of the body, renders it more capable of withstanding the effects of cold than otherwise would have been.— *Popular Errors Explained.*

October 24, 1846
PATRONS OF THE PACKET!
Packet *founder William Harris's departure from his newspaper after two years at the helm was accompanied by a self-serving letter to readers. In addition to boasting of his success bringing liberal ideas to Bytown, it also contained one last attack on Ogle Gowan, an Orangeman, Tory and Harris's former business partner at the Brockville* Statesman. *Here's an excerpt:*

Kind Friends,—
It becomes my duty to inform you that with this day's publication my connection with this Journal wholly ceases; a duty I am about to perform with a mixture of pleasure and pain—pain to relinquish a pursuit to which the best portion of my life has been ardently devoted; and pleasure to get rid of the continuous cares and anxieties always attendant on the joint occupation of Editor and Publisher of a public Journal

in this Country. I have disposed of this establishment without reserve; and, before consigning it to other hands, deem it proper to say a few words to you at parting. I part with you on the best of terms—grateful to you for your munificent patronage, and conscious, from your many expressions of private esteem, that you are satisfied I deserved it. The establishment is in a flourishing condition, and has done much better than I at all anticipated it would when I commenced it on the Ottawa.

To the public of Bytown, and the valley of the Ottawa generally, I am indebted for handsome support; and to three classes of the community, distinguished as Free Church Scotch, Franco-Canadian and liberal Irish Catholic, I am so peculiarly indebted that even at the risk of being invidious it would be ungrateful of me not to particularize. Regard for that public virtue which is derived from a strong sense of our own interest in the preservation of prosperity of free Government, I believe to be the actuating motive of the two former; while with the latter— the liberal Irish Catholic—I believe that, with a national bias combined, stimulated him to an enthusiastic support, and he is too impulsively honest to know any other. To the latter I consider myself deeply indebted. Their warm friendship I shall never forget, and shall always be anxious to acknowledge. Who is it that says the Irish Catholic is religiously bigoted? Let him step forward. Reeking with and embarrassed from an unfortunate connection with Ogle R. Gowan—the interested instrument of a bigoted and brutal hostility towards Catholics and the dirty satanic and public scourge of all Irishmen, Protestant as well as Catholic in this Country,—I came amongst them. They saw me—heard me, and believed me. And all the questions asked were, "Is he liberal"!—"Is he honest"!—"Is he competent?" Satisfied on these points, there were no further questions asked, and the most enthusiastic confidence given. Always, and everywhere, have intelligent Irish Catholics had confidence in Protestant public men who deserved it;— but never—oh! never,—have Protestants, as a people, shown a like impartiality towards Catholics. Let us hear no more, then, of Catholic bigotry—let us first examine ourselves.

The young man who has purchased this establishment—Mr. H. J. Friel—is well known in Bytown, where he has been brought up; and the patrons of The Packet out of Bytown will, of course, form their opinion of him by his management of this Journal. He is a Catholic, a native of Canada, of respectable Irish parents; and I only wish that the Protestant community will extend that support to him which Catholics have generously given me. If honesty of purpose, rectitude of conduct, and good intention, are appreciated as they deserve, I am confident he will merit it. And, while on this subject, I would be ungrateful were I to pass unnoticed the excellent merit of the printer of this paper, Mr. Bell. The superior mechanical appearance of this paper

The advertiser no doubt meant to say "strayed." A 21st-century spellchecker would have missed this one, too.

is creditable to his taste, industry, and management.

And now, kind friends, having taken some pains to address you, and perhaps unwarrantably transgressed on your attention, I have but one word more to say to you as a public writer.

Farewell.

WM. HARRIS

April 7, 1847

DEATH OF TWO WELL KNOWN CHARACTERS.—Most of our readers in Town are probably aware of the death of James Smith, better known as "Happy Jimmy." This eccentric character deserves a passing notice. He was a Scotchman—a native of, if we are rightly informed, Paisley. He enlisted in the Light Artillery some 30 years ago, and was discharged after a service of some ten years, since which time he has been in and about Bytown. In the trying seasons of Cholera, "Jimmy" was of great service here, for he was the only person who could be had to attend upon the sick and bury the dead. For the past few years he subsisted upon the charity of the Towns-people. He was an unfortunate but harmless specimen of human nature. Patrick Whelan, commonly known as "Paddy Whelan"—a man of great strength of body but of weak intellect, whose peculiar conduct and droll antics in our street have been a source of amusement to some and pity to others—has also paid the debt of nature. He died in the Township of March on Tuesday last. This unfortunate individual was possessed of a good prosperity, and has left a large family.

May 1, 1847

In its early days, The Packet *was fascinated with science, especially astronomy. During most of the late 1840s, the paper ran a regular feature on the night sky written by astronomers at Britain's Royal Observatory, as well as frequent articles on general science. Here are two typical examples, including an item on the newly discovered Brorsen-Metcalf comet.*

THE NEW COMET.—W. Cranch Boad, in a letter to the editor of the *Boston Courier*, dated Cambridge Observatory, March 26, 1847, says: "The comet of March 4th is fast approaching in its parhelion; it was seen last night near the star Sigma Andromedea, the trail is hardly perceptible to the naked eye, although it is six millions of miles in length, and increasing at the rate of half a million of miles a day—the appearance of the comet, when seen through a telescope of sufficient light, is very interesting, from its rapid increase in size and brightness, and frequent changes of focus. The distance from Earth is about eight millions of miles. It will pass its parhelion on the 30th inst. at which time it will be moving at the rate of eleven millions of miles daily. It will remain south of the ecliptic for only two days and in passing its nodes, will be near the Earth and Sun.

May 1, 1847

CENTRAL FIRES IN THE EARTH.—The increased temperature, found at increased depths in digging the Artesian wells, more particularly that of Grenelle in France, has been adduced by M. Arago, and other philosophers, as proof of central fires in the earth. Commander C. Morton, of the Royal Navy, known as the propounder of the "electrical origin of hail stones," and the vegetable origin of the basaltic columns of the Giant's Causeway, and those of Staffa, merely regards the increased temperature at increased depths as the natural consequence of the increased pressure of the atmosphere, and as much a matter of course as the increased cold or diminished temperature found to exist on ascending mountains, according as the atmospheric pressure diminishes in the ascent. The beautiful simplicity of this theory may, perhaps, induce the conviction of its alliance with nature. In corroboration, we may justly remark that the artificial compression of air does elicit heat.

May 22, 1847

Although editor Henry J. Friel was known to take a drink—there is an account of him visiting a tavern—his newspaper was an enthusiastic supporter of temperance. But in a town full of lumbermen (Bytown was reputed to have more taverns per capita than any place in British North America), Friel's hope for abstinence was little more than a dream.

TEMPERANCE.—We are gratified in being able to state that the temperance movement is fast gaining ground in Bytown. It is pleasing to us to know that the French Canadian portion of our population have now nearly all taken the Temperance pledge. Such a pleasing information must sow the seeds of future morality and happiness. The Rev. Mr. Chiniquy—who has been styled the Father Mathew of Canada, and who has written a work entitled *"Manuel de Temperance,"* which has been favourably noticed by the Montreal Press— was here on Sunday last, and made an eloquent appeal to his countrymen, which had much effect upon his hearers. We understand he intends having an English translation of his work published.

May 22, 1847

MOTIONS OF THE EARTH AND HEAVENS.—While we are apt to imagine we are sitting in absolute rest in our apartments, we are in reality whirling round towards the east at the rate of hundreds of miles

FURIOUS DRIVING.—On Friday the 12th instant two ladies driving on the Richmond Road towards the residence of John Thomson, Esq., were met by some ruffians in a sleigh, who, regardless of the consequences and the presence of females, drove against the vehicle in which they rode, upsetting it, and causing severe injury to one of them. Such brutal conduct deserves severe punishment.

March 27, 1847

The last *Official Gazette* contains a proclamation creating the Allumette Island a Township, under the name of the Township of Allumette Island.

The "Union Railroad" is completed, and will, we understand, be opened as soon as it is possible for Steamers to ascend the Ottawa.

A portion of the Dam at Burritt's Rapids on the Rideau Canal has been carried off. It is expected that the breach will be filled up before commencement of the Forwarding season. We observe that the *Kingston Argus* states that a part of the Deep Cut, near Bytown, had given way. This report is altogether without foundation.

We have much gratification in being enabled to state that upwards of fifty pounds have been subscribed during the past week for the purchase of a piece of Plate to be presented to Mr. Hopper, late Agent of the Bank of Montreal at this place. Such an evidence of respect on the part of the inhabitants must be peculiarly grateful to the feelings of that gentleman.

It is rumored that in the event of a general election taking place G. B. Lyon, Esq., of Bytown, and John Egan, Esq., of Aylmer, will be candidates for the County of Ottawa.

May 1, 1847

an hour and are, at the same time, carried through the regions of space with a velocity of sixty-eight thousands miles every hour, so that, during every moment, or every pulse that beats within us, we are carried nearly twenty miles from that portion of space we occupied before. When we lie down to sleep in the evening, we are seldom aware that, during our seven hours repose, we have been carried along through the space of four hundred and seventy thousands miles! When, amidst the gloom of winter, we look forward to the cheering scenes of spring, we must be carried forward more than a hundred millions of miles, before we can enjoy the pleasures of that season; and when spring arrives we must be carried, through the void of space, hundreds of millions more, before we can enjoy the fruits of harvest. During every breath we draw, and every word we speak, we are carried forward in our course thirty, forty, or fifty miles, unconscious of the rapidity of our flight; but the motion is not less real because we do not feel it. What should we think of if we beheld one of the largest mountains in Scotland flying through the atmosphere, across the island of Great Britain, with a velocity which would carry it from John-o'-Groats to the Land's End, a distance of seven hundred miles, in seven minutes? It would, doubtless, excite universal wonder and astonishment.—But this is not one-tenth part of the velocity with which the great globe of the earth, and all it contains, flies through the boundless regions of space. Were we placed on a fixed point a thousand miles distant from the earth, and beheld this mighty globe, with all its magnificent scenery and population, and carrying the moon along with it in its rapid career, such a spectacle would overwhelm us with astonishment inexpressible, and even with emotion of terror, and, would present to view a scene of sublimity and grandeur beyond the reach of our present conceptions. To angels, and other superior intelligences, when winging through flight from heaven to earth, and through the distant world, such august scenes may be frequently presented.—*From the Solar System, in the Monthly Series of the London Trust Society.*

June 12, 1847
THE OTTAWA SLIDES–STEAMERS–RAILROADS
NECESSARY IMPROVEMENTS

This excerpt is the lyrical opening section of a lengthy editorial urging improvements along the Ottawa River to increase the waterway's commercial potential. The item is not only a fine example of the embellished prose style popular in the press of the 1840s, it offers a perspective on the river's great influence on life in Bytown.

This noble river may be seen to much advantage at this season of year. The spring floods increase its dimensions, and add more strength and swiftness to its current. The great falls of the Chaudiere present a beautiful appearance under the influence of "high water." This rapid, one of the largest upon the Ottawa, can hardly be equalled, whether we take for our standard of perfection the beautiful or the terrific. At a distance the view is light, smooth and pleasing, resembling in effect a painter's sketch, but as you near it "the war of the waters," and the sight of a river bounding from rock to rock, heeding nothing in its onward progress, till its passion seems to be exhausted in the quiet basin below, is sufficient to strike the beholder with awe and wonder. Over the rocks, which seem daring enough to dispute its passes, it dashes and the whole waters of a stream which has not its equal in Canada, if we except the proud St. Lawrence. Over its enraged bosom a human creature has not dared to pass in consciousness, though many have made their exit from this stage in daring to approach the scene of conflict between two great rivals of inanimate nature. Often have large quantities of timber passed through its midst, coming out below all broken and destroyed. And often, too, have men been carried with them, their mangled corpses uncovered perhaps weeks after the sad occurrence. To view the maddened feature of this awful rapid, and imagine a fellow mortal struggling in the midst, is thought in itself excruciating. There are several channels, but the main one, over which the Union Suspension Bridge is erected, forms the subject under notice. The channel heretofore termed by timbermen and voyageurs the "Schnief," is now known as the Government Slide. This slide it is said works well, and is likely to add much to the large revenue collected upon the Ottawa by Government, and distributed in every quarter except that which requires it, and from whence it is derived. The next channel as you approach the bridge is the old slide passage, formerly owned by the late George Buchanan, Esq., whose enterprise and exertion effected many improvements in this quarter. This slide is now closed up we believe through the intervention of Government. The next object which attracts notice is the Union Suspension Bridge. It is a beautiful piece of work and reflects great credit upon the builder, Mr. Wilkinson, who, it is said, is an American. The view from the centre of the bridge is enlivening. You have here a sight of the spot from which the rapid takes its name, the Chaudiere or Big Kettle, an immense trough into which the body of water falls, and spray rising from which has much the appearance of steam, hence the name.

June 12, 1847

THE IMPORT OF LADY'S DRESS.—Let no woman suppose that any man can be really indifferent to her appearance.—The instinct may have been deadened in his mind by a slatternly, negligent mother, or plain, maiden, low-church sister; but she may be sure it is there, and

THE PACKET.

OUR COUNTRY.

BY-TOWN: SATURDAY, OCT'R. 16, 1847.

Notices of Births charged 2s. 6d.—Marriages 5s.

SINGULAR CASE OF CORRUPTION! —THE GATTINEAU FERRY!

It has seldom been our lot to expose a more gross case of corruption on the part of individuals or government than the one we are just now called upon to notice.— For a certain number of years—from 1843 up the present time—Mr. James Hagan, of Gattineau Point, Township of Templeton, about three miles below Bytown, has held the Ferry crossing the Ottawa at that Point to the opposite side of the River, in the Township of Gloucester, in Upper Canada. During the years 1843-'44 and '45 Mr. Hagan enjoyed uninterruptedly exclusive right to the Ferry; but in 1846 Mrs. Mc-Nab, whose land lies on the opposite side of the River, cast an eye upon it. She first threatened, through her Attorney, to prosecute Mr. Hagan as a trespasser upon her Lands, and afterwards offered to take £20 a-year from him for right of landing. Mr. Hagan—resting secure on his License from the Government, which prohibits any other person from the right of Ferrying at the

The Packet published an early piece of investigative reporting in 1847.

with a little adroitness, capable of revival. Of course, the immediate effect of a well-chosen feminine toilet operates differently in different minds. In some it causes a sense of actual pleasure; in others a consciousness of passive enjoyment. In some it is intensely felt while present; in others only missed when gone. None can deny its power over them, more or less; or for their own sakes, had better not believe if they do.—Such being the case, the responsibilities of a wife in this department are very serious. In point of fact, she dresses for two, and in neglecting herself, virtually defrauds her neighbour. Nature has expressly assigned her as the only safe investment for his vanities, and she who wantonly throws them back from their natural course, deserves either to see them break out on his own person, or appear in that of another. But independent of the plain law of instinct, there is one for the promotion of dress among ladies which may be plainer yet to some—and this is the law of self-interest. It is all very well for bachelors to be restricted to a costume which expresses nothing beyond a general sense of their own unfitness to be seen—since they can be safely trusted for publishing their characters to the world with that forwardness which is their chief element; but heaven forbid that the spinsters should ever take to the same outward mentality. With their habitual delicacy of mind, and reserve of manner, dress becomes a sort of symbolical language,—a kind of personal glossary—a species of body phrenology,—the study of which it would be madness to neglect. Will Honeycomb say he can tell the humour a woman is in by the color of her hood? We go farther, and maintain that, to a proficient in the science, every woman walks about with a placard, on which her leading qualities are advertised.

June 12, 1847

HUMANISING INFLUENCE OF CLEANLINESS.—A neat, clean, fresh-aired, sweet, cheerful, well-arranged, and well-situated house, exercises a moral as well as a physical influence over its inmates, and makes the members of a family peaceable and considerate of the feelings and happiness of each other; the connexion is obvious between the state of mind thus produced and habits of respect for others, and for those higher duties and obligations which no laws can enforce. On the contrary, a filthy, squalid, noxious dwelling, rendered all more wretched by its noisome site, and in which none of the decencies of life can be observed, contributes to make its unfortunate inhabitants selfish, sensual, and regardless of the feelings of each other; the constant indulgence of such passions renders them reckless and brutal, and the transition is natural to propensities and habits incompatible with respect for the property of others or for the laws.—*The Tropic*.

BYTOWN MARKETS.

Bytown, 2nd December, 1848.

	£.	s.	D.
Hay per ton,	2	10	0
Oats per bushel,	0	1	1
Flour per brl.	1	2	6
Indian Corn, per bushel,	0	0	0
Oatmeal per kentle,	0	0	0
Peas per. bushel,	0	2	0
Beef per cwt.	0	15	0
Pork per cwt.	1	3	9
Butter per lb.	0	0	6
Potatoes per bushel,	0	1	2

JOHN DARCEY,
Clerk of the Market.

BYE-LAW No. 40, TO AMEND BYE-LAW No. 39, TO ESTABLISH MARKET REGULATIONS IN THE TOWN OF BYTOWN.

BE IT ENACTED by the Mayor and Town Council of the Town of Bytown, that the second and third Section of the 24th Clause of the Lye-Law No. 39, to establish Market Regulations in the Town of Bytown, be amended as follows, viz :—

That the sum of six pence be inserted in place of one shilling, and the sum of three pence be inserted in place of seven pence half-penny in each of the said sections.

Given under the Seal of the Corporation this 25th day of November, 1848.

J. B. LEWIS, Mayor.

September 4, 1847

*In a town built almost entirely of timber and surrounded by
thousands of stacks of cut wood, fire was a constant threat in Bytown.
Virtually every edition of* The Packet *contained several fire stories,
although few were as detailed—and opinionated—as this one.*

FIRE.—A fire which threatened to make much greater ravages than
we have at present to deplore occurred on Monday last about one
o'clock in the Upper Town.—It originated in the premises occupied by
Mr. T. M. Blasdell as a Foundry and Blacksmith's Shop in Wellington
Street. This building, with an adjoining one, occupied by Mrs. D.
Bosquet, was totally consumed in such a short time as to prevent the
possibility of saving even the furniture. The wind being high, fears
were entertained that the fire would cross the Street and communicate
with the Post-Office, &c. This was, however, prevented by some exertion; but unfortunately a few flakes of fire were carried by the wind to
the rear of Wellington Street, and fell in a quarter where no such disaster was expected.—Chaudiere Cottage—the residence of John Burrows, Esq.—was soon a sheet of flame, and other buildings connected
with it, to the number of four or five, were reduced to ashes in a few
minutes. The houses consumed were all built of wood, with the exception of the Blacksmith's Shop, which was of stone.

The wind being unfortunately high, it was utterly impossible to save
any of the above buildings but owing to the active exertions of the
Hook & Ladder Company and the Fire Companies the fire was stayed,
and many buildings in the same quarter were saved. A body of the Rifles attended, under Lieut. Gale, and having with them the Government Fire Engine, were of material assistance. The Hook & Ladder
Company—which is composed of active young men, who made themselves conspicuously useful on this occasion—is not well furnished
with implements for the purpose. They have Axes, Saws and Ladders,
but they want Hooks. Clearer evidence of the want of those Hooks
need not be required than that presented at the fire on Monday. The
inhabitants should see to this matter, and by furnishing this Company
with Hooks, &c., render them truly efficient in case of need. With a
contemporary, we are of the opinion that means should be adopted to
secure a sufficient supply of water when fires occur. By a little management this desirable arrangement might be effected.

The losses by this fire are considerable. Mr. Blasdell we believe to be
the heaviest loser. The value of his property has been computed at
about £1,400. The house occupied by Mrs. Bosquet was owned by Mr. J.
C. Blasdell of Gatineau Mills, and was worth about £400. Mr. Burrows
was also a heavy loser. We are informed that Mr. Burrows lost the
greater part of his furniture, &c. His houses were for the most part

THE PACKET.

OUR COUNTRY.

BY-TOWN: SATURDAY, JAN'Y. 15, 1848.

DOWNFALL OF TORYISM!!!
HURRA! HURRA!! HURRA!!!

THE DAY IS OURS!
BYTOWN HAS DONE ITS DUTY!!!

Majority for Scott, 39.

With feelings of honest pride
we congratulate our readers on
the triumph they have just achieved. The Reform Candidate is
returned by a large majority,
when we consider that the electors are but 300 in number; and,
also, that the Tory Candidate was
the most popular man in the Tory
ranks. But the people of Bytown
struggled for honest principles,
and the result has been such as
to reward them fully for their exertions.

The peace has been pretty well
preserved. Several little scrim-
ages took place, of which we will,
if necessary, give the particulars
next week.

We will not bestow much time
upon matters affecting the defeat
of our opponents this week— we
will give them breathing time,
and then start a-fresh. All we
need say is, that Reformers have
nobly done their work, and

A glorious victory is ours!

small wooden buildings, and we, therefore, imagine that his loss is not so extensive as is reported. No insurance was effected upon the property consumed. A Mr. Harrison, a lodger at Mrs. Bosquet's, lost a large amount of property, and his case is more to be regretted, as we are informed, in consequence of his having lately arrived in this country—his wife being then ill, had a narrow escape from the flames. Mrs. Bosquet also lost all her property.

There is a circumstance connected with this fire which should be known, and if possible measures should be taken to prevent a recurrence of like complaints. The bell hung in the tower of the English Church was silent as the grave during the time the fire raged, although the Church is situated in the immediate vicinity. In the absence of alarm bells, it would have been no great sacrilege to cause even a church bell to rouse the inhabitants to a sense of their danger.

A man named Greene, who left Lower Town to assist the Firemen, was found the next morning at the foot of the Barrack Hill dangerously hurt. The night being very dark, he is supposed to have fallen over the precipice. He is since dead.

October 16, 1847

John Scott, who became Ottawa's first Reform MP in 1848, was the courageous mayor featured in the item below. Given The Packet's *strong Reform leanings, it's interesting to ponder whether a Tory mayor would have received the same glowing coverage.*

On Saturday last, one John Mahon was arrested for an assault upon a person named Sproat. Several of Mahon's friends rescued him from the Constable, and the Constable was severely beaten in the scuffle. His worship the Mayor, hearing of the affray, left the Court House, where he then was, and immediately proceeded to the spot accompanied by James Johnston, Esq., Mr. Powell and one or two others. One of the rioters was in the act of making his escape, where he was pursued by the mayor; he made his way into a house at some little distance and immediately fastened the door. His worship immediately smashed in the door, and securing the culprit by the neck, dragged him to the Gaol, and a true Bill having been found against him by the Grand Jury, he was tried and sentenced within forty-eight hours. The Hon. the Attorney General in his address to the Jury, in the case of the Queen vs. McLeary, paid a high compliment to our newly elected Mayor for his praiseworthy conduct on this occasion.

November 13, 1847

The following item, reprinted from a newspaper in Buffalo, N.Y., is believed to be the first account of a sports event published by The Packet.

BYTOWN FEMALE SEMINARY.

TERMS, PER QUARTER, OF TWELVE WEEKS:

	£	s.	d.
English Branches, according to age and progress of pupil, 10s.: 15s. or	1	0	0
Boys under eight years of age,	0	15	0
Needle-Work,	0	5	0
French,	1	0	0
Drawing,	1	0	0
Music,	1	10	0
Use of Piano,	0	10	0
Board, including English studies, room, Furniture, fuel, and light,	6	0	0

Boarders provide their own bedding' and towels. No deduction made for occasional absence, and no Pupil received for a shorter time than a quarter. The next quarter of this Institution will begin April 2nd, and at its close there will be a vacation of three weeks.

M. FRASER.

Bytown, 7th March, 1849.

FIRE.—On Sunday night last, about eleven o'clock, the large wooden building and premises known as the residence of the late PHILEMON WRIGHT, Esq., the first Settler in the Township of Hull, was discovered to be on fire, and notwithstanding every exertion, this valuable property—erected, we understand, some forty years since—was totally consumed. The Furniture, &c., was saved with great difficulty. The fire is supposed to have originated from some breakage in the Chimney.

April 21, 1849

*It would be another 50 years before the newspaper set aside
a space for daily sports coverage.*

The ten-mile race for $200 was won on Saturday last by Charles Si-
mon, alias Smoke, a Cattaraugua Indian. The competitors were Gildersleeve, John Canada, John Armstrong and Charles Simon, or Smoke,
Steeprock not appearing on that ground. The first mile was made, in 5
minutes, 25 seconds, Gildersleeve keeping the lead. The running was
about the same until the first quarter of the eighth mile, when Simon
darted ahead of Gildersleeve and was followed by Armstrong and
Canada beating Gildersleeve by 28 seconds, and, accomplishing the
mile in 5 minutes, 32 seconds. On the ninth mile, the Indians had it all
their own way, the strife being between Canada and Simon. The tenth
mile was made in 5 minutes and 30 seconds, Simon leading Canada
about four yards, and Armstrong some six yards behind. Whole time
of running, 58 minutes, 17 seconds. Gildersleeve succeeded in getting
in two seconds before the expiration of the hour.— *Buffalo Commercial Advertiser.*

May 12, 1849

Returning from the Church-Yard yesterday, where we had been to assist at the last demonstration of respect to one departed, we were
shown where some excavation had been performed, a Coffin protrud-
ing, containing the remains of some person who had been interred in
the old Church-Yard on Besserer Place, and which had been left when
the removal of the bodies there deposited took place some years since.
As this disagreeable sight must be met with passing through Rideau
Street, we are surprised that the Corporation authorities have not
heard of it. Some attention should be paid to this matter.

September 22, 1849

FATE OF BYTOWN DURING THE PAST WEEK

Over the years, the first major local news story covered by The
Packet *has come to be known as the Stony Monday riots. But the
confrontation—between the English of Uppertown, supported by Tory
farmers, and the Irish and French of Lowertown, Reform-Liberal
backers, over an upcoming visit by the governor general—lasted all
week. The Packet devoted half its news space, roughly 8,000 words,
to the battle, using a diary-like approach of daily segments. Here's an
excerpt covering a standoff on Wednesday, September 19, 1851:*

Early on Wednesday the friends of the Liberals poured into the Lower Town in great numbers from all sides. On the other hand, the Tories
from the settlements of March, Huntley, Goulbourn, Nepean, Fitzroy,

INFORMATION WANTED.
OF MARGARET BUCK, aged 42, and her
three Children—Margaret, aged 18; Mary
Ann, aged 16, and William John, aged 10 years.
They arrived at Quebec by the Ship "Sir Charles
Campbell" on the 6th of October, 1847, and were
last heard of in Montreal, when on the 8th of Oc-
tober they proceeded to Bytown.
  Should this notice meet the eye of any person
who can give information as to their present resi-
dence it will be most thankfully received by the
distressed Husband and Parent, Robert Buck, at
Messrs Drusmore & Kyie's, No. 124, Prat Street,
Baltimore, U. S., or by the Chief Agent for Emi-
gration, Quebec.
  ☞ Upper Canada Papers will confer a favor by
giving this notice a place in their papers.
  Quebec, 12th July, 1848.   4w-23

KILLED BY THE FALL OF A TREE.—A melancholy and mest distressing accident occurred at
Black Rapids, in the township of Nepean, on
Tuesday the 16th inst. Mr. Thomas Moore, a
farmer of that place, was employed, with some
others, chopping in a piece of woods. After falling several trees, he was engaged chopping one of
them in pieces, when a sudden gust of wind threw
down a dry topless trunk, standing near by,
which struck him on the head and almost deprived
him of life. He was unable to speak after receiving the blow, and lived but four hours. The
deceased was a native of Tipperary, Ireland.

April 27, 1850

THE HULL SLIDES.—We would beg to inform the Lumberers on the Ottawa above Bytown that the Slide on the North side of the Chaudiere Falls, on the Ottawa River, late the property of Ruggles Wright, Esq., is this season narrower than it has been heretofore. Cribs of Timber intended to pass through it should not be wider than twenty-two feet over all, from outside to outside.

April, 1850. The job of keeping mistakes out of print was no easier in the 19th century than in the 21st.

IMPORTANT—HULL SLIDES.

We have to correct an error made last week in reference to the width of the Hull Slides. Instead of the width of Cribs being twenty-two feet, as we stated last week, they should be TWENTY-FOUR FEET in width from outside to outside The entire width of the Slide is twenty-four feet and nine inches.

Marlborough &c., flocked in in wagons, all armed in great numbers. Indeed, both parties were as completely armed as if the Country were in a state of civil war. Fortunate, indeed, was it on this occasion that the Town is divided into two parts, at some distance from each other—fortunate was it for the Mayor [Robert Hervey, a Tory supporter] issued a Proclamation to suppress the meeting he had so improperly invited occasion to call, fortunate was it that the peaceable and well disposed inhabitants of the place that some of Her Majesty's troops (handful though they are) were stationed on the ground, drawn up in line across the Sappers Bridge, to prevent a collision of the hostile parties; so but for any one or all of these fortunate incidents one of the bloodiest tragedies on record would forever hereafter have blackened the character of this fair Town, and made it unfit for civilized society. As it was, the day,—and we trust the day will be marked as an event—an event by which it will be remembered that with such an inflamable population as that now surrounding us no Political Meeting can hereafter be held with safety in Bytown,—the day was spent by both parties in hostile array; the one (the Tory party) drawn in line on the brow of the Government Hill overlooking the Canal Locks; the other (the Liberals) in the Market Square of Lower Town, well armed with guns and fixed bayonets, and, we are told, with two pieces of Cannon. Here, then, stood two hostile parts of our population, perhaps 1,000 men in all, armed for battle, within sight, and almost within firing distance of each other for the greater part of a Summer's day. The stranger may well ask,—"Can this be true? Is this the mere painting of a pencil revelling in tragedy? Can such a scene have occurred in the middle of the 19th century, in enlightened Canada"? Alas! "'tis, 'tis true, and 'tis pity 'tis true."

January 12, 1850
MR. CHARLES DICKENS' SUGGESTION
FOR PRIVATE EXECUTIONS

Nineteenth-century newspapers routinely reprinted articles from other publications at no cost. The practice enabled a newspaper like The Packet, *with its limited resources, to throw open a window on the world by carrying articles from the metropolitan dailies in London, New York and Boston. Although* The Packet *could not afford the fiction of a celebrated writer like Charles Dickens—who by 1850 had serialized* Oliver Twist, Nicholas Nickleby, David Copperfield *and* A Christmas Carol *in newspapers around the world—it was able to pick up some of the writing he did for British newspapers. This letter to* The Times of London *was carried on* The Packet's *front page:*

Sir,—My positions in reference to the demoralizing nature of public executions are—First, that they chiefly attract as spectators the lowest, the most depraved, the most abandoned of mankind; in whom they inspire no wholesome emotions whatever. Secondly, that the public infliction of a violent death is not a salutary spectacle for any class of people. From the moment of a murderer's being sentenced to death, I would dismiss him to dread obscurity. I would allow no curious visitors to hold any communication with him. His execution within the walls of the prison should be conducted with every terrible solemnity that careful consideration could devise. Mr. Calcraft, the hangman (of whom I have some information in reference to this last occasion), should be restrained in his unseeming briskness, in his jokes, his oaths and his brandy. To attend the execution I would summon a jury of 24, to be called the Witness Jury, eight to be summoned on a low qualification, eight on a higher, eight on a higher still; so that it might fairly represent all classes of society. There should be present likewise, the governor of the gaol, the chaplain, the surgeon, and other officers, the sheriffs of the county or city, and two inspectors of prisons. All these should sign a grave and solemn form of certificate (the same in every case) that on such a day, at such an hour, in such a gaol, for such a crime, such a murderer was hanged in their sight. There should be another certificate from the officers of the prison that the person hanged was that person, and no other; a third, that that person was buried. These should be posted on the prison-gate for 21 days, printed in the Gazette, and exhibited in other public places; and during the hour of the body's hanging I would have the bells of all the churches in that town or city tolled, and all the shops shut up, that all might be reminded of what was being done. I submit to you that, with the law so changed, the public would (as is right) know much more of the infliction of this tremendous punishment than they know of the infliction of any other. There are not many common subjects, I think, of which they know less than transportation; and yet they never doubt that when a man is ordered to be sent abroad he goes abroad. The details of the commonest prison in London are unknown to the public at large, but they are quite satisfied that prisoners said to be in this or that gaol are really there and really undergo its discipline. I am, Sir, your faithful servant,

Charles Dickens.

March 30, 1850
NOTICE
To the Drunkards and Dram Drinkers, Tavern-Keepers and Tiplers

Myself I'm pledged in the teetotal cause,
Strictly adhering to its stringent laws;

List of Letters remaining in the Bytown Post-Office.

	s.	d.
A		
Ashfield, James	0	1
B		
Barns, Richard (J. Skead)	0	9
Beatty, Elizabeth (J. Milligan)	1	4
Bell, Mm. (Nepean)	0	7
Blake, Jno.	0	9
Blue, John	1	4
Bourke, John	1	4
Bradley, Clements	0	7
Bradley, Joshua	0	9
Brady, Mary, Margt. or Bridget	1	4
Brennan, Thomas	1	1½
Brian, James	1	4
Baker, Abraham	0	0
Brownlee, Thomas	1	1½
Bruli, Honore	0	9
Buisson, Louis	0	9
Burn, Edward	0	7
Butler, Ann	1	4
C		
Cameron, William (Gilmour & Co)	1	4
Cane, Mary	0	9
Carew, Judith	1	4
Cass, Charles	1	10½
Caton, Miss	0	0
Chalou, Lucy	7	0
Chambers, James	1	4
Chaput, Baptist	0	9
Clerke, John	0	0
Corcoran, Jeremiah	0	9
Corcoran, Elizabeth	0	0
Cowan, John (P. McTavish)	0	0
D		
Davie, Patrick (Mr. Perkins)	0	0
Demonlin, Honore	0	9
Doxey, Thomas	0	4½
Duffy, Michael	1	1½
Dunning, Mary [2]	1	6
Durand, Genvieve Dame	0	9

Therefore take notice, all ye tipling crew,
No more I "treat"—no more I drink with you.
Henceforth resolved to make expenses less—
I'll save my cash, and patronize the Press.

DANIEL BENNETT

Woodhouse, Feb. 12, 1850

THE PACKET.

"Our Country."

BYTOWN: SATURDAY, FEB'Y. 15, 1851.

The present number closes the sixth volume of *The Packet*. It is a source of pleasure to be able to congratulate the numerous friends of this paper upon the liberal support it has received, and its extensive and steadily increasing circu'ation. The great aim has been to render it wo·thy of support, and very substantial evidence has been afforded that the efforts bestowed upon it have been duly appreciated. The style and appearance of the paper will be immediately improved, and its name changed. This is the last number that will appear under the present name.

The paper will be called the "OTTAWA CITIZEN," and will be published regularly every Saturday morning as usual. The "CITIZEN" will be ornamented with an appropriate vignette, designed and engraved expressly for it, by the best artists in the country. It is hoped that within a short time the sheet will be made equal to any in Canada in respectability of appearance, and with increased experience every means will be employed to increase its value and usefulness.

With hope and confidence we push forward, trusting that our patrons will appreciate the exertions put forth to render the paper in every way worthy of their support.

April 20, 1850

THE WEATHER.—During the past two weeks the weather has been generally fair, but remarkably cold. The snow is gone, excepting a small patch here and there, where shaded from the sun, and the roads are already dry and dusty. The ice is leaving the Ottawa by degrees, but a good deal remains yet. At Bytown, persons on foot can still cross the river. Some fifty miles from Bytown up the Gatineau, the snow is still deep in the woods, and the ice in some places fit for crossing. Up the Ottawa there is still considerable snow in the woods.

May 24, 1851
A LADY'S EXPENSES
This article was published on Queen Victoria's 32nd birthday.

Some of our modest female readers may like to know the difference between what it costs to keep them, and what Victoria spends: The Queen's salary was fixed by the reformed Parliament, in 1837, at £385,000—nearly two million dollars! This is distributed among a number of titled persons, the Lord Chamberlain, Grooms in Waiting, Gentleman Ushers, and Sergeant-at-Arms, whose duties are to hold watch outside the King's tent, dressed in complete armour, and armed with a bow, arrows, and a sword, and the mace of office. This is in the 19th century! In the Lord Steward's department, the butter, bacon, eggs, and cheese consumed, equals in cost President Filmore's salary. The butcher's bill is nearly $50,000. The Lord Steward gets about $6,000. The kitchen takes about $50,000—the chief cook getting nearly $3,000 salary. This department costs annually £128,386, about $600,000. The department of the Master of the Horse, who gets $15,500 a year, costs £335,000 a year. On one occasion, recently, $335,800 were voted for the Queen's stables, and the same session refused $150,000 for National Education. God save the Queen.

August 16, 1851
THE CIRCUS.
This most respecting company, that have delighted us for three days, left here yesterday morning, carrying the best wishes of the people of Bytown, for their future success, wherever they may go. We are at a

loss to appreciate justly the various performances, and the decent and becoming manner with which it was carried on. We were little prepared to be so innocently amused after the sortie the Bytown Gazette thought proper to make against this Circus, which according to its Editor, was not to be countenanced on account of the immoral effects produced by such exhibition on the mind of men, children and women especially. Really, the Editor of the Gazette is impayable, when forgetting who he is, he robes himself in the garb of an essayist, and decides for the spiritual benefit of his townsmen, what sort of amusement they are to have, and what are those which might prove to be detrimental to their morals. It is a great pity to see, that notwithstanding all his efforts to indispose the public against the Circus—that he has contributed to their success, and he must now acknowledge the fact, that no company of actors has received such an encouragement as the Oriental Circus has received here—and that he has been preaching in the desert when he thought of influencing the people of Bytown, who would be very sorry to take his advice on this, or on that. We would have been happy to given full account of the various performances which have been the delight of all that have witnessed them—and pay our tribute of admiration to the different actors; but want of time and space prevents us from doing so to-day.—We may, if possible, in our next issue give our readers some idea of the impression produced by the lady-like, and admirable horsemanship of Mrs. Cole, who can have no superior in the elegant manner with which she sits in the saddle, and the ease with which she manages her spirited animal.—Mrs. Sherwood will also commend our notice as a good equestrian performer. The gentlemen of the company are also deserving of praise, and were it possible, we would give each and every one of them their due share; but as we have said want of space prevents us. Nevertheless, we cannot conclude this short and imperfect notice without alluding to Mr. Gossin, who as the spirited and merry Clown of the troupe, has kept us constantly in fits of healthful laughter, his bon mots and quick reparties have made him quite a favourite with Bytown, and its inhabitants will long remember the well deserved castigation he gave during the last performance to the Editor of the Bytown Gazette. It elicited from the audience a roar of laughter at the expense of Mr. Powell which we hope (if that is possible) will teach him that his position amongst us is not such as to warrant his giving us advice as to what is morally becoming to the ladies of Bytown.

October 18, 1851

DREADFUL ACCIDENT. A very severe injury was inflicted on an interesting child, eight years old, a son of Mr. Louis Penard of Sussex Street, Lower Bytown, during the early part of the present week, by a

POPULATION OF BYTOWN.

	East Ward.	Centre Ward.	West Ward	Total
Total population,	1905	2587	1767	6259
Natives of				
England,	47	72	165	284
Scotland,	88	76	118	282
Ireland,	529	576	612	1717
Canada French,	677	693	69	1439
do. British,	560	572	744	1876
United States,	3	19	28	50
Other Countries,	1	3	5	9
Not ascertained,	0	576	26	602
	1905	2587	1767	6259
RELIGIONS,—				
Church of England,	146	364	465	975
do. Scotland,	106	130	234	470
do. Rome,	1386	1285	635	3306
Free Presbyterian,	140	64	117	321
Other do.	1	11	2	14
Wesleyan Methodists,	88	64	246	398
Episcopal do.	31	47	3	81
Other do.	0	2	0	2
Independents,	0	18	38	56
Other Denominations,	6	2	27	35
No Creed or do.	1	1	0	2
Not ascertained,	0	599	0	599
	1905	2587	1767	6259

☞ Owing to several errors in correcting the proof of the above return last week, and which escaped notice, we publish it now corrected.

September 28, 1850

kick from a horse, which took the effect on the forehead immediately above the right eye driving in a considerable part of the skull, and lacerating the brain so that parts of its substance escaped through the wound. It was deemed necessary to trepan the little sufferer by the Surgeons in attendance, Drs. Hill and Beaubien, and we are informed that this important operation, which consists in the entire removal of entire parts of the skull, was sufficiently performed by these gentlemen, affording speedy relief to the little patient who was in a dying state; and we are happy to be able to add, he is since doing well, at present there being every prospect of his perfect recovery.

January 11, 1851

January 3, 1852

The sickness during the past week of two of the compositors engaged in the office of this paper is the cause of *The Citizen* appearing only on half a sheet to-day. Under the circumstances no apology is necessary.

March 20, 1852

In 1852, the Citizen *hired V. B. Palmer as its first foreign "agent." Although part of Palmer's job was to drum up advertising in New York, Boston and Philadelphia, his main task was to supply articles from his New York base. Most of his stories, a mix of news, politics, gossip, fashion, arts and crime, were rewritten from other papers. Here's an early dispatch:*

By V. B. Palmer

BY TELEGRAPH

Reported for The Citizen

Via the Bytown & Montreal Line.

New York, March 13.—Mrs. Forrest's reading at Metropolitan Hall last evening, we are sorry to report, was a complete failure. The Hall was well filled, but Mrs. F. broke completely down in her reading.

New York, March 16.—The Steamship El Dorado with the California Mails to February 18th, and 11 millions of dollars in gold arrived at half-past five o'clock, with 130 passengers.

The most important item is the loss of the Steamer *General Washington*, at the mouth of the River Columbia. Passing the bar she become unmanageable in consequence of the roughness of the sea, and drifted towards Clatson-Spit, where she finally struck, the sea breaking over her with great fury. She parted her whole hull, and before assistance could be procured by a host's crew, despatched with extreme difficulty to the shore, every vestige of the wreck had been swept away, and all on board perished, including Captain Thompson. The event caused much gloom among the people. She had on board a cargo of produce valued at $80,000, and was owned by Garrison and Frets of Panama.

April 10, 1852

In the mid-19th century, letters to the editor, especially from travellers,
often provided newspapers with their most fascinating material.
For fine writing, splendid detail, environmental prescience—and
sheer bravado—nothing exceeds this rambling letter from an
unnamed lumberman.

To the Editor of the Bytown Citizen.

MASTER CITIZEN,—I dare say you will be astonished to receive a communication from one of my craft. You and your readers will wonder what in the world can a Raftsman have to write about; and some good natured among them (I mean your readers) may even consider it a piece of presumption on my part to appear in print at all. Well, I own that I am much more accustomed to wield the axe than the pen, but the very nature of my employment for at least six months of the year away in the green woods of the Ottawa leads me to commune with my own thoughts, and reflect on what is passing in the outer world; and although my "few remarks," as Mr. Sparks would say, may not be put down in "well set phrases," I hope I shall meet all indulgence from a "discerning public." Last year, after delivering our Raft in Quebec and getting our hard-earned wages honestly paid us;—last year was a grand year for us Raftsmen for getting paid;—no "due bills payable on the sale of the Raft:" nothing but the cash down;—well, as I said, after getting our money we went into town to make a few purchases, and an off mixture our purchases were;—calico shirts and dancing pumps, Jews Harps and ginger bread. Batiste Fallardeau, one of our broad axe then paid 7s. 6d. for an imaginary likeness of Kossuth [a Hungarian revolutionary], because, as he thought, it bore a striking resemblance to our own Bourgois. When we got clear of a good many dollars in this way, it behooved us to take good care of our goods, and although many of us had trunks already, it was unanimously agreed upon that new ones must be bought,—for, as our Cook said, who is a "bit of a wag," in his way, it would never do to "put new wine in old bottles," so we each bought new seal-skin trunks, and to keep our flashy calico shirts from the rain we must of course have umbrellas. I myself wanted a trunk very much to keep my notes and memoranda from the prying eyes of our Cook, who, I found out, used to read them last winter while I was out in the woods, and worse than all, divulge my "sayings and doings" to the whole Chantier afterwards. So I was determined this should not happen again, and although the lock of my new trunk is not by any means a "Hobbs'," this winter I have heard none of my "wild wood notes" detailed in the "camp." The umbrellas, however, were a bad bargain. The loon of a shopman assured us the ribs were whalebone; instead of that they were nothing but painted wood, and after using mine

BY TELEGRAPH.

Reported for the Citizen.

Via the Bytown and Montreal Line.

Arrival of the Africa.

NEW YORK, March 14.

The *Africa* arrived at this port at half-past three, P. M. yesterday; she brings 58 passengers, and $17,000 in specie. She spoke the *Canada* on the 27th abrest of Sherries, going on. The *Franklin* arrived off Cowes on the 25th, at noon. The *City of Glasgow* from Philadelphia arrived at Liverpool at 10 P. M. on the 25th. The *Africa* was delayed in consequence of a terrific storm at Liverpool, which prevented her mails getting on board.

LIVERPOOL, Feb. 25.
Bright, Grady & Co.'s Circular.

In the absence of speculative enquiry our market continues to wear a quiet aspect. Demand very limited to immediate requirements of dealers. At to-day's market rather less was taken to effect sale, say 2d per 70 lbs for Wheat and 6d per brl. for Flour. Indian Corn nominally the same as last week. Ashes—demand very moderate at 26s 9d per Pots and 28s for Pearls. Lard—sales 50 tons on the spot at 59s and to arrive at 56 per cwt.

Baring's London Circular quotes Wheat and Flour rather cheaper to sell, but not to any quotable extent. Corn held firmly. Iron firm.

In American Stock no material change. The demand has been limited, and in some cases a slight reduction has been submitted to.

In provisions no material change since last month. Transactions in Beef and Pork to a moderate extent at last week's rates.

The most singular feature in the news is that France, while professing to act in conjunction with Australia in the Montenegrin difficulty, is ever on terms of the closest friendship with Turkey.

Apprehensions are entertained of an outbreak in Hungry.

Mazzini is supposed to be at Milan.

Liverpool Cotton Market ⅛d lower. Breadstuffs dull.

ENGLAND.

On Thursday, an important debate took place in the House of Lords, on the subject of war with Ava. Earl Ellenborough moved for the production of a letter written in 1829, by the East India Company, to the Governor General, giving instructions as to the minor operations to be made in any future war with Ava, especially with reference to the proclamation for the annexation of Pegu. Earls

April 9, 1853

in Montreal, where we remained one day on our way up to see the Circus, I found out there was a most perverse disposition on the part of the ribs to retain their last bend. I must acknowledge we were served right in the umbrella business. If we really wanted such articles, we should have purchased them from our own honest Bytown shopkeepers, who would not have cheated us so; besides, if our object was to keep our calico shirts from the rain, I opine parasols would be just as suitable, for the "fast colors," as the rascal called it, were in as much danger from the sun as the rain. I wish, Master Citizen, you could have seen our Cook's calico shirt after the first and only washing it ever had—the sewing was "no where," and the "colors" went "fast" enough, I assure you. I believe now the fellow was poking fun at us when he spoke of these "fast colours." I think I hear you say, what the ——— would this Raftsman fellow be at? Well now, don't get in a passion; just hold on one minute until I tell why it is I have been so particular in my introduction to you and your readers. The fact is, I have a great many things to write about, and if you will so far favour my "few remarks" as to give them place in your paper, the chances are you will hear from me very often. I would just say here, that however much I like your paper for your capital "Editorials" upon the Ottawa country and its capabilities which occasionally appear in your columns, yet your politics and mine do not exactly dove-tail. I know you will be sorry to hear that. Never mind,—I have good hopes for you yet: But the Ottawa is *the* thing—hang politics.

"Revenons a nos moutons"—I found that phrase in a French book I bought from Hew Ramsay in Montreal. He did not cheat me, honest man, altho' Batiste Fallardeau says the Francais in my book is "ver bad," for the simple reason, I suppose, that it does not agree with his own. But we are at my "Notes." On opening my seal-skin trunk, I find the first thing presenting itself has reference to my most intimate friend—the Pine tree. The "Pine tree!" Is there not something poetical in the name of the towering monarch of the forest?—well may the inhabitants of the Ottawa feel grateful to a beneficent Providence for this same Pine tree. Is he a Farmer,—he has a ready market for all his productions, besides employment for himself and horses, should he wish it. Is he a Mechanic,—he has ample work to do. Is he a Store-keeper,—he sells his goods. Is he a hard-working man like myself, he is employed on good wages,—and all on account of the Pine tree. Now, master Citizen, I say that this, my best friend, is ill used,—in fact, shamefully used; and my object solely in addressing you at present is for the purpose of saying something in its defence.

Many a noble White Pine have I helped to "kiss the dust," and it often struck me that if a little more sound judgment and common sense were brought to bear upon the conversion of a White Pine tree into

White Pine Timber it would be of immense service to an Ottawa people. Did you, Sir, ever see the operation of scoring and hewing? If you
did, you will agree with me that the waste of valuable timber is perfectly shameful. I have often made calculations on the loss arising from
our system of "dressing" timber, and I know I am within the mark
when I say that one-third of the most valuable part of the tree is scattered in chips from the axe of the scorer and hewer. Any one who
knows timber will say that the most valuable part of a White Pine is
next the sap, and why arbitrary scales laid down for our present mode
of manufacture compel us to waste this best portion of our Pine, is to
me incomprehensible. We are now "hacking" down White Pine at the
rate of eighteen to twenty millions of feet annually, and altho' our
forests are vast, yet we may have to deplore some day the improvident
system we have hitherto adopted. Let us, therefore, bethink ourselves
in time, and see what can be done to remedy the evil. I will give you my
plan, and if any of your readers can desire one better, I shall be very
glad—only let the subject be brought under consideration at once. Instead of making timber square, I would suggest that it be made Octagon—*that is all.* I am quite aware that great prejudice exists against
radical changes like the one now under consideration, but if I can shew
that the manufacturer can send 33 1/3 per cent more timber to market,
of a better quality, and at a cheaper rate than he is now doing, and that
the consumer will profit in an equal proportion,—it will surely become the bounden duty of all parties interested seriously to give the
matter their consideration. Let any one who doubts my assertion that
one-third of the best timber is lost in squaring the tree just take the
trouble to go into a saw mill when they are sawing logs, he will then
see the quantity of pine timber produced before the log is made
square. An octagon would take off very little more than the sap, and I
am sure timber thus shaped would descend rapids less injured than if
it were square. I don't think the rafting would be more expensive. The
only difficulty would be transport to England, but even this might be
got over by getting some public-spirited Shipowner to take a cargo or
two, even at a higher rate of freight. The House of Gilmour & Co. is
deeply interested in the trade, and I think they would give my plan a
trial, by sending home one or two cargoes. By the way, your Correspondent "Mercator" in your last issue states that the vast operations
of this House in this country are of not much benefit to us. "Mercator"
is on the right track on many points, but he will pardon a Raftsman for
telling him that he ought to be more cautious in giving to the public his
ideas of the "wealth of nations." Our Bourgois when up at our Chantier
last winter told us that the House I am speaking about pays out in one
season on the Ottawa alone £120,000. Who gets this money?—Let the
Farmer, the Mechanic, and the Labourer answer the question, Mr. Mer-

THE CITIZEN.

Our Country.

BYTOWN: JULY 30, 1853.

NEW ADVERTISEMENTS THIS DAY.

County of Carleton Grammar School.
Toronto School of Medicine.
Tailoring, &c.—Stovel & Baines.
Sons of Temperance Demonstration in Aylmer.
Strayed Horse,— Thomas Byrne.

Lord Elgin's Visit to the Ottawa.

His Excellency the Governor General left
Quebec on Tuesday evening last in the
steamer *John Munn,* and arrived at Montreal
between five and six o'clock on Wednesday
morning. Notwithstanding the earliness of
the hour, a considerable concourse of spectators was present to witness the debarka-
tion of His Excellency, to whom several
gentlemen paid their respects. Gen. Rowan
and his staff attended. The troops were
drawn up, and received him with the usual
honors. Shortly after His Excellency proceeded to the Lachine Railroad Station, and
left at the usual hour by the passenger
train and procceded on their tour by the Ottawa River. The steamer *Lady Simpson*
received the party, with passengers and
mails as usual, at Lachine, and leaving that
place at eight a.m. arrived at Carrillon a
few minutes after twelve. A carriage and
four horses had been sent from Bytown the
day before to convey the distinguished vis-
iters over the road to Grenville, and were
accordingly turned into the service. The
day was beautiful, and all parties appeared

cator. Would that we had many more such establishments upon the Ottawa. I must now really have some regard for your nerves, and "stop the steam." I am on a visit to Bytown engaging additional hands for the spring, and must be off to-morrow morning, but there is a great deal more in the "Seal-skin," and any drafts upon it will be duly honoured. Meanwhile. I am, with much respect,

   Master Citizen, yours

      A RAFTSMAN

      Bytown, 8th April, 1852

July 3, 1852

ACCIDENT.—As the Hon. Thos. McKay's carriage was passing over the Sappers' Bridge on Wednesday evening last the pole straps broke, and the horses became unmanageable. The consequence was that the carriage was hurled with great violence against the log railing, and the inmates of the vehicle precipitated over the bridge,—a height of about 15 feet. Mrs. McKay, and Mrs. Parker from Montreal, Miss McKay, and a nurse and child, were in the carriage at the time. Mrs. McKay fell upon her head, and was very seriously hurt. The others received greater or less injuries, with the exception of the nurse, who was but slightly bruised, and the child, which, by the presence of mind of the nurse who disregarded her own safety, was protected from harm. The parties were immediately taken up and medical assistance obtained. They were shortly afterwards sufficiently recovered to be carried home on litters.

DREADFUL.—On Wednesday night last a man by the name of Rossineault, employed in the New Edinburgh Mills, in attempting to light his pipe from the gas light immediately above one of the circular saws, slipt and fell upon the saw. In a moment he was a ghastly corpse,—the saw in a single revolution exposing the poor man's heart and lungs to view.

March 12, 1853

STEAM ENGINE MANUFACTORY IN BYTOWN.—Amongst the growing manufactories of our rising City, we have much pleasure in noticing Mr. T. M. Blasdell's establishment in Upper Bytown, and especially we wish here to draw attention to the fact that Steam Engines are now manufactured by Mr. Blasdell and can be furnished here of such description and at such price as to enter this manufactory an advantage to this part of Canada. Mr. B. is now finishing a horizontal bed-frame engine for the new steam sawmill at the Gatineau point, opposite Bytown, owned by A. Leamy, Esq. The engine is computed forty-horse power, with three feet stroke and seventeen inches bore. It is intended to make sixty revolutions per minute. The fly-wheel is twelve feet diameter, of cast metal throughout, and weighs two tons. The boiler is tubular and is fully in proportion to the cylinder. Another engine is also in progress of being made to order. Mr. Blasdell is prepared to execute orders for steam engines of almost any description up to eight feet stroke and seventy-horse power, either high or low pressure, and for all kinds of mill machinery. While we congratulate the people of Ottawa country on the increase of important facilities for furthering enterprise, we trust Mr. B. will receive the liberal encouragement to which, for his enterprise and perseverance, he is fairly entitled.

June 11, 1853

Not surprisingly, the Citizen *championed the idea of selecting Bytown as the permanent capital. Here's an excerpt from an editorial written as the impracticality of rotating Parliament between Quebec City and Toronto was becoming increasingly unpopular with politicians and the public.*

On the question of the final location of the seat of government there are several opinions afloat, some of which are no doubt considerably influenced by the interested position of the parties who give expression to them. If we were to record our disapprobation of the antiquated and expensive system of travelling parliaments, it would of course be suspected that the welfare of Bytown constituted our principal motive for so doing. We can, however, support the claims of this town to become the permanent seat of government, and at the same time keep the general interests of Canada in view. A person living in another country and having the map of the province before him, and having no interest in one part more than another would, if the question were submitted to him, reason thus:—The inhabitants of this country are settled not in a circular space but in a long and narrow belt of territory, extending nearly east and west from Lake Huron to the Gulf of St. Lawrence, a distance of over one thousand miles. In a north and south direction this chain of settlements is in no place much more than one hundred miles in width. It is ten times longer than wide. The people at one end are entitled to as much consideration as those at the other end or in the middle. The object of furnishing them with a government at all is to provide for the general welfare of all, and not for the especial benefit of any particular number living or being privately interested in any one locality. All have more or less business to transact at headquarters. If the seat of the legislature, where all the public business of the province is transacted, be placed at one end, then all the people at the other extremity will be obliged to travel the whole length of the country to attend to their affairs, while their more favoured countrymen would have the public offices at their own doors. One portion of

By-Law No. 99.

By-Law to Tax the Town of Bytown for the Year of our Lord 1853 for the payment of the County Rate, and for other purposes therein contained.

BE IT ENACTED and ORDAINED by the Town Council of the Town of Bytown, and it is hereby by the said Town Council Enacted and Ordained, That there shall be Rated, Assessed, Levied and Collected during the present Financial Year upon the whole taxable Real and Personal Property within the Town of Bytown (over and above the Rates and Taxes already imposed by special By-laws) the following Rates and Taxes for the following purposes for the present year, that is to say,---

For the payment of the County Rate to the Municipal Council of the County of Carleton the sum of Eight Pence Half-penny in the Pound.

For the payment of the sum required for Common School purposes the sum of Five Pence and One Farthing in the Pound.

For the payment of the sum required to be levied for the Provincial Lunatic Asylum the sum of One Penny in the Pound.

For the payment of the Salaries of the different Officers of this Municipality, for improving and maintaining the Streets and Side Walks in the said Town, and for general purposes chargeable by Law against the said Town, the sum of One Penny in the Pound.

And be it further Enacted and Ordained, That this By-Law shall take effect immediately after the passing thereof.

Given under the Corporate Seal of the Town Council of the Town of Bytown this Eighth day of August in the year of our Lord one thousand eight hundred and fifty-three.

J. B. TURGEON,

By 1853, Bytown had adopted a more sophisticated emblem featuring a pine and a river.

the people will thus be better dealt with than the others. To give them this advantage would be practising that species of favouritism so odious to all free nations. No reason can be assigned for such a course of proceeding, unless it be that the parties who advocate so unfair a measure are influenced by the most disgusting partiality, and by the desire of increasing the value of their own property, and those of their relations and supporters. The general interests of the country cannot be the cause of such a course of public conduct, for the reason that common sense proclaims that to locate the seat of government at one end instead of in the centre, is not the best way of conserving those interests. The centre of the province, no matter who may be personally interested in that spot, is the place for the seat of government. We think that we can venture upon this statement without rendering ourselves liable to the charge of saying anything contrary to the interests of the country. When the contrary is proved then we shall undergo a recantation of our opinion in this respect, but not until then.

September 10, 1853

BRUTAL OUTRAGE.—It is not often that we have to record an outrage in our town of so gross a character as that which took place upon Wednesday night last. About midnight several men armed with clubs broke into the house of a man named Nahill, in Rideau street, Lower Bytown, and nearly murdered him and his wife while lying in bed. Nahill was so brutally beaten that his life is despaired of, but his wife and a child who was in bed with them, escaped without any very serious injury. A girl who was sleeping in the next room was the only other person in the house, but she was in such a state of fright that she gave no alarm. We understand that some clue has been got towards the detection of the low-minded and cowardly ruffians who have perpetrated this inhuman act; but as yet they have not been arrested.

May 13, 1854

Long before Ottawa had professional musicians, concerts by amateurs represented the pinnacle of local culture. The Citizen *rarely missed one of these events, and usually provided an enthusiastic account.*

MR. FRASER'S CONCERT.—Mr. J. Fraser's second Concert came off on the evening of Wednesday, the 10th inst., with great *eclat*. The performers were as follows,—

Mr. Fraser and his two sons on Cornets.
Mr. R. Lyon, Violin
Mr. Marsan, Piano
Mr. Duff, Flute.

GRAND PIC-NIC EXCURSION,
UNDER THE PATRONAGE OF THE
Young Mens' St. Patrick's Association.

THE Members of the YOUNG MENS' ST. PATRICK'S ASSOCIATION beg most respectfully to announce that they intend to treat the Sons and Daughters of Old Ireland, and their Friends in Bytown, to a GRAND PIC-NIC EXCURSION, on

THURSDAY, the 7th instant,

They will leave Bytown at HALF-PAST FIVE O'CLOCK in the Morning, on board the Steamer PHŒNIX, and proceed down the Ottawa, to a beautiful and romantic spot, where they will spend the remainder of the day, until the return of the *Phœnix*, in the enjoyment of all the amusements and comforts customary on such occasions.

The Splendid BAND of the Society will be in attendance, together with other accomplished Musicians.

Tickets, to admit a Lady and Gentleman, 10s.— To be had at the Stores of Messrs. J. O'Meara, Wellington Street, Upper Town; E. Smith, York Street, M. Loughran, Patrick Street, F. Doherty, E. Cunningham, and H. Craig, Sussex Street, J. Heany, George Street, Lower Town, and at the Hotel of Mr. Daniel Goode.

By Order,
M. O'BOYLE,
Secretary.
Bytown, August 31, 1854.

September 2, 1854

Mssrs. Duff and Marsan sang several songs, which were loudly applauded and encored, as also was the singing of Mr. Paisley, who sings Scotch songs with great effect. The instrumental performances of Mssrs. Fraser, Lyon, Marsan and Duff were beautiful. The house was crowded with a highly respectable audience, who testified their satisfaction by most rapturous applause. These two entertainments, consisting altogether of native talent, were exceedingly creditable to the amateurs by which they were conducted.

August 26, 1854

A crib of timber with nine men upon it, on Tuesday morning last, missed the proper channel and was carried to the very verge of the cataract of the Chaudiere. When within thirty or forty feet of going over it grounded on a rock and stuck fast. The river here tumbles over a precipice into a deep chasm, from the depths of which there usually rises a cloud of deep spray, like the steam from a boiling cauldron, and hence the name Grand Chaudiere, or "big kettle," bestowed upon the place by the old French voyageurs, who first ascended the stream. The position of the crib was upon the edge of this gulf, and to have been precipitated into it would have been certain death to the whole crew. Fortunately, the water is so low that the people from the shore could approach the other side of the ravine, and by slinging a fishing line across with a stone which was caught by the men, a small rope was first drawn over and then a hawser.—A derrick was then erected, and a bridge consisting of a single rope, like those sometimes used for crossing chasms in mountainous regions, was thus formed. An iron ring was so arranged that it could slide from one end of the rope to the other. To this ring the men were slung and hauled across, one at a time dangling over the yawning gulf below, and at times enveloped in the spray. Their escape has been almost miraculous.—By the merest chance the crib was arrested within five seconds of taking the leap, when all would have been launched into eternity. The gentlemen who were the most active in their exertions to rescue those men from the peril in which they were placed, were the Messrs. Alphonso and Charles Wright, and Mr. Waggoner, of Hull; Mr. Wm. Mackay, of Bytown; and Mr. Baldwin, (of the State of New York) proprietor of one of the sawmills at the Chaudiere. To these gentlemen all praise is due for their exertions in saving the lives of a number of their fellow creatures under circumstances which required a great deal of courage, coolness, and not a little of engineering skill.

Willam S. Hunter, Jr.'s engraving of the Chaudiere heroism described in the Citizen was reprinted far and wide.

sympathized with the ......
South." The New Yorker replied
through Adams & Co.'s Express, a
e "City Directory."

almerston has been distributing meri-
nsions from the civil list, much to the
n of the English literary world. The
e been particularly favored. Among
ents of his favor are the daughters of
outhey, of Leigh Hunt, Professor Bell,
s of Mrs. Jameson, the widows of
aydn, Professor Henfrey, Lady Bren-
Mrs. Barber. They have received
000.

. BEECHER AND HIS CHURCH.—One
and twenty-five members of Plymouth
Brooklyn have enlisted—among them
echer's oldest son, and the bethrothed of
t daughter. A member of the church
ged to furnish every one going from
ch with revolvers, up to the number of
he church will make ample provision
utfits of its members. In the church
every day, from 9 to 1 o'clock the
the congregation meet for the purpose
ng up articles necessary for soldiers.—
avery *Standard.*

REBEL LOSS AT CHARLESTON.—A native
nont, residing in Charleston wrote to his
in Windsor County Vt., that in one
fter the attack on Fort Sumpter, he as-
n carying more than *two hundred dead*
away from the Floating Battery and
umming Point Battery. From the tes-
of many witnesses, it appears certain
e accounts of the attack on Fort Sumter
road by the authorities of South Caro-
ere false in regard to both the living and
ad.

E CONSOLIDATED STATUES.—It has been
nced in the *Leader* that a copy of the
olidated Statues will be forwarded to every
ied magistrate in Canada. The Gover-
ought to have come to this determination
ago. How can magistrates be expected
minister the law when they have no access
e recent statues? The public money could
e more usefully employed than in circulating
s of the Consolidated Statues throughout
Province to the qualified magistrates. We
ct the supply for this County will be re-
d shortly.

OW TO GET EARLY TOMATOES.—An emi-
gardner thus writes :—A good large turnip
r better than any hot-bed for propagating
y tomatoes. Cut off the top, and scoop out
shell three quarters of an inch thick. Fill
cavity with rich mould, plant half a dozen
ls, and place the turnip in a box of loam.—

IT IS READ BY ALL CLASSES,

—AND—

Political Parties.

It has no Forced Circulation !

Though more extensively taken in the Ottawa

country, and especially in the adjoining town-

ships, than any other local journal which gives

it a preeminence as an

ADVERTISING MEDIUM !

VALUABLE

To the Man of Business !

WHEN YOU ASK FOR

GLENFIELD PATENT STARCH,

SEE THAT YOU GET IT,

As inferior kinds are often substituted.

WOTHERSPOON & CO., Glasgow & London.

September 11, 1860.   [99]†

ORDNANCE LANDS,
OTTAWA.

Change in the Air

The Second Decade, 1855-1864

"ELEMENTS OF CHANGE are swirling in the surrounding air," Robert Bell wrote on Dec. 29, 1854, the day the Bytown & Prescott Railway's first scheduled train pulled in to Bytown. Little did the *Citizen* owner—and railway president—realize how right he was. To be sure, the railway signalled new opportunities for the backwater lumber town, opening it to the outside world in ways steamer and stagecoach could not. But even bigger changes were swirling for Bytown. Before the decade that began Jan. 1, 1855 with a new name for Bytown drew to an end, Ottawa would be Canada's capital, the city's population would triple to 14,000 and the job of remaking Barrack Hill with a series of magnificent stone governmental buildings would be well under way.

The decade meant significant change for the *Citizen*, too. By the close of 1864, the *Citizen* still sold the most papers in town, but it faced competition from six newspapers, half of them recently established in hopes of cashing in on Ottawa's potential as the capital. Of course, the *Citizen* had the same idea, and was already well ahead of the game. In 1859, Bell had imported a state-of-the-art Taylor steam-driven cylinder press from New York, a technological leap that allowed him to run off 2,000 papers an hour and publish the *Citizen* twice a week, Tuesday and Friday. By the early 1860s, the *Citizen* was also putting out a Saturday edition, a sort of "Best of" issue for readers without the time, or money, for two papers a week. (An annual subscription to the *Citizen* semi-weekly sold for $3. The Saturday edition cost $1.50 a year.)

The new press further enabled Bell to dramatically increase his general printing capacity, so that by 1861, the newly incorporated Citizen Steam Job Printing Office was the busiest in the capital, turning out almanacs, advertising sheets, catalogues, calendars and posters for businesses across the city. The printing office, located in the same building

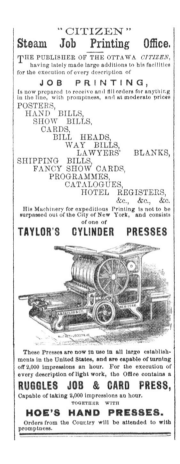

Opposite, May 14, 1861: An editor with a sharp pen and rust-brown ink scratched an angry message to the printer that a line (called a "rule" in the print shop) should have separated the Citizen ad from the one below it. The error in "political" may have first awakened his annoyance. The editions that survive from this era appear to be the newspaper's own markup copies, punctuated by scrawls and clippings.

as the newspaper on Rideau Street, also began to attract government work, starting with the City of Ottawa's book of bylaws. In late 1863, with Bell now sitting in Parliament as the Conservative member for Russell County, the *Citizen* printing office was awarded the lucrative contract to handle the bulk of the national government's printing jobs.

The next year, amid the charges of pork-barrel politics that followed, Bell decided he had too many balls in the air—he was also operating a book and stationery store in addition to his duties as an MP, major railway investor and newspaper publisher—and put the *Citizen* up for sale. It was a decision that would bring momentous change to the newspaper scene in Ottawa.

January 20, 1855

LECTURE ON WOMENS' RIGHTS.—On Wednesday evening Mrs. Cridge from Ohio, delivered a very instructive and interesting lecture on this subject at the West Ward Market Hall to a crowded audience. The views of the advocates of womans' rights, as explained by Mrs. Cridge, are in substance that women are not in general inferior to men in mental power, and that with the same amount of education, they would be quite competent to labour in a more extended sphere of action than that to which they are by the usages of this age confined. She contends that it would be well for the general happiness of society if industrial schools were established in all parts of all countries, and that in those schools should be taught, by competent teachers, aided by philosophical apparatus, the principles of chemistry, natural philosophy, geology, and agriculture, and that girls should be instructed in all those branches as well as boys. They should be taught to be useful as well as ornamental, and the consequences would be that in life the cares of the mother, the wife, and governess of the household, would fall more lightly upon them. The fashionable system of education is faulty, inasmuch as it is not of a practical nature unless supported by wealth.

Should poverty overtake persons thus educated, they become helpless and miserable creatures. Women, no matter what may be their rank in society, have many difficulties to overcome; and it would be well for them if in early life, their intellects were supplied with every species of knowledge which might become of service to them in their day of trial. Yet according to the present system they are not thus fortified to fight the battle of life, and the advocates of women's rights contend that to leave them this mentally destitute, is a great injustice. We think so too; but while in favour of educating the ladies, we think it would be of no great service to them to take part in elections and politics generally,—matters which most naturally belong to the rougher sex. There is no reason that we know of why they should be prohibited the right of doing so, but we would recommend them rather to turn their whole attention towards making their homes as happy and as comfortable as possible. We are somewhat in favour of the division of labour. Let the woman reign in her own kingdom—the house, and strive to make it a delightful resting place for those who look to her for comfort and love, and she will be blessed. Let man's department be to go abroad and buffet the storm, and provide the materials of support, and bring them home for woman to expend her ingenuity upon them, and if she succeed he also does well. But let either undertake both of these labours and neither will be done well. This is our view at present. Mrs. Cridge delivered one of the best and most instructive discourses ever heard in this city. She was listened to with the greatest attention, with one or two ignorant exceptions, which were promptly silenced by the respectable part of the audience.

January 27, 1855

It is with much regret that we feel ourselves called upon to notice a very disgraceful proceeding which took place in our city during the last week. A French Canadian by the name of Sicord, a master carter, died after a painful illness of several weeks.—During his sickness it is said that he was frequently disturbed and annoyed by parties who had taken offence at his having become a Protestant. The people who attended his funeral on Thursday were also insulted while following his remains to the grave, and during the evening a "charivari" [the banging of drums and pans to drive away evil spirits] was got up in front of a house in which some of Sicord's relations were residing. The names of the parties engaged in this outrage upon the common decencies of humanity should be ferretted out, and handed down to posterity with disgrace. Several persons were arrested upon a charge of having been concerned in this brutal row, but brought forward evidence to show that they were not guilty, and they were accordingly discharged. The promptness with which this matter was taken up by the city authorities shows it to be their intention to put a summary end to all proceedings of this kind. For the credit of our rising city, we hope that not only they, but all future Councils, may persevere in this determination. It is bad enough to insult the living, but after life's fitful fever is over, no matter in what faith a man may die, his enemies have no more to do with him. He is no longer in the hands of man to be judged.

October 14, 1859

For reasons lost to time, only a few issues of the Citizen *published between early 1855 and late 1859 have survived. Perhaps fire destroyed back copies of the paper kept by journalists for reference, or perhaps they were lost during renovations in the late 1850s. Whatever*

The Ottawa Citizen.

OTTAWA: DECEMBER 20, 1859.

Breaking Ground for the Parliament Buildings.

GRAND DEMONSTRATION IN HONOR OF THE EVENT!!!

This morning the ceremony of breaking ground for the commencement of the Parliament Buildings is to take place on Barrack Hill, in presence of Commissioner Rose and Assistant Commissioner Keefer, who arrived here yesterday from Quebec, for the purpose of approving of the marking out of the site, and being present at the ceremony of turning the first sod. To mark so important an event in the history of Ottawa, and the dedication of one of her noblest cliffs to the permanent occupation of our provincial rulers, it has been determined by our spirited citizens to get up a grand demonstration on Wednesday evening, in honour of the occasion. A torch-light procession, bonfires, and a display of fireworks, form a part of the programme. A great time generally may be looked for.

the reason, this three-and-a-half-year period pre-dates the establishment of the Library of Parliament, which was later to gather most of the early Canadian newspapers that exist in collections today. It also explains the gap in articles contained in these pages.

A PARAGRAPH FOR BOYS.—It is one of the besetting sins of the young man in this extravagant age, to endeavor to get rid of work by seeking for easy and lazy employment; and the consequence is, that many of them turn out worthless vagabonds. Boys, avoid this whirlpool as you would a plague spot; banish your dangerous desire to live without work. Labor is honorable, dignified, it is the parent of health, wealth and happiness; look upon it as an invaluable blessing and never as a burden or a curse. Shun idleness and sloth; pursue some honest calling and be not ashamed to be useful.

November 4, 1859

LADY FRANKLIN

Fascination with the last days of Arctic explorer Sir John Franklin continues to this day. But in the years after his mysterious death in 1847, Franklin was practically an obsession with newspapers and their readers, as this decorous homage to his widow demonstrates.

Before the fate of Sir John Franklin, which held the world so long in suspense, fades out of men's minds, we feel impelled to a duty, strangely neglected by our contemporaries, to say a few words of one of the noblest human beings that has ever illustrated the passable excellence of humanity. It is not of the hero, whose bones are bleaching on the Arctic coast, that we would speak, but of her who, by the shores of the Mediterranean, thinks of him only.

If it were not for fidelity such as Lady Franklin's we should begin to doubt the value of humanity itself. It is great passions that ennoble our race. It is unselfish attachment to something out of one's self that brings back our lost faith in human excellence. In general, men illustrate the nobleness that is in them by devotion to some great cause—to liberty, to science, to philanthropy, to a party, a church, or a nation. But women are created to show the exquisite beauty of their natures, by an utter devotedness to one.

While we would not disparage a Joan of Arc, or a Florence Nightingale, we confess that Lady Jane Franklin is, to us, nearer the ideal of a woman, and so more truly noble. We think that every one feels this, and it is strange to us that it has not been more freely said. The great dramatist thrilled the heart of the world when he made his heroine say:

"Thither where he lies buried;

EXTENSIVE CONFLAGRATION!

DESTRUCTION OF McKAY BROS.' FLOURING MILLS!

$60,000 worth of Property Destroyed!

About 12 o'clock on Wednesday night the extensive Grist Mills belonging to the Messrs. McKay, and situate in the village of New Edinburgh, contiguous to this city, were discovered to be on fire, and shortly afterwards became, with its valuable machinery and other contents, a mass of ruins. The fire companies, owing to the inefficiency of the alarm, were not upon the ground until all hope of saving the buildings had been abandoned; but they exerted themselves in preventing the spread of the flames to the adjoining outbuildings, and were successful. Owing to the extensive operations going on in the mills at this season of the year, the stock of grain was necessarily large, and the loss in consequence greatly increased. There were in the

January 13, 1860

That single spot is the whole world to me."

This is woman, as God made her. So long as there was the faintest shadow of a belief that her husband might be suffering anywhere on earth, the wife could not rest. Her heart was not in any of the beautiful homes of England.

She could not enjoy the fragrance of flowers, nor the beauty of the rich parks where ages of cultivation have spread around an earthly paradise. She was silent in society, and sad when alone. Forever she saw in waking musings and midnight dreams wide wastes of frozen waters, grinding packs of ice floes, wrecked vessels and worn-out men lying down to die. Rising up from an enforced quiet that became unendurable, she compelled her world to arouse itself to rescue her husband. Old sea captains, men to whom the north star had been nearly vertical; whalers who had chased their prey along the coast of Greenland; lords of the Admiralty, the Queen on her throne, all were overborne by the love of this lone woman to listen to her paramount demand for her husband's rescue. The British parliament paused in debate upon war abroad and reform at home, to vote supplies for Lady Franklin; the American Congress hushed its stormy conflicts over the destinies of the linked States of its Western world to give its attention and its sympathy to Lady Franklin. Rich merchants and bankers in England and America offered their wealth, and the noblest seamen and gentlemen on both sides of the broad ocean volunteered to risk their lives at the pleading eye and voice of Lady Franklin. Surely the world has not seen a more touching spectacle.

For twelve years she went patiently forward. The veterans of the ice-world went to the frozen ocean, and returned to report that all was in vain. Our gallant Kane offered up his life as a sacrifice; Van Dieman's Land even sent a contribution of eight thousand dollars to help in the search. At last the British government lost all hope, and the name of Sir John Franklin was stricken from the rolls of the navy. All men urged the one heart to give up the search. But she listened, unpersuaded. When they all wearied, there was one thing, there was one more thing that she could do. She still possessed property of her own, and piece by piece it was sold to penetrate into the regions of eternal ice, to find her living or dead husband.

The love's sublime; but the intellect also. It was not helpless clinging to the heart of the world; it was not mere tears that moved the sympathy of stalwart men. This great love laid under contribution the energy of a strong and comprehensive intellect. No chart of the icy Ocean that she did not pore over. No volume filled with Arctic details of glacier and berg, and ice-foot and the strange possibility of an open sea enveloping the pole, that she had not learned by heart. No possible

March 27, 1860

method of examining any square foot of that mysterious region, yet unsearched, that she had not considered. No trait of Greenlander or Esquimaux that she had not studied. More familiar than England itself were these waters of perpetual desolation.

She had succeeded. His fate is ascertained. As in the beautiful story told by Mrs. Jameson of the heroic German girl who travelled to Eastern Siberia to save her brother, she found "only a grave;" but still she found it. Sir John Franklin does not suffer anywhere on earth. She has done what she could. She has stopped at the utmost limit of human effort. She has stopped where Omnipotence intervened and said, "Thus far shalt thou come and no farther."

We do not know how this strikes our readers, but we confess that it affects us profoundly. The English people should do homage to this lady. She has exalted her nation; she has added new lustre to human nature itself. A pension larger than her expenditures should be given her by the British Government and women throughout the civilized world should unite in some testimonial to her. She has not led armies; she has not made discoveries in science; she has not nursed wounded men in hospitals; she has not gone to teach Christianity to savages. But she has done something nobler still. It has been said of the greatest genius that the world has yet seen, that his greatness consisted in this, that of the commonest materials he constructed most magnificent structures. It is so with Lady Jane Franklin. The most common duty of woman, in her hands, has become the sublimest of human virtues. (*From the Boston Traveller*)

By the 1860s, ads were appearing with increasingly sophisticated engravings as illustrations. The Victoria House, above, sheltered the Prince of Wales during his 1860 visit. Pictured in another edition was Campbell's Hotel, below.

CAMPBELL'S   HOTEL,
SUSSEX STREET. OTTAWA

November 8, 1859
INQUEST

A death of a most extraordinary character took place in this city on the 2nd, the particulars of which, as they came out in the inquest are these: some of the men in Mr. Yedling's employment were about to slaughter an ox, and had attached one end of a rope to the horns, and passed the other through the door, into the slaughter house, and were driving the animal in.

The boy, Simon O'Donnell,—on whom the inquest was held,—held a candlestick in one corner of the shed, to throw light on the proceedings. When the beast was driven in, it appears that it made a sudden movement towards the corner where the boy was, and was instantly seized by the nose, by one of the butcher's dogs, when it roared out loudly, and the boy dropped to the ground in an instant, perfectly dead. The jury returned a verdict that the death of the boy was occasioned by "fright," and recommended that in future boys should not be admitted into slaughter houses, while the killing of cattle is going on.

November 18, 1859
John Brown's unsuccessful effort to arm slaves with weapons he and his
followers had stolen from a federal arsenal in Harper's Ferry, Virginia,
set off a flurry of anti-slavery indignation in Canadian newspapers.

GAGGING THE PRESS.—The slave hunters of Virginia, not satisfied with gagging their runaway negroes, have undertaken to muzzle the press; and to this end, have excluded the New York *Tribune* from their State. If it be a true maxim, that drowning men catch at straws, the Southern slaveholders must be in a sinking condition. The State trials of Brown and his colleagues have aroused the slumbering sympathies of the North, and already the traffickers in human flesh, anticipating danger to their "peculiar institution," blindly rush to the rescue, and commit enormities which they determine shall not come to light through the medium of a fearless press. But, they are like the little boy who shut his eyes and imagined himself invisible. On every Christian altar a light will burn to shew the accursed tendencies of slavery, both on the oppressor and the oppressed, and ere long the very tyrannical exertions now put forth to maintain and perpetuate the institution must aid in crumbling its bloody pillars into dust.

December 30, 1859
MODESTY AND MERIT SUFFERING BADLY
Henry J. Friel, a former mayor and Packet *owner, started a rival paper, the* Union, *in 1858 to help his political aspirations. When the* Union *shamelessly promoted Friel's run for mayor in the 1860 election—not an uncommon practice in that era—the* Citizen *couldn't resist the chance to mock him as a would-be saint, and to plug his rival, Alexander Workman. The item is a fine example of the spirited rivalries among newspapers of the day. As it turned out, Friel lost badly. However, he would become mayor again in 1863.*

We feel in duty bound to give due consideration to the following extracts from an article in Mr. Friel's paper, the *Union*, of the 28th instant, on the subject of the Mayoralty:

"The candidate upon whom the public voice unites in reference to all the requisite qualifications is unquestionably Mr. Friel. No one dreams of comparing him in this respect with either of his competitors. The present time requires extraordinary energy, capacity, activity, reliability and determination of purpose. To Mr. Friel or any other man the Mayoralty can be but a heavy burden and a serious responsibility, which he would do well to repel did he not desire the general welfare, rather than his own case or personal gratification."

The conclusion is a gem. Here it is:—

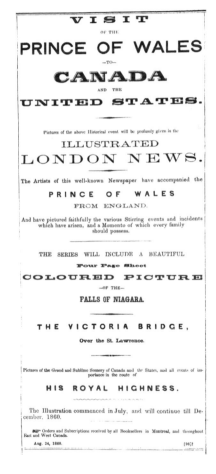

September 1, 1860

Brough, Brother & Co. sought attention in the 1860s with ads turned sideways, running nearly the full depth of the page.

"Amongst all classes he has warm friends; and unfettered as he is by intrigues, dodges, pledges or prejudice, his cause is the purest, and deserves, consequently, to be the most successful. Monday and Tuesday next will decide which shall triumph—Friel and the public interest, or weakness, intrigue and deception."

A perfect man is a rare sight. Such a person is not fitted for this world, and should leave it as speedily as possible. It is quite clear to us, and must be so to the public as well, that if the above extract be correct, Mr. Friel is totally unfit to be mayor of this City. He should be canonized as a saint. Such a paragon of perfection—so pure and free from all dodges, intrigues and prejudices, it would be grossly wrong to put him in the way of temptation. This new condition of ignorance of evil-doing on his part, and sublime superiority, it appears only commenced last Wednesday,—at least the public had no earlier notice thereof;—and as it cannot as yet have acquired much strength from habit, we cannot assume that this "greenhorn" in perfection would be proof against a severe shock of any kind in the way of temptation. Besides, we have reason to complain that the public have been taken by surprise. The notice is too short. A month's notice, at least, should have been given by Mr. Friel of the happy and auspicious change in his quality and condition.

To say that Mr. Friel's abuse of Mr. Workman,—direct and indirect,—is evidence of his remaining imperfections, must go for nothing. Under other circumstances it might avail, but it is nothing against Mr. Friel's declaration of his own excellence. He publicly professes a character that nobody supposed he ever owned, or ever will own by right. But it is quite clear that either Mr. Friel is a perfect mortal, as he professes to be, or he is not. If perfect, he is unfit to meddle in election matters, and if not perfect his profession is not correct, and he must be as he has been heretofore—a very frail mortal especially as regards elections. For him to assail Mr. Workman is only adding so much to the farce perhaps that is necessary to make it complete, but we can scarcely believe that the people of this city are yet prepared to play it out for him as desired at his bidding.

February 17, 1860
PROGRESS OF THE PUBLIC BUILDINGS
The Citizen's *excitement over the construction of the governmental buildings undoubtedly reflected the pride of Ottawa residents, but their erection was also good for the newspaper's business. The government chose the* Citizen *and Toronto* Globe *as its main vehicles to call for construction tenders, a significant and regular source of revenue for the papers between the start of construction in 1859 and the buildings' completion a decade later. During that time, the* Citizen

carried regular progress reports, and as an 1860 New Year's gift to
subscribers, published an architect's engraving of the buildings.

With a view to satisfy a very natural and proper curiousity on the
part of our readers out of the city, we yesterday visited Barrack Hill—
the site of the Public Buildings. But it is not now the picturesque and
beautiful promenade our citizens were wont to resort to.—Its surface
lies hidden beneath immense heaps of building materials, or upturned
for foundation walls. Indeed, so completely does confusion reign that
it requires a stretch of fancy to imagine that out of the chaotic mass
now spread over every available spot of its forty-three acres, the architects' elegant picture will be realized. Still, these very signs betoken
the completion of the undertaking, and that, too, at an earlier day than
is generally imagined.

But to be more precise. During our visit we ascertained on examination that the excavation for the Departmental Buildings will be completed during the ensuing week, and that there is on the grounds a sufficient quantity of stone, sand and other materials to complete the
basement storey, which will be immediately and vigorously pushed on.
The Parliament Building itself is likewise progressing rapidly although
the nature of the work renders the excavation more tardy, as it is in
part composed on solid rocks, which have to be removed by blasting.
Even in view off this obstacle, the work goes bravely on and will be
completed about the 20th proximo. For this building there is also on
the ground a sufficiency of the various kinds of material required to
raise the first storey. The Library excavation, which is being made in a
bed of solid rock, will also be ready for the masons in three or four
days, and there is plenty of the requisite material on hand to keep them
busy for some time to come. In an incredibly short space of time there
have sprung into existence on the grounds—carpenters', blacksmiths',
and stonecutters' shops. The old barrack buildings, too, have been ren-
ovated and turned into offices for the contractors and their attaches.—
Five or six stone quarries are also being worked in various localities
contiguous to the city. From these, teams are constantly drawing rubble stone. Indeed, when we say that there are at present employed on
the works not less than between four hundred or five hundred men,
and two hundred teams, some idea may be formed of the amount of labor that has been and is now being performed on the works in question. On the opening of spring this force is to be considerably augmented. Taking the severity of the weather and the character of the
work being executed into consideration, the undertaking in every part
is progressing most favourably, and betokens an earnest desire on the
part of those interested to push it rapidly on to completion without
any unnecessary detention.

November 9, 1860

February 29, 1860

DISORDERLY.—A poor, emaciated, elderly woman named Jane Sullivan, from the Township of Nepean, was charged by officer Ross with disorderly conduct in the streets. She was fined $2 and costs, and being without funds was committed for 12 days. This poor woman is the same that we alluded to the other day as wandering through the streets, shouting at the top of her voice. Although said to be insane, she was a picture of meekness while being tried, and admitted that she had been disorderly in shouting through the streets. The authorities of the County of Carleton should surely do something for this unhappy creature and not allow her to go about as she has been doing. Giving her temporary shelter even in the jail is a charity, and we hope ere the term of her imprisonment expires she shall be properly cared for.

November 6, 1860
NEW BOOKS

Although book reviews had been a feature of newspapers since the early 1800s, the Citizen *didn't begin the practice until 1860, and only then because of a deal with local bookseller John Durie. In return for the promotion generated by the almost always favourable reviews, Durie supplied the books and became a regular advertiser. These are believed to be the first reviews published by the* Citizen.

A CHILD'S HISTORY OF ENGLAND.—Boston: Hickling, Swan, and Brewer. Ottawa: John Durie.

STORIES OF SCOTLAND AND THE ADJACENT ISLANDS.—New York: Sheldon & Co.—Ottawa: John Durie.

The "Child's History of England" is by Charles Dickens. That fact alone is sufficient to secure it for extensive circulation. It is hardly necessary to say that it is eminently readable. The same may be said of the "Stories of Scotland," by Mrs. Thomas Geldart. Many of our readers will remember the eager interest with which, in the days of their youth, they pored over "Tales of a Grandfather" by Sir Walter Scott. Some will acknowledge that, for what they remember about "Robert the Bruce" and "Wallace wight," and about the more ancient kings and thanes of Scotland, they are more indebted to these "Tales" than to profounder works studied in maturer years. The two little books under review are similar in design. It would be too much to say that we consider them equal to Sir Walter's Tales. But they are both good; and either of them would be an appropriate and acceptable Christmas present to the young for whose benefit they are intended.

November 9, 1860

SMALL POX IN OTTAWA.—Several of our Western contemporaries [newspapers in southern Ontario] have asserted that small pox is raging very violently in Ottawa, and that it has been spread by inoculation. We have made every enquiry into the truth of this, and although we find there have been a great many cases and that some yet remain under treatment, we are gratified to hear that the disorder assumes the mildest possible type. So mild, indeed, that the cases have been very rare in which the patient has been necessitated to remain in bed. Our utmost exertions have not enabled us to trace out a single case in which the practice of inoculation has been resorted to. We trust that our medical practitioners would not lend themselves to the perpetuations of this dangerous and illegal operation.

November 9, 1860

FEARFUL RIDE OF A LOCOMOTIVE

The author of this delightful piece is unknown, as is the train that took him on his breathtaking ride. Because trains rarely exceeded 40 miles an hour in 1860, Ottawa railway expert David Knowles speculates the writer took his much faster journey along a stretch of a main line, possibly between Hamilton and Windsor.

Twenty-nine miles in thirty minutes! Describe it? Impossible. I have always noticed that engineers were quiet, dignified, sober people, and now I understand it. I should regard a trilling engineer as I would a jolly whistling undertaker. Describe my ride on the Huron? Never! The whistle nearly blew my ears off; the rushing air wore out my eyes; the jogging of the engine leaping from rail to rail all but broke the end of my backbone off; my hat, which was blown away in less than a minute after we started, was caught by the fireman in a miraculous manner; and every nerve in my body jumped, squirmed and wired, as relentless as the iron horse kept up to time.

Now the head of a luckless hen was nearly shaved away; then two Hibernian gentlemen who were quietly smoking by the roadside were apparently frightened out of their wits, and before they had recovered them, we rushed, frantically, fearfully by a station, in such close proximity to a freight train that I had held my breath and trembled lest the next second should be my last. I had no idea before of the manner in which an engine jumps but I have now. While we were going at this terrific speed—while the mile posts succeeded each other so swiftly that they seemed like fence stakes, and while the various growths of wheat, oats, potatoes and corn looked as if they were planted in a heap, the engine would jump, leap, skip and roll like a frightened horse, and in a "dreadful uncertain" manner. After a little, I became used to the

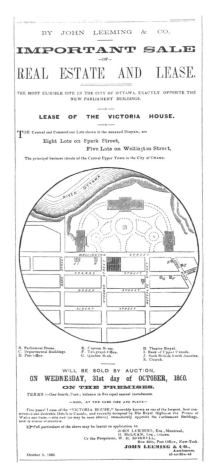

October 6, 1860

unnatural rush with which we were going, and I had more leisure to watch the engineer. He was as calm as a May morning. He pulled a rod and an unearthly scream was heard. He pushed another one, and the speed, already like an arrow's dart, became that of the lightning's flash. All was under his control, and I could but admire his coolness, the firmness of purpose, and quickness of execution which he unconsciously exhibited. No wonder that he is a quiet uncommunicative person; he deals with facts, between which and an unrevealed horror there is but a hand's breadth, and coming at any moment can only be warded off or remedied by his skill. I was glad and yet sorry, when the twenty-nine miles were finished; glad, because physically I was about used up; sorry, because I was mentally charmed, and fascinated by the novel sensation experienced during the ride.

November 13, 1860

APOLOGETIC.—We owe an apology to our readers for the large amount of space occupied just now by our advertising patrons, and the paucity of reading matter our paper contains in consequence. For some time past we have been obliged to exclude matters of local and general import; but we hope soon, with the indulgence of our friends, to make up for all the deficiencies in this respect. This is the season to advertise, and our business people seem alive to the importance of calling public attention to their wares through the medium of our columns. From to-day's issue we are reluctantly compelled to exclude several articles and one or two communications, which must lie over till our next.

November 16, 1860

MELANCHOLY AND FATAL ACCIDENT.—An accident occurred on Wednesday afternoon, resulting in the death of a promising lad, named James Burns, who was employed in the Ottawa Soap and Candle Works. It appears Mr. Fuller, of the firm of Fuller and Jones, had some business with Mr. Walsh, one of the proprietors of the Soap Works, and left his horse in charge of the boy with instructions not to mount him; the lad, however, disobeyed the order and the horse running away with him, he fell off. Unfortunately one foot stuck in the stirrup, and he was dragged nearly a hundred yards over the stones, causing instantaneous death. It is a singular coincidence that the boy's Father was killed in the same manner about ten years ago.

November 27, 1860.
THE STATE OF OTTAWA

It's difficult to imagine in today's placid capital, but in its early days, Ottawa—a town rife with Protestant-Catholic and French-English-

Irish animosities, transient lumbermen and dozens of taverns—was considered one of the most dangerous cities in British North America. In 1860, with Ottawa preparing to assume its place as a capital, the Citizen *couldn't help but lament the city's rough-and-tumble reputation.*

We have refrained for some time from making any allusion to the state of society in some parts of our city, but it is quite impossible longer to remain silent. After dark, and through the whole night, in many portions of Lower Town, an utter state of lawlessness prevails. There is safety neither for life, limb nor property. There are organized gangs of ruffians, numbering from five to forty each, prowling about, intent on plundering and ruffianism, during the night. Many of them have their faces blackened and shirts over their clothes, and they are armed with formidable bludgeons and other deadly weapons. Doors and shutters are battered in, passengers assaulted and most cruelly maltreated, and threatened with death if they attempt to defend their persons or their property. This is not a picture from a new Mysteries of Paris; it is an actual and by no means overdrawn sketch of the state of things in the City of Ottawa in this November, 1860. Can such things be and no remedial measures in progress?

An occurrence took place in Dalhousie street on Saturday night last, which we believe will call forth such an expression of public opinion that further supineness will be impossible. A very respectable trades-man of the name of Brown, residing in that street, had on Saturday night closed his shop, and was sitting with his wife taking his supper. Suddenly he heard a clamour at his door, and a voice asking for protec-tion and admission. He went to the door and found there an old man whom a dozen ruffians were most cruelly maltreating. Mr. Brown got the poor old man inside and secured the door, and it was considered his assailants had dispersed. After resting for a time it was thought he could safely go home, and the door was opened and he was let out. He had scarcely got outside before the ruffians were on him again and this time with ten-fold ferocity. Mr. and Mrs. Brown, alarmed for the man's life, opened the door again, for they heard the villains threatening to murder him on the spot, and from the blows that were delivered, they were convinced that this would be carried out. The old man managed again to get inside, and the wretches then turned with fury on Mrs. Brown, and threatened to murder her. Mrs. B., justly alarmed, called on her husband, who had a pistol in his hand, to fire. He was about to do this when the old man, who stood by him, begged him not to fire and pulled his arm. The result was that the bullets—the pistol was charged with three—passed, two of them into Mrs. Brown's arm and one into her side. The ruffians, it appears, then decamped for that night. Mrs.

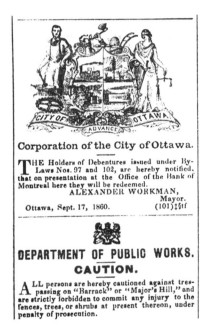

November 13, 1860

Brown remains in a very precarious state, and one of the bullets in her arm is yet unextracted.

We trust that, things having arrived at this pass, something will be done for the protection of our peaceable inhabitants. A great many are arming themselves, and many others are thinking of leaving the city. We would suggest that a public meeting be at once called to take these matters into consideration, and we have no doubt, but that the public spirit which led to the formation of the fire brigades, rifle companies &c., will induce our citizens to come forward as volunteers for the preservation of the peace of the city. We propose this in case no other remedy is applied, for immediate action is indispensable.

WITHIN the last few days we have had three or four fires in the city, all arising, as we understand, from overheating consequent on the extreme severity of the weather. One in the neighbourhood of Sussex Street, which took place on Friday last, appeared to be exceedingly alarming, but was put out fortunately without much damage having been done. The others were very easily suppressed.

LAMENTABLE ACCIDENT.—Yesterday afternoon as two of the Sisters of Charity were passing along Sussex street, a fall of ice took place from the house of Mr. Varin, which struck the ladies, one of whom, Sister Hagan was, we much regret to say, so seriously injured that her life is despaired of. The other lady fortunately escaped with only a broken finger.

February 12, 1861

A PUBLIC PARK
January 18, 1861

A movement is now in progress in this city having a very desirable object in view, viz:—the formation of a public park or pleasure ground. The originators of this project deserve great credit at the hands of their fellow citizens, and are entitled to expect unanimous support and encouragement. Now is the time, while there is yet plenty of unoccupied ground about us to raise this question. Of the great advantages of a public park there cannot be any difference of opinion we should presume, and those who are aware of the difficulties which such an undertaking has to encounter in old cities will rejoice that it has been taken up here in this early stage of the existence of Ottawa. That there are certain sites preferable to others we are all aware, but Major's Hill is not the only suitable place which might be selected; there are several charming spots in our environs which at a very moderate outlay could be made available for this purpose. For instance, where could a more beautiful situation be found than the west bank of the Rideau? We trust that the originators of the movement will persevere: they may safely calculate on the support of all those whose countenance is of any consideration and they may safely venture to treat the petty snarling with which this patriotic purpose has been greeted in a certain quarter with the contempt it so richly merits. Some persons are such inveterate jobbists that they smell a job in everything, and so intensely conceited that nothing can be good where their fingers have been—and most wisely—kept out of the pie.

February 8, 1861

Some of the New York journals are still laboring under the Canada annexation hallucination and appear to think that we will readily seize the bait with which they are fishing. Never before did we see so perfect a realization of the surly old English moralist's remark respecting angling and anglers—that the angler's implement has a worm at one end a fool at the other. Some of these journals assume quite a pitying and patronising tone; the *Herald* [of New York] in particular, and were not its remarks smothered by their absurdity, they would be insulting in the extreme to the good sense of our fellow countrymen. The fool may hold the rod but the Canadians will turn away with derision from the worm. What has the United States to offer us, a chronic condition of disorder, anarchy, mob law, lynching, filibustering and a state of society where the expression of opinion, unless coincident with the views of my lords of the majority, endangers life and limb. And what should we give in exclusive for those rather questionable blessings?—peace, happiness and freedom, perfect liberty of speech and writing, and all the mighty benefits for which a long line of free ancestors have toiled and fought and bled. Can there be a doubt as to the selection which Canada will make? We can hardly look at this question or write about it with coolness, so gigantic is its folly, so stupendous its misconception of the temper and feelings of the people of Canada, and of the relative position, prospects and advantages of the two countries and their institutions. More than this, where is the demand for union on the part of Canada? And is it not well known, to take the reverse, that there are portions of the States which would rejoice to be able to throw themselves into our arms. The *Herald* has a farcical horror of annexing the British isles and his main objection is their pauperism. How stands this question? Pauperism in Great Britain has of late years been rapidly diminishing—in the States it has been as rapidly increasing, and at this moment New York is probably the most pauperized as well as the most criminal city in the world. The nonsense to which we have referred is scarcely worthy of notice, and we have done it with the sole purpose of showing to what extraordinary heights absurdity can reach.

March 8, 1861

THE NEW PRESIDENT.

It will be seen by our ample telegraphic reports that the inauguration of President Lincoln passed over without any disturbance of the public peace. This was more than a great many persons had anticipated, for rumours of all sorts of outrageous projects had been floating about for some time past, and sober-minded men feared that the fanatics of the party might not confine themselves to mere vapouring and threatening. The beginning of the end, however, was quiet and this, conjoined with other indications, leads the hopeful to think that the American situation may yet be ameliorated, and that, although it may not be possible to restore the former order of things in their entirety, a compromise may be effected which will prevent the further spread of disaffection and disunion, and restore peace to that distracted country.

The policy of the new President with reference to the Secession

GENERAL PROTESTANT HOSPITAL.

DISEASES.—OMITTED IN ANNUAL REPORT.

Diseases.	Admitted.	Died.
Abscessus	1	
Amenorrhœa	1	
Anasarca	1	
Asthma	1	
Catarrhus	1	
Caries Vertebræ	3	
Cerebritis, Chronic	1	1
Contusio	4	1
Congelatio	10	
Cynanche Tonsillaris	2	
Cynanche Maligna	1	1
Diarrhœa	1	
Delirium Tremens	2	1
Dyspepsia	1	
Erysipelas	1	
Feb. Com. Cont	8	
Fractura Simplex	4	
Furunculus	1	
Hypochondriasis	2	
Haemorrhoidea	1	
Morbus Coxæ	1	
Morbus Cordis	1	
Ophthalmia	3	
Phthisis	5	
Paraplegia	1	
Rheumatism, Acut	4	
Scrofulosis	3	
Sclerotitis	1	
Syphilis	3	
Synovitis	1	
Ulculcus	10	
Variola	15	1
Vulnus	5	
Vermes	1	

Mr. J. W. Sootheran's extensive carding mill in Cavan, was destroyed by fire last week. There was no insurance.

February 15, 1861

VOLUME II.—No. 41.

Bury me in the Valley.

Bury me in the valley,
    Beside some rippling stream,
Where blooms the modest lily
    Amidst the emerald green ;
And where the feathered songster
    Will build its downy nest,
Amid the fragrant rose-tree
    That blooms above my breast.

Bury me in the valley,
    Where early comes the spring,
And where the towering holly
    Will lasting beauty fling ;
And let the distant sunset
    Its gold and crimson shed
Upon the murmuring water
    That glides beside my bed.

Bury me in the valley,
    Where tender breezes blow,
And let them murmur gently
    My requiem soft and low :
And let the glistening dewdrop
    Be pearls upon my breast ;
With quaintly carved though humble slab
    To mark my place of rest.

February 19, 1861

movement, does not appear as yet to be distinctly understood. His inaugural address is on all hands admitted to be an able state paper, but it is most variously interpreted, and receives as many different meanings as there are parties and interests. Some see in it clear indications that no attempt at coercion will be made; that the Seceding States will be permitted to pursue their own course unmolested if they refrain from becoming themselves assailants. On the other hand it is regarded as tantamount to a declaration of war, and some of the implicated States are maturing their measures of defence. There can be no doubt that the crisis is of the most serious and alarming character, and that Mr. Lincoln's task is second only in peril and importance to that which the great Washington so successfully performed. We have from the first deplored the unhappy dissensions of our neighbors, and viewed with regret the disruption of a great and powerful empire. There is the bare possibility of moderate counsels and measures being effective; the institutions of the United States are not framed for coercion, and could not be applied to sectional domination. In our own mind we have no doubt that Mr. Lincoln's policy is pacific; we do not believe that he will try to reconstruct the Union by force. He and the enlightened men of his party foresee a disastrous failure in such a course, and will wisely forbear from making the attempt.

March 15, 1861

Thomas D'Arcy McGee, best known today as a Father of Confederation and the victim of an assassin's bullet on Sparks Street in 1868, was famous in the 1850s and '60s as an exceptional orator and a skilled poet. As this story demonstrates, his lectures were major local events.

LECTURE BY D'ARCY McGEE, ESQ., M.P.P.—The lecture by Mr. McGee, M.P.P., on the American crisis which has been twice postponed in consequence of the severity of the weather, was delivered in the Ottawa Theatre on Wednesday evening last. Notwithstanding the unfavourable condition of the streets, and the previous disappointments, the reputation of the lecturer attracted a large audience. The fact of the disruption of the States, the lecturer considered was a fait accompli, and he regarded the fact with extreme regret, calculated to make despots sneer, and cause those who hoped and struggled for the cause of liberty to shake their heads in doubt. But he still looked upon the constitution and system of republican government in the United States with confidence, and attributed the untowardness of its working not to any imperfection in the constitution itself, but to the degeneracy of the people. Patriotic and private virtues were no longer looked upon as qualifications for political promotion but the country's rulers were chosen from those who promised most and pandered most to the vices of the mob. He attributed this state of things, not to the physical, but to the mental emaciation of the present day caused by the universal absorption of the light and frivolous literature which is so extensively disseminated throughout the United States. The stern virtues and patriotism of the men of the revolution were thus forgotten, and their strength sapped by the morbid matter which formed their intellectual subsistence. The system of government was good, but the people were demoralized, and unworthy of the system. The subject of American slavery, to which he, of course, attributed the disruption of the now dis-United States, the lecturer treated in the most moderate manner. While much fanaticism, and insincerity might be charged against the abolitionists of the North, still they had the right upon their side, and he hoped they would not abandon their ground. The existence of a Southern Confederacy he viewed as a political paradox, the holding of property in man being incompatible with the principle of constitution that all men are born free and equal. While he denounced in the most uncompromising terms the system of degradation in which slavery held those images of God, because they were made not exactly in the "Ivory but in the Ebony likeness of their Divine Creator," he exonerated the States from having either as colonists, or in their condition of Independence, introduced the evil. The slavery traffic was inaugurated and conducted under the flags of old Europe, and he instanced Liverpool, Lisbon and Holland as having largely participated and profited by that branch of commerce. And the framers of the constitution of Independence regarded the evil as temporary, and to be got rid of gradually. The fanaticism of the South appeared determined to frustrate this intention, but if the question did not receive a peaceful solution, it would receive a bloody solution. We regret being unable to give a fuller and more lengthened report of this lecture. Mr. McGee's pleasing and impressive delivery are now too well known to require any eulogy from us. The lecture was listened to throughout with marked interest and attention, and except in one instance, without interruption. The St. Patrick's Band was in attendance, and played several appropriate airs.

THE LATEST SECESSION DISCORD.—The California mail brings a report from San Francisco, to the effect that a dreadful quarrel took place between the Siamese twins at the American Museum on the 7th inst. It seems that Chang who is a North Carolinian and a secessionist, had insisted on painting the ligament black which binds them together. To this Eng objected, preferring the natural colour, whereupon Chang resolved to "sever the union" with Eng, which he declared to be "no longer worth preserving." Eng, who is of a calmer temperament, finally persuaded him to wait a little—untill the 4th of March next. A system of non-intercourse will probably be adopted : each party reserving to himself the privilege of biting his own nose off. —News.

February 19, 1861

March 15, 1861
MELANCHOLY AND FATAL ACCIDENT
With deep regret we have to record the occurrence of one of the most melancholy and heart-rending accidents, which has ever come under our notice. Yesterday Mr. and Mrs. J. M. Currier and some friends left Ottawa to visit Mr. Currier's mills at Long Island [in the Rideau River at Manotick]. On their arrival there, according to the best accounts which we have been able to obtain, Mr. Currier, having occa-

sion to leave the building, deputed Mr. Merrill to show the ladies—
Mrs. Currier and Mrs. Merrill—over the premises. They had ascended
to the upper part of the building, and were returning down when the
frightful accident occurred. It seems that an upright shaft revolves
very near the bottom of the staircase. Mr. Merrill preceded the ladies
down, and as he reached the lower floor cautioned them to be careful
with their dresses, but scarcely were the words spoken before the unfortunate lady, Mrs. Currier, had ceased to exist. A portion of her dress
came in contact with the shaft, and she was torn round with a frightful
velocity and crushed against a pillar or support which was fixed within
a few inches of the shaft. It will be remembered that it is yet but a brief
month since we announced the nuptials of this lady and gentleman,
and already has this fearful separation divided them for ever as far as
this world is concerned. We are sure that poor Mr. Currier, in this great
affliction, will receive the heartfelt sympathy of every inhabitant of
this city and of every other individual by whom either he or his amiable lady was known.

April 9, 1861
DEATH OF MR. CHARLES JOHN FORD.

*In the interests of privacy, Canadian newspapers have refrained from
reporting on suicides since the 1960s, except in rare cases, such as
those involving prominent figures or someone in police custody. In the
1800s, however, suicides were routinely reported, often in great detail
and often accompanied by passages from a suicide note.*

To-day it falls to our lot to speak of the melancholy end of perhaps the
oldest working printer on the American continent—we mean the late
Mr. Chas. John Ford, who for the last 60 years has been a devoted and
by no means an obscure follower in the footsteps of Faust. Yes, 60
years ago the subject of this obituary notice commenced his career as a
printer, and from that moment to the present, with but brief intermis-
sions, he applied himself to his avocation with an earnestness and diligence which seemed to exclude almost everything else from his
thoughts. On arriving in this country from Great Britain,—the theatre
of his early efforts,—he found employment in Quebec, where for many
years he was engaged in the Government Printing Office, of which he
had charge. On the removal of the Canada *Gazette* establishment to
Toronto in 1845, he accompanied it, and remained there until the Office was again taken to Lower Canada. Shortly afterward he came to
this city, and became connected with the *Citizen* establishment, in
which he has worked for the past ten years. Latterly, his loneliness in
the world—death having some time since removed his only relations
on this side of the Atlantic—seemed to weigh heavily upon him, and

Latest News by Telegraph.

By Special Telegraph to the Citizen.

LATEST FROM CHARLESTON!

HOSTILITIES COMMENCED!

Bombardment of Fort Sumter!

FORT SUMTER IN FLAMES!

PREPARATIONS AT THE CAPITAL!

Surrender of FORT SUMTER!

FORT SUMPTER GARRISONED BY
PALMETTO GUARDS.

Explosion of Magazines in the Fort!

THE PRESIDENTS REPLY TO THE
VIRGINIA COMMISSIONERS.

*WAR DECLARED BY PRESIDENT
LINCOLN!*

INUNDATION IN MONTREAL!

(*From the N. Y. Herald's Correspondence.*)
WASHINGTON, April 11, 1861.

The men of West Point Flying Artillery received orders to keep their revolvers constantly
loaded, to be ready for immediate action. Part
of the volunteers will be stationed at the bridge
across the Potomac, so as to defend it from an
invading force. Nearly 1000 men are now enrolled for regular service from the ranks of the
District militia. Those who refused to take the
oath of allegiance were marched back to the
armory, disarmed and their names stricken from
the roll. Hisses from the spectators accompanied

April 16, 1861

induced a melancholy turn of mind which his advanced years, and waning strength, were incapable of shaking off. For months past life had for him no charm, and he often wished the summons to another world. But his robust, erect, and vigorous frame forbidding his hope of speedy dissolution, he sought a solace for his grief in the inebriating cup—to which he formerly had been a bitter and avowed enemy. But in the maddening drink he found no joy—deeper and deeper it sunk him in despondency until it robbed him of all self-respect—and then he sought to destroy a life which to him had become a burden. A heavy dose of strychnia furnished the means; but not till after enduring its effects for the extraordinary period of ten hours did the well-knit frame of the deceased succumb. Though he retained his reason until the last spasm deprived him of life, he murmured not at the terrible sufferings he endured, and closed his earthly career without making any declaration further than that he died by his own act. Deceased was about 75 years of age.—He was at one time Vice-President of our Mechanics' Institute, and for years an intelligent and worthy member of the Masonic fraternity, and a rigid and faithful Son of Temperance.

> "His life was gentle: and the elements
> So mix'd in him, that nature might stand up
> And say to all the world,—This is a man."

An inquest held upon the body on Friday morning last resulted in a verdict: "That Chas. John Ford came to his death through the influence of strychnine, taking during a period of mental depression, induced by continuous intemperance, with the intention of producing death."

May 7, 1861
GREAT DESTRUCTION OF SHEEP BY A BEAR.
—THE BEAR KILLED.

For a few years back a bear has infested the farms in the 2nd Concession South March, County of Carleton, and has destroyed much stock—calves, sheep and pigs. This spring he has been very destructive, killing and injuring on four farms convenient to each other, 35 sheep and a large hog. On the night of the 2nd of May he visited the farm of Mr. Wm. McLaughlin and tore open a strong stable door where Mr. McL. had his sheep and a span of horses enclosed for safety; he injured five of the sheep badly and carried off one. The next day Mr. McLaughlin set a gun in the bush where the bear had left a part of the sheep he had carried off. In a few hours afterwards a report of a gun was heard, when four men started off in pursuit of the bruin with axes. They soon came in view of his bearship, who showed not the least sign of fear, and proved to be an enormous large male, weighing nearly 400

SNOW-BALLING IN PARIS.—Snow-balling in the Tuilleries-gardens was carried on to such an extent on Christmas day that it became necessary to send for troops to protect the public. A parcel of young scamps systematically assailed every well dressed person, particularly ladies who wore bonnets worth spoiling. One young man, supposed to be an Englishman, used his cane in self-defence, and a regular row was the consequence. Many bearskin caps belonging to the Grenadier Guards, who came to restore order, were seen rolling about in the snow. The troops were unarmed and could do but little, but ultimately a body of *sergents de ville* cleared the gardens, and arrested several of the snow-ballers.

January 15, 1861

October 1, 1861

lbs. After a little time the bear started off at a brisk pace, and an animated chase ensued, which lasted an hour and a half, when suddenly, in a very thick part of the bush, he stood at bay, with every demonstration of anger. The men now closed on him, when one of the men very skillfully gave him a heavy blow of an axe on the head, which so stunned him that he was easily dispatched. The inhabitants are quite rejoiced at his being killed. Great credit is due to Mr. McLaughlin for his zeal and well directed efforts to destroy such bold and crafty marauders, which are at once the plague and terror of the settler, and year after year impoverishes him. We hope the example of Mr. McL. will be generally followed in like cases, instead of lamely submitting to injury which a little well directed resolution may prevent.

August 9, 1861
HER MAJESTY'S THEATRE.
Completion of Her Majesty's Theatre on Wellington Street at O'Connor in 1856 ushered in a new era of entertainment for Ottawa audiences, attracting a variety of professional touring companies— opera, drama, minstrel, even small circuses. After several ownership changes and renovations, including those mentioned here, the theatre closed in 1866.

It is a positive treat to attend the Theatre, under its present management. Unfinished it is, "unannointed, unannealed"—with "all its imperfections, on its head." Mr. Fleming has called order out of Chaos, and the result is,—we are charmed to find, that Ottawa has evinced good taste enough to second the manager in the most tangible form. Plays, such as "Richelieu," "Hamlet," and "Ingomar," are eminently qualified to elevate the public taste, and any one who has the happiness of knowing Mr. Fleming always feels secure that whilst in his hands, the Theatre is safe from ungenerous assaults of either fanaticism or bigotry—such could only recoil upon the assailants. The company has been so long working together, at a few plays, that everything goes like clockwork; all are capable of doing what they are "engaged" to do, so that for the lovers of the Drama, a rare gratification is presented. We deem it unnecessary to enter into a detailed critique; suffice it that those who spend an evening with Mr. Fleming—"Dolly" Davenport, Mr. Scallan, Mr. Kingsland, and the bevy of beauties who constitute the female corps dramatiques—are not very likely to grumble at the outlay, but on the contrary, are sure to repeat their visit.

October 8, 1861
In 1842, Charles Stratton was a four-year-old midget living in Connecticut when P. T. Barnum transformed him into General Tom

Thumb, training him to sing, dance and imitate famous people. Until
he died in 1883, Tom Thumb performed around the world, and gave
four shows in Her Majesty's Theatre, Ottawa.

GENERAL TOM THUMB.—This *Multum in Parvo* [Much in Little]
played to crowded houses at our Theatre during the two occasions,
Friday and Saturday last, he appeared amongst us. It is unnecessary to
remark that he fully carried out the universal reputation he has acquired, and that he proved by his acting, singing and dancing in conjunction with readiness of wit, through self possession and perfection
of manners and form, that he is indeed one of the wonders of the age.
He is accompanied by some excellent vocalists, who added greatly to
the enjoyment of the little Gen'L's "levees;" and all these attractions,
combined with the business fact and gentlemanly bearing of the
Agent, render General Tom Thumb's exhibitions the very best of the
kind now travelling. We have every reason to believe that this one is
the "original" Tom Thumb, but whether or not, both he and his "aides,"
form a perfect array of rational and attractive entertainment.

December 27, 1861.
DEATH OF PRINCE ALBERT

Newspapers in the 19th century inverted their column rules to mark a
significant death. Instead of printing a thin line between columns, the
much wider base of the rule was inked and filled the gap between
columns with black. The death of Queen Victoria's husband, Prince
Albert, provided the first known occasion for the Citizen *to invert its*
rules. Readers still had to open the paper to learn who had died.

Amidst the excitement of passing events which involved the most
important interests of great nations, and cause the minds of men to be
moved with deep emotions, and at the moment when in social life the
Christmas festivities and associations are being enjoyed, we have the
solemn announcement that death has visited the family of our Sovereign, and we are forcibly reminded that, sooner or later, we must all
pay the debt of nature. His R.H. Prince Albert expired on the 15th instant. We are informed that the immediate cause of death was gastric
fever. The particulars of his illness are not yet forthcoming.

His Royal Highness was born on the 25th August, 1819, and was married on the 10th February, 1840. At the age of forty-two years, while apparently in the prime of life, after a very short illness, he has been
stricken down. The season of festivity is changed to a time of mourning, but if aught could alleviate the sorrow for his loss, it would be the
reflection that throughout the British Empire every heart will sympa-
thize most deeply with Her Majesty and family in their afflictive be-

reavement. During the last twenty-one years Prince Albert has occupied a position of the most important and delicate character, and his conduct has always been marked by sound judgement, sterling good sense, and liberal principles. We are indebted to him for the great International Exhibition of 1851, the first effort of the kind recorded in history, and also for the promotion of literature; and many most useful improvements of a practical kind in the liberal arts, and agriculture, were originated by him, and carried out under his direction. This sad event will cast a gloom over every portion of the widely extended dominions of Her Majesty. However illustrious the position, or however surrounded by all the advantages that human agency can afford, the stroke will be deeply felt in the family circle, and there they will mourn the loss of the husband and the father. Dignity and honours cannot repair their loss or remove their sorrow. The prince and the peasant, the rich and poor, must alike bow before the Sovereign Law of the Creator, and go down to the narrow house appointed for all living.

December 27, 1862

HAVING YOUR PHOTOGRAPH TAKEN.

There are few periods of a peaceable man's life more deserving the proverbial name of "*un mauvais quart d'heure*" than the space of time he is beguiled into spending in a photographer's studio. Of itself, the attempt to select your own best expression of countenance is a perplexing effort, and the consciousness that the face you put on, whatever it may be, will be the one by which, in all time, all who look into your friends' albums will know you, does not diminish the embarrassment. You have a vague expression that to look smiling is ridiculous, and to look solemn is still more so. You wish to look intelligent, but you are hampered by a fear of looking sly. You wish to look as if you were not sitting for your picture, but the effort to do so fills your mind more completely with the melancholy consciousness that you are. All these conflicting feelings pressing upon your mind at the critical moment, are very painful; but they are terribly aggravated by the well meant interposition of the photographer. "Just a little expression in your countenance, if you please, sir—perhaps if you could smile," is a most distressing admonition to receive at such a moment, just when you know that the photographer has his hand posed upon the cap. If you are weak enough to listen to him, and extemporize "a little expression," you come out upon the plate with a horrible leer, looking like the Artful Dodger in the act of relating his exploits. If as is more probable, you are too much absorbed in the uncomfortableness of your own position to regard his exonerations, you are immortalized with an expression of agonized sternness upon your features, unpleasantly suggestive of a painful disorder.

March 4, 1864

MR. JACKSON HAINES, the champion skater of New York, arrived here on Wednesday night, and yesterday exhibited his singular skill and dexterity at the Subscription Skating Rink on Col. Aumond's premises, Nicholas Street. He exhibited at three o'clock in the afternoon, and at half-past seven in the evening. Mr. Haines is a short, slightly made young man of gentlemanly address and appearance, and is quite an artist as a skater, performing the most incredible feats, and that, too, without any apparent effort. He cuts all sorts of figures, turns, somersaults, skates on one leg backwards, and turns and twists in the most extraordinary manner. Further, he dances a hornpipe or a jig with as much ease as if he had his pumps on. He is funny as well as active and graceful. Part of his performance yesterday was the role of the novice in skating taking his first lesson, and it was rendered in a way which excited the risible faculties of the spectators to the utmost tension. The exhibition, taken altogether, was really wonderful, and it is a pity that circumstances did not permit of more notice being given of it. Hundreds more, we are satisfied, would have flocked to see him, and his success here, pecuniarily, would have not been less than it was in Toronto and Kingston. As it was, great numbers were present. The proceedings were enlivened by the performances of a band. Owing to the weather, the Rink was in excellent order, Mr. Haines observing that he had not skated on finer ice this winter.

June 14, 1864

The second Excursion of the Ottawa Natural History Society took place, according to an announcement, on Saturday last, their destination being the Iron Mountain in Hull, some ten miles distant. Independent of the members of the Society who assembled on the occasion, were a few scientific strangers. The party went by the Gatineau road, and returned by the western side of the Mountain. At half-past eleven it is reported to us that a shower, followed by a severe hailstorm, took place, so severe, indeed, that the excursionists were compelled to seek for shelter in Mr. Gilmour's cottage, and remain there for a full half hour. During the rest of the tramp, however, both out and home, the weather was all that could be desired, or even hoped for, the slight storm having only served the great and good purpose of allaying the onslaught of the mosquitoes or, in scientific parlance, *culex pipiens*. Some of the scientific guests, recently from Europe, found much to excite, if not to admire, in the way of bush roads, windfalls and swamps, but were more than recompensed at the same time on reaching the goal of the excursionists, where, after doing full justice to the contents of the knapsacks, the party scattered. A few, consisting of the juvenile portion, betook themselves to a trout stream in the vicinity and were made happy by the capture of the finny tribe. Mr. Billings, and several of his allies, were off with their entomological nets and vasculums, in search of insects and flowers. Others, again, went in pursuit of birds; whilst Professor Winter, with a few veteran naturalists, with geological hammers, made a minute inspection of the Iron mine, and came back to the appointed station heavily laden with spoil. When the prolific character of the region is taken into account, it is scarcely necessary to say that the gentlemen composing the staff were well rewarded by the results of their otherwise toilsome scramble; and after, in true naturalist character, partaking of a luxurious abluting and invigorating tea at Donney's, they, after three hearty cheers, separated to meet again, however, on the second Saturday in July; some crossing by the ferry to the Lower Town, and others returning by the Suspension Bridge to the Upper Town. An eye-witness, when he saw them start, dressed as they were in coats of all cuts and all colors, and accoutered with guns, vasculums, knapsacks, geological hammers, fishing baskets, hatchets, and haversacks, could not help repeating the words from Charles Mackay's "Garden Gate:" "Stand back ye pomps and let me wear, the liberty I feel./I have a coat at elbows bare, I love the deshabille." Conscious that "there was no tinsel in the grove" they divested themselves of all state and after a day of glorious enjoyment returned home both better and wiser men.

The Battles before Richmond.

Accounts from Eye-witnesses.

Seven days fighting !

The Federals retreat to James River.

THE GUNBOATS BROUGHT INTO ACTION.

Confederate Loss said to be 30,000.

FEDERAL LOSS ADMITTED TO BE 20,000.

We devote a large portion of our space this morning to the publication of the accounts of correspondents of the New York *Times*, and by telegraph, of the late bloody events before Richmond. The fighting, according to the latest reports, lasted seven days. The Federal loss is put down by themselves at 20,000, and they represent the Confederate loss at 30,000.

On board the Gunboat Stepping Stones, James River, Monday, June 30th, 1862.

The right wing of our (Federal) army has at length been attacked by the enemy—an event which was not wholly anticipated by us. For several days previous to the attack, preparations were being made by the right wing to resist, if possible, to some extent, any advance movement of the rebels from the direction of Hanover, or Mechanicsville, but the extent of the preparations were not sufficient to justify the belief that a vigorous stand was to be made on the west side of the Chickahominy.

THE CONFEDERATE'S ADVANCE ON THURSDAY, THE 26th JUNE.

July 12, 1862

August 30, 1864
Most of the Citizen's *coverage of the U.S. Civil War came from American and British sources. Sometimes, though, the war came closer to home.*

Facts are daily showing that the activity of the secret agents, sent out by the Federal Government in Washington to entice Canadians into the Northern army, has not a whit abated. We could point to a good many instances that have recently occurred, not far from this neighborhood either, of young men being inveigled down south, but one, a young man named DANIEL MCDONALD, from Fitzroy, will, we think, be sufficient to show what treatment those who leave their homes for the States, may expect. It seems he had been somehow led to believe he would succeed better in the States, and he accordingly started from home for Detroit on the 14th inst., which he reached on the evening of the third day, about seven o'clock. Ignorant of the existence of the draft in that city, he immediately went to a hotel, and having secured a room, went to bed shortly after. About 4 o'clock in the morning, he was awakened by the beating of drums, the sounding of bugles and the mournful cries of women and children in the streets. Almost immediately after, a troop of soldiers broke into the hotel, and captured amongst the rent our unfortunate hero, who was immediately escorted to the guard-house and there confined. He writes that he made all the resistance he could, at the same time declaring that he was a British subject, "but it was no use speaking to them." On the following morning, he was hand-cuffed and sent with the rest of the company by the care to Evansville, where they were all compelled to take the oath of allegiance and then enrolled in the 42nd New York regiment. This regiment was to leave for Washington on the 28th of next month, so the young man has deter-mined to effect his escape by some means or other before that time. After regretting that he ever left Canada, he says, in conclusion, "I would not advise any person to come here just now—merchants are offering as high as $1,200 for a substitute."

September 9, 1864

Signor FARINA's tight-rope performances to-day at the Falls will doubt-less attract immense crowds. The rope on which this fearless man is to execute his dangerous feats was laid across the chasm on Wednesday, and the spot has since been visited by hundreds of the curious. It seems hard to realize that any one could walk over a slender pathway of such length and at so giddy a height much less that he could do so with baskets on his feet, or enveloped in a sack and entirely blindfold-ed. But the thing having been repeatedly done by this extraordinary man, in the presence of thousands, all doubt on the subject is set at rest. By the courtesy of Messrs. PERLEY & CO., Mr. JOHN BOOTH, Messrs. PARRIS and SMITH, and Mr. J.L. WHEELER, arrangements have been made by which some hundreds of people may be provided with an especially good view of the exhibition. The flume at this end of the rope has been reserved by these gentlemen for FARINA's benefit. It is to be safely cov-ered over, fenced in, and fitted up with seats; and for the privilege of admission a charge of twenty-five cents will be made. There will be two entrances to it—one beside the Brewery; and the other through MR. BOOTH'S NEW MILL.

November 1, 1864
POETRY
For "The Ottawa Citizen"
No Federation.

One of early Ottawa's most colourful figures, William P. Lett was a newspaperman, strident Orangeman, outdoorsman, amateur playwright and long-time city clerk, the first after Ottawa's incorporation in 1855. But today he is best remembered for "Recollections of Early Bytown," a book-length poem recounting his memories of growing up in Bytown. His poetic commentaries on news events were also a regular feature of the Citizen, *which published his*

work prominently even when the newspaper did not agree with his views. His poem opposing Confederation is an example.

We've lived beneath the aegis
Of the brave old British Crown,
We've prosper'd, aye, and flourished
In this country of our own;
With British Institutions,
Red battalions at our back,
We've lived in freeborn happiness,
Then let us still look back.

We want no "Federation,"
No snapping of the bond,
That links us to the old red-cross
In kindred feeling fond.
We want no imitation
Of the anarchy which reigns
With unabated horrors
Over fair Columbia's plains.

What is "Confederation?"
A visionary dream,
A dim utopian project—
A democratic scheme;
A lesson which no Briton
Should ever seek to con,
A rock, I trust, which Canada
Will never split upon.

We've flourished since the day that Wolfe
Expired on Abraham's plain,
Beneath the FLAG he planted
On the spot where he was slain!
We glory in our union
With our mother o'er the sea,
Then down, say I, with tinkering!
Let our Constitution be!

Wm. P. Lett.

Ottawa, Oct. 29, 1864.

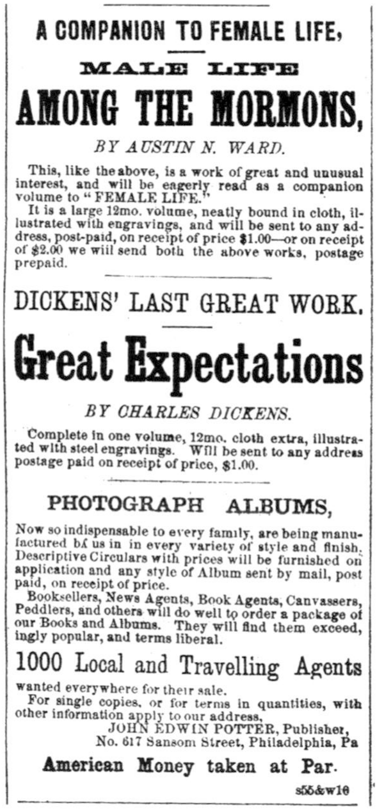

May 6, 1863

CORRESPONDENCE

December 28, 1864

To the Editor of "The Ottawa Citizen"

SIR—The manner in which the public are treated at the Post Office of this city is becoming more and more intolerable every day. It is not by any means an unusual thing, in all sorts of weather, to be kept standing on the foot-path during the sorting of the mail. That may be all very well in tolerable weather, although I doubt very much the right of Mr. Baker or any other Post-master to close the doors of his office against the public at such a time. Last night the mail was delivered at the Post Office, from cars, before six o'clock, and I among many others went between half past six and a quarter to seven o'clock. Surely it could not take all that time to sort so small a mail; or even granting that it did, why not allow the public the privilege of a little protection from the intensely cold wind and frost? By finding space for the above in your paper, you will confer a favor on.

Yours, most respectfully

COSMOPOLITE

Ottawa, Dec. 23, 1864

October 3, 1863

bacco, and had a quid in her mouth when arrested. Such a woman is safer within the walls of a prison than at large in the city, and it is probably she will spend a term in the county jail.

We publish to-day a portrait of Louis Riel, who is now in Montreal, and is expected to arrive in Ottawa to-morrow. It is a fair picture of

THE NOTORIOUS HALF-BREED,

engraved by Mr. George Cox, from a photograph taken shortly after the murder of Scott. It will be recognized at once by any-one who has ever seen him.

A Serious Complaint.

Complaints are heard from all parts of the city against the Gas Company for the disgraceful manner in which the street lamps are lighted. Rideau street lamps are seldom alight until 8.30 or 9 o'clock in the evening—a serious inconvenience considering the darkness of the nights and the muddy state of the streets. In no other city in the Dominion would such a state of affairs be tolerated, and it is a matter of surprise that the question has not

---

A Real Newsman

The Third Decade, 1865-1874

WHEN HIS OFFER to buy the *Citizen* finally went through in April 1865, Isaac B. Taylor knew he had to move quickly to retain the paper's No. 1 standing in Ottawa. As the *Citizen*'s editor under owner Robert Bell since 1861, Taylor had watched as two of the city's six rival newspapers—the *Union* and *Daily News*—began to publish at least five days a week. The *Citizen*, still putting out two editions weekly, was starting to lose readers and advertisers.

So within weeks of taking control, Taylor not only plunged the paper into daily journalism, he made it the city's first morning daily. With characteristic enterprise, he bought exclusive Ottawa rights to midnight telegraph dispatches, allowing him to fill the *Citizen*—delivered by 6 a.m.—with the latest news from Canada and around the world.

But Taylor wasn't finished. With Canada edging toward a newly defined nationhood and Ottawa as its capital, he wanted a respected journalist to edit his paper. In August 1865, Taylor convinced Francis Ridgeway, a prominent American-based war correspondent, to become his editor in chief. Ridgeway, British-born former owner of the *Richmond Gazette*, had sold his Virginia paper at the start of the Civil War and travelled to the front to report the war. "Ridgeway was the first of the real newspapermen . . . who were to place the *Citizen* in the forefront of the national daily press," William MacPherson wrote in *No Claptrap*, his short 1995 history of the paper.

The next few years brimmed with great events, and Ridgeway, a literate and curious journalist who took an immediate liking to Canada, put out a lively paper that reflected the excitement. When Thomas D'Arcy McGee, a Father of Confederation and national icon, was assassinated on Sparks Street in 1868, the *Citizen* published a supplement providing intricate details of the shooting and analyses of its political

MIDNIGHT DESPATCHES.

BY SPECIAL TELEGRAPH.

CAPTURE OF

JEFFERSON DAVIS & ALL HIS STAFF.

The Official Notifications on the Subject.

A Strong Guard to convey them to Washington.

PROCEEDINGS AT THE ASSASSINA-TION TRIAL.

REPORTERS TO BE ADMITTED.

The Case of Surrat taken up.

Nature of the Evidence Adduced.

Singular objection to Mr. Johnson, the Counsel for Mrs. Surrat.

FULL REPORT OF HIS SPEECH IN REPLY.

MOVEMENTS OF THE ARMY OF THE POTOMAC.

Departure of Ocean Steamers for Europe and Southern Ports.

OFFICIAL.

WAR DEPARTMENT, }
WASHINGTON. 13th. }

Maj. Gen. Dix :—
The following despatch, just received from Gen. Wilson, announces the surprise and capture of Jefferson Davis and his staff by Col. E. Pritchard and the Michigan cavalry on the morning of the 10th inst., at Irwinsville, Irwin Co., Georgia.
(Signed,)   E. M. STANTON.
Secy. of War.

May 15, 1865

Opposite: Although advertisers had been using illustrations to amplify their messages since The Packet's early days, this image of Louis Riel appears to have been the first illustration in the news pages. It appeared October 21, 1873.

and social implications. The next year, the paper produced a section that featured a hair-raising account of the execution of McGee's assailant written by a reporter who watched from under the gallows.

Although the *Citizen* remained a devoted supporter of John A. Macdonald's Conservatives—especially during the 1872-73 Pacific railway scandal—during Ridgeway's tenure, the newspaper was much less a political weapon and much more a balanced journal than at any time in its history. The Ridgeway era ended in late 1869 when he left for Montreal to edit a new paper, the *Star*. Soon after, Taylor sold a half-interest in the *Citizen* to Ridgeway's successor, George Holland. In 1873, Taylor sold his remaining shares to J. M. Currier, the Conservative MP for Ottawa. Within a few years, it would prove to be a move that set the *Citizen* on a new course of political activism lasting into the 1890s.

May 15, 1865

In issuing the first number of *The Ottawa Citizen* as a Daily Newspaper, and thinking of the undertaking to which we are thus committed, we are naturally led to reflect upon the progress of this place in which no fewer than three daily journals now solicit the patronage of the public. Scarcely a generation has passed away since the district in which the City of Ottawa now stands was comparatively a wilderness. The timber which covered the face of the earth was unvalued. The waterfalls, with their mighty hydraulic power, were unappropriated. The river, on which the city stands and whose name it bears, rolled its dark waters towards the ocean, undisturbed by the keels of civilization and commerce; the wolf and the bear roamed through dreary and infrequented wilds; the red man, who alone disputed their dominion, wended his way through the mazes of the forest, guided only by the course of the sun, the position of the stars, or the current of the streams. But the European came and, before him, the aboriginal possessors of the soil, along with the wolf and the bear, have almost disappeared. The forests have been cleared away; and luxuriant crops have waved where a short while ago, trees of gigantic growth lifted their towering summits to the clouds. The noise of waterfalls is now commingled with the din of hammers and the rattling of machinery. The steamboat bell and the railroad whistle proclaim the efforts of energetic colonists to keep pace with what is called "the spirit of the times." Within these few years past, this place of our habitation, lately a wilderness has been successively, first, an insignificant and, as was thought by many, a mere temporary settlement—then, a flourishing village—and then an important town. More recently, being elevated to the status of a city, the old name of Bytown, still the most familiar to some of the old settlers in the surrounding country, was superseded by the present name of the city, Ottawa. And, besides all this there is

the still more remarkable and important fact of its having been elected by her Majesty's Government as the permanent Capital of Canada, a country destined to exert, in one way or other, a mighty influence upon the future of the American continent. We admit the responsibility of journalists in such a place to be great. It is our desire to prosecute our work under this conviction and to do our best to promote the material and moral well-being of our countrymen in the region of the Ottawa, and in the whole country, East and West, of which that region forms a part.

February 13, 1866

YOUTHFUL DEPRAVITY.—At the Police Court yesterday three little boys, (the oldest of whom is not much over twelve years of age,) named respectively Malcolm Macdonald, Sidney Mott and John Cooper, were charged with disorderly conduct on the streets at 12 o'clock on Saturday night. They certainly were beginning early to lead a life of depravity. Young Cooper gave evidence by floods of tears of his contrition, and was let off with a warning. The mothers of these little hopefuls were in court and with faces of pain and eyes suffused with tears watched the progress of the trial. Macdonald and Mott were committed each three days to gaol. Perhaps this will serve as a warning to the many young rowdies who swagger about our streets with cigars in their mouth, impudence in their faces and a care-for-nothing in their manner; and who, to judge them from their demeanor, are older than their fathers, wiser than their teachers, and more honored than the President of the Board of School Trustees. These young fast ones ought to be stopped in their speed. They are legion—the shame of families, the disgrace of the city, the sad and solemn reproach of themselves. Stopped ere tobacco shatters their nerves; ere the loafer masters in the man; ere good ambition and manly strength give way to low pursuits and brutish aims.

August 30, 1866

A RAID AMONG DISORDERLIES.—DESCENT
UPON PROSTITUTION DEN.—A LARGE NUMBER
OF PERSONS ARRESTED.

At the Police Court yesterday morning, quite a number of "frail" creatures were brought up to answer for being inmates and frequenters of houses of ill fame. The policemen for some time past have been indefatigable in bringing to justice the keepers and inmates of the many vile dens of infamy which abound in our city, and yesterday the scene at the Police Court told that they were determined to root out the evil if possible. On Monday night a posse of police made a descent upon a house somewhere in Lower Town kept by a Mrs. Julie Bennett.

The house referred to has the reputation of being a favorable resort for the worst sort of characters. In fact the place had become so noisy that the neighbors were very frequently disturbed of their rest, and complained to the police about it. When the policemen surrounded the house, those inside were engaged in drinking, carousing and dancing, and were taken completely by surprise. Julie was ordered to be committed three months to gaol and to pay a fine of fifty dollars. In default of paying the fine she will have to remain in gaol three weeks longer. Emeline Dube was fined $20 and two months; Jane Deri, $20 and two months; and Mary Laverne $20 and three months. Julie was also charged with the monstrous crime of child desertion. The latter case was remanded till to-day. John Parrie and Jos. Gelina were charged with frequenting Madame Bennett's and were fined each $4 and costs. Edwin Seguien, for a like offence, was fined to the extent of $20 and costs. Paul Gravelle was up for keeping a house of ill-fame. The charge was not proved and the case was dismissed. Mr. Ross appeared for the defendant. Nearly all of the above parties were sent to gaol in default of payment of the fines. They formed quite a procession down the street.

October 9, 1866
Although the Citizen *failed to mention it, War of 1812 veteran
Hugh Byres was 74 years old when he died.*

'ONE BY ONE THE STARS ARE FADING.' The old veterans of Canada are fast going to "that bourne whence no traveller returns." There are but few now left, and it is only occasionally that it falls to the lot of the journalist to chronicle the death of one who figured in that troublous time when Canada had to fight her way through great internal difficulties and oppose, by armed force, the endeavors of her more powerful neighbor who sought to force her into an alliance at once distasteful to her people and detrimental to her interests. On Saturday last the funeral of one of these veterans was seen wending its way slowly through the streets of this city. The body that was being conveyed to its last earthly resting place, was all that remained of Hugh Byres of Black Rapids, a man who, as bugler, sounded the charge at Lundy's Lane, the attack at Fort Niagara, and took part at the battle of Queenston Heights, where the noble Brock fell fighting for his country. Nothing delighted the veteran loyalist, whose remains were on Saturday followed to the grave by a large number of his friends and neighbors, so much, during his declining years, as recounting the incidents of his younger days. His loyal heart beat high, and his failing limbs gained strength as he heard and thought of the dastardly attempts upon Canada by the cut-throat Fenians, and it was not without strong

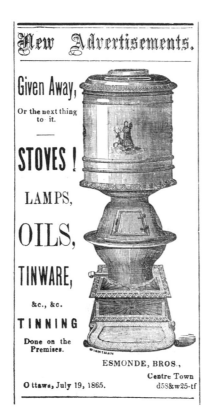

persuasion on the part of his friends that he could be induced not to enroll himself as a volunteer and go forth once more to fight for the liberty and integrity of his country. Another instance added to the many we daily hear of the true spirit of loyalty which exists in the breasts of the majority of the Irish and Roman Catholic portion of the population of these colonies. The deceased had lived for upwards of half a century in Canada, and at the close of an eventful life, during which he had secured the esteem of very many, his remains were interred in the Roman Catholic cemetery here. May the spirit which animated these old veterans exist for ever, and become intensified by years, in the breasts of their descendants.

February 14, 1867

THE DELIGHTS OF SHOPPING. Reader, did you ever go a-shopping for wife, sister, aunt, cousin, or any other lady? If you have, the system inaugurated by some of our large dry goods stores will hardly cause you to exclaim, "How delightful!" The ladies may like it, but for a gentleman on an errand of this kind, one trial is sufficient. You enter a store and ask the nearest attendant if he has a certain article. "The other side of the store," is your answer. You proceed on. "The other aisle you will find it." "Farther down, if you please." "We sold the last one we had yesterday," answers the fourth, and so on, until you begin to think you are shopping in earnest.

"Everything in the right place" is a very good maxim, but why keep a fellow trotting around to find out whether he can obtain the article in question and be obliged to go to another store afterwards, only to go through the same process? That's what we want to know.

April 22, 1867

"HOW ARE YOU, BILL?" On Saturday last our "local" took a stroll up Sussex street with an oleaginous and good-looking young friend from the country. Our objective point was to show him the "lions" of the city. Just after passing George street we were considerably astonished and our friend, who, without exception is the most modest man in Canada, taken "all aback" by a young and lovely lady rushing out of a store and throwing a pair of the whitest, roundest and plumpest arms about his neck. Warm, earnest and heavenly kisses fell upon his own from lips that would tempt a bee to search there for honey. Between the pauses of the kisses she exclaimed: "Why, Bill, how are you? (Kiss.) When did you get back? (Kiss.) Where have you been all this time? (Kiss.) Why have you not been to see us, you old queer duck you? (Kiss, kiss, kiss.) Ma-a-ad? (Kiss, kiss, kiss.) There, there you darling (kiss) I'm not going to scold you!" (Kiss, kiss, kiss, kiss.) Our friend's face turned as red as boiled lobster. His eyes stood out from his head

THE ATLANTIC CABLE.

ARRIVAL OF THE BRITISH WAR STEAMER "TERRIBLE," AT NEWFOUNDLAND.

Report of Captain Napier.

CABLE PARTED ON THE 2ND INST.

The Great Eastern returned to England for Stronger Grappling Gear

MR. VARLEY VERY SANGUINE OF SUCCESS.

By Special Telegraph to "The Ottawa Citizen."

Heart's Content, 15th, via Aspy Bay, 17th.

The British man-of-war steamers "Terrible" and "Galata," from Heart's Content, 2nd, arrived at St. John's, N.F., at 9 o'clock on Tuesday evening, 15th inst.

The steamship "Great Eastern," returned to Sheerness on the 11th inst.

Capt. Napier reports as follows:

The cable parted on Wednesday, the 2nd instant, at noon, in nineteen hundred and fifty fathoms of water. It was then grappled for three different times, and raised twice, nine hundred and six hundred fathoms respectively. Each time the grappling broke, but the cable remained unbroken. The 'Great Eastern' returned to England for stronger and better grappling gear.

Mr. Varley, one of the electricians, writes most encouragingly in regard to the cable. He says: "We found no difficulty in grappling the

August 18, 1865

like the horns of a yearling calf. Perspiration poured down his cheeks in drops as large as partridge eggs, and in sufficient quantity to thoroughly wash his shirt. At last, by concentrating all his strength for a single decisive effort, he wrenched himself from the lady's embrace, exclaiming as he did so: "Madam, there's some mistake here!" "Good gracious!" cried the lady when she discovered that she had been wasting her sweetness upon a stranger. "I thought it was Bill Davis!" And in a second a vision of crinoline disappearing through a neighbouring door was all that was visible of the charming young creature.

May 10, 1867

Rumour having been busy to the effect that the Hon. John A. Macdonald desired to represent Ottawa in the House of Commons, a number of influential gentlemen waited upon the hon. gentleman on Tuesday, by appointment, for the purpose of ascertaining his feelings on the subject. The deputation was received with the utmost courtesy, and Mr. Macdonald frankly stated that, while highly appreciating the compliment implied in the mention of his name as a candidate for the representation of Ottawa in the House of Commons, it would not be in his power to accept the position. He had now represented the City of Kingston for twenty-four years; he had been returned eleven times at general and special elections; and, having been requested by his old constituents to be a candidate for the House of Commons, he felt that it would be ungrateful on his part if he did not accede. He had been waited upon only that morning by a deputation from Kingston; and strong as had been the support he had hitherto received there, he had been assured that it would be even greater in the future.

July 3, 1867

Given the Citizen's *enthusiasm for Confederation, the paper's coverage of the celebrations marking Canada's birth as a Dominion on July 1, 1867 was surprisingly understated. However, the paper did express its disapproval—to a point—of Governor General Lord Monck's decision not to make a public appearance on the big day. Here's an excerpt from the editorial:*

It is a matter of the greatest regret that His Excellency the Governor General deemed it inexpedient to receive the public demonstration which our citizens were prepared to give him upon his return to the seat of government, after a protracted absence. His Excellency has probably missed one of the heartiest and most enthusiastic receptions ever tendered to the Representative of Her Majesty, and the disappointment of our citizens at being denied the opportunity of tendering their greetings and congratulations is severely felt. It was the earnest

wish of the city authorities, the members of our national societies and the citizens generally, to congratulate His Excellency—and, through him, Her Majesty—upon the accomplishment of Confederation. Lord Monck's name is closely identified with the history of the closing period of the old Union, and it is the pleasure and will of Her Majesty that his name shall appear on the opening pages of the history of the incoming Union. Our people believe that with Confederation a glorious future is opened to the country, that the material progress of all the Provinces will be greatly accelerated, and that the British connexion which they so much esteem will be cemented afresh. In Lord Monck they recognize that representative of Her Majesty who has been amongst them during a critical period of our history, who has watched the progress of the measures for Confederation, and who has been selected to inaugurate the new order of things. With these feelings and acting upon these considerations, it is only natural that the citizens of Ottawa should desire to extend to His excellency their heartiest congratulations upon his return to the Seat of Government, and that the disappointment should be keenly felt. But this disappointment could not very easily have been avoided. His Excellency appears to have forwarded his request—that the public reception should be put off—at the earliest possible moment after receiving the conventional notification of the intended demonstration, but for personal reasons and public considerations he did not consider the present an opportune time for public demonstration . . . . (Lord Monck's) visit to Ottawa at the present time is connected with purely business matters; his stay here will be short for the reason that Rideau Hall is not yet in a state of readiness. His Excellency believes that a more suitable opportunity for a public demonstration would be when he comes to take up his permanent residence at the Seat of Government. We feel assured that it is far from His Excellency's thought or intention to do anything towards unnecessarily frustrating the demonstrations of loyalty and respect which the people may choose to exhibit.

Local Intelligence.

ACKNOWLEDGEMENT.— The Treasurer of the County of Carleton General Protestant Hospital, acknowledges per honor of O. T. Thomas, Esq., the receipt of ten dollars, Subscription from the St. George's Society of the city of Ottawa, in aid of said Institution.

No OIL YET.—The announcement made by us and the other city papers on Saturday that oil had been struck in North Gower was premature. Of course the strongest kind of hope exists of striking the "substance" at an early day, but the reality has not yet, by any means, outrun the hope.

January 1, 1866

SIR JOHN FRANKLIN,S EXPEDITION—The *New York Times* states that a second part of Captain Hall's report on his search for fuller information about Sir John Franklin's Arctic expedition has been received, The wrecked ships of Franklin appear to have been visited, the remains of a large number of their crews seen· frozen and multilated, and the valuables left in the ships appropriated by the Exquimaux. They encourage Capt. Hall to believe that some of the men may still be living.

February 13, 1866

July 12, 1867

Organized hockey was still two decades away, and lacrosse far and away Canada's most popular game, when the Citizen *carried this spirited—and, by today's standards, insensitive—account of a game held in Montreal on the first Dominion Day.*

A LACROSSE MATCH. We have received the following account of the Lacrosse Match at Montreal between the Montrealers and Indians on Dominion Day:

It is 8.40 when, amid cheers and clapping of hands, the players enter the field. The Montrealers are, Maltby (Captain), A.

Davidson, A. Tate, E.A. Whitehead, R. McDougall, F. Dowd, Watson, McDonald, Ralston, Middlemiss, Henderson and Thompson. The Indians' names defy pronunciation on the part of any one who fears lockjaw. The Montrealers wear their natty uniform, white caps, white jackets with red cuffs, grey Knickerbockers with red cord, and black stockings. The Indians appear in varied costume, barefooted, for the most part, with trousers of modest dye, scarlet and yellow predominating, motley headgear, and shirts to match. They stand much higher than their opponents, several of whom are only boys in size, and whose beards scarcely average two-fifths of a whisker each.

That Lacrosse is a popular game this excited crowd of four or five thousands testifies. There are many reasons why it should be so. "Why," growls a cricketeer at our left, "can't we raise a crowd of a hundred to see a cricket match?" For the simple reason that lacrosse is a popular game, easy of comprehension, always of thrilling interest, while Cricket, barring four-hits and catches at longfield, is slow to all but the players, or to understanding lookers-on. Cricket, like billiards, requires an educated audience; lacrosse, like a horse-race, is red jacket against blue, the excitement is more intense, and the suspense is soon over.

While we are moralizing, the players are stationed, the ball is in motion, and sent at once to the Montrealer's goal, followed by a rush from the Indians, and a lively rally, the whites a little nervous. After a pretty close thing of it, the white jackets get it away into the middle of the field, then a long-legged aborigine, like a pair of tongs or a starved greyhound, gets it back, another helps it along, a white jacket goes tilt into the melee, scatters the contestants, loses the ball to another Indian, the goal keeper tips it away cleverly into the crowd. But even crinoline is no sanctuary, for half-a-dozen players rush over the crowd, a clashing of crosses, and then the ball is driven half way down the field, then in to the Indian's goal; but Dowd was hardly quick enough and it goes up in the field again. Then a fifty yard sprint between Whitehead and an Indian, but the Montrealer is the quicker, and the ball is thrown to another white jacket. A ten-second rally, and the ball is thrown squarely through the flags, Montreal scoring the first goal, amid wild cheers. The victors come back triumphantly to the refreshment room, ready to turn somersaults in their exuberant spirits, the Indians stretch themselves in the field, and the crowd yawns and criticizes the game.

THE FENIANS

SPECIAL FROM TORONTO.

Special to " Citizen " per Provincial Line.

TWO THOUSAND FENIANS AT FORT ERIE !

THEY CAPTURE AND DESTROY A LARGE AMOUNT OF PROPERTY.

THEY HAVE CUT THE TELEGRAPH WIRES !

BRIDGE DETROYED BY THE FENIANS.

THE QUEEN'S OWN LEFT THIS MORNING FOR THE SCENE OF ACTION !

THE 10TH ROYALS ARE GETTING READY !

Toronto, 1st.

News has been received at Toronto of the Fenians crossing, about 2,000 strong, at Fort Erie, and destroying a great deal of property

They cut the telegraph wires.

The Queen's Own left this morning, about 500 strong, for Port Colborne.

The 10th Royals are getting ready to leave by this morning's train.

Refugees from Fort Erie at Brantford report the burning of the Sourwines Bridge five miles west of Fort Erie. Nothing new elsewhere.

June 2, 1866

July 26, 1867

NO PLACE FOR THEM. Two unfortunate imbecile children were brought in from Osgoode by their friends, on Friday afternoon, with the hope of getting them placed for safe keeping in the gaol, but the authorities had no power to admit them, the gaol being preserved for criminals and not open to unfortunates. Both of them—a boy aged eleven, and a girl of thirteen—brother and sister, are fine healthy-looking children, and their robust physical condition makes their mental infirmity appear the more deplorable.

November 8, 1867

OPENING OF PARLIAMENT

As the largest circulation paper in the capital, the Citizen *took its self-assigned role as Parliament's "paper of record" very seriously. It provided long, often verbatim accounts of debates and, when significant bills were being discussed, printed the legislation in its entirety. This excerpt from a lengthy item on the opening of the first Dominion Parliament is typical of the detail the* Citizen *provided in its coverage.*

The opening of the first Parliament of the Dominion of Canada was a day long looked forward to as a culminating point in the Union of British North America—a day which witnessed the first assembling of the legislators of a new nation, and a day which will be forever notable in the history of the country. The weather was clear and pleasant, and the sun shone brightly and brilliantly, as if smiling approval on the proceedings of the day. During the afternoon business in the city was almost entirely suspended, the streets were crowded with people in holiday attire, and in obedience to the expressed wish of His Worship the Mayor, B. Lyon. Esq., the houses were decorated with flags and banners. Seldom has the Capital City worn a gayer and happier appearance. Early in the afternoon the military companies assembled at their several rendezvous, and then proceeded to the various places allotted to them in the day's programme. At the main entrance of the Parliament Buildings was stationed the Band of the Rifle Brigade, and a guard of honor, furnished by the same regiment, which also furnished a detachment to line the passage of the building. From the main tower to the entrance on Elgin street was lined with troops. The right of the line was occupied by the Rifle Brigade, after which were the 17th regiment the Garrison Artillery, Ottawa Provisional Battalion of Rifles, and the Civil Service Rifles.

Long before the appointed hour, the galleries of the Senate Chamber were crowded with spectators, among whom were many ladies, to witness the event. A more brilliant and fashionable assemblage was per-

SPECIAL FROM HEARTS CONTENT

ARRIVAL OF THE

"GREAT EASTERN"

Atlantic Cable Successfully Laid ! !

IT IS WORKING PERFECTLY ! ! !

THE OLD CABLE TO BE TAKEN UP AND COMPLETED ON THE 15th AUGUST.

Special to the CITIZEN per Montreal Line.

Montreal, July 29.

We have received reliable information this morning from Hearts Content, New Foundland, via Sackville, New Brunswick, that the Atlantic cable was successfully completed at 9 a. m. on the 27th, and signals through it were perfect. The "Great Eastern" will return immediately to pick up the cable lost last year, and Mr. Field is confident of having a second cable complete by the 15th of August.

STILL LATER

Heart's Content, New Foundland, 27.—The "Great Eastern" left Sheerness Saturday noon, June 30th, arrived at Beerhaven Thursday morning July 5th, and there received the balance of her coals and provisions. The other steamers accompanying the telegraph fleet joined the "Great Eastern at Beerhaven are as follows : The "William Cory" and "Terrible," Friday the 6th: "Albany" on the 7th ; "Medway"

July 30, 1866

haps never before convened in Ottawa. Occupying prominent positions on the floor of the House were Chief Justice Richards, Monsr. Guigues, Roman Catholic Bishop of Ottawa, Judge Armstrong, Rev. Mr. Lauder, Rev. Mr. Bliss, Rev. Mr. Higginson, Mayor Lyon and others.

About half-past two the House was organized by reading the proclamation calling together the Senators, after which the proclamation appointing Hon. Mr. Cauchon as Speaker of the Senate was read. The commission of Mr. Fennings Taylor, Clerk, was then read and the oath administered by the Hon. Mr. Cauchon. This was followed by the reading of prayers by the Rev. Dr. Adamson, Chaplain of the Senate. Shortly before three o'clock a salute, fired by the Field Battery on Major's Hill announced that His Excellency had left Rideau Hall for the Parliament Buildings, and at the hour appointed he entered the Senate Chamber, attended by a numerous and brilliant suite. A message was then dispatched from His Excellency that the House of Commons had been assembled in their own Chamber where the oath of office was administered to those present, by the Clerk of the House. Upon receiving the summons of the Governor General, they proceeded to the Upper House, where His Excellency informed them that exigencies of State required the summoning of the representatives of the people to meet him in Parliament—that he would not explain the reasons which induced him to call Parliament together until they had chosen a Speaker, but that on Thursday he would meet them at the same hour and explain his reasons for so doing. He then dismissed them, and shortly after the Senate adjourned.

The members of the House of Commons returned to their own Chamber and proceeded to the election of a Speaker....

February 14, 1868

AWFUL TRAGEDY.

A WOMAN KILLS HER FIVE CHILDREN WITH AN AXE

Seldom does it fall to the lot of a Canadian journalist to have to chronicle an occurrence equalling in horror and magnitude that which we are to faintly describe, and happy it is that such events are exceedingly rare in the history of this country. Murders, it is true, are only too common in this civilized age, among civilized people, but rarely is humanity shocked by hearing of the destruction of a family by the hand of a parent. In the Township of Alice, near the town of Pembroke, live, or rather lived, a German family by the name of Webber. The family consisted of a father—a tailor, who earned his living by working round among his neighbours—his wife and six children. The father is said to be a peaceable and industrious man, and his wife had the reputation of being a kind and affectionate mother though some years before she had exhibited symptoms of insanity; two daughters, the eldest fifteen

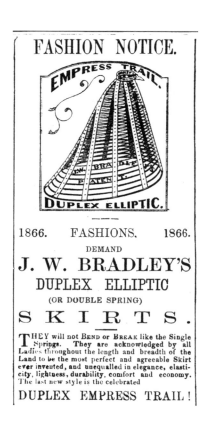

August 14, 1866

or sixteen years of age, and four sons made up their family. On Friday, last, 31st ultimo, the father being out at work, the eldest daughter went out to milk the cows, but before she got through was called in to the house by her mother. On reaching there she was startled to find her mother standing in the entrance with an axe and remarking to her, they are all dead. Or words to that effect. But on looking into the house, the horrible sight of her younger sister and brothers lying around the room, gashed and bleeding, met her eyes, and she fled in wild terror to one of the neighbors. It is said that the mother was making demonstrations to make her a victim also, but she got out of her way in time to prevent it. Word of the horrible affair was soon afterwards received in Pembroke, when Dr. McKenzie, coroner, repaired to the place, and held an inquest at once, after which the woman was conveyed to the jail in Pembroke, to await further proceedings on the part of the authorities. Three of the children were dead when the coroner arrived at the scene of the tragedy, another died while the inquest was being held. Four of them were buried on Sunday last.

Insanity, as will at once be inferred, was the cause of this awful and unnatural act. About ten years ago, while yet in Germany, her husband tells of her killing a cow with an axe, while in a similar frenzy. Up to Friday last, the derangement in her mind seems to have slept, as there appears to have been no danger apprehended by her friends, of violence on her part; on the contrary, those who know her speak of the great amount of affection she always manifested for her children. On the morning in question, the children, it is believed, from the circumstances gathered, had just got up out of bed, and were standing round the stove when the old demon of insanity returned with redoubled power, and urged the wretched woman to the committal of the most unnatural act the mind can conceive. The axe was seized, and rapidly the deadly blows descended on the heads of the poor children, cleaving their skulls and scattering their brains in a horrible manner. Awful indeed must be the power of this unknown agency, which thus drove a mother, naturally tender, to the destruction of her nearest, and dearest! It is strange that no screams or other noises were heard by the daughter outside, who was only a short distance from the house. The horrid work must have been accomplished almost in a moment, with all the vehemence and cunning that insanity engenders, preventing alike any unusual noise and escape on the part of the bewildered children,

The spectacle, on entering the scene of the butchery, when the inquest commenced, is described as sickening and pitiable in the extreme. Three of the children were already cold in death, and the other two, barely alive, were lying where they had fallen, with ghastly wounds in their heads, precluding the possibility of recovery. One of those yet alive had in addition, part of one hand cut off, the little thing

August 30, 1866

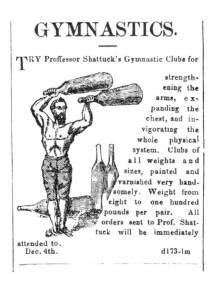
December 28, 1866

having, probably on the same principle that drowning men catch at straws, mechanically clasped its hand over its head to ward off the descending blow. Altogether, it was a shocking sight, and taken in connection with the cause and circumstances it was no wonder that the strongest nerves were unstrung, and those accustomed to view death and suffering in every shape turned from the sight with shuddering. We will spare our readers from further details. After the inquest, the coroner, Dr. McKenzie, committed the woman to the county gaol in Pembroke, where she now is waiting the further actions of the legal authorities. Since her commitment, the wretched being has come to her usual sense, but save a few half meaningless expressions, has said very little in connection with the affair, and is not apparently disposed to speak at all on the subject. Her mental agony appears to be excessive as evinced by her constant moaning and rocking to and fro, while the tearless eyes seem to denote an extremity of inward suffering too great to be relieved by tears.

Since writing the above we learn that one of the children is still living—the one with the mutilated hand—though it cannot recover, so dreadful is the wound inflicted.

According to Alice Township death records, the five children attacked by their mother were Carl, 10, Maria, 7, Eduard, 5, August, 3, and Franz, four months. Maria, the child who survived the attack, died three days after this story appeared. The children's mother, Caroline, died in jail five weeks later. No cause was given, although suicide seems likely, since there are no accounts, in newspapers or in official files, of a trial or execution.

April 10, 1868
STARTLING & DIABOLICAL MURDER
Hon. Thos. Darcy McGee Assassinated.
The Fatal Shot Enters Behind His Ear and Escapes Through His Mouth. Death Almost Instantaneous.
THE ASSASSIN STILL AT LARGE

This morning shortly after two o'clock the city was thrown into a state of horror and alarm by a report that the Hon. Thomas Darcy McGee had been assassinated at the door of his boarding house in Sparks street. At first the dire intelligence was scarcely credited. But few who heard it could resist the desire to enquire into the correctness of the statement, which upon investigation turned out to be only too true. During the evening the appointment of Dr. Tupper as High Commissioner to England had been under discussion in the House, and the honorable gentleman had addressed the Commons at some length on the subject. After the adjournment he must have left the Parliament

April 12, 1867

Buildings almost immediately, as the House had not risen more than twenty minutes before he was found lying murdered on the sidewalk in a pool of blood in front of the Toronto House, where he resided. It appears that a servant in the boarding-house heard someone at the door and a shot fired. Going to the door at once she discovered the body of the murdered man lying on the planks, and at once gave the alarm. From the nature of the wound and the position in which the body lay there can be no doubt but that the murder was coolly done, and that instantaneous death ensued. The deceased was found lying on his back, his hat not even displaced from his head and his walking cane under his arm. The bullet entered at the back of the neck and came out of his mouth and destroyed his front teeth, lodging in the door about two inches above the latch-key hole. It is evident, from these facts, that the honorable gentleman must have been in the act of opening the door, stooping to find the keyhole with his head close to it, and his cane under his arm, and that the assassin must have approached him cautiously, and putting the pistol to his head behind his ear, discharged it and fled.

The fearful news soon spread among the members of the Legislature, few of whom had retired to rest, and ere long the place was filled with his sorrowing friends and admirers, whose deeply expressed detestation of the cowardly crime will find an echo in every honest breast. The Premier and the Premier of Ontario, with many others, hastened to the spot, and every effort was at once set afoot to discover the perpetrator of the crime, which for audacity and cool-bloodedness stands unequalled in our history.

July 31, 1868

A VISIT TO THE GAOL.

INTERVIEW WITH WHELAN, BUCKLEY

AND THE OTHER PRISONERS

Nearly four months after McGee's shooting, the Citizen *was granted the first interview with Patrick James Whelan, the man charged with the murder. The interview took place during a* Citizen *reporter's "inspection" of the county jail, a ruse arranged by jail authorities to ward off requests for interviews by other newspapers. The* Citizen *repaid the favour by praising the condition of the jail. Whelan was eventually convicted and hanged for the murder, partly on the controversial testimony of Jean-Baptiste Lecroix, who claimed he saw Whelan leaving the crime scene. This is an excerpt from the* Citizen's *lengthy story on its jail tour:*

On Thursday we paid a visit to the County Gaol, and through the courtesy of the Sheriff and Governor of the institution, were allowed

PROCLAMATION !

WHEREAS it will greatly conduce to the health and comfort of the Citizens of Ottawa generally, to have the City cleaned of all filth and nuisances : And whereas the introduction and spread of Cholera, Typhus and other contagious diseases is, and will certainly be influenced by the sanitary condition of the city : And whereas

THE BOARD OF HEALTH

Under and by virtue of the Powers conferred upon them by various Acts of Parliament, establishing "Boards of Health," and in accordance with various By-Laws of the City of Ottawa, have deemed it advisable that immediate steps should be taken for cleansing the City.

NOW KNOW YE THAT I,

ROBERT LYON,

Mayor of the City of Ottawa,

Do hereby order and direct, that all

YARDS, CELLARS,

STABLES,

Out-houses & other Buildings,

And Enclosures,

Lanes or Alleys

Shall be thoroughly cleansed of all

FILTH, DIRT, NIGHT SOIL,

Or other impurities by the owners or persons occupying the same.

Before the 20th day of April,

1867 : and I hereby give notice that the Chief of Police and the Constabulary of this City are enjoined to proceed, at once, to have all Privy Pitts, Cesspools, &c., thoroughly cleansed, and to see this order carried into effect, and all and every person or persons disobeying or neglecting to observe the same, on or before the Twentieth day of April, 1867,

WILL BE PUNISHED ACCORDING TO LAW.

Given under my hand at the City of Ottawa, this 23nd day of March, A. D., 1867.

ROBERT LYON,

MAYOR.

d273-td

April 17, 1867

REQUISITION.

To His Worship the Mayor, of the City of Ottawa:

WE, THE UNDERSIGNED, being Rate-payers of the City of Ottawa, respectfully request your Worship to call, as early as possible, a PUBLIC MEETING, for the purpose of considering the best means to be employed for protecting the City against a repetition of the late INCENDIARY FIRES.

Jas G Robinson	M McNaughton
C W Bangs	D Murphy
Alex Mowat	J T & W Pennock
Grant & Henderson	H W Bate
Ch P Cunningham	Thomas & W Hunton
Isidore Traversy	E Jessup
L Winters	Jas Peacock
James Jarvis	G H Preston
Patrick Casey	J G McLachlin
Jas Bailiff	R J Bowles
Kearns & Ryan	R H S Hardy
Fingland & Draper	Chas Austin
L N Nye	A Cowan
Alex Heney	Thomas Birkett
George May	Peter Kilduff
D P Williams	Thos Patterson
P Wright	Alex Workman
Hugh Williams	Andrew Wilson
O'Connor & Waller	Robert Lees
W A Lamb	J G Whyte
J A Pinard	Chas Rowan
Angus & Huckell	Joseph Ward
James Buchanan	John Hill
A Graham	T Cavanah
Samuel Graham	Michael'Connell
E F Joyce	Thos G Burns
Chas Hirsch	John Lang
Dan Goode	Michael Welsh
Edward Bowique	A I Dunning
T Burns	W C Wood
Wm J Lamb	J Robert
John Kehoe	John Patterson
George Patterson	Whiteside & Walker
Wm Sutherland	S P H Borbridge
C H Burpee	G R Russell
P O'Meara	James Fraser
Th Friedrick	J Powers
Herrick, Brush & Co	G E Elliott
Samuel Christie	Wm Hamilton
John Thompson	Jas L Gillespie
I B Taylor	George Angus
Chas Sparrow, sen	W H Tracy

April 24, 1867

to inspect the whole establishment. The manner in which the building is at present kept reflects great credit on the staff employed about it. From basement to attic everything was in a most orderly condition and a state of exquisite cleanliness, and we were pleased to learn from Dr. Sweetland, the Gaol Physician, who chanced to be present during our visit, that though there were a large number of prisoners in the building, he seldom had occasion to practice the healing art upon them, all being generally in a healthy condition. The number of prisoners in the building at the present time is forty-three, fifteen of them being women. These latter are all, with one exception, committed as vagrants or disorderly characters, and are undergoing short sentences. The parties now in custody charged with Fenianism naturally will attract most attention, and of those whose names have been publicly connected with the sad tragedy of last April, first we encountered was

THE WITNESS LECROIX

who certainly seems none the worse for the easy life he has been leading for some weeks past. We met him in the kitchen where he was enjoying himself with his wife and little boy, a youngster of about two years of age, the whole forming a more merry family group than a visitor would expect to meet within the walls of a prison. Lecroix recognized us at once and during a short conversation expressed himself quite satisfied with the treatment he experienced, though he confessed he would like to be at liberty again. Both he and his wife appeared in capital health and spirits, he in particular having grown quite plump since his detention. His wife evidently wants for nothing, she having been allowed $6 per week from the Government for the support of herself and child since his incarceration, while he has his meals supplied from the Albion Hotel; and but for the name of being a prisoner, he is better off probably than he has ever been before. As we entered he was bestowing what attention he could spare from his family, on some very fine and over-ripe cucumbers, one of which he was very anxious we should take away with us when we were prepared to leave. We would not, however deprive him of the treasure, but left him in undisturbed possession, while we ascended to the prison corridors. In the first of these which we entered we found

PATRICK JAMES WHELAN.

When we entered the corridor the prisoner was walking up and down with that nervous agile movement and step peculiar to him. He was in his stocking feet, and had on a light flannel shirt and a pair of black trousers fastened about the hips with a piece of calico. Since his imprisonment he has not been shaved, and has now somewhat of a full and long beard. His hair has also been uncut for some time, so that his appearance is a good deal changed from what it was at the time of his arrest, although he appears in excellent health and seems, physically, none the worse for his confinement. No other prisoners are kept in the same tier of cells with Whelan, nor is he allowed into the prison yard. He is permitted, however, to take what exercise he wishes in the long hall or corridor, but has a man on guard with him night and day. As soon as he saw us he stopped in his walk, and when we spoke to him entered freely into conversation on various topics. He recognized us as the reporters of the *Citizen*, and expressed himself by no means pleased at the publication of his supposed confession in our columns. He also told us he had several extracts from the *Citizen* as mementoes of our opinion of him. He enquired about the general state of affairs in the outside world, complained of the heat of the weather and assumed a most easy and unembarrassed manner. He made no allusion to the other prisoners implicated in the assassination of Mr. McGee, nor to his own treatment in gaol, but he is evidently made as comfortable as the circumstances of the case will permit. We noticed that he had several newspapers in his cell, and remarked to him that he was well supplied with literature. He laughed and replied, Yes; they allow me to see the city papers now, but would not give me the privilege for the first six weeks I was here. The Governor of the gaol subsequently informed us that Whelan spent the greater part of his time in singing and whistling, and was in general very restless; indeed, as we were about proceeding to the adjoining range of cells, and after we had left his own, we heard him singing in a loud voice that good old English song, The Death of Nelson. Leaving Whelan's cell we proceeded to the adjoining corridor, where we found several other of the prisoners . . . .

August 7, 1868

ELOPEMENT.—On Tuesday evening Detective O'Neil received a telegram from Mr. Madere, of Aylmer, complaining that a plasterer of that place had eloped during the previous night with his sister. He describes the Lothario as about thirty-six years of age, and requests that the fugitive couple might be taken in custody. The bereaved brother forgot, however, to prepay his telegram, and when Detective O'Neil answered him he refused to pay for the answer. The Detective naturally considers his affliction cannot be of the deepest kind, and declines to take any active measures till he can discover who will pay the expense.

WHELAN'S FINAL MOMENTS.
February 12, 1869

Part of the Citizen's coverage of Whelan's execution in the killing of McGee included a detailed account of the prisoner's final hours in the Nicholas Street jail. Here's an excerpt on the hanging itself.

The gallows, which had been for the past two days a subject of curiosity to many, are situated at the eastern end of the gaol, and so constructed that but a partial view of the condemned can be obtained from outside. A door opening from the topmost corridor leads to it, and was constructed when the gaol was first erected, though, happily never required for use till now.

After 10 o'clock the crowd rapidly filled up, and in the course of the following twenty minutes must have increased to upwards of five thousand, a large proportion of which was composed of women. The lower part of Daly street and a large part of Stewart street which faced the gallows was completely filled. Even where the crush was greatest, however, the police had no difficulty in keeping clear the alley in rear of the gaol. The utmost order and decorum were preserved, and there was a total absence of that levity and rowdyism which, in general, mars such events. As the time passed and the fatal moment drew near, many who had waited for a considerable time to witness the final scene abandoned their purpose and left the ground.

At the door of the gaol a considerable number of persons were assembled, waiting for admission, consisting of officials, medical men, and members of the press. The doors were opened at half-past ten precisely, and those who were entitled to enter admitted. A guard of sixty men of the P.C.O. Rifles, under the command of Captain Bunburry, entered the gaol some five minutes before, and lined the stairs and passages. The rope was ready, swung over a pulley and fastened to the stair post inside. It was not new, but looked as if it had seen service on previous occasions whether in similar work or not it was not possible to tell. Allowance was made for a fall of six feet. Only the officials and Reporters could be admitted to the confined space inside the gaol and near the drop.

The last ten minutes before leaving his cell were passed by the prisoner in reciting prayer in company with the Rev. Dr. O'Connor and three other clergymen. At 11 o'clock the Sheriff entered the corridor accompanied by Governor of the Gaol, Mr. Lace, County Attorney, Mr. James Frazer, Clerk of the Court, and Dr. Sweetland, Gaol Physician. The executioner followed almost immediately closely covered so that it was impossible to recognize him. Whelan had drank a little tea just before. He looked pale, and as if controlling his emotion by a strong exercise of that will. He shook hands with all present and said, "I part from you in peace and good will, I bear no ill-will to my men. I wish God to bless me and to bless you." He was pinioned by the hangman in perfect silence, after which he was conducted to the place of execution. He walked to the place and stood upon the drop, before the vast crowd, with more firmness than could have been expected.

He then in a loud tone, but evidently with much suppressed feeling addressed the assembled crowd in these words: "Friends and fellow-

EXECUTION OF WHELAN !

This morning Patrick James Whelan, convicted at the last Fall Assizes in this city of the murder of the late Honorable Thomas D'Arcy McGee, suffered the extreme penalty of the law. And now that the curtain has fallen on the last act of this awful tragedy, it may not be out of place to review, from the opening to the closing scene, the episodes of a drama which, happily for our country, stands without a parallel in its criminal annals.

THE MURDER.

The atrocious murder for which the hardened criminal this morning paid the forfeit of his life, was committed between midnight on the 6th of April last and daylight of the morning of the 7th, under circumstances of such daring cold-bloodedness as excited unspeakable horror, not only in the community of this city, where the deed was unhappily committed, and in every section of the Dominion to which the electric wires flashed the distressing news, and in which the talents, patriotism and kind-heartedness of the unoffending victim were known, but throughout the civilized world. The Canadian Legislature was at the time in session, and owing to the pressure of the business then before it, the debates of the Commons were in general prolonged until some time after midnight. On the night of the 6th an unusually animated discussion had taken place, which lasted till shortly before 2 o'clock in the m___ __ which hour the House rose ___ ___ ___ ___

February 12, 1868

countrymen, I humbly acknowledge the sins and wrongs that I have committed. I ask all whom I have injured to forgive me, and I heartily forgive those who have injured me. I have got nothing further to say. God save Ireland and God save my soul." The last sentence was uttered with more force and energy than the previous part of the speech. Short as were the words the wretched criminal did not venture to deny his guilt, and the justice of the sentence which in a few moments he was to suffer. Standing on the brink of eternity, and surrounded by the Ministers of his Church with the prayers of that Church, just as it were on his lips and in his ears, he could only acknowledge his sins and ask for pardon. The words spoken could hardly be heard by those outside the gaol walls, but were audible enough to those inside and in the court yard below. Immediately after, the executioner drew the cap over the felon's eyes. Again he joined in prayer with the Rev. Dr. O'Connor, the last rites of the church administered and with the words of Ave Maria on his lips, the bolt was drawn, and the murderer of Mr. McGee was launched into eternity.

In the court yard below were assembled about twenty-five persons, chiefly members of the press, who anxiously waited for the appearance of the prisoner on the drop. A slight noise above, and the appearance of the prisoner's spiritual advisers told that his last moments were come. With upturned faces all anxiously watched and listened silently to the prayers and the ceremony going on above. All being completed, precisely at six minutes past eleven o'clock, the body of Patrick James Whelan fell through the drop with a dull, heavy thud which caused a start among those assembled below. Immediately after the fall the body whirled rapidly round, and from the nervous twitching of his hands and fingers, coupled with the contraction and drawing up and crossing of the legs, which were not tied, it was evident that the prisoner died very hard, there being a nervous twitching of the muscles plainly visible for the space of four and three quarter minutes. Then there was a stiffening of the limbs, and a discoloration of the finger ends and nails, and the lifeless body hung an inanimate and dull and uninviting object. In the passage way leading to the court yard, and immediately under the drop, there was standing a rough pine coffin ready to receive the body. After hanging about twenty minutes the body was cut down in the presence of Drs. Sweetland, Bell and Beaubien, who pronounced life extinct. Outside the gaol a hearse was in waiting to convey the body thence to his friends. Application was at once made to the Sheriff for his remains but an immediate answer was not given as to what disposition was to be made of the body.

PROCLAMATION.

THE CITIZENS OF OTTAWA

Are hereby requested to observe

THURSDAY,

THE FIRST DAY OF JULY, 1869,

AS A

PUBLIC HOLIDAY,

BY THE

SUSPENSION OF BUSINESS,

THE

DISPLAY OF FLAGS,

And such other

DEMONSTRATION OF REJOICING

as may be appropriate to the

due and proper

CELEBRATION OF THE ANNIVERSARY

OF THE

INAUGURATION

OF THE DOMINION OF CANADA.

GIVEN under my Hand, the 28th day of June, 1869, at the City of Ottawa, aforesaid.

JOHN ROCHESTER, Jr.,
Mayor.

July 1, 1869

The Ottawa Citizen

I. B. TAYLOR, PROPRIETOR.

DAILY EDITION

THURSDAY, SEPT. 9, 1869.

Sir JOHN A. MACDONALD and family arrived last night.

His Excellency the GOVERNOR-GENERAL is expected at Rideau Hall on Friday.

Our Halifax news of Monday last stated that the prospect of the union cause in Newfoundland was not as bright at present as it was some time ago. We would very much regret anything which would retard the entrance of Newfoundland into the Dominion. It is well known that several of the wealthy merchants in St. John's have opposed Confederation from the first. Two of these, Messrs. BENNETT an GRIEVE, must entertain very strong feelings on the subject, w..

The new capital's newspaper was soon posting the whereabouts of government personalities.

August 1, 1871

CORRESPONDENCE.

To the Editor of THE OTTAWA CITIZEN.

Dear Sir; I am a grumbler and a communist, if you like. In my humble opinion we have had too much sunshine, too much rain, the weather is too fine and warm, it engenders house flies, which trouble me, particularly my nose, when I am endeavoring to sleep. Whose business is it if my nose is a little red? Is it any one's business whether I paid for the dye or not that colored its extremity? The crops are too promising, and potatoes are growing outrageously large. Under such circumstances, flour, pork, and every other necessary of life will be cheap. I don't like cheap things. What if I do purchase expensive articles, is it any body's particular business whether I pay for them or not? I do not like the aspect of affairs; it is too promising; people are too happy, and however others may be satisfied with this general prosperity, I am not; and I sincerely hope that the people of Jackasstown, where I live, will call an indignation meeting and earnestly protest against this rain and substance—big potatoes, heavy wheat, luxuriant oats and barley—this threatened general prosperity which everywhere appears to abound. I solemnly protest against the farmer having any right to such an abundant fortune for his labor, while I, and others like me, have no such prospects. If I don't choose to work, whose business is that? The world owes me a living and I will have to stand and deliver. I protest against the whole framework of society. I don't like religion, temperance, and such antiquated notions. I protest most solemnly against everything but myself and my inalienable right to eat well, wear good clothes (whose business is it if the tailor is not paid?) and drink as much whiskey as I can get without paying for it. I am a philosopher, and go smack in for living by my wits. What's the use of brains, if they don't enable you to live without working? I dive straight for communistic privileges respecting other people's earning. What right has any man to anything of his own? What right has any one to talk such nonsense as the rewards of honest labor? I don't believe in this nonsense about honesty.

Yours truly,

PETER GOSSAN

Jackasstown, Aug. 9th, 1871

September 15, 1871

THE WRATH TO COME.

This tongue-in-cheek editorial was part of a decades-long crusade to convince city council to improve the quality of Ottawa's water supply and deal with an increasingly serious sewage problem. It was a struggle that continued well into the next century, although it

*produced early results in 1875 with the construction of the city's
first large sewer main.*

It is rumored around town that a vigilance committee, composed of
the most influential and respectable citizens of Ottawa, is about to be
organized, with the avowed object of calling at the City Hall next Monday evening and collaring each and every member of the corporation
by the scruff of their necks, lifting them from the corporation chairs,
and then carrying them in a body around the city, to visit and taste the
different sources of the present water supply of Ottawa after which the
whole crowd are to be immersed in the slimiest part of the Bywash, to
take the wool out of their eyes. Each man will then be presented with a
free pass to the Rocky Mountains, with a warning that if they are ever
found inside the limits of this city again they will receive a full suit of
tar and feathers, free, gratis, and for nothing. The programme as laid
down is as follows: The Aldermen are to drink a pint of water from the
bay in the vicinity of the brewery sewer, which is supposed will be sufficient to create a vacuum in their stomachs five minutes after it is
swallowed, and prepare them for the following tests. One pint of water
from Perkins quarry, one quart of Bywash abominations, one pint of
Canal Basin rot gut, half a gallon of saw dust soup from the foot of the
locks, one gallon of essence of cat from the LeBreton's flat pump, half a
pint of grave-yard juices from Sandy Hill, one quart of distilled pig sty
juice from Clarence street, one gallon of swamp water from Ottawa
ward, and one pint of Bank street putrid. After which the dregs of a wa-
terman's barrel is to be divided amongst them, which is expected to be
about as much as human endurance can stand. Should there be any
danger of death overtaking them at the close of the process they will
be conducted to O'Mear's where cocktails will be supplied at the May-
or's expense as such are a certain cure for extreme cases like theirs, the
Vigilance Committee being aware that the generosity of an act on behalf of His Worship will prove too much even for the City Council.
This operation it is supposed will be a sufficiently frightful warning to
the new City Council that is to be elected next January to deter them
from following the foolish, idiotic, gassing, stupid, wasteful, vexatious,
quarreling, and scandalous course adopted by their predecessors, the
occupants of the Ottawa City Municipal Bear Garden.

January 6, 1872
OUR BACHELOR'S LIST.

Since the publication of the list of some of our well known, well preserved bachelor residents of this city, in the *Citizen*, we have had a
number of communications from our lady readers calling for a continuation of our list. Our correspondents have sent us the names or de-

Advertisers tried to capitalize on
current events, in this case the visit
by Prince Arthur. Below is the menu
for his dinner on Oct. 12, 1869.

THE BILL OF FARE:
SOUP.
Potage a la Royale.
Dishes Ornamented.
Gilatine de Dinde a la Gelie.
Gelatine de poulet a L'astic.
Pates de Gibieraux Truffes.
Mayonnaise de Homard.
Salade a la Russe.
Mayonnaise de poulet a la Reine.
Salade a la Canadienne decorie.
Jambon ornes a la Royale.
Round de Beouf Glaces a la Moderne.
Roulade de Lapin en Bellevue.
Chicken pot-pie a L'Americaine.
Relishes.
Roast.
Poulets, Perdreaux Dindes, Farcies.
Canard Sauvage.
PASTRY.
Biscuits decories, Blanc mange, Galeaux
a L'espagnol, Charlotte Russe a la Vanille,
Gelie au Rhum, Pyramids, Gelie aux Fruits,
Patisseues Francaise, Gelie au Mareschino.
MOTTOES.
FRUITS.
Pommes, Poires. Grapes, Raisins de Serve,
Figues.
CRYSTALLIZED FRUITS.
Champagne, Carte Blanche, Sherry, Amou-
tillado, Claret, Chatean Lagrange,
Port T. G. Saudemannis.
The luncheon, which was done ample jus-
tice to after the exertions of the previous
few hours, was provided by the lumbermen,
whose names are given in another place.

scriptions of several tough cases, who are to receive a notice gratis, but a great many of the gentlemen are too young to be placed on the list of old bachelors subject to leap-year overtures. As we intend to comply with the wishes of our lady friends and publish the remainder of the incorrigibles next week, we would request our contributors when sending any additions to our list to give the name, occupation and address of each victim. No person being considered worthy of a notice unless he is either a widower or a bachelor over twenty-five years of age. Ladies will govern themselves accordingly. God save the Queen.

February 27, 1872
A TOTAL ABSTINENCE TAVERNKEEPER.

The spacious dining-hall of the Dominion House, corner of Sussex and Clarence street, was last evening the scene of one of the happiest anniversary gatherings we have had the pleasure of hearing of for a long time. The occasion was a social celebration of his twenty-seventh anniversary as a pledged total abstinence man, of the highly esteemed host, Mr. William McCaffery. It certainly was something out of the usual way to see the landlord of hotels, where liquors are sold, celebrating such an anniversary. We very much question whether anything similar has ever taken place in this city for the landlord of a tavern to have been twenty-seven years a pledged teetotaller, and honouring the anniversary of his pledge by such a pleasant gathering in his own saloon. What a blessing it would be to unfortunate inebriates were all tavern or hotel-keepers of the country in the hands of men as temperate and honourable as the proprietor of that excellent and well-managed house. It is too often the case that tavern-keepers have no scruples about selling liquor to all who ask for it, but we have known from personal observation that Mr. McCaffery has refused to sell liquor in many instances to persons who are victims of intemperance. A man who, rising above the love of gain, is actuated by such unselfish motives, well merits the eulogies of the community.

About nine o'clock the guests were ushered into the dining-hall, where a sumptuous repast was spread. Amongst the guests present were Chief Langrell, Alderman Heney, Mr. Battle, Mr. J. Desloriers, Mr. Groulx, Mr. H. S. Watson, Mr. Donahue, Mr. Devlin, and several others. The cloth being removed, the usual round of toasts and speeches followed, which were pledged in hot coffee, tea and cold water, no intoxicating liquors except a couple of glasses of wine being used. The company adjourned at a late hour after passing a pleasant evening. As a temperance meeting we consider this to have been one of the greatest novelties of the season.

August 11, 1871

June 13, 1872
POLITICS AND FANATICISM.
(Excerpt from an editorial)

It is very hard to know how to deal with a fanatic. There is no use talking reason to him, for the more reasonable a proposition appears in your eyes, the more intolerable does it appear to him. There is no use in calling his attention to facts. Facts to him are non avenues, that is to say, have no existence, if they are not to his liking. He will not surrender the smallest detail of the system he worships, and in which he is shut up, for all the facts in the world. Talk to him of conciliation and compromise and he will call you a traitor; talk of constitutional rights and he will call you a heathen; say that you cannot do what he wants and he will threaten you with hell.

There is a journal in the Province of Quebec whose apparent aim is to show the people of this hitherto happy country to what extremes of unreasonableness and violence religious bigotry can lead men. Strangely enough this journal, instead of being called *Le Moyen Age*, is called *Le Nouveau Monde*. Its doctrine may be briefly described as everything that the New World repudiates. It puts forth pretensions for the Church that the most Catholic countries in the world would not tolerate for a moment, and tries to persuade a gullible circle of readers that Canada is the highly favoured land in which ecclesiastical absolutism is to display itself in the most imposing forms; that here we are to have the edifying spectacle of the complete triumph of the spiritual over the secular; of the church over the State.

We do not attempt to argue with our mediaeval contemporary. His modes of thought are not ours, nor are his standards of true and false, such as the modern world recognizes. What we are concerned with is that this Canadian Universe is devoting itself to the task of running down in the opinion of their countrymen, two of the most loyal Canadians who have ever figured in public life in this country, Sir Georges E. Cartier and Mr. [Hector-Louis] Langevin [both Fathers of Confederation from Quebec]. Everyone who knows these two gentlemen knows that, in any matter in which the interests of their countrymen are concerned, they are never found wanting either in vigilance or zeal. It might be a question whether they have not secured advantages for their native province somewhat in excess of what it could rightfully claim; and it is a matter of common belief that upon more than one occasion, they have been prepared to resign their positions, and become again simple representatives of the people, rather than yield points for which they felt it their duty to contend. The thanks they get from this Ultramontaine journal is to be held up to execration, because they refuse to be guided solely by natural sympathy for their co-religionists, but try to look at the matter as lawyers, as statesmen, as men who,

CHICAGO IN FLAMES

A GREAT CONFLAGRATION.

Fire Engines and Water of no Avail.

One-half the City Destroyed.

150 Thousand People Homeless,

MILLIONS OF PROPERTY DESTROYED

THE FIRE STILL RAGING.

Chicago, 8th.—About 11 o'clock last night a fire broke out in a block situated between Clinton Canal, Van Buren, and Jackson Streets, and before it was extinguished four blocks, bounded on the north by Adam Street, on the south by Van Buren, on the west by Clinton Street, and on the east by the Chicago River, were destroyed.

Chicago, 9th, 1.45 a.m.—To-night is the most fearful in the annals of our city. The fire which commenced at 10 p.m. has already swept over a space of at least three miles, as large as that of last night, and is still rushing on with greater fury than has marked any stage of its progress, the engines

October 9, 1871

though they are French by descent, and Catholics in faith, yet feel themselves responsible for wider interests than those of one nationality or one creed. . . .

The *Nouveau Monde*, by taking up the absurd position that the only thing a Catholic member of the Government has to do, is to find out what makes for the advantage of his co-religionists and insist on that, puts forward a theory that would throw all government into chaos. The country, fortunately, has too much good sense to accept such notions, and the journal that puts them forth, will find that the effect of its tirades against the two staunchest representatives of French Canadian Conservatism will be to cause their supporters to rally round them with more devotion than ever.

May 16, 1872

August 8, 1873

By the early 1870s, baseball was quickly emerging as the most popular summer sport in Canada. In Ottawa, some of that fervour can be attributed to the Boston Red Stockings, the greatest team of the 19th century, which visited Ottawa in 1872 and 1873 for exhibition games against local amateurs. Boston won both games easily.

IMPROPER.—A number of boys amused themselves last evening on Sparks Street by playing base ball. Now while pedestrians have no objections to boys engaging in this exhilarating exercise in the proper place, still they do think that it is dangerous practice in a crowded thoroughfare like Sparks Street. It is sufficient to run the risk of being liable, at any moment, to have a fragment of stone from the waterworks explosions bulge in your crown, without running the danger of having your visual organs draped in mourning for a month with a baseball. The police will bear this fact in mind.

August 19, 1873
DAN RICE'S CIRCUS.
AN EXCITED CROWD TRAMPLED ON BY MULES,
CAMELS, AND HORSES.

Dan Rice's circus was advertised to perform last evening, and although he endeavored to do so, he didn't succeed. Neither Dan Rice nor all the showmen since the days of Darius, who sent Daniel to see the lions, could have conducted a performance in an orderly manner, with a tent so crammed as the pavilion was last night. Our reporter went to that circus, and took a friend with him. They secured high seats with a view to seeing the elephant, but although the animal was a Saul among his fellows, nothing could be seen of him but an occasional glimpse of the top of his ears through the vistas of swaying heads. The animal with his trunk and attendants, would have gone without the knowledge of the *Citizen*'s representative, but for the fact that his mightiness dropped one of his feet on a boy's corn, and immediately there arose shrieks of pain from the sufferer. When the elephant had passed, the boy's foot was dug out of the ground, and he was taken home for repairs.

The tent was full, but Dan Rice had come here to make money, and he never refused to sell a ticket while there was anyone ready to pay for it. The crowd continued to pour in, and pressed the dense mass under the canvas, further towards the centre, until there wasn't space enough for a cock fight. Dan contrived to find room for a stool, on which he stood, and in the most self composed manner imaginable informed twelve thousand people, in a tent that could accommodate not more than five—that owing to the immense multitude of people he dared not introduce the rhinoceros. He wouldn't from his love of the human race, hazard the lives of so many people. The rhinoceros didn't come, and nobody saw him, and couldn't have seen him if he had been introduced. Two mules and a kicking horse were brought into the ring instead, and made a general and unexpected raid upon the heads of many of the audience. The greatest excitement prevailed for a moment, and there was a prospect of the Quadruple Combination being broken up and scattered to the four winds. The wild horse trampled on a young man in the crowd who retaliated by kicking the horse in the side and the two bare-back riders, who had attempted to run through the dense mass of perspiring humanity, were dismounted. The ring manager rushed after that man and dealt him a heavy blow over the eye with his whip, and then told the entire crowd that he was open for encounter. All this time the two mules had been exercising their hooves on the heads of the spectators, who, after enduring it for a while, turned the long-eared animals on their backs at the feet of the manager. Cheers were now heard outside, and it soon spread through the pavilion that the crowd had threatened to mob the ticket office if their money was not returned. But, notwithstanding the violent threats, the treasury department managed to elude them, and no action was taken. After its mules had done trampling and a few acrobats tried to get tumbling room, the manager announced that there would be another performance to-day, but with better order. An hour and a half later the tent was empty. Our reporter thinks a force pump judiciously applied, will expand him to his normal dimensions.

February 13, 1874
HOW SHALL A WOMAN FASTEN HER STOCKINGS.

How shall a woman fasten her stockings so as not to interfere with the circulation of the blood, or spoil the shape of the—let us see—of the *honi soit qui mal y pense*. After the most careful research, as far as

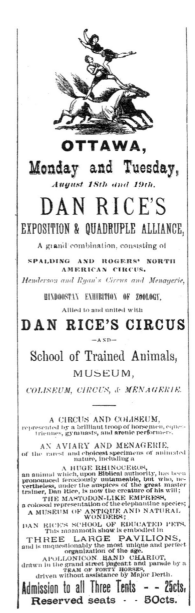

August 16, 1873

our limited faculties would allow, we arise from our humble explorations, and humbly tender the following suggestions:

Wear them short, and let the top bubble over the shoe in the form of lace, a la beer mug.

If you have 'em long, put mucilage inside and stick 'em to you.

Have them long enough to tie about the waist, and use the top for a pannier.

Edge the tops with steel and fasten a load stone to your corset.

Fasten a strap to each stocking, extend them gracefully up each side of the body and attach, with blue ribbons, to the earrings.

Pin them in some other articles of clothing in the immediate vicinity.

Fasten them to a nail and go bare-footed.

Attach a small balloon to each stocking.

Make them out of material that will draw up.

If you are thirty-five and unmarried, make a hole near the top of each stocking and button it to your knee cap.

These are all the methods that suggest themselves to us at present, and of the number some are or more may be deemed worthy of anticipation. We have taken a sudden lively interest in this matter, and shall not rest until the needed reform is brought about. Women's limbs shall not be hampered, and knotted, and deformed, if we have enough inventive faculty to bring about new and healthful ways of wearing the stockings, and we think we have. We shall continue our investigations into this subject. What women of this country need most is not suffrage, but symmetry; not rights, but rationality; not a place in legislative halls, but a place to fasten their stockings.

CORPORATION
—OF THE—
CITY OF OTTAWA.

TO ARCHITECTS

ARCHITECTS are invited to prepare and send in Plans for a New City Hall for the City of Ottawa.
The estimated cost of the building, complete, not to exceed sixty thousand dollars (60,000).
Information relative to site and general size of building may be obtained, on application, at the office of the City Engineer, Ottawa.
Plans to be sent in addressed to the City Clerk, Ottawa, on or before the TENTH day of APRIL next.
The Corporation will not necessarily accept any of the plans submitted, or bind itself in any way to remunerate, or to afterwards employ, either or any of the authors of the plans submitted.
JOHN P. FEATHERSTON,
Mayor
City Hall, Ottawa,
March 9, 1871   dtd.

March 6, 1874
Reporters and Reporting.
SOMETHING CONCERNING THE LOCAL PAGE
OF A DAILY PAPER
A Few Facts in Relation to Phonography
Whether the author of this amusing, if slightly cynical, account of a day in the life of a reporter was a Citizen *staff writer is unclear. There are no obvious local references, and the item could have been reprinted from another newspaper. It is worth noting that by 1874, the* Citizen *was publishing both morning and afternoon editions.*

The life of a reporter for a daily paper is a varied one, especially in large cities. He rises about 8 o'clock a.m., and after breakfast goes to the office of the paper with which he is connected, examines carefully the local pages of all the city papers of that morning in order to post himself with regard to public exercises of any kind which are to take place during the day or night. Then he gets his instructions and goes out on the streets, returning to the office in time to prepare his copy for the evening edition.

The results of his day's tramp may be found briefly jotted down in his note book, and are of a heterogeneous character, and it is now his task to elaborate and write up the items thus collected, which usually keep him employed until three o'clock in the afternoon. In that time he has written upon almost all subjects imaginable, his note book containing items relative to marriages, dog fights, horse races, runaway teams and runaway matches, accidents, arrests, murders, suicides, stabbing affrays, drunken brawls, funerals, proposed city improvements, complaints of citizens on various subjects, forthcoming entertainments, fires, burglaries, etc, etc.

A reporter hears lectures and other discourses upon theology, medicine, law, astronomy, physiology, painting, sculpture, education, politics, and various other subjects, but, viewing both lectures and lecturers in a business light, is seldom interested. If he is a short-hand man and has instructions to take him in full he cares more for a speaker's pronunciation than for his graceful gestures (which he never sees), and would much rather he would be distinct than *distingue*. To him the discourse is but a mass of words and the speaker a talking machine by whom he cannot be impressed, as he loses the effect of the expression, gestures and manner which form an important part of the discourse.

He finds by experience that speakers who carefully write out what they have to say, speak too rapidly, while those who do not, repeat themselves, occupying a great deal of time to no purpose, and delivering themselves in a loose disconnected way which necessitates an immense amount of doctoring on the part of the reporter in order to make the speech presentable. This is especially the case at banquets and public dinners to which ladies are not admitted, but wine is. The solids having been disposed, the liquids are brought on, and then toasts are in order. The average Canadian is eminently a speech-making animal, and when loud cries are made for Jones to respond to the toast, The day we celebrate; or The Thingumbob Society, (at whose expense the company is being entertained,) that individual arises and holding a glass of wine in one hand, while he steadies himself with the other, branches out with a mass of very trashy buncombe, which he would be ashamed to see in print the next morning but which, under the circumstances, passes for sense and is loudly applauded. He is followed by Brown, Smith, Robinson & Co., all of whom have been imbibing freely, and are even more than ordinarily impressed with the conviction that they possess oratorical abilities of a high order.

The entire host of local lights having exhausted themselves, the reporter puts his notebook in his pocket and wearily winds his way to the office. He knows that the speeches are very silly, containing but a

April 18, 1874

grain of sense to a bushel of rubbish, and it is his duty to go through that mass of rubbish, find that grain of sense, and tacking on a little here and a little there, presents his readers the next day with speeches which might have been made but were not.

There are many unpleasant features connected with the business of a reporter. He never has any time for himself, is liable to be sent any-where at a moment's notice and is constantly greeted with the enquiry, Well, what's new to-day? by those among his acquaintances belonging to that large class who invariably end their brief letters with a request to sit right down and tell me everything about everybody. Then the compositor wounds his sensitive spirit at times. For instance, he will originate an innocent little joke, the point of which centers in the mis-spelling of a word, and in order that the reader may see it indicates that the mis-spelling is intentional by the use of quotation marks. The printer, having an antipathy to incorrect orthography, spells the word properly, but leaves out the quotation marks. Then the heart of the re-porter is filled with sadness and he wishes he was a Government clerk.

On wet days his lot is a hard one, as he cannot shirk his regular rounds, be the weather ever so disagreeable. When fire bells ring he rushes after the engines with the speed of a wild gazelle, and in the midst of the excitement and uproar learns the names of the owners of the property, amounts of insurance, names of the companies and the amount in each probable loss, supposed origin of the fire, and hastens back to the office studying up startling headlines with which to em-bellish his report, if the fire should prove to be a large one and under these circumstances it is a difficult matter to get his questions an-swered correctly. A few years since, the writer was endeavoring to get for his paper some information relative to a startling evening. Never you mind: you read all about him in the morning papers, was the some-what discouraging response of the Teutonic gentleman to whom he applied.

Experienced reporters are paid from twelve to twenty dollars per week. A competent shorthand writer, who has a talent for making ac-quaintances, who can ask questions without giving offence, is able to condense, keeps sober, and can write up his items after he gets them, has no difficulty in securing a position in any of our large cities for such men are not plentiful.

Notwithstanding the fact that phonography is now taught quite ex-tensively, first class shorthand writers are very scarce, while the de-mand for them is rapidly increasing, and it is a remarkable fact that those who are able to take a speaker verbatim, seldom have any liking or aptitude of ordinary local work. The long reports of meetings held the night before said reports appear in the morning paper are usually written by professional shorthand men, who make a business of taking

May 22, 1874

testimony in the courts, and such reports are paid for at the rate of three to five dollars per column. As it will take a rapid writer five hours to transcribe an hour's work in short hand, several reporters are required in order to get out a long report in time for a morning paper.

Phonography is of inestimable value to the newspaper reading public, and in this age of railroads and telegraphs, could not be dispensed with. But it is an intricate study, hard to master, and easily forgotten. A rapid longhand writer can write forty words per minute while an expert phonograper writes two hundred, but years of practice, a good memory and nimble fingers are indispensable requisites to this rate of speed, and out of ten thousand phonographic students, but one will get beyond a hundred words per minute.

September 22, 1874
DEER HUNTING IN THE CITY.

Yesterday evening, about six o'clock, a deer hunt extraordinary took place in the Rideau near St. Patrick street bridge, or rather, close to Mr. John Terrance's slaughterhouse. A handsome buck of five tines was seen on the opposite side of the river coming from the neighborhood of McKay's bush, and looking as if he was fagged out. He was no sooner seen than about a couple of score people turned out, armed with all sorts of weapons wherewith to capture the game. They got round him and headed him off in all directions, being afraid to shoot for fear of hitting one another. Finally, the animal, driven to desperation, made a charge, and took to the water, swimming a great deal stronger than he could run. In the meantime, Mr. Terrance, who was engaged in the slaughterhouse, heard the hub-bub and, on discovering its cause, called out some of his men and, launching two canoes, gave chase. They soon managed to get close enough to their quarry to deal it several severe blows on the head with a paddle, and when the animal was pretty well stumped, they dragged him into one of the canoes, and cut his throat, rather a ticklish experiment to try in a canoe; however, he did not struggle much, and Mr. Terrance landed his game without any further trouble. He proved to be in splendid condition—fat, and altogether the handsomest animal of his genus we have seen for some time, weighing, when drawn, 200 lbs. Messrs. Satchell Bros. purchased it off Mr. Terrance for $20—not a bad evening's work—and the captor says he would not mind if a few more would come along that way. The carcass is hanging up in Satchell's stall in the market.

GOLD FLAKE CUT. PLUG SMOKING.

MANUFACTURED BY GLOBE TOBACCO CO., WINDSOR, ONT.

GOLD FLAKE CUT PLUG.

ITS MERITS.

We claim that this is the best Smoking Tobacco ever produced in this country and present a few facts to substantiate our claim:

1. It is made from the very best selections of Bright Old Virginia Leaf.
2. It is absolutely pure, and entirely free from the noxious properties so common to other smokings.
3. It will not gum the pipe. This fact alone proves its superiority over any other tobacco made.
4. It burns free and sweet to the very last, and leaves no bitter taste in the mouth.
5. It gives a cool and pleasant smoke, and does not parch the throat or dry the tongue.
6. Its lasting properties equal that of any plug made, and being cut ready for use is much more convenient.
7. It does away with the thraldom of the knife and tobacco-cutter, and saves much valuable time and material.
8. It is put up in neat and convenient packages, handy for the pocket, and warranted to keep in any climate.
9. It forms a live coal in the pipe, and will keep its fire in the strongest wind, making it the best in use for sportsmen.
10. Its pleasant aroma and fragrant smoke makes it a favorit with the ladies.
11. It is superior in every point of ECONOMY, CONVENIENCE and EXCELLENCE to any smoking ever introduced in Canada.
12. It is made by a responsible concern, which makes no assertions that cannot be substantiated.
13. It is put on the market at great expense, entirely on its own merits, and at so low a price that only large sales can give a fair return.
14. It shall be kept up in every point of quality and excellence so long as it is manufactured by us.

ANNOUNCEMENT.

We would respectfully inform our many friends and the Tobacco using public generally, that while we may soon to confine our attention largely to manufacturing the Gold Flake Cut Plug, that we are still supplying a constantly growing trade with all the various brands of Cut Goods, both Chewing and Smoking.

Our Globe Fine Cut Chewing, so justly popular in the United States, is also manufactured in our Windsor Factory, and having the same stock and material, as well as equal facilities, we make here, as in the States, the Best Chewing Tobacco in the World.

The "Victoria" brand, known to chewers for the past twenty years in Canada, has been so improved by us that it is growing in popularity every day. We have also cheaper grades of "Cut Chewing" and Smoking Tobaccos.

The "Wig Wag," a common smoking, is also well known, and gives universal satisfaction.

It is expected that the Government will require all Cut Goods to be put up in packages of one pound, or less, and we are now as rapidly as possible perfecting our arrangements to comply with this new requirement.

This new law, while entailing upon us an amount of additional labor, will be a great convenience to both dealer and consumer, and result in having our Goods reach the Consumer in much better shape than at present.

HOW AND WHERE OUR GOODS ARE SOLD.

We employ no travellers and sell only to responsible Wholesale Houses. The saving of the cost of selling Retailers is given to the Wholesaler, who is thus enabled to sell at Factory Prices.

We give below the names of prominent merchants who keep our goods in Stock, and from whom dealers may order as they need

WINDSOR.
Samuel Stover

LONDON.
Edward Adams & Co.,
M. Masuret & Co.,
J. Smith & Co.,
Wm. Kelley & Sons.

ST. THOMAS
J. & J. McAdam

BRANTFORD.
A. Watts & Co.,
George Watt & Sons

HAMILTON.
Alexander Harvey & Co.,
Stuart & McPherson,
James Turner & Co.,
Lucas, Park & Co.,
Lumsden Brothers,
Reid, Goering & Co.,
W. H. Gillard & Co.,
Simpson, Stuart & Co.,
Brown, Routh & Co.

KINGSTON.
A. Gunn & Co.,
George Robertson & Sons

OSHAWA.
W. H. Gibbs, Jun.

OTTAWA.
C. T. Bates & Co.

ST. CATHARINES.
W. J. & J. McCalla.

TORONTO.
F. Smith & Co.,
Nerlich & Co.,
Moore & Warren Bros.,
James Lumbers,
Hill McIntosh & Co.,
J. W. Scales,
F. McHardy & Co.,
John Morrison,
W. J. Ramsay & Co.,
W. Ramsay & Co.,
E. Gordon & Co.,
P. G. Close & Co.,
Perkins, Ince & Co.,
James Burns,
Smith, Keighley & Co.,
Eby, Blain & Co.

J. RATTRAY & CO., Montreal, Sole Agents for the Province of Quebec.

JARDINE & CO., St. John's, Sole Agents for New Brunswick.

S. H. SYMONS, Halifax, Sole Agent for Nova Scotia.

We shall be pleased to have you give our goods a trial and report to us if not entirely satisfactory.

GLOBE TOBACCO CO.,
DETROIT, MICH., AND WINDSOR, ONT.

The above cut is a fac-simile, except in size, of our four ounce package, of GOLD FLAKE CUT PLUG.

The following letter speaks for itself:

(handwritten letter)

THE GLOBE TOBACCO WORKS,
OF DETROIT,

Formerly conducted under the corporate name of Walker, McGraw Co., has changed its name to the GLOBE TOBACCO COMPANY, with the same Shareholders, Officers and Management as before.

This has been done partly on account of incorporating their branch at Windsor Ontario, which for the past two years has been carried on in the name of J. E. Saxton the secretary and treasurer of the Detroit company.

The name of the Windsor concern—

GLOBE TOBACCO COMPANY

With J. E. Saxton as President, and A. A. Boutell, Secretary and Treasurer.

'We Need You, Sir'

The Fourth Decade, 1875-1884

AS HE WALKED across Sappers' Bridge on his way to an interview at the old chieftain's home on Chapel Street, Charles Mackintosh mulled over the questions he'd drafted in his Russell House hotel room the night before. Little did he know he'd be the one answering the questions.

It was late autumn 1874, and Mackintosh, the 31-year-old managing editor of the *Chicago Journal of Commerce,* was responding to a summons from Sir John A. Macdonald. He assumed the former prime minister, still bitter from his recent electoral defeat, had a message he wanted to get out. The *Journal of Commerce* was widely read in Canada and the U.S., and the young Mackintosh was known to Macdonald from his years as owner of the Conservative *Strathroy Dispatch* in southwestern Ontario. But Macdonald had something else in mind.

One of his MPs, J. M. Currier, was part owner of the *Citizen,* and Macdonald had convinced him his paper required a dynamic Conservative sympathizer at the helm. "We need you, sir," Mackintosh recalled Macdonald saying soon after he came through the door. "Will you accept the task?" Mackintosh agreed to become lead editorial writer, but that was only the start. Within six months, he was promoted to editor-in-chief when George Holland left for a job in the Senate. By 1877, he was the *Citizen's* principal owner, a stake he held for the next 14 years.

As Macdonald had hoped, Mackintosh soon became a power in Ottawa, first through the *Citizen*—he appointed himself chief parliamentary correspondent—but later as a politician. In the 1878 election, which returned the Tories to office, Mackintosh travelled the country delivering passionate speeches for Macdonald. The next year, he was elected mayor of Ottawa, a post he won again in 1880 and 1881 before turning his ambitions to national politics. In 1882, he was elected MP for Ottawa, and he remained the member for most of the next decade.

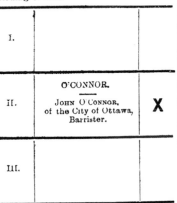

The following form of ballot paper is given for illustration. The candidates names are placed in alphabetical order according to law.

I.

O'CONNOR.
JOHN O CONNOR, of the City of Ottawa, Barrister.
X

II.

III.

Under section 24 of the Ballot Act, any elector at any polling place may, in the absence of any person authorized in writing to act as the agent of an absent candidate, declare himself to be and may act as the agent of such candidate without producing any authority in writing.

January 14, 1875. The secret ballot was a new enough idea that it needed explanation.

Opposite: Full-page ads began appearing during the fourth decade and one of the first was for Gold Flake tobacco, May 29, 1880. A century later, the Citizen was the first daily in North America to close its pages to tobacco advertising.

The press gallery of Parliament, 1870s.

February 15, 1875

In the late 19th century, it was still acceptable—even common—to run a newspaper and hold political office. And while Mackintosh's *Citizen* remained unwaveringly loyal to the Conservatives in its editorials and news columns, it also attempted, not always successfully, to present other political viewpoints, including verbatim accounts of speeches by Liberals.

It also developed into a better local newspaper. Partly that was a response to the emergence of *The Free Press*, a daily that had grown steadily since its 1869 launch by concentrating on Ottawa events. But years of working in small towns had also shown Mackintosh the value of local coverage—crime and tragedy, society events, municipal politics, health and moral issues, business and sports. It was an approach that would serve the *Citizen* well for the next century, and beyond.

March 25, 1875
DEATH OF DR. VANCORTLANDT

Perhaps no one cut a wider swath in Bytown and early Ottawa than Dr. Edward Vancortlandt. In addition to his renown as a surgeon and man of strong opinions, he was an avid amateur scientist whose Bytown Mechanics Society museum contained thousands of specimens eventually passed on to the Canadian Museum of Nature. Before Ottawa had a municipal library, Vancortlandt also lent books from his own collection to the public. This is an excerpt from his obituary:

The expression used by Dr. Vancortlandt a few weeks ago, that he would "last out until March," has been verified, for he breathed his last this very morning at 8 o'clock. The lamented gentleman was well known in scientific and other circles as a mineralogist, geologist, botanist and physician of great repute throughout the Dominion. He was born in Newfoundland in 1805, and was the son of a retired military officer who was connected with some titled families in England, his sister having married Sir G. Butler, and her grandson now is Lord Elphinstone....

At fourteen, the doctor commenced the study of medicine under the late Dr. Hacket, with whom he remained until he left for England in 1825. In 1827 he passed his examination at the Royal College of Surgeons, and was complimented by Abernethy [eminent surgeon John] and Sir A. Carlisle upon the creditable manner in which he acquitted himself. In 1829 Dr. Vancortlandt was chosen librarian to the Royal Medical and Chirurgical Society of London, there being a large number of English candidates for the office. He was elected as a recognition of the brilliant examination he had passed at the Apothecaries Hall, at which after thirteen minutes of questioning he was allowed to retire, the examiners stating that if he stayed any longer he would puzzle them. This the doctor used to relate with great gusto.

Three years afterwards he returned to Canada and settled in this place, then Bytown, where during the subsequent years up to the time of his death, he practiced and pursued his researches in the geological, archeological and natural historical world, holding offices in many of the Scientific and Literary associations. His museum and library are extensive, and both contain specimens or works upon subjects more especially in relation to this section of the country. He always took to himself a measure of credit for the Parliament buildings being built of Nepean sandstone. He pointed out to Lord Elgin the locality of the stone with which they are built; subsequently, at the request of the City Council, he published *Stone of the Ottawa Valley*, and on another occasion he published a brochure on the production of the same.

The Doctor will be greatly missed in the city, notwithstanding his eccentricities, and brusque manner which savored strongly of the old Abernethian school. He was looked upon as a man of genius. He was a clever surgeon, cool, decisive and of wonderful nerve, and as a physician there was scarcely his superior in the Dominion. He was surgeon of the Ottawa Field Battery for many years, and no doubt he will be buried with military honors.

He leaves a widow and several children. He was in the 70th year of his age, and up to the time of his demise was in perfect possession of his faculties.

February 15, 1875

March 27, 1875
THIS SEASON'S RHUBARB—Mr. John Thompson, of the Metropolitan Tea and Coffee Warehouse, Rideau street, is thinking seriously

of entering an action for damages against the *Citizen* for omitting to insert his advertisement on Thursday evening about the arrival of fresh rhubarb, lettuce, &c., from Col. Rhodes' Farm, Quebec. The majority of the stalks are quite thick and measure three feet in length. The lettuce are as full grown as summer stocks. They were purchased solely for Easter dinners, and orders left any time today will be attended to.

May 6, 1875

From a regular feature commenting on Canadian and world events:

An exchange says that most men, when undertaking suicide, try to make it as horrible as possible, some going so far as to kill their wives or sweethearts before shuffling off their own mortal coil. But this could not possibly apply to one Henry Diehen, of Cincinnati, who evidently was another sort of man. He got drunk last Saturday and took it into his head that he had lived as long as necessary, in which conclusion he was probably correct.

Now what does Henry do? Does he go slashing around with knife and pistol, stabbing his wife, cutting his babies' throats, shooting the dog and setting the house on fire? Not a bit of it. Like a considerate husband, who realizing that his wife must know the inevitable, still wants to make it as pleasant as possible, he sits down, reads his life insurance policy to her comfort, and then lets out his own life's blood with a butcher knife. Could anything be more graceful, more heroic, or better calculated to make otherwise depressing circumstances cheerful and buoyant? His policy was a sweet reminder to himself in the last hour of duty performed, and the fact that he did not go off like a surly dog and read it alone speaks volumes in his praise as a model husband.

July 20, 1875

SORE THROAT—Complaints are heard from all parts of the city that the sore throat is very prevalent among the female portion of the community. The cause is attributed to the constant sprinkling of the sidewalks. The practice has become an intolerable nuisance, and it is high time that the Chief of Police should interfere. Sewing girls on going to their work in the morning get their feet wet through their thin shoes, and while sitting at their work they catch cold and sore throat. Ladies who go out in the evening to make calls or to attend entertainments or religious meetings, get their feet wet in the same way through the unnecessary wetting of the sidewalks, and suffer in consequence from sore throat, inflammation of the eyes and other complaints which delicate constitutions are prone to. It is all very well to have the streets watered to keep down the dust, but the sidewalks should not be kept wet. In rainy weather ladies wear rubbers to protect themselves, but they

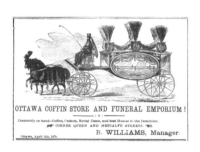

April 17, 1875

September 19, 1875

protest against having to wear them in dry weather also.

September 4, 1875
PRIZE FIGHT!
IRISHMEN VS. FRENCHMEN

Three Thousand Spectators—How the Fight was Arranged
and how the Police Interfered and Spoiled the Fun!

About one o'clock to-day Sussex street, near Murray street, was literally jammed with an excited crowd of men endeavoring to settle how,
when and where a fight would come off between one Cormory, an
Irishman, and Guilaume Gagneau, a Frenchman, from Saguenay district. Cormory had, it appears, made a statement on Murray street this
morning that he could

WHIP ANY FRENCHMAN THAT EVER GRACED SHOE LEATHER

Several French shantymen who happened to be within hearing of the
remarks, entertained a rather different opinion, and regarded the boast
as an insult to their nationality. They thereupon held a consultation
and chose one of their number, a man named Gagneau, to fight Cormory. Gagneau expressed his willingness to come to the scratch, and
sat down while his backers arranged bets and a place of meeting. They
finally decided that McKay's grove afforded desirable accommodation,
and fixed 1:30 p.m. as the time at which the fight should come off. At
one o'clock both men were ready for the fray and left Murray street for
the scene of the contest. The crowd at the time numbered a few hundred persons, but before they had gone two blocks, the sidewalks on
both sides of the street were

LITERALLY JAMMED WITH BOTH MEN AND WOMEN

anxious to witness the battle. The pugilists, fearing that the crowd was
getting too large, endeavored to "steal a march" by taking a circuitous
route, traveling up unnecessary streets, etc., in the hope of getting separated from the excited crowd. It had the reverse effect, however, for
every street they passed through added to the number. Finally a direct
course to McKay's Grove was taken and before it was reached fully

FOUR THOUSAND PERSONS HAD GATHERED.

Bets were then taken on the result while the men were getting ready,
and there were some very large ones among them. One man was so excited over his choice (Gagneau) that he staked his house and lot on St.
Andrew's street against $250 that he would win. Another enthusiastic
admirer of Cormory, who happened to have no cash with him, pulled
off his coat and hat and offered to bet them against 50 cts; and to crown
all an Irish woman in the crowd offered to "wallop," as she put it, "the
best French woman that ever ate leeks if Cormory didn't beat Gagneau." In the meantime, while all these opinions were being ventilated,
the police got wind of the affair and appeared on the scene just as the

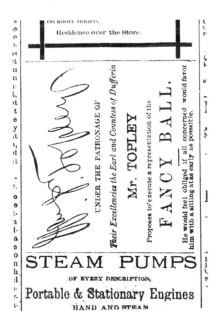

January 16, 1876

April 6, 1876

men were coming to position, and arrested Gagneau and Cormory.

THE CROWD PROTESTED

against the fight being spoiled. They held that the police had no jurisdiction outside of the city, but the police wouldn't listen to their protests, but took the men away to the station, where they are now. Instead of getting excited, as crowds generally do under such circumstances, they argued quietly for the police to let the fight go on, but the police "couldn't see it." Both Gagneau and Cormory are strong able-bodied men, and would make a wicked fight. Had the police not interfered in time, there might probably have been loss of life.

ADVERTISE.
———
IF YOU
Want a CooK
Want a situatioN
Want a servant girL
Want to rent a storE
Want to sell a pianO
Want to sell a horsE
Want to buy or sell a housE
Want a good boarding housE
Want to lend or borrow moneY
Want to buy a second hand buggY
Want to find anything you have losT
Want to find strayed or stolen animalS
Want to let the public know anythinG
You can do it through the columnS
Of the DAILY or WEEKLY CITIZEN.

☞ The Largest Circulation of any Paper
☞ published in Ottawa or Central
☞ Canada.

February 12, 1876

The Citizen had long given rifle matches greater coverage than any other form of contest except elections. On September 15, 1877, it even reproduced the shooters' targets.

November 15, 1875

THE MISSING GIRL.—The girl Mary Henderson, reported to have been thrown over Cummings' Bridge, has turned up. She refuses to give any explanation. In answer to questions she merely says she knows nothing about the story, or where she has been. From her general appearance it would appear that she has been exposed to the weather, and since returning home she has been ill. Mrs. Munro should be hunted up and punished for giving publicity to such a base and sensational story. If it was intended as a practical joke it certainly was a success.

December 9, 1875

BOSS TWEED

New York Detectives Think He is in Ottawa—A Run Around the City.
After his escape from jail, Willam Macy Tweed, whose sensational New York forgery trial sparked headlines across North America, eventually found his way to Spain, where he was captured in 1877. It's unlikely he visited Ottawa, although the Citizen *and other local papers continued to report the possibility for several weeks.*

The New York police having received information which would lead them to suppose that "Boss Tweed," who escaped from Ludlow street jail on Saturday, succeeded in making his way to Ottawa, despatched three detectives to this city in pursuit. They arrived here to-day by the morning train, and have since been strolling around the city in search of the notorious fugitive. Up to a late hour this afternoon they had neither seen nor heard anything that would confirm the reliability of the information furnished them. What time may develop, however, remains to be seen. If the "Boss" is here, no doubt the detectives, with assistance of the city police force, will ferret him out.

December 9, 1875

A SAD SCENE.—A gentleman saw a crowd of people gathered on

Dalhousie street yesterday afternoon, and upon making enquiry found that they were offering their sympathy to a poor woman who had, by force of circumstances, been obliged to give away her only child—a little thing of two or three years—to save it from starvation. She said her husband had deserted her, and it was impossible for her to earn sufficient to keep herself and child. The poor woman was crying bitterly when our informant passed.

FUN

February 3, 1876

In early 1876, the Citizen *began to publish a regular column of what it considered humorous items—straightforward jokes, amusing anecdotes, distasteful stories—collected from here and there. Here's an excerpt from a typical collection:*

Man—"Do you think it would be safe for me to cross the pasture?" Maid— "Well, the old bull don't like red very much, but if you will chalk your nose I guess he won't attack you."

•

The London Rothschild is dead and every poor devil of an editor remarks with satisfied complacency that "money could not save him." Poverty don't save a man, either.

•

"You ain't afraid to die?" said the clergyman, tenderly. "No," replied the sufferer, "I'm only afraid if I do that the old woman will go snooping among my private papers the first thing."

•

Twelve hacks went over the 4:45 tram yesterday afternoon and brought back one passenger, which is an average of four cents a hack. And yet people wonder why hackmen are profane.

•

A Chinaman in California, whose life was insured for a large amount, was seriously hurt by falling from a wagon. There was some doubt of his ever getting better, and at length one of his friends wrote to the insurance company, "Charley half dead, like half money."

•

"Will your Honor please charge the jury?" asked an Arkansas lawyer at the conclusion of a horse thief trial. "I will," replied His Honor, "the court charges each juryman one dollar for drinks, and six dollars extra for the one who used the court's hat for a spittoon during the first day of the session."

•

At Saratoga, the other day, a bridegroom stepped off the cars for a moment and the tram went off with his bride. He followed by the next

October 1, 1877

train down, and she on the other hand returned by the next train up, and they passed each other on the road. This operation was repeated, each trip leaving them at different ends of the route, until a peremptory telegram kept the bride stationary until her husband reached her.

•

The boys of Winnemucca, Nevada had some fun with a showman. They formed a line from the ticket office extending around a near corner. Each asked the price of admission, and when being told that it was fifty cents, shook his head, said it was too dear, retired, and fell in at the rear of the line. This was kept up until the showman, astounded by the unanimity and the seemingly great number, reduced the charge, and then every boy cleared out.

•

A fellow in Kentucky ran away with a farmer's daughter and horse, and was hotly pursued. The farmer got within close range, and flourished a revolver. "Don't shoot, for heaven's sake!" shouted the lover, "I won't," was the reply, "cause I'm afeared I'll hit ther hoss. Just leave ther hoss and take ther gal." The compromise was accepted by the young folks, who walked on to the preacher's house, the father riding home on his horse.

March 24, 1876

THE NEWSBOYS' CONCERT.—The newsboys of the city have arranged the following programme for their concert, which is shortly to take place: Double clog by the Gorman Bros., Pete and Mick; balancing on the trapeze, Johnny Guinan; bar act by the company; double Dutch song and dance, Guinan and Gorman; bending act by "Ginger" Gorman, the "boneless boy;" the wonderful flying trick by Guinan and Gregory; double Irish jig, Gorman Bros.; comic song, "Mulchay's Home Again," Mick Gorman; stump speech, "What shall we do with our Girls," Johnny Guinan; Irish comic song, "The Shoes that Dennis Wore," M. Gorman; the whole entertainment to conclude with hat spinning by the little clowns Guinan and Gorman. Master Guinan announces that he will tumble two back somersaults in the air before coming to the ground—a feat never before attempted. A number of gentlemen are advancing the urchins the necessary funds for completing the arrangements. They will, no doubt, draw a crowded house. The proceeds are for the benefit of the poor—the newsboys.

May 13, 1876
SPORTING!
Foot-Ball—Harvard vs. Canada—Description of the Match—
The Teams—A Warm Struggle—Harvard Wins
Canadian and American football grew out of a series of 1874 games

THE AGE OF BALLOONACY

THE LEGEND OF BARNES AND HIS ÆRONAUTIC EXPERIENCE.

AS TOLD BY HIS SORROWING FRIEND.

MACK MERRYMAN.

RAY, do not for a moment entertain the suspicion that it is my desire to cast a gloom over Professor Grimley, or any other Professor's balloon expeditions; it simply devolves upon me to chronicle a somewhat heart-rending case which occurred quite lately. Do not for a moment imagine I am actuated by a covert desire to awaken feelings of melancholy in the minds of æronautic experimentalists, or that I expect any charitable society to prepare a monument, or provide for a number of bereaved relations. But

BARNES IS NO MORE!

He was an enterprising reporter, an original, deep-thinking, philosophic, companion. Saying this is but telling one-half! When he started in life, literary pursuits enthralled him; he first was of opinion that his forte was humor, he wrote an article, but could get nothing for 't; he showed it to a Celtic friend, asking him if he could appreciate the joke; but his Scotch friend read it through and looked at him with dismay, remarking, "Hech! Rabbie, ye dinna want to wricht sic dolefu' discoorses at your time o' life; try mon an' gi'e the pooblic a gleg an' winsome skyte!"

January 1, 1878. The Citizen took an interest in balloon flight, above and opposite.

between Harvard and McGill universities. McGill played rugby football while Harvard played the "Boston Game," which was more like soccer. The teams alternated rules to give both a fair chance. The Harvard players liked running with the ball, and by 1875 persuaded Yale University to adopt slightly altered rugby rules for their annual game. By 1876, the year of this Harvard-Canada game, those rules were used exclusively. It is unclear who wrote the article excerpted here. 'Correspondent' could refer to a reporter sent from Ottawa, or to a freelance writer—likely a Canadian, judging by the article's tone—attending the event.

(From our Correspondent.)

BOSTON, 9th.—The international foot-ball match which has excited so much interest and attracted so much attention was played on Jarvis Field, Cambridge, near Boston, last Monday afternoon. Punctually at three o'clock the Canadian team made their appearance on the ground, and were greeted with great applause, their forms and athletic frames eliciting much admiration. The day was pleasant, rather cloudy, but still good foot-ball weather. About 5,000 spectators were on the ground, among whom were many ladies. The ground itself though not very level, is fair enough for foot-ball and rather sandy in several places. The names of the teams are as follows:—

HARVARD—Whiting, Captain; Wetherbee, Lostbard, Faucon, Austin, Curtis, Hall, Bacon, Leamans, Keys, Russell, Cushing, H.W.; Cushing L.; Blanchard.

CANADA—Perram, Captain; Hope, Kerr, Palmer, Murray, Hare, Greenfield, Helliwell, Young, from Ontario; Gough, Cross, Eardley, Wilmot, Campbell, Smith.

The game was to be played for one hour and a half. Ends to be changed at half time. Canada won the toss and elected to play with the wind. The ball was kicked off with the Harvard Captain, but Canada with a strong rush, forced it down to the Harvards' goal, and in a few minutes Harvard had to touch down in self-defence. Again the ball was started. Faucon made a plucky run but was tackled and Smith took the ball, and again Harvard had to touch down. The Crimsons were now beginning to feel that matters were looking dangerous and made a great rush down the field. Bacon dodged several players very prettily but Perram laid him low and back went the rubber to Harvard's goal, only to be sent back where Palmer caught it and ran about 30 yards until held by Cushing. Harvard punted the ball away down to Canada's goal. Stuart Campbell dropped it back again. Cushing ran with it, Canada chuckled him. Harvard passed and Canada dropped, and the ball went hither and thither over the field, whilst the crowd of spectators were in a great state of excitement.

"He'll die game," at last said the medical man, "and when a fellow's got to do it, he may just as well use a popular color, eh?"

I answered not. The companion of poor Barnes—the only member of his household—had been a cat—a Maltese cat—domesticated; gentle and tender. As Barnes inflated, the animal's back bone gradually hooped; then there was a sudden snap and her corsets gave way!

"Regui his-cat-in-pace," said the doctor solemnly.

"Can I be of further service doctor?" I asked.

"I'm not aware that you've been of any particular service, yet," was the gruff reply. "The balloon will soon be ready to go up— a new direction for reporters to travel!"

I looked at Barnes;

HE WAS NOT AS HE USED TO BE!

Poor Barnes! he was an enterprising reporter!

"*Sic transit gloria Mundi,*" or Tuesday, I cannot be positive as to the precise day or hour!

WHERE THE PEOPLE'S MONEY WENT.

Millions of Dollars Squandered Upon Favorites

THE TRUE STORY OF THE STEEL RAIL TRANSACTION.

Facts For the Electors.

RESULTS OF FIVE YEARS GRIT-ROUGE RULE IN CANADA.

No subject has been more discussed since Mr. Mackenzie came into office than his unfortunate purchase of steel rails. A simple record of the facts in this case is all that is necessary to show, first, that the purchase was a most unwise one; nex', that it was without the authority of Parliament; and, last, that it was open to the grave suspicion of having b en prompted by a spirit of nepotism. It will be remembered that Mr. Mackenzie's first proposal in relation to the Pacific Railway was to utilize the water stretches. All the railway, therefore, to be built by him was about 45 miles fiom Lake Superior to Shebandowan. and about 100 miles from the northwest angle to Fort Garry, and the Pembina Branch of about 70 miles, making altogether a little over 200 miles of

August 31, 1878

One of the prettiest pieces of play of the day was some very scientific passing by Bacon and Seamans, who succeeded in bringing the ball near Canada's goal, till Gough with a most plucky charge, overthrew the Harvard men. Stuart, of Quebec, Perram, Gough, Smith, Wilmot and Helliwell were all working hard as forwards, whilst the fine kicking of Young, Hope, and Kerr did good service. On the Harvard side, Bacon, Hall, Curtis and the Cushing brothers distinguished themselves. So matters continued until a scrimmage formed within 8 ft. of the Harvard goal. Every player was at his place and the moment the ball touched the ground it was passed back to Hope, who tried a drop kick at goal but failed. The kick was a difficult one to make. Immediately the Harvards pushed out the ball, Hall making a fine run till collared and thrown by Campbell. The play now was very even. The fine tackling and kicking of the Canadians more than outbalanced the splendid running powers of Harvard, but no decided advantage was taken. Time was now called. Harvard had been forced to touch down seven times in their own defence, whilst the ball had never been behind the Canadian goal. Thus far all the men showed well. Every man played with the determination to win, and did his best.

After about two minutes rest, the ball was again kicked off, ends having been changed. Soon the Harvards began to reverse the position of affairs and gradually the ball was worked down to Canada's goal yet so strong was Canada's defence that the Harvards were unable to score a touch down. It soon became evident that Canada had a great disadvantage in not having practiced together and several of the Ontario members showed lack of training. The condition of the Montreal men was excellent and a notable exception to the statement regarding the Ontario men was Mr. Perram, who played a splendid game. His magnificent physique and cool judgement make him the foremost foot-ball player of Canada and there was admittedly no rival for him on the Harvard side.

Harvard continued to force down the ball, and a scrimmage was formed about three or four yards from Canada's touch-line. The ball was sent into side-touch, thrown out at side angles, caught by a Harvard man and thrown back to Seamans, who dropped a goal amid intense excitement and great applause.

Notwithstanding their most determined efforts Canada failed to score anything more, but the ball was kept in the middle of the field, for the rest of the game. Canada played under the great disadvantage of not having practiced together and under the circumstances the defeat ought not to discourage the Canadian team, but should rather incite them to more earnest efforts in the future. . . .

October 13, 1876
A BRUTAL HORROR!
Two Brutes Abuse a Woman and Cut Out Her Tongue
Because She Threatens to Expose Them.

One of the most shocking tragedies that has ever been perpetrated in the Ottawa Valley is reported in Ramsay township, where two murderous villains are said to have ravished a school mistress, and then because she threatened to expose them turned upon her and severed the tongue from her mouth.

Neither the names of the parties implicated in the outrage, nor that of the victim, have transpired at this writing, but rumors of the frightful horror were quite current this morning on the road between this city and Fitzroy Harbour. A *Citizen* reporter having heard that Mr. Kenny, of Goulbourn, knew the particulars of the tragedy, interviewed him on the Byward market this morning. In answer to questions, that gentleman said he was coming to the market this morning when he heard that a murder had been committed somewhere in the vicinity of Fitzroy, the details of which were of the most harrowing description. Naturally anxious to learn the particulars he made inquiries along the way and learned from a farmer, whose name he could not recollect, that two young men had entered a school house in Ramsay, after the scholars had been dismissed for the day, and without any explanations seized the mistress. She attempted to scream when they gagged and outraged her. The unfortunate woman in her excitement threatened that knowing both the men she would bring them to justice, and the villains seized her again, and on her attempting to scream one of them caught her tongue in his hand and cut it out. The poor woman fell to the floor unconscious, and the murderous ruffians succeeded in making their escape. Some time afterwards the woman recovered her sense and crawled towards the blackboard. Here after much struggling she managed to write on the blackboard the names of her murderers and a brief account of the affair. At last, weakened from the loss of blood, she fell to the floor and died. The body remained in the school house until morning, when it was found by some of the scholars lying in a pool of blood. The brief description of the horror she was enabled to write remained undisturbed.

If you thought that story was too horrible to be true, you'd be right. No doubt the Citizen *accurately portrayed the tale as it was told by Mr. Kenny. But none of it happened, and the newspaper didn't bother to check. In the era before telephones, it might have required a day to confirm a story in Ramsay Township, 70 kilometres southwest of Ottawa. But as the* Almonte Gazette, *Ramsay's largest newspaper, noted in a scathing criticism the next week, "Without first taking the*

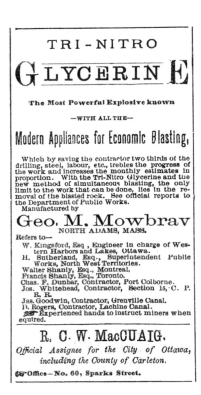

January 27, 1879

time to verify the very vaguest of vague rumours, the Ottawa Citizen *prostitutes its columns to gratify the prurient curiosity of its readers."*
To make matters worse, the Citizen *never published a correction,*
or apology.

October 13, 1876
HAIR-PULLING MATCH.—Two female residents of Nicholas street yesterday afternoon engaged in a hair-pulling match for the benefit of the people of that locality. The disgraceful exhibition was witnessed by a number of men, many of them being perfectly delighted with the cruel sport, and not at all desirous of putting a stop to it. Considerable hair was sacrificed. Both of the combatants will be obliged to get a few switches from Miles before they can make a respectable looking appearance in public. Whiskey was the cause.

August 16, 1876
RAFTSMEN ON THE RAMPAGE!
A Disgraceful Attack on a Gipsy Camp.—One Man's Leg
Fractured and a Child Seriously Injured.
Raftsmen, as a class, are a law abiding people when sober, but when they indulge in "the cup which cheers and doth inebriate" they have no more respect for the statutes than a hungry dog has for the family roast. Last night a number of them went out on a "jamboree," and after fighting among themselves near Mechanicsville, bore down in a body on a Gipsy camp situated in that vicinity. One of the men acted as captain of the ruffianly gang, and on approaching the Gipsy enclosure called one of the band by name. The Gipsy, on hearing his name mentioned, went out. No sooner had he exposed himself than he was struck in the face with a club and felled to the ground.

Then the ruffians commenced to destroy everything they could lay their hands on. Not satisfied with this they attacked men, women and children, throwing them around and kicking them in a most heartless manner. A member of the Gipsy band who was only recovering from illness occasioned by having had his leg broken, was pounced upon, and in the scuffle had the limb fractured again. A little child was also abused. Her injuries are internal, and may yet prove serious. Then, as if they had not committed sufficient outrage, the ruffians actually drew revolvers and fired them in the air to add greater terror to their outlandish proceedings. After this they left the camp, and one of the gipsies came down to the police station and informed the police of the affair. Prompt measures will doubtless be taken to capture the gang of scoundrels and bring them to justice. We understand the gipsies know the name of the ringleader. If such is the case it is more than likely arrests will be made to-day.

March 28, 1879

May 22, 1879

May 8, 1877

THE TAXERS OF THE PEOPLE

This excerpt from an editorial was likely penned by
editor-in-chief Charles Mackintosh, whose stirring speeches
on behalf of Sir John A. Macdonald's Tories in the 1878 election
usually rang with these same anti-Liberal sentiments. It is also likely
Mackintosh wrote the Dominion Day editorial that follows and the
July 12 account of Macdonald's campaign-style trip through Quebec.

When the Government of Sir John Macdonald were in power they expended from income, that is, from ordinary revenue, several millions of dollars in the construction of useful public works, giving employment to thousands of working men and helping to promote the general prosperity and progress of the country. During their period of office they also remitted about three million of taxes, and thus lessened the burdens of the people. When they left office the country was happy, contented and prosperous; trade was good, manufactures flourished, employment was abundant, bank notes were a circulating medium, the public exchequer was overflowing, and things generally were in a satisfactory condition. But when the present Government came into power there was soon a change. Gross jobbery became the order of the day. Steel rails were purchased for years before they could be used, the country losing thereby one million of dollars. Contracts were given to political supporters without tender, in defiance of law and public decency, the money of the people was squandered in a most reckless fashion on political favourites, and there was a carnival of plunder and spoliation of the public treasury and public morality. The debt of the country has been increased, a deficit of some millions appears between revenue and expenditure and the burden of taxation has been increased. And yet the present Government has boasted of their economy, their retrenchment, and of their purity!!

July 2, 1877

DOMINION DAY!

Yesterday the Dominion of Canada had completed the first ten years of its history, and it was fitting that the anniversary should be celebrated with suitable demonstrations of public rejoicing in all the great centres of population—and in none more so than the city of Ottawa. Confederation, it had been generally admitted, was an experiment in "State making" and the working of the new system has been watched with interest not unmixed with grave apprehension. There are many who have had their conscientious doubts whether the scheme to bind together Provinces which had little in common but their allegiance to

The Hull Disaster.

THE SMOULDERING RUINS.

INSPECTED BY THOUSANDS OF CITIZENS.

A DESOLATE SCENE.

AID FROM THE GOVERNMENT.

A $7,000 CONTRIBUTION.

THE WORK OF RE-BUILDING COMMENCED.

Yesterday's morning's sun broke on a desolate scene in Hull, a scene that moved to pity all who gazed on it, and made an impression on the memory that time cannot soon efface. Only a few hours before hundreds of families were gathered in their homes chatting cheerily, unconscious of the approaching danger that was sweeping down upon them; now the smouldering ruins stand out as a monument of misery and desolation, and a striking exemplification of the uncertainty of things worldly. Throughout the day thousands of citizens flocked to the scene and poured out their sympathy for the

April 23, 1880

their Mother Country, would be successful, and even those who took a prominent part in framing the compact of Union have on many occasions been tempted to feel as if their work must be in vain. And during the decennial period which has just elapsed since the Government of the Dominion first assembled on the banks of the Ottawa, the country has passed through many dangers which seriously threatened the perpetuity of the Union. But very fortunately there was a Government at the head of affairs which, pursuing a patient, forbearing and conciliatory policy, succeeded in overcoming or warding off the dangers and in establishing our young Confederation on a firm foundation. The people may look back with pleasure on the great material progress which the Dominion has made in the first ten years of its life, and, although there is now a cloud of commercial depression hanging over the country, they may reasonably look forward to the time when business prospects will improve, and the Dominion start forward once more in the race of progress like "a young giant refreshed." The country of the Ottawa, the city in particular, no doubt owes much to Confederation, and in the great progress which the Dominion has made towards autonomy and stability the people of the valley have reason to rejoice and feel proud.

The demonstration held yesterday was no doubt an indication of the feeling with which the people of the Ottawa Valley, and may be the people of the whole Dominion, regard the anniversary of Union and the progress which has been made towards cementing the people of the various Provinces into the new northern nationality: and such demonstrations, it is to be hoped will be repeated, if not from year to year, at least on the occurrence of every decade of the Union.

THE END AT LAST.

Death of the Hon. George Brown

A VISIT TO HIS MURDERER.

Special to THE CITIZEN.

Toronto, 9th.—Hon. George Brown died this morning at 2.20 o'clock, but the news of his decease was not communicated beyond the immediate household until this morning at 9 am. Dr. Johnston has given notice of his intention of holding an inquest, which will commence at 10 a.m. to-morrow. Hon. Mr. Brown had been unconscious for a long time prior to his death, and passed off quietly in the presence of his family and medical attendants.

Toronto, 9th.—Upon learning of the death of the Hon. George Brown this morning, your correspondent visited the gaol for the purpose of seeing the prisoner, Bennett. He was courteously received by Governor Green, and brought into the presence of the murderer. He had not yet been made acquainted with the death of the Senator, but was aware of his fatal condition for some days past, and showed the marks of anxiety in his haggard countenance and nervous manner. He remains entirely apart from the other prisoners confined in the same corridor, and employs most of his time in writing on sheets of paper, which he as constantly tears up.

Already there is talk in the city of giving the Hon. Geo. Brown a public funeral, but so far the wishes of the

May 10, 1880

July 12, 1877
SIR JOHN MACDONALD'S PHYSICAL ENDURANCE
(From our Correspondent.)

Montreal 10th.—For some time past it has been the policy of the Grits, and of a few weak-kneed Conservatives as well, to declare that Sir John Macdonald's constitution is run down, that he has lost his intellectual vigor, that he is now too old for active public life, and that he should retire and make over the leadership of the party to some younger and more vigorous man. Conservatives who are not personally acquainted with Sir John will be as gratified, as the Grits who do know him will be disappointed, to learn that the Conservative chieftain was never in more vigorous health in his life than he is at present. In his recent tour through the Eastern Townships he displayed a physical endurance, vigor and vitality that amazed those who accompanied him. Few public men of the present day could have gone through what Sir John did on Saturday last, and shown so few symptoms of fatigue after it. On Friday he drove from Compton to Senator Cochrane's farm and from there across the country to Stanstead, some thirty-five miles in all, in an open carriage; received several addresses, to which he replied, and wound up with a banquet in the evening. On Saturday morning he had to be up in time for the early 7 a.m. train, and he ate no breakfast. At Sweetsburg, in the afternoon, he delivered a speech of an hour and a half in length; at West Farnham and St. John's he also replied at length to addresses. The train arrived at Montreal at 9 p.m., where he was met by the monster procession that escorted him to Dominion Square, where he delivered the speech, that was published in the *Citizen* of yesterday. During the delivery of that address the heat and smoke from the torches, rockets, Roman candles, red lights, and other fireworks was intense, yet notwithstanding the fact that he had eaten nothing the whole of that day—the only nourishment he had taken being a couple of glasses of Burgundy, the speech which he delivered was full of fire and vigor. On Monday morning he was as fresh as a daisy and he received visitors in the St. Lawrence Hall the whole day. As he says himself he's not much to look at but "he's a rare'un to go."

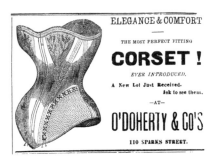

May 25, 1880

September 29, 1877

AN UPROARIOUS MEETING!

A MOST DISGRACEFUL SCENE.

Messrs. Clancy and Kinsella Fight on the Stage.

Dating back to the 1830s, wild public meetings were a staple of life in 19th-century Ottawa, often leading to drunken brawls, injuries and arrests. This meeting, called by opponents of Mayor Waller and city council to whip up sentiment against plans to finance a railway to Toronto and a new bridge over the Ottawa River, eventually spilled into the street, where it erupted into fisticuffs. Among the many colourful aspects of this excerpt is the spectre of the mysterious Moses the Inkman trying to calm tensions.

One of the most disgraceful and uproarious meetings ever held in this city took place last night in the Market Hall. There were about four hundred persons present, some of them ratepayers and others who attended with the express purpose of having some fun. The meeting was called to discuss municipal matters.

Dr. Hill was called to the chair, and among those on the platform were Messrs. Clancy, J. D. Dwyre, L. Perkins, R. Lees, Q.C., P. A. Eggleson, Sen., J. M. Goulden, Lang, Tom Kinsella and Moses the Inkman. Mr. Clancy was required to act as a secretary.

The Chairman explained that the meeting was called by advertisement to discuss the affairs of the city generally. He said this was an important crisis in the history of our city, and, meetings like this should

June 26, 1880

be held in every corner of the city, as an opportunity of ventilating the proposed railway bonus, and characterized it as a wild goose scheme, an insane project. He held that we had to pay annually £32,000 on our debt in addition to what was required for local improvements, and it was high time that the people were setting their faces against the useless and extravagant expenditure. Then again, another $50,000 was asked to aid the construction of a bridge over the Ottawa River, a scheme which would in no way improve the trade of the city. He proceeded also to show that the Toronto & Ottawa Railway would in no way benefit the city. It was a perfect humbug. With respect to the bridge over the Ottawa, nature never intended that the river should be bridged at New Edinburgh. It was a ridiculous project and would interfere with the navigation of the river. He said it was argued that manufacturers would come to the city if the railway was built. This was absurd, the heavy taxes would drive them away. He proceeded also to condemn the extravagance of the School Board, and said they were as mad as the members of the City Council.

After a brief silence the chairman said it was now in order for any ratepayer to address the meeting. Loud cries were heard for Kinsella. He refused for some time to come forward, but was finally induced to address the meeting. His appearance before the footlights was the signal for deafening applause, intermingled with hisses, caterwauls, etc.

Mr. Kinsella, after the storm had subsided, proceeded to say that Ottawa was a Conservative city, bad luck to it, and that Gladstone was the greatest statesman on earth, God bless him, when the boys behind interrupted him with deafening yells. He refused to be put down, and asked for a wiss of straw to be put in the mouth of one of those calves, which brought down the house. Coming to the questions he said he objected to the salaries of the firemen and policemen being cut down, the former, because they reduced his insurance, and the latter because they prevented a man from shooting him on one occasion. (Tremendous cheering).

At this point, Mr. Kinsella, who appeared to be warming to the subject, turned round to the gentlemen in the platform, and asked the audience to "take stock of the men who wanted to cut down the wages of their officials." There was Mr. Clancy who charged 100 per cent for his money, and who was the greatest enemy the poor man had. (Cheers and hisses). There was Dr. Hill who charged the poor $5 for a dozen of pills. (Great confusion). And there was Mr. Dwyre who wouldn't be there at all if anyone gave him two dollars and a half to keep away. (Cheers and laughter). When . . . . Dr. Hill caught him by the arm and tried to prevent him from speaking, this created great confusion. Some shouted, "Bounce him;" others roared "go on Tom," and between them there was a lively time. The chairman appealed to the audience to keep

June 26, 1880

quiet for a few minutes until he had the opportunity of saying a few words but they had no such intention, and continued shouting and whistling for some minutes.

Finally a lull occurred and Mr. Kinsella said he was worth $30,000 and had more political influence in By-Ward than Dr. Hill, Mr. Clancy or Mr. Dwyre, or any of that crowd, and he wasn't going to be put down by any nonentities. (Great cheering.) He would sit down of his own accord, but by the Board of School Trustees he wouldn't be put down. (Cheers.) This was a free country, and no one could put a padlock on his mouth. (Applause.) This was an age of science, but science mustn't sit on the poor man. (Applause.) If she does the poor man may some day sit on science. (Cheers.)

At this point, Mr. Clancy rose and said it was time this disgraceful conduct terminated, and throwing his arm around Mr. Kinsella's neck tried to pull him off the stage. The crowd rushed for the stage, and the wildest confusion of pushing and punching prevailed for a time. Mr. Kinsella managed, after a hard struggle, to get his arms around Mr. Clancy's neck and after giving him a squeeze he got his digits in his hair and made matters lively for a time. Ald. Lang came to Mr. Clancy's rescue and with the assistance of several others parted the two men. Mr. Kinsella was taken to one end of the stage and Mr. Clancy to the other where they were allowed time to cool off. Then Mr. Kinsella again appeared before the footlights, more determined to be heard than ever amid cheers and hisses, when Moses the Inkman attired in a new suit of broad-cloth, white tie and new plug hat, stepped up behind and counselled him to "cut it short."

Loud cries were now heard for "Moses." Moses advanced and Mr. Kinsella pushed him back and advised him not to cross his path or he would hurt him. At this, Moses assumed an offended air, and said, "You, what for you say dat to me? Have I not been your brudder in de circumstances which surrounds our fleeting existence?" (Applause.) While this reproach was being uttered the confusion was terrible.

Dr. Hill, at this point, vacated the chair and Mssrs. Eggleson and Lees left the room, with a number of others. Moses came up to speak again, but had hardly opened his mouth when he felt a hand grasp him by the coat collar and slide him over to the side of the stage. The crowd rushed up to the stage again, and for a time it looked as though the affair would terminate in a large row....

June 30, 1880

December 5, 1877

IN THE CELLS.—Some time ago, it will be remembered, a young man from Plantagenet came to this city, in search of a girl named Mary Shea, whose charms had captivated his heart. To his great astonishment he found that she had wandered from the path of virtue. He loved the girl to distraction, and said he was willing to sacrifice his life for her. He proposed that she should leave her haunts of vice and board in a Sussex street hotel for two weeks and in the event of good behaviour during that period he would make her his wife. She finally consented, and at the end of the stipulated term the Plantagenet young man expressed himself thoroughly satisfied with her conduct and felt that she had seen the error of her ways, and would yet make a good wife. The wedding day was fixed and the happy young man bought the object of his affection a $30 pea green silk dress and other expensive articles. The appointed time of the wedding arrived, and the bridal party, arrayed in all the colours of the rainbow, set out for the church. They reached the door of the sacred edifice without anything taking place to mar the happiness of the hour, but before the altar was reached Mary had changed her mind, and rushed out of the church as though she had been suddenly stricken by an idea that her presence was required elsewhere. The bridegroom followed in pursuit but failed to capture her until her hotel was reached, when she quietly told him that she had made up her mind to put up with the name of Mary Shea for some time to come. Without further explanation, she handed him back the wedding trousseau, gifts, etc., and departed. The young man returned to his home resolved never again to yearn for a bride. Nothing more was heard of the girl until yesterday when she was arrested for being an inmate of a house of ill fame.

The Pacific Railway

SUCCESS OF THE MISSION.

NEGOTIATIONS CONCLUDED.

A Contract Made Subject to the Approval of Parliament.

The Syndicate Composed of English French, and American Capitalists.

Special by Cable to THE CITIZEN.

London, 15th.

All previous statements with reference to the Canadian Pacific Railway negotiations, including the *Times'* article, were premature. A contract has been made to-day by the Dominion Government, with capitalists in London, Paris and America, for the construction and working of the Canadian Pacific Railway,— the contract to be subject to the approval of the Canadian Parliament.

August 16, 1880

December 21, 1877

FOR THE POOR.—The second of the series of entertainments in aid of the poor was given last night in the basement of Christ Church. The attendance was good and the entertainment throughout most enjoyable. Capt. McCuaig was called to the chair, and discharged the duties in an admirable manner. The first item on the programme was a well executed piano solo by Miss Wright, which was applauded. Mr. Lanctot gave an amusing reading, "Meeting House and Missionary Work," which kept the audience in roars of laughter, and drew forth round after round of applause. Mr. Lanctot is a pleasing reader, and the Committee of Management will doubtless make an effort to secure his services again. Miss Bishop delighted the audience with a pretty song sweetly sung. She was encored and responded. Mr. Wicksteed next gave a concertina solo with piano, accompaniment by Miss Wright, and received an encore. Mr. Smellie gave a humorous reading about the young man who took his lady love up in a balloon and scared her into promising him her heart and hand. When she got down she gave it to him in the shape of a box in the ear with all her heart. The piece was well received. Mr. Bishop entertained the audience with several comic

songs which created much amusement. Besides being a source of relief to the poor of the congregation these entertainments have a tendency to engender that spirit of sociability without which a church seldom progresses.

May 25, 1880
A HUSBAND OF THREE.
JOHN BAPTISTE FORTIN'S FEAT.
He Marries Three Maidens, All of Whom
Mourn their Sad Fate.
Perhaps the only subject that attracted the attention of 19th-century
newspapers more than prostitution was bigamy, seemingly much
easier to achieve in the age before electronic record-keeping.

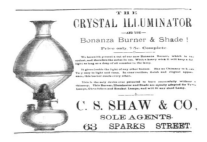

October 16, 1880

Artemus Ward, or some other funny fellow who had the misfortune
to marry a strong-minded woman, once made the remark that where
life was so short, and the cup of happiness so hard to fill, one wife in a
life-time was enough, and in many cases more than enough.

But this is a world of contradictions, and it is no wonder that we find
one Jean Baptiste Fortin, differing widely from the aforesaid Artemus
Ward. To him all women are angels of mercy, and no one of them capable of filling his cup of happiness. So when they came floating around
him to minister unto his love, it is no wonder that he clipped their
wings and "made them one with himself." He has, after a series of brilliant manoeuvres, succeeded in captivating three, and reducing them
to that state of "oneness" that the poet tells us is the outcome of love.

November 1, 1880

That John Baptiste acted wisely in being so much married, is a question which he has considered very carefully, although very reticent in
discussing the delicate question, still he exhibits an exterior that betrays his feelings. His countenance is very sad, sad enough in fact to be
the countenance of a "husband of a thousand" as "Ruth" might say
were she a man. Then his head is bald. The vast area being as smooth
and as bright as a piece of polished Parisian marble. There is undoubtedly a lack of vegetation, but whether that has been superinduced by
the too-frequent laying on of hands, or whether it is a freak of nature,
the reader must judge for himself. It is enough, however, to know that
he has three wives, and with this volume of circumstantial evidence
before the reader, it is unnecessary to express an opinion.

In 1868, at nineteen years of age, his boyish heart beat lovingly towards one Amelia Chartrand, who resided in St. Ren, a girl who, he
says, was as beautiful as a picture to look upon, with a face that made
simplicity a grace; and having seen her he could not bear to longer remain alone. The more he pondered on it, the more the form of the fair
one haunted him and the more he thought with the poet:—

O, lost in virtue, lost to manly thought,
Lost to the noble pathos of the soul,
Who think it right to be alone.

That settled it; he popped the question and they took each other for better or for worse, for richer or for poorer, and all that sort of thing. As the years rolled on little olive branches made their appearance from time to time until a family of five found shelter around the parental roof.

Being a raftsman Jean Baptiste had occasion to be away from his wife four months at a time, and during one of these protracted stays, he met one Josephine Dumoulin, of this city, whose eyes were as captivating as the raven orbs of Queen Isabella. She gazed on him but once and he wilted; he told his love; she reciprocated, and a matrimonial alliance was formed at once. The nuptials were performed at St. Anne's Church. He lived with Josephine for a short time, but getting tired of her he bid farewell to her, and returned to his first love in St. Rose.

Subsequent to this he went to Aylmer where he was engaged by the Messrs. Klock Bros. to work on the farm. About six months ago, he returned to the city and located in Champagne's hotel, where he was smitten by the cook, a buxom lass of twenty-eight summers, named Nora Macnamara. To her he poured out his love, and his pleadings were rewarded with victory, for he carried her off triumphantly to the cathedral, where the third matrimonial noose was tied. They lived together for a short time, until the first wife wrote to Mrs. Champagne, making enquiries about her husband. This led to the revelation, and the arrest of Jean Baptiste.

The case will come up before the Police Magistrate to-day. It is said, however, that wife No. 1 has refused to prosecute since laying the information, but that will not protect the bigamist, as the law must take its course.

Fortin was eventually convicted on two charges of bigamy and sentenced to three years in prison. His marriages to Josephine Dumoulin and Nora Macnamara were declared invalid, freeing them to marry again.

August 24, 1880
A SAD STORY.
AN OTTAWA GIRL DIES FROM MALPRACTICE IN CHICAGO.
Her Last Letter to Her Mother.
Chicago 21st.—Two weeks ago a sick woman, identified by letters as M. A. M. Faulkner, of Ottawa, Canada, took a lodging on West Madison street, and was attended by Dr. Cream. On Thursday he entered the

November 6, 1880

house with a case of instruments. Yesterday the keeper of the house, Mrs. McKay, left. This morning a boarder attracted by an unpleasant smell, notified police and then broke into Miss Faulkner's room, where he found the body on the bed—which was suffused with blood—and rapidly decomposing and bearing evidence of abortion. Through a description by the boarders, Dr. Cream was identified and in his drug store was found a note addressed to him from Mrs. McKay saying, "The Woman is dead, I have left the house." Both the doctor and Mrs. McKay have been arrested.

On receiving the above despatch on Saturday, a *Citizen* reporter started out to discover the friends of the unfortunate girl, if she had any. After considerable trouble he found a widow named Faulkner, living on St. Paul street, and questioned her regarding her family. The woman is very poor, being supported by her little son who sells newspapers. She has other children grown up and married, besides a 22-year-old son, a printer, residing in Boston. The family came to this Country about ten years ago from the island of Guernsey where they had evidently been in very comfortable circumstances. The reporter having discovered an entry in the family Bible corresponding with the name found on the deceased, asked Mrs. Faulkner if she had a daughter named Mary Ann, in Chicago. Without giving a direct reply the poor woman cried out, "Oh, what has happened to my child? I had a dream last night and saw her lying dead." After attempts to pacify the old lady the reporter finally broke the sad news to her. The poor creature's grief was distressing to behold, and it was some time before she could be induced to answer further questions. It appears that when the family came to Canada the daughter Mary Ann was left behind on account of a sore leg for which she was being treated in a hospital. When she had recovered she followed the rest across the Atlantic and arrived here just before her father's death. That sad event appears to have caused a breaking up of the family, and Mary Ann left home to go out to service. She went to Chicago a couple of years ago, and has since kept up a frequent correspondence with her mother, often sending her money. The last letter her mother received shows pretty conclusively how matters stood with her, and is proof either of treachery or cowardice or both on the part of the man on whom she had set her affections.

The following is a copy:-

CHICAGO, June 10, 1880.
DEAR MOTHER.—I received your welcome letter and was very glad that Mickey came home. I hope that he will not run away again. I send you four dollars this time. I hope it will be of some service to you. I would send you more but it is all I

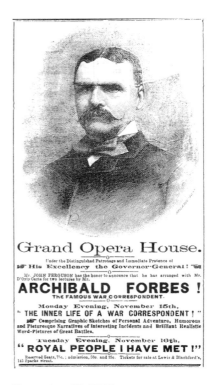

Grand Opera House.
Under the Distinguished Patronage and Immediate Presence of
His Excellency the Governor-General!
Mr. JOHN FERGUSON has the honor to announce that he has arranged with Mr. D'Oyly Carte for two lectures by Mr.
ARCHIBALD FORBES !
THE FAMOUS WAR CORRESPONDENT.
Monday Evening, November 15th,
" THE INNER LIFE OF A WAR CORRESPONDENT ! "
Comprising Graphic Sketches of Personal Adventure, Humorous and Picturesque Narratives of Interesting Incidents and Brilliant Realistic Word-Pictures of Great Battles.
Tuesday Evening, November 16th,
" ROYAL PEOPLE I HAVE MET !"
Reserved Seats, 75c. ; admission, 50c. and 25c. Tickets for sale at Lewis & Blachford's, 141 Sparks street.

November 15, 1880

GREAT EXCITEMENT IN ST.
PETERSBURGH.

Struck Dead on the Street

NITRO-GLYCERINE THE AGENT.

The Troops Indignant—His Successor Proclaimed.

"God's Will be Done."

By Telegraph to THE CITIZEN.
St. Petersburg, 12th.—As the Emperor
was returning from parade in the Michel
Menege, about two o'clock this afternoon,
a bomb was thrown which exploded under
the Czar's carriage, which was considerably damaged; the Czar alighted unhurt,
but a second bomb exploded at his feet,
shattering both legs below the knee, and
inflicting other terrible injuries. The Czar
was immediately conveyed to the Winter
Palace, where he died at 4·30 o'clock this
afternoon. Two persons were concerned
in the crime, one of whom was seized immediately. The explosion also killed an
officer and two Cossacks. Many policemen and other persons were injured.
St. Petersburg, 12th.—The imperial carriage was attacked on Kakrinofsky Canal,
opposite the imperial stables, while the
Emperor was returning with the Grand
Duke Michael, from the Michael Palace in
a closed carriage, escorted by eight cossacks. The first bomb fell near the
carriage, destroying the back part of it.
The Czar and his brother alighted unin-
jured. The assassin, on being seized by
the Colonel of the police, drew a revolver

March 14, 1881

have got. Let me know who sleeps in my bed. I hope Ned is
better. What is the matter with him? As soon as I can I will
send you some more money. It is Lizzie's birthday. Tell her I
think of with her joy. Dear Mother, cheer up. I shall come and
see you perhaps in a month and surprise you. But I shall not
tell you how. We will only stay a short time. Tell Mickey to be a
good boy till I come home. Tell you the truth mother, if I do
not change my mind, I shall be married next month. Would
you like it. I inhabit such a nice place at present and the people
are so kind to me. I feel close with them. I sit to one table with
them and they make no more difference than if I was in their
own family. Dear mother send me a nice letter and if you have
anything to say put it on a little slip of paper for my mistress
would like to see my letter sometimes. So, dear mother, I hope
you will receive this all right. Answer as soon as you receive it.
I wrote to Aunt Ellen last night. How is your leg? Give my best
to George. How is his wife? How is Nellie? I never heard anything about her in your letters. She ought to be able to write a
letter herself. How is Eliza and family? Give them my love. Tell
all my brothers and sister to write me. No more. I remain your
affectionate daughter, with love and a thousand kisses.

M. A. FAULKNER
Care of Mrs. Fairman,
Illinois Central Depot, Chicago.

The entry in the family Bible is as follows—Mary Anne M. Faulkner,
born 8th August, 1851. This shows her to have been 29 years old, but
from a recent photograph which she had sent her mother she looked
much younger, possessing a very pleasant, intelligent face. Unfortunately she has never mentioned the name of her intended husband in
any of her letters, and, unless he is discovered through the doctor and
boarding-housekeeper he will doubtless escape unpunished. Her married brother here, on being informed of the terrible occurrence, immediately telegraphed to his brother in Boston to go on to Chicago, he being unable to go himself for want of means. It is a sad story, and the
hope of all well-thinking people will be that the parties implicated may
receive the full limit of the law.

September 17, 1880
THE VALUE OF A COMMA

There is nothing like correct punctuation sometimes. Here is an illustration: Among the additions of the free list of the tariff bill enacted
two years ago is the following: "Fruit plants, tropical and semi-tropical,
for the purpose of propagation and cultivation." The clerk who en-

grossed the bill, smiling probably at the ignorance of the legislator who drew it, thought to improve upon this copy by inserting a comma after fruit, making it read "Fruit, plants," etc., thus changing materially the sense of the bill. The committee did not observe the change, and the bill with the clerk's amendment became a law. The Treasury Department, however, administered it according to the intention of its framer, until some shrewd importer of fruits planted himself firmly upon the comma, and refused to pay duties on his import, except under protest. Insisting upon his construction of the law, he at last obtained the return of the duties, and ever since fruits have been admitted free. The comma is said to have cost the government two millions of dollars. Among other merchants who benefitted by the insertion of that comma were the Boston dealers, who have had $500,000, gold, refunded to them, paid under protest. The honest engrossing clerk ought to be remembered by the dealers in foreign fruit. They can afford to unite in presenting him with a brownstone front house, filled with gorgeous furniture and things, and if he doesn't remind them of such a thing, it will only be on account of his excessive modesty.

May 17, 1882
OSCAR WILDE
Lecture in the Grand Opera House.

There was a fairly good audience last night to hear Mr. Oscar Wilde on the subject of "Art Decoration." It would be unfair to say that the audience was disappointed, for a very considerable portion of those present assembled as much out of curiosity to see the Esthetic leader as any desire to hear what he had to say on the subject of decorative art.

Dr. Grant in a few terse sentences introduced the lecturer, who was dressed in the fanciful costume which is so familiar to the public eye wherever a photographic gallery exists. He was clad in a suit of black velvet of the last century style, with black stockings and low shoes, with heavy lace cuffs and collar. Of more than ordinary height and a rather good figure, he would present a fine appearance were it not for the outre manner in which he wears his hair. As a lecturer Mr. Wilde is anything but an unqualified success. His style of speaking resembles very much the dull monotone so common in some of the pulpits of the day, while there is an absence of animation which is also characteristic of some of our modern sermonizers.

Although a native of the capital of the "green isle" in the eastern Atlantic, Mr. Wilde's speech resembles the English Cockney more than it does that of the Dublin born and educated gentleman. He said he would speak of what was being done in England to search out those who had a real love for the beautiful and to bring the artist and the handy craftsman in closer union. The ideas promulgated by this gen-

LOCAL WEATHER REPORT.

TUESDAY, April 9th.

Thermometer.   Barometer.

8 a.m. 56 deg. above zero.   8 a.m. 29.80 in.
1 p.m. 61 deg.   "   1 p.m. 29.83 in.
6 p.m. 60 deg.   "   6 p.m. 29.85 in.
Maximum, 61 deg. above zero.
Minimum, 53 deg.   "
Minimum previous night, 50 deg. above.

Remarks—8 p.m.—Rain descended at an early hour this morning, but the storm-clouds wept themselves away soon after sunrise and the weather became clear and bright, as the sunlight danced and shimmered downward through the sky, as with the very overcharge of vitality it came to bring. The fields are looking bright with spring verdure, the trees are pushing out their small swelling buds, and grasses and mosses are springing forth in every variety of brown and green, the first of the spring. Atmospheric pressure was lower but steady notwithstanding a strong northeasterly wind. The air is musical to-night with the dulcet strains from the frog ponds.

May 10, 1882

tleman might be excellent if all people were either millionaires or savages, but in the practical 19th century, and in a practical country like Canada, he is not likely to find many followers. His local suggestions were by no means new, though no practical man would have expressed them so extremely. That it is a pity that the Ottawa should be dirtied with sawdust has been long admitted, and that pure sky should be dirtied with smoke may also be a pity, but Mr. Wilde goes too far when he advocates that no man should be allowed to carry on a business which produces either of these results. His complaint about the hideousness of the majority of stores, is one which has appeared time after time in every American manufacturing journal in America, and the difficulty to surmount which has occupied the attention of the best practical men. His objections to putting a landscape on a soup plate, or a sunset scene on a saucer, are hardly in accord with those of Charles Dickens, and the veteran novelist probably knew human nature as well as Mr. Wilde. He will of course draw large audiences wherever he goes.

September 15, 1882
AN ASTRONOMER'S WARNING
The Greatest Storm of the 19th Century Coming

Editor of the Citizen:

Sir.—The *Asia*, Her Majesty's steamship *Phoenix*, and many others have been wrecked in the great storm which I announced two months ago would pass from east to west over this continent during the month of September....

My warnings were unheeded and hundreds of poor souls who know nothing of the great laws by which nature governs the world have gone down to the bottom of the sea....

Owing to the advice of friends and to the fact that every man should feel an interest in his fellow, I now make the following announcement:—

A great storm will strike this planet on the 9th of March next. It will be felt in the Northern Pacific, and will cross the meridian of Ottawa at noon (5 o'clock London time) of Sunday, March 11th, 1883. No vessel smaller than a Cunarder will be able to live in this tempest. India, the South of Europe, England, and especially the North American continent, will be the theatre of its ravages.

As all the low lands on the Atlantic will be submerged, I advise shipbuilders to place their prospective vessels high upon the stocks, and farmers having loose valuables, as hay, cattle etc., to remove them to a place of safety. I beg further most respectfully to appeal to the honourable Minister of Marine that he will peremptorily order up the storm drums on all the Canadian coast not later than the 20th of February, and thus permit no vessel to leave harbour. If this is not done hun-

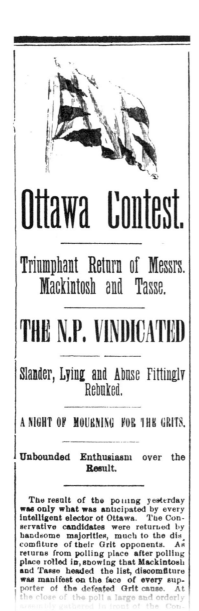

Ottawa Contest.

Triumphant Return of Messrs. Mackintosh and Tasse.

THE N.P. VINDICATED

Slander, Lying and Abuse Fittingly Rebuked.

A NIGHT OF MOURNING FOR THE GRITS.

Unbounded Enthusiasm over the Result.

The result of the polling yesterday was only what was anticipated by every intelligent elector of Ottawa. The Conservative candidates were returned by handsome majorities, much to the discomfiture of their Grit opponents. As returns from polling place after polling place rolled in, showing that Mackintosh and Tasse headed the list, discomfiture was manifest on the face of every supporter of the defeated Grit cause. At the close of the poll a large and orderly assembly gathered in front of the Con-

June 21, 1882

dreds of lives will be lost and millions worth of property destroyed.

E. Stone Wiggins, LLD
Astronomer, Ottawa

Wiggins was not an astronomer, but rather an amateur weather forecaster with a day job in the Finance Department. Even so, his letter sparked a worldwide sensation after it was picked up by The Associated Press and published in U.S. and European newspapers. Experts dismissed his forecasts as silly and his seemingly correct earlier warnings as coincidence. But as the date of the predicted disaster loomed, newspaper coverage intensified. Advertisers cashed in on the hype, using "Wiggins' Storm" to help sell everything from hats to tea. When the day arrived, hundreds of East Coast fishermen hedged their bets and stayed home. However, apart from stiff winds here and there across North America, Wiggins' great storm simply blew over.

March 6, 1883
These are the very first of millions of words about hockey published in the Citizen. *The Ottawa Hockey Club was an informal group of men, some of them public servants, who got together for occasional games of shinny. The Royal Rink, one of the first covered facilities in Ottawa, was located where Confederation Park is today.*

HOCKEY CLUB.—The Ottawa Hockey Club had its first contest on the ice at the Royal Rink last night. There was good play made on both sides.

April 13, 1884.
EASTERTIDE.
A Splendid Display of Beef by Our Butchers.
A CHOICE SELECTION.
By and Wellington Ward Markets
Competing for the Supremacy.

As usual at Eastertide, the chief attraction in the city, next to the churches, is the magnificent display made by the butchers. The knights of the cleaver have had a busy week of it between purchasing cattle, slaughtering them and fitting up their stalls in an appropriate manner. Some of the decorations are very fine.

WELLINGTON STREET MARKET,
at this end of the city, our old friend Mr. A. Bufton, comes well to the front. He has a magnificent display, including two enormous steers from Mr. David Moore, weighing about 1,900 pounds each, besides many other choice cattle from the most celebrated breeders in the Ot-

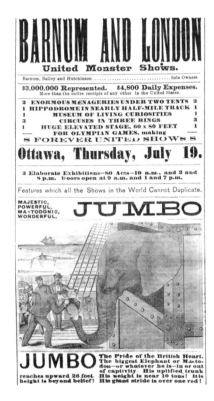

July 7, 1883

tawa Valley. Some fifteen or twenty calves, fed by Messrs. Butler and Armstrong, both renowned for choice cattle, are reputed to be the best ever raised by these celebrated breeders. Mr. Bufton's decorations are very tasty indeed, the more ornamental which have been admired by everybody, have been, we understand, supplied by Mrs. Bufton, and reflect the very greatest of credit on that lady. If a good Old English roast beef cannot be supplied by Bufton this Easter, none can be procured.

THE HANRAHANS.

This is a huge display. Barnum would call it "the biggest show on earth," but we do not wish to exaggerate. We will simply say that it is very large, and choice, well-arranged and tastily decorated, and furnishes a complete choice from which the most choosy housekeeper can select his Easter dinner. Seventy-six of the choicest of mutton, twenty-five Guelph prize cattle, eight calves, forty-five fat porkers, six spring lambs, hams, bacon, sausages, etc. If you want to thoroughly recover from the demoralizing effects of a forty days' fast, by all means call at the palace stalls of Messrs. Hanrahan.

MR. E. GLOVER.

Between the stalls of the above mentioned butchers stands that of Mr. Glover. Mr. Glover's display is, indeed, not so large, but it is tasty, and he has evidently spared no effort in catering to the Easter wants of his customers, of whom he has many.

MR. GEO. WHITE

has as usual a good display, and is evidently determined not to be behind in his endeavours to supply the wants of his customers at Eastertide. Several very choice cuts are on view and no lack of variety is noticeable in his selections, which are very choice.

RICHARDSON.

We cannot pass over our old friend Richardson. Competition is the life of trade, and we presume that it is also a healthy stimulant to butchers.

KIMPTON,

the pork man, is bound to be the front man in his line, seeing that his is the only pork butcher on the Wellington Ward Market. Anything that "Tom" cannot supply you in the way of fat hogs, either at Easter or Christmas, or any other time, is not worth having.

BYWARD MARKET.

Mr. Duhamel, at the Clarence street corner stall, has a beautiful display. A dozen choice steers, the very choicest possible selection of mutton, calves, porkers, spring lambs, hams, sausages, puddings, etc., all are here, beautifully displayed and tastefully decorated. Mr. Duhamel has within the past year suffered heavy losses by fire, but is evidently not at all crushed, and his many customers and personal friends will rejoice to see him doing well this Eastertide.

GREAT CALAMITY.

Terrific Volcanic Disturbances in Java.

FIFTEEN CRATERS IN ERUPTION.

Towns and Islands Overwhelmed with Rocks and Lava.

A MOUNTAIN SWEPT OUT OF SIGHT.

Thousands of Persons Killed by the Catastrophe.

By Telegraph to THE CITIZEN.

Batavia, 29th.—The volcanic eruptions in Java began on the Island of Krakatoa, in the strait of Sunda, 100 miles from the coast of Java, on Saturday night. At Sunda the disturbances had extended beneath the water of the strait, causing great waves and a rise of twenty degrees in the temperature. The sea disturbance was felt 500 miles away. By noon Waba Meru, the largest volcano in Java, was in violent interruption, and shortly after Galunggong, the crater of which is the largest in the world, and fifteen out of the forty-five craters in Java, were either in active eruption, or seriously threatened. At dusk Galunggong sent out streams of white sulphurous vapour. With the

August 30, 1883

THORBAHN,

the Pork Prince, comes solidly to the front. We cannot imagine many concerns in the city that do as large a business as that of H. Thorbahn. The whole of the Lower Town nearly, and a portion of the residents of Centre and Upper Town buy their supplies in the pork line all the year round from this enterprising dealer. Making a specialty of the pig business, he is able to do justice to it, and has always some beauties in stock. He has now a magnificent display.

SLATTERY.

This well known old butcher has a grand display this Easter. For a long time caterer to Government House, it is needless to inform the public that what Mr. Slattery keeps is of the choicest and best. Several magnificent animals are displayed this week at his spacious stall, and the decorations alone are worth a visit to see. They are delightful.

ROBERT & CO.

make their usual excellent display. No man in the business on either market takes more pains to thoroughly supply the wants of his customers than Mr. Robert, and his customers know it.

MR. E. GAUVREAU

had also a very choice selection, the particular of which will be found in his advertisement is another column, Mr. Gauvreau has spared no pains, and his efforts will not doubt, meet with proper appreciation from his customers.

MR. POMINVILLE

has also made extensive preparation for Eastertide. His display is very choice and reflects the greatest of credit upon him.

MR. J. MARTEL,

also of By Ward Market, is "last but not least." Mr. Martel has made extensive purchases this Easter, and is prepared to supply the wants of the public in the beef line, no matter how extensive their wants may be. We wish Mr. Martel all success in his laudable efforts, and predict for him a prosperous Easter business.

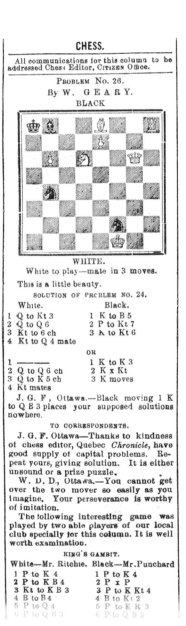

CHESS.

All communications for this column to be addressed Chess Editor, CITIZEN Office.

PROBLEM No. 26.
By W. GEARY.
BLACK

WHITE.
White to play—mate in 3 moves.
This is a little beauty.

SOLUTION OF PROBLEM No. 24.

White.	Black.
1 Q to Kt 3	1 K to B 5
2 Q to Q 6	2 P to Kt 7
3 Kt to 6 ch	3 K to Kt 6
4 Kt to Q 4 mate	

OR

1 ——	1 K to K 3
2 Q to Q 6 ch	2 K x Kt
3 Q to K 5 ch	3 K moves
4 Kt mates	

J. G. F , Ottawa.—Black moving 1 K to Q B 3 places your supposed solutions nowhere.

TO CORRESPONDENTS.

J. G. F. Ottawa—Thanks to kindness of chess editor, Quebec *Chronicle*, have good supply of capital problems. Repeat yours, giving solution. It is either unsound or a prize puzzle.

W. D. D., Ottawa.—You cannot get over the two mover so easily as you imagine. Your perseverance is worthy of imitation.

The following interesting game was played by two able players of our local club specially for this column. It is well worth examination.

KING'S GAMBIT.

White—Mr. Ritchie. Black—Mr.Punchard

1 P to K 4	1 P to K 4
2 P to K B 4	2 P x P
3 Kt to B 3	3 P to K Kt 4
4 B to B 4	4 B to Kt 2
5 P to Q 4	5 P to K R 3
6 P to Q B 3	6 P to Q B 3

September 13, 1884

His Excellency's Government does not intend to submit to the Legislature during the present session a bill for the immediate settlement of the Clergy Reserve " Then ensued what may not inappropriately be termed a fierce, uncompromising debate. With infinite skill Mr. Macdonald permitted one after another of those—who, though against Mr. Hincks, were opposed to the Conservative party—to commit themselves and put upon record opinions adverse to the Ministry; then rising in his place, whilst the galleries were crowded by spectators from every section of the country, he delivered a speech of the Clergy Reserves; the Opposition, however, contested it, clause by clause and stage by stage, until it finally received the Royal sanction. The chief objection taken was that the proposed Act took a certain sum of money and gave it as commutation to the English, Scotch and Roman Catholic clergy which by the action of the Imperial Government had been a charge upon the fund. The Canadian Clergy Reserves were settled by an Act of the Imperial Parliament in 1840; that Act gave preferences to certain churches. An appeal, however, growing out of the agitation preceding the downfall of Mr. Hincks' Government, became necessary, the Imperial Government consenting,

which at once placed him in the foremost rank of parliamentary debaters and, at the same time

SOUNDED THE DEATH KNELL OF THE ADMINISTRATION.

Mr. Hincks resigned, and in a speech that was highly distasteful to the majority, Lord Elgin dissolved the Assembly. Mr. Sandfield Macdonald (afterwards Premier of the united provinces and Premier of Ontario under Confederation) as Speaker of the House protested against members being dismissed —holding that "the passing of a bill through all its stages, according to the laws and customs of Parliament, is considered necessary to constitute a ... with this proviso, that the position of those individuals having stipends, charged upon the fund and guaranteed by the pledge of their Queen, should not be affected in any changes inaugurated. Instead, then, of paying out to each clergyman his annual salary, Mr. Macdonald conceived the idea of calculating the total value of each stipend, and thus discharging the debt in full. Nothing could have been more creditable than the behaviour of a large majority of those interested. They accepted without a murmur the amounts allotted them, and after discharging all dues, the Attorney-General was in a position to say that not only were the ...

Modern Times

The Fifth Decade, 1885-1894

HE WASN'T A SUPERSTITIOUS man, but when Charles Mackintosh looked back on the events of June 30, 1891, many years later, he decided they were meant as a sign for him to move on. He was approaching 50, his political hero, Sir John A. Macdonald, was dead nearly a month—and now the newspaper he'd owned for 14 years was consumed in flames.

Mackintosh, also Ottawa's MP, was on his way from his parliamentary office to the *Citizen* building at 106-108 Sparks Street when he heard the late night alarm. "He clambered up a ladder and made a brave attempt to reach his private office where valuable papers were stored," the Toronto *Mail* reported. The flames and smoke drove him back, although firemen later saved his desk, a few papers—and a large, signed photograph of Macdonald, a gift from the former PM that survived undamaged while portraits of Robbie Burns and Napoleon Bonaparte, hanging alongside, were destroyed.

"It was a strange freak, a circumstance to give pause," he told a reporter 30 years later. And so it did. After putting the paper back on its feet, Mackintosh turned the editorship over to Robert Shannon and went to see the new prime minister, Charles Tupper, to announce his plan to quit politics. To his surprise, Tupper asked if he'd consider becoming Lieutenant-Governor of the Northwest Territories, then a vast region that also encompassed Saskatchewan and Alberta.

By 1892, Mackintosh was gone from Ottawa, and the *Citizen*'s cosy relations with the government were gone with him. He sold the paper to Shannon, an experienced, hard-nosed journalist who remained editor, and his brother Lewis, who took over as business manager.

In many ways, the Shannons were an ideal fit for the times, a period when electricity and the telephone had begun to speed the pace of life.

The Ottawa Daily Citizen

TUESDAY, FEBRUARY 2, 1892.

TO THE PUBLIC.

I beg to state that I am no longer connected with the Ottawa DAILY CITIZEN, which has hitherto been under my editorial management. In withdrawing from what was for so many years to me a labour of love, if not pecuniary advantage, I have to thank those who, through cloud and sunshine, extended their support, sympathy and confidence.

My successor will be Mr. R. W. Shannon, a gentleman in every way qualified to assume the responsibilities of the position.

Ever faithfully,
C. H. MACKINTOSH.

Ottawa, Ont., Feby. 1st, 1892.

February 2, 1892

Opposite: The front page of Sunday, June 9, 1891, proclaimed the death of Sir John A. Macdonald. Nearly a century would pass before the Citizen would publish a regular Sunday edition.

113

Sometimes called Canada's first "modern newspapermen," the brothers were determined to make up ground lost to the *Free Press* and *Journal,* now in its second decade, since the fire. To signal new owners were in charge, they renamed the paper *The Ottawa Daily Citizen.* Robert Shannon, a robust editor with an eye for lively stories, added reporters to increase local coverage, and broadened the paper's scope to include more foreign, business and sports coverage, and topics thought to interest women. His brother ran an aggressive marketing campaign, using billboards (a newspaper first in Ottawa) to praise the *Citizen's* merits—"spicy, fresh news" and "the only morning daily between Montreal and Toronto"—and offer deals to new subscribers.

The Shannons' time at the helm was to be short. But it proved successful enough to attract the attention of another family, one that would shape the destiny of the paper for a century.

January 12, 1885
A LEADER WANTED.

Two years later, the Citizen *probably wished it hadn't run this job ad-cum-editorial mocking the talents of Liberal leader Edward Blake. In 1887, Blake was replaced by Wilfrid Laurier, who was to become one of Canada's great prime ministers—and precisely the kind of leader the* Citizen *said the Liberals required.*

WANTED—By the Grit party of Canada, a young man of prepossessing appearance, gentlemanly address and having some courage and ability, to take the position of leader of the party in the Dominion House of Commons. Only those who are warranted to stand fire and not to run at the approach of an opponent need apply.

We give the above publicity in our editorial instead of our advertising columns, in order that it may be as generally seen as possible, and that no aspiring young Grit who is a reader of the *Citizen* may lose the opportunity of applying for a position which must shortly become vacant. That Mr. Blake has signally and utterly failed as a leader is beyond question. When he and his clique conspired the—shall we say "removal"?—of Mr. Mackenzie from the position of leader of the party, the event was blazoned with a great flourish of trumpets. We were told that great events would follow the change of leaders, that the triumph of the party was to be immediate, and that Sir John was to be knocked out of office in less time than it would take the proverbial lamb to give ten wags of its proverbial tail. But years have tolled away, one general election and scores of by-elections have taken place, and the new leader instead of gaining strength and popularity has led his small force from one disastrous defeat to another until it is no wonder they at last rebel and want another change. Mr. Blake as a leader has devel-

HON. WILFRID LAURIER.

Notice.

The company of sharpshooters for service in the North-West will muster for parade in full marching order with kits, at the Drill Hall at 9 O'CLOCK SHARP this morning.

A. HAMLYN TODD,

Captain.

March 31, 1885

oped an amazing and alarming power of wind, and very little else. His terrible harangues of three, four, five and six hours duration have got to be a bore to his friends and a nuisance to everybody else; and for all the talking he does it is really remarkable how little he accomplishes. From a Conservative standpoint we, of course, wish him more wind power, for the more and the longer he talks the greater assistance he unconsciously is to the Conservative party. A striking instance of this is to be found in the Lennox election, where Mr. Blake's three hour speech in Napanee, coupled with his gallant conduct in refusing to meet his opponents in fair discussion, was largely instrumental in converting a Liberal majority of two in that town into a Conservative majority of forty-three. A few more such triumphs of oratorical skill and there will be no Grit party left for Mr. Blake or anybody else to lead.

March 30, 1885
A MURDEROUS ATTACK.
An Unoffending Citizen Stabbed Three Times
on a Public Thoroughfare.

For some months past there has been a small Italian colony in Lower Town, composed of workmen discharged from the work of construction on the C.P.R. It is very difficult to make those who compose it understand that the climate of Canada is not a congenial one for many of the little peculiarities which distinguish the bravos of sunny Italy, and that the use of the playful stiletto and the gay and festive dagger is contrary to the laws of the Dominion.

In consequence of this obtuseness on their part, these Italians have been a constant source of trouble to their neighbours and to the police ever since they arrived here. They not only stab each other on the slightest provocation but often take it into their hands to practise the same method of assault on the ordinary citizen. An instance of this occurred on Saturday night last. About half-past eleven o'clock as Mr. Frank Rossignol, a one-armed man, was coming out of Malone's grocery store near the corner of Clarence and Cumberland streets, a man whose name he does not know, but who he recognized as one of the Italians, hustled up against him. Mr. Rossignol asked him what he wanted, and the Italian replied by stabbing him three times with a sharp stiletto. The blows were delivered with lightning-like capability, the first taking effect in the breast, the second in one of the shoulders and the last in the back of the victim. Mr. Rossignol shouted for help and the Italian made off at top speed and was soon out of sight. Some passers-by, having heard Rossignol's cries, ran up and found him lying in a pool of blood.

He was at once conveyed to the residence of his brother-in-law, Mr. Favrell and medical aid was summoned. The blood flowed heavily

The Riel Revolt.

Extensive Military Preparations to Crush it.

INTENSE FEELING IN CANADA.

Magnificent Outburst of Loyal Enthusiasm.

VOLUNTEERING VERY ACTIVE.

Particulars of the Duck Lake Encounter.

FLAG OF TRUCE OUTRAGED.

Burning and Evacuation of Fort Carlton by Mounted Police.

STORES SEIZED BY INSURGENTS.

Situation Becoming Very Serious—Attitude of the Indians—A Riel Emissary Captured in the Saskatchewan—Menacing Demeanour of the Crees.

By Telegraph to THE CITIZEN.

The news published in THE CITIZEN on Saturday morning announcing that a conflict had taken place in the North-West was the chief topic of conversation all day long. Many wild stories got afloat, and some of them gained credence, but no additional reliable news was received during the day. At the hotels, in the Parliament Buildings, in the Departments—in fact all over the city scarcely anything else was spoken of, even the Anglo-Russian situation

March 25, 1885

BAD NEWS

Town of Battleford in the Hands of the Cree Braves.

A PRECARIOUS SITUATION

Threatened Attack on the Barracks by Hostiles.

TWO INSTRUCTORS MURDERED

Plunder of the Stores by Half-Breeds and Indians.

THE STONIES UP IN ARMS.

Louis Riel Urging the Red River Metis to Join Him.

BATTLEFORD IN ASHES.

Advance of General Middleton's Forces to Qu'Appelle.

SETTLERS PILLAGED AND KILLED

Embarkation of the Ottawa Sharpshooters at the Union Depot.

AN ENTHUSIASTIC SEND-OFF.

The Contingent Greeted with Ovations all Along the Line—The Battalions on the Way—The Ministerial Statements in the Commons Yesterday—Lieutenant-Governor Dewdney has a Pow-Wow with the Crees—Continued Enthusiasm Among Volunteers Throughout Canada.

The excitement in the city yesterday over the North-West *emeute* was unabated, although it did not find expression in any public demonstration, unless the large crowd of men, women and

April 1, 1885

from the wounds and it was only with great difficulty that they could be staunched. Although serious it is not thought that the wounds will prove fatal, but the coward that committed the act has succeeded in evading arrest although the police have a clue to his identity.

April 6, 1885

THAT SNOW STORM.—The snowstorm which commenced on Thursday morning is said by the proverbial "oldest inhabitant" to be the longest he ever experienced. It commenced shortly before ten o'clock on Thursday morning and continued to rage without intermission until two o'clock on Saturday—thus making a continuous snowstorm of fifty-two hours.

April 7, 1885
ROUGH ON THE ROYAL.
The Roof of One of Ottawa's Theatres Collapses Yesterday.
How a Prospective Ottawa Audience
Had a Narrow Escape—A Terrible Crash.

A loud report resembling the explosion of a powerful magazine followed by an immense cloud of smoke caused the men on duty in the Central Fire Station yesterday afternoon to think that a conflagration was in progress. The consequence was that Box 41 was sounded, and equipment from all the stations promptly responded to the call. There was, however, no necessity for the run, and the members of the brigade returned to their stations without having to lay their hose. The alarm was due to the falling in of the roof of the Royal Museum Theatre on York street, immediately adjoining the Central Station.

It seems that about half-past three Mr. William Plant, the property man of the house, was engaged in replenishing the fire in the stove situated immediately under the gallery, when he heard a rumbling sound, which was followed by the fall of plaster. Instinctively suspecting that danger was impending, he beat a hasty retreat to the rear of the building. He had hardly gained the stage when that portion of the roof which covered the auditorium crashed in, smashing the seats and breaking its way down through the ceiling of the basement, which is occupied by the Canadian Institute.

The building was immediately surrounded by a crowd of eager sightseers, most of whom were doomed to disappointment, as no signs of the accident were observed from the exterior of the building. When a *Citizen* reporter through the courtesy of Mr. Cain [the owner] visited the wrecked building yesterday afternoon a sorry sight was presented to his view. The auditorium was open to the sky, while the flimsy structure which once had covered it lay heaped in indescribable confusion, mingled as it was with the remains of the chairs allotted to the use of the audience. What was formerly the apparently massive stone tower which once graced the front of the Canadian Institute Building, appeared on the floor of the auditorium a most humiliating and undignified looking mass of zinc and paint; while what had previously passed for a substantial piece of architecture proved to be but heaps of useless wood and plaster. In short, there was a complete wreck.

Broken chairs, damaged scenery, and general dilapidation was what met the eye of the spectator. Luckily there was no matinee yesterday afternoon owing to the fact that the Mendelson Comedy company was delayed owing to the recent heavy snowstorms. Had the company been here as early as expected and held their usual matinee a frightful loss of life would no doubt have resulted from the caving in of the roof of the building. As it was, the only persons in the building at the time of the accident were Messrs. William Plant, Henri Junot and Alfred Cusson, all of which were in the rear of the building and escaped the accident.

Messrs. Cain and Hartray having promised the public of Ottawa a week's performance of the above company determined to fulfill their promise. With commendable enterprise they immediately secured the Grand Opera House for the week. To all who witnessed the interior of the building after the accident it was apparent that the collapse was due to faulty construction. The owners of the building held a meeting last evening, and it was decided to repair the damage and make the building better than ever it was before. The total damage will amount to not less than two thousand dollars.

The storm that delayed the Mendelson Comedy team — and was the longest in the "oldest inhabitant's" memory — dumped nearly 70 centimetres of wet snow on Ottawa. Could it also have been a factor in the roof collapse? The Citizen *never said.*

PRIVATE OSGOODE.

The above cut is an excellent likeness of Private Osgoode, of No. 1 Company, 43rd Battalion, who was killed in the engagement of May 3rd between the troops under Col. Otter and the Indians under Poundmaker. He was 23 years of age, and the only son of Mr. Jeremiah Osgoode, of New Edinburgh. He went to the North-West with the Ottawa Sharpshooters.

PRIVATE ROGERS.

The above is a portrait of Private John Rogers, of the Governor-General's Foot Guards, who was killed in the engagement at Poundmaker's reserve on May 3rd. He was born in Barbadoes, and was 27 years of age at the time of his death. He had been a resident of Ottawa for a little over two years, and on the outbreak of the rebellion went to the North-West with the Ottawa Sharpshooters, under Capt. Todd.

May 16, 1885

May 18, 1885
RIEL A PRISONER

As this editorial shows clearly, the Citizen *had little patience for Louis Riel, the Métis leader of the Red River and Northwest rebellions. Indeed, the paper repeatedly called for his execution, even before the trial that sentenced him to death a few months later. In an interesting twist, just days before his hanging, Riel sent a letter to* Citizen *editor James Johnson to thank him for "his leniency," for urging clemency for Riel's followers. The* Citizen *purchased the original letter from Johnson's descendants in 2002.*

The announcement of the capture of Riel yesterday created a great deal of excitement throughout the city and throughout the country.

THE METIS

Progress of the Insurrection in the Northwest.

LOUIS RIEL AND SCOTT

Communication with the Scene of Trouble Again Cut Off.

RIEL DECLARES WAR.

And Says that He is Bound to Rule or Perish.

VOLUNTEERS FOR THE FRONT

Battleford Again to be in Imminent Danger.

AMERICANS ON THE ALERT

The Canadian Authorities Roused by Threats of Fenian Raids.

THE OTTAWA SHARPSHOOTERS.

Incidents of Their Trip Over the C. P. R.

By Telegraph to THE CITIZEN.

THE OTTAWA SHARPSHOOTERS.

(FROM OUR REPORTER.)

North Bay, C. P. R., April 1st.—The first day's experience of the Ottawa detachment of sharpshooters under Capt. Todd has been very pleasant, no untoward incident occurring to interrupt the harmony. The railway accommodation was as comfortable as could be desired, the rate of travel was rapid, the running proving very smooth. At nearly every station passed there was a large turnout to see the volunteers, and many men offered their services being . . .

April 4, 1885

The regret is general that after putting the Dominion to so much expense and having caused the loss of so many valuable lives, the arch-rebel escaped the bullets which disposed of so many of his deluded followers, leaving him a living man while their bodies lie scattered over the ravines and bush from which they fired upon our Volunteers. The sentiments expressed in Saturday's issue we echo to-day. If law and order are to be maintained in Canada; if our military organization—the value of which has been so fully demonstrated in the present crisis—is to be kept in existence, Riel must be made to pay the penalty of his crimes. For months previous to his putting armed men in the field against the Government he incited the territories including the Indians and Half-breeds to rebellion, not, we hold for the purpose of securing the resisting of any grievances, real or imagined, which existed, but with the one object in view of exalting himself. He used the misguided people who trusted him, but now to-day exonerate his name, to advance his own ends; and after many of them had been killed he deserted them, leaving them to their fate, while he looked after the safety of his own person. The clemency of the Crown might be judiciously exercised in the case of Riel's betrayed dupes; but to his own case, nothing less than a fearless prompt and vigorous administration of justice will satisfy the country.

September 7, 1885
A HORRIBLE TALE.
An Aged Scoundrel Outrages
a Number of Little Girls.

The usual quiet of the little village of Grenville, which is situated about sixty miles down the river from Ottawa, has been disturbed and the population thrown into the wildest state of excitement by the discovery of the fact that a series of outrages on little girls has been committed by an old man fifty years of age, named Seguin, who lives in that vicinity. So far as is known his latest victims were three little girls whose ages range from nine to ten years.

Upon Sunday night last one of them was taken ill, and upon being questioned by her mother her answers gave rise to grave suspicions as to the cause of her illness. Upon being further pressed by her mother the little girl admitted that she and two other little girls who are members of another family had been coaxed away to a secluded spot by Seguin, who offered them candy, and then were outraged by him. Further investigations brought to light the fact that the aged scoundrel has been carrying on this sort of thing for some time, and that a number of young girls had fallen victims to his fiendish lust, but had been afraid to tell their parents what had happened.

Upon learning these facts the indignant mothers of the three first mentioned victims, whose fathers were absent from the village, went to Seguin and taxed him with his crime. He admitted his guilt in the most nonchalant manner, and treated the matter as one not worth casting a thought upon. The women then left him and proceeded to the residence of Mayor Prudhomme, before whom they laid the whole matter. He immediately issued a warrant for Seguin's arrest, but before a constable could be found to execute it the miscreant took alarm and managed to make good his escape.

Up to latest accounts no trace of him had been discovered. He is a married man and father of a large family. Great indignation exists among the villagers, and threats of summary justice, should he be caught, are heard on all sides.

Seguin was eventually captured and sent to prison.

November 12, 1885
READY TO HANG RIEL.
Or Twenty Men for $25—A Very Accommodating Executioner.
(Special to The Citizen.)

Hamilton, Ont., 11th.—In conversation with this reporter to-day, Chief Steward, who assisted at the Riel trial, was asked if he thought there would be any trouble in securing a hangman for Riel. He replied that it was likely they would get Henderson, an old hand, to do the job.

He is a cool, nervy one, the most nonchalant executioner I ever saw. He is the man who hanged Connor, the murderer. The hangman who had previously been engaged to do the job lost heart and disappeared on the day of the execution. The authorities thought of Henderson and a messenger was despatched to his house to secure him. The old man was eating his breakfast, with his wife.

"Do you want to make $25 this morning, Henderson?" asked the messenger. "How?" asked the old fellow.

"We want you to hang a man."

"Yes, I'll hang twenty men for $25. Wife, give me my boots."

When they arrived at the place of execution, Henderson, who wore no mask or anything to conceal his identity, asked where Connor was and when the murderer was pointed out to him he beckoned to him and said, "Come along," and forthwith began pinioning him. Connor was almost as cool as the hangman. He had a sore on his neck, and Henderson was not very gentle in adjusting the rope.

"Take care," said Connor, "you hurt me."

"That's all right," said Henderson in a slightly offending tone, as much as to say, "I'm running the business and know how to do it."

Depend upon it, if they get old Henderson to hang Riel there will be no bungling.

Cree Scalpers !

Their Bloodthirsty Work in the North-West.

A SHOCKING CHAPTER

Sickening Details of the Frog Lake Assassinations.

THE VICTIMS' STRUGGLES

General Middleton and Troops Camped at Humboldt.

THE FORCES IN GOOD SPIRITS.

And Ready for an Immediate Advance on the Saskatchewan.

THE HALIFAX CONTINGENT.

Right Royal Welcome to the Plucky Haligonians.

LOUIS RIEL'S PROGRAMME.

David Glass's Views — The Manitoba Legislature's Timely Step—Letter from Captain Todd—Crowfoot's Message. .

It having been understood that the Halifax Provisional Battalion would arrive here about noon en route for the front, a large number of citizens assembled at the C. P. R. station at that hour to welcome them. Upon arriving there, however, they were disappointed to learn that the special train with the battalion had not left Montreal. A tel-

April 14, 1885

HURRAH!

Government Triumphant in Yesterday's Contest.

THE N. P. SUSTAINED

The Party of Union and Progress Sweep the Country.

ALL MINISTERS ELECTED.

Several Important Losses and Gains.

GREAT VICTORY IN OTTAWA.

February 23, 1887

November 16, 1885
THE DEATH WARRANT.
Riel Informed that He Will be Executed To-day.
The Prisoner Said to be Perfectly Resigned to his Fate.

Like most of Canada's major newspapers, the Citizen *sent a reporter to Regina to cover Riel's trial and execution. It's unlikely the* Citizen's *correspondent was actually in the prison cell to witness Riel's reaction to the news that the Marquess of Lansdowne, the governor general, had approved his execution. More likely, he waited outside the prison and obtained the details, excerpted here from a lengthy story, from Sheriff Chapleau, who gave similar accounts to other papers.*

(From our Correspondent.)

Regina, N.W.T., 15th.—The special messenger bringing the warrant signed by the Governor-General of Canada directing that the execution of Louis Riel should take place, arrived here on a special train at 8 o'clock to-night. There is no longer a doubt that Louis Riel will meet his fate at some hour to-morrow. The arrival of the warrant was a surprise to even many of the officials, who, owing to the late hour and previous delays, had argued that another respite would follow.

Riel received the formal intelligence at 9 o'clock to-night in his cell in the guard-room of the Mounted Police barracks, three miles west of this city. The intelligence was conveyed to him in person by High Sheriff Chapleau. The scene was in many respects remarkable. The famous rebel's cell is immediately adjacent to the guard room of the troops doing night patrol duty, fully five of whom occupied the room. Through the iron gate in front of the cell was seen an armed sentinel on duty and outside the building a cordon of armed men were pacing their beat. The iron gate was thrown open on the approach of Sheriff Chapleau and Col. Irvine, commandant of the Mounted Police.

Riel, who had been conversing with the surgeon of the post, arose and welcomed the Sheriff in a hearty and thoroughly unconstrained way. His voice was modulated, and he displayed no sign of excitement. His initial greeting was, "Well, and so you have come with the great announcement. I am glad." Sheriff Chapleau replied that the death warrant had come. Riel, continuing in the same cheery way, said: "I am glad that at last I am to be released from my sufferings."

He then broke off into French and thanked the Sheriff for his personal consideration. He proceeded again in English: "I desire that my body shall be given to my friends to be laid in St. Boniface." (This is the French cemetery across the Red River from the City of Winnipeg.) The Sheriff then asked him if he had any wishes to convey as to the disposition of his personal estate or effects.

"Mon cher," replied he. "I have only this," he said touching his breast above the region of the heart, "this I gave to my country fifteen years ago and it is all I have now." He was asked as to his peace of mind, and replied, "I long ago made my peace with my God. I am as prepared now as I can be at any time. You will find that I had a mission to perform. I want you to thank my friends in Quebec for all they have done for me."

He continued, in reply to another question, "I am willing to go. I shall be permitted to say something on the scaffold," he said in a tone of inquiry. When told that he would be allowed to do so, he said, smilingly, "You think my speech will be too long, that it will unnerve me. Oh, no! I shall not be weak, I shall feel that when the moment comes I shall have wings which will carry me upwards."

Then reverting again to the French tongue and in an inimitably winning way, for which he is famed to all those who have known him closely, he spoke again of the glad remembrance he would retain of those who had espoused his personal cause. He closed by saying to Sheriff Chapleau, as he held out his hand in parting,"adieu mon ami." His eye was clear and unflinching, and his bearing throughout was such as to evoke a sense of admiration by the absence of any tremor of excitement. If he ever showed the white feather under fire, or on any occasion he succeeded in keeping himself admirably under command in the presence of his own approaching fate. Pere Andrew, his spiritual adviser, then arrived, and he was left with him to celebrate mass. . . .

April 14, 1885

March 25, 1886

A MESSAGE FROM MARS.—A startling discovery has been reported from Italy, tending to the inference that the planetary system is in direct communication with the earth. An amateur astronomer of Teramo, in the Abrusi, named Pemignani, has ascertained the presence on the face of the planet Mars of several luminous points of exceeding brilliancy, which shift from place to place with methodical regularity, as if they were controlled by some intelligent action. The observer has therefore concluded that the sparks are telegraphic signals sent on speculation by the inhabitants of Mars to their neighbour the earth. Up to the present the meaning of the signals has not been interpreted, but those interested in the discovery do not despair of finding their signification, and are engaged in attempting to answer the astral messages.

October 24, 1887
A $25,000 RACE.
Harry Bethune, the Sprinter,
Beaten by an Unknown.
POTS OF MONEY CHANGE HANDS.

Mystery was writ large on the faces of the boys around town on Saturday morning. Whispering gangs were congregated on every street corner and it was evident that there was something in the wind. What that something was was hard to gather but by-and-by it began to be whispered abroad that a big foot race was to be held.

One thing was apparent—a number of sports from Montreal and Toronto had arrived in town. Billy Bingham of Toronto was one of the first recognized, and Toby Elliott of Montreal soon after had to say, "How d'ye do," to a number of friends. Then Harry Bethune turned up and was greeted heartily by a host of people who had seen him run and knew, or thought they knew, what he could do. When Bethune appeared on the streets it speedily became a matter of public notoriety that he was in Ottawa to run a foot race and the news spread among the boys like chain lightning gone wild.

Then the cry went around—"Who is going to run Bethune?" Some said Smith, some said Brown, and all who talked knew nothing at all about it. The men who knew were few and they kept their knowledge dark. In fact, they wrapped themselves up in a cloak of mystery, trimmed with the very quintessence of vagueness....

Not a line of notice of the approaching event had appeared in any of the local papers, because not a word of warning had been allowed to be uttered by anybody connected with the affair. That something extraordinary was on the tapis was evident, when the *Citizen* reporters started out in the morning. The groups on the street corners, their animated talk and gestures, gave the clue which, on being followed up led to the discovery, pregnant with significance that Bethune and the unknown were matched to run a race for $1,000 a side. The money was put up in Sam Cassidy's hands and the race was run on Saturday.

Bethune arrived in town, looking bright and fresh, on Saturday morning. He was accompanied by S. S. McKay, Toby Elliott and others from Montreal. Mr. Bingham, of Toronto, with his unknown, also arrived early in the morning and registered at the Russell House. Speculation was rife as to the identity of the unknown, and he turned out to be an unknown in very deed. Nobody knew him, nobody could place him. He was seen in the Russell House and on the street before the time fixed for the match, and failed to be recognized by anybody.

As four o'clock, the time fixed for the race, drew near, a general move was made toward the Exhibition Grounds, where it had been arranged that the event should come off. Everybody was on the grounds. There was Chief McVeity and a posse of police; proprietors of hotels and proprietors of peanut stands; old men and aldermen; young men and boys; sports of all sorts and conditions. The attendance was not large but it was very representative; all classes of the community had samples on the ground and all were ready to bet the last dollar in their clothes on

WASHINGTON'S LARGEST MAN.

He Is a Negro Porter, and Is on Good Terms with All the Big Statesmen.

Willard's hotel, at Washington, has one of the most unique hotel porters in the country—a veritable black Falstaff in more ways than one.

He is almost as broad as he is long, weighs nobody knows how much, and is said to be the greatest man physically at the capital. He has been unable to look upon his knees for a good many years. But he is tremendously powerful, and the ease with which he shoulders a Saratoga trunk and bounds lightly up four pairs of

WASHINGTON'S BIGGEST MAN.

stairs with it, makes the effete and flat chested dudes of the capital city turn green with envy. This porter is further noted for the fact that no one has ever seen him without a most astonishing grin on his ebony countenance. His mouth looks like a coal mine, and when he laughs he always draws a crowd. Clerks from the treasury department up the street rush in breathlessly and ask what's the matter. He has known nearly all the celebrated statesmen of the past generation, and is on terms of intimacy with the leading legislators of the present day. It is amusing to watch the air of importance he assumes when Tom Reed, of Maine, buttonholes him and carries him off to a corner to talk politics—for the fun of the thing. The witty Tom maintains a most solemn demeanor all through these discussions, and nods his head gravely and says "That's so!" whenever his African opponent makes a "strong point." Sunset Cox, too, will occasionally hold high converse with this favored darky about the limitations of the infinite, or some other equally light and airy subject, and some of Cox's most

July 25, 1888

Bethune—or the unknown. It was known that there was a big pile of money up and everybody on the track could see that it was going up all the time. Thousands of dollars were involved and the crowd stood right up on the tiptoe of expectation.

The day was cold but speculation was pretty warm and the hundreds were put up one after the other until Stakeholder Cassidy's pocket bulged out like a balloon. By and by the stentorian voice of Constable Mackenzie was heard shouting: "Clear the track," and pretty soon the runners appeared. The track, which was on the south side of the regular trotting track on the home-stretch, was measured by Ald. Lewis, who had been agreed upon as referee.

Bethune was the first of the runners to make his appearance and when he came on the track he was closely wrapped in a heavy coat and a buffalo robe, in which garb he quietly paced about until the unknown appeared. Two minutes after Bethune the unknown showed up, attended by Ike Weir, who carried a heavy blanket. Throwing off his overcoat the unknown let himself go for thirty yards in a heavy suit of white woollen underclothing. He proved to be a well-built young fellow, with heavy shanks and the style of a flyer, and though there were many who snickered at the form he displayed in his preliminary spin, the majority of those on the track, who noted his easy stride and the confident air which he wore, without whiskers, recognized a flyer from Flyerville. After the unknown had had his spin, Bethune stripped down to a bronze vest and showed his paces for a short distance. His appearance was greeted with cheers, and he seemed to be in the pink of condition and confident of winning. Both men then retired beneath the shelter of friendly blankets and shortly emerged stripped for the race, each wearing trunks, shoes and "nothing else."

It was agreed that the start should be by mutual consent, which means that the first time both men go over the line it is a race. Not more than a minute elapsed after the men were stripped when they were away. In scoring they struck characteristic attitudes. Harry Bethune stood, toe to scratch, with arms stretched to the utmost and looking as he felt, eager to get away. The unknown was well balanced over the mark with his arms pretty close to his body, and watched his opponent with all his eyes. Both over the mark and it was a go!

Both men got into their stride right away and went for all they were worth. The unknown made the pace and Bethune, who ran to win, had a stern chase from the start to the tape. Up to the half distance the unknown led Bethune handily. When fifty yards had been covered Harry pulled himself together for a desperate spurt and did his level best to catch the unknown, but it was no good. The mysterious runner was going like a deer, and though Bethune closed upon him he could not catch him, and was left at the finish by about twelve feet.

APPALLING.

Eight to Ten Thousand Lives Engulfed

IN THE AWFUL FLOODS

Which Carried Death and Disaster in Pennsylvania.

800 PERSONS BURNED ALIVE.

Passenger Trains Swept Off by the Mighty Torrent

AND PASSENGERS DROWNED OR KILLED.

The Terrible Scenes Witnessed—Children and Women Crushed or Drowned before Helpless Onlookers—The Thrilling Battles Against the Resistless Flood—5,000 Houses Swept to Ruins—Partial List of the Dead.

By Telegraph to THE CITIZEN.

Pittsburg, 2nd.—A despatch from a point near Johnstown says 200 houses are still standing at Johnstown and the main street is under twenty feet of water. The natural gas pipes burst, setting fire to the wrecked buildings and adding horror to the scene. The Alleghany River at Pittsburg is rising at a frightful rate, and is black with debris. The police and fire departments are out looking for bodies.

June 3, 1889

There was considerable kicking. It was said that Bethune had thrown the race, a charge that nothing seems to justify. Bethune was anxious to win. He had his own money staked on the race and declared after it was over that he was beaten by a faster man. He also said that he ran in good condition and expected to win. He did not know the unknown, but thought he was Gent of England. Anyway, said Harry, "I have been beaten by a man who has beaten the champion of America."

Just who the unknown is nobody knows, except his backer. He is a clever runner and knows his business—that is evident. One thing is certain, he is the most mysterious unknown who ever engaged in a foot race in Canada. Just as the race was the greatest that has ever been run in the Dominion. More money changed hands over the race on Saturday than in any foot race on record in the Dominion.

The unknown, in conversation with a *Citizen* reporter, stated that he was under engagement not to reveal his identity, and no amount of blarney and soft soap could shake his determination to keep himself wrapped up in his incognito character....

September 22, 1887
OUR MUNICIPAL RAMBLER.
"New is the Line, Let the Chips Fall Where they May."
"LOOK OUT FOR THE STEAM ROAD ROLLER!"

"Our Municipal Rambler" was the first "signed" column to appear regularly in the Citizen. *The identity of Raglan, the author, is unknown. It's possible he was Welsh, and took his moniker from the famous castle. Whatever the case, his mandate was to wander the city looking for ways for council to improve the quality of life. Here's an excerpt from one of his first columns:*

Whether one can read or not, whether one is short-sighted or not, the municipal authorities evidently imagine killing to be no murder, so long as a twelve by ten board, with a printed warning is rested against a telegraph pole or lamp post. I know of no city in the United States or Canada where the steam roller is used on the principal streets during the busy hours of the day—save and except in Ottawa, the Capital of the Dominion. Usually the work is done between 11 p.m. and 2 a.m., or 3 a.m. to 6 a.m., when carriages and wagons and horses are having a rest, and the labouring man getting a rest, too. When it is necessary to perform roller work on a prominent street in the day time, obstructions are placed at either end of the street operated upon. Not so in Ottawa; "You pays your taxes and you takes your chances," is the maxim. Hence, life is imperiled and limbs are treated with indifference. On Elgin street lately several hairbreadth escapes from shying and running

JACK THE RIPPER.

Whitechapel Again the Scene of His Bloodthirsty Operations.

A WOMAN FRIGHTFULLY CUT UP.

Salisbury on Colonial Federation and Irish Affairs.

BALLOONIST LENNOX'S FATAL FALL

By Telegraph to THE CITIZEN.

The Whitechapel Fiend.
London, 16th.—The community has been startled by another murder, thought to have been committed by Jack, the Ripper. The body of a woman, mutilated in the usual frightful manner, was found to-day in Castle Alley, in the Whitechapel district. There is no trace of the murderer.

Servia's Preparations.
Belgrade, 16th.—The Servian Government

July 17, 1889

horses were noted. Some day Death will lay his cold hand on a few innocent victims and the steam roller manipulator may be shot!

At all events, the city exchequer will be badly mulched when an action for damages is brought. The steam roller, like various grades of
poison, is a good thing when properly used—but it should not, for the
sake of saving money, be made a standing, or moving, municipal nuisance. Life is short at any time, but why should the authorities tax a
man, and then jeopardize his life. Thousands upon thousands of dollars have by means of local assessment and Local Improvement By-
laws, been raised and expended—or rather squandered—upon poor
planks and consequently poor sidewalks. Some of the heaviest taxed
ratepayers on prominent streets are obliged to make a sort of Dick
Swiveller circuit to get to their homes in the evening with sound
bones. Along Daly street it is horrible; on some portions of King street,
towards Stewart and streets south, it is positively outrageous. In some
parts of Upper Town, there is a cry against the disgrace of neglected
sidewalks. Where is the Board of Works? Where is the City Engineer?
Poverty cannot be pleaded, for the city now saves about $10,000 per
annum, by reason of the Dominion Government taking over the
bridges and a part of Wellington street, Major's Hill park and other
civic points. Added to this the revenue from general taxation is greatly
increased, and the city should be in a position of thorough repair. Let
some Municipal Tribune stand up at the Council Board and speak on
behalf of the Corporation. Who will be the man?

•

I dropped down to New Edinburgh yesterday, just to see where those
fine horses owned by Mr. Cunningham, of Rideau and King streets,
were injured by falling into the Waterworks trench. Truly, it is marvellous the lad who drove them escaped. He is evidently reserved for
some special work in this world. But what should be said of, what done
to, the authorities who failed to have a warning light suspended over
this destructive pit?

Whoever the negligent party was, should be punished severely. Well,
the municipal authorities save coal oil—that's a great thing! Economy
is a splendid thing until it lands a Corporation before Judge and Jury,
and when Mr. Cunningham asks for damages, the municipal Solons
should not turn the whites of their eyes heavenward and whimper,
"Good Lord, deliver us from such an unpatriotic ratepayer." Better far,
take time by the forelock and provide for the protection of both human
and animal life. There is too much locking the stable door after the
horse has escaped, or been killed. As it was in New Edinburgh so may
it be in any other portion of the city to-night or tomorrow night....

RAGLAN

PUGDOM !

Two Sluggers Fearfully Punished in the Ring.

SULLIVAN GETS THERE

With Both Feet, But a
Badly Bruised Mug.

KILRAIN'S MAGNIFICENT FIGHT

The Result Evenly Balanced for
Nearly Two Hours.

75 ROUNDS CLOSELY CONTESTED.

Special to THE CITIZEN.

New Orleans, 8th.—Intense excitement
existed throughout the city to day, and to-
night the hotels, barrooms, and resorts of
this character are crowded to excess. Kilrain's defeat is claimed as a virtual victory
by his friends, such immense staying powers did he evince. All admit that he will
yet be champion, as with a little more hard
training and further developments

July 9, 1889

May 17, 1890

January 9, 1888

THE WANDERING ARABS.—For some days past little parties of foreigners have been seen in different parts of the city. They are said to be Arabs, but whether they are or not is not known, as no one as yet has turned up who can understand them. All they can say is, "Arabia from Jerusalem" and "money," and have the Arabs' weakness for begging, which comes to them like second nature. A woman and two children were taken into custody on Saturday afternoon and lodged in the cells. They will be brought up this morning on a charge of vagrancy, when an effort will be made to get an interpreter. It is said that food and clothes given them by the charitably disposed have been thrown away, only money being wanted.

August 13, 1888
HOW SHE BATHES.

The methods of the bathing girl are unique. After lying for a glad half-hour at full length in the soft, hot embrace of the sand she gets up courage enough to go teetering down the slope of the beach for a look at the water. She pecks about for a few moments like a sand piper, and after many feints and backward jumps she touches a wasted wavelet with the tippy tip of her unwilling toe. Then she looks up quickly to see if any one at the pavilion caught her doing it. It takes fully 15 minutes for the girl to get out as deep as her knees, and when the swells float up to where the pantalets begin you can see the short gasps that she has to make for breath. After many trembling wide-eyed moments of doubt the girl makes an important decision. She watches for a nice, gentler wave, and when she finds one that pleases her, turns half round and sits on it. Oh! She jumps from off it as though it were red hot. Then she goes up on the beach and lies prone on the velvety sand for another delightful season.

September 10, 1888
ON THE ROAD.
Pencil Jottings by the Way.
THINGS WE SEE AND HOW THEY ARE SEEN
Sporadically over several months during the summer and fall of 1888, the Citizen *ran a series of delightful travelogues from a writer identified only as "The Old Man" or "The Old Canuck." Here's an excerpt from one of his adventures after he signed on with a travelling horse and rodeo show:*

Today, I am located at the Town of Indiana, Pa.; about centrally placed on the map of this wonderful State. I say wonderful, for its great prolific resources in coal, oil, natural gas, coal, glass and iron make it so. This town has a population of about 5,000, and almost every twelve or twenty miles, on an average railroad run, such are to be found; all humming hives of industry changing each to some.

Here, planing mills, door and blind works, machine shops, steam tanneries, are the principal features. At Warren, where I last wrote you from, a span of the largest and best draught horses belonging to the show, with harnesses on, were stolen off the lot. The night was dark and a heavy damp fog hung over the valley and the thief had made a good retreat before the team was missed. Being rather tired, I had turned in quite early. Mr. Charles Drum, the boss hostler, had been out searching for the horses, and the train all loaded ready to pull out, now 1:40 a.m., and the run to Mercer, our next stand eastward down the Allegheny, about 96 miles, made it necessary for an early start. Mr. Frank Miller, becoming uneasy at the delay, made enquiry as to cause, and Mr. Stowe told him about the stolen horses, and Drum's vain efforts to find them. Here was a dilemma; the train must put out; who to leave to

PLAY HAWKSHAW.

That was the query, Stowe suggested the old Canuck. Mr. Frank Miller endorsed the suggestion with the remark: "Yes, he's the man; but it's too bad to ask an old man like him to tackle such a job." Stowe woke me and in a few words explained; I jumped out, and on leaving pocketed my bull dog, ready for the worst. Frank says: "Good, Old Man; you are the only man we have that can do this, and I am confident

YOU WILL GET OUR HORSES."

My response was, as the train pulled out: "I'll never come back without the horses." Here I was on the railroad track—a dark and damp night—fully a mile from the business part of Warren. I struck out on the way there, the brain clear and active, shaping plans. First hunt up a policeman, then a detective, then put the telephone and wires to work, and, if possible, hem the thief in. Now came the trouble—no policeman—there being only

A CHIEF AND ONE ASSISTANT

in the town, the former doing duty in the day, the deputy at night. After a long search I found the latter, and he, in reply to my questions, told me the name of the Government detective—Darius Magee—and where to find him. I roused Magee out at 3 a.m., and being a keen hustler, we proceeded to search for a thread. Over the lot, around the lot, across the side tracks by the oil tank lines, then along the river's edge, where it was fordable; through woods studded thickly with vines and tall ferns—a heavy damp fog hanging over all—away we went.

EVERY POINT OF ESCAPE

was carefully looked over for a track or thread that would lead to the main point. Rather on the weary side, and very wet, 6:15 a.m., a clue or starter was obtained from a Mrs. Maddison. Her story led to a search at

PRICE $29.00 FOR $19.75.

PRICE $33.00 FOR $21.25.

PRICE $15 00 FOR $9.00.

May 17, 1890

a point near the main street. While here searching for foot marks, another thread was picked up, and then Magee—who I looked upon as the right man—with me proceeded to work the wires. Out in a hurried flash to some fifteen points I sent the following message:

"STOP THAT THIEF!

Stolen from the circus lot, Warren, Pa., Monday night, August 27th, a span of dun coloured horses, with harness on studded with brass nails. One a dark dun, white mane and tail, with a white stripe on face. Darius Magee, Government Detective."

Whilst these were going out, Magee had been getting out a span of horses to take the road. Before leaving town I ran up into the telephone office, and on entering was told that a man had been trying to sell a span of horses at Kinqua, as described, with a harness on. I requested her to wire: "Have some one arrest him; those are the stolen horses." To this the answer came, "Gone back towards town." Out we went on the Kinqua Road at a rattling good gait. About three miles out, a long wooden bridge crosses the river, and on which a toll is collected—15 cents for a span each way.

Whilst paying the toll I asked the lady if she had seen anyone pass during the night or morning, leading a span of horses. She quickly answered, "Yes, near eleven o'clock last night a man leading horses with harness on, studded with brass nails, crossed here; he would not pay toll as he said the horses were bought by Mr. Rogers, who lived on the other side, and he was going to deliver them." This made it apparent that

THE THIEF WAS A LOCAL MAN

else he would hardly have known that the Bridge Company had for some reason awarded Mr. Rogers the right of free toll. She then gave an elegant description of the fellow, and Magee said at once, "I know him." On we went, and when about two miles further, found the horses, just turned into a barn, with only a halter and collar on. The fellow had been so closely pressed, that he made away with the harnesses, turned them loose, and took to the woods. Glad to get the horses so quick—now near noon—I started back to Warren and left the harness to the detective. I wired Mr. Miller of my success. When the news reached the show everybody rejoiced over the Old Man's work. As soon as possible I got a car and started, with a bundle of hay, in the same grain box car. My experience of a tough pull through for three days and nights on railroad might be interesting, but will keep for this winter's fireside at home. Enough to-day. . . .

THE OLD MAN.

Indiana, Pa., Sept. 3rd, 1888.

September 27, 1888
HORRIBLE TRAGEDY!
A Human Being Drops from the Clouds in Mid-Air.
THOUSANDS PALE AT THE SIGHT.
How Thomas James Wensley Met His Death
Yesterday—With Slender Hold He is Taken up
by the Balloon and Drops from a Height of 500 Feet.

"A drop from the clouds" was included in the advertised programme of diversions for the fair-goers yesterday afternoon; but little did anyone dream of the fearful descent which would indeed be witnessed—a drop from an altitude of close on a thousand feet—a dive to horrible death, made by a human being before the gaze of fifteen thousand awe-stricken men, women and children. This was the sad end of poor Tom Wensley, who, in a mad freak took uninvited passage to cloud-land, hanging at arm's length from the hem of Professor Williams' balloon.

The Professor's daring drop from an altitude of two thousand feet, with nothing but his parachute—little more than a great umbrella—to break the force of the descent, was to have been the great event of the afternoon. It was the first feat of the kind to be performed in the capital, and all day the people had awaited it with anxious expectancy. The great canvas of the balloon lay flat upon the ground in a reserved circle roped in across the arena directly opposite the grand stand. The Professor kept vigilant guard over it, and patiently answered the oft-repeated question, "Will there be an ascent this afternoon?" "Yes, at five o'clock," he would quietly answer.

Shortly before that hour the work of inflation was commenced. Hot air was used, as usual, and the canvas quickly took on the shape of the treacherous air ship. By this time thousands had gathered about the ring, watching every move with curiosity and impatience and anxious for the voyage to begin. To hasten the work of inflation,

VOLUNTEERS WERE CALLED FOR

to straighten out the canvas, and prevent its overlapping and lying in folds. The call was eagerly responded to, among others by Tom Wensley, and as many hands as could be applied to the task soon had firm grasp of the canvas. Prof. Williams superintended the work, constantly moving round and directing where fresh holds should be taken; as the canvas gradually swelled and rose high above the heads of the crowd. Up, up it rose, until, the work of inflation nearly completed, the top of the balloon must have been fifty feet in the air. Beneath it were probably thirty volunteer helpers, many more children, holding the canvas. Up to this time the balloon had been secured by a stout cable stretched immediately above it and effectually preventing ascent, whilst substantial guy ropes prevented its escape to either side and consequent freedom from the restraint of the top ropes. As the

HOW TO DRIVE
The Proper Way to Hold the Hands and Reins.

How to drive—of course everybody says they know how to drive, but how many are really stating facts. There are various kinds of driving. The experienced and the inexperienced—the scientific and the unscientific—the graceful and the ungraceful. There are many ways of handling the reins, but only one right and proper way. Driving is a pleasure. It is very enjoyable to be bowling along behind a spanking team, if you happen to be a good driver and have thorough command of your horses. This however is almost impossible, unless you know how to handle the "ribbons." For the benefit of the uninicitiated, therefore, the following illustrations and directions have been compiled:

In driving you must hold your hands as in Fig. 1, whether you have one horse or two:

FIG. 1—GOING STRAIGHT.

FIG. 2—TURNING TO THE RIGHT.

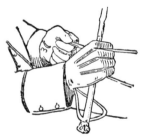

FIG. 3—TURNING TO THE LEFT.

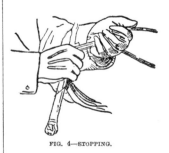

FIG. 4—STOPPING.

June 14, 1890

The Bad Painters and the Poor Old Gentleman.

An early comic strip, (continued opposite) July 2, 1890

MOMENT FOR THE ASCENT

arrived, the fastenings were loosed, and the Professor entered his tiny basket, first having passed round the balloon with the caution distinctly uttered to the live anchors:

"WHEN I SAY LET GO, LET GO ALL TOGETHER."

"Let go," he quickly shouted, and all hands released the balloon. No; not all. One slower than the rest was rising from the crowd! The balloon was scarce moving, and the crowd laughed at the tardy man.

He still holds on, however, and the laugh is silenced. The crowd grows anxious. Up he goes, to six, eight, ten feet, still hanging there, firmly grasping with both hands a slender rope running around the base of the balloon much in the fashion of a drawing cord about a bag.

"Let go! Let go!" shout a score of voices, and the startled aeronaut joining in the cry calls from the basket, "Let go, for God's sake."

But all for naught. The unwelcome passenger retains his grasp; he gives

A SICKLY CHEER,

the weird sound of which sends a horrible suspicion through the mind of the hearer. It is the note of triumph of a madman about to accomplish an act from which he half shrinks, yet will not flinch. Up, up goes the doomed man, to twenty, forty, sixty feet—to death, for to relax his hold now means sudden, horrible death. There he is, hanging high above the head of the master of the balloon, who, safe enough in his basket below were it not for this extraordinary outside passenger, has absolutely no power to control their flight through space. The wind catches the balloon and whirls it westward, away from the awe-struck thousands, and its upward flight is hastened.

THE MAN'S FALL

is breathlessly awaited. The rope he grasps is strong, but it is no thicker than a clothes line and must lacerate the hands, and even with giant strength no man could long hang suspended from it. But the doomed man is apparently full of vigour. After his parting cheer, his goodbye to the world, for not another note did he utter, he kicked his legs in a lively manner. Not as in a death struggle, but as if to give the impression of his strength and self-reliance. He soon grew rigid, however, but a moment later there was another change. Now he seemed to seek to change his position, to struggle towards the net work fastening the aeronaut's basket to the balloon.

HOPING AGAINST HOPE.

The crowd actually breathed more freely, all but those who had been close to the spot of ascent, as the *Citizen* reporter had been, and realized only too well the horrible truth. "See," some said in effect, "he intended to go up, and is going to get into the basket now."

Further away, up by the grand stand, another theory was advanced:

"It's a dummy they've hung on. But how dreadful to frighten the people so!" Others still had a different idea: "That's the man that makes the parachute descent. He'll come down presently."

A DROP TO DEATH.

And come he did. This was no dummy, all realized. It was a live man, and he had no parachute to save him, as those who advanced that theory speedily discovered. Straight as a bolt he came, feet down for a couple of hundred feet; then there was a wild wave of the hands and feet, and the body turned horizontally to the earth, the rapidity of the fall being noticeably checked. Off came the hat, a soft felt, and half buoyed up by the air, and the motion of the hands to the head and the removal of the hat were so simultaneous that one half fancied he had hurled it away. An age seemed to be occupied in the descent of the body, but at last it passed down out of sight, and the witnesses of the tragedy just enacted turned from its contemplation to gaze upon each other. Every face was blanched; nigh every tongue was speechless. Standing still as if rooted to the ground, the thousands watched.

THE AERONAUT

was still aloft. After the fatal drop of his strange passenger the balloon had shot up several hundred feet, and it had gone considerably further west before Professor Williams cut free, and he too commenced a terribly swift descent. But in a moment the parachute opened above him, and he came gently to the earth. When the basket had been cut adrift, the balloon turned bottom up, and putting out a volume of thick black smoke was soon quite empty and it too came floating down.

A HORRIBLE SIGHT!

Seeing the direction the balloon had taken, and anticipating the fatal fall, hundreds had rushed from the grounds, across Bank street and over the fields to the west. The foremost were not far from the spot where the body fell, and heard the sickening thud as it struck the earth.

It had fallen about four hundred yards west of the Bank Street Road, along side the residence of Farmer Hott, and as the party from the fair grounds hastened to the spot, a horrible sight met their view. Of course life had been extinct long before the earth was reached. The body was found sitting in a half upright position, one arm being badly broken, the extremities between the thighs and upper part of the legs were horribly crushed, and the fractured bones were driven through the flesh. The bowels protruded also, and other horrible injuries had been sustained. The head, however, was not disfigured, and bore a natural expression, except for the unnaturally upturned eyes. . . .

A coroner's inquiry later determined that Thomas Wensley, 21, plunged about 250 metres to his death. What it couldn't say for sure was whether his fall was an act of bravado gone bad—another story

described him as "a daring lad, at times more wild than prudent"—or whether he'd found an unusual way to commit suicide. Whatever the case, Wensley was the first aviation fatality in Canada. Professor Williams, based in Cincinnati, was cleared of any blame.

April 30, 1890
EXECUTION BY ELECTRICITY
(Excerpt from an editorial)

Joseph Kemmler will be the first murderer in the United States to suffer the death penalty by means of electricity. In March, 1889, Kemmler attacked his mistress, as the result of a quarrel, inflicting upon her body no fewer than twenty-six cuts with a hatchet. She died the following day. He was arrested, tried, found guilty of murder in the first degree, and sentenced to death under the new law of the State of New York providing for the execution by electricity of persons condemned to death by the courts....

Since the passing of the death sentence upon Kemmler many tests have been made by experts upon animals for the purpose of determining the effectiveness of this new mode of execution, and the result in the case of a human being will be awaited with no ordinary interest in the scientific world. The manner in which the execution of Kemmler is to take place is thus briefly described: Death will result just as speedily and surely with the new apparatus as with the old, but there are fewer horrible features. The chair in which the condemned man will be placed is a comfortable one with an upright back and arms that are adjustable to those of the man who sits in it. There is a leather-covered pillow for the head to rest against. Fastened to the back is an adjustable figure which can be raised or lowered so as to come down over the head of the condemned.

The technique of the thing is very simple, and argued to be humane. Through the lower outer angle of the chair there is a hole, and through this will pass a rubber tube containing a rod of steel or copper, to which a wet sponge is fastened. This sponge will touch the crown of the condemned man's head. Another pipe, with webbing and a sponge inside, will pass up so as to touch the base of the spine when the man is strapped firmly in his seat. This will be accomplished by the use of several straps, one passing around the chest, another around the abdomen, which will draw the webbing against the spine, while the arms will be firmly strapped to those on the chair on which they will rest. The feet will rest on a comfortable foot-rest, after the fashion of those in use in a barber shop.

The electricity will be generated by a dynamo, which has been placed near to the power room, a thousand feet away from the place of

DEAD!

Tillie Zeigler's Murderer Pays the Penalty!

KILLED BY ELECTRICITY.

Kemmler when first arrested for murder.

Graphic Details of the Awful Event at Auburn.

(Special to THE OTTAWA CITIZEN)

Auburn. N.Y., 6th.—Kemmler, who so foully murdered Tellie Zeigler nearly two years ago, died this morning from an electric shock, under the new law providing this method of inflicting death. Strong efforts were being made secretly to save Kemmler. From the most approved

August 6, 1890

execution, and the insulated wires which will connect it with the rods and sponges, which have all been strung in readiness for their work.

Kemmler was finally executed on Aug. 6, although no one could have predicted his gruesome end. For 17 seconds, a 2,000-volt current was sent through his body, causing him to convulse against the straps and turn bright red. But it wasn't enough to kill him. As officials worked frantically to recharge the generator, Kemmler groaned and struggled for breath. When the current was finally restored, it was left on for more than a minute, causing smoke to rise from his head.

September 17, 1890

THE STRAUSS CONCERT.

A Rare Musical Event—The Rideau Rink Crowded.

Eduard Strauss was never as popular as his famous brothers, Johann Strauss II and Josef Strauss, who dominated the Viennese light music world for decades. But his appearance in Ottawa was a major cultural event. Here's an excerpt from the concert review:

A large and enthusiastic audience heard Strauss in the Rideau Rink last evening, and it is safe to say that all would like to hear him again. Strauss's music, by his own orchestra and under his own direction, is something wonderful and enchanting.

Hardly less enjoyable than the music itself was the conducting of Eduard Strauss; promptly at eight o'clock he hurried to the front and waved his baton for the opening number, and from that to the last strains of our National Anthem, his gestures were a continued marvel; now beating time with head, hands and feet, again holding his breath for a moment to intensify a diminuendo but with his body always swaying more or less in rhythm with the music.

Some of the oldest and most popular waltzes were held in reserve for encores, and were brought out with greater effect because unexpected, among the number being Johann Strauss' "Beautiful Blue Danube," which was received with rapturous applause. The major part of the programme consisted, however, of the compositions of Eduard Strauss, or arrangements by him from other composers. Beethoven and Mendelssohn also appeared on the programme, the former in the "Adagio from the Sonata Pathetique" arranged by Josef Strauss, and the latter in the song, "On Wings of Song"; and, after all, none of the brilliant dance music, charming though it was, produced the feeling of satisfaction that followed these classical numbers.

Among the instrumentalists was a particularly skilful and pleasing flautist, who produced tones of rare volume and richness; a lady harpist also added much to the effect of the lighter passages. The es-

**STRAUSS
AND
HIS
FAMOUS
VIENNESE
ORCHESTRA.**

RIDEAU RINK,
TUESDAY, 16th Sept'r.

Reserved Seats $2.00 and $1.50. General admission $1.00.
Sale of seats now open at Nordheimer's.

September 13, 1890

prit of the orchestra and their almost electric response to the leader's slightest signal were simply marvellous, and the result was the precision of a machine inspired by emotional intelligence. Altogether it was a treat of a rare description not soon to be forgotten. . . .

September 27, 1890
SOCIAL LIFE IN CANADA.
LEADERS OF SOCIETY AT THE CAPITAL.
Her Excellency Lady Stanley of Preston—Mrs. C. H. Tupper—
Mrs. J. A. Chapleau, Lady Middleton—Madame Wilfrid Laurier
and Mrs. Mackenzie.

Throughout its early history, the Citizen *cultivated a close, even fawning, relationship with official Ottawa, especially the inhabitants of Rideau Hall, as this excerpt shows. The author, C.H.T., remains a mystery. Could it have been Charles H. Tupper or Mrs. Tupper?*

The Capital of the Dominion,—Ottawa,—is far from being a lively place excepting in one season of the year. Then everything is life and bustle. The drowsiness of the lumbertown is cast off, and the gaiety and rush of a Capital takes its place. This is the season when Parliament meets. Then politicians high and low, members, ex-members and would-be members, with a vast throng ever hanging on the skirts of Parliament, reach Ottawa, many of them accompanied by wife and daughters, sister or some other relatives belonging to the gentler sex.

This assemblage from all over the Dominion gives wonderful impetus to the social life of this Capital. But social life in the Capital is unlike that in Toronto, Montreal or other big cities. It resembles more closely that of Washington. It savors too much of red tape and court etiquette, of officialism. That is what society is there, it is official. But the presence of the Vice-Regal court, and the Departmental offices, probably renders this imperative. There are some really charming women who adorn and lead the social circles at the Capital.

Lady Stanley of Preston, wife of His Excellency the Governor-General comes first. She is by right of her position the "first lady in the land." Lady Stanley belongs to the famous Villiers family, and is the eldest daughter of the Earl of Clarendon. She is one of those women, of whom there are too few in the world. She is a tall, handsome woman with wavy brown hair. Queenly in her walk and manner, but gentle and gracious withal, Lady Stanley has endeared herself to all Canadians with whom she has come into contact. As a hostess she is simply delightful. Her invitations are much sought for and give certain distinction in local circles to the receiver.

The hospitalities at Rideau Hall, the Vice-Regal residence, have been

THE WORLD OF FASHION.

SOME PERTINENT POINTERS ABOUT
PRETTY SUMMER TOILETTES.

Latest Manifestations in Dress and Dress
Materials—A Handsome Vigogno Dress
With Surah Guimpe — A Travelling
Cloak and Hat—Fashions in Paragraphs.

The dress here illustrated is of forest green vigogne relieved by pale pink surah. The bell skirt is untrimmed. The round bodice is cut open in jacket shape at the front and back on a pleated guimpe and

high collar of surah, and an apparent continuation of this guimpe is a surah pleating that comes from under the lower edge; the lower half of the bodice is in corselet shape, with one front edge slashed, pleated in two points, and ornamented with two large buttons.—Harper's Bazar.

June 21, 1892

proverbially enjoyable and charming affairs. During Lady Stanley's regime they have become more charming than ever. Half the dinner parties at Rideau Hall are official ones, the remainder are Lady Stanley's own particular affairs. Balls, dancing, private theatricals, and in season garden parties, tobogganing, snowshoe and skating parties are among the attractions at the Hall. During the winter season an outdoor, "At Home" is given every Saturday; curling, skating, hockey, tobogganing and sometimes dancing are indulged in by the five or six hundred guests. Lady Stanley is blessed with seven sons and one daughter—Hon. Isabel Stanley, who is about 14 years old, and the youngest. Hon Edward Stanley, of the Grenadier Guards, is the heir of the house of Derby. He is A.D.C. to his father, and a year or so ago married Lady Alice Montague, youngest daughter of the late Duke of Manchester. Lady Alice is a most charming woman, with a perfect figure. She assists Her Excellency in the giving of entertainments. . . .

Lady Macdonald, wife of the veteran Premier is the "second lady in the land." She entertains occasionally at "Earnscliffe," Sir John's residence, and is popular in local and political circles.

One of the younger leaders of society, who should take one of the highest places on the list is Mrs. C. H. Tupper, the charming wife of the Hon., the Minister of Marine and Fisheries. Mrs. Tupper is a daughter of Chief Justice McDonald of Nova Scotia. She is a tall woman with a superb figure, dark with a most graceful carriage. Her greatest charm however lies in her manner. She entertains a great deal and her recherche affairs are well known and greatly appreciated.

Mrs. J. A. Chapleau , wife of the Hon. the Secretary of State is a dainty little woman, very popular in her set. She entertains considerably during the session.

Lady Middleton who has recently left the country with her husband the ex-commander of the Militia, was possessed of many of those qualities which lead to recognition in the social world. The Middletons entertained on a small scale at their house, situated almost at the back gate of the Governor-General's residence. Lady Middleton was a Miss Doucet of Montreal and possesses the dark coloring, and lively and vivacious ways and manner of the French-Canadian. She was a popular little woman, but was apt to fall into military pompousness of manner, acquired by contact.

There are two ladies, leaders of the clans who make Ottawa their home when Parliament sits. They come right out into the front rank of the official circles, and their joint weekly reception is already famous in the land. Madame Laurier boasts of ancient lineage. She is French to the backbone, and has that inherent grace and manner so marked with all her well bred country-women. She is the wife of the Hon. Wilfrid Laurier, the great Liberal leader. Madame is of medium height, dark

HE IS DEAD !

The Father of Confederation is No More.

THE CHIEFTAIN GONE

" THE STATE - ORACLE IS MUTE!"

CANADA'S FAVOURED SON.

The Great Conservative Chieftain Passes Away.

MARVELLOUS CAREER OF SIR JOHN.

Portraits of the Late Premier and of Lady Macdonald.

Death claimed his own last evening at 10.15 o'clock when the Right Honourable Sir John Macdonald passed away at the family residence, Earnscliffe.

[The following sketch of the Right Hon. Sir John Macdonald's career from his early years to his becoming leader of the Oppos...

June 7, 1891

complexion, ruddy coloring and gray hair.

Mrs. Alexander Mackenzie, the wife of the ex-Premier of Canada, is a tall stately old lady, with silvery hair and quiet and dignified manners. She assists Madame Laurier at the Liberal "At Homes," and has done so for years.

There are others yet to be mentioned in the category of dames of high degree and leaders of Canadian society but space does not permit it here—C. H. T.

January 30, 1892

March 19, 1892
THE CHAMPIONS DINED.
An Enjoyable Gathering
of Admirers of the Hockey Team.

Judging by this excerpt, the banquet held to honour Ottawa's hockey team for being the best in Canada was a roaring success. Almost forgotten amid the alcohol and song, however, was the evening's big news—the announcement that the governor general, Lord Stanley, had decided to donate a trophy to the country's best team.

The members of the Ottawa Hockey Club will always hold dear to their memory recollections of the banquet tendered them last evening in the Russell House. It was under the auspices of the Ottawa Amateur Athletic Club. About seventy-five of the team's most enthusiastic admirers were seated at the table. The president of the association, Mr. J. W. McRae, presided, with Mr. Russell, captain of the team, at his right, and Mr. Jenkins at his left. The vice-presidents' chairs were occupied by Mr. P. D. Ross and Mr. Desbarats. When all appetites had been satisfied, Mr. McKay proposed the health of the Queen. Mr. Ross next proposed the toast of the Governor-General, and in a few remarks referred to the great interest manifested in hockey by His Excellency.

THE GOVERNOR-GENERAL'S PRIZE.

Lord Kilcoursie [a hockey enthusiast and one of Lord Stanley's top aides] responded, and read the following letter from His Excellency:

March 18th, 1892

I have for some time just been thinking that it would be a good thing if there were a challenge cup which should be held from year to year by the champion hockey team in the Dominion.

There does not appear to be any such outward and visible sign of championship at present, and considering the general interest which the matches now elicit, and the importance of having the game played fairly and under rules generally recognized, I am willing to give a cup which shall be held from year to year by the winning team.

I am not quite certain that the present regulations governing the arrangement of matches are entirely of satisfaction, and it would be worth considering whether they could not be arranged so that each team would play once at home and once at the place where their opponents hail from.

Lord Kilcoursie stated that Capt. Colville, who was at present in England, had been commissioned by the Governor General to order the cup. It would be held here by trustees till the end of the next season, and then presented to the champions. The reading of the letter was greeted with enthusiastic applause.

THE CHAMPIONS.

The president proposed the health of the Ottawa hockey team, which was drunk by their friends, who stood upon their chairs. The first of the team to respond was the amiable captain, Mr. Russell, who did great honour to his team in a speech, that was full of humour, and which was heartily appreciated by all present. The other members of the team then spoke in the following order: F. M. S. Jenkins, H. Kirby, J. Kerr, W. C. Young, A. Morel and C. Kirby. The last mentioned delivered his oration while mounted upon the table....

The president here read a telegram received from the Quebec team as follows: "Quebec regrets that she cannot send a delegate and do honour to the finest hockey team in Canada." The toast of the ladies, proposed by Mr. Russell, was responded to by Mr. Stowe and by C. Kirby and C. Bethune.

After the toast of the press had been disposed of, Mr. J. W. de C. O'Grady proposed the toast of the O.A.A.C. which brought the president and Mr. P. B. Taylor to their feet. Lord Kilcoursie sang a song appropriate to the occasion and all joined in the chorus, which was as follows:

> Then give three cheers for Russell
> The captain of the boys,
> However tough the tussle
> His position he enjoys.
> And then for all the others
> Let's shout as loud as we may
> O-T-T-A-W-A.

Mr. Garvin, of Toronto, and Mr. Colson followed with songs, and the pleasant gathering dispersed after singing the national anthem and Auld Lang Syne.

March 27, 1893

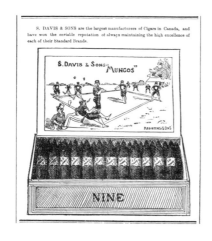

July 22, 1893

August 8, 1892
STUART DICKEY'S SUICIDE.
THE OTTAWA CRICKETERS TOUR CULMINATES
IN A TRAGEDY.
One of Their Foremost Players Shoots
Himself Through the Head in a Halifax
Hotel—The Inquest and Verdict.

Halifax, Aug. 6th—F. Stewart Dickey of the Ottawa cricket team shot himself in his room at the Queen's Hotel to-night and died two hours afterwards. He was playing on the cricket field Friday but his place was taken by another and it is said that he was disappointed with the play of his team and also much worried that Fleming was substituted for him on the team to-day. The late Mr. Dickey was 27 years of age. He was a son of Senator Dickey and a brother of Mr. Dickey, M.P. for Cumberland. He recently came to Ottawa from Toronto, where he had been a reporter on the staff of the *Mail, News* and *Empire* at different times. Recently he was in the Civil Service. He was one of the best cricketers in Canada.

Further particulars of this sad affair state that Mr. Dickey shot himself twice in the temple, and did not recover consciousness before he died. At dinner in the hotel there was nothing in his behaviour to indicate that he had any intention of putting such a sad and ill-timed end to his life. He was to have gone that night to his home in Amherst with Col. Stewart. After dinner he went straight to his room and when his friends, alarmed by the two revolver shots, rushed in to see what had happened, they found him unconscious upon the floor, with blood streaming from the double wound in his temple.

A coroner's inquest was held late Saturday night, and the verdict returned upon Mr. Dickey's death was that it was due to temporary insanity. The body was sent on to Amherst for burial. Senator Dickey is in London, Eng.

August 15, 1892
PROGRESS OF PHOTOGRAPHY.
Scientists Expect Soon to Be Able to
Take Your Picture by Telephone.

A map of the heavens is being prepared at a cost of £1,200,000 (which the leading nations have agreed to raise), as an example of what telescope photography can do. Instantaneous photography seems to have attained perfection, for it is now possible to affix the image of a cannonball flying through the air. Even microbes are now being photographed. A young French chemist, M. Henri Courtonne, is credited with a new discovery, for which we have been looking to Mr. Edison.

Sounds being transmissible by telephone, M. Courtonne argues by a rigorous analogy that light might be transmitted, too.

As the telephone consists of a transmitter, a wire, and a receiver, so there was reason to believe that these three organs might be adapted for transmitting light vibrations, and for this purpose the transmitter and receiver should be prepared chemically for receiving and giving out light instead of sound vibrations. This was done by substituting sensitized photographic plates for the ordinary telephone piece. One of the plates was placed in front of an aperture through which an image was cast and this image has been forwarded by wire and has been seen at the other end. The first apparatus was very imperfect, and M. Courtonne having heard that Mr. Edison was on the track of a similar discovery, resolved to publish his experiments, a description of which he, however, sent in a sealed letter to the Academy in 1889. This letter is only to be opened at the sender's request.

The *Figaro* says that the consequences of the telephotography cannot be over estimated. Tomorrow it says, you will see in Paris the image of a man smoking in St. Petersburg.—*London News*

The Canadian Cheese Trophy at Chicago.

July 22, 1893

September 30, 1892
A MONSTER CANADIAN CHEESE.
IT WEIGHS ELEVEN TONS AND IS PRIME STUFF.

Canada will send to the Chicago World's Fair a cheese that will beat the world for size. It was made at the Experimental Dairy Station at Perth, Ont., under the skilful direction of Professor Robertson, Dominion dairy commissioner. The cheese weights twenty-two thousand pounds and contains the curd of a day's milk from one thousand cows.

A gigantic baking press was first erected and two hundred tons of pressure applied to the mass of curd, the mould or hoop to resist this immense strain consisting of steel boiler plate five-sixteenths of an inch thick. Twice a week from now until the time comes to send it to Chicago this great cheese will be turned upside down until thoroughly cured. The cheese has been tested already and pronounced perfect in texture, flavor and color.

It will form the base of Canada's dairy exhibit which will be arranged in pyramid form, and will be afterwards cut up in pound pieces and sold either at Chicago or in some large city in Great Britain. So exact was Professor Robertson's calculation as to the quantity of curd required to fill the great mould that not so much as an ounce was wasted in the process of manufacture.

The cheese was declared largest in the world, and was the subject of numerous stories in newspapers across the United States.

November 4, 1893
FOR OTTAWA WOMEN.
PARAGRAPHS TO PLEASE THE CITIZEN'S LADY READERS.
To Marry or not Marry : The Right way for a Woman
to Decide the Momentous Question.
(Excerpt from a regular Citizen *feature started in 1892:)*

Sometimes you hear a chivalrous and admirable gentleman say this: "In the ideal state of society no woman will have to work for her living. Men will do all the work at high wages and take care of women."

The chivalrous gentleman is quite unaware that he is merely repeating in another form that miserable old trades sentiment which to this day would, if possible, keep women out of all the money earning occupations, simply because the men want all the money for themselves to dole it out to women as they like or do not like. Experience shows that mostly they do not like it. Our trades idealists go further, and declare it is woman's business to mother her children and that her place is in the home taking care of them.

Once more, at heart this is merely because men want all the money for themselves. Woman was created with moral, spiritual and intellectual faculties. Development is the end and aim of existence. It is a woman's duty to develop these moral, spiritual and intellectual faculties, whether she has any children or not.

If she is kept at home, knowing nothing of business, the world or the earning and care of money, she will remain in a state of intellectual childhood. Young children are very sweet, old children are not. Only through struggle, through hustling, through experience, does the human race become ripe and rich in wisdom, beauty and power.

A woman who is not the mother of little children that demand her immediate care is under the same obligation to earn her own living that a man is, and she will be ten times the woman for doing so. But the human race would run out, say the trades idealists, if they permitted women to do anything else than be the mothers of children. Well, did you ever think of it—the fact is, the race would be considerably better off if about half of it would run out.

If a woman's domestic tastes are stronger than her other tastes, then she should marry and devote herself to domestic life, if she can get a husband to suit her. But if her tastes for professional and business life are more powerful than the domestic instinct, then she should stay single, at least until she has achieved her career. That seems to decide the momentous question—to marry or not to marry?

September 18, 1893

November 4, 1893
EARS AND CHARACTER.

You never saw a poet or a painter with large, coarse ears that stand out from the head like extended wings. That kind of an auricular appendage betokens coarseness of mind. A long, narrow ear that lies flat to the head is a sign of punacity. Never trust a man with a thin, wafer-like ear. He was born a hypocrite, if not a thief. A very small ear betokens a trifling mind, lacking decision. Ears set very high on the head indicate narrowness of mind. A large well shaped ear, that does not spread itself to the breeze, is indicative of generosity. Most of the World's compellers had large ears and well-developed noses. Although there are so many millions of people in the world, no two pairs of ears are alike. Each has a marked individuality.

December 22, 1893

The Citizen
September 1901

First Section

Pages 1–12

T.R.H.
DUKE OF YORK — DUCHESS OF YORK

ROYAL SOUVENIR NUMBER

Sir Wilfrid Laurier

R. L. Borden M.P.

Capt. Bell, ADC

Capt. Graham, ADC

GOVERNOR-GENERAL

Major Maude
Military Secretary

COUNTESS OF MINTO

Price 10c

28 Pages

All in the Family

The Sixth Decade, 1895-1904

WITH A BIT MORE CASH, Robert and Lewis Shannon might have won the newspaper war in Ottawa at the close of the 19th century. Since taking control of the *Citizen* in 1892, they had increased staff, expanded coverage and vigorously marketed the paper. Circulation and advertising were on the rise, but not quickly enough. In early 1897, the *Citizen* was still running a poor third to the *Journal* and *Free Press,* and it was going to take a serious infusion of cash to change that. Even cranked to the breaking point, the *Citizen's* old flat bed press could only churn out 900 copies an hour, a fraction of its rivals' capacity. The paper's Queen Street offices were cramped, and its reporters were receiving the lowest wages in town. To make matters worse, the Liberals' 1896 election victory had severely reduced government advertising and patronage printing for the *Citizen*. Far from wealthy, the Shannons required a loan to get back on track. And the banks were having no part of it.

Instead, they turned to William Southam. For decades, he'd run a successful printing business in his home town of London, Ont.. and since 1877 had owned the Hamilton *Spectator.* Southam was interested in a stake in the *Citizen,* but only if his eldest son, Wilson, was put in charge. The Shannons agreed and the new publisher quickly went to work. He moved the paper to 112 Sparks St. and outfitted it with a press capable of producing 10,000 copies an hour. That opened the way for an evening *Citizen*—the morning edition would continue—to sell for one cent, half the price of its competitors. By early 1898, circulation of the morning paper had increased from 1,800 to 2,226 and the evening *Citizen* was selling 3,728 copies, the most in the city.

Realizing the *Citizen* was no longer really theirs, the Shannons sold out entirely to Southam, who soon sent another son, Harry, to Ottawa

Opposite: The Citizen began promoting its souvenir supplement two months ahead of the visit of the future King George V and Queen Mary Sept. 20, 1901. Page after page of photographs were reproduced by the lavish rotogravure process and are still impressive a century later. This decade would also bring the simpler halftone photo reproduction process to the daily news pages.

to help increase advertising. By 1902, the brothers had nearly doubled retail advertising and were putting out the largest classified ad section in Canada. Two years later, the paper moved into a new building—the first in Ottawa constructed specifically for a newspaper—at 136 Sparks just east of O'Connor, a location it retained for 69 years.

Their commercial success notwithstanding, perhaps the Southams' biggest achievement was the hiring of Edward Whipple Bancroft Morrison—Dinky to his friends—as editor in 1898. Just 31, Morrison, later a decorated Boer War veteran, was a splendid writer, watercolourist and avid outdoorsman. He was also a tough-minded newsman. Until he left in 1908, Morrison not only ran a paper of broad scope, he raised its standards at Sunday afternoon tutorials on reporting skills, political writing, arts criticism and journalism ethics. "Getting it right is more important than getting it first," he once said. "Getting both is our goal."

Only Morning Paper Between Toronto and Montreal

50 Years Old and Still Leads. Try It.

January 26, 1895

February 4, 1895
A TRAMP ON TRAMPS.
A TRAMP'S NARRATIVE AND
HOW THE "COPY" WAS SECURED.
The Story of a Vagabond's Life—Hard Lines that Became
Second Nature to an Educated Man Who Liked
Strong Drink—His Remedy for Tramps.
(An excerpt:)

He slipped in unannounced.

"Excuse me," he said, faltering, "but I want to see one of the writers on this paper—a man who was a schoolmate of mine twenty-five years ago. I don't remember his name for whisky has taken my memory."

The man was a tramp—a little fellow with piercing black eyes, gray hair and unkempt beard. He stood quietly in the *Citizen* doorway as two or three names were suggested to him. At the mention of the fourth he stepped forward.

"That's it," he exclaimed. "Where is he?"

When the little tramp learned that his boyhood companion was in another city, a prominent and prosperous citizen, he shook his head and put out his hand. "Well," he said, "I will humble myself at your feet—a stranger's—and ask for a dime. And say," he went on, "wouldn't you like to buy the story of a tramp's life? I am an educated man and I can give you an article worth printing."

He received little encouragement and he went away. At 4 o'clock in the afternoon the tramp had returned with a manuscript that was "respectfully submitted." The story follows:

Born to a good name, educated at a college whose colors are famous on many an athletic field, I have been for the better part of a quarter of a century now a common tramp. I have been thoroughly identified with every phase of the haphazard, reckless vagabond life embraced by that term. I have spent seemingly interminable hours of bitter winter nights turning myself like a spitted chicken by a tie fire over against the railroad track. I have infested back doors in quest of fragments of cold victuals. I have been the occasional patron of nickel lodging houses, sharing the wretched shelter they afford with thousands of nameless bedfellows. I have utilized the talent bestowed for nobler purposes to coax coin from the sympathetic with which to satisfy the insatiable appetite which has been my destruction. In fact, I have lived, and according to all evident probabilities, shall die a thorough vagabond.

You have asked for a recital of some of my experiences. They have been so varied and extensive that it is difficult to make a selection. Tramps, as a body, are a divisible quantity. There are the altogether vicious and irredeemably depraved, who inherited the vagabond instinct, born to prey upon society and entering upon the career as does a just-hatched duck seek the nearest pond of water; but it is a great mistake to class all nomads with this unbruited specimen.

It has become so generally known that tramps can and do traverse great distances by fast trains without surrender of any financial consideration to the corporations providing the rapid transit that when a single man finds himself unemployed and behind with his board bill, the suggestion is at hand that the continent is large and the means of traversing it in search of betterment easily available.

And so he loads his already ruined fortunes into the first convenient freight car and starts upon an aimless journey, often only terminating with the close of his life. Presently a stopping place is reached and the trainmen eject him at some lonesome wayside station. About this time the demands of hunger assert themselves, and since they will have no denial he timidly approaches the nearest house with a plea for food. As may well happen, the substantial fragment of a chicken or a quarter section of a porterhouse steak is handed out, with perhaps some toothsome cake and a piece of delicious pie on the side. In many cases that preliminary experience settles the man's future. At the best of times, when in employment, he is not regaled with such fare as this, and so elects to enjoy it without any other physical exertion than is involved by asking for it.

And then another recruiting agency of tramphood is promoted by the growing indisposition of discriminating people to feed robust, able bodied beggars. This has led to a systematic practice of decoying young children away from their homes with enticing promises of alluringly adventurous travel—eventuating only in compulsory begging and petty theft for the support of the kidnappers. . . . .

How to rid the world of vagrants? It is, of course, useless and impracticable to suggest the formation of a universal league to withhold food

Traveling Incognito In 1915.

—Judy.

A cartoonist envisions the motorcar, April 6, 1897.

THE EASTER BONNET.

ITS MUTATIONS AND ITS MARVELS
FOR TWENTY-FIVE YEARS PAST.

1871.

1876.

1881.

or other material aid from all applicants, therefore, as the next best and reasonably possible thing I should say to apprehend all vagrants everywhere, at whatever temporary cost, subject them to the hardest and most humiliating labor upon the most meager and uninviting dietetic regimen consistent with health, and my belief is that the nearest possible abatement of the tramp nuisance will be accomplished which is achievable this side of the millennium.

July 19, 1895
A LADIES TENNIS COURT.

Editor, *Citizen*: I propose that a new tennis club be organized by the ladies of Ottawa. It is unpleasant for us to feel that we are only admitted to the grounds of the present club on suffrance. Mamma tells me that the men call Monday the "petticoat" day—horrid. Just fancy. I for one cannot stand it any longer, and some of these men avoid coming to the grounds on Monday because it is what they term "women's day." Did you ever hear of such impudence? If a new club is formed, I for one will join it on condition that not one of the members of the present club be admitted,

Yours, etc.

MAUDE, Ottawa, July 18, 1895.

July 20, 1895
THE LADIES AND TENNIS.

Editor *Citizen*: Will you please tell your correspondent "Maude" that if the ladies organize a new tennis club I shall subscribe $5 to assist the enterprise. The sooner they will not require our grounds, the better for us. As to her threats that none of us will be admitted to this female club, she should wait till any of us asks for admission. Yes, "Wait till you are asked" is a motto that "Maude" should adopt.

CHRISTOPHER, Ottawa, July 19, 1895.

My dear Maude,—Your letter in yesterday's *Citizen* has almost driven us all to despair. You know very well, sweet Maude, that we will do anything to please you. I shall propose at the next meeting of the club that the grounds be reserved exclusively for the ladies on every afternoon except Mondays, the club to provide every day for tea, ice creams, etc., also for racquets for all of you, besides the nets, balls, etc. as usual. A couple of paid attendants might also be provided for by the club to run for the balls for you. Will that be satisfactory to you, dear? If we can do more for you, please tell us, darling.

Your best friend,

"X," Ottawa, July 19, 1895.

October 2, 1895
TOBACCO CHEWERS BEWARE.

On June 15, when the Capitals and Shamrocks met in their first match here, C. D. Rochester, a railway mail clerk attended with his wife. When they left the stand Mr. Rochester found that the back of his wife's dress was covered with tobacco juice and ruined as far as further wear was concerned. On enquiry he learned that Charles Durkin and William Burns sat behind his wife and he entered suit for damages for injury to his wife's dress. The case was tried yesterday morning and Judge Mosgrove gave judgment for plaintiff for $5 and $6.50 costs.

July 30, 1897
EXCESSIVE NOVEL READING.

The Citizen *never shied away from telling readers what*
was good for them, as this excerpt from an editorial shows.
The Homiletic Review *was a popular Catholic journal.*

The *Homiletic Review* discusses what it considers one of the great vices of the age, namely, inordinate novel reading. It holds that three results directly follow from this bad habit. The first is that the intellect is weakened, the novel reader losing the power to grapple with the great truths that underlie the realities of life. The second is that true feeling is deadened. The novel reader is subject to the weak impressions created by the actions and passions of fictitious personages. These impressions being constantly repeated their subject loses the power of responding justly to the demands made upon his sympathetic nature by the actual facts of life. The third evil result is that novel reading cultivates mental indolence, relaxes the tone of the mind and prevents us from grappling with serious study which is so essential if we are to grow intellectually.

There is no doubt that all this is very true, and when the same writer indicates an intimate connection between the prevalent passion for novel reading on the one hand and sensational journalism, political corruption and moral laxity on the other, no doubt he is not going further than the facts warrant.... As mental excitement becomes our habitual condition the habit of contemplation is lost and we become unable to sink to the deeper sphere of consciousness where moral law and religious conviction reign; in other words we become incapable of leading a spiritual life....

The remedy is to avoid those habits which produce the disease, to be careful that our best strength is given to the mastery of deep and solid works containing the best thoughts of great men, that our minds are informed with true and permanent ideas, that we leave ourselves sufficient leisure amidst the hurry and turmoil of life for quiet meditation,

1886.

1891.

1897.

Above, opposite: April 21, 1897

and that when we have resort to fiction we shall be careful to partake sparingly of it, knowing that, however alluring, it has a tendency to absorb too much of our time and thought.

May 21, 1898

HE SAW SNAKES IN HIS GLASS,
And Decided Prohibition was Badly Needed in Ottawa.
BUT NOW HE IS AN ANTI,
For There Were Two Leeches in the Water
and His Eyes Did Not Deceive Him.

Although this item has a decidedly light tone, it forms a small part of the Citizen's *decades-long crusade for pure drinking water in Ottawa. Indeed, when the city's first filtration plant was finally opened in 1932, the* Citizen *celebrated with a 24-page supplement.*

A gentleman went into a well-known butcher shop on Queen street west for a drink of water yesterday. He drew a cupful from the tap, but on looking at it, gave a gasp, and mentally resolved to vote for prohibition. There in the limpid water was what appeared at first to be a couple of sea-serpents. Recovering from the fright of the moment he made an examination and found the intruders to be a couple of horse leeches about two inches long. Then he decided that if this was the alternative perhaps prohibition might be a mistake.

The reptiles were properly secured and sent to the police station, where they now are, presumably, awaiting trial on the charge of bathing in public without a proper costume. Meanwhile their captor thinks how near he came to swallowing the little, wriggling, black things, and turns ill at intervals.

A well-known physician was asked as to what would have resulted had the man imbibed before looking, and while he did not seem willing to admit that the dose would have been fatal, he agreed that it would not have been beneficial to the health.

The water with which the city is supplied is not exactly filtered, but it is strained through a wire netting, and, although the mesh is fine, yet the soft, slimy, flexible body of a small horse leech would naturally pass through a very small hole, especially when aided by the pressure on the outside and the suction from within. It, therefore, behooves all water drinkers (of whom, it is rumored, there are quite a number in the city) to take a good, careful look before they drink.

September 2, 1898

A DISGRACE TO OTTAWA

There is one reason why it is imperative that Ottawa should have a patrol wagon at once. And that is for the transference of prisoners from the police court to the jail, and vice versa. It is a disgrace to the city of Ottawa that these unfortunates are marched through the streets chained. The police do the best they can to spare their feelings by taking an unfrequented route to and from the jail, but the mere idea of men and women being walked in a chain gang through the public streets is abhorrent to all sense of decency.

In other cities they take them in a cart or patrol wagon, and where the latter is the case agitations are afoot to have these wagons closed in. Of course, it should be explained that the women are not handcuffed here or put on the chain with the men, but they are walked with the gang; and on Wednesday morning the degrading spectacle might have been witnessed of a young and pretty girl convicted of stealing 25 cents from her employer being paraded with a prostitute and a lot of drunks and petty thieves over the canal, to serve one week in jail. It was her first offence. The case was an extreme one, perhaps, and does not happen often, luckily. But the matter is one in which the ladies of Ottawa should interest themselves and bring their influence to bear to have such a blot on the fair fame of the city removed.

The police are not to blame. They do the best they can, but the police commissioners should remedy it at once by getting a patrol wagon.

At the same time, if it is not rushing the march of civilization too much, a matron should be secured to attend to female prisoners in the cells. In the case of this same girl already referred to, the fright of her arrest made her very ill and there was none but men to minister to her in the cells. Some woman living near could be retained as a matron for a small sum to act in such emergencies, to search female prisoners and perform other similar duties. Other cities have them.

After the city's other newspapers joined the chorus, a patrol wagon was purchased for the police in 1899.

December 31, 1898
BEER FLOWED
Scene in Ex-Ald. Stewart's Committee Rooms.
A GANG OF BOOZERS
A *Citizen* Reporter Witnesses Liquor
Freely Distributed in New Edinburgh.

Beer flowed freely at Mayoralty Candidate Stewart's committee rooms for Rideau ward at 115 Creighton street last evening. It is said to have been on tap since Monday last. A *Citizen* reporter, learning these facts, dropped in on the German electors gathered there last night and shared in the election drinks.

At other times the residence, which is used as a committee room, serves to house Charles Rudowski and his family. Now all is changed,

August 10, 1897 (and opposite)

in the first flat at least. The ordinary furniture has been removed from the front parlor, and in its place one finds three goodly-sized card tables. The walls are planted around with chairs, supporting planks, which in turn support the crowd of beer-bought electors.

Last evening between forty and fifty-seven—by actual count—of the Rideau ward electors were ranged around the rooms. Every table had its quota of card-playing enthusiasts and on-lookers. The atmosphere was filled with thick tobacco smoke and German was the language spoken on all sides.

At frequent periods an attendant would make his way through the willing crowd, bearing aloft a tray supporting ten, twelve, and even fifteen tumblers of "beer, beer, beautiful beer." To give some idea of the quantity that was put away by the electors, it may be stated that the large stock of bottled stuff laid in for the occasion gave away early in the evening, and a five-gallon keg and its mate had to be called upon and copious drawings made therefrom.

A visit to the kitchen revealed a startling state of affairs. In one corner sat a venerable grand dame; in the other, which is of more importance, nestled a keg of McCarthy's ale flanked in by a regiment of the bottled kind. As the beer flowed freer, the crowd drew nearer to the keg, where an ex-brewer operated the tap.

Cigars were also freely provided for the crowd, and the provisions taken full advantage of. But the beer was in such abundance as to exceed the output of an average hotel.

No elector was allowed to be idle—either a glass of beer was pressed to his lips or a cigar placed in his hands. Everybody was given to understand that "open house" reigned day and night; all were made to feel at home.

As the evening wore on the crowd received many additions, who, hearing of the good things provided, had come for their share. As time passed the crowd become noisier, the smoke thicker, and the beer beautifully less, in quantity, but not in effectiveness. By the time the reporter left the crowd were in a position to discuss nothing but that all absorbing topic, beer.

In conversation with some of those present who seemed to be taking quite an active part in extolling Mr. Stewart's qualifications for the mayoralty, the reporter was informed that the liquor was sent there under circumstances with which Mr. Stewart was familiar and that that gentleman knew the liquor had been sent and was being distributed in his committee room.

The free beer and cigars didn't do the job for Robert Stewart, who lost the mayoral contest to Thomas Payment. Not surprisingly, given the tone of this story, Payment was supported by the Citizen.

April 29, 1899
A NEW FACE.
Boy Has Another Chin and Lip Grafted.
A SURGICAL TRIUMPH.
A Wonderful Operation Successfully Performed
at Protestant Hospital.

Surgery is certainly advancing! A boy supplied with a new chin and lower lip is the latest evidence of this.

Three weeks ago a lad named Harold Kennedy was taken to the General Protestant hospital from Martin's Lake, suffering from the total loss of his lower lip and chin, part of the bone being destroyed, also part of the cheeks and neck as the result of a bite from a horse. Now he is the proud possessor of a renewal of these lacking parts of his face.

The operation was performed a week ago yesterday by the attending surgeon of the hospital and the union of the new members of the artificial face as the result of the plastic transplantation was so perfect that the stitches were removed on the fourth day after the operation. The boy, though marked, will have a good face and almost perfect mouth and lips.

Just where the flesh grafted was obtained would not be divulged.

July 15, 1899
CIGARETTES
Smoking the Fashionable Woman's Latest Fad
in American Society.—The Princess of Wales Alleged
to Have Set the Fashion in England.
(An excerpt:)

The anti-tobacco league may continue to pronounce physical and mental doom on the cigarette smoke, but never has the cigarette been more distinctly fashionable than now. There has grown up a legend at Newport, R.I., and other summer resorts that in the presence of women especially the cigarette is far more agreeable and complimentary than the cigar; while the pipe is barred out entirely. Cigars are the privilege of the older men and a pipe is only possible when a yachting, riding or driving party is made up of masculines only.

Since the cigarette has secured an additional strong hold on the average smoker's affections, a preference has arisen for very slender rolls of tobacco, and this is attributed to the fact that a man nowadays is expected to pass his well-filled case to the women, as well as those of his own sex that may form a group, and the women show a marked liking for the delicate cigarettes.

In consequence of this feminine influence on tobacco, the gilded youths have fallen into the expensive habit of importing their cigarettes at no less price than $3 a hundred, from a well known London to-

**EARDLEY MYSTERY
SHOULD BE PROBED**

Riopelle Was Not Called at the Inquest to Tell How
He Came to Leave His Companion Dead
on the Road.

Evidence That They Were Quarrelling on the Wagon
a Short Distance from Where the Body
of Boyer Was Found.

LEON BOYER.   ANDRE RIOPELLE.

August 8, 1898

bacconist who is purveyor by special appointment to Her Royal High-ness the Princess of Wales, an inveterate but fastidious lover of the weed. The princess prefers Turkish tobacco and a small cigarette, with a cork mouthpiece, and exact duplicates of Her Highness' own you can see in the cases of any smart young man who offers you the hospitality of his supply . . . .

No man, in these enlightened days, makes the egregious sartorial mistake of wearing a smoking cap. There is at present a more or less popular lounging coat that can hardly be called a smoking jacket, though it can be put on for a home smoking concert. Usually it is of rough black Tuxedo cloth having a collar of black velvet and black frogs on either side down the front. A man is privileged to wear this in the morning when he retires to his den. . . .

April 27, 1900

April 27, 1900

THE FIRE.

Citizen publisher Wilson Southam, generally a dour man, was *reportedly moved to tears by the devastation created by the fire that roared through parts of Ottawa and Hull, killing seven and leaving 15,000 homeless. Although he wrote rarely for his paper, Southam penned this plea for the community to pull together and rebuild.*

This is an hour for deeds not words. Fifteen thousand citizens are houseless, homeless, their effects, their accumulations of a lifetime are consumed, and worse, the industries by which they have had their living, are destroyed.

These thousands, however self-reliant and willing to provide the ne-cessities of life under normal conditions, are today dependent upon the benevolence of the public for food and other requisites.

To these thousands, words, mere words, are but a mockery, as little comforting as the fierce wind which yesterday urged forward the flames in their mad fury to devour their substance. They ask, and rightly, that we shall prove our sympathy by deeds of kindness that we shall minister to their necessities.

Fire chief Peter Provost

The scenes of desolation which were witnessed during the day as the arms of flame embraced new districts and, with little warning, compelled the terrified wives and children to flee, leaving their mea-ger stores to be burned, were frequently of the most heart-rending de-scription. At best, in many cases, they had but little to lose, but in near-ly every case they lost their all.

Nineteen hundred homes and business places in Ottawa and as many more in Hull burned to the ground suggest a picture of ruin complete enough to sadden the heart and cause the fountain of benevolence to flow.

The first, the supreme duty of those who have fortunately escaped the calamity which has befallen their fellow citizens is to consider and attempt the relief of their distress. This morning ten thousand and more wearied, worn people in this city and its suburbs will find a new meaning in their prayer for daily bread, and their Father in Heaven will expect you to answer for Him their cry and send them relief.

As you surround your well furnished breakfast table think of those who have none, and decide what you owe to their necessity. The double impulse of gratitude for your good fortune, and sympathy with those who have not, should inspire you to devise liberal things.

While individual effort may meet a pressing need, the whole subject of relief will have to be systemized. A strong committee must be formed, charged with the responsibility of organizing the benevolence of the people, so as to most effectually relieve the inevitable distress.

A special meeting of the council has been called for eleven o'clock this forenoon to consider the situation. The board of trade, doubtless, will be ready to co-operate with the council, and they jointly will be able to so organize the system as to command public confidence and ensure the best result.

Though the people have been heavily taxed for benevolent purposes during recent months, yet in the presence of such a disaster it will be found that the streams of their liberality have not run dry.

The *Citizen* believes, however, that it will be better that what the people have to give should be given through a central, responsible committee. Pending the creation of such committee, the *Citizen* will be glad to receive and acknowledge contributions for this purpose and duly hand them over.

Late last evening the following subscriptions were authorized:

Sir Charles Tupper $100.00
Mr. Charles McGee $100.00
Mr. John Coates $100.00
Ottawa Citizen Co. $100.00

Any other amounts, large or small, will be gratefully received and acknowledged in these columns. Let every citizen bear his share in this work nor delay doing his duty because he can not give as largely as others.

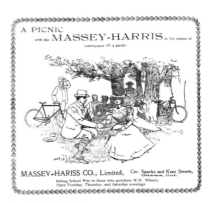

April 28, 1899

June 16, 1899

December 5, 1900
DAWN OF THE 20TH CENTURY
A century later—or, to be exact, 99 years later—the world
marked the passing of the 20th century with considerably
more fanfare, and trepidation, than it did in 1900.

A Rubber and its History.

We are putting on a rubber exhibit in our store here, both interesting and educating. This is a display showing how

e here. botl

A thoroughly pedestrian ad on November 16, 1899, appears to have been the Citizen's first use of halftone reproduction of photographs. The same process is used today, tricking the eye into seeing shades of grey in an array of black dots of varying size. Before this, the newspaper used an artist's pen hatchings to suggest shades of grey, as shown below in an ad from the same day. In many cases, the artists were already working from photographs, which were now prevalent.

In both cases, though, the Citizen *paused to consider the moment.*

As the hand of the dial of Time points the hour of 12 a.m. on Jan. 1st, 1901 the Nineteenth Century will expire and the Twentieth Century be born. This is an event of such rare occurrence and stupendous significance that it should not be allowed to pass unobserved or unemphasized. As a moment of time it is no more big with fate than any that shall have preceded or shall succeed it; but as marking an epoch as registering a transition from one century to another it summons men to thought and action, to recollection and resolution, to repentance and reformation, to gratitude and service.

It is inconceivable that the churches should ignore the event. They may be expected to reap the largest advantage possible for an occasion that must so powerfully appeal to the moral man—to man in his relation to the Great Creator who ordained nature, fixed its bounds and projected the start upon their courses, by which we shall measure time till Time shall be no more.

But shall the state that is so largely indebted to the expiring century not watch beside its couch and gratefully acknowledge its indebtedness? Shall it not wait expectantly the accouchment and hail with acclaim the latest born century, heir of all the ages that is to wield so beneficent a scepter over our sons and their sons and sons' sons to the latest hour?

What can be done to properly mark the event? The *Citizen* does not think it necessary or even desirable to go to any considerable expense to celebrate. Toronto will at that hour ring for the first time its new chime of bells, just placed in the tower of the new city hall, and in Philadelphia the mayor favors the illumination and decoration of the city hall and the holding of a reception there in from 9 p.m. Dec. 31 to 1 a.m. during which music shall be supplied by one of the best bands of the city.

There may not be much in either of the above plans to guide Ottawa. The *Citizen* does not favor any extravagance in this connection. It may be a good beginning of the century for the city to practice economy in this matter. By way of leading the public thought, the *Citizen* would propose a concerted ringing of the bells of the city at the midnight hour; possibly the guns at Nepean Point might join in waking the echoes. Might there not also be a revival of the choral singing so familiar and delightful a feature of Old World festivities? Many such bands might be organized, and in various portions of the city their cheerful music would serve to brighten the feeling of welcome experienced by the citizens at this rare moment in Time. . . .

January 23, 1901
BRITAIN'S QUEEN IS DEAD
THE EMPIRE IS MOURNING ITS REVERED SOVEREIGN
Her Gracious Majesty Passed Peacefully Away Surrounded
by Those Who Loved Her Best and on the Anniversary
of the Death of Her Father, the Duke of Kent.
Messages of Sympathy Pour in to the Royal Family
From All Parts of the World.
Ottawa City Council the First to Wait on His Excellency
With a Resolution of Regret.

Probably no event in the Citizen's *history prior to 1901 received
as much coverage as the death of Queen Victoria, whose reign began
eight years before the newspaper appeared in Bytown in 1845.
Here's a excerpt from the main Page 1 story, which ran
under a giant black headline and banks of sub-headlines.*

Cowes, Isle of Wight, Jan. 23.—Queen Victoria is dead and Edward
VII reigns. The greatest event in the memory of this generation, the
most stupendous change in existing conditions that could possibly be
imagined, has taken place quietly, almost gently, upon the anniversary
of the death of Queen Victoria's father, the Duke of Kent.

The end of this career, never equalled by any woman in the world's
history, came in a simply furnished room in Osborne House. This most
respected of all women living or dead, lay in a great four-posted bed
and made a shrunken atom whose aged face and figure were cruel
mockery of the fair girl who in 1837 began to rule over England and her
Empire.

Around her were gathered almost every descendant of the line. Well
within view of her dying eyes there hung a portrait of the Prince Consort. It was he who designed the room and every part of the castle. In
scarcely audible words the white-haired Bishop of Winchester prayed
with his Sovereign, for he was her chaplain at Windsor. With bowed
head the imperious ruler of the German empire, the man who is now
King of England, the woman who has succeeded to the title of Queen,
the Princes and Princesses and those of less than royal designation listened to the bishop's ceaseless prayer.

January 23, 1901

Six o'clock passed. The bishop continued his intercession. One of the
younger children asked a question in shrill, childish treble and was immediately silenced. The women of this royal family sobbed faintly and
the men shuffled uneasily. At exactly half-past six Sir James Reid held
up his hand and the people in the room knew that England had lost her
Queen. The bishop pronounced the benediction.

The Queen passed away peacefully. She suffered no pain. Those who
were now mourners went to their rooms. A few minutes later the in-

evitable element of materialism stepped into that pathetic chapter of international history for the court ladies went busily to work ordering their mourning clothes from London.

The wheels of the world were jarred when the announcement came, but in this palace at Osborne everything pursued the usual course. Down in the kitchen they were cooking a huge dinner for an assemblage the like of which has seldom been known in England and the dinner preparations proceeded just as if nothing had happened.

The body of Queen Victoria is being embalmed tonight and will probably be taken to Windsor, Saturday. The coffin arrived last evening from London.

An incidental characteristic of the Queen's solicitude for others occurred two days ago when in one of the intervals of consciousness she summoned strength to suggest to her dressers who had been acting as nurses to take the opportunity of getting some fresh air. On Monday afternoon she asked that her little Pomeranian be brought to her bed.

It was feared the Queen was dying about nine in the morning and carriages were sent to Osborne cottage and the rectory to bring all the princes and princesses and the Bishop of Winchester to her bedside. It seemed then very near the end, but when things looked the worst the Queen had one of the rallies due to her wonderful constitution, opened her eyes and recognized the Prince of Wales, the Princess and Emperor William. She asked to see one of her father's servants, a member of the household. He hastened to the room but before he got there the Queen had passed into a fitful sleep.

The Prince of Wales was very much affected when the doctors at last informed him that his mother had breathed her last. Emperor William, himself deeply affected, did his best to administer to the comfort of his stricken uncle, whose new dignity he was the first to acknowledge.

From all points of the world there are still pouring into Cowes messages of condolence. They come from crowned heads, millionaires, tradesmen and paupers and are variously addressed to the Prince of Wales and the King of England. . . .

January 24, 1901

January 11, 1902

LETTER FROM OTTAWA

A Quartet of Charming Girls—Middle-Aged Men
More Interesting Than Young Men.

Ernestine was the pen name used by the editor of the women's pages to sign her letters to a friend published weekly by the Citizen *in 1901 and 1902. The letters were a clever, chatty way to comment on social events in the capital, and often sparked a flood of letters from readers. Here's an excerpt from a typical Ernestine letter, and some reader response:*

My Dear Janet—At the skating party given by Their Excellencies a week ago, of which I wrote you a short account, I noticed something rather strange, namely, that so few ladies ventured on the ice. It may have been that they were not good skaters, or, more probably, that there was a scarcity of gentlemen. I hope it was not the latter reason.

Why I mention this is that on Saturday afternoon at Government House a similar state of affairs prevailed. The same dozen gayly-dressed, graceful skaters, and practically the same men that were on the ice on Thursday monopolized the rink all forenoon. I can't understand why it should be so. You know there is certainly more sport on the ice than in a crowded dressing-room, and if young gentlemen are in the minority don't you think the ladies ought to have courage to venture on the ice without a gentleman.

I wonder why the young men here stand "shivering on the brink"—not only at the skating rink. Do they think that their courteous, gallant manner will be misconstrued or is it that they are specially careful not to compromise themselves lest breach of promise cases should arise. Their motto is not "nothing venture, nothing win." The young men there would compare very unfavourably with the manly, fearless men one meets in New York. It is evident Ottawa possesses more spectators at a dance and skating party than I have seen anywhere else....

I wonder if I have seen the average young man of Ottawa. The middle-aged men are gentlemen in the truest sense of the word. They are men of fine physique and gallant at all times. Probably all the uninterested young men will be irresistible old men. That's just the conclusion one must come to here. I must not say anything more about the men. Yes, one word more, and that is, that if I could judge every man in Ottawa from the standard of one whom I have met at the Russell, I would have a very high opinion of the gentlemen at the Capital.

There are four perfectly charming ladies here. As you do not know them I will not mention their names, but I will describe them. One lives on Daly avenue. She is tall, has soft golden-brown hair, and a bewitching smile. Her manner is charming. Another one lives on Vittoria street. Her eyes are soft and brown as is her seal sacque. She has a pink and white complexion, and perfect white teeth. I am sure her disposition must be as bright and happy as is her smile. It would be a pity if her Romeo should have to come from far off lands. Still another lives on Elgin street. She is pretty, dresses daintily, and has a most captivating manner. The other lady lives on Metcalfe street. She is of medium height, has bright eyes, a pink complexion, pretty teeth, and dresses with excellent taste. I am going to watch the career of this charming quartet. I wonder what the months of May and June will tell. All know those are the months of roses and weddings. If Ottawa cannot boast of its young men it certainly can of its maidens....

THE CITY'S VANITY FAIR

WHAT FRILLS CONFIDES TO HER FRIEND KATE.

Something of the O.A.A.C. Tombola— Madame Taschereau Entertains— Some Advice to Mothers as to the Treatment of Milk.

9/12/97.

Dear Kate:

The curtain fell after the last act of the interesting and successful Tombola. The drawing of the prizes, on Tuesday night, and after a strained silence which bespoke the evident anxiety of the holders of lottery tickets, for there were many valuable prizes to be drawn for, congratulations were in order to those who had been successful. The great prize of the occasion was the thousand dollar horse most generously presented by Mr. Joseph Seagram, M. P., and said to be one of the gems of his famous stable. This coveted prize fell to the lot of Miss Mabel Woodburn, the daughter of our much esteemed, fellow-citizen, Mr. A. S. Woodburn. Those who like myself know, how much the success of the Central Fair, which brings so many visitors and so many dollars to the city yearly, has been due to the untiring exertions of Mr. Woodburn, will appreciate the appropriateness of his daughters' good fortune. Not less was my pleasure that

the process of sterilization recommended by Prof. Robertson, our great authority on dairying, in Tuesday's Citizen ought to be adopted, the process being as follows: Place the can or jar of milk in a pot of water, and allow the water to come to a boil, and as it is best that the milk itself should not boil but be brought to a scalding heat it should be carefully watched until that point is reached. Try it.

* * *

The air is still full of political rumors, but as Gloria, in the Christian, puts it, tempus is fugiting, and as I must say good-night, I shall reserve particulars till my next epistle. Much love.   Ever thine,
                    FRILLS.

December 10, 1897: An early society column by "Frills," the pen name of Helen McIntyre, wife of prominent Liberal lawyer Alexander McIntyre, and a writer "widely and popularly known in political and social circles in the capital."

Dear Janet, I wish you were here, just to hear your opinion about the people of Ottawa, for I know that people interest you more than scenery. There may be little to write about, but we could find quite enough to talk about....

—ERNESTINE

February 15, 1902
Letters in Defence of Our Young Men
To the Editor Woman's Page.

Dear Ernestine,—You say we are not gallant. What do you mean by that assertion? Do you imply we are not like the Yankee boys? No, I know we are not and I don't think we have any desire to be like those romantic young men.

In one of your letters you stated a young lady fell on the rink, that five young men sat on the platform, not one of them went forward to assist the young lady. If you had noticed more closely you would have seen that not one of said five young men had on their skates. If they had there is not a doubt but they would have gone to the rescue.

DICK
Metcalfe street

In saying that the young men of Ottawa are not gallant I mean that they do not avail themselves of their privileges as young men. I fail to see why Dick has no desire to be like the American young men. I would like to know what are his reasons. My impressions are that the Ottawa young men could improve themselves very much. Probably they realize that they are in the minority, and that it makes very little difference whether they are gallant or not; they will always meet with a cordial reception from the ladies.

To say that if the young men had had on their skates only makes matters worse. As far as I can see they would have incurred no rush by going on the ice without their skates. That one event impressed me that the young men were not as gallant as they might have been.

•

Dear Ernestine,—All my friends are indignant because you speak so uncomplimentary about our Ottawa boys. They asked me to write you if you would make a public apology, and state in which edition you would publish it. Before I close I wish to say that all our boys are very gentlemanly, gallant and considerate.

MAUD
Daly Avenue

I regret that all Maud's friends are indignant at my "uncomplimentary" remarks. No doubt said young men have received nothing but compliments since they left college. But that does not prove that the un-complimentary remarks were untrue. I cannot, however, comply with your request to make a public apology. If I meet a more manly class of young men, or if the young men of whom I have written should be transformed into gallant, independent young men I will be only too glad of the opportunity to make it known. The "boys" of Ottawa evidently have a strong admirer and champion in "Maud."

June 14, 1902
THE CAPITAL DURING NIGHT
How the Hours Pass When the Residents Sleep.
THE CITIZEN'S OPERATIONS
Some Interesting Scenes
and Sounds Recorded.
(An excerpt.)

Does Ottawa Sleep? A stroll through the Capital's streets between midnight and dawn would frame a negative answer. At no hour can the city be said to rest from its ceaseless round of brain-racking, money-making activity. True, there is at times a jog in the never ending race, a breathing spell, but a halt, never. The average law abiding citizen should mislay his latch key some night just to steal an excuse to study his civic home, during the hours it is commonly supposed to be at rest. He will be surprised and enlightened.

Ottawa is a strange city in many ways. It is unique in the manner in which it empties its streets. Take a Sabbath evening for instance. During the hour following the dismissal of the congregations of the different churches, it is impossible to move along the business streets at a brisk pace. One might as well try to run a foot race at a bargain counter. Sparks and Bank streets seem to attract the crowds like a magnet holding the steel filings. Fifth avenue and Broadway may harbor gayer throngs but none more interesting. The villages and country side for miles around contribute their quota to the stream of humanity that reaches the high water mark. One moment Sparks street will be crowded with a close set procession of easy strolling citizens and visitors out to see and be seen.

Almost the next moment it would seem, so rapid is the transition, the stream has dwindled to a rivulet, only a few late stayers or callers homeward bound appearing in sight. The pavements might have opened and closed on the irregular army of sight-seers and strollers, so rapidly do they take themselves to their different homes. In less than fifteen minutes the main streets clear themselves, and the city settles down, apparently, to a well-earned rest.

The minutes lengthen into hours, and midnight draws near. The regular car service becomes irregular and finally comes to a close in the

lines of hustling trolleys which, having made the final "run," race to the sheds. Looking eastward from the corner of Bank and Sparks streets, a rare sight now presents itself as the cars with brilliant varied colored lights swing into view around the Russell House corner, a dozen or more in line at once, filling the deserted street with their clang and clatter. The last belated car bumps along, leaving the street in possession of the slow-stepping cop. He with a conscientious regard for duty and a wholesome fear of the night sergeant tries every office and store door. Woe unto the absent minded tradesman who has neglected to "lock up." From slumber and pajamas he is roused, and hustled down to rectify his error....

Scarcely has the last car lost itself in the distance, emitting sparks and clanging calls from the gong, when the mail car darts out from the post office siding and races down to the Union station to catch the Soo express. The motorman on the mail car is lord of the road. He looks neither to right nor to left for he carries no passengers, and has no fear of being held up by waving umbrellas and canes at the street corners. He has right of way and he takes full advantage of the privilege, a fact borne out by the rate of speed at which the car is raced along.

For the next hour or more the cabbies keep the pavements ringing with the steel-shod hoofs of their wearied chargers. It is a living illustration of the once popular English music hall song, "The Cabby Knows His Fare." This is the hour when the Jehus [Jehu was a biblical chariot commander] "cash in" on the merrymakers bound for or returning from the road houses. The distant creaking of a heavily laden wagon tells of the approach of the wood carver, who during the small hours of the morning hauls from the Chaudiere mills the slabs and edgings thrown aside by the singing saws in the daily manufacture of lumber....

Still long before the night has paled to dawn, the traffic which like vitality has been at its lowest ebb, takes on new life. The gardeners from the suburbs and villages can be seen urging their steeds along, on the home stretch maybe of an all-night trek. Piled high with vegetables are the wagons, and eager is the driver to secure a prominent place on By Ward market. There, when the first frugal housewife makes her appearance, he will be seen with his load displayed in tempting array on the van backed up to the curb.

Other sights and sounds there are. Through the hours of night and early morning can be heard the steady song of the Merganthaler linotype machines in the mechanical department of the *Citizen* office. High above the street they are situated, molding with magic touch into type the news that greets the reader when he picks up his *Morning Citizen* at the breakfast table a few hours later....

Across the way at the northwest corner of Metcalfe and Sparks

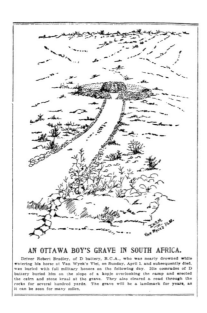

AN OTTAWA BOY'S GRAVE IN SOUTH AFRICA.

Driver Robert Bradley, of D battery, R.C.A., who was nearly drowned while watering his horse at Van Wyok's Vlei, on Sunday, April 1, and subsequently died, was buried with full military honors on the following day. His comrades of D battery buried him on the slope of a kopje overlooking the camp and erected the cairn and stone kraal at the grave. They also cleared a road through the rocks for several hundred yards. The grave will be a landmark for years, as it can be seen for many miles.

May 8, 1900

THE ECLIPSE OF KRUGER.

The despatches announce that Kruger had fled from Pretoria, and that the British forces would enter the Transvaal Capital at noon Wednesday. The eclipse is total and permanent.

May 31, 1900

streets, and farther east at the southwest corner of Sparks and Elgin streets, the steady click of the telegraph instruments answer the call of the Merganthaler machines. There in the Great Northwestern and Canadian Pacific Telegraph offices, operators through the long night receive the news carried for the *Citizen* from every quarter of the globe. On the night air every word spoken by the telegraph and lino-type machines sounds clear and distinct, whereas in the clatter and confusion of noonday traffic, their message descends to the passerby as a whisper only. They tell of life in other lands and cheer the lonely pedestrian as he trudges homeward, praying fervently for the day when the O.E.R. [Ottawa Electric Railway] will inaugurate an all-night service.

The air chills and from the bakeshops comes the appetizing odor of plump loaves fresh from the oven for a city's consumption. Dawn is at hand. The cats that held their amateur bouts and political discussions on the sheds and fences, meander to the rest they've robbed from many a light sleeper. The vagrant dogs foraging for stray bones take themselves off. The vanguard of the army of early workers appears out of the struggling light. Another day is at hand freighted with its joys and jangles, its cares and cheer. If any doubt rests on this score it is re-moved by the clarion call of the city rooster. For be it known that Ot-tawa possesses a widely scattered colony of birds, that in vocal powers can put their fellows of the country barn yard to shame.

The cop on the night beat draws his cloak closer about him in the chill of the new born morn, and paces impatiently along the street looking for the "relief." While the west is still wrapped in darkness, the light breaks clear in the east, outlining spire and steeple sharp in the morning sky. The full clear note of the night hawk, flute like and reso-nant gives way to the chatter of the irresponsible sparrow and the early notes of the feathered songsters. The patient, industrious charwomen, trudge along with mop and pail to wage war on dirt and disorder in the business section.

Most interesting of all the early morning scenes is the rally of the *Cit-izen* carriers. Along the streets from all directions hurry the lads who deliver the morning edition. There's an army of them, bright eager faced lads, exulting in the very joy of living. They are businesslike chaps and wait with impatience on the monster press that turns off the thousands of copies of the people's paper.

Each lad is provided with a strong canvas bag and each has his "route" along which he delivers his papers. No time is lost by them in moving off on their rounds. The majority are provided with bicycles, a couple ride blocky little broncos, a few drive, others deliver their pa-pers on foot. They are well on their way before sunrise and old Sol smiles on their errand of enterprise.

LORD ROBERTS

OTTAWA, CANADA, THURSDAY, MAY 31, 1900.

PRETORIA IN THE HANDS OF GEN ROBERTS' ARMY

Despatch States the Forces Would Enter in Two
Hours, And The London Times Accepts
The Cables as Fact, Though
Bobs is Silent.

Earl of Rosslyn, a Prisoner, Sent Out The News—Kruger Has Gone to
Waterfall Boven and Burgomaster Sousea Will
Receive the British—Many Prisoners
Are Released.

May 31, 1900

Creaking carts pass along the streets bound for the various hives of industry. The bustling milkman rushes the can at every turn. Out of the sheds speeds the early car. Thin wreaths of smoke cut the morning air. Everything is in readiness and the wheels of industry at a standstill during the night prepare to revolve once more.

In league with hygiene
. . .
Hygiene demands absolute cleanliness in the bath room.
No room seems to soil with greater ease.
Nothing will clean and brighten with equal ease like SOBRITE.
No dirt escapes it—no germs can live where it goes—it is nature's own
dirt exterminator—beautifies, brightens and cleans.

SOBRITE 10 CENTS
rapid action cleaner
will not scratch

June 16, 1900

August 20, 1903
AT BRITANNIA BAY.
Permanent Illuminations Were
Inaugurated There Last Night.

The permanent illuminations of the electric railway terminus at Britannia on the Bay were inaugurated last night and the pretty little resort has been transformed into a miniature fairyland of electrical decoration. Over two thousand bulbs have been arranged on the pier, the lookout at the end of the pier, the elevated crossing over the railway tracks and the arches opening into the grounds. All of these are outlined in electric lights and the whole arrangement is most artistic, setting off the place to great advantage and producing a vivid reflection in the bay. There was a big crowd out last night and the illuminations won many favorable comments from the spectators. The Guards band rendered a choice program.

September 4, 1903
GATINEAU HEAD WATERS A HARD ROAD TO TRAVEL.
The Difficulties and the Hardships of the Portage—Climbing Rapids and Trekking Against Current—Incidents of the Journey.
Legend of Far North—Meeting With Missionary—Remarkable Natural Phenomena — Awful Results of Electric Storm.
Citizen *editor E. W. B. Morrison's lively travel adventures were eagerly awaited by readers in the early 1900s. Some of his series, including a diary of his 1902 journey to London as head of the Ottawa contingent to the coronation of Edward VII, were repackaged and sold as souvenir sections. So, too, was a four-part series on his trip to the headwaters of the Gatineau River. Here's an excerpt from Part 2:*

The idea of going to the Height of Land and back in a fortnight appeared to strike our Indian guides as a good joke and for the first two or three days they did not take the trip seriously, evidently thinking we would soon get enough of it and change our minds. The first morning at Des Eaux, before we broke camp Jocko reeled off the menu for the day: St. Joseph portage (over a mountain), Castor rapid, Big Eddy, Two mountains, Brule chute, but the list conveyed little to our unsophisticated minds at the time. Before evening we knew better.

Prior to that I entertained an hallucination that paddling all day against the current would be the worst we would be up against, but subsequently I found that that was the easy part of the up trip. At the end of the days that followed the retrospect was more like one long portage and climbing of rapids, interspersed with intervals of clear paddling against the current and brightened by Simon's assurance that if it was hard going up we would come down "lak a weddin'."

There were three ways of getting up—rapid-paddling, towing and portaging. Paddling a rapid meant cunningly picking a way through the eddies and backwater as far up as possible and then making a dash, pitting the strength of the paddlers against the force of the current at the critical point. The danger in this was that in case of failure to stem the current the canoe would be probably rolled over and we would go down "lak a funeral." Towing up meant that line was attached to the bow of the canoes and some of us scrambled along the slippery rocks on shore or waded knee-deep in water pulling, while a couple of men in the canoe warded her off rocks and poled her up with stout poles cut in the bush for that purpose.

But portaging combines more misery to the square inch than any other mode of progression. In the first place it came as a rude shock the discovery that the portages were long, that they were so rough and cluttered up with fallen logs, rocks and morasses as to be really no paths at all and; worst of all, everybody was supposed to carry his own stuff. The method of carrying stuff over portages is with a tump line— a broad leather band which passes across the forehead while its ends are attached to the burden on the back which rests over the hips. . . .

Having got your load on your back and your rifle, fishing rod, rain coat, paddle and a few other goods and chattles in your arms you struggle up the steep bank of the river with the round stones rolling from under your feet and plunge into the underbrush through which the path is traced with difficulty. It is suffocatingly close, and the humid heat makes the perspiration break out in beads on your mobile countenance as you struggle up the steep rocky bed of a partially dry torrent, then strike a section of stumps, undergrowth and fallen trees; next slipping and edging down a steep hillside to find yourself staggering knee-deep through an oozy bog like a hamstrung pack mule.

By this time the oppressive heat has got in its work, red balls of fire dance before your eyes, the tump-line feels like a steel compress on your temples and round your head hovers a cloud of black flies and mosquitoes fattening on their helpless victim. The perspiration drops off your eyebrows and trickles down your nose as you stagger desperately on exhausted but not daring to stop lest the flies and mosquitoes eat you up entirely. At last a glimmer of light through the bush ahead indicates that the other end of the portage is in sight, and reaching the river bank again the pack is dropped with aching relief.

MR. R. L. BORDEN, M. P.
The New Conservative Leader.

February 8, 1901

•

During the first two or three days we had as many as half a dozen portages daily in addition to the paddling and poling up rapids. The packs averaged from fifty to eighty-five pounds and it was extremely exhausting work until we got into good condition. We usually started at 7 a.m. and camped about 5 p.m.... We did not see much game except ducks up to that point, but the bears and deer were said to be plentiful and we saw any amount of fresh tracks and places on the banks where bruin had been trumping through the blueberry bushes.

Just below Baskatong the river Jean de Terre enters the Gatineau from the west. At Baskatong we exchanged our two canoes for one large one and cut our baggage down as much as possible to lighten the load. Very little definite information could be obtained regarding the river further north except that there was a rapid about 25 miles long. By this time our Indians came to the conclusion that we meant business and they settled down to hard work. There was very little fishing in the Gatineau itself but in Lake Bitobee, to which we portaged to avoid some heavy rapids, we got half a dozen very large pike in half an hour. I hooked one so large that we had to paddle ashore to land it, but as soon as it found itself in the shallows it lashed about like a young whale until it broke the trolling line and got away. It must have weighed about—well, as much as most fish that get away....

•

February 22, 1902

October 20, 1902

The following day we met two trappers in a canoe—one old half-breed with a muzzle-loading Hudson Bay gun, a powder, horn and a cloth haversack, looking very much as if he had stepped out of one of Remington's pictures. Later on we heard a religious chant and down the river came a large canoe travelling rapidly with the current. There was a squaw, paddling in the bow and her husband at the stern, while amid ships surrounded by a number of children sat a tall man, bearded to the eyes and wearing spectacles. The black cassock proclaimed his calling, and paddling with a long sweeping stroke looking straight to his front, he passed us chanting sonorously, the Indians joining in again after pausing a few moments to look at us. It was a strange and impressive sight, this missionary from the far north on his parochial visits. Far down the river at the Indian village we heard them firing a salute in honor of his arrival. This day we made a number of portages over the Sturgeon, Bols, Franc, Ceesor and Serpent falls and rapids. The latter is a magnificent fall about forty feet high and constitutes a magnificent water power....

It was here I made my record as a star marksman. Four big ducks came winging their way swiftly down the river and Joe Commando, who hadn't much respect for Lee-Metford carbines as a sporting weapon, remarked: "Dere fine duck; mak' good bouillon if we only had gun." This was too much. I pulled my carbine and buzzed a .303 at the swiftly moving game and down toppled a fine, fat duck. "Ba tam, that good shot!" said Joe, and the other Indians grunted. The duck could not have been half as surprised as I was, but I never blinked an eye. We paddled across the river and Joe dived into the underbrush, quested about like a hound and retrieved the game. At every Indian village after that they showed the carbine and told the story of the duck to admiring aborigines. But the glory was too much for me. I was afraid to fire another shot during the trip while the Indians were about lest I ruin my hard-earned reputation.

•

The last two days before reaching the Forks were taken up in ascending 21 miles of continuous rapid. The canoe had to be towed and pulled all the way. Sometimes we trudged along the shore, sometimes in the water, or in the brule on the top of the banks. Our feet got sore with the water and bruised by the stones, and the mosquitoes and black flies nearly finished us. The black fly is about the size of a midge but shaped like a wasp and when it bites it takes the piece out and draws blood. The mosquitoes have no song—they just swarm onto you and get down to business. Unlike the 'skeeters of civilization they never attempt to dodge the hand of the smiter. They die in their tracks and their places are immediately occupied by another batch.

At the Logue lumber shanty fifteen miles below the Forks we were hospitably entertained, and there we heard for the first time of a remarkable natural phenomenon. They told us that a couple of miles above there had been a tremendous landslide which had almost blocked up the river. We examined the place the same evening and sure enough the side of a hill seemed to have slid down and deposited a mass of gravel, trees and earth several acres in extent, in the river. Later on we counted 71 similar landslides, big and little between there and the Forks. What caused them was a mystery. In some places great hills had scars on their flanks and the trees and earth ripped off from the top to base, often a hundred or two hundred feet wide and piled in a heap of debris at the foot. On our arrival at the Forks the trader there, a Scotchman, named John Forbes, explained that one night last June there was a dreadful electric storm lasting about an hour. The lightning smote the hills in every direction and it was these lightning bolts that scarred the hillsides and brought down the landslides. He showed us where three bolts had struck the hill behind the trading post, one opening up a beautiful spring of water. It was a most terrifying experience and the Indians thought the end of the world had come. The storm seemed to have centred just over that region and the lightning fairly bombarded the hills for hours.

—E. W. B. MORRISON.

November 17, 1902

THE CITIZEN'S NEW HOME

E. L. Horwood, Architect.

On November 17, 1902, the Citizen published an architect's drawing of its new building at 136 Sparks St. The newspaper moved there in 1904 and stayed until 1973.

December 30, 1903
HOT ON THE FLATS
ELLIS AND VINCENT RAISE THE RACIAL ISSUES.
Audience Didn't Respond to Mr. Vincent's
Sentiments—A Warm Mayoralty Meeting
in Boileau's Hall Last Night.

*Tension between French and English speakers has been part
of Ottawa's political scene since its early days. But the campaign
leading up to the January 1904 mayoral election was particularly
nasty, as this story excerpt from an all-candidates meeting in LeBreton
Flats demonstrates. The election was won by James Ellis. His main
opponent, D'Arcy Scott, eventually became mayor in 1907.*

Joseph Vincent, lawyer and ex-alderman, champion of the French, and supporter of Ald. Ellis on the mayoralty contest, raised what was regarded as a race cry at the big meeting in Boileau's hall on the Flats last night. Speaking in French, he accused D'Arcy Scott of having signed a petition to have more English-speaking professors at the University of Ottawa and have the French put out. This allegation denied in part by Mr. Scott raised a tempest, the disturbance being so great that Mr. Vincent had to sit down. The meeting was arranged by D'Arcy Scott and seemed largely in favor of the candidate....

Mr. D'Arcy Scott denounced the appeals to racial prejudices made by Mr. Ellis and said that in a mixed community a man who resorted to such tactics admitted thereby that his cause was a weak one. He desired a clean campaign on the municipal issues of the day. Mr. Scott devoted considerable time to disputing Ald. Ellis' claims as to surpluses which he said were attributable to borrowed money. The other improvements in the finances were the result of the work of ex-Mayor Morris in which he had assisted. He denied emphatically that there was any politics in this contest.

Ald. Ellis who followed dwelled at length on the telephone and, lighting questions and claimed credit for the financial management of the city.

Then the eloquent orator from By ward, "senator" Devlin [clothing store owner R.J. Devlin], spoke in support of Mr. Scott. "I was asked to run for mayor myself," he observed, "all creeds and nations promised me support, but I decided not to run and gave you ample canvas and a smooth sea to pick out your own representatives. In this unique contrast I find that the whole fight is between Mr. Scott and Mr. Ellis.

Mr. Devlin made a very eloquent appeal against racial prejudices being raised by Ald. Ellis or his "man Friday," as he called Mr. Vincent.

Geo. Kidd, candidate for alderman, asked for the floor. "If I couldn't run for a public position without raising these miserable cries of racial prejudices," said the speaker, "I would stay at home. Irish Protestant that I am, I don't want these religious, national issues trotted out at any time. We are Canadians—that's good enough for me."

Ex-Mayor Morris supporting the candidacy of Mr. Scott, charged that Ald. Ellis was taking credit for his (Mr. Morris') work in the city council and he also claimed that that gentleman (Ald. Ellis) being a law clerk at Caron and Sinclair's, solicitors for the Bell Telephone, shouldn't be mayor when that company was seeking a franchise in the city. Ald. Ellis replied that he hadn't been a law clerk for three years and that Caron and Sinclair were not acting for the Bell company. . . .

Then came Mr. Vincent, received with a chorus of boos. Speaking in French, he said that Scott had signed a petition to Rome to have the French priests removed out of the university.

"It's a lie," said Mr. Scott.

At this point there was a storm of hisses and shouts and the chairman had difficulty in keeping order.

Shouts of "fire brand" and "traitor" could be heard all over and there was a sort of pandemonium.

Honore Charlebois got up and exclaimed, "Go home, Vincent, we don't want any fire brands down here."

The furore lasted half an hour and only with difficulty was order restored. Mr. Vincent cut it short by appealing above the din of support for Ald. Ellis.

Mr. Scott said that when English-speaking instructors were repeatedly being removed from the university and replaced by French he had signed a petition to the French head of the order asking that the English language get more consideration and the request had been granted, two of the new English-speaking instructors sent out having perished in the late fire at the university.

It was after midnight when the meeting ended.

Emblematic of the Hockey Championship of the World. It was won by the Ottawa Hockey Club last night, when they defeated the Montreal Victorias, 8 goals to 0. Rat Portage will play the Ottawas for it Thursday and Saturday nights.

CHAMPIONS AGAIN ARE THE OTTAWAS

Defeated the Victorias, 8 to 0, and Won the Stanley Cup and the C. A. H. L. Championship— A Hard Game.

Ice Covered With Water but Play Was Exciting— Record Crowd Attended—Rat Portage Thistles Here.

March 11, 1903

February 6, 1904
MORGAN'S OTTAWA VISIT
AMERICAN FINANCIER'S HURRIED TRIP TO CAPITAL
Called at Government House and Spent an Hour
and a Half With Their Excellencies—Received
Numerous Telegrams on Trains.
(An excerpt.)

J. Pierpont Morgan, multi-millionaire, maker of monopolies and trusts, king pin of American finance and commercialism, spent a few hours in Ottawa on Saturday. He came at three o'clock in the afternoon and went away at ten in the evening, in the meantime paying his respects to the vice regal household and incidentally viewing the Parliament buildings.

THE LATE POPE LEO XIII.

July 21, 1903

It had been arranged that Mr. Morgan would lunch at Rideau Hall, but the special train on which he traveled through from Quebec was delayed by snow at Outremont, and only pulled into the central station at 3.30. It consisted of a locomotive, baggage car and three sleepers—Mr. Morgan's own car, the Magnet, the New York Central parlor car, Genesta, and the C.P.R. sleeper Sandon. Accompanying the great trust king were Mrs. Morgan, the Misses Morgan, Dr. and Mrs. Markoe, Mrs. Douglass, Miss Riller, Mr. Young and a small retinue of servants and valets along with a private detective . . . .

As Mr. Morgan walked down the platform, a small crowd of people who had been attracted by curiosity, were on hand to get a peep at the Wall street financier. Tall in stature, rugged in appearance, broad shouldered and with an inclination to stoutness, Mr. Morgan's step is quick and active, and the general expression of his face is shrewd and intelligent, giving evidence of keen foresight and business talent.

But though Mr. Morgan may figure in the hall of fame he scarcely will ever rank as the ideal among types of American beauty. An otherwise well featured countenance, is overbalanced by an abnormal nose about which there is something unnatural, but then nature has amply compensated in a material way for any defect in his physiognomy. The magnate wore a heavy furlined overcoat and a seal cap, drawn down in protection of his ears.

Sleighs were called and about four o'clock Mr. Morgan and his party went to Rideau Hall, where they met the Earl and Countess of Minto and the vice regal household and also attended the skating party, a number of the guests being presented to the distinguished visitors.

Mr. Morgan subsequently drove to the Union station whither his train had been transferred, and in doing so passed in front of the Parliament buildings. He had arranged to go to Toronto and Niagara Falls late at night but countermanded that order and decided to leave at ten o'clock. During the evening, however, numerous telegrams came and Mr. Morgan ordered his train to Montreal from which city he was to return to New York . . . .

Mr. Morgan was somewhat uncommunicative, but he remarked that during his Canadian trip he had enjoyed himself immensely and hoped to return. He dropped a ten-spot to Mederic Landgraville's man who drove him to Rideau Hall.

February 16, 1904
A LONG FELT WANT.

The quick lunch idea has struck Ottawa and seemingly it is entirely welcome. At No. 152 Sparks street, immediately west of Poulin's departmental store, is located the Boston lunch room. Its fittings are of the finest, its service excellent and its charges moderate. The proprietor is an experienced man and his establishment is one that the Capital can be proud of run as it is on the lines of the best lunch centres in the States. The European system prevails. Lunches as ordered are served at separate chairs, a broad arm on each serving as a table. In full view is the scale of prices, and the list provides alike for the modest and the fastidious appetite. The Boston should prove popular with business men, shoppers, civil servants and others for whom time is a consideration. A special feature is made of the excellent coffee served. A night and day service will be maintained.

February 18, 1904
THE POLICE COURT.
Even the Naughty Ones
Find It Too Cold to Be Bad.

Yesterday was an off day at police court and there was comparatively little grist for the mill of justice. It was not a case of low water or anchor ice as with the Chaudiere mills, it was simply a falling off in business. Apparently the below zero weather has frozen up the crime germ as well as the city water services. Magistrate O'Keefe is still wrestling with la grippe, and it devolved on Ald. Askwith to measure out justice.

Edward Ledoux, a stranger in a stranger land, found his due in a charge of drunkenness. Eddie promised to turn the other cheek when passing the tempting barrooms hereafter and to hie himself to his American home forthwith. On these conditions he was allowed to sniff the free freezing air once more.

Ledoux, who had the appearance of a mechanic in hard luck, blew into the police station yesterday afternoon. He asked for a night's lodging and was told to return at seven o'clock. He gave evidence of having made the acquaintance of Johnnie Barleycorn. Ledoux looked him up again with the result that on his return to the police station in the evening he came to a landing on the window sill. He might have been frozen into the likeness of a cigar shop statue had a passing cop not noticed him and assisted him to the cells.

John Douglas, the colored man "bohn in Zululand your honah," was again arraigned on a charge of stealing a watch from Thomas Brenhan. He was allowed his chilly liberty on bail, $100, furnished by himself, and $100 suret

August 15, 1904
SLATTERNLY WOMAN.
Type of Woman Who Blames Her Intolerable
Slovenliness On the Heat.

She is an eyesore to her husband, a bad example to her daughters, and an offence to society—the slatternly woman. She claims to be a

ICE-CLAD RUINS   CITY POST OFFICE.

January 7, 1904

MAKING THE SNOW FLY.

February 1, 1904

product of the dog days—poor dog days, everything is blamed on them—the ice man, the garbage system, the street flooder and sunstroke. She says the heat is simply awful, and she "can't dress to-day."

So she goes clad in a wrapper of hideous pattern and design or else she wears a blouse with a rip under the shoulder and a skirt very up in the front and down in the back, and looks miserable but feels happy. She goes without corsets, often, and wears the oldest, most disreputable footwear she can rake out of her ash heap—they're so loose and comfortable, she says, those old shoes. Her hair is done up hastily, two hairpins or maybe three, confining the bulk of it at an impossible angle, on her head. She rolls up her sleeves, sits on the doorstep and scrapes her neighbors character.

She may have and probably has a great deal to do; she may be and very probably is tired out when evening comes. But can anything short of paralysis excuse her attire throughout the day, and the neglect to change before the evening meals. Go down any back street in this city in the morning and if you are a book agent, go round to the back door and take a look at the mistress, the do-your-own-work kind who toils within. The odds are large that she won't be dressed fit to answer a ring at the front door bell. Her excuse is usually the heat; then, stress of work. But in spite of heat or work, if her husband or sons were to go down town to business or office looking relatively as she does at an early morning hour, she would be shocked, yea, verily.

There is no excuse for any woman in Ottawa being a slattern; prints are cheap, dirt cheap, and if she can't buy enough to make herself a morning gown, she ought to be in the poor house. Some women have an idea that "any old thing will do in the kitchen." But one who is constantly doing housework in slatternly attire soon loses her self respect, and certainly, that of her family. Office girls, clerks, factory girls, all dress for their business, and neatness is the primary requisite of their attire.

Perhaps the reason why householders do not pay more attention to their clothes, is because they do not regard housekeeping in the light of a business, as serious, as real, and, far more important than any other vocation into which a woman can enter. The making of a home and the husband and the thousand and one little details which go to make up a well kept house constitute a business and ought to be so regarded by every woman who shoulders this responsibility. Household labor, and the daily round of duties, have long been looked upon as lower work, requiring little skill or intellect to perform than anything else.

But a beautiful home is the expression of the highest daily ideals, and the woman who creates and maintains a beautiful home is doing a much more important and difficult task than her stenographer sister or saleswoman cousin is aware. And to make the home beautiful, a

CREW OF A RUSSIAN BATTLESHIP.

February 18, 1904

woman cannot be a slattern. She is a blotch on the face of nature and ought to be removed. The dog days should offer no excuse for frowziness and untidiness and the hideous back kitchen attire should give place to something far removed from it. Truly it is an infatuated husband who loves a slattern wife.

October 8, 1904
LEAVING OTTAWA
Fang Tung Going Back to China,
He was a Citizen Subscriber.

Tired of Canadian life and anxious to rejoin his family in the faraway Flowery Kingdom, Fang Tung, a Bank street celestial, is leaving for China and the Capital is about to lose one of its many progressive orientals. Balloon-like are his sleevelets and large are his sandals, but Fang Tung, taken all round, is a businesslike citizen and many regret his unexpected leave-taking. Fang Tung always enjoyed life, and one of his many pleasures was derived from reading the news columns of the *Citizen*. Since Fang became a resident of the Dominion's capital city he has been a subscriber to this great family journal and it was with regrets that the Chinaman waltzed into the *Citizen* office yesterday and ordered his paper stopped. "I'm going home," he told a reporter. "Back to the scenes of my boyhood days. Does the *Citizen* go there?" Fang speaks fluent English, has been educated and writes a nice hand. He will visit points in Canada en route and his local business [a laundry] will still continue, managed by Fang's cousin.

ZULU PRINCE WED
Nephew of Cetywayo the Noted Zulu Chief.
FINDS WIFE IN OTTAWA
He was Brought to England, with Five Others
and Prince Cetywayo in 1882—A Sketch.

Nearly half a century ago in a native village in Zululand a bouncing baby boy made his debut to charm a proud papa and a dusky mamma. All through the long fly infested summer days he squawked and smiled in turn as babies do the world over. As he grew in years and yearnings, he wandered off and got lost in the jungle and tempted the crocodiles in the near-by stream. He seemed destined to live a life like that of his fellows who cared not for clothing.

But a day came for Deroweidia, for that was the name the little chap answered to when he answered at all, when he turned his back on his jungle home. He was scion of royalty, a nephew of Cetywayo, the celebrated Zulu chief, and along with four others he was taken to England. Deroweidia at the time was thirteen years of age and his knowledge of English about as scant as his native apparel.

April 8, 1904

On Tuesday night Rev. F. C. Reynolds pastor of the West End Methodist church, united in marriage one John Douglas and Mrs. Annie Booth, a hard-working widow who numbers amongst her early possessions a small contingent of lusty youngsters and a neat little restaurant on Wellington street, immediately east of Bank. Her husband is an honest looking chap, decidedly dusky of countenance and nearing the half century mark. He is none other than Deroweidia, the child of the African jungle, the man of royal connection.

The story of his life from the time he left Sunny Africa to the time he captivated and captured the Ottawa widow reads like a chapter from a story book and a good story book at that. Deroweidia, or Douglas as he is now known, left his native land, where clothiers would go bankrupt in a week, in 1884, the year that his uncle Cetywayo, prince of the Zulus, made his unsuccessful attempt to buck the line against the British. That effort on his part, it will be remembered, resulted in the disastrous Zulu war. Deroweidia's father was also mixed up in the little fracas, occupying in the native ranks a position corresponding to that of lieutenant in the British army. The son of course was rather young to take up his little war club, but anyway he didn't get a chance, for, as has been said, in company with four others, he was taken to England at the request of "the great white Queen."

It is hardly likely that Queen Victoria knew that such a little colored chip of royalty who shied rocks at alligators and wore his necktie around his waist, existed, but in any event Deroweidia got the call and the trip to England. Victoria the Good, always interested in the welfare of her subjects, black, white and otherwise colored, saw that the visitors from the jungle were introduced to the white man's burden, fashions and education.

Deroweidia, or Douglas as he was called in English, "made good" and picked up everything in the way of learning that honestly came his way. In the sights of the Strand and the pleasures of Piccadilly he forgot to grow home sick and seldom even in his dreams did the pleasures of a crocodile chase haunt him. As he reached man's estate, he received an appointment as butler at Alexandria palace, still enjoying the protection of the Queen, whose protege he was. Tiring, however, of life with royalty as a neighbor, he came out to Canada about five years ago, arriving in Ottawa shortly afterwards. His liking for the new country caused him to spend his money freely, but he eventually came to the end of his purse strings.

Then he struck a job as a cook, turning out flap jacks and steaks at the Russell hotel during Charlie Genslinger's regime. He was afterwards employed as cook on the C.P.R. transcontinental trains, but it was only quite recently that he made the acquaintance of the Widow Booth.

"No, I was never married before," he said yesterday to a *Citizen* reporter. "I like this woman; she was honest and hard working and I thought we could make it. I asked her and she thought we could make it, too; so we got married."

"Do you ever intend to return to Zululand?" he was asked.

"I will when I get money enough," was the reply. "I never had much hankering to go back after I got in the way of wearing clothes and eating bread and such like. Out there they wear hardly anything and cook very little and I couldn't go back to that life."

Where he first came to Canada, Deroweidia, or Douglas, as he prefers to be called now, bore a letter of introduction from the Queen to Lord Minto, according to his own story.

"I often talked with the Queen. She asked me many questions about my people and seemed greatly interested in them. I've seen the present King and talked with him, too," stated the "prince."

Douglas is a member of the masonic order, one of the few Zulus in that august fraternity. He also makes the boast that he is the only Zulu residing permanently in America. In appearance he resembles a negro very much and appears to be an active, sensible chap. His Canadian courtship was a short one, for brevity in matrimonial matters is the rule with his people. Out in Zululand a girl is valued not on the strength of her personal charms so much as on the weight of brass and other metal ornaments she wears. Sometimes she'll be a regular junk shop, carrying around with her a weight of forty or fifty pounds of wire and ornaments about her neck and ankles and in her nose and ears. Before he can call her his own, her admirer has to turn over to his future father-in-law an agreed number of cattle.

From this it can be seen that Prince Deroweidia in seeking a wife in Canada made a much better bargain than he would have under the sheltering palms of his native village. He intends to establish a restaurant in Ottawa.

Supply Company of Canada   The Independent Coal Co., Limited.   Thos. Birk

BUTTERWORTH FOUNDRY, LIMITED

The Gulston School

GEO. M. MASON, LIMITED

University of Ottawa.

THE ST. ANTHONY LUMBER CO. LIMITED

Wm. J. Murphy

ION WAREHOUSING CO., Limited.

J. Oliver & Sons Limited.

The C. C. Ray Compa

The Western Canada Cement & Coal Company L't'd.

THE OTTAWA Forwarding Co., Limited.

THE LAURENTIDE MICA COMPANY, LIMITED

S. J. MAJOR, LIMITED

WATSON AND TODD, LIMITED

MURPHY - GAMBLE LIMITED

W. C. EDWARDS & Co. Limited

Sun Life

A. A. FOURNIER

Tie and Timber Company

The CHAUDIERE LUMBER Coy, L'td.

P. J. POWERS Co., LIMITED

The Bell Telephone Co. of Canada.

ITE MINING Co LIMITED

OTTAWA LUMBER CO'Y, LTD.

The Canadian Railway Accident Insurance Co.

A. G. ACRE

ORME & SON, Limited.

AMERICAN BANK NOTE Co.

ASHBURY COLLEGE

THE OTTAWA SANITARY LAUNDRY CO. LIMITED   FOR BOYS

THE RIDEAU LUMBER CO. Limited

THE HULL WALL

THE HULL ELECTRIC CO.

Library Bureau

Modern Mac

CALEDONIA FOUNDRY AND MACHINE SHOPS

ALEXANDER FLECK, Limited.

of Canada Limited
Head Office

INTERNATIONAL HARVESTER COMPANY OF AMERICA

THE BRONSON COMPANY

THE OTTAWA GAS COMPANY.

The Hurd

LOW'S MACHINE SHOP

CO., LIMITED   THE WINDSOR

OTTAWA, ONT.   THE HOTEL VICTOR

174

Brothers in Arms

The Seventh Decade, 1905-1914

THE NAMES AND IDEAS that were to shape the *Citizen*—as an influential newspaper and a thriving business—for the next 50 years settled into place during the first decade of the new century.

Leading the way with their peculiar mix of high-minded moralism and tough-minded capitalism were Wilson and Harry Southam, brothers, neighbours, partners and Christian Scientists—"the two-headed publisher," as the rival *Journal* once put it. The jibe wasn't far off the mark. Years of joint decision-making had forged a remarkable like-mindedness between the brothers that extended to religion, literature, politics, business, dress, even alcohol (they both became teetotallers the same week). When Harry discovered the writings of Mary Baker Eddy, he persuaded Wilson to join him as a Christian Scientist. When Harry fell under the sway of the single-tax doctrine of economist Henry George, he and Wilson embarked on a tax reform crusade that lasted both of their lifetimes. When Wilson built a home in Rockcliffe, he called it Lindenelm. Harry built one next door and called it Casa Loma.

Not surprisingly, all this had a profound impact on the *Citizen*. In 1909, the paper stopped accepting liquor and patent medicine ads, a practice that lasted 40 years and cost $5,000 in revenue in the first year. The Southams also pushed hard, in editorials and by personal lobbying, for Ontario tax changes giving municipalities the power to set up a single tax system the Southams believed would encourage growth.

Because newspapers have the potential to do harm, the brothers asked their news staff to eschew "unsavory news unfit for home reading" and to strictly adhere to the ideals of fairness, accuracy and reliability. "A newspaper of such character would have a tremendous moral influence in its constituency and its material prosperity would be greatly enhanced," they wrote in a 1907 memo to staff. And while the

We believe that The Citizen's policy of rejecting all objectionable and sensational medical advertising has done much towards winning and holding the confidence of its readers and has been the means of interesting the public generally in clean newspapers as a whole and The Citizen as such particularly

July 12, 1911

Opposite: The Citizen's striking Business Proclamation issue of December 1, 1909, featured signatures and business stamps from all phases of the city's commerce.

Citizen supported the Conservatives editorially, the Southams insisted their reporters "should not allow this to interfere with their giving . . . impartial copy dealing with political matters."

The task of putting these ideals into print fell to editor-in-chief E. W. B. Morrison—replaced in 1908 by Charles Casson, a one-time Unitarian minister—and a crew of budding young talent whose names remain bound to the *Citizen* a century later: city hall reporter Charles Bishop, later dean of the Parliamentary Press Gallery and a senator; evening editor D'Arcy Finn, who rose from teenage errand boy to long-time managing editor; sports editor Tommy Gorman, seven-time Stanley Cup winning coach; veteran parliamentary reporter Robert MacLeod; and beat reporter R. K. (Andy) Carnegie, legendary press gallery chief for The Canadian Press.

MAJOR E. W. B. MORRISON, D.S.O.

On March 23, 1907, the Citizen ran this photograph of its editor-in-chief when he was put in charge of recruitment for the Ottawa Field Brigade. Morrison later commanded Canada's Gunnery Artilleries in the First World War and was knighted in 1919. Mount Morrison in Banff National Park is named for him.

February 12, 1906
E. B. EDDY IS DEAD.
A BUSY LIFE ENDED.
The Great Manufacturer, Practically the Builder of Hull,
Passed to His Reward on Saturday Afternoon. Illness Was Brief.
Mr. Eddy's Career, Something of His Sterling Worth,
His Character and the Upbuilding of a Great Industry.
(Excerpt from a lengthy Page 1 obituary.)

Flags are lowered to half-mast all over the city of Hull today. The ponderous machines of the big factories are motionless and still. There is an unwonted calm over the city and many evidences of mourning. E. B. Eddy is dead; E. B. Eddy, who was the founder of Hull's industrial enterprise and whose vast works are the main spring of that city's material prosperity. A captain of industry, the match king of America, a business man of rare ability, a whole-souled, generous, good-natured personage, Mr. Eddy passed to his heavenly reward on Saturday afternoon. He died at ten minutes to two, at his home, Standish hall. He was 79 years of age.

A man of strong physique, he had been in good health comparatively till the last year or so when decline in his physical powers became noticeable. At the same time he retained to the last an unimpaired mental vigor. Though ailing for several weeks he was daily at his office, the last occasion being on the 25th of January. He left that night complaining of not feeling very well and took to his bed a day or two afterwards. He was suffering from an ailment of the stomach which developed a catarrhal condition of a virulent type. The patient gradually sank, though to the last he was conscious. The end was peaceful. . . .

The noble life which ended on Saturday began 79 years ago. Ezra Butler Eddy was born on August 23rd, 1827, near Bristol, Vermont. His father was of Scotch descent; his mother a direct descendant of Miles

Standish. Like many other great men he was born on a farm. He got his education in a little red school house. When but fifteen years old city life held out its usual attraction for the country lad and he went to New York. There he secured a situation in a mercantile house at a low salary. His ability won him promotion and ere long he rose to a position of trust in the financial management of the house.

But E. B. Eddy was shaped for greater things. A few years in New York and then he went back to his native Vermont. In 1851, he commenced on a small scale the manufacture of friction matches. In this undertaking, he was successful but with that keen foresight which always characterized him he saw better prospects in Canada. He came here. He sized up the latent potentialities of the Chaudiere and decided to locate in Hull in 1854.

His enterprise and endeavor there are synonymous with the development of the place from a mere hamlet to a city of considerable proportions. To the upbuilding there of a great industry he brought and applied those virile qualities that the ancestral blood might be expected to produce. When he came the population was under two hundred. It is today over 15,000 and with that growth Mr. Eddy had much to do.

The beginning was humble. In an old cement shop belonging to Ruggles Wright, Mr. Eddy began to make friction matches of the comb variety. He worked at the machines himself. His first wife, though not working, used to instruct women how to make the paper boxes. Mr. Eddy in those days was his own salesman. He used to peddle his output, travelling with a team, from Ottawa as far west as Hamilton and Sarnia. There was never a better whip than he. He could make his horses cover as much territory in a day as any living man and this without unduly tiring them. Making one of the necessities of life and without a great deal of competition, Mr. Eddy's business grew and prospered.

Then he branched out. He went into manufacturing pails. Afterwards Ruggles Wright built a circular saw mill and Mr. Eddy, at first renting this, subsequently bought it and started to saw lumber. Then he built another saw mill himself and a sash factory and acquiring limits up the Ottawa started actively in the lumbering business. Success attended his efforts and as a lumberman his output became about the heaviest of all along the river—as much as 175 million feet a year. At the same time the match and pail factory was being extended and increasing its output. All Hull, so to speak—and by that time the city had commenced to grow—was working for him. Some were in the shanties, others in the factory, while in the homes the women and girls used to make the paper boxes. . . .

Soon the city became a hive of industry. Each year saw some new building going up or else an addition to one standing. The number of

February 2, 1906

March 19, 1906

THE CARNEGIE LIBRARY.

April 30, 1906

ON THE LIBRARY STEPS.

"I want you to remember, as the last words of Andrew Carnegie, that this is the library of the people."

Ottawa's first public library was built with a $100,000 donation from U.S. philanthropist Andrew Carnegie. On May 1, 1906, the Citizen ran a sketch of him at the library's opening.

employees increased; so did the output and the demand. But reverses were still in store. It is stated that no less than twenty-seven fires have occurred on the premises. Twice they were wiped out.

The ordinary man in the face of such disaster or reverse would have quit. Not so with E. B. Eddy. His persistent tenacity of purpose, his dogged perseverance, always came to the rescue. Before the smouldering ruins were cold he would be out with plans for rebuilding. He had an unwavering faith in the country. He foresaw its growth and development and the business that would follow as a result. He always restored what fire or flood laid low, influenced by a sense of keen and shrewd perception. He was one of those cool and calculating men who meet the responsibilities of today and measure up the possibilities of a greater future. He soon became the largest manufacturer of matches in the British dominions ....

What an industry has grown and expanded from a beginning so humble! Stand on Parliament hill and look across the river to the long stretch of stone structures, each with its costly equipment, from those of the most delicate mechanism to the ponderous paper and pulp machines; go over in Hull and see the mass of humanity that pours out when the shrill siren blows at evening; hear the incessant roar day and night from the great machinery halls; see the homes that have grown up about it—and you form some conception of the extent of an industry that owes its establishment to E. B. Eddy's enterprise; its growth and development to his great generalship, his iron strong will and his remarkable business talent.

July 28, 1906
THE CALL OF THE WEST
LURES AMBITIOUS MEN
Miss Katherine Hughes, The Citizen's Special Correspondent,
Concludes An Exceptionally Interesting Series.
Some of the Features and Conditions Which Attract
in the Great Canadian West. The Mounted Police.
As a female journalist covering "men's issues"—that is, anything not related to recipes, fashion and social events—Katherine Hughes was a rarity in the early 1900s. Equally unusual was editor E. W. B. Morrison's decision to buy her freelance series—the final part is excerpted here—on the emergence of the Canadian West. Soon after, Hughes was hired by the Edmonton Bulletin *to cover politics. She later became Alberta's first provincial archivist.*

Some years ago there was in the Federal ministry at Ottawa, a very able, very unassuming man who, after organizing the unwieldy department of the interior, was selected as first governor of the Northwest.

To his friends at home in letters he spoke of the big western wilderness, quaintly, as "my parish." Governor [David] Laird's "parish" of the seventies is our golden west today, with the potential wealth of an empire. It is a magnet of prosperity drawing thousands of new settlers weekly, and fortunately for the west, it is drawing, on the whole, a better class than any new country has done before.....

This year I learned why our west (apart from its opportunities of money making) is so potent now in its call to men of spirit, so strong in the ties it makes to them. It is just its youth, its unspoiled youth, its buoyancy, the field it offers to make or mar, and the eternal impulse in spirited manhood to do and know and achieve for himself. Who, being offered his choice of the ages fifty or twenty would choose the former? The United States is comparatively mature, western Canada is still gloriously radiant in her youth, a new Ceres with her hands full of gifts and golden sheafs of grain for her emblem.

It is still, too, as much a land of mystery as of promise. What may not her metropolis, Winnipeg, be in thirty years? What part is the west destined to play in the administrative future of all Canada? What men will it produce?

An American magazine, now giving the story of Andrew Jackson's determined strides up from the humblest station to the highest in the nation, touches lightly on his life as an attorney in the frontier town at Nashville. At the same time, the writer says, Webster was playing about his father's farm, Martin Van Buren in his father's taproom, Clay a boy in Virginia, John Quincy Adams a youth at college—all ignorant of the other's existence; all destined to meet one day and know each other's mettle in great issues. May not our Canadian west, to frontier towns and lonely farms, hold a group of spirits as rare, developing to "make good" some day the aspirations of the nation, as their fathers are doing now with individual aims?

Winnipeg, as the metropolis of this "last west" is growing splendidly. Last year it spent $10,000,000 on new buildings. This year, according to the present rate of increase in expenditure, estimates place the total at $12,000,000. A number of its business-men are Americans, and commercially it is somewhat American—that is, quite enterprising in spirit. But it is thoroughly Canadian and British in sentiment ....

So, the east need not doubt the loyalty of the west. Western Canadians are a practical race. They are welcoming Americans; they treat them fraternally, fairly, and adopt every up-to-date method suggested by them. But they mean to keep Canada for the Canadians, native or adopted. Many of the farmers coming in from the western states are, according to authorities at different points of the west, natives of Great Britain and Ireland who emigrated to America in their youth. And these find, as one of them said to me, "It is pleasant to come back to the

CANADA WINS AGAIN.

BEATS THE WORLD IN THE MARATHON RACE AT ATHENS.

May 2, 1906: The Citizen celebrates Canadian William Sherring's win in the Athens marathon.

old flag, and be able to make as good a living under it."

They like the old flag, and every man of them has unstinted admiration for the Mounted Police. I was struck with this comment, by a young business man at Regina, the descendant of three generations of Americans, and who, coming last year from a south-western state, intends to be a Canadian citizen soon. "One thing I remark here," he said, "is the interest men take in politics. It seems part of their life, and they enjoy talking about it all the time. In our state we used to take a fierce interest in politics around election time, but dropped it to go on with our work again. What do I find most striking in Canada? Its wheat; its opportunities generally—and, of course, the Mounted Police."

It was at their headquarters in Regina that I first saw the Mounted Police in force, though at every town we had heard of their splendid work.... The adventurousness of the plains—now becoming limited— has drawn, for a few years, young men with life fresh before them, and, for a lifetime often, men wearied or sated with life in the old world. These have not wasted time descanting on the beauties of old cultured England nor bewailing the amenities of life left behind them. They simply set manfully about their voluntary work for Canada, and did it in a way that has challenged the admiration of two continents. The unique body of men they formed, their enforcement of the law and their respect for it, their deeds of daring and of endurance, the traditions of fidelity and fearlessness imparted to the Service—these would make a rare story; one worthy of gentlemen....

Since its organization in the seventies, this efficient force has maintained perfect order and a most wholesome respect for the law on our frontiers and in the wilderness. As a practical instance of their effectiveness, I would quote Miss Marle Gilroy, the bachelor-maid farmer who was often obligated to remain alone on her farm some miles out of Regina. She is a native of Australia, a bright, self-reliant, educated and capable woman; she said: "I have never felt any fear out on this prairie, even when quite alone. I would have been afraid in a similar position in the Western States or Australia but here the country is so well patrolled by the police one has nothing to fear. Unless it is the scarcity or inefficiency of labourers," she added laughingly.

July 1, 1906

February 28, 1907
GREAT FIGHT FOR HOCKEY TICKETS
Early Morning Scenes In The Struggle.
WINDOWS SMASHED
Method of Ticket Distribution Criticised By Public.
The city's first riot over hockey tickets occurred part-way
through a three-year Stanley Cup drought for the Ottawa Hockey
Club, popularly known as the Silver Seven. When the team was given

*a chance to play the Kenora Thistles for the Cup by defeating the
Montreal Wanderers, Ottawa fans went wild for tickets. Montreal
won the series, and eventually took the Cup from Kenora.*

A mob of excited hockey enthusiasts numbering nearly 3,000 besieged the Elgin street entrance to Allan & Cochrane's drug store at eight o'clock this morning. The greater part of the crowd had been there for several hours and a considerable section of it had arrived a trifle of eight or nine hours before. . . .

The trouble had its inception yesterday afternoon. As is well known, the Ottawa Hockey Club has a season ticket list, each holder being entitled to two seats for every game. It is believed the tickets thus disposed of would reach 1,000, leaving about 1,200 seats for the general public, exclusive of the bleachers. The seats left after the club's 1,000 had been laid aside were presumably to be offered for sale at eight o'clock this morning. But the Ottawa Hockey Club, the public say, decided to protect their patrons and extend a helping hand to the friends of their patrons and to the friends of the friends of their patrons. In order to do so without any fuss the club seems to have marked off an additional 850 seats, leaving 350 for the public when the "plan" would be opened.

The aforesaid public were not aware of this yesterday, so about midnight of last evening the advance guard of the speculators arrived. These consisted of small boys hired to stay up all night by various despatch agencies and private individuals. At 12:30 this morning 150 boys and men were in line. An hour later there were twice that number, and at three o'clock fully 500 were on the scene.

About two o'clock when everything was going well and the line was unbroken and patiently waiting, the law arrived and forced the head of the line away from the narrow doorway. Those thrown out of their positions fought to get back and in a few minutes everything was in confusion, so that at three o'clock all the elements required for a small-sized riot were in evidence.

The crowd steadily increased in size and disorder and the theory of the survival of the fittest began to be demonstrated in a practical manner. Small boys nearest the building were lifted up and heaved away, while everybody fought for positions. The police had been reinforced but could do nothing, and about five o'clock things looked serious. The crowd swayed and swung and finally attempted to push those in front through the building. They succeeded in a sense, as the crashing of plate glass indicated that something was giving way, and in an instant later the real work began.

The police drew their clubs and commenced to belabor the smallest and most inoffensive individuals within reach. As a result gore was

Ex-Mayor W. D. Morris, Candidate for Mayor 1907

Morris a sure winner
Ownership of public utilities
Ratepayers know his record
Reduction of taxation
Independent of corporations and cliques
Says things and does them

Freedom from outside influence
Ottawa an industrial center
Retrenchment and economy

Manufactures will be encouraged
An equitable assessment
Your interests will be conserved
Ottawa advance
Retirement of "ringsters"

December 8, 1906

soon in evidence and a young man named McEwan and another named McKay were placed hors du combat. Several people fainted in the heart of the mob and amid a terrible uproar the crowd, which now numbered about 1,500, kept charging against the building and the blue-coats. The latter laid about them with clubs right and left and when the dawn merged into daylight the siege was still on.

In the meantime, the mob was growing and at seven o'clock, one hour before the advertised time for the opening of the emaciated plan, 2,500 people blocked the street from Sparks to Wellington. The calmness that the daylight brings had fallen on the mob and patient waiting had taken the place of excitement and physical exertion.

As eight o'clock approached signs of restlessness began to be once more manifested. Just here a diplomatic move was decided upon. An outbreak by the disappointed crowd could be safely expected when the doors opened, so it was thought better to take the bull by the horns. An upper window was raised and the announcement made that no tickets would be placed on sale owing to the inability of the staff to handle such a rush. The crowd was informed that the plan would be transferred to Dey's arena, where the sale would open at one o'clock. The announcement was taken good naturedly when understood by all and the street began to slowly clear .

The departure of the crowd revealed the extent of the damage caused by the bad handling of the affair. The plate glass fronts in the offices of John Culbert and Son and C. W. Bangs were smashed in, while the basement windows in both establishments were kicked from their sashes. On the road were rubbers and hats.

A member of the Ottawa Hockey Club executive when asked for an explanation of the way the plan was handled said: "We gave everybody in Ottawa a chance to get a season ticket at the beginning of the year. They were for sale without favor or restriction. We are protecting our friends who have stood by the club throughout, from speculators and ticket sharks, and in so doing are accomplishing what no other club in Canada has ever attempted to do. That a number of people want to see one game—the best game—in a year is all right, but the club's patrons will be protected from speculators and I think the fair-minded public will agree with us that we are right in acting as we have."

March 7, 1907
HOCKEY PLAYER SUCCUMBS
Owen McCourt, Struck in a Mix-up by
Charles Masson, died this Morning at Cornwall,
where Ottawa Vics Had Gone.
Cornwall, March 7.—(Special)—Owen McCourt, "Bud," the famous rover of the Cornwall hockey club, died about 8 a.m. today in the Hotel

Dieu as the result of the injuries he received in last night's hockey match. The Victorias of Ottawa and the Cornwalls were replaying a Federal league game, which was ordered to be played over in consequence of McCourt and Degray having played a couple of unauthorized matches with the Shamrocks.

The game was becoming rather rough and full of cross checking, tripping and slashing as a result of the referee's leniency. Early in the second half McCourt and Throop exchanged blows and separated. As they came to the side Throop seemed to strike again at McCourt, and as the latter went to retaliate, Charles Masson of the Ottawa team struck him on the head and he went down like an ox while Rumons cut Throop across the cranium. It all happened in a second or two and both men were helped off the ice and a doctor sent for.

McCourt returned to the game for a few minutes, but complained that he was "all in." He shortly retired to the dressing room. These were his last words, as he was unconscious when Dr. D. O. Allguire reached his side a minute or so later. He was taken to the Hotel Dieu, where an operation by Doctors Allguire and Hamilton revealed a broken blood vessel in the brain. The fracture was almost in the same place as that of Alcide Laurin, the Alexandria player who was killed two years ago at Maxville. McCourt never regained consciousness and passed away about 8 o'clock this morning.

When it was discovered that McCourt's condition was critical Chief of Police Smyth laid an information before Hill Campbell, J.P., charging Masson with assault with intent to do grievous bodily harm, and this morning just before McCourt breathed his last, Chief Smyth arrested Masson at the Hotel Duquette and conveyed him to the lockup. Masson, who is a son of ex-Alderman Masson of Ottawa, wanted bail, but this was out of the question when it was known that McCourt had passed away. The charge against Masson will be amended today. . . .

The deceased was a fine young man, standing over six feet in height. He was a splendid player, fast and clever and his work was always clean. He had a hot temper, but was never deliberately rough. He has been playing hockey and lacrosse since his earliest school days and has been in senior company four years, playing in Woodstock in 1905 and the other years in Cornwall. He was the eldest son of the late Patrick McCourt and was born in Cornwall 22 years ago. Last fall he had a severe attack of typhoid fever, but recovered and was able to take part in recent matches. Last night he seemed to have a premonition of something and did not want to play. He did not come to the rink till nearly 9 o'clock and only went on at the last minute because the local team were handicapped by the absence of several other men. . . .

Charlie Masson, the young man who has been arrested as the result of the death of McCourt, was not a regular player of the Victorias, and

LOOK ME STRAIGHT IN THE FACE.

"I am the Y. M. C. A. Campaign Clock, I Am Getting There. But it Is Tedious Waiting for Your Contribution. I Desire to Move My Hands But Am Helpless Without Assistance. Push me Along to $200,000."

March 18, 1907

MOGUL

Egyptian Cigarettes
(Cork Tips)
15c PER BOX

July 28, 1907

was called up to play at Cornwall on account of the inability of Capt. Bob Harrison. Masson had been playing at Truro, Nova Scotia, this season and returned to Ottawa about three or four weeks ago. He played cover-point for the Victorias and was seldom ruled off for rough work; in fact he had been looked upon as a very clean player. Masson was well known and liked about town....

Masson, eventually charged with manslaughter, was acquitted at trial when evidence showed another Ottawa player had also struck McCourt. However, the death set off a national discussion about hockey violence, including the Citizen *editorial excerpted below.*

March 8, 1907
THE HOCKEY FATALITY.

The expected has happened. A young hockey player at Cornwall has been killed, not as the result of an accident of "rough play" but in a fight with hockey sticks which took place during an interval when the players concerned were not actually engaged in play....

During the past two seasons so-called rough play in hockey has been becoming rife to a dangerous extent. The newspapers have declaimed against it and have insistently warned the players against the consequences liable at any time to ensue as a result of either a chance or deliberate blow, but to little or no purpose. Primarily the responsibility rests upon the associations who have refused to make and enforce rules which would stop rough play. It is a disagreeable thing to have to say, but nevertheless true, that it is the sordid management of clubs who encourage roughness in sport because it makes for a good "gate."

While the better class of people who enjoy clean sport have been drawing away from the game it has increasingly attracted the element which would flock to a prize fight were such allowable under the law. As the management of clubs control the associations they take good care that proper rules are not made and carried into force which will stop "scrapping." These are the men who are morally responsible for the fatality at Cornwall....

Whatever the outcome of this case may be so far as holding the assailant responsible for the death of his victim, it is to be sincerely hoped that it will result in bringing hockey players and hockey enthusiasts to their senses.

CITIZEN GOT FIRST WIRELESS

On Opening of Trans-Atlantic Service.

DEPARTMENT NOTES

Geological Survey Operations. Movements of Ministers and Members.

In connection with the successful inauguration on a commercial basis yesterday of the Marconi wireless telegraph system, it is interesting to note that the Evening Citizen was the first Canadian newspaper to receive a direct wireless message. It will be found on another page of this issue.

October 17, 1907

November 22, 1907
IS HYPNOTIZED BY STRANGER
Peculiar Experience of Geo. French, Bank St.
CONDITION SERIOUS
Physician Worked All Night

To Save Life. He Tells Strange Story.

George French, a well built boy of nineteen, late of the Grand Trunk Railway, was hypnotized by a strange man yesterday in the early afternoon, near his boarding house, 202 Bank street, while walking with a companion, and collapsed. A Somerset street doctor was called in and worked over the lad all night, barely saving his life.

The hypnotizer, described as a tall dark man with a "peculiar face," disappeared when the boy fell to the pavement and cannot be found. The case is one of the most mysterious that ever came under the notice of the medical fraternity in Ottawa. The police have been notified, and are on the watch for the stranger, but as none of the parties concerned know the man, or ever saw him before, the chances of apprehending him are very slim.

When seen this morning by a *Citizen* reporter, young French was so weak and exhausted that it was with difficulty that he could turn over in bed. He told a most amazing story of the peculiar incident. Of a husky physical build, with a keen intellectual face, French does not look the part of a man liable to be subject to hypnotic influences.

"Yesterday, about noon," said he, "I went out with Mr. E. W. McDonald, a friend of mine who boards here in the house, to go across to Mc-Cracken's store, McDonald having business there. He went inside the store, and I remained out on the street, waiting for him, and while waiting a brakeman of the G.T.R. whom I know, came along. We chatted for a while and then the stranger passed.

"I never saw this man before and even now I can't give any description of him. All I remember is that he had a most peculiar look on his face. He stared at me, and I looked rather hard at him in return. As far as I can say he was big and dark. I felt my face flush, my head began to ring, and then the stranger's face lit up in a flash. I felt myself grow weak and turned to the G.T.R. brakeman and said that I'd better go home. Then I fell, and I don't remember any more. They say I was brought home unconscious and babbled about the stranger for hours. Where the man went to or who he is I don't know at all."

French further said that he had dabbled a little in hypnotism as an amusement, but had never had any great success with the science. Why he collapsed is a mystery to him, a mystery he lays to the door of hypnotism.

In speaking of the peculiar case, one of the leading physicians in Ottawa said that, while he had not studied hypnotism to any extent, he fancied that French's case was one in a thousand, as a subject of hypnotism could not be sent into a trance very easily the first time by a man whom he had never seen before. It would take time to get control of the optic nerve. However, French might be a very easy subject, and might have been in weak health. This, French says, is not quite the fact,

THE MEN TO VOTE FOR.

FOR CONTROLLERS.

Ex-Ald. CHARLES HOPEWELL.
Ald. JAMES DAVIDSON.
Ald. ROBERT HASTEY.
Ald. CHARLES G. PEPPER
or
P. M. DRAPER.

FOR ALDERMEN

Victoria ward.
Ald. W. W. BOUCHER.
Ald. S. ROSENTHAL.

Dalhousie ward.
Ald. W. FARMER.
Ald. E. P. McGRATH.

Wellington ward.
Ald. GEO. H. WILSON.
Ald. R. K. FARROW
or
T. A. SHORE.

Central ward.
Dr. IRA BOWER.
Ald. G. A. LITTLE.
or
F. A. MAGEE.

St. George's ward.
WILLIAM FORAN.
J. M. MACOUN.

By ward.
Ald. A. W. DESJARDINS.
Ald. C. E. LAPIERRE.

Ottawa ward.
Ald. C. S. O. BOUDREAULT.
Ald. E. GAUTHIER.

Rideau ward.
Ald. W. SHORT.
Ex-Ald. BREARY SLINN.

VOTERS, Attention !

For the board of control one vote for each of four candidates only is allowed and each ratepayer is requested to exercise his four votes. There must not be more than one cross (X) after each name voted on or the ballot will not be counted.

For aldermen only two are to be elected from each ward—instead of three as in the past—and if more than one cross (X) is applied after a candidate's name the ballot will not be counted—being spolled.

Ratepayers may however vote for aldermen in each ward they have the proper assessment.

January 4, 1908

as he was in perfect physical condition yesterday....

Mr. McDonald, who was with French at the time, when seen today, bore out the story in toto. French, says McDonald, was with a man named Jack Gouin, while he (McDonald) went into McCracken's store. When he came out, both Gouin and French were pale and trembling. "I'm going to fall dead," murmured French; "hold me." Both Gouin, who had partly recovered, and McDonald took the man home. He raved all yesterday afternoon about a man who stared at him with flaming eyes.

Although several others reported seeing the strange hypnotist around town over the next few days, the case was never solved. Or explained.

March 28, 1908
JEWELRY CLERK WAS A WOMAN
But Passed Herself Off as a Man Here.
STRANGE STORY
How the Real Sex of Clerk Was Found Out.

Some years ago a popular novelist named Gunter published a tale entitled *A Florida Enchantment* wherein a young man, by the simple process of swallowing a mysterious pearl, could change himself into a rather awkward young lady. The complications that arose in polite society when the transformation was affected and the young woman would absentmindedly fish out a cigar, place her feet on a table and attempt to strike a match formed, among other things, the basis of an amusing, if somewhat improbable, story.

Something along these lines recently happened in Ottawa. At least the main character, hero or heroine as the reader may prefer, evinced a strong liking for pearls and became enchanted with them to such an extent that she (better make it she right now) became a man in order to get as close to the plunder of the oyster burglars as possible. Else why should a young woman have her hair clipped short, don a coat, vest and a pair of—well, anyway, why should she, if it wasn't just to let the management of a big Sparks street jewelry store think that she was what she appeared to be, a nice neat, polite new clerk?

The management did think so and the new clerk with the small hands and the little trubies took his place (let's use the masculine gender; it may help make a man of this clerk) behind the show cases while the wise pearls blushed in their purple velvet pods. He was a big success, was the new and soft spoken young assistant, and the lady customers in particular seemed much attracted by his manners and general appearance.

And thus everything went off well until, after a while, numerous arti-

February 6, 1909

cles of jewelry began to disappear in the most mysterious way. The thefts, despite the utmost precaution kept up, to the consternation and chagrin of the staff who felt that their reputations and honor were being seriously compromised. None, moreover, seemed more distressed than the new man who was rapidly forming a pleasant circle of friends and whose conduct was above suspicion.

But one day a little trap was set and that same day a strange man visited the house where the pleasant clerk roomed and searched all over and found pearls and things. While he was looking at the jewelry and perhaps wishing that he had a cultivated taste like the person who lived there, the door opened and the clerk came in and asked him if he didn't think he had made an awful mistake and wasn't he in the wrong room? The stranger began to explain, but didn't get any further than saying he was a detective when the clerk dropped off in a dead faint. The detective—like all detectives—was warm-hearted and when he realized that he had been a little abrupt he got sorry and went to get some water to bathe the clerk's head. Besides, it is easier to walk down to the station with a friend than to have him like a lot of spare time hanging heavy on one's hands. So he went for the water.

But when the detective, rejoicing in his good deed as indeed he might seeing how sadly the profession is often misjudged, knelt down with a little prayer of thankfulness that he had been given the opportunity to be of some service to his fellowman, he experienced one of the greatest surprises in his long and romantic career. The detective was just about to percuss the patient when the clerk opened his mouth and uttered a scream. Even now when the whole thing is past and gone, the detective sometimes hears that scream in his troubled sleep and awakes to find his trembling limbs bathed in a dampened perspiration. He knew as soon as his trained ear heard the sound that it could not possibly emanate from any other but a female larynx.

There isn't much more to this story, which, considering the present price of paper, has already cost a good deal. The jewelry firm, whose place of business is located on the north side of Sparks street between Metcalfe and Elgin (no, not a word more, it wouldn't be fair) didn't care to prosecute under the circumstances; the police kept silent and the young lady left town. She didn't go back to Carleton Place because she had carried out her little plan successfully in that town before coming to Ottawa. Instead, she went to Ogdensburg where, rumour says, she has once more assumed the distinctive attire of the male clerk and is a popular man with the ladies.

May 23, 1908

CHILD CULTURE.

For several years, the Citizen *and the local Council of Women*

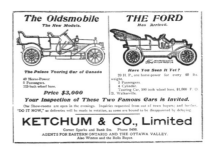

April 24, 1909

November 20, 1909

urged city council to create supervised playgrounds for children. The persistence paid off in 1912 with the opening of Gladstone Avenue Park. Here's an excerpt from an early Citizen *editorial on the idea, remarkably progressive for the times, and likely inspired by the Southam brothers' Christian Science beliefs.*

The greatness of a country is not found in its trade, but in its production of child life. The wisdom of a country is not to be gauged by its books, but by its care of its children. The defence and safety of a country is not in its army, but in its schools and other institutions that are designed to enlarge and improve the character of the child. At the base of all civilization and achievement is the babe, and wise indeed is the city and the country that recognizes the fact.

Not the least among these institutions is that of the modern city playground. Like oases in the desert, these green spots are appearing, each with its spring of joy for the refreshment of the children. In many cities may be found great playgrounds, with swings, ball fields and gymnastic apparatus, awaiting the boys and girls whose muscles are astir with the restless energy of young life.

Children are bound to play somewhere and somehow. The satisfaction of the play instinct is as essential as the satisfaction of the hunger instinct. Man may "be made to mourn," as some plaintive poet once put it, but the child was made to be joyful and make merry. The mere idea of discipline as being the thing of imperative importance in the training of the child is wholly wrong and foolish. Not repression, but expression, is the fundamental need. That a child does not work is never as serious as the fact that it does not play, and the truant boy, gambolling colt-like out of bounds, has in him more promise than the other boy who mopes through alleys on his way from school . . . .

Many of our modern cities take no cognizance whatever of the real needs of child life. They are built absolutely without regard to the demands of children. Everything is made to serve the purposes of business. Trade becomes a tyrant. Business blots out every fair spot. Vacant lots are fenced, or barred from use by prohibitive signs. Home grounds are so small that they just give the suggestiveness of the open, and the child's appetite for it, without adequately satisfying the desire.

Parks are not enough. Generally they are show places. Often they are absolutely useless from a child's standpoint, because of the lack of liberty. "Keep off the grass" is not a good sign, so far as the child is concerned. A park is to the child what the home parlor is, a place to sit primly where movement is dangerous. The child needs useable, scratchable, walk-on-able things and places.

And supervision is also absolutely needful. To permit children to engage in play in some faraway field, without any suggestion as to the

February 2, 1910

ethics of sport or inculcation of the ideal of playing fair, is the height of folly. Many a baseball field is sulphurous with oaths and foul speech. It may confidently be predicted that the time will come when every city will have its superintendent of amusements, who will have charge of the sports of the children of the city.

Let us be of the number awakening first to a consciousness of the imperative demand of the child upon us. Let us realize that no expense is too great if it secure greater privileges for the young citizens. Better is it that we lose our trade than that we lose the opportunity afforded us to make the life of the future stronger, healthier, happier, by giving to the child that which he needs today.

October 9, 1908
PESTERING THE BUSY HOUSEWIFE
Complaints of the Persistent Line of Pedlars
Who Haunt Front Doors and Flurry Women.
Tradesmen Too Suffer from Their Piracy.

The nuisance of the pedlar—it is a sort of ever continuing tragedy in Ottawa. Their persistence, impudence, and the amount of damage they do the domestic temper is incalculable—at least so householders and tradesmen combine in thinking.

A *Citizen* man came upon a woman Thursday who was vainly bidding a man with dirty boots and laden with wares, begone. The woman was guarding her own doorway and as the smile of the pedlar grew she cast an appealing look at his boots and at the reporter, to whom this state of affairs was no revelation. The housekeeper was only too pleased to open her mind on the subject of pedlars.

"I am simply tired to death of them," she said. "This is the third I have had at the door this morning. They're all the same, and if you hadn't come up in time I daresay I should have been obliged to buy something before he went."

"Is this morning's annoyance exceptional?"

"Oh, no; not at all. It is almost a daily occurrence, and the impudence of the men surpasses all bounds. They keep one running up and down the hall answering their rings and waste no end of time. Some talk English—others get terribly tangled in trying to talk it. I believe some of them adopt the broken style of talking in order to keep you at the door, listening to them a little longer. Of course there are genuine foreigners, and many of them. They speak all accents but Canadian and it takes about half an hour sometimes to understand their errand. After fathoming it one gets disgusted. I think I shall put in a claim against the town for repairs to the verandah, the damage being caused by countless of these fellows. They are absolutely wearing it away. Just look at the state it is in this morning."

July 5, 1910

September 13, 1910

Published by The Ottawa Citizen Co.,
Ltd., Ottawa, Canada.
Southam Limited, Proprietors.

TORONTO OFFICE:
Southam Press Building, Duncan Street.
F. W. Crabbe, Representative.

Advertising and Subscription Rates for
all editions on Page 4.

OTTAWA, SATURDAY, MAY 7, 1910.

EDWARD THE PEACEMAKER.

Not only the British Empire but the
civilized world mourns today the passing away of Edward the Peacemaker.
The ruler of millions of subjects, an
imposing figure in contemporary history, a wise and tolerant monarch,
has been called from the scene of his
earthly power and majesty.

The nation mourns today. But the
splendid consolation remains that
Edward VII. to the last upheld the
nobility and loftiness of character
that endeared him and the traditions
of his royal house to his people and to
the world.

To Britain's dead King, to his firmness of purpose and to his abhorrence
of injustice the peace of Europe is and
has been due. In his short reign of a
decade, national prejudices have in a
great measure been wiped out, the
differences of nations adjusted, and
the amity and harmony of a continent
assured.

Edward VII. has passed from earth,
but the world is the better for his
having lived. Surely no greater reward can be achieved by man.

May 7, 1910

The *Citizen* man looked and saw many mud marks and appreciated the woman had good cause for indignation.

"Work, worry and waste. That is what these fellows mean to the unfortunate householder."

Then she went indoors to attend to the neglected work and the reporter called at another house in the district. The tenant had little time to spare. "Oh, it's all true," she declared when he told her what he had heard. "I used to listen to them once upon a time, but I won't be bothered with them now. As soon as I discover what they are I shut the door promptly. Some are so impudent they commence ringing the bell.

"I once had a great fright from one fellow. It was a dark night and well on in the fall and all my boarders happened to be out. There came a ring and then the door was opened. I thought the ring was peculiar and went into the passage to see. It was a stranger—a pedlar—who seemed perfectly at home. Then the door opened—a welcome boarder came in, and the pedlar disappeared in wonderfully quick time. Such things are apt to make one nervous."

The reporter agreed, and called upon a tradesman. He had heard much of the pedlar—too much—and did not hesitate to condemn him as doing a great deal of harm to the trades people and taxpayers of the city. "I believe they pick up their goods in the market—who knows if not before hours. They get rid of a great deal of fruit, and I daresay their piracy has cost me many dollars, for I deal in fruit."

Similar complaints were made by other tradesmen and the *Citizen* man was curious to ascertain what sort of people the pedlars were. So he went down into the district they haunt and found them of a variety of types, their principal stock in trade being persistence. There were women and men of all nationalities. Mostly they live in groups all in one house. A particularly enterprising type was the dark Syrian woman.

Then when the *Citizen* man got down to write this article, a bearded, clean-looking man walked into the office and placed under his very nose a cardboard box full of weird buttons. He said he was from the old country, but had worked as a carpenter on the G.T.R. at Toronto for many years until an attack of locomotor ataxy disabled him. At the age of 64, he continued, he was obliged to find this method of gaining a living. He was not the sort who disturbed householders—his victims were the business men whom he caught at their offices. This was his story and the reporter asked him if he needed a license—not for the telling of the tale, but for the selling of the buttons. He smiled knowingly. "Did he need one?"

March 5, 1910

"SMOKING STRICTLY FORBIDDEN"

Ottawa Hockey Club Has Declared War Against Tobacco
for Tonight. Police Being Instructed To Eject Anyone
Found Using Cigars, Cigarettes or Pipe During Ottawa-Wanderer
Struggle. Smoke Would Spoil Match.

No smoking in the Arena this evening. The rule was made yesterday at a conference between the Ottawa Hockey Club and Manager Dey at the Arena. And it will be enforced to the letter.

It is not on this occasion a mere bluff at putting a stop to the nicotine nuisance; on the contrary it is a genuine, dyed-in-the-wool, O.K. crusade to stamp out the chief annoyance at hockey matches.

At a number of big games played in the local rink this winter the smoke, towards the close, has become so dense that one could not tell, from any distance, the players apart. When the weather was cool the smoke was not so conspicuous, but on damp nights it has been the source of a great deal of annoyance.

Hundreds have pleaded with the hockey club to put a stop to it, and if possible the lid will be put down tonight, the fact that it is going to be soft prompting Ottawa officers to issue the order. Consequently you may roast the referee, break the furniture or your neighbours' hats, cheer yourself hoarse, or split your gloves clapping; but you must not smoke. The "No Smoking" sign will be displayed bright and early, and anyone found enjoying the fragrant weed will be politely "bounced."

It is a good move, and the Ottawas deserve encouragement in their effort to stamp out the greatest existing hockey nuisance. Chief of Police Ross has instructed his men to be on the lookout, and bluecoats and plain clothes men will pass among the spectators at intervals with a view to stopping smoking should any be attempted. Ushers will be enrolled as special constables and—well, goodness only knows what isn't being done to put the smoker under cover for tonight at least.

There was plenty of grumbling, but the smoking ban worked—to a point. Many smokers, keeping a wary eye out for police, still lit up during the game. But the overall level of smoke was cut dramatically. A cigar smoker himself, owner Edwin Dey retained the ban in 1911.

March 10, 1910

LAST DAY WAS MEMORABLE ONE

Police Assisted in Handling the Murphy Gamble Crowds.
So Great Was The Rush in the Firm's Old Quarters.
Established in New Building This Morning.

The Ottawa housewife appreciates a bargain just as much as the housewife of any other city, but the way they invaded the old Murphy-

Coronation Day.

KING GEORGE V.

June 22, 1911

George V. Crowned to-morrow

The King!

In the days of George the Third, this welcome toast was pledged in many a glass of USHER'S WHISKY, and to-day the loyal subject, at home and abroad, in the same whisky, drinks to

HIS MAJESTY KING GEORGE V.

July 1, 1911

Gamble store yesterday afternoon proved too much for the big staff of clerks, and the aid of the police had to be summoned.

The store was packed with women, and for an hour and a half the doors were kept locked with the bluecoats on guard. By that time the immense crowd in the store had been served, and the doors were again opened to admit another throng.

At 5:40 yesterday afternoon the old Murphy-Gamble store was closed and at eight o'clock this morning the firm was ready for business in their handsome new block. There were large crowds in the new store today, and the management made special efforts to show everyone over the building.

Wednesday night the entire staff worked until midnight getting the stock in place in the new store, and this morning it was in perfect order. There was no stock lying around, and the very first customers were served with promptness and despatch. The entire block is occupied by Murphy-Gamble, and all except the top storey is now in use.

Just what is to be made of the top floor is as yet undecided. There has been some talk of a restaurant but just now that floor is being used as a stock room. The new store is well lighted and equipped with all the most modern cash and parcel-carrying devices.

*Even before it moved up the block to 118 Sparks St., the
Murphy-Gamble department store reflected the dominance
of Sparks Street as Ottawa's commercial centre. For years, the
store's top floor tea room was one of the city's social high spots.
The store was eventually sold to Simpson-Sears.*

June 13, 1910
BOY SENT TO BEG.
Arrest of Lad on Somerset Street Was Exciting.

The arrest of a boy on Somerset street, near Preston, on Saturday created a furor of excitement in that district. It appears that the boy had been sent out by his parents to beg. Constable Cooke, of the Children's Aid Society, discovered the game, and promptly got on the trail. The boy started to run, but the constable proved more fleet footed and soon had the little fellow in charge. The boy put up a desperate fight. A curious crowd consisting of the nearby residents and a score of boys on bicycles were interested onlookers. As the penalty for sending a boy out to beg is heavy it is probable that the case will be given an airing in the juvenile court on Wednesday. The boy, who is about nine years of age, is held at the detention home on Bronson avenue.

Hero of Aeroplane Flight
Across Straits of Florida.

JOHN McCURDY.

John Alexander Douglas McCurdy, the Canadian aviator, is a protege of Dr. Alexander Graham Bell, the inventor of the telephone. For the past few years McCurdy, with F. W. ("Casey") Baldwin, had been engaged at Baddeck, N.S., in experiments with heavier than air craft. The "Silver Dart" and "Baddeck No. 2," which came to grief in the trials at Petawawa two years ago, were the invention of Mr. McCurdy.

January 30, 1911

July 29, 1910
COCAINE VICTIM IN HULL TELLS POLICE
HOW DRUG IS OBTAINED.

Girl Under Arrest Confesses To Chief Marcoux That Man Who Claims To Be Doctor Issues Prescriptions for Cocaine Which Are Filled In Hull. A Father Tells of the Case of His Son. Said To Be More Than 300 In City Addicted To Drug.

That a man who poses as a qualified physician in Hull issues prescriptions for cocaine promiscuously to all who apply for it, and that the prescriptions are duly accepted by a Hull drug store, is the astonishing confession made to Chief Marcoux by a young girl who was arrested while in a crazed condition from the effects of the drug.

A *Citizen* reporter was present this morning while a girl giving the name of Leontine Lambert, Inkerman street, was questioned by the chief. She was still partially under the influence of the drug and presented a pitiful picture, being hysterical and the nervous twitching of the muscles of her face betraying to what an awful extent cocaine had obtained a hold on her.

The girl stated that she has been using the drug for over two years continuously and had first taken it at the suggestion of a girl friend of hers, who had recommended cocaine as a means of relief from illness. Questioned by the chief as to where she obtained the drug she became hysterical and for a time refused to make any statement, but after some hesitation she named a man in Hull who had supplied her with prescriptions which she had filled at a drug store there, the name of which she gave. She stated that the man had called himself a doctor, but investigation by the police indicates that he is not a qualified physician of the city.

Asked as to whether the "doctor" demanded any reason for supplying her with the drug, she said it was very easy to obtain it by simply saying she had trouble or was sick.

Miss Lambert stated that she obtained as much as $1.50 worth at the time. It was supplied in small pill boxes which would contain about half an ounce. The drug is in the form of a powder which is emptied onto the back of the hand and sniffed up the nostrils the same as tobacco snuff. She stated that it made her feel jolly and created a craving for cigarets. She said she was aware that it would kill her in time but did not care as long as she had the cocaine.

Chief Marcoux stated that the girl had been arrested at the instigation of her brother, who had tried in vain to stop her use of the drug. She was absolutely uncontrollable and violent when under its influence. The girl alleged that there were more than three hundred persons in the city who were addicted to the use of cocaine which could be easily obtained both in Ottawa and Hull, she said.

March 4, 1911

March 11, 1911

The *Citizen* reporter afterwards accompanied Chief Marcoux to a house on Bridge street, where a boy only 17 years of age has also been using the drug for over a year. On Thursday, while under the influence of cocaine, which his father states he obtains by stealing money from him, he was seized with a fit of rage and plunged his fist through a large window in his room, cutting his hand so badly that Dr. Tasse had to render aid, and even after the injured hand was bandaged he repeated the performance. The boy has spent six months in the Hull jail and his father states he can do nothing with him. The windows in the room were broken, the floor covered with blood and furniture smashed, showing the state of frenzy to which users of cocaine are brought.

Chief Marcoux will take immediate action on the information supplied by the Lambert girl and the arrest of the supposed doctor will shortly follow. He, however, expects great difficulty in bringing home the charge owing to the secrecy which is evinced by "cocaine fiends" who refuse in almost all cases to give any information of the person from whom they obtain the drug.

March 11, 1911

June 13, 1911
MOVING PICTURE SHOWS.

Regarding the local discussion whether moving pictures have a pernicious influence on the minds of their patrons, it is interesting to note that Wm. A. Brady, one of the shrewdest theatrical managers in the United States, does not hesitate to say that the moving picture theatre has reached its climax of popularity and that within a few years there will be 75 per cent less of these theatres, simply because the people will have tired of them.

Mr. Brady thinks that pantomimic performances will not satisfy the people for long especially as the figures are only representations of the originals. The moving picture lacks the ability to create what is technically known as "heart interest." The situations may be thrilling enough but the human element is missing and human sympathy cannot be invoked by the unreal.

We cannot agree. It is quite true that many of the subjects are more or less designed to make the task of following the story meant to be conveyed as easy as possible, that, in other words, they are hardly worth the time wasted in setting them out. But it is undeniable that the moving pictures have provided cheap, clean and altogether enjoyable relaxation for a large percentage of the people in every community. And invariably attacks upon them by well meaning but misinformed citizens have been shown to be without reason.

April 5, 1912
ABOLISH THE PIE

Although its owners were teetotallers and the paper refused
to accept liquor advertising, the Citizen *believed a proposal*
to restrict alcohol sales and consumption in Ontario was excessive,
as this satirical editorial suggests.

Some astute politician should bring in a bill to abolish the consumption of pie. It would meet a long felt want. It is impossible to estimate the suffering and misery that has been caused by pie. Some people can eat pie or let it alone; but there are thousands of otherwise respectable and useful citizens who ruin their digestions with pie and drag on a miserable existence as victims of dyspepsia.

Not only is it a case of unhappiness to themselves, but it has rendered many homes unhappy, because the dyspeptic victim of the pie habit is too often the cause of unhappiness in others. Pie, while not useful for medicinal purposes, is still a fascinating article of food, so long as it is used and not abused. However, so great is the number who fall victim to the consumption of pie and become dyspeptics, that those who use pie temperately must be prepared to consent to its abolition in the interests of the few who are carried away by this unfortunate appetite. As the consumption of pie is most prevalent in the country, it would be a matter of some difficulty to establish local option districts outside towns and cities. But in the latter there is no doubt that local option for the abolition of pie would secure a two-thirds vote, and this might lead to total prohibition of pie in the rural districts.

Public feeling has not yet been sufficiently educated to prohibit the manufacture and sale of pie, but the consumption might be seriously restricted by abolishing the pie counters. In any case a person detected in the act of selling pie to a minor should be prosecuted, and the pernicious habit of treating to pie should be made an offence punishable by fine and imprisonment, or both. The ravages of pie in the land are indicated by the widespread advertisements of patent medicines and cure-alls for the treatment of dyspepsia and kindred diseases, all directly or indirectly traceable to this unhappy appetite.

Unfortunately our time-serving politicians would shirk dealing directly and manfully with this issue, well knowing the storm of protest that would go up from the thoughtless majority, who by reason of superior will power or gastronomic strength, continue to revel in pie, careless of the well-being of their weaker brethren who fall victims to this pernicious edible. Some day, however, there will arise a courageous statesman who will take up the white man's burden of heavy piecrust and emancipate the nation from its ravages.

April 1, 1911

May 11, 1912

Back in the Game.

TL COBB, smiling because his suspen-
sion has been lifted by President
Ban Johnson of the American
League.

May 28, 1912

May 22, 1912

THE AUTOMOBILE PERIL.

*(Excerpt from an editorial. On most city streets,
the speed limit was 15 miles per hour in 1912.)*

The automobile season has not been long open, but already there have been entirely too many accidents in Ottawa due to carelessness or worse. At a late hour on Monday evening a machine said to have been travelling at the rate of forty miles an hour on Sussex street, dashed into a carriage, throwing the driver out on the street, while the automobile continued on its way without any attempt to ascertain what damage had been done, and the chauffeur's identity only discovered by aid of an eye witness.

Only a short time ago a driver knocked down and seriously injured an elderly lady and did the same trick, but luckily his number was noted and his apprehension secured. In this case the guilty person jumped his bail and disappeared. A few days later an automobile ran into a carriage standing at the curb and knocked over two ladies who were on the far side of it. On Monday a chauffeur was fined $50 and had his license cancelled for killing a cab horse.

Apparently the police magistrate is determined to deal severely with people who thus show disregard for the safety of the public, and especially in the case of automobilists who drive away from the scene of an accident in order to escape detection. It is a question whether joy riders who injure people and then endeavor to escape punishment by racing away, should be admitted to bail when apprehended. In doing so they place themselves beyond the pale of ordinary offenders and it is a just question whether fining has any effect on such reckless individuals. Accidents may happen in which the driver of the automobile is manifestly to blame, but if he stands by and shows a willingness to accept the responsibility of his act and make good the damage, he is entitled to the consideration which such action deserves. But joy riders who endanger lives and property by speeding and attempt to escape the consequences, should be treated no better than ordinary criminals.

Incidentally, the police might show more energy in the suppression of automobile speeding. There has been a great deal too much of it already this season, especially late in the evening on Sussex, Rideau, Bank and Elgin streets, and the Driveway. Yet the *Citizen* believes it is correct in saying, that except when an accident has occurred, there has not been a single case of prosecution on the part of the police....

June 15, 1912

THE ANTI-FLY CAMPAIGN GIVES BOYS AND GIRLS
CHANCE TO EARN MONEY.

Prizes Offered by Local Council of Women Should

Arouse Ottawa Children to Activity Against Household Pest.
War Will be Waged During First Two Weeks of July.
Some Useful Information on Most Effective Methods
of Fly-Catching. All "Catches" Will be Officially
Computed at the City Hall.

Arrangements are about completed for the great anti-fly campaign which the Public Health Committee of the Local Council of Women is inaugurating in Ottawa. It will officially open on July 1 and continue to July 15, though children may begin operations now if they wish.

Prizes are offered to children under 16 years of age who catch the greatest number of flies and produce them at the city hall, where the medical health officer is making arrangements to receive the proceeds of the hunt, weigh or measure them, and after computing the number take the names of the successful hunters. There are nine prizes in money allotted as follows:

First Prize	$10
Second Prize	$5
Three prizes, each	$2
Four prizes, each	$1

The rules governing the contest are very simple: Any method of fly-catching is permitted save the use of tanglefoot paper, and children are permitted to organize clubs. Judging from the demands made on the *Citizen* personally as well as by phone and letter for information regarding the competition and the most successful methods of capturing and exterminating the great household pest, Ottawa will this summer be a most unpopular resort for the fly.

There is to be no formality about getting into the contest. Just go to work and capture your flies. Then collect them in a can, bottle, box or other handy receptacle to be turned in at the city hall. The health officer will probably set an hour for the receipt of flies daily. Each consignment will be measured up and receipt given for the number of flies turned in. These receipts must be kept until the close of the contest.

One of the most effective methods of corralling the fly is the employment of traps, marvellous little wire screen houses to be baited with milk, wherein a fly once entrapped is doomed. These may be placed on porches, window sills, garbage pails or anywhere that flies are likely to congregate, but always on the outside of the house—always outside. Catch the fly outside the house before it has a chance to come inside and spread its poison and disease.

The number of ways in which flies can be caught is only limited by the ingenuity of the catcher. Poison, however, is another very good method—that is, fly poison—but perhaps one of the best killers is

OTTAWANS ON BOARD ILL-FATED STEAMER.

So far as is known there are four Ottawans on board the Empress of Ireland.

They are:

Mr. and Mrs. Edward Seybold. Mr. Seybold is one of Ottawa's best known citizens and president of the Eclipse Manufacturing Company.

Mr. and Mrs. J. W. Black. Mr. Black is an accountant at the J. R. Booth Co.'s works.

MR. EDWARD SEYBOLD.
Ottawan on board the Empress of Ireland.

May 29, 1912

made from a simple recipe which seems to be very tasty and therefore popular with the fly. It is made thus:

Beat together the yolk of one egg, one-third cupful of sweet milk, one level tablespoonful of sugar and a level teaspoonful of black pepper. Put on plates and set where flies abound. This is a very attractive fly dish and soon the floors will be found covered with dead flies, which should be collected at once.

Formalin is a very successful poison for flies and has been used extensively with excellent results. Probably the best way of using it is in milk, with the following proportions: One ounce (two tablespoonfuls) of formalin; 16 ounces (one pint) of equal parts milk and water. In this proportion the mixture seems to attract the flies much better than when used in sweetened water. The mixture should be exposed in shallow plates. A piece of bread in the middle of the plate furnishes more space for the flies to alight and feed and in this way serves to attract a greater number of them.

"I first used this poison in a milk room where the flies were very numerous, and poisoned over 6,000 flies in less than twenty-four hours on several occasions," says Prof. R. J. Smith, entomologist of the North Carolina agricultural station. "Over a pint of flies were swept up in this room each time the poison was used.

"Another experiment was used in a large calf barn where the flies were numerous. I exposed six ordinary sized plates of the formalin poison mixture and killed about forty thousand (four quarts of flies) between 12 o'clock noon and 8 the next morning. This is only an illustration of what can be done with formalin around the stables where flies are breeding. I could cite a number of cases where the formalin poison mixture has been used in unscreened kitchens and dining rooms and resulted in killing practically all the flies.

"A good place to use this formalin is on the front and back porches, where flies are frequently numerous and waiting to enter whenever the doors are opened."

Hundreds of children participated in this bizarre, and mostly ineffective, effort to lessen the spread of disease. The winner was a 14-year-old Lowertown lad who collected nearly 65,000 flies. Similar contests were held in communities across North America.

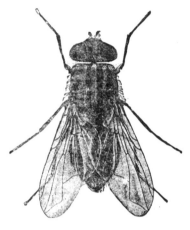

Here He Is! Swat Him!

July 1, 1912

January 16, 1913
A POLICEWOMAN TELLS OF HER SPECIAL WORK
Where Women Are Needed
In Police Work and Results of Innovation.
Small and slender where one would look for size and proportion; quiet and low voiced and above all essentially feminine is Mrs. Alice

Stebbins Wells, of Los Angeles, Cal., the first policewoman in America, who is here to lecture this evening in the Y.M.C.A. hall under the auspices of the Local Council of Women.

The comic supplement representation of the eagerness of all the men in a woman-policed town to be arrested must have some foundation in fact after all; Mrs. Wells is womanly in all her manifestations, so much so that one would scarcely credit to her her two years' record of police work on the Los Angeles department in the pursuit of which she has visited dance halls and cafes and served warrants on proprietors who have violated civic ordinances.

Mrs. Wells thinks Ottawa, too, should have its "women policemen," that is, policewomen. She expressed much interest in the police regulations of this city and was very pronounced in praise of the law which prevents the purchase of revolvers without a permit.

"I am the first regularly appointed policewoman in America," she said. "They are becoming more numerous now, however, and we have three on the Los Angeles force while other American cities have commenced to employ them. A police department is primarily a preventive agency and the real work of a policewoman is in preventing crime. The women and children with whom I deal are not necessarily criminals; I don't recognize the term. In the handling of women in various capacities there is need of women policemen and this includes the enforcement of police ordinances in places of amusement. It is not our idea to invade the field of men but to do that which we can do best.

July 8, 1912

"Have I ever arrested anybody? Yes, I have made arrests, though I do not attempt to apprehend men on the streets, but have never had any very exciting experiences; I avoid them as much as possible. I understand you have a law here prohibiting the sale of firearms without a permit. I must congratulate you very warmly on that; I think it is a distinct step forward.

"What is the proper proportion of women in a police force? Well, that depends largely on the nature of the problems you have to deal with. They will always be in a minority, of course, but in large cities there should be proportionately more of them than in small.

"You tell me you have a 16-year age limit in Ottawa for children attending moving picture shows unattended. Well, it is 14 years in Los Angeles and we enforce it very rigidly. We have the same trouble as you experience here of children seeking the company of chance strangers in order to procure admittance, but we have enforced the exercise of discretion on proprietors of such places by fining them when they admitted these children."

Ottawa hired its first policewoman in 1914.

March 10, 1913
THE SUICIDE OF THOR.
The practical idealism of the Southams and their editor,
Unitarian minister Charles Casson, ring everywhere in the
optimistic pre-World War One editorial excerpted here.

It has been popularly supposed that if ever Thor, the god of war, should die, it would be before the triumphant forces of the armies of Peace. And while this may be true in the larger sense, there are increasing signs that the end of war will come by reason of the suicide of Thor. War shall die by its own act.

Striking evidence of this is found in several quarters today. It is known by all that the war-debts of the past press heavily upon all nations. Every national debt is in large part caused by past expenditure for war, and every cent paid in interest is a reminder of its costly evil.

On July 15, 1910, Mr. Lloyd George, referring to naval expenditure, told the House of Commons that "the countries of the world are spending annually 450 million pounds upon this machinery of destruction. In twenty years there has been an increase of 200 millions per annum in this expenditure. All nations seem to be infected with an epidemic of prodigality, which seems to be sweeping over the world, and sweeping it to destruction." He might have added that Great Britain and Germany were responsible for 40 per cent of the whole naval cost, and every cent of it a tax on German and British toil. . . .

The most striking illustration is supplied by the most recent act of Germany in regard to her military development. In addition to extraordinary expenditures for naval purposes, which alone impose heavy burdens upon the people, the Emperor has announced that a special levy of several hundred millions will be raised for the improvement of fortifications and the army. This sum is to be paid by those having a capital exceeding $5,000, from one-half to one per cent of their possessions being practically forfeited for this militarist purpose.

The result of this latest act is just what one might have guessed. The protest against war is greater than ever before, and voiced by a class who have thus far not felt the direct pressure of the tribute burden. The taxation of fortunes is something hitherto undreamed of in times of peace, and its effect throughout the German Empire is said to be tremendous. It is further stated that many Germans are planning to leave the country to escape what they believe to be an unjust and needless imposition.

Then France, catching the militaristic fever of the time, has decided to increase the term of military service from two to three years, and to abolish the exemptions which before existed. While this manhood tax cannot be computed in money, it means a tremendous sacrifice and

HOW SEWAGE LEAKED ONTO THE INTAKE.

The men in the picture are standing on the concrete clear water pipe
Sewage is shown pouring from the leaky 12-inch sewer pipe embedded in the wall of the aqueduct.

September 5, 1912

expenditure. The men whose labor is thus withdrawn from industry must be supported, to say nothing of the direct loss suffered through their industrial inaction. A protest against this new military measure is certain to exist and to increase.

All of this means that the alarmist reports that come across the sea to Canada, telling of enormous expenditures for naval and military purposes, bring with them the secret germ of their own antidote. War is becoming so expensive a luxury that the people of any nation cannot afford it. And presently, under the stress of financial oppression, they will ask what it is all about, and discover the hollow absurdity of the whole thing. Every additional increase of military expense hastens the repudiation of war by the people who in every case constitute the life and will of the nation.

June 29, 1914

July 28, 1914
WAR IS DECLARED BY AUSTRIA.
FORMAL NOTICE SENT SERVIA TODAY SOON
AFTER COLLAPSE OF MEDIATION PLANS;
SERVIAN STEAMERS CAPTURED.
Royal Rescript Created Tremendous Excitement
in Hungarian Parliament and Members
Are Inflamed With War Spirit.
*The Evening Citizen announced the trigger that set off the
First World War in a series of bulletins from telegraph and news
agencies around the world. It was an approach that had been used
by newspapers to cover major events for the previous half century.
While it generally provided the scope of the news, it was
less satisfactory for readers looking for depth and analysis.*

LONDON, July 28.—Announcement of the declaration of war by Austria-Hungary on Servia came today almost immediately after Germany and Austria had notified Sir Edward Grey, the British foreign minister, of their refusal to attend a mediation conference.

It is assumed here that the efforts of the European nations will now be directed toward localizing the area of hostilities.

SERVIAN VESSELS SEIZED.

NISH, Servia, July 28.—The Servian steamers *Deligrad* and *Moravia* were seized today at Orsova on the Danube by Austrians. The Servian colors were hauled down and the Austrian flag hoisted. The passengers were detained.

ANOTHER RUMOR.

LONDON, July 28.—A newspaper despatch from Semlin, on the Danube, says the Servian parliament, after a prolonged debate, is reported to have accepted all the demands made by Austria-Hungary.

CAUSE OF CONFLICT.

LONDON, July 28.—The actual cause of Austria-Hungary's decision to enter into hostile conflict with Servia was the reply sent by the Balkan state to the note from Vienna demanding that Servia take steps to put a stop to the pan-Servian propaganda on Austrian territory and also punish these Servians indirectly concerned in the assassination in Bosnia on July 28 of Archduke Francis Ferdinand, heir to the Austro-Hungarian throne.

The response of Servia was considered by the foreign office in Vienna "unsatisfactory" and in a semi-official communication made public yesterday the Austro-Hungarian government said that the reply was "filled with the spirit of dishonesty."

WHEN WAR DECLARATION WAS ANNOUNCED.

NEW YORK, July 28.—(Wall Street, 2 p.m.)—Stocks were unloaded on an increasing scale when Austria's war declaration became known. Blocks of 1,000 to 3,000 shares changed hands and the whole market bent under the weight of the enormous offerings. International shares were forced down violently, selling orders pouring in from all quarters. Canadian Pacific lost almost 9 points and Union Pacific, Southern Pacific, Reading, Amalgamated and Smelting 3 to 5. The sharpness of the decline brought hurried support and prices rallied, but only temporarily.

THE OFFICIAL DECLARATION.

VIENNA, July 28.—The declaration of war was gazetted here late this afternoon. The text is as follows:

"The royal government of Servia not having replied in a satisfactory manner to the note remitted to it by the Austro-Hungarian minister in Belgrade on July 23, 1914, the imperial and royal government finds itself compelled to proceed itself to safe guard its rights and interests and to have recourse for this purpose to force of arms.

"Austria-Hungary considers itself therefore from this moment in a state of war with Servia. (Signed) Count Berchthold, Minister of Foreign Affairs of Austria-Hungary."

EXCITEMENT IN THE DIET.

BUDAPEST, July 28.—A great patriotic demonstration took place in the Hungarian diet today when the royal rescript was read proroguing parliament. The deputies cheered for the king, the country and the army. Speeches were made by prominent deputies during which every patriotic word was loudly applauded.

RUSSIAN TROOPS ADVANCE.

BERLIN, July 28.—An unconfirmed despatch from Gumbinnen, eastern Prussia, to the *Taegliche Rundschau* today says Russia has occupied Wirbatten, Russian Poland, with a force of engineers, cavalry, and

August 5, 1914

artillery while Russian guards have been placed along all roads on the frontier. The despatch adds that a squadron of German Uhlans has advanced to Eydtkyhnen on the Russian frontier.

August 7, 1914
THE GERMANS IN CANADA.
By the end of the war, the Citizen's *position on the treatment of Germans in Canada hardened considerably beyond the view expressed in this editorial, written two days after Canada entered the conflict.*

London is respecting the feelings and the material interests of Germans resident in the British capital. This is only what could be expected of a great people whose real character and sentiments are shown best in times of national stress or in face of unknown dangers.

Canada should not be less civilized. The destruction of a German consulate in one of our Pacific coast cities reflects no credit on either the community concerned nor on the Dominion. Germans in Canada are among our best citizens. They are hardworking, inoffensive and law abiding. In many centres, such as Ottawa, they are regarded as among our most intelligent ratepayers, taking a deep interest in municipal and other government.

It is only natural that Germans in Canada, or elsewhere, should retain much of their old affection for the fatherland. Irish and Scotch and English citizens are none the less desirable because of their old country attachments. It is likewise only human that the expatriated Germans in Canada should be interested to a more or less degree in the success of German arms abroad. If, therefore, our German fellow citizens should express themselves on occasion along these lines surely the people of Canada are big enough and intelligent enough to take all the facts into consideration, and instead of reviling and insulting good neighbors to overlook what is merely an indication of the love of country, which is world wide and exists in the breast of every real patriot however humble his situation in life may be.

Canada is too young a country to have completely assimilated its various elements. A generation form now the sons of old country or European nations will be Canadians in name and fact. To treat their fathers with respect, to honor them for their love of home, will do more towards making them and their children true lovers of this new country than all the legislation that could possibly be bestowed upon them.

August 11, 1914

"Your Heart Sounds All Right, Ottawa"

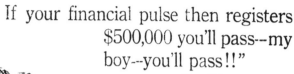

"BUT--we'll have to wait till the returns come in on Thursday night to see if it is in good working order.

If your financial pulse then registers $500,000 you'll pass--my boy--you'll pass!!"

Dr. Finance,
C.P.F. & R.C.

$500,000 in 3 Days---March 5-6-7

Thursday is the Last Day Let's run over the mark!!

$500,000 is what we are looking for as Ottawa's share--but --no harm will be done if we make it a lot more. In fact--the need is so much greater--and growing still greater--as the war progresses--that we cannot give too much. There is no nobler cause--as all the money is used in upbuilding and protecting against the ravages of war. The Patriotic Fund looking after the dependents of those fightng overseas--and the Red Cross Fund caring for the wounded and the sick.

All Together---Now---For a Red Hot Finish!!

The twenty teams of men and women workers have been working hard. They have been meeting with cheerful reception from all--as befits the great heart of Ottawa. It has been their intention to call on everybody--but if you have been overlooked--don't lose your opportunity to help. Sit down now and send in your cheque or promise to pay. Thursday is going to be a very busy day. With a final burst of enthusiasm all are going to do their best. Let us all show the "boys" abroad that the heart of Ottawa is in the right place--and working fine.

"See it through!!"

Canadian Patriotic & Red Cross

A Man for the Times

The Eighth Decade, 1915-1924

PROBABLY NO 10-YEAR span in the *Citizen's* history has been as packed with momentous events, at home and abroad, as the decade that began amid the ravages of war in Europe: 60,000 dead, 155,000 injured, conscription, Union government, parliamentary fire, influenza, Russian Revolution, Winnipeg strike, the emergence of Mackenzie King and radio and flappers, the heroics of King Clancy and Babe Ruth.

Harry Southam remained at the helm during the entire decade—Wilson stepped down as publisher in 1920—but increasingly the *Citizen* was being shaped by a doughty engineer who arrived almost by accident in late 1913. Fired from his job at the Department of Railways and Canals for being outspoken, Charles Bowman was departing for England to spend his severance when he was seized by a romantic notion. He dropped into the *Citizen* to ask whether the paper might like some articles from overseas. Within a year, he was lead editorial writer; within two, he was the paper's editor. Before he left the job an astonishing 30 years later, he'd befriended five prime ministers, served on two royal commissions and influenced the policies of a dozen ministries. He'd nudged the *Citizen* away from its 60-year association with the Conservatives and, for an unsteady moment, into the arms of Social Creditism. And he'd hired the journalists—E. W. Harrold, Austin Cross, A. C. Cummings, Jack Scott, Isabel Armstrong, Jack Koffman—whose writing drove the paper until well after the Second World War.

In Bowman, raised in a British family with trade labour sympathies, the Southams had found a man with the skill and charm to turn the *Citizen's* editorial pages into a place where liberal, even radical, views were welcome. His crusades against war production patronage earned him the enmity of Tory ministers but the admiration of Prime Minister

Still Getting Them.

"Babe" Ruth, great slugger of the New York Yankees, who is keeping his team up in the American League pennant race. He slammed out two homers yesterday and made his record to date 41.

August 7, 1920

Opposite: Ads to raise funds for the war effort were a recurring feature in the Citizen's eighth decade. This one appeared March 1, 1918.

Robert Borden. And his innovative suggestions to lessen the distrust between Tories and Liberals helped to create the wartime Union government.

The decade also brought the end of the *Free Press*—after 48 years, it was absorbed by the *Journal* in 1917—and the start of the era of the two (English-language) newspaper town, a situation which remained, more or less, into the 21st century. Unlike the bitter rivalry that characterized relations between the *Citizen* and *Journal* after 1950, the two actually entered a partnership in 1917 to end cutthroat competition. For two years, they each held 40 per cent of the other's stock. For 30 years, they operated a bureau that controlled the circulation of both papers and, even more remarkably, entered an agreement to share advertising profits. The arrangement, which Southam family historian Charles Bruce later called an "armed truce," allowed both papers a level of stability that would sustain them for decades to come.

SURROUNDED, FIGHTING BACK TO BACK, THE CANADIANS ALONE STOPPED THE GERMAN ONRUSH

British Correspondents Tell How the Canadian Soldiers, When the French Line Was Forced to Break by the Poisonous Gases Used by the Enemy, Were Attacked on All Sides but Managed to Hold Their Lines and Force the Germans Back, Retaking Captured Guns.

(Canadian Associated Press Cable.) LONDON, April 25.—Under the caption of "avenging Canadians" the Morning Post correspondent describing Friday's engagement says: "This battle is unique as being the first great event of its kind in the history of Canada, for Canadian troops can claim it as their own and the glory of it. They were holding the extreme left of the British line preparing the ground. By means of their poison bombs the Germans driving through Langemarck and Pilkem forced a passage across the canal between Stenstraet and Hetsas, reaching the village of Lizerne. "French Zouaves and Fusiliers Marines with Belgian Carabiniers, caught in the stupefying fumes of gas bombs, were taken at a disadvantage and despite valiant efforts of their supporting lines were forced to give way. Pouring their masses across the canal, the German then swung to their left and attacked a considerable portion of Canadian

the division of Canadians held in reserve to the north of Ypres. The division was compelled to retire, leaving the four guns in enemy hands but the troops responded to the call with a magnificent dash and spirit and with two brilliant bayonet charges they forced the enemy to retreat in disorder. They not only recovered the lost guns but took many prisoners and drove the enemy out of Pilkem. Such deeds cannot be done without heavy loss and the loss of the Canadians in this brilliant action are heavy." The whole of Paris press pays homage this morning to the admirable and marvellous dash of the "glorious Canadian contingent." Lord Charles Beresford, inspecting the Northamptonshire volunteers yesterday said their hearts had been thrilled by the story of the gallantry of the Canadians. "The Canadians saved the day," he said, "and the story of their glorious achievement would run through the Empire, giving a fresh stimulus to our patriotic sons across the sea." They

April 26, 1915

March 13, 1915

OTTAWA SHOULD BE NATIONAL SCHOOL OF TOWN PLANNING.

A Beacon to Sociological Betterment, as Experimental Farm is to Agriculture. Opportunity for a Splendid Park System Here at a Relatively Low Cost.

Soon after becoming lead editorial writer, Charles Bowman convinced one of Canada's pre-eminent urban planners to pen a regular column for the Citizen. *Noulan Cauchon, an exponent of the theory that beautiful surroundings breed a healthy population, later became Ottawa's chief planner. His 1922 report was the first to advocate the creation of federal capital district.*

BY NOULAN CAUCHON

One of the needs of the present and no less a requirement of the future is a system of adequate parks—breathing spaces; lungs for the city as they are sometimes called. Ottawa, destined to be the show place of the nation, must have the best that can be devised and obtained—and treated in the most efficient and effective manner.

Ottawa in fact should be our national school of town planning, a beacon to sociological betterment as the experimental farm is to agriculture. This does not mean making spectacular plans to be pigeonholed but a permanent and competent body to plan practically and see to its carrying out—continuously on the watch to safeguard public interests.

Under the most approved modern view, the functions of parks and parkways are also for the ventilation of a city. They should encircle the city like ramparts against congestion and disease—providing therewith rest and recuperation for the tired and repose for the weary.

Apart from encircling parkways, long wedges of parks should con-
verge toward the centre, less and less so as they widen and recede towards open country till they revert to primitive forest. A system of numerous such park wedges bound together by hands of encircling parkways, the whole reached at convenient points by adequate transportation, constitutes ideal conditions.

Ottawa has the opportunity for a splendid system at relatively low
initial cost. As referred to many times and pointed out at lectures, on
the topographical maps of the district there are a certain number of
high areas disposed in a circle around the city. These areas constitut-
ing elevations of 300 feet and over above sea level are, in the nature of
things, particularly fitted for park purposes. These high areas will always remain at a disadvantage for water pressure for domestic and
particularly for fire purposes—therefore least desirable for building
purposes, but by reason of their very elevation particularly desirable
for parks. They are cheaper lands to purchase from lack of possible
proper domestic use and fire fighting facilities.

There are also other areas within the city which by reason of low-
ness lack facility of easy drainage—drainage that would require un-
warranted general city expense and perpetual pumping of sewage.
Such low areas should likewise be expropriated for park purposes.
There is an area in Ottawa South and portions of Ottawa East and also
facing both these districts across the Rideau River, all of which suffer
from floods, which could to better advantage be developed as modern
prototypes of Venice—be converted into parks with islands and
dredged channels for "canoedling."

The successful treatment of parks in this fashion is well known and
its peculiar charms appreciated by those who are familiar with Belle
Isle park in Detroit. There, hundreds of canoes and their pleasure
seeking occupants may be seen thronging the flower-bordered channels and sometimes congregating in wider water areas to listen to civic
music. Here is a vision for Rideau River Valley in Ottawa South and
East: consider the advances of adapting the low lands in such a manner
that this system of water parks could be connected with the Rideau
River, itself improved by dikes and dams so that one could canoe or
"put-put" from Porter's Island to Bronson avenue, about five and a half
miles of lake, and in the many pleasure channels suggested for the park
embellishment of the low lands.

Adjuncts to such a park would be botanical gardens, a zoo and aquar-
iums. It is not necessary, nor is it contended, that these things should
be undertaken at once—let them however be kept in view and planned
for and all things be broadly determined and buildings prohibited
where the city would have to pay for and pull them down later on. The
areas mentioned for great circle parks and parkways and swamp lands

WIDE EULOGY
OF CANADIANS
NEW TRIBUTES

F u r t h e r List Casualties
Among Officers. Names
of the Men Begin to
Filter In.

After four days of continuous
fighting, the Canadian division was
in reserve yesterday, according to a
cable from Col. J. J. Carrick, M.P.,
to the minister of militia.

The list of casualties which continues to filter through from the
front furnishes additional evidence
of the intense character of the fighting north of Ypres. The fact that
several officers of the 15th battalion
appear in the list disposes of the
rumor that this regiment, which had
not figured previously in the casualty list, had fallen captured into
the hands of the Germans.

Col. Carrick wired General Hughes
—"Canadians covered themselves
with glory. Their heroism most
highly appreciated at headquarters.
In reserve today."

April 27, 1915

reclamation would not exceed roundly about five thousand acres.

The scheme of parks outlined for the south side of the Ottawa River comprises a semi-circle beginning below the Rockcliffe rifle ranges and following for many miles a southerly arc ending up at Britannia.

There will eventually be a crossing from Britannia to Deschenes, the most westerly point feasible for many miles, and then the parkway would run from the crossing up to the five hundred foot level and follow the crest of it in its natural curve towards the foot of the mountain back of Fairy Lake. From that point there are two routes back to the Ottawa river which should both be taken. The first comes down the valley by the lake known as Fairy Glen—right into the city of Hull—and the second runs from the mountain easterly towards the river ....

Town planning is a matter for ceaseless activity—not just to plan things right for once—but to keep them going right all the time. It is the broad principle of self preservation in its many manifestations.

June 30, 1915
WAR AND ITS CAUSES.
Bowman's upbringing in a family with British labour sympathies was often reflected in his editorials about the war, as this excerpt shows:

A year ago a poor misguided man killed a pampered, hereditary crown prince and his wife, and thereby ignited a fuse, which, in burning, has caused the explosion of thousands of tons of ammunition, killing and maiming hundreds of thousands of men. The fuse still burns, and its burning may ultimately cause the destruction of the lives of more than a million men, women and children. Not one of these people who have been killed, or who are going to be killed, has desired that any of his fellow men be killed.

What has caused, and is causing, this destruction of life? Why does not someone extinguish or destroy the deadly fuse? Is it not because the majority of the leaders of the people who live in the countries now at war fear the burning of the fuse less than they fear its extinguishment? There can only be one reason that can justify men to carry on war, and that is that they believe by means of it, life and happiness can be sustained in the future by a lessening expenditure of effort. Therefore, the problem of the abolition of warfare can find a solution only in a method to satisfy as nearly as possible the appetite of mankind with the expenditure of the least possible effort.

Human experience has shown that the least effort is required of men towards satisfying their appetites when the labor of some is applied to produce one kind of product and the labor of others to produce other kinds, and these products are exchanged. Is it not absurd that almost all of the inhabitants of Europe are divided into two great camps, both striving to their utmost to destroy not only the products of labor that they could exchange but to destroy life—potential labor—the product-use of which could be exchanged, and thereby also help satisfy the appetites of the belligerents?

What is it that the inhabitants of one country want that belong to another? It is not the possession of persons—the day of slavery has passed. It is not the possession of the product of labor—the day of piracy is over. It can only be the right to trade with the inhabitants of other countries, by the expenditure of less effort, for the possession of the products of labor and the privilege of using land. Therefore, each of the nations at war must believe that, after the coming of peace, trade will be carried on by its inhabitants with less expenditure of effort than if the nation had not engaged in the war.

It is the day of restricted and fostered trade, and this war is being waged because some men want to have advantage in trade over others, either through lessening of comparative restrictions of trade or through comparative advantage in the fostering of trade. In other words, the people of each nation at war are fighting for the purpose of making the people of other nations, to a greater or less extent, trade slaves, and to obtain for themselves the loot that they expect will result from this trade slavery. Thus, Europe is fighting to enlarge national boundaries so that men in some countries will be forced by men in others to trade the product of their labor.

Nations cannot trade freely so long as taxes are collected upon that part of the value of the product of labor which is caused by the individual performing the labor. Nor can men trade freely so long as any of them possess the power to collect, through trading of the product of their labor, any value not created by that labor. Wars and rebellions will continue to occur until trade is free, and in order for that, society must collect and use for social purposes all of the values created by it.

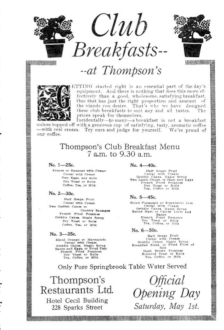

May 1, 1915

July 10, 1915

WHEN YOU PROPOSE.

(A Complete Guide to Openers
for the Use of Tactful Persons.)

"Shall I draw my chair closer? I am afraid that what I am about to say to you, if overheard by others, might be the cause of vulgar comment."

"Do you remember the first day we met? Ah! How vividly it rises to my mind! Well, since then——"

"Don't be startled, but would you mind if I called you darling?"

"Doesn't it seem rather warm to you? But perhaps I feel it more because I am about to perform an action which has the most momentous consequences of a lifetime—for both of us."

"Do you know this is the twenty-third call I have made? I suppose we must both begin to realize that this cannot go on forever. Well, dear—"

"How cold your hand is tonight! Ha! It isn't much like my heart I can tell you! Speaking of hearts——"

" I hope you don't mind my coming so early. But the fact is, I have a terrible evening before me. That is, I mean —oh——"

"Struggle as I will I can no longer conceal from you the fact that——"

"Isn't that a new rug? Oh, no! You must pardon me but ever since we first met, nothing has looked the same to me. And now...."

April 3, 1916

PEOPLE LIVE IN HOUSES THAT ARE NO CREDIT
TO THE CAPITAL.

Families Who Perforce Can't Pay High Rents Have
To Put Up with Unsightly, Cold, Damp
and Dilapidated Dwellings. Specific Instances.

There are many houses in Ottawa which are no credit to the capital city of Canada. People live in them and pay rent, but any rent is high for such houses. A *Citizen* tour reveals the fact, however, that there has been an improvement in housing conditions over those which existed not so very long ago. The health department of the city has been active, as is indicated by the great number of houses which have been closed up and labeled "insanitary." Nevertheless, there are many still inhabited which are not worthy of the name of dwelling houses and are certainly not conducive to health and happiness.

One of the worst examples of bad housing was discovered not far from St. Patrick street. Here is a court, a parallel to which it would be hard to find. There are half a dozen tenements and five families occupy rooms, the sixth being empty. The approach is through a morass of half-melted snow and the accumulations of the winter. The sun does not penetrate, save at high noon. In one of these places an Italian household lives. There are ten of them in the four-roomed "apartment," access to which is gained up a creaking stairway. The ceilings are low and little light and air can get in. The verandah of this section is a menace to life and limb. The rent is $10.

Below, a French-Canadian family lives in three rooms which on a sunny afternoon are dark and dismal. The lady of the house said it had been awfully cold through the winter and the water pipes had frozen whenever there was a severe cold spell. It was reached by stepping over a pool of water bridged by pieces of timber. The rooms were low and the air humid. There were three other families, two on the ground and one on the upper floor, each in a poor condition. Many of the windows would not open, and the walls were peeling. The rents for apartments in this rookery were $10, $11 and $12.

Another bad example was a house in a row of four in which there were two rooms down stairs and two up, occupied by a family of six. The rent was $14. There was no cellar and the floors and walls were damp. The upstairs rooms were reached by a ladder-like flight of stairs and the roof was so low that on the side one had to bend down to move about. There was a shed at the rear which was called a summer kitchen. It was occupied by a French-speaking family which sat round the stove in the middle of the two down stairs rooms.

Not far from the one just mentioned were several other rows of "houses" several of which had "to let" signs on them, although they looked like anything but fit for occupation. The rent of the houses was $10 for four rooms. Quite a few windows were missing and through these could be seen dark rooms with discolored walls and ceilings, with the paper off in many places and an appearance of dampness.

In a row of timber structures which looked as if a good puff of wind would blow them down, the roof was in a bad condition, but a pile of shingles on the sidewalk intimated that the owner was at last going to put on a much needed new roof.

There were many other places the appearance of which condemned them. Many of the occupants were very reluctant to say anything for fear of "getting in the wrong" with those "higher up." There are scores of houses which are allowed to be occupied simply because they comply with the requirements of the law in having inside sanitary arrangements, and not because they are decent places to live in.

May 10, 1915

September 13, 1916

CANADIANS' GRAVES BY THE WAYSIDE.

Capt. Rex Vickers Writes of a Trip Up

to the Front and His Introduction to Enemy Shellfire.

Mr. H. H. Vickers, 420 Gilmour street, has received an interesting descriptive letter from his son, Capt. Rex Vickers, who is at the front with an ammunition column. He writes—

"I am writing this letter to you in order that you may have a fair idea of what things are like and how wonderful and yet dreadful everything is. In this job after you know the lay of things, you choose where to go and the best time. Everything is done at a certain time both by us and the Germans, so you can pretty well pick your way.

"The other day I got word from the trench mortar battery that some of their men had come out of the trenches and would I come up and pay them. They are closer up than we are. I went up in the afternoon with another officer from the column and paid them. We got word that things were rather quiet up the line, so we decided to go up and see just what the front was like. I will try and tell you just as much as I can in keeping with censorship.

"It was about 6.30 when we started (on horseback with our grooms.)

Major C. L. Sharman and Lieut. H. T. C. Whitley of 1st Artillery Brigade in the Casualty List.

The following casualties among officers were reported last night in a private cable to Major Gen. Hughes, minister of militia:

1ST BATTALION.
REPORTED WOUNDED, NOW RE-PORTED NOT WOUNDED.
Capt. G. J. L. Smith, Chatham.
WOUNDED.
Lieut. F. J. G. Chadwick, Moncton.
5TH BATTALION.
MISSING.
Lieut. W. M. Hart, M.D.

1st BRIGADE, FIELD ARTILLERY
MISSING.
Major C. L. Sharman, Ottawa.
Lieut. H. T. C. Whitley, Ottawa.
MAJOR C. H. L. SHARMAN.

Major Chas. H. L. Sharman, who is reported missing was the com-mander of the 2nd field battery when the war broke out and was one of the leading officers of the Can-adian artillery. His father lives in England but Major Sharman came to Canada when a young man and serv-ed for a time in the North West Mounted police. He later came to Ottawa, where he entered the civil service and rose to the position of chief clerk in the health of animals branch of the agricultural depart-ment. He joined the 2nd battery as a lieutenant and was later promoted

January 3, 1916

We had our gas helmets with us, of course, and a shrapnel helmet, something like a tin wash basin. We had to wind in and out, and as we went up on each side of the road you could see the small graves each with a little wooden cross of the Canadians who had fallen. One had the broken propeller of a plane (which had been brought down) stuck up to form a cross to mark the poor chap's resting place. On these graves nearly all have a sealed bottle with the name, etc., inside on a bit of paper to identify them.

"All the way up you could see the marks of war. Big farms and fine houses deserted and most of them blown to bits. After we had gone a mile or so we got off our horses and left them with the grooms at an old chateau which is now an advance dressing station. Our own batter-ies were in the fields around here, and the horses don't take to it very kindly when they fire. We walked up. On each side of the road the shell holes were almost close enough to jump one to the other. Under every bush and in every field there seemed to be one of our guns. One by one they started to bark, sometimes several at a time, which would almost deafen you. And then on the next road to us, which was about two city blocks away, and is quite noted for its shelling, Fritz started to drop them in. You could hear them whistling through the air and then— bang! and a pale, yellowish-green cloud of smoke would rise up. It was very wonderful to see them.

"This was shrapnel bursting just above the road, so we went on up the road we were on. Then a few high explosives fell also and you would see the earth fly up. Nearly every tree around was dead or on its way or blown down. We then came to the outskirts of the city that was what we were going to see. You would not imagine how lonely and dreadful that place looked. Can you imagine a city about the size of Ot-tawa with not a person or house or building of any kind with four walls standing, and debris piled each side of the road? Then we came to the centre of the place and it was even worse. We went into the ruins of an old hall, one of the grand old places you hear about. Your heart would have broken to have seen it.

"Those flying corps men are all flying right over our heads, they are banging away above with the high explosive and it would make the shivers run up your neck (if shivers ever do that.)

"Then the evening "hate" started. Our batteries opened up and you could feel the earth shake under your feet, and of course Fritz came back with some also. So by this time we thought it time to clear out, as we had no dug-out to get into. On the way back we passed a large building which seemed in a little worse shape than the rest, so we looked in. In the centre one of those huge German shells had landed. It made a hole about forty feet across and looked like a young lake. It had cleared the entire centre of the building out. Down in the basement of some of the buildings (they would be reinforced with sandbags) you could see a little group of chaps playing poker or something of that nature. You see, it's not such a bad little war after all.

"We sent word to one of the seconds to send a man to us with a sleeping outfit. They got it twisted up and the fellow arrived with a broom and shovel. The captain asked, "What in blazes is that for?" (we talk that way at war.) And he said he was to report to us with "sweeping outfit." Some army!"

April 10, 1917
CANADIAN TROOPS CARRIED FAMOUS
VIMY RIDGE. GREATEST CONCENTRATION
OF GUNS SINCE WAR BEGAN, BOOMED OUT
AS BRITISH AND CANADIANS "WENT OVER."
After an Oppressive Silence, Timed to the Minute,
Hundreds Upon Hundreds of Pieces Broke Loose
in the Greatest of Cannonades. The Entire Country-side
Became an Inferno That Dazed and Stupefied the Germans.
*The identity of the "staff correspondent" who filed this gripping
story from the front at Vimy Ridge is unclear. It is possible
the writer was engaged by the Southam company on behalf of its four
newspapers (in Hamilton, Calgary, Vancouver and Ottawa).
More certain is that the writer obtained some of his information
from former* Citizen *editor E. W. B. Morrison, the major-general
who led the Canadian artillery assault at Vimy Ridge.*

(From a Staff Correspondent.)
WITH THE BRITISH ARMIES IN FRANCE, via London, April 9.— The war on the western front which has been moving more rapidly in the past five weeks broke into full swing today. Widening their attacks which they have been directing against the retreating Germans in the sector of the Somme, the British, Canadian and Scottish armies struck still farther north, and in a series of assaults on a broad front, with Arras more or less the pivotal point, they drove the Germans from scores of important positions, penetrated far in to the enemy lines and inflicted heavy casualties.

April 11, 1917

A visit to corps headquarters this afternoon indicated that the number of prisoners taken in the past 12 hours will exceed five thousand. The barbed wire "cages" or compounds built to receive prisoners, which were expected to be taken, were overcrowded long before noon, although the principal attack did not begin until shortly after dawn.

The heaviest fighting today developed along a line from a few miles southeast of Arras in a northerly direction to the neighborhood of Lens, but the actions extended far south, in the direction of St.

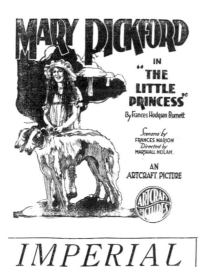

Quentin. The fighting on Vimy Ridge was carried out by the Canadians, who had retained a footing on the ridge all winter, but always higher up was the enemy. On either side of the Canadians were English and Scottish battalions, and in today's battle there was glory for all.

One position captured to the north of Arras was a sort of labyrinth of trenches enmeshed in multiple bands of wire, called "the harp" because of its shape. Prisoners had proclaimed this strong point practically unassailable, but, sweeping over it today, the British took within it nearly a thousand prisoners, and they captured also during the day, three German battalion commanders, who compare in rank to colonels in the British army. The Canadians took two thousand prisoners.

It was said everywhere along the attacking line, that the Germans appeared to have been taken by surprise, and only in a few instances did they put up a strong fight. One reason for this was that they had been fairly dazed by the British artillery fire of the past ten days.

From the high ground, overlooking Arras, a panoramic view for many miles of the British attack was presented. The concentration of guns for this operation was probably the greatest, for a given amount of front, since the war began. Almost countless guns had taken part in the bombardment, since the beginning, but it was not until last night that many masked batteries joined in the grim chorus.

Approaching the battlefield well before dawn, the reflection of the gunflashes against the low hanging clouds gave the inevitable impression of a continuous play of sheet lightning along the horizon. But when this wonderful night picture of modern warfare came into full view, it seemed as if suddenly one stood on the brink of an overwhelming inferno. Looking down into the valley, tongues of flame could be seen flashing from hundreds upon hundreds of gun mouths, like so many white-hot serpents' fangs. The guns were playing upon the ridges looming up in the distance enveloped in darkness, upon which lay the German lines. There was, as yet, no alarm. The Germans had become accustomed to receive daylight strafes from the British and they were sending up only routine star shells and trench flares.

As dawn approached, the British batteries one by one became strangely silent. For half an hour, the stillness was almost oppressive. The hot pit flashes disappeared. All this time, however, the German star shells and flares were ascending with the same monotonous regularity which marks the German positions along the entire front. The glorious weather of Easter Sunday had disappeared, and from menacing black clouds overhead, rain began to fall. It was driven along by a stinging gale left over from the abundant storms of March. The storm delayed the coming of dawn to such an extent that it was still quite dark when the moment set for the British attack arrived.

Then, as if the myriad of guns had been synchronized to the tick of a watch, they broke the foreboding stillness with a volcanic roar. The earth trembled from the shock. The licking tongues of the inferno appeared now to have been multiplied a hundredfold. The objective hills began to writhe under the tortures of the screaming shells. Most of the distress rockets burst to great showers of golden rain; others looped high into the air and broke into flaming balls of red and green. It was difficult to realize that this was not simply a stupendous, almost supernatural, pyrotechnic spectacle, arranged for the pleasure of the Gods. It was more difficult still, to realize that it was the actual reality of war and that the thousands of flashes and quick flames, playing into the dawn, were funeral torches lighting the way of souls into eternity.

From the moment the great crater erupted along the horizon, the whole world seemed red. Under the glare of exploding mines, which had been dug under the enemy lines, and out under the shells could be seen the British soldiers trudging—trudging, across No Man's Land to a hand-to-hand encounter with the Germans. They moved closely behind the protecting shell curtain sent up by their guns.

As this barrier fire moved forward, the men kept pace. It will ever be an amazing feature of this war, the absolutely cold valor with which the men go into action. Never the old shouting or the impulsive rush to victory—just a slow, deliberate trudge, not more than two or three men grouped, and each silent, with his own thoughts, until actual fighting with the hitherto unseen foe begins. Then it is a quick surrender, a shot or a bayonet thrust, and the attacking wave moves on.

The coming of day changed the magic pictures of night completely, and with almost naked suddenness. Now the horizon was dull, with accumulated smoke. Shells, which had burst into pillars of fire by night, now appeared as black fountains springing from the earth. There was an occasional flash to the shrapnel bursts, but generally they flew in, merely as puff balls of smoke. The roar, however, was always the same.

The sun broke through the clouds just before noon, as the British were breaking through the third and fourth German lines.

July 10, 1918
GREASE TO ELBOWS AND SMUDGE OVER EYES,
OTTAWA GIRLS LEARN MECHANICS.
(Excerpt from a feature story.)

Not so many years ago, men scoffed at the idea, some women laughed and went on with their teas and tangoes, but a few just looked wise and with their visionary minds saw into the future and visualized the possibility, not so very remote, of female Henry Fords and a lady Thomas Edison, despite the prevalent incredulity about feminine minds grasping the mechanism of anything more complicated than a sewing machine or a fireless cooker.

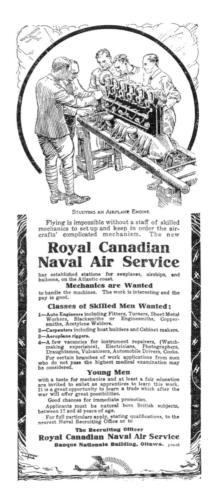

October 14, 1918

October 14, 1918

The war and the consequent opening up of man-manipulated industries to women, of course, exploded this theory of the skeptics, and . . . . women covered up their petticoats with coarse, practical jeans and veritably dug into the mechanical world, grease, dirt and all, with patriotic vim. Today the scoffers bow with admiration, the tea tangoers have cast aside their useless flippancies, and many have joined the ever increasing army of women who are working behind the men behind the guns.

But not until the mechanical transport class for girls started was Ottawa able to boast of her part in this world-wide move. Can you imagine fourteen of the city's "youngest and fairest," whom one used to watch daintily pouring tea at the Chateau or skirting the ballroom in ante-bellum days, inside of a pair of dusty khaki or navy blue overalls, sleeves rolled up and grease, yes, black, greasy grease, almost up to the elbows, with a smudge over one eye, and a streak on the back of the neck that used to carry a circlet of pearls? This is what these girls are doing twice a week over in the Mechanical Transport headquarters on Albert street. And because Major Cameron, who is their instructor, has been so thorough in his work, every one of these girls knows every one of the 4,980 parts that the ordinary motor car is credited with, can take them all apart and put them together again, from removing the full floating axle in the differential on a Ford or Briscoe chassis to dissecting the steering wheel.

It's all real work, too, and everyone in the class is as earnest about it as a good soldier in the army. Altogether they have had five lessons on the practical side of the work, which was preceded by a lecture course, and not one of the girls would miss a class without the greatest of provocation.

"I'd rather do this than eat," said one girl last night, and that just about sums up the enthusiasm that prevails and which, in the end, will no doubt do much to influence the Canadian government that they mean business and want to be recognized. They are eager, anxious to do their bit in this mechanical line—the same as the girls in England and the United States are doing, and although the class is unofficial as far as the government is concerned they are determined to put their knowledge into patriotic usage . . . .

To prove their sincerity and bulldog determination, the whole class has signed up with Lieut. Bowen at the base recruiting office for mechanical transport work in Canada in order to release men for the same work in France.

Some of these girls never drove a car before in their lives, many of them did nothing more strenuous than a few homely duties, or coaxing a golf ball over a bunker, before the war . . . but they all caress carburetors, axles, radiators, steering gears, valves, differentials, and the countless other queer looking nuts and bolts that make the wheels go around in a buzz wagon that formerly would have meant so much junk to them. Handling a monkey wrench comes as quick and naturally as wielding a pair of ivory knitting needles, and timing valves is not more trouble than turning a heel and "purling two."

Did you ever see a lot of bees around a comb of honey? That's just what these mechanicesses looked like last night in their blue print bordered workshop digging into the vitals of a Ford, Briscoe and Russell chassis, and the "buzz, buzz, buzz" wasn't missing, either. Occasionally a comb or a hairpin slipped from its native rest into the transmission gear box, or in the process of grinding valves, and getting back the exhaust and intake manifolds, a finger nail plugged up with soap, bent to the quick, or a wrench just jumped off its perch and dropped on a tapering finger, but the worst one heard was an "ouch" or a yell pitched in a high G. The story goes that last week one of the fourteen met with some phase of this fate and just sat on the floor and kicked her feet and "squeaked" while the rest of the chorus laughed. . . .

Miss Laura Saunders and Miss Aileen Maxwell had a playful time with a "camshaft" and timing valves and there wasn't a bump of a hook or a nut that hadn't found its "home and rest" when they finished the job. Incidentally they discovered "la raison d'etre" for a piece of wire which was buried in one of the infinitesimal parts of the whole.

Miss May Brophy was fiddling with the Ford, and having had past experience with the Canadian Club truck, etc., the extra knowledge she gained will no doubt play her in good stead, on a country road some day. Her particular interest last night was centered around the piston and valve to the engine, making those little "griddle-like" discs that convert the duty, minus the "gas."

The steering wheel held charms for the Misses Jean Bryson, Edith Baird and Mae Brock. They turned it up side down and inside out, and then put it all together again.

Oh, the differential on the "Briscoe" chassis! Miss Marguerite Conn, who, by the way, did a little driving in England, and was just about to be sent to France to drive an ambulance, when she was called home, with her sister Miss Jessie Conn, Mrs. Allan Horwood and Mrs. Philip Barnshaw had a beautiful time discovering why some of the teeth on the crown wheel were missing and why this differential had so much to do with the movement of the rear wheels of the car.

EDITORIAL.

THE WORLD SET FREE.

Kaiser Wilhelm II, German Emperor and King of Prussia, has been stripped of the trappings of superstition and barbarism. As William Hohenzollern, he has no more divine right than any other man. It is a fit occasion for rejoicing, for flag-flying, singing and cheering. The kaiser represented nothing worth saving from the wreck of autocracy. He reigned as an opponent of goodwill towards men. It is not an eclipse when the kaiser is eliminated, it is the passing of one of the deepest of the dark forces of evil.

The mesmerism of authority by divine right has been shown to be a fraud in the present war. It has failed. It is not worth one thought of regret. As the German people free themselves of their belief in kaiserism, or sentimental memory of it, they can become the more free to enthrone goodwill and right in the place of the diabolical "divine right" of an autocrat.

Hohenzollern, Hapsburg, Romanoff, the thing they represented can have no place in civilization. When people ceased to believe in the werewolf, it disappeared from humankind. The very word is forgotten. So let the kaiser, the apostolic king, the czar, be forgotten.

When peace is signed, and the war ended, the great crusade towards the reign of goodwill is just beginning. The way is being opened for world freedom

November 11, 1918

December 4, 1918
THE RETURNING MEN DO NOT TAKE KINDLY
TO HOME SOLDIERS.
Incident at Halifax Shows That They Resent Guards

at Docks to Make Them Keep in Order.

That the boys returning from overseas don't like the idea of being "bossed" too much now that the war is over, is illustrated by a little story of what occurred in Halifax station the other day when men from the steamship *Aquitania* were being placed on trains bound for inland points. The story was related by an official of the militia department as an illustration, he said, of the difficulties which are confronting the department in handling the returning men because of their feeling that the restraint they have been under in the past should be lifted now that the war is ended.

A detachment of military police, many of them men who had not been overseas, was placed at the station to keep order while the soldiers were entraining, and evidently, from stories which have filtered through to Ottawa, the veterans didn't like the idea of "home soldiers" bossing them. Some of the fellows organized a raid on the unfortunate military "cops" and their rifles were taken away from them, the bayonets detached and thrown away and the rifles handed back. Having done this the newly arrived soldiers got on the train feeling that they had righted an injustice. "You see what we are up against," said an official of the militia department today when speaking of the incident.

The department is also having a lot of trouble with bootleggers. At Halifax they slip through the guards despite all the precautions that are taken and the returning soldiers are supplied with liquor, which the department has ascertained, is only a vile concoction calculated to get the men in such a condition that they are hard to control. The same thing happens at Montreal, where, although there are orders against the serving of men in uniform, bootleggers, out to get as much of the soldiers' pay as possible, ply their nefarious trade with bad results to the men on their way home.

It is pointed out that the men are not entirely to blame. They are just come from overseas, where they have been through the mill and have suffered all kinds of hardship—and the opportunity of getting a little of this off their minds, and celebrating their return, is afforded by the circulation of the bootleggers with their bottles among them while they are at the station.

With regard to the transportation of the Ottawa men home, a militia department official stated today that public opinion, demanding the sending home of the troops as speedily as possible, resulted in the change of the original plans which was to send all troops home through the military district headquarters. The Ottawa men are now placed on trains at the disembarkation points, bound for Kingston, but the department has bowed to public opinion and in order to save the triangular trip which would have been necessary if the men had to go to Kingston and then back to Ottawa, furlough papers and pay checks

CANADA MUST BE REPRESENTED AT PEACE CONGRESS

Premier Borden Says It is not Only Right But Necessary Dominion Should Have Voice.

TELLS OF COUNTRY'S PART IN STRUGGLE

London Daily Telegraph Eulogizes Our Effort in World War.

(Canadian Associated Press Cable) LONDON, Dec. 2.—War effort and the future of Canada are subjects of an interview with Sir Robert Borden which fills a column in the Daily Telegraph. Speaking of the peace conference, Sir Robert said it was not only appropriate but necessary that the dominions be represented. On behalf of Canada he said that the Dominion was prepared to co-operate in the task of reconstruction of the devastated countries.

Canada had contributed over 450,000 men to the war and her soldiers had been since February, 1915, in the forefront of the struggle. At

December 3, 1918

are issued to the local men before the train reaches Montreal, which is the transfer point of the journey.

December 15, 1919
SIR ROBERT BORDEN TO RELINQUISH PREMIERSHIP.
PREMIER TO GIVE UP OFFICE OWING TO STATE OF HEALTH;
CAUCUS ON SUCCESSOR NEXT MONTH.
UNIONIST LEADER RELUCTANT TO QUIT BUT PHYSICIANS
CLAIM HE MUST LEAVE ALL ACTIVE DUTIES.
Sir Thomas White, Sir Henry Drayton, Hon. Mr. Meighen,
Hon. Mr. Calder and Hon. Mr. Rowell Mentioned as Successors.
*Because of Charles Bowman's close ties with the Union
government, and his friendship with Sir Robert Borden,
the* Citizen *was first to report details of the prime minister's
failing health and his impending retirement. Here's an excerpt:*

Suffering from impaired health in the wake of the war and enjoined by his physicians that retirement is absolutely necessary, Sir Robert Borden, Prime Minister of Canada since 1911, and one of the outstanding figures in world politics, is about to retire from public life.

It is understood that a caucus of ministerial supporters is to be held early in January to select a new leader who will become premier. Sir Robert afterwards will resign and, in doing so, counsel the Governor-General as to whom he should call upon to form a ministry.

The semi-official intimation of the premier's retirement came to the *Citizen* on Sunday and it is known that already steps are being taken to summon the party caucus upon which will devolve the selection of the man upon whom the mantle of Sir Robert is destined to fall.

This sudden development is not a surprise to those who have learned of the premier's condition, but the climax has come a little sooner than was expected. Normally strong and rugged in constitution, he applied himself with an unwavering fidelity of purpose in all the period of work and worry incidental to the war. Before the armistice came, he had been summoned to England to discuss the terms of peace and for months was in attendance at Paris. He came home last spring to be confronted with a multiplicity of peace problems and, then, came the autumn session of parliament. It had not progressed far when his health gave way. A cold developed with influenza and, badly shattered, the premier was forced to go south in October.

Two months spent in Virginia resulted in improvement, but not to the extent hoped for. The prime minister's constitution has not responded to the exactions of the work that attaches to his high position and he is not able to continue. Physicians in consultation are understood to have counselled his retirement and reluctantly, Sir Robert

May 14, 1919

May 15, 1919

purposes to follow their advice. He has no organic ailment, but simply is not able to carry on the duties which involve so much of physical, mental and nervous strain. Away from public life his normal health it is believed will return.

Who will succeed to the premiership will be for the party caucus composed of Unionist members and senators to determine when they convene here for that purpose as early as possible next month. There is a fairly wide field of possible selections and a corresponding opportunity for speculation.

There is Sir Thomas White, Hon. Arthur Meighen, Hon. N. W. Rowell, Sir Henry Drayton, Hon. J. A. Calder and Sir James Lougheed, but with chances not necessarily in the order mentioned. All of them but Sir Thomas White are now in the government, and all are in parliament....

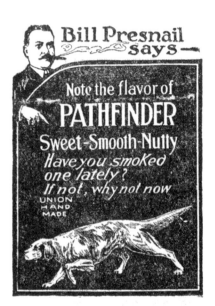

May 14, 1919

May 15, 1919

December 23, 1919
HUNDRED OTTAWA SOLDIERS ARE GIVEN
WARM WELCOME TO CAPITAL.
Men From the Steamer Regina Reached
the Capital Late Last Night.

E. W. (Ernie) Harrold, among the returning soldiers mentioned in this excerpt, became one of Ottawa's most loved newspapermen through his delightful column, Diary of Our Own Pepys, *which ran in the* Citizen *for nearly two decades in the 1930s and '40s.*

Scenes of unprecedented enthusiasm were witnessed at the Central Station at midnight last night, when over a hundred men from Ottawa and district at last returned from the front, including sixty-seven sons of the Capital, the names of whom, with a brief biographical sketch of their war history, are given below. Nearly ninety per cent of the men had seen service in France, most of them had been wounded, many of them several times, several wore decorations for bravery. They were a jolly bunch of fellows, looking fit and smiling broadly and happily at being home for Christmas.

A tremendous crowd welcomed them, and military police had to be used to keep lanes open for the heroes to pass out to the waiting automobiles. The cheering which was let loose as the Grand Trunk train from Montreal steamed in with two coaches loaded with soldiers can only be described as pandemonium, and many were the touching little episodes staged in various parts of the station as mothers clasped long-absent sons to their hearts and wept over them .... The boys were glad to be welcomed so splendidly, but they were in a hurry to get home, and they lost no time doing so.

We have a little welcome of our own to relate. Gunner Ernie Harrold, a well known Ottawa newspaperman, and a young member of the edi-torial staff of the *Citizen*, was one of the party. Every newspaperman at the station was on the watch for "Ernie," and when he hove into sight, he was given a very impromptu but most effective welcome. The po-lice court reporter relieved him of one dunnage bag and his trench hel-met, the "sub" grabbed something else, and arm-in-arm, or rather in arms, because there were seven reporters to this returned soldier, "Ernie" Harrold was escorted in triumph to a car, and transported to the *Citizen* building, where another celebration was in order. The capi-tal can join the *Citizen* in welcoming back a newspaperman who is the "real thing."

Judging from the happy-looking fellows the *Citizen* reporter chatted with coming up from Montreal on the train, they had a swell time on the trip. Far from making any kicks the men were full of praise for the treatment on the boat, the wonderful reception given them at Halifax, Moncton and Truro, where the good-hearted citizens turned out en masse and plied the chaps with apples, fruits and candy, smokes and matches, and the wonderful despatch which marked their clearance at Halifax and Quebec ....

One of the funniest stories heard from the boys on the train was the way veterans fooled "rookies," as the draftees from Canada were called, at the training grounds, Kinmel Park, Wales. The "vet" broke up a lot of old stoves and sold the pieces as scraps of shrapnel brought back from France, as high as ten shillings being received for the pieces. The late arrivals in khaki from Canada were fooled completely. One boy on the train rather gloated as he told how he palmed off on a rook-ie an old cigarette case that he had punched a hole in with a knife, for ten shillings, the rookie believing the story told him, that the case had saved the seller's life and the hole in it was caused by a bullet. Another boy sold a dirty, greasy old cap for "five bob," a rookie being taken in by the story that it had seen three years' service in France.

June 7, 1919

April 4, 1921
HON. MARY E. SMITH SPEAKS OF HONOR WOMEN RECEIVED
Says Pride Not Personal But She is Gratified
at Recognition Given Women by B. C. Legislature.
*Until the 1970s, it was common practice for newspapers to send
reporters around to the major hotels to see what famous people
might be visiting town. The* Citizen, *like the* Journal, *often
provided hotel staff with alcohol and cigarettes
in exchange for access to the guest register.*

The modest signature "Mrs. Ralph Smith, Nanaimo, B.C.," on the Chateau Laurier register this morning, was far from telling that Hon.

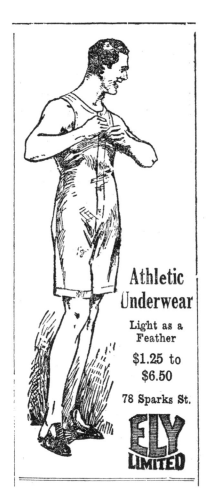

Athletic
Underwear

Light as a
Feather

$1.25 to
$6.50

78 Sparks St.

ELY
LIMITED

July 26, 1920

Mary Ellen Smith, the first woman in the world to become a member of a responsible government, had arrived in Ottawa. Mrs. Smith was sworn in as member without portfolio in the government of British Columbia a few days ago. A couple of days later she left for Ottawa to attend the sessions of the Canadian Council of Immigration for women, which open in Ottawa tomorrow.

Mrs. Smith chatted with a *Citizen* man in a delightful and informal way this morning, in her rooms at the Chateau, of the significance of the inclusion for the first time of a woman in a British ministry. She is a middle-aged woman with a charming and well modulated voice. There is nothing in the slightest about her appearance to denote a woman whose life has been devoted to the public good. She was attired in a blue serge gown, of modern design, and wore a necklace of topaz with earrings to match. She also wore a gold brooch, evidently a family heirloom. She had nose glasses on a string attached to her dress but only wears these when reading. Mrs. Smith expressed cheerfully her willingness to answer any questions. Asked about her elevation to the British Columbia ministry, she said:

"Yes, it is a great honor that has come to women that one of us should be sworn in to a British ministry. I do not accept the position with any feeling of personal pride but simply from the point of view of the triumph it is for women in general. You know we have not been enfranchised so very long."

Mrs. Smith was asked why she declined the speakership of the British Columbia legislature, which position, that of first commoner, she was first offered.

"I declined," she said, "for reasons which I think were justifiable. I felt keenly the honor, but also that the position would shut me off from all public debate. As speaker, I would not have been free to express public opinion and so I did not think it was the right thing to do to accept, especially when the women of the province had entrusted me with missions that so keenly affect their sex, their homes and their children. And my attitude was justified by the very many letters I have received both from the highest and lowliest in the land.

"You ask if women have a place in public life? I say emphatically yes. I believe the right type of woman can influence legislation, but she must be broad enough to understand and to influence the male man.

"You know, I don't think of men as men. I simply regard them as human beings. Sex barriers are likely to create sex antagonism. We are enfranchised and must be willing to take and receive hard knocks.

"The ballot for women is only a step on the road towards getting the amount of legislation that women still need. It is the last court of appeal for women as well as men, insomuch as through it we express ourselves as the kind of people we want to represent us. And the right type of woman in our legislatures is badly needed."

"How have you found public life in British Columbia?" she was asked.

"The finest thing I have found," Mrs. Smith answered, "is that the men in the government of British Columbia are willing to listen to women and to the demands of women not only sympathetically but practically. Today we are putting in force as practical legislation things that a few years ago were regarded as the merest dreams."

And here Mrs. Smith spoke of her ultimate dream. "The women of Canada," she said, "should bind themselves together in some national way; they should get together on the problems that affect them and consider them from their own angle. By doing this they would be able to influence and direct legislation affecting them in the various Canadian provinces and ultimately have a big effect on federal legislation.

"In British Columbia we want more immigrants. We want people who will go on the land and who are used to the land. There are millions who want a new start in a new country and there is room for them in our valleys. We, too, want Canadians to buy Canadian goods. Last year we sent out of Canada between twenty and thirty million dollars to buy goods in foreign countries. Had that money been kept at home it would have done much to prevent unemployment and to have kept our factories going. In British Columbia last year we sent $11,000,000 out for imported cigars, yet we grow excellent tobacco."

Mrs. Smith here said smilingly that she knew she was treading on dangerous ground. "I do not smoke," she said, "but men who do tell me there is something about the flavor of an imported cigar that our domestic ones do not possess. At any rate our own tobacco factories turned out only a million and a quarter of cigars in the same year.

"Older countries build themselves up by loyalty to their own industries. The sooner we learn this lesson in Canada the better for all."

MISS D'VORAK
PERFORMING EVERY AFTERNOON AND EVENING
AT
GLADSTONE ROLLER RINK
SPECTATORS AND SKATERS, ADMISSION 25c.

August 27, 1920

May 31, 1921
THE TOWER OF PARLIAMENT.

Editor Bowman was being a touch immodest when he praised architect John Pearson's plan to carve words of inspiration on the walls of the Peace Tower memorial chamber. The idea might have been Pearson's, but it was Bowman who chose the Bible quotations. He also selected the quote from Lord Byron's Don Juan *inscribed in stone over the Parliamentary Press Gallery fireplace. Neither contribution is mentioned in the editorial excerpted here.*

Generations to come will thank the architect of the Canadian Parliament Buildings for a thoughtful act of justice to the Canadian people of this day. During the early years of the building of the new national edifice, the years of war and revolution, it has been made plain that the true spirit of the people of Canada is above materialism and mere superficial display. The memorial chamber in the great tower of Parliament will contain a record of sacrifice by Canadian men, without thought of material reward, that should make it a hallowed place in the heart of this nation.

Around the windows of the tower the architect has carved into the stone, for all time, words of truth that reflect something of the higher idealism for which more than fifty thousand Canadian men gave their lives on active service overseas. Carving in stone is part of the principle of architecture. It is the proper work of the architect to unite truth and beauty in the design of a building. . . .

Architect John Pearson has conceived the splendid idea of adorning the tower around the windows of the memorial chamber with words of spiritual aspiration. On the front facing Wellington street, the words are: "Give the King thy judgements, O God, and thy righteousness unto the King's son." This is the first verse in Psalm 72.

Around the window on the east side of the tower, the words are from the same source: "He shall have dominion also from sea to sea." On the side looking to the west is the following appropriate quotation from Proverbs: "Where there is no vision, the people perish."

While the thoughts expressed in the above architectural features of the tower of Parliament would seem to be particularly timely, at the present period of Canadian national unfoldment, they can be interpreted metaphysically to apply to all time. . . .

The expressed faith in God can hardly be offensive to religious opinion in Canada. Jew and Gentile can surely view the tower in a spirit of harmony, designed as it is to elevate thought above conflicting human elements to contemplation of the Great Architect of the Universe.

Some petty criticism of the tower and other features of the new national divide occurred in the House of Commons during the warm weather last Friday and Saturday. The unhappy utterances of the critics are not worth repeating. It is enough to turn back to Hon. George Brown's criticism of the original buildings in 1864, to note how history is liable to repeat itself where there is lack of vision. Hon. Mr. Brown had been visiting Ottawa to inspect the Parliament Buildings. When he returned to Toronto, he wrote to Hon. John A. Macdonald, as follows:

" . . . The buildings are magnificent: the style, the extent, the workmanship are all surpassingly fine. But they are just 500 years in advance of the time. It will cost half the revenue of the province to light them and to heat them and to keep them clean. Such monstrous folly was never perpetrated in this world before. But as we are in for it, I do think the idea of stopping short of completion is out of the question. I go in for tower, rotunda, fountains, and every conceivable embellish-

July 8, 1921

ment. If we are to be laughed at for our folly, at least let us not be ridiculed for a half finished pile. I go in for making it a superb folly that will bring visitors from all countries to see a work they can't see elsewhere. . . . "

In less than fifty years from the time Hon. George Brown wrote thus of the original buildings, Canada had grown in national stature far beyond the narrow vision of the critic. Is it too much to expect that in the next fifty years the Canadian nation will continue to grow in spirit and substance up to the high standard of idealism expressed in the architecture of the great tower of Parliament?

February 22, 1922

A CANADIAN ARTIST.

Excerpt from an editorial written nearly five years
after Tom Thomson's mysterious death in 1917:

For the first time in Ottawa a number of the best works of Tom Thomson, Canadian artist, have been brought together and placed on public exhibition. They will be found in two of the smaller galleries of the National Art Gallery and deserve a visit from all Canadians, particularly those interested in native art.

Tom Thomson painted for twenty years, but his best work was done during the last eight. He was not only an artist but a lover of the northern places where nature's handiwork is revealed on a grand scale. Each year he would go into the woods, along the rivers and past the edges of cool lakes. And each year he would bring back in the form of sketches in oils some of the rugged beauty and wild charm of that Canadian lakeland. Twenty-five of these are in the collection now on view. The small sketches are augmented by six larger canvases, one or two of which are already familiar to Ottawa art followers.

With due thought for those other Canadian artists who have done so much to build up the authentic Canadian school, it is not too much to say that Tom Thomson was the first to display individual genius as a native artist. His work is redolent of this country, expressing its characteristics as few other national artists have succeeded in doing. It is vigorous and colorful, highly decorative and distinctly original. Yet with its bold technique, its lack of soft lines, its solid masses, there is a charm of composition and harmony of scheme that is unsurpassed.

The painting, "The Jack Pine," is known to many. As a composition in color it is a work of genius. And it is typical of his method and style. With pure color and pointed light he has transfigured wonderful skies, woods and waters. There is, indeed, something brilliant about his work besides color. It is clear and vivid and strong, whether it portrays upland snows, naked trees, northern promontories, autumn woods, ice-dotted rivers, wind-flecked lakes or fantastic clouds.

TRAFFIC SIGNALS
CODE ENDORSED

LEFT TURN or SWERVE

SLOW DOWN or STOP

RIGHT TURN

THIS SIGNAL NEED NOT BE SEEN FROM REAR, BUT IS MAINLY INTENDED TO WARN PEDESTRIANS AHEAD AT STREET INTERSECTIONS.

Illustration of proposals approved by the Ottawa Police Commission.

July 8, 1921

March 30, 1922
RESPECT FOR THE LANGUAGE.
*Another of editor Bowman's passions was grammar
and language, evident in this editorial excerpt:*

At present it is not illegal to pronounce "yes" as "yah," but many will be inclined to agree with Mr. Justice Latchford that it is an offence against good taste. When a witness in the courthouse made answer to certain questions, he used that abomination "yah" while indicating the affirmative. His lordship, no doubt suffering exquisite mental discomfort from hearing the language so maltreated, sharply told the witness to say "yes." "There is no such word as 'yah' in the English language," he said.

There is reasonable excuse for mispronouncing or faulty enunciating big and uncommon words, but none exists for corrupting the everyday one- and two-syllable words that occur in almost every sentence spoken. Yet this is just what happens. The variations of the word "yes" range from "yeh" to "yup" and sometimes "uh-uh." The word "no" suffers from similar distortion at the hands of the careless. So do hundreds of other common words, and for no justifiable reason....

One need not be a pedant or grammarian to resent the habitual violation of the language. One sad aspect of the subject is that the murdering of the King's English is not confined to one class. Judge Latchford might listen to a Parliamentary debate one evening.

Nor must it be believed that those who like to hear the common words of the language spoken pleasantly and correctly want everyone to become a declaimer of majestic blank verse or epic prose, a walking Shakespeare warbling his wood notes wild, or a voluble and glorious Milton. It is simply a matter of treating the language with that ordinary respect it demands. And it costs so little to exercise that respect.

SIR SAM HUGHES, FORMER MINISTER OF MILITIA, DIES AT LINDSAY HOME

Passing Occurred at One O'Clock This Morning (Standard Time). Had Been in Failing Health Since Return From Old Country Last Winter, Suffering From Pernicious Anaemia. Notable Career, Both Civil and Military, of Outstanding Figure in Canadian Public Life.

LINDSAY, Ont., Aug. 24.—Sir Sam Hughes, former minister of militia in the federal government, died at one o'clock this morning, standard time, at his home here.

Sir Sam did not rally conscious during the night, and passed away peacefully. Those at the bedside when the end came were Lady Hughes, Mrs. (Col.) Green of Chatham, daughter; Miss Aileen Hughes, daughter; Dr. McAlpine, brother-in-law; Miss Burke of Bowmanville, sister-in-law; Bernie McAlpine, nephew and T. H. Stinson, an old friend of Sir Sam.

Advised Against Trip.

Sir Sam had been in failing health ever since his return from the Old Country last winter. He made this trip despite the earnest advice of his physicians, who realised that his health needed the extremest care.

In April last in Ottawa he suffered the second attack of pernicious anaemia. Constantly attended by two physicians, who at many periods during his illness regarded his case as hopeless, that he ever lived to see out the session and return to Lindsay was in the nature of a miracle. For weeks his condition was so grave that the least thing might have turned the scale, and yet he lingered on, optimistic and interested by everything about him, despite his extreme weakness.

Two transfusions of blood were given him while in Ottawa, and one soon after he returned to Lindsay. All three were regarded as successful, and after each Sir Sam's feeble condition seemed to improve somewhat.

A few weeks ago the former minister of militia suffered a severe relapse. Dr. J. McAlpine, his physician, holding out no hope for his recovery. This occurred during the extremely hot weather and with the advent of cooler days Sir Sam ral...

LATE LT.-GEN. SIR SAM HUGHES

...sin, through the arrest of a Turk. Letters found on the Turk pointed out not only the plot to assassinate, but declared the victim was to be "one of Canada's biggest military men."

General Hughes was knighted in August, 1915, during an audience with King George in Buckingham Palace. He was made a Knight Commander of the Bath, which conveys civil as well as military honors.

Conferring of Knighthood.

The story of the conferring of...

August 24, 1921

April 5, 1922
MISS AGNES MACPHAIL DESCRIBES
HER EXPERIENCES IN PARLIAMENT.
Is Impressed By Amount of Work There is to Do
and the Little Time Available to Do It In.
Excerpt from a lively interview with Canada's first female MP:

(Special to The Citizen.)
PETERBORO, Ont., April 5.—Miss Agnes C. Macphail, M.P., has lost ten pounds during her first month's stay in Ottawa. This much was revealed in an interview given last evening in this city following an address to the U.F.O. [United Farmers of Ontario] club. Miss Macphail has an intense passion for achievement in a chosen field in which she

is often inclined to wonder if the game is worth the candle.

"Sometimes it is and sometimes it isn't," said the member from South East Grey. Miss Macphail said she had few illusions concerning the task before her. The men in the House are getting used to her presence there; she says she is not the sort of woman who wants a man to throw away his cigarette and jump to his feet every time she appears on the scene.

The amount of work there is to do and the little time there is to do it in impresses Miss Macphail very much. She wonders what it will be like when the committees get down to business. She is a member of three important committees. Some of the members say Miss Macphail doesn't do anything but chat with friends and answer letters from constituents. Requests for favors of all kinds pour in, but the Progressives are not so badly harassed in this connection as the two old parties.

Miss Macphail has developed a strong regard for Hon. Arthur Meighen. At one time she disliked the former Conservative premier with a feeling that amounted almost to an obsession. She likes the Hon. Arthur's courage and his ability, but at the same time asserts that she is peeved over his defeat . . . . Miss Macphail thinks Mr. Mackenzie King is a sweeter tempered man than Mr. Meighen and that he looks much better with his hat on. "You see the trouble is with his hair. There is that lock in front." However, the member from Grey is quite firmly convinced that Mr. Crerar [leader of the Progressives, Macphail's party] is quite the handsomest of the three.

Miss Macphail likes the conveniences afforded members at Ottawa and considers the civil service, although over-manned, very obliging and efficient. "There are some sort of flunkies down there and you don't even have to stamp your letters. . . . But I always insist on carrying my grip myself," added Miss Macphail.

Miss Macphail has the frank desires of the girl in her professed love for skating, dancing and fun, but not for society. "No, society does not appeal to me," she said. . . .

Miss Macphail insists she is the Progressive member for Grey, rather than the only lady member of Parliament, when attending a caucus or committee meeting. And because of that fact, the comfort of "mere male" members of committees, who like to smoke during their committee work, is not interfered with. When Miss Macphail appeared in the committee on banking and commerce some of the members began tucking pipes and cigars away, but seeing the Progressives still smoking, brought them out again after a few minutes. . . .

April 25, 1922

March 19, 1923
KU KLUX KLAN NOT NEEDED IN CANADA.
However, Rev. Dr. Wyllie Claims
Conditions in U.S., Justify the Organization.

Every Monday for half a century, the Citizen *ran coverage of a
Sunday sermon from one of the city's many churches. Because of his
penchant for speaking out on issues of the day, Rev. Wyllie, minister
at Erskine Presbyterian Church, became a* Citizen *favourite.*

An able sermon was preached last evening in Erskine Presbyterian
church by Rev. Dr. Wyllie. His subject was Citizenship and he dealt
with the Ku Klux Klan and asked Canadian citizens to forever make
impossible the conditions that have made the Klan a factor in the life
of the United States.

Dr. Wyllie said the origin of the Klan was due to the atrocities practiced against the vanquished south by the politicians of the north after
Lincoln's death. The south was overrun by "carpet-baggers" who dis-
enfranchised the whites and put the negroes in sole control of political
and social life. Conditions became so intolerable that among the
Southern Veterans the Klan was organized to control by fear and swift
and relentless justice the hordes of blacks and their debased political
masters. The south owed whatever of Reconstruction was effected to
the vigilance of the Klan. Its work accomplished, the Klan became almost non-existent.

With the past war period its activities were renewed. Again the
cause is to be found in the peculiar social and political conditions of
American life. Dr. Wyllie expressed his highest admiration of American people while deploring the dominance of the political machine.
This largely alienates the active interest of the best classes in political
life, and frequently throws the control of all legal machinery in the
hands of gangs, religious societies, etc.

The Klan is not anti-Catholic, nor anti-racial, he claimed, except insofar as such bodies attempt to control life and thwart law-enforce-
ment. Against such it has proved effective. . . . He ridiculed the creduli-
ty of the Canadian officer who tried to settle on the Klan such things as
burning churches and threatening orphanages. This is the result, he alleged, of propaganda by certain societies and bodies who seek to dis-
credit the Klan and put on it the opprobrium of decent people. . . .

The Klan, Dr. Wyllie declared, stands for Americanism and enforcement of law and order—failing the established means, they employ
concerted efforts of the members, generally the best citizens of the
community, but there is no sanction to violence, murder or ruthlessness. . . . Apart from religious tolerance, political and social purity and
high souled devotions to the good of all, the evil conditions that pro-

duce the Klan and justify it, said the speaker, will ever appear, and with them all evil brood of mob violence and secret machinations.

April 3, 1923
OTTAWA SENATORS ARE WORLD'S
HOCKEY CHAMPIONS.
Stanley Cup Holders Defeat Edmonton 1-0
in Final Game, Broadbent Scoring Winning Goal.
"KING" CLANCY SETS UNIQUE RECORD
OF PLAYING EVERY POSITION ON TEAM, TAKING
BENEDICT'S JOB WHEN GOALER IS RULED OFF.

It was far from Ottawa's first Stanley Cup victory, but the 1923 win over Edmonton is still considered by many to be the team's greatest. Coming off a gruelling four-game series with Vancouver, and without two key defencemen, the Senators rode to glory on the shoulders of their sensational young star, Francis (King) Clancy, and wily veteran forward Frank Nighbor. The team was coached by former Citizen *sports editor T.P. Gorman. Here's an excerpt from the Cup-winning game story by one of his successors:*

May 20, 1922

BY ED BAKER
Sports Editor of the Citizen.

VANCOUVER, April 7.—By the time this story is in print Tommy Gorman and his gallant band of super-hockey stars will be going through the Rockies over the Canadian Pacific on their way back to the Capital, proud possessors of the famous Stanley Cup, emblematic of the World's Hockey Championship. They won the second and final game of their series with the Edmonton Eskimos last night in Frank Patrick's Arena by 1 to 0, after displaying for one more time courage and resourcefulness almost unbelievable.

That the Senators should defeat the Eskimos naturally would not be surprising to eastern hockey followers, but to defeat them without the services of their two defence men, Captain Eddy Gerard and George Boucher, and especially after coming through a victorious four game series with Vancouver, Pacific Coast Hockey League champions, stamps the feat as nothing short of wonderful.

True, George Boucher took part in the first match against Edmonton Thursday night, but his effectiveness was sorely diminished early in that game by a wicked clout on his foot, and it was only a marvellous exhibition of gameness that kept him on the ice. Captain Gerard, sickened with injuries, was unable to get on the ice in that game . . . .

Eastern followers of hockey know what the Senators had to go through before connecting with the National Hockey League championship, but one had to be in Vancouver and witness these series with

April 23, 1923

April 2, 1923

April 2, 1923

the Vancouver and Edmonton teams to have a knowledge of their rocky road to the world's hockey title.

Leaving Ottawa on the night of March tenth with the Senators, I have witnessed about every move the boys have made since that time, and I have seen the acid test applied to them as never before applied to a set of athletes, at least to my knowledge. They're the pure quill without the slightest sign of alloy in their make up. From their honored leader, Thomas Patrick Gorman, the club's secretary and manager, through to Frank "Cosy" Dolan, the trainer, there has always been an air of confidence even when one misfortune after another fell to their lot.

They are fitting representatives of the Capital of this great Dominion, and while Ottawa in years past has honored some great teams, rugby, lacrosse and hockey, the Senators, world's hockey champions of 1923, will go down in the history of sport as one of the greatest, if not actually the greatest, band of athletes ever assembled.

As I stated in a previous article, it was asking much of a hockey team to travel in excess of two thousand miles from the east to the Pacific Coast and play two teams of champions. The weather conditions in the east and west at this time of the year are greatly different and coming from zero weather into almost summer in the course of a few days could but have a deterrent effect on the players. The Senators had gone through a strenuous season in their regular N.H.L. schedule, and then two trying play-off matches, finishing the latter just twenty-four hours before taking their train for the west. . . .

Last night's game was largely a repetition of the first clash with the Eskimos, the only difference being that the Senators started their offensive earlier. After playing cautiously for ten minutes, that famous "pinch-hitter" of hockey, Harry Broadbent, found an opening and sent in one of his bullet-like shots, which resulted in a counter. Then, for fifty minutes of play, that lone tally was guarded as faithfully as the Royal Mint on Sussex street.

The Ottawas started out with the one and only Clint Benedict in goal. Capt. Gerard and Frank Clancy on defence, Frank Nighbor at centre and Cy Denneny and Harry Broadbent on the wings. Lionel Hitchman was on several times to give his ailing captain a breather. Harry Helman, who had been seriously injured in practice ten days ago, was on for a short time relieving Broadbent. . . .

Frank Clancy completely won the hearts of the Senators' supporters and the plaudits of seven thousand spectators by his great exhibition. The Lower Town youngster took up the burden laid down by George Boucher, one of the game's greatest defence men, and came through with flying colors, turning in a game that any seasoned veteran could only envy. . . .

The match was cleanly played. There were a number of penalties but a rough-housing call against Benedict in the final period sent him off the ice. Clancy was a substitution in the net, and that gave the young-ster the unprecedented distinction of having played every position on the lineup in a single match. He had previously subbed in both defence positions, centre, and on right and left wings....

Despite the fact the Eskimos felt their defeat keenly, the players all went into the Senators' dressing room after the match to congratulate the world's champions. They were all loud in their praise for the Sena-tors, and really consider it an honor to hold the champions to a one to nothing score....

November 23, 1923

SOCIAL HYGIENE FILM IS SHOWN.

(Excerpt from a short news item:)

"After a child reaches the age of ten, who has been brought up in a quarrelsome home, it is almost useless to make her believe that mar-riage is a sacred rite made in heaven," said Miss Edna Moor, when ad-dressing a largely attended meeting held under the auspices of the So-cial Hygiene Council in the Little Theater last night.

Miss Moor, of Toronto, who is a nurse in the Social Service Depart-ment in the provincial department of hygiene, stated that .... it was only since the war that social hygiene workers could bring their mes-sage to the public. Miss Moor spoke strongly on the value of sex educa-tion to children and stated that a child absorbs its education from the first minute it is born.

An interesting picture on The Gift of Life was shown, demonstrating the various phases of life in plants, animals and human beings.

Miss Hazel Todd, at the conclusion of the film, made an appeal to members of the Social Hygiene Council. She announced that a lecture on bathing would be given Sunday evening in the Center Theater, for women only, by Dr. Heagerty and also that the annual meeting of the Hygiene Council would be held in the Chateau Laurier Wednesday.

January 3, 1924

IT MUST BE BOLSHEVIK PLOTTING.

(Excerpt from an editorial:)

Skiers in Ottawa are watching with mixed feelings the lengthening days and the continued mild weather. At best there is only about ten weeks left this winter for ski-ing. The sun is growing warmer. Yester-day morning it seemed almost to hint at the return of spring, with the birds chirping and icicles dropping from the eaves. Unless something is done very soon by President Ted Devlin of the Cliffsides, and Presi-

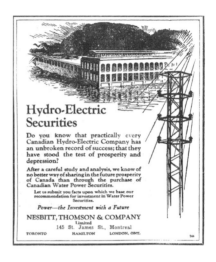

dent C. E. Mortureaux of the Ottawa Ski Club, to bring on some real winter weather—anything may happen.

People who wish to can easily see the hidden hand of Bolshevism in this subtle interference with Canada's normal weather. The information has leaked out from Moscow that warm weather is the order of the day in Russia. The thermometer there has actually registered seventy degrees of heat on an alleged winter day. Now, just as the Germans are suspected of sending out radio waves to put the magnetos of French aeroplanes out of commission, some people will readily believe that Bolshevik plotters are transmitting balmy drafts of Russia's weather to Canada to keep Ottawa skiers away from the Gatineau hills. The Bolsheviki must have heard that ski-ing is counter-revolutionary.

Gliding through the hills and along the wooded paths inspires feelings of good fellowship with every one. When a real tingling blue and white day comes along, with a good foot of snow for the hickory blades to glide over, nobody cares about any -ism. No one worries about the iniquities of capitalism; the C.P.R. is hailed as a boon and a blessing, as the Gatineau train carries the ski parties, brimming over with joyous youth, up to the hills. Such days are positively demoralizing for Bolshevik plotters. Hence, the evidence is against the Soviet—as evidence against Russia goes.

June 11, 1923

February 12, 1924
MARRIAGE OF MISS LOIS BOOTH
TO PRINCE ERIK CAUSES UNPARALLELED SCENES
OF ENTHUSIASM IN CAPITAL.
Glorious Weather Favored Happy Event Yesterday When
Ottawa Born Girl Became Princess Erik, Countess of Rosenborg.
Ceremony Performed by Right Rev. J. C. Roper, Bishop of Ottawa,
in All Saints Church, Before Brilliant Assemblage, Including
His Excellency the Governor-General and Lady Byng
of Vimy, Who Represented British Throne.
Excerpt from coverage of the social event of 1924:

The marriage day of Ottawa's Princess has come and gone. It was a perfect day. And when Miss Lois Frances Booth, the only daughter of Mr. and Mrs. J. Fred Booth, and granddaughter of Mr. John R. Booth, was united in marriage with His Royal Highness Prince Erik of Denmark, son of His Royal Highness Prince Valdemar of Denmark, and a cousin of His Majesty King George the Fifth, of Great Britain, the sun's rays from a western sky shone beneficently through the wide windows of the little gray stone church of All Saints, casting a golden glow over the beautiful scene. The flowers were fragrant, the benediction solemn, and throughout the audience of guests one detected tears of sympathetic gladness.

It was fitting that All Saints church, at the corner of Laurier avenue and Chapel street, should have been chosen for the event. Here it was that the Royal Prince and his bride, during his visits to Ottawa, attended divine worship. Small in proportion to other sacred edifices is All Saints, yet every guest was comfortably seated and every arrangement in detail at the church carried out well.

An hour or more before the appointed hour of four o'clock for the ceremony to commence, guests began to arrive. It is the first time in Canada that their Excellencies The Governor General and The Lady Byng, attended a wedding, and yesterday they represented Their Majesties King George and Queen Mary. And it is the first time at All Saints church that the National Anthem preceded the Bridal March.

And did it not stir all hearts when they realized that at the chancel steps stood H.R.H. Prince Valdemar, he who had witnessed the crowning of his sister at Westminster Abbey, to give his son in marriage to an Ottawa born girl?

Nor is it exaggeration to assert that never in Ottawa was a sacred edifice more beautifully adorned than for this occasion. The whole interior of the church appeared as a Southern garden. The walls, windows, pillars and chancel were completely hung with southern smilax and white lilies. At the chancel steps, where the bridal party was, stood a very high arch of greenery and lilies from the centre of the bow of which was suspended a huge wedding bell composed of purest white spring blossoms, and to each side of the arch were tied with wide white satin ribbons large clusters of white lilies. To each side of the arch at the front of the chancel were bankings, fifteen feet high, formed of ferns, fancy crotons and palms with stately vases of lilies....

As the guests assembled Mr. John W. Dearder, F.R.C.O., the organist of All Saints, who presided, gave beautiful interpretations to the Wagner music. When, at a few minutes before the hour, Their Excellencies the Governor General and the Lady Byng of Vimy arrived, the National Anthem was played, with all the guests rising in greeting.... Her Excellency was wearing a sapphire blue gown of crepe de chine, a blue velvet cloak trimmed with skunk and her hat was of jacquard tinsel with a white plume....

From outside the guests caught the chorus of cheers from the crowd which announced the arrival of the bride. Softly and then fully and firmly came the stirring strains of The Bridal March from Lohengrin, and at the main door entered the charming young bride who was so soon to be acclaimed a princess. She held firmly to her father's arm while the bridal procession was being formed....

All eyes were centered on the lovely vision of girlish charm in her richly simple wedding gown. Of softest whitest duchess satin, straight

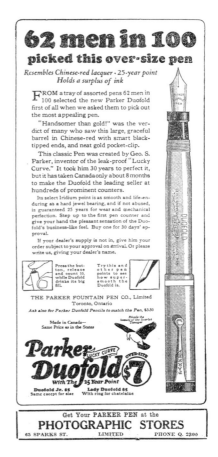

Over 36,000 last year

"Hello, Mrs. Brock, do you know who's speaking?"

"No, I haven't the faintest idea."

"It's Irene — we just had our telephone installed and I thought you would like to know our number."

"Why, that's fine, Irene, I've often wished your mother had a telephone."

And so Mrs. Brock returns to her paper with a new and greater appreciation of the fact that "every new subscriber adds to the value of YOUR telephone."

Of the net gain of 52,018 telephones in Ontario and Quebec in 1923, over 36,000 (or 70%) were installed in residences.

Merchants and shop-keepers should not overlook this large addition to the number of householders they can reach by telephone.

J. A. Gorrie Jr.,
District Manager.

Every Bell Telephone is a Long Distance Station

February 6, 1924

of line except for a slight fullness in the back, this exquisite gown was the workmanship of an artist. A bit of seed pearl embroidery at the yoke, and a large pearl ornament with long single strands of pearls were the only adornments. Long plain sleeves reaching to the wrists were edged with a stitching of pearls. The court train, also of satin, was carried by the pages, and over the train and nearly as long was the real lace veil, the filmy folds of which were held in place with a bandeau of pearls and rhinestones. The veil was the same as adorned the bride's mother on her wedding day. Her only jewels was the rare corsage ornament of rubies and diamonds which had been presented to the bride by R.H.R. Prince Valdemar, and also a diamond bracelet which was a gift from her own father. . . .

July 31, 1924
OTTAWA AS WINTER RESORT.

The movement afoot to bring more of the benefits of winter tourist trade to Ottawa should appeal to the public. There are possibilities of making Ottawa as attractive to tourists in winter as Jasper Park is in summer. There is no more favorably situated city in Canada for maintaining a steady stream of visitors during the months when snow is on the ground. Many people go to Banff for the winter sports. Where hundreds are sufficiently keen to travel so far west, thousands could be attracted from the populous cities of the United States to a Canadian resort which could be reached in one night's train journey.

The plan to attract winter tourists to Ottawa would have to be on a different basis from the winter carnival which the city experimented with a few years ago; instead of one week's spectacular display, to become a winter resort, Ottawa would have to compete with popular places like Lake Placid. There are so many natural advantages in Ottawa, and strong local clubs to give the winter sport season the necessary publicity, it would require only the hearty co-operation of local organizations to turn the tourist tide to this city.

There are few cities where it is possible to step out of the train into such a commodious hotel as the Chateau Laurier, combined with the possibility of skating, tobogganing and ski-ing right at the hotel door. It would be necessary to build the toboggan slide again from the Plaza to the Ottawa river. An ice track could be kept open on the river for skating and sleigh driving, and the ski tower would have to be built at Rockcliffe Park again for the jumping contests. The Gatineau line of the Canadian Pacific Railway makes it possible to step right off the train into a most delightful ski country, with a variety of trails to suit all grades of skill, from the beginner over the mica-mine trail from Kingsmere to the veterans who look for new hills to conquer over the Wakefield Cascades and other ski routes.

In the coming winter it is probable there will be heavy demands on the public treasury and on private firms for unemployment relief. It would be very much better to invest some of the money which must be spent in any case to give employment along such lines of enterprise as the winter tourist trade would stimulate in Ottawa. A strong committee of citizens could at least canvass the possibilities of developing Ottawa as a winter resort. With the co-operation of transportation interests, merchants, newspapers and clubs, within a very few years it is probable that Ottawa could be made popularly known on this continent as the city of winter sport.

September 2, 1924
THE WAR IS ON AGAIN.

A dastardly plot against bobbed hair has been uncovered, which is likely to lead to a renewed outbreak of guerrilla warfare between the bobbed and the anti-bobbed. Last year the storm over bobbed hair was at its height, and while the bobbed army seemed for a time to be on the brink of defeat, it eventually won out, and clipped locks took on a new lease of life. The shingle and the new boyish bob came in, and everything seemed fine.

But the bobbed haired protagonists were over-confident. They were lulled into a false security. They counted too little on the cunning of their opponents. For the discovery has been made that a great majority of those who are winning the summer beauty contests at the beaches this year are the possessors of long tresses! At first glance, there is nothing sinister in the discovery. But the bobs have proclaimed that this phenomenon is no accident. With subtle ingenuity, it now appears, the anti-bobbers have been getting themselves and their friends appointed judges in the beauty contests.

The result is obvious. The long-haired queens have been chosen as winning beauties, and the short-haired ones have therefore been crowded off the prize lists and the rotogravure sections. And so the war is on with renewed fury. The bobs are up in arms against the antis, and the fur, or the hair, is flying. Their first action is to destroy the rumor that the Prince of Wales prefers girls with elongated locks and views with disfavor the curtailed coiffure. So long as that rumor is allowed to spread, it is plan that the bobbed warriors are fighting under a frightful handicap.

June 26, 1924

THE CITIZEN

OTTAWA CENTENNIAL

Industrial section

THEN · CHAUDIERE FALLS · NOW

Charlie and Bill

The Ninth Decade, 1925-1934

"THEY WERE QUITE the times," Charles Bowman would marvel 20 years later, "and it still makes me a bit dizzy to think I was allowed there in the middle of things." It was typical of the *Citizen's* editor to be immodest, just as it was typical for newspapermen to get close to the politicians they covered during the first half of the 20th century.

Even so, Bowman's relationship with William Lyon Mackenzie King took things to a new level. Their friendship began in 1911 when Bowman arrived in Ottawa as a government engineer and King was Liberal labour minister. Fifteen years later, amid the constitutional crisis we know today as the King-Byng affair, Bowman had been editor a decade and King prime minister for half as long. And Bill, as Bowman called his friend, had been relying on Charlie for advice just about as long.

When King couldn't convince Lord Byng, the governor general, to dissolve Parliament rather than turn the reins of power over to Arthur Meighen, the PM brought Bowman into his inner circle to plot strategy. Years later, Bowman recalled he was writing a Dominion Day editorial when King called: "Charlie, we're in my study and need your outside views on this turmoil," Bowman remembered King saying. He quickly turned in his editorial and grabbed a cab to Laurier House.

After a short period out of office, King returned as PM later in 1926. As a reward for his help, King asked Bowman to travel with him to London as an official delegate to the Imperial Conference being held to shift more autonomy to the colonies. Bowman agreed, and although the *Citizen* covered his expenses, he sat at King's elbow at the conference, and wrote a major speech King delivered on the BBC. And, of course, he sent insider stories back to the *Citizen,* so enraging correspondents from other Canadian papers that King had to ask Bowman to invite them to his room at the Ritz Hotel to feed them a few crumbs.

February 12, 1925

Opposite: The Citizen marked the centennial of the founding of Bytown with a comprehensive anniversary supplement, August 16, 1926.

The cosiness didn't end there. In 1929, King named Bowman one of three members of the Aird Royal Commission on broadcasting, which eventually led to the creation of the CBC. This time, Bowman accepted government pay, although he took a year-long leave from the *Citizen*.

All of this was done with the blessing of the Southams, who were Conservative by inclination but also friendly with King. Besides, they liked the idea of having influence on Parliament Hill, and weren't shy about using Bowman to carry their views to King. Obviously, no one pretended the *Citizen's* political coverage was as balanced as it might have been. Certainly it would be unacceptable today.

But the bias wasn't enough to scare away R. B. Bennett, who called on Bowman for advice after he became Conservative prime minister in 1930. There's no record they called each other Bob and Charlie. But Bennett came to admire Bowman's ideas on monetary policy, and Bowman respected Bennett's tenacity in the face of his Depression critics—even as he wrote his editorial calling for Bennett's ouster in the 1935 election.

March 21, 1925

July 20, 1925
"PROGRESS" AND THE BIBLE.
Although this editorial on the famous Scopes "Monkey Trial" in Dayton, Tennessee, accepts a few of the basic tenets of Darwin's theory of evolution, its overall thrust is permeated by Harry and Wilson Southam's Christian Science beliefs—especially the Bible's stature as the supreme guide to eternal life. This is an excerpt:

Whatever the verdict may be in the sensational trial of a school teacher in Tennessee for teaching the doctrine of evolution contrary to the law of the state, thinking people will keep clearly in mind the fact that the Bible is not on trial. Nothing that anyone on the side of the defence, or the prosecution, may say can alter the truth contained in the Volume of the Sacred Law, which is an inexhaustible well of truth.

In modern times, popular esteem for the high priests of the altar has been largely displaced by faith in the high priests of the chemical laboratory. People bow before the golden standard much as they used to bow before the rood.

In *The Times of London's* report on the state opening of the British Empire Exhibition at Wembley, as an example, the list of dignitaries commenced with the King and Queen, quite properly, members of the royal family and high officers of the court; then came the names of eminent bankers, including the governor of the Bank of England; and then the pillars of the church, including the Archbishop of Canterbury—following the pillars of finance.

Along with the glorification of the golden calf, including the eclipse of modern church edifices by the architecture of great banking institutions, has emerged the cult of pseudo-scientific progress. It is quite the thing to believe in evolution. Many of the modern believers are no more familiar with the content of Charles Darwin's *Origin of Species* than the faithful flock in earlier times were with the contents of the Bible; but to express doubt about the doctrine of evolution would be almost heresy, like being old-fashioned or antiquated. So the popular thing is to accept the general belief in evolution, without understanding what is implied in "the survival of the fittest" and the theory of "natural selection."

Nothing in the noble life's work of Darwin would justify some of the devious philosophies that have been built upon it. The leaders of German culture were not alone in believing that war is the human method of making progress, that man is subject to the same law as the beasts of the jungle, "nature red in tooth and claw." So long as such beliefs are accepted as true science, it is possible that the human race will continue to suffer the consequences....

Certainly no one need feel ashamed, or old fashioned, in stoutly maintaining that the story of creation as recorded in the first chapter and the first three verses of the second chapter of Genesis is scientific. The doctrine that man evolved from protoplasm or slime is, to say the least, incomplete. It is also being undermined by more advanced discoveries regarding the structure of the atom. The evidence in support of much materialistic theory is insubstantial. The more the opening words of Genesis are tested by science, the truer they ring....

It has been well said of the Bible that it contains the truth for all mankind for all time. As man becomes more ready to grasp the truth, through growth of spiritual understanding, so the truth is unfolded, as it is to be found in the Volume of the Sacred Law.

July 9, 1925

October 22, 1925
GREAT CHANGE FROM OLDEN DAYS
COMES OVER ELECTION CAMPAIGN.
PERSONALITIES A THING OF PAST.

Those who worry that 21st century politics is too much about personality and not enough about policy will find it interesting to note that 80 years ago some people were concerned there wasn't enough personality in politics. This wistful reminiscence on the glory days of cutthroat campaigning, written in the leadup to the Oct. 29 election, was probably the work of veteran Citizen *parliamentary reporter Charles Bishop, who was appointed to the Senate in 1945.*

The "good" old times, when politicians abused one another, and per-

sonalities were considered valuable campaign aids are apparently
gone forever.

The old time election was a great occasion for evening up scores.
There was no talk of libel or slander actions when one candidate
would give the public his personal opinion of his opponent and the
party to which he belonged. The other fellow had the same privilege,
and the most popular was most often the man who could turn out the
most sarcastic phrases or the most fitting epithets.

The "faithful" followed suit, and the party press put forth its best efforts along the same line. Frequently, election meetings ended up in
the time honored "free for all" when the side with the bigger biceps
came off victorious.

Election day was a strenuous time, but nothing compared to election
night when the results were announced. While all the bars were
closed—at least the front doors were shut—the winners as well as the
losers had generally provided against this contingency. The winners
invariably celebrated with a grand parade. Torches and red fire were
features, but quite paled against the red hot oratory of the occasion.

But gradually there came a change. It was first evidenced in the way
the results were received. The victors seemed to take their responsibilities more seriously, while the losers appeared to realize that it was
all over but the cheering. Then the candidates began to tone down in
their methods. The conviction seemed to grow that the people were
no longer misled by the tumult of the mob and the shouting of the captains. Personalities, too, grew fewer, and finally ceased altogether. It
became bad form to abuse one's opponent. His policy and the policy of
his party were still, quite legitimately, open to attack, but his individual
qualities, his record and his private doings were regarded as altogether
outside the question.

Today there are practically no personal attacks, there are no insinua-
tions of corruption, no charges that the other fellow's chief qualification was his ability to beat his wife, or defraud his creditors. This is not
an altogether welcome change inasmuch as it has removed some of the
exciting attractions of political discourse.

Perhaps the reform filtered down from the upper stratum of politics.
In the old days the leaders in Parliament set the example to their followers throughout the country. There, language was more polished,
and the innuendo was couched in more delicate phraseology. One did
not call one's opponent a horse thief on the floor of the house although
one might suggest that the honorable member opposite had a reputation for acquiring equines in a way that promoted much speculation
among those who were aware of this peculiarity. But it took some time
for this change to manifest itself in the chief council of the nation.

Peculiarly enough, the tone of legislative discussion in the earlier

July 9, 1925

Parliaments of the Dominion was much higher than in those of a score of years later. Indeed, the biting retort and the personal allusion were the flowers of a later oratorical period, chiefly in the '80s and early sessions of the next decade. It was during this period that Sir John Macdonald was always referred to as "Old Tomorrow," from his alleged tendency to stall off office seekers until the next day. It was an excellent formula because it could be employed continuously, without quenching the hope that arose eternal within the office-seeking breast.

Similarly Sir Richard Cartwright was known as "Blue Ruin Dick" because of his habit of predicting national disaster unless there was an immediate change of administration and the Liberals restored to the offices of power.... J. B. Rykert, member for Lincoln, was referred to as "Scrap Book" Rykert. He always kept a scrap book and compiled damaging speeches against his opponents, which contained many injudicious and forgotten opinions by his political enemies.

On one occasion in the '80s Sir John quoted a passage of Scripture to the house and Alexander Mackenzie at once demanded to know from what volume the speaker was taking the passage.

"I do not wonder the honorable gentlemen does not recognize it," replied Sir John. "The extract is from the Scriptures."

"Oh, mon ye shouldn't do that," retorted Mackenzie. "Ye are na well acquainted wi' the author."

In the same session Sir John introduced a measure that the Liberals had long advocated themselves. At once a Liberal member arose and accused the premier of stealing the brains of the opposition. Sir John promptly arose to a point of order.

"Mr. Speaker," he said, "I have been accused of many offences in my life time, but this is the first time I have ever been charged with petty larceny."

But these exchanges were trivial compared to a famous clash in the Senate on one occasion when Senator Miller, in an angry speech, referred to Senator Ross as a "toothless old viper." Senator Ross at once countered with a challenge to Miller to run a 100 yard race around the parliamentary grounds for a side bet of $100.

"I can't bring myself to compete with an individual who is so far advanced in senility that he stumbles into this chamber and collapses into the first seat he encounters," replied Miller....

April 20, 1926
AMERICANIZING OURSELVES.

Fifteen United States publications have, according to the Canadian Printer and Publisher, a combined yearly circulation in Canada of 23,858,612. Those fifteen are but a few of the six hundred odd American magazines and weekly newspapers that circulate in Canada and carry

LINERS OF THE SAINT LAWRENCE

Canada Steamship Lines *Limited*

Spetember 7, 1925

on the work of Americanizing us.

One United States magazine that has built up a tremendous circulation by printing inspiring articles on the rise of successful go-getters has thousands of readers in Canada, and yet has never printed a story about a Canadian who made good in his own country. It has published stories of Canadians making good in the United States—of the Toronto boy who became a hotel king, of the Nova Scotia lad who became a woollen magnate, of the Eastern Canadian who became a Washington cabinet minister, of the Canadian who changed the face of a great city, of the boy who became a millionaire meat packer, of the Toronto girl who became the darling of the screen—but not one, as stated, of a Canadian in Canada.

With so big a circulation of their products in Canada, one might expect the publishers to be less provincial in their nationalism. But they even insist upon the same policy in the novels that they print. "Wild Geese," by Martha Ostenso, was written in Canada by a resident of Canada, but mention of Canada has been carefully eliminated. The locale of the novel becomes a vague "north west." Other books have been treated the same way. Thus Canadians are made reluctant agents in the Americanization of their fellows. And what the remedy is, nobody seems to know.

September 7, 1925

September 21, 1925

July 22, 1926
DISGRACEFUL SCENES IN GATINEAU TOWN;
ORGY OF DRUNKENNESS.
After Lapse of Twenty-one Years Licensed Sale Gets Away
to Bad Start. Three Jailed. Man in Hospital in Grave Condition.
LICENSEE BEHAVES IN ATROCIOUS MANNER.
Judging by the names of the brawlers mentioned in this excerpt,
it seems the return of alcohol to Maniwaki exacerbated
tensions between the town's French and English citizens.

The opening of licensed hotel bars in the town of Maniwaki, Que., for the first time in twenty-one years, which happened yesterday, was attended by the most disgraceful scenes and orgies of drunkenness which have ever been known there, even in the palmiest days of the open barroom.

As a result of the day's "festivities," three men are in jail, one of whom may be tried on a murder charge; another is in hospital in such a serious condition that he is expected to die, and one of the new licensees behaved in such an atrocious manner that he was hauled into court and given a month's hard labor, which, however, was suspended, otherwise his license, only a few hours' old, would have gone by the board.

Such is the story brought to Hull this morning by Judge Roland Millar, who held police court at Maniwaki yesterday, and was most disagreeably impressed by the scenes which characterized Maniwaki's departure from the dry list. There were pitched battles in all parts of the town, and Yves Tremblay, chief of police, had his hands full....

Joseph Riel and Georges Malboeuf, two of the principal offenders who appeared before Judge Millar, were given fifteen days in jail without any option of a fine for their prominent share in the disturbance, when they thoroughly beat another citizen named Stevenson.

Aloide Barbe is awaiting trial in the Hull jail on a charge of having committed grievous bodily harm upon one Patrick Heeney. The latter suffered a broken nose, dislocated jaw and features almost unrecognizable, plus visible footmarks on his body. He's in the Maniwaki hospital in very serious condition. In fact, so serious is his condition that Judge Millar remanded Barbe without bail for eight days to await the outcome of Heeney's injuries.

Joseph Myrand, proprietor of the "Chateau Laurier" at Maniwaki, drew a sentence of a month in jail which was suspended for very boisterous conduct.

"It took you more than twenty years to get your liquor licenses in this town," said Judge Millar, addressing a crowded court room, "but it won't take you that number of days to have them cancelled, if this kind of thing is kept up. Representations will be made to the Quebec Liquor Commission if liquor licenses here, and there are only three of them, are going to cause such disturbances."

May 5, 1926

August 12, 1926
PHONOGRAPH RECORD STARTED REAL RIOT.
Aftermath of Pamilla St. Battle in Court.

The playing of a Victrola on Pamilla street the other night at nine o'clock started an argument which ended in police court.

Mrs. Lucy Dinardo, 56 Pamilla street, was in bed when she heard a tune which she thought she recognized as being produced by a record which she owned but which had not been returned to her after having been loaned by the daughter of Antonio Girotte, 65 Pamilla street.

Mrs. Dinardo then went to the Girotte home and demanded the record. Miss Girotte said the record did not belong to Mrs. Dinardo and the argument was in full swing when Mr. Girotte arrived and took a hand. It was given in evidence that he threatened to smash the record over Mrs. Dinardo's face if she persisted in saying that it was hers and also that he had tried to shove her away. One side went further and said he had hit Mrs. Dinardo and had caught her by the throat.

Into the argument then came Mrs. Dinardo's mother, her sister and her brother-in-law. Mr. Girotte and his daughter claimed that he was knocked down and kicked, breaking his teeth. In support of this he produced a dentist's bill for $40. The other side claimed he had his teeth loosened some time ago when he got into an argument with his daughter's "first lover." Mr. Girotte also claimed the women jumped on him like wolves and tried to scratch his face. There was also evidence that unsavory epithets were used in the argument.

The aftermath was that Mrs. Lucy Dinardo charged Mr. Girotte with assault. Mrs. Rosie Calagie, 517 1/2 Rochester street, daughter of Mr. Girotte, charged Alexander Asquini, brother-in-law of Mrs. Dinardo, with assaulting her father, Antonio Girotte, and Mrs. Dinardo and her mother, Rosie Arcuri, 66 Pamilla street, with being disorderly on the street. Magistrate Hopewell found all four guilty and imposed fines of $5 and $2 costs in each case.

•

Matthew Saikeley, 269 Bay street, pleaded guilty to an infraction of the Lord's Day by selling ice cream on Sunday and was fined $5 and $2 costs. Detectives Johnson and Frost laid the information.

•

Emile Maisonneuve, 27 Desjardins street, Hull, paid $30 and $2 costs for exceeding the speed limit of 15 miles per hour in his automobile when passing the corner of Bank street and Clarey avenue.

Here's The Right And Wrong Way To Drive Your Car

RIGHT

WRONG

The right way and wrong way of passing a slower vehicle, with another approaching on a narrow road, are shown here. The safe method is to permit the approaching driver to pass, and be sure of a clear road before going ahead.

August 16, 1926

Centenary and Exhibition Visitors

will enjoy a visit to Weldon Graham's. It is a distinctive example of the model tea room and fountain.

There's a restful, good-fellowship atmosphere at Graham's that makes delicious dishes and cool, refreshing foods and drinks, doubly inviting.

When uptown shopping your visitors will appreciate dropping in for lunch or afternoon tea.

Weldon J. Graham
Limited
90 SPARKS ST.   Near Metcalfe.

August 16, 1926

September 18, 1927
SEES WORLD WITHOUT ANY BEAUTIFUL WOMEN.
Scientist Gives Dire Picture of Future.

It will be a sad world indeed in two or three centuries, for present indications are that there will be practically no beautiful or brilliant women, wrote Professor Ellsworth Huntington, of Yale University, and Leon F. Whitney, executive secretary of the Eugenics Society of America, in a book, "The Builders of America," published today.

This is but an aspect, they said, of the alarming decline in birth-rate among the brain worker or builder class. In five generations, 200 fathers of the brain worker type will leave but 28 descendants, while an equal number of unskilled workers will leave 472—unless something is done, their statistics revealed, to check this present trend, through which the creative, artistic and imaginative faculties of the race are said to be dying out.

The Follies girl and the college girl have been equally remiss in failing to have children, the authors found. Of 800 attractive Follies girls they found but 500 married, and only 25 were known to have children. The average child per graduate of 2,294 Vassar graduates was but one and one tenth.

Professor Huntington and Mr. Whitney reached conclusions directly opposite from the common argument that the upper class is being constantly built up from the lower classes. A study of "Who's Who" lists indicated that those who rise from the lower classes are usually childless or have very small families, they said.

They found kitchenette apartments and difficult economic conditions for professional workers among the primary causes for the decline of the biological vigor of the creative class.

The fledgling U.S. eugenics movement, which advocated the use of artificial selection to improve humans, was an inspiration to the Nazis, whose radical adaptation of the theory culminated in the Holocaust.

March 17, 1928
WHAT A ROBOT THINKS ABOUT.
(Excerpt from an editorial:)

"Mr. Televox," the mechanical man, is "here to stay," says his inventor. What is more, he will be perfected from time to time so that no home of the future will be complete without him. He already performs chores, and soon he will be made to speak. All that remains is to make him think.

And when he is able to think, what will he believe in? It is our guess that when "Mr. Televox" at last submits to being interviewed by the press, he will have some pronounced views on a number of things. He'll be for liberty, but not for licence. And of course for evolution, but not for revolution.

In his opinion, no doubt, the opinions of Mrs. Dora Russell [British feminist and wife of philosopher Bertrand Russell] are an Insult to American Womanhood. And, naturally, people who don't like it here should go back where they came from. He will be for Coolidge, and more than likely will share the opinion that Sacco and Vanzetti [U.S. anarchists] got what was coming to them. Inevitably, he will be for constructive and against destructive criticism, adding, "Anybody can tear down; it is harder to build up."

When Mr. Televox is asked whom he considers the three greatest living men he will just automatically reply that they are Edison, Rockefeller and Ford, with Lindbergh getting honorable mention. In the field of literature and drama he will favor those books and plays which bring gladness into the world. "There is enough sadness as it is, without going looking for it," he will add safely. He will not exactly object to women smoking, but he will certainly believe that real womanly women will not want to smoke. And as for the younger generation, why, it seems to have no realization of the way it is heading. What is wanted, he will say, is more old-fashioned family worship. He will be for free speech, but there are limits, etc., etc....

One might go on. But sufficient indication is given of the mentality of

MISS WHITTON ON JUVENILE COURT'S IMPORTANT WORK

Says Amazing Thing Is That Delinquency Among Young Not Greater Than It Actually Is Today.

In an address on social delinquency, given before the Ottawa Social Workers' Club, Miss Charlotte Whitton, executive secretary of the Canadian Council on Child Welfare, stressed the importance of the juvenile court.

Referring to the increase in juvenile delinquency, Miss Whitton said the amazing thing is that the increase is not greater in view of the breaking down of traditional codes and the need of readjustment of modern life to the precepts taught, or the adjustment of precepts to actual practices.

Probation is the cogwheel in the mechanism of the juvenile court, and in this connection Miss Whitton emphasized the qualities required in the judge of the court, the peculiar requirements for probation officers and the interest which should be taken by the Children's Aid Society or a juvenile court committee in the community. As far as possible, children should be kept in their own or other private homes, and institutional treatment should be for only problem cases, or cases where other methods have failed time and time again. No child should be held for more than twenty-four hours without its case being dealt with by the court. Miss Whitton endorsed the statement made by Judge Julian Mack that practically every normal boy or girl who comes into the juvenile court may be saved to a life of good citizenship.

There was a good attendance of members of the club at the luncheon.

January 6, 1927

the perfect Robot. If it were otherwise, he would not be a Robot.

June 4, 1928
THE GIBB SIAMESE TWINS,
Whom Doctors Were Going to Separate Some Months
Ago In Order That One Could Marry
Are Appearing at Keith's Starting Saturday.

Think of it: Two sixteen-year-old girls, well educated, accomplished and vivacious, joined together since birth at the base of their spines, with death certain if any surgeon should attempt to separate them. These are the famous Gibb Twins, the world's most unusual natural attraction who will appear at B. F. Keith's theatre [on Bank Street near Albert] commencing next Saturday matinee.

One would think the Gibb girls as afflicted and one would naturally pity their plight. But the girls—Mary and Margaret, keenly intelligent and witty—would smile at the idea, for they have the best of times together and they are never unhappy.

It is literally true that the Gibb Twins have never had a cross word. They are two distinct personalities, but they can walk, play, work, read, study and amuse themselves with complete accord and perfect understanding and synchronization. Mary may fall asleep while Margaret sews or reads—and that is alright with them both. One may play checkers with a friend while the other plays Mah Jong with another visitor. They play the piano together and one will accompany the other's singing. They run, play, stroll and motor in perfect harmony, only Margaret, the left-hand twin, must needs drive the motor with Mary always at her side.

During their engagement at B. F. Keith's, the Gibb Twins will hold a reception for theatre patrons every day in the lobby of the theatre, immediately following their appearance on the stage.

September 12, 1928
WILL PRESENT RADIO AUDIENCE
WITH BOTH SIGHT AND SOUND OF THE PLAY!
Broadcast Television Makes Initial Appearance
as Vehicle of the Drama. Engineers of General Electric Co.
Give Demonstration at Schenectady, N.Y.
(Special to the Evening Citizen.)

SCHENECTADY, N.Y., Sept. 12.—Broadcast television yesterday made its initial appearance as a vehicle of drama. In a one act play, having a cast of two characters, engineers of the General Electric Company here demonstrated to a party of newspapermen that television, synchronized with the regular form of radio broadcast, can be used to present the radio audience with both the sight and sound of drama.

The drama appeared on a screen a few inches square and displayed only the head of the characters with the moving images of small stage portions introduced as effects. The spoken portion of the drama was broadcast through regular radio channels by the company's station here WGY.

The broadcast of television scenes, with figures in full length and background in some detail, is in the not distant future, the engineers indicated.

The image of the television screen possessed the clarity of the average newspaper photograph. Movements of the head, lips and eyes were registered as natural motions.

The play chosen for the broadcast was J. Harley Manners' "The Queen's Messenger."

April 16, 1929
OLYMPIC WINNER RIDICULES
TITLE 'FASTEST HUMAN'.
Percy Williams Thinks It Absurd to Assume
No One Has Beaten His Time. Ethel Catherwood
"Too Intelligent" to Get Married.
*The arrival of the stars of Canada's 1928 Amsterdam Olympics
team was big news in Ottawa. The event sparked bitter competition
between* Citizen *and* Journal *reporters for access to the athletes,
including sprinter Percy Williams, winner of two gold medals,
and Ethel Catherwood, winner of high jumping gold and "the prettiest
girl athlete in the world," according to* The New York Times.

Canada's Olympic heroes came to Ottawa at noon today, headed by the fleet Percy Williams and the beautiful Ethel Catherwood.

A large crowd of civic authorities, other officials and friends and several thousand people met the visiting athletes, who proceeded through to the Chateau Laurier where they registered. They will be entertained by the city this afternoon, by a drive around the Capital. Most of them evinced a keen interest to see Parliament in session. Surprising as it may seem, many of the team have never been to Ottawa before, and showed a lively anticipation over their impending visit. They will all participate in the big sports meet at the Auditorium tomorrow night.

Percy Williams was the first person sought by the *Citizen*. As the reports indicate, he is a quiet and retiring youth, and has to be coaxed to talk to our reporter.

"Please don't describe me as the fastest human," he said at the outset. "That's absurd. Do you mean to say that nobody has traveled as fast as I have!"

"Do you think you can beat your time?" he was asked.

Above and opposite: Images of fashion from March 11, 1927

"I don't know," he replied.

"Of course he can," interjected Miss Alexandrine Gibb, Toronto sports writer, coach of women's athletics, who is in charge of the girls on this trip, and who also looked after them at the Olympics in Amsterdam. Miss Gibb has traveled nearly 100,000 miles in connection with women's sports. "Of course he can—he is just too modest to say so," she repeated. . . .

Earlier in the interview, Mr. Williams stated that very few newspaper reports of races were correct.

"Take last night for instance," he said. "The paper said that Fitzpatrick was two yards ahead of me. He is a very fast man. Now how could I possibly catch up two yards on him? The answer is that I couldn't. He was only about half a yard ahead of me."

"How about your reputed slow start—can you improve on it?"

"Of course I can. That's something I've got to learn. We are learning all the time. Practice and competition will do that."

Meanwhile, quiet and stately, Miss Ethel Catherwood, the "Saskatoon Lily," and world's champion high jumper, sat nearby. She stated confidently that she could beat her own world's record high jump. Miss Gibb cut in to say that Miss Catherwood needed competition to bring out the best she could do, and even the Olympics could scarcely provide that.

She also remarked, about matrimony: "I am not going to get married. I've got intelligence."

"How about those movie contracts? Are you going into the movies?"

"No. That was denied by me next day. When I got back from Amsterdam, I got lots of them. But I paid no attention to them. I am taking a commercial course in Toronto," she said. . . .

March 11, 1927

November 3, 1930
CORONATION OF RAS TAFARI
WAS BARBARIC SCENE
Titles Are Lord King of Kings of Ethiopia, Conquering
Lion of Tribe of Judah and Elect of God. Estimated
Ceremony Cost Some $3,000,000. Gargantuan Open-Air
Banquet Given By Emperor To 25,000 Tribesmen.
*In the early days of the Great Depression, news of Haile Selassi's
lavish coronation as Ethiopian emperor supplied
an exotic counterpoint to the grim news at home. The* Citizen
splashed the story, excerpted here, across its front page.

(Special to the Evening Citizen.)
ADDIS ABABA, Abyssinia, Nov. 2.—Amidst barbaric splendor and lavish pageantry, Ras Tafari Makonnen, the 39-year-old prince who has

been regent of Abyssinia for fourteen years, was crowned at dawn to-day as Emperor Haile Selassi I.

The coronation gives Ras Tafari, who claims descent from King Soloman and the Queen of Sheba, the titles of Emperor, Lord King of Kings of Ethiopia, Conquering Lion of the Tribe of Judah, the Elect of God, and the Light of the World.

Simultaneously, the royal consort, Princess Waziru Menen, a short, rotund woman of 40, was crowned as Queen Etega Menen, Queen of Queens of Ethiopia. This was virtually the queen's "coming-out party," as she has heretofore been confined to her housewifely and motherly duties in the royal household. She has five children, one of them married, and has taken no active part in court and state affairs.

The coronation ceremony, performed by the venerable Coptic arch-bishop of Ethiopia, was unparalleled in modern times for quaintness, color, magnificence, and expenditure. The cost to the government was estimated at $3,000,000. For six months the nation has been preparing holiday garb for the occasion.

As their majesties rode to the church through the dusty, rubble streets of the mountain capital, which were packed with tens of thou-sands of their braves and chieftains, the masses thundered forth cheers and wild, savage cries of acclaim. Scores of natives were trampled in the dust as the crowd surged to catch sight of the coronation party.

On either side of the colored potentates, acting as escorts of honor, were olive-skinned, black-bearded and curly-headed Ethiopian tribal chiefs. They wore multi-colored costumes of silk and satin, embroi-dered in gold and silver. Their shields were of hippopotamus hides, and they had medieval swords and scabbards. Behind the monarch and his queen were the high priests in vestments of scarlet, green, yellow, or purple, and carrying gold and silver crosiers and incense lamps. Fol-lowing the ecclesiastics were groups of princes and grandees in black silk ceremonial capes, and the members of the cabinet and govern-ment in their national shammas.

Ras Tafari and his queen rode in the imperial chariot which once be-longed to former Kaiser Wilhelm of Germany. The carriage was drawn by six snow-white horses.

Arriving at the Church of St. George, they descended from the chari-ot, their coronation robes of scarlet and gold flittering in the sun. The sunlight was reflected fiercely from the gold and diamonds on their crowns, where the figures of the Lion of Judah symbolized the national power. The foreign princes, ministers, and delegates had already taken their places in the church, which proved too small, in spite of recent additions, for the throngs which clamored for admission. Their majesties found difficulty in making their way through the crowd to the inner sanctuary, where the Coptic archbishop performed the reli-

SIR WILFRID LAURIER MONUMENT

The site chosen for the Sir Wilfrid Laurier monument is at the south-east corner of East Block overlooking Wellington street and Connaught Place. The location is a commanding one, being on an elevation—the lawn falling away towards the entrance to the grounds near the Lovers' Walk, opposite the Post Office. The situation lends itself to very effective treatment in the way of terraces and steps approaching the monument.

The total height from the ground is 13 feet 4 inches, the bronze figure being 9 feet high, standing on a granite base 4 feet 4 inches. This base takes the form of a monolithic block standing on the sub-base of two broad steps which extend to a width, across the front, of 10 feet 11-2 inches, and 9 feet back to front.

There is no elaborate inscription; the only lettering is on the front of the base and reads:—

"LAURIER"
1841—1919

The simplicity of this inscription is aptly expressed by the Prime Minister when he said: "The absence of accessories is always a tribute to the individual whom the monument is extended to portray."

The sculptor's fee for this work is $25,000, exclusive of the founda-tions which are now being put in place by the Department of Public Works.

Canadians will be gratified to know that the design is the conception of a Montreal sculptor, Mr. J. Emile Brunet. Mr. Brunet is a young sculptor who was born in Montreal and received his education and early training in Canada. He was engaged for sometime in his pro-fession in the United States, and while there, won the competition for a War Memorial to be erected at Longueuil, Quebec. He then entered the renowned School of Arts in Paris (Ecole Nationale des Beaux-Arts), where he attained great distinction in his chosen profession, successfully competing against European sculptors. It is also of interest that Mr. Brunet was for a time in Ottawa and contributed to the ornamental sculpture of the New Parliament Buildings.

The unveiling ceremony will take place in July, during the Jubilee of Confederation.

May 6, 1927

gious rites and ceremonials. The atmosphere was murky, almost suffocating, with incense and the thick, stifling smoke of tallow candles.

Small of stature, thin, frail, with delicate, almost feminine features, Ras Tafari nevertheless assumed a look of dignity and solemnity as the archbishop placed the crown upon his head. Yet the emperor seemed dwarfed by Queen Waziru Menen, who is of Amazon proportions....

The coronation was followed by a dance of the high priests in front of the church. To the time of low, rhythmical chants, accented by monotonous drumbeats and the clash of cymbals, the priests, bearded and mantled, swayed their bodies violently to and fro according to the peculiar Ethiopian ritual, and waved their long, gold-headed "prayer-sticks" like wands.

After the royal pair left the church, they were driven, amidst fresh outbursts of applause, to a great, lavishly decorated coronation dais in the big square in front of the palace. In front of them, tethered to the platform and growling like captive beasts in a Roman arena, were a quintet of fierce-looking lions with beautiful golden-brown manes, guardians of the throne of Ethiopia and national symbols of power.

The ruling princes and chiefs from the outlying provinces were admitted to their presence in processional order. As they approached the rulers, they prostrated themselves, touching the earth with their foreheads as an indication of their submission and homage. Beside the sovereigns stood the crack guardsmen of the palace, tall, stalwart youths, brilliantly uniformed, who guard their monarchs' lives and lead the way into battle.

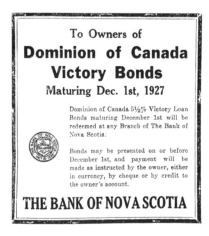

January 24, 1931
UNCLE RAY'S SATURDAY MAIL BAG.
Motto: "O.U.R.S.—ON UNCLE RAY'S SERVICE.

For more than two decades, "Uncle Ray's Corner," published Monday to Friday, and Uncle Ray's Saturday Mail Bag were fixtures in the Citizen. *Unknown to the column's legion of young readers—called nephews and nieces—Uncle Ray was actually Isabel C. Armstrong, who for years was women's editor and was later in charge of entertainment news. Here's an excerpt from a typical column:*

WAS BUSY HELPING MOTHER.

Dear Uncle Ray: I wanted to write you before Christmas to wish you a Merry Christmas, but my three sisters were ill and mother asked me to amuse them, and I was unable to write. I am nine years of age and I will be 10 on March 16. I was wishing you a prosperous and happy New Year. Poor Uncle Bim is sad all right. Maybe Freckles is getting along all right and I am glad Farbar is caught. I will write you again.

Your nephew, ROGER TRUDEL, 27 Rockcliffe Way, Ottawa.

Well done, Roger. It was splendid of you to help mother by amusing your sisters. You were doing even more than the Scout's "good deed a day." Did you tell them stories and play games with them? I feel sure you "read" the funny page pictures to them, you seem know Freckles and Uncle Bim and the rest so well. Do you like Sneezix and Annie Rooney also?

—UNCLE RAY.

THANK YOU FOR GREETINGS.

Dear Uncle Ray: This is my fourth letter to your Cosy Corner. I thank you very much for the birthday greetings although my name was spelled wrong. I should be M-a-i-r not M-o-i-r. I hope you will correct it in your Birthday Book. This is the second time my name has been spelled wrong. I will close now with wishing you and all the corner cousins a Happy New Year.

Your loving niece, MAIR DAVIES, 95 Holmwood Ave., Ottawa, Ont.

The name is M-A-I-R in the Birthday Book and the error was what is called a "typographical" one. Next time we will tell the printers to watch very carefully. You see, you are the possessor of a very unusual name.

—UNCLE RAY.

NIGGER AND BLUEIE PETS IN THIS HOME.

Dear Uncle Ray: This is my first letter to the Cosy Corner, and I hope you will put it in the paper. I read the Cosy Corner letters every night and enjoy them very much. My name is Dorothy. I am twelve. Please put my birthday in your book. It is on Oct. 6. My sister is writing too. I have two sisters and two brothers. We have a dog named Nigger because he is black and a cat name Blueie because he is a grayish blue. I love them both very much. I will close now as my letter is getting long.

With love, DOROTHY JOHNSTON, Ottawa.

Pets are wonderful friends. It's so nice that you can have two such good friends.

—UNCLE RAY.

TOO COLD FOR SCHOOL SO WE STUDY AT HOME.

Dear Uncle Ray: It's a cold stormy afternoon and as I cannot go out skiing I will write a few lines to you. I hope you had a very merry Christmas and wish you all kinds of good luck in the New Year. Santa Claus was very generous to all of us. He brought me books, toys and several other presents from my friends.

When it is not too cold my sister and I ski. We enjoy it very much and hope some day to join a ski club. There are no hills close enough to ski on, but I think we do not fall as often as we would going down hills. The weather is too cold for us to go to school, but we study at home.

We had a small concert at school before Christmas. My sister and I had parts in it. We had to sing a song called "Spotty and Dotty." I do not want to take up too much space so I will say goodbye.

Your loving niece, MARGARET DALY, Breckenridge, Que.

I can imagine you have a cosy time studying at home when it is cold and stormy outdoors. Did you ever see anyone make a big jump skiing? It is very thrilling. Did you notice that a former champion jumped 217 feet at Lucerne last week? Thank you on behalf of cousins, as well as myself, for your kind wishes.

—UNCLE RAY.

June 16, 1931
TAN GIVES WAY TO LILIES.
(Excerpt from an editorial:)

Women, it seems, will have pale complexions this summer. The word has gone forth—who sent it is not disclosed—that it will be fashionable henceforth for the fair sex to be white and not brown. To put it plainly, the day of tanned skin has gone out and the new day of the lily-white complexion has come in. "White faces and white arms are absolutely in fashion this season," declares a "beauty doctor."

On the whole, we are satisfied with the new complexion trend. It is true that a smooth, tanned skin—delicate bronze with a suggestion of gold in it—has its esthetic appeal, and some women looked really charming when tanned. But most of the others did not. They either turned a grayish brown or became simply scarlet, which was anything but prepossessing. . . .

Now white can be all things to all women. It is really their true color. And white is not only more becoming to a larger number of women, but it is more natural. After all, it is not natural for human beings to seek exposure in the sun and bake their bodies. Why, otherwise, do we always walk on the shady side of the street and find shelter under trees? The reason, of course, is that our distant ancestors were arboreal. They lived in shady trees—and it was a sign of intelligence.

Therefore, we claim, this sun business is un-human. Tanned skins may be attractive to some, but the more civilized tint is white—with a suggestion of rose petals at appropriate places.

June 17, 1931
PSALM OF BENNETT.
Bennett is my Shepherd, I am in want.
He maketh me to lie down on park benches,
He leadeth me beside still factories,

July 15, 1929

He restoreth my doubt in the Conservative party.
He leadeth me in the path of destruction
For his party's sake.
Yea, though I walk through the valley of the shadow of debt,
I will fear much evil, for thou art against me.
The politicians and the profiteers they frighten me.
Thou preparest a reduction in my salary before me,
In the presence of mine enemies.
Thou anointest my income with taxes,
My expenses runneth over my income.
Surely unemployment and poverty,
Will follow me all the days of the Conservative administration.
And I shall live in a rented house forever.
                            —ARTHUR S. JOHNSON, Ottawa, June 8, 1931.

June 27, 1931
YO-YO TIME IN OTTAWA.
TOY-CRAZE HIGHLY POPULAR.
Playgrounds Commission Arranging to Stage Yo-Yo
contests at the Twelve Respective Playgrounds.
Young Expert Here to Demonstrate.
(Excerpt from a news feature:)

The Capital of the Dominion has begun to "yoo-hoo" for the yo-yo.
And in the event that you are unaware of what a yo-yo constitutes, it is
the latest toy-craze to hit the continent.

Ottawa was struck with it today and for those children, boys or girls,
who cannot leave the city for their summer holidays, they will find unbounded joy and amusement in mastering the recently discovered fad.

It is more than difficult to describe the yo-yo, but it is something like
the old monkey-on-the-string toy of a few years ago. But it's not a monkey; it's monkey business or something to that effect. At any rate the
sole idea of yo-yoing is to keep your yo-yo bouncing; it's a bouncing
ball or a bounding block providing you are sufficiently skilful to make
it bob . . . . It isn't exactly a game or an indoor sport. It is a fascinating
novelty that will capture the city by storm and no preventative measures by the police, firefighters or health authorities will arrest the unusual attack on the minds of the city's children.

But that's not all. What youngster, boy or girl, is going to be recognized as the champion yo-yoer in the city. You don't know and neither
do we. But we will all know soon enough.

The Playgrounds Commission of the city, through its supervisor, E. F.
Morgan, is arranging to stage yo-yo contests at the 12 respective playgrounds. Following the competitions the yo-yo champions of the dif-

July 15, 1929

ferent parks will be announced and later on a city-wide contest, at which the winners of the preliminary battles will compete, will be held, Mr. Morgan promised.

Parents would be well advised to send their children to the playgrounds, where they may receive tuition and practice with their yo-yo. It will be a smart young lad or miss, who will win the title of "yo-yo champion of Ottawa."

Harvey Lowe, a Chinese youth from Victoria, is in the city now and will make a complete tour of all the playgrounds, instructing all in the art of yo-yoing. Harvey is Canadian champion and to see him perform "Atlantic hops," Walking the dog," and other intricate maneuvers, will make you want to yo-yo from morning till night. . . .

August 12, 1931

TIES.

(Excerpt from an editorial.)

We have no sympathy with the young gentleman in *Punch*, who, entering a haberdasher's to buy a tie, informed the salesman that he wanted one in school colors. "What school, sir?" "Any good school," replied the purchaser.

That attitude is recklessly criminal, it is not condoned, and yet we recognize there is some justification for boldly challenging the right of any two or three people gathered together to call themselves a club and to arrogate to themselves the monopoly of certain colors or arrangements of colors in ties. There are, after all, only a limited number of wearable colors in the spectrum and it is inevitable, irrevocable, there should be a clash of interests between high-powered tie monopolies claimed, say, by athletic clubs and other clubs or individuals. In such a clash, what is moral? To what standard of his thinking and clean living must the tender-souled wearer of some other club's tie turn for guidance?

For ourselves, we suffer from righteousness in ties. We would not, like Mr. Punch's young man, deliberately of malice aforethought, purchase the tie of a school to which we had not gone, or of a club to which we could not afford to belong. Yet for all this righteousness, we are constantly suffering from cutting comments and almost rude challenges—even those who wear club ties may be rude.

One day, for example—it was the day after pay day—we saw a silk tie of superbly regal blue. It was beyond our means, but it could not be resisted. We spent a large percentage of our pay check and proudly wore it. Alas, we met what is called an Oxonian—an example of race transcending races, something individual and different, like kings— individuals who have acquired by inoculation or environment racial char-

acteristics superseding those of color, creed, language, and the cephalic index. Such a one cuttingly inquired if we had rowed for the Varsity or if we had earned the "blue," signified by our tie, on the rugger field.

Our blue tie, pride of a few brief days, now reposes in the cupboard, a bread line for unemployed moths, and a lesson in cravatic deportment. Our own righteousness, and our fear of Oxonians, had destroyed our rash investment. Conscience had made a coward of us. On receipt of the next pay check, we are going to buy twenty-four safe inches of lamp wick. No club that we can imagine has adopted that useful textile as a tie.

August 11, 1930

August 31, 1931
THE BEGGAR AT THE DOOR.
Isobel Robertson Currier frequently sent letters to the Citizen,
which often published them as columns.

We have lately had a most unfortunate experience. Any men's old clothing which collects about the house, we send to the men's Mission. Well, we had a bundle all nicely tied up, a blue serge suit that had been knocking around for some time and a couple of shirts and socks we were tired of mending, just awaiting an opportunity to deliver it, when a young chap came to the door and he explained that he had torn his only pair of pants and he had been to nineteen houses that morning asking for an old pair and no one had any.

Yes, he knew the Mission—had spent last night there, but they had none either. Yes, he was a Scotchman and he gave his name. He had a sister married in Alberta and he was on his way out to her. Maybe he could get a job there. Yes, he might have done better to have stayed at home. Oh, yes, he had been well taken care of at the Mission. All he wanted was an old pair of pants.

Perhaps it was the Scotch accent, or perhaps the fact that he spoke well of the Mission—anyway we gave him our bundle, and we noted the bad tear in his pants as he walked away. He was most appreciative, and for a week we thought that, for once, our help had gone to a really deserving case. Then, we read in your columns that a young Scotchman with the same name as our young fellow was about to be deported, having been three times convicted of petty thieving. It rankled a bit to think that we had probably been had, and that our still serviceable clothing was likely decorating the front of some second-hand store, but we were somewhat reconciled when we heard some of the experiences of a charitable neighbor.

One man's plea was that he was forced to beg on account of having a sick wife and a family of seven small children to provide for. So he was

December 29, 1930

well fed at the house, and given an armful of clothing particularly suitable for children. This chap became a regular caller, until one day a tell-tale smell of strong drink aroused suspicions. He was asked why he spent money so foolishly instead of buying food and things for the needs at home. He replied that his friends treated him just to cheer him up out of sympathy.

A good suit of underwear that had been given to him had disappeared on his next visit, and his maudlin condition led to further investigation with the result that he was found to have no wife and no family. He was a healthy chap, well able to work, who had been refused admission to one shelter in the city on account of his disorderly conduct following the spending of his pension each month. It was an easy guess as to what had become of the suit of underwear that had disappeared.

When asked why he told such lies, he laughed and said, "Oh, you've got to pitch a good yarn to get anything in these hard times," and when told that he had better tell his treating friends to give him food instead of booze, he gave our neighbor a reproachful look and shambled off.

Our neighbor, like ourselves, is becoming much less credulous of sad stories told at the door. She has been to the Mission, on the corner of Daly and Waller streets, and learned how the men are received and fed, with due attention to good conduct and discipline, how they are given soap and warm showers to get clean, how their clothes are all fumigated over night and the men provided with clean nightshirts and clean beds in bright well-aired wards, and how each man can get advice and help from the workers at the Mission if he so desires.

One youngster, just three days out of a job, discussed the question of begging from door to door quite frankly.

"I'm new to this sort of thing, and I don't like it. I've only been around here a couple of days, but the men have been telling me things, and I know the kind of story to tell the police, and the kind to tell a kind-looking gentleman on the street, and the kind to tell a lady at the door, and the kind to tell here at the Mission to get the best treatment, and—aw—I don't want to do that sort of stuff. I want a job." This was some weeks ago, and the Mission got him a job on a farm right away, and he is still there.

Our trust in human nature is becoming sadly frayed. We will pass our responsibility on to the Union Mission, where they know more about the tricks of the begging trade, by handing out only Mission tickets at the door.

—ISOBEL ROBERTSON CURRIER.

March 5, 1931

January 8, 1932
ON DOING WITHOUT.
(Excerpt from an editorial:)

R. J. C. Stead, the novelist, said some very wise things to the fruit and vegetable jobbers' convention in the city on Wednesday. But with his general conclusions with respect to the current difficulties, we would enter a mild demurrer. As we understand him, Mr. Stead feels that the post-war slogan, "Why do without?" has been made the ruling philosophy of modern life. "Look where it has left us," he said.

Another novelist recently gave expression to similar views. According to the *Golden Book*, Sir Philip Gibbs says: "The source of all our present troubles lies in the illusion that we could live more luxuriously after the war than before the war, in spite of all that wasted wealth and the four and a half years devoted to destruction."

That sounds like what is called sense. So does Mr. Stead's belief that not doing without has left us where we are. But with all due respect to these two gentlemen, the trouble is not that the world has not learned to do without so much as that the world has not yet devised a means of bringing the people who have had to do without in touch with the abundance available.

What should we do without? Wheat? The elevators bulge with it. Motor cars? The factories are running half time. Coffee? They are burning it in Brazil. Caviar? It is rotting in Russia. By "doing without," what possible good can come? And why should we live "less luxuriously" when never before in the history of mankind were luxuries so plentiful? There is no virtue in "doing without" when there is abundance for all. We have passed the age when people believed there would always be a shortage. We are in the age when goods are piled in lavish array in storerooms and warehouses waiting for the consumers to consume them.

The practical solution is not to do without. It is to apply the means whereby consumers can consume by having purchasing power restored to them.

September 7, 1932
BEARDS NO LONGER HOLD POPULARITY
OF MEDICAL PROFESSION.

Van Dyke beards and other hirsute facial adornments which in former days gave an air of dignity to the professional men, especially doctors, are no longer the vogue, according to many of the famous medical men attending the twelfth congress of the French-speaking doctors of North America in session at the Chateau.

The doctor no longer has to wear a beard to give him the appearance

March 5, 1931

March 25, 1931

of an important man in the profession, one doctor said. The scientific mind is in the ascendant and a doctor's record, rather than his appearance, is what counts today.

Out of the 400 doctors registered at the convention, there are not more than a dozen wearing beards.

April 25, 1933

OTTAWA WOMEN SHOWING KEEN INTEREST IN COOKING SCHOOL.

Capacity Audience at R.K.O. Theatre This Morning When Miss Frances Thompson Began Demonstrations in Culinary Art.—Fashion Show Also Drawing Large Crowd.

In the 1930s, the women's pages rarely missed an opportunity to shamelessly plug Citizen *advertisers. The story excerpted here promotes no fewer than two dozen products.*

It is a long time since the women of Ottawa have had the privilege of spending such a profitable morning as they did today. Promptly at half-past nine o'clock, at the R.K.O. Capitol theatre, a capacity audience of women of Ottawa listened with interest and amazement to little tricks in cooking which banish the drudge from housework.

Miss Frances Thompson of the Canadian School of Home Science, who is no stranger to Ottawa women, is in charge of the demonstration of home cooking and with her are her two associate dieticians, Misses Ruth Crawford and Helene Chagnon....

A most attractively set stage greeted the eyes of those in the audience. The director and her assistants, in their crisp uniforms, which they told had been laundered at Vail's, and their hair, freshly trimmed and finger waved, which they confided had been done at Maxwell's, were wholly at ease. Miss Thompson explained that one reason she and her assistants do not tire, although they stand so much, is because they are wearing Lockwedge shoes, obtained at A. J. Freiman, Ltd.

Such a modern kitchen was on the stage that every housewife was envious. There were two Canadian General Electric refrigerators and stoves, as well as a sun lamp, all of which had been loaned by Robertson Pingle and Tilley Ltd. and Ogilvy's. A tastefully set dinner table, the table being loaned by A. J. Freiman, Ltd., the damask linen by the Canadian Departmental Stores, and the silver and china by Nettleton's. Community silver and china in the same design made a most attractively set table and the center of flowers was given by Wright's, the florist....

For the program this morning a number of breakfast dishes were given. A quick bread for breakfast was shown in the making, Miss Thompson explaining that for this recipe it had been discovered that

January 27, 1931

Opposite, below: March 25, 1931

Egg-O baking powder could not be too highly recommended. When adding her egg to the batter she explained that all the dairy produce was purchased at the A. and P. Stores which assured them of its quality, and their dairy products from the Ottawa Dairy.

A most appetizing beef and ham loaf was made from left overs, however, as she had none, she explained she had purchased her cooked meats from R. Hector Aubry. For the breadcrumbs she had used Standard Bread Ltd., and mentioned their special loaf, which contains a cup of milk.

When company comes in unexpectedly and a cake is needed Miss Thompson advised again the use of Egg-O mixed cake flour for muffins, cakes and small biscuits. The recipe given was one of the most quickly made and the results were amazing. Then to make the little cakes for company an easy recipe for magic frosting was given which was made simply with Eagle Brand condensed milk, chocolate and water. . . .

During the various phases of her cooking Miss Thompson washed her hands, and in each instance she spoke highly of Lux soap for the softening of the hands.

Then breakfast snacks and cheese biscuits were made, the latter having Chateau cheese used for the filling. In a delightful new dish named Kedgeree, Miss Thompson used the Baumert cheese which is prepared by the same company. In the Kedgeree, St. Charles evaporated milk was used.

During the course of her talk a cleaned coat was brought to Miss Crawford which had been done thoroughly and cheaply by Parker's cleaners and dryers. Miss Thompson also demonstrated the use of Rinso in soaking clothes. . . .

There was an intermission from the cooking school for a short time and models appeared in the most delightful spring costumes supplied by Chas. Ogilvy, Ltd. There were early spring costumes, filmy summer dresses and hats, bathing suits and pajamas and negligees. The flowers on the stage added to the attractive setting for the fashion show and they had been supplied by Wright's.

Vi-Tone, highly recommended by Miss Thompson as a drink which was rich in protein, was made and passed to the audience. Vi-Tone ice cream, made by the Ottawa, Central and Producers Dairy, was also on display.

As a break in the morning's talk Miss Thompson made a pot of tea from Salada, Orange Pekoe, and a number of the ladies enjoyed it. It was only steeped for three minutes then poured from the pot it was made in into a community silver pot. Miss Thompson advised any who were staying down town to lunch following the school, to visit the Venetian Sweets. She showed a can of Otter Brand coffee which she

said she would make and allow any who wished to sample.

Then the morning's school was over and Miss Thompson had to run as a Chevrolet car was waiting to take her to another appointment . . . .

November 16, 1933

November 16, 1933

EXCLUSIVE TALK WITH HITLER BY CITIZEN WRITER

Lukin Johnston's interview with Adolf Hitler set off one of the strangest weeks in Citizen *history. Strictly speaking, Johnston was Southam's London correspondent, but like all of the chain's papers, the* Citizen *laid claim to him as its own. After writing stories from Germany for a few weeks in the fall of 1933, Johnston was given 30 minutes with Hitler. He filed a lengthy story via his London assistant, ex-*Citizen *reporter A.C. Cummings, and said he was heading home. Two days later, Cummings cabled the* Citizen *with the news that Johnston was dead. He'd fallen overboard on the ferry crossing from Holland to Britain. Because a British naval officer had vanished from the same boat a few weeks before, an evil plot was initially suspected. But an inquiry revealed Johnston had fainted in his Berlin hotel room four days earlier, and reported feeling sick aboard the ferry. Coverage of the incident follows in the three excerpts below.*

BY LUKIN JOHNSTON
Special Correspondent of The Evening Citizen.

Berlin, Nov. 16.—Germany stands ready to consider favorably any invitation from the other great powers to recommence negotiations for disarmament or limitation of armaments. She does not care whether negotiations take place within or without the framework of the League of Nations. Her only condition is she will enter only on terms of absolute equality. She waits the call to Geneva or elsewhere . . . .

Such were the unequivocal statements made to your correspondent by Chancellor Hitler in an exclusive interview here. This is the first statement of Germany's future policy made since Sunday's monster referendum constituted Hitler absolute master of Germany.

Incidentally, it was the first interview he has ever granted a Canadian newspaperman. There was a complete absence of formality about our meeting. He received me in his private office in the Chancellory, in a room panelled in mahogany, without pictures and without ornamentation. As I entered he rose from his desk and came forward, clicking his heels together as the introduction was made and we shook hands. He wore a light fawn tunic of military pattern with an Iron Cross on his left breast and on the left arm a band bearing a swastika sign, and black trousers.

For the more than half an hour our conversation lasted the chancellor submitted to a barrage of questions. The conversation ranged over many topics of the international situation, reminiscences of many occasions on which he came face to face with Canadians across the barbed wire of No Man's Land, and took in the question of alleged militaristic training given the youth of Germany as well as the matter of the concentration camps. As we talked we sat in armchairs on either side of a small table.

Answering my questions, Hitler stated that last Sunday's great vote did not alter by one iota Germany's claims regarding disarmament.

"Our position is just as it was before," he declared. "We demand absolute equality in negotiations which we undertake with other powers—no more, no less. Given these conditions we are prepared to resume negotiations at any time."

When I asked whether he considered it was up to Germany to make the next move or to the other powers, he replied: "It is difficult to answer that at this moment. But my opinion is that the initiative should come from those states which have not disarmed. Germany after all cannot disarm because she has disarmed already," he said....

I asked him if he had ever met any Canadians during the war. He at once forgot he was the chancellor of Germany and became the war veteran, talking reminiscences. He smiled and gesticulated as he reeled off dates and places when he had been opposite Canadians. In effect, he said: "You bet I met Canadians in the war, at Armentieres in 1915, at Bapaume on the Somme in 1916, and in France later."

To my suggestion that he should know Canadians as a virile people he laughed and thoroughly agreed. These reminiscences brought a flood of words to his lips. "As a Canadian who was in France and Flanders you ought easily to understand the attitude of Germany after the revolution," he said. "Soldiers who actually faced each other across No Man's Land must surely have a clearer view of each other than politicians who never fought. From what I know of the Canadians and the British as soldiers I cannot imagine that if they had been defeated in the war they would have submitted tamely to the treatment handed out to Germany."

I told the chancellor Canadian opinion was much exercised by statements that school children and storm troops were given military training which went far beyond what could reasonably be considered as defensive training, also that a grave danger to world peace was seen in the new doctrine of race supremacy being taught in Germany. It was considered retrograde and even savage by other nations.

With much vehemence of gesture he declared the training he was giving young Germany was not militaristic nor aggressive but merely educative. It took the form of strict discipline.

"When in opposition," he said, "I had to work with a great mass of

August 13, 1931

men and fight Communism in its most violent form. Do you think I could have done that with a crowd of street preachers?" Striking the table with his fist, he stated: "Now with the success of the revolution I want to keep up that spirit of discipline but insist again it is not militaristic. You cannot have a huge following without some forms of organization, and that naturally takes on a military appearance."

He declared utterly untrue statements made recently that storm troops have been told secretly that the leaders of the nation were making pacifist speeches for foreign consumption, but that they were to be disregarded. "I should like to have before me the man who made that statement. It should be clear that if we have succeeded in uniting forty million people on a platform of peace and equality, it would be impossible to give out secret instructions to the contrary," he said. . . .

Finally I asked the chancellor if he could indicate when he thought the concentration camps which had aroused so much criticism abroad would be abandoned. Here again he became voluble.

"People abroad have not realized the seriousness of this question to us," he said. "In no other country has the government no power to fight against six million organized Communists. Other countries can deport undesirable citizens, but Germany has had no such opportunity, such as France for instance.

"We should be most happy to get rid of our troublesome people and would gladly pay their fares to Canada if Canada would take them. But Canada would be rather astonished at the kind of people they would have to welcome. Canada has always had strict immigration laws and Germany has admitted too many people who have abused the privileges of citizenship."

According to the chancellor there are now only seventeen thousand persons in the concentration camps.

On August 13, 1931, an ad in the Citizen announced the completion of renovations to the R.K.O. Capital Theatre on Queen Street at Bank. Built in 1920, the 2,530-seat theatre was the largest in Ottawa history. It closed in 1970.

November 18, 1933
LUKIN JOHNSTON ACCIDENTALLY
DROWNED OFF SHIP.
Citizen London Correspondent Lost Overboard.
Had Been in Germany Covering
The Recent Election Campaign There
And Was Returning To London.
Notable Career As Writer And Soldier.

The Evening Citizen regrets to announce the tragic death of Mr. Lukin Johnston, chief of the London News Bureau, which occurred when he was accidentally drowned off a steamer while returning from Germany, where he had been covering the German election campaign.

A cable early today from Mr. A. C. Cummings of the London staff announced the grave possibility of Mr. Johnston's death, and a later message received stated: "Captain North Sea steamer confirms beyond doubt Lukin Johnston accidentally drowned."

Mr. Johnston was travelling by the London and Northeastern steamer *Prague* en route from the Hook of Holland to London. . . . The steward collected Mr. Johnston's second class ticket, allotting him two cabins and last saw him at 12:50 a.m. when he finished and went on deck.

"A seaman saw Major Johnston at 2:20 a.m. sitting on the promenade deck. Just before the boat arrived at Parkeston quay today the steward went to call Mr. Johnston and found he was missing. His bed had not been slept in. All the spare cabins were searched but no trace of him was found," a Canadian Press dispatch said. . . .

Mr. Johnston visited Ottawa a couple of years ago, and during his stay addressed the Canadian Club, giving a very impressive talk on "Glimpses of England," creating a favorable and happy impression. . . .

The staff of the *Citizen*, with whom the late Lukin Johnston was in daily contact through his cable service, join with all other members of the Southam organization across Canada in expressing their deepest sorrow to the family of a beloved confrere.

October 21, 1931

November 20, 1933
CHANCELLOR HITLER PAYS HIGH TRIBUTE
TO LUKIN JOHNSTON.
Deeply Moved By Tragic Loss of Man
Who Had Fully Lived Up To High Responsibility.
BY A. C. CUMMINGS.
From The Evening Citizen's London News Bureau.

LONDON, Nov. 20.—In a statement to the *Evening Citizen*, Dr. Hanfstaengl, foreign press chief for Chancellor Hitler, expressed his sincerest regret at the tragic fate of Mr. Lukin Johnston. He had met him, he said, the evening before he left for London, and discussed with him his impression of Germany.

Both this time and two years ago when he met Mr. Johnston for the first time he was struck by the fair and loyal character of this Canadian journalist who so frankly pointed out those things which he found worthy of criticism and those features which he found praiseworthy.

Dr. Hanfstaengl said he was authorized to speak in the name of Herr Hitler when he pointed out that the chancellor was deeply moved by the news of this tragic loss not only to Canada but to world journalism, because anybody who had come in contact with Lukin Johnston could not help but realize that he was dealing with a man who had fully lived up to the high responsibility of his profession.

April 11, 1934
HOCKEY AND POPULATION.
Ottawa had been home to high-level professional hockey for 40 years
when the National Hockey League Senators moved to St. Louis at the
end of the 1933-34 season. The NHL returned to the capital in 1992.

Announcement that the Ottawa hockey team will no longer operate in the N.H.L. will not come as a surprise to local followers of the winter game. For long it has seemed to be but a matter of time before circumstances forced the Senators out of the big time company. The owners of the team have finally bowed to the inevitable.

The question reduces itself to costs and population. In his statement intimating the withdrawal of Ottawa from the national league, Major Burpee said that "the cost of running a team does not differ by more than a few thousand dollars if it is run in Ottawa instead of a city like New York." This being so, the key to the situation is furnished by the following figures.

Population
Ottawa 126,000
Toronto 631,000
Montreal 818,000
Boston 781,000
Detroit 1,568,000
Chicago 3,376,000
New York 6,930,000

It will be seen that Ottawa has but one-fifth of the population of the smallest city among those others operating N.H.L. teams, and only one fifty-fifth of the largest.

In proportion to population, of course, Ottawa remains the "best hockey town." By this we mean that on a pro rata basis a 5,000 crowd in Ottawa is equivalent to a 25,000 crowd in Toronto and a 250,000 crowd in New York, and a five thousand gate is fairly frequent here.

But unfortunately, a dollar in Ottawa is worth the same as a dollar in any other city, or almost the same, and so it is the cash that finally determines policy. There will be genuine regret at the hockey league's decision, and not only in Ottawa. It cannot, however, go on losing money, and so local fans must accept the situation as gracefully as they can.

July 13, 1932

June 6, 1934
BRITAIN MAKES SECRET TEST OF POSTAL ROCKET.
Witness Says Experiment Successful But Postmaster
Does Not Consider It Practical Yet.
BY A. C. CUMMINGS.,
Citizen London Bureau.

LONDON, June 6.—The world's first postal rocket was tried out to-day near London by the British postal authorities. A witness reported that the experiment was successful. From an authoritative source, however, it was learned that the postmaster did not consider the rocket practical in its present stage.

Deep secrecy veiled the experiment with the rocket which, invented by Gerhard Zueker, German expert, is said to be the forerunner of a service calculated to give Great Britain one-minute postal contact with France and three-minute contact with Ireland.

The rocket will carry 1,200 letters, bearing special stamps, it was learned. It will be trained on Calais from Dover, or else across the Irish Sea, and the letters will be posted at the nearest postal point to where the rocket falls.

The speed of the rocket is estimated at 20 miles a minute.

April 26, 1934

As First Food Reached Men Trapped in N.S. Mine

Rescue workers, with Mrs. Robertson and Mrs. Magill, hear the first words from the entombed men through the diamond drill bore.

Plane drops supplies, including funnels and rubber hose to carry liquid food to the prisoners.

Two miners, penetrating the Reynolds shaft, report just room enough to squeeze past timbers.

Men receive hot soup, first food to reach them since being trapped Easter Sunday night. Coffee was then sent through the tube, and first messages were exchanged.

How the 186-foot tube was sent through the 103-foot bore made by the diamond drill, enabling the men to receive vital, nourishing liquids, and to inform workers on the surface of their condition. The tube is pictured being received by Dr. Robertson and passed to Magill, reclining, and Scadding.

(Drawing by Charles R. Snelgrove, Evening Telegram staff artist. Copyright, 1936.)

A War of Words

The Tenth Decade, 1935-1944

"GET TOO CLOSE to the quarry and it'll turn 'round and bite you," goes the old newspaper adage generally attributed to American journalist H. L. Mencken. It was a lesson the *Citizen* learned the hard way in 1941—hauled up in court by Mackenzie King's Liberals on a wartime charge of subversion. Twenty years of cosy dinners, backroom advice, government sinecures and back-slapping, all of it forgotten in an instant because of one critical editorial.

The incident had a harmless beginning. In early 1941, barely 18 months into the Second World War, editor Charles Bowman returned to the subject on which he'd made his name in the First World War—arms supply patronage. This time, he fired a volley at the government's fishy contract with a Toronto company to make Bren guns, the light machine gun used by Canada's troops. After questioning the deal's secrecy, Bowman ended his editorial with a flourish: "When the lads come home from overseas, after years of service at the real business end of the Bren gun, they may know better where to shoot than Canadian veterans did in the years of debt and privation after the last war."

The editorial raised a few hackles and would probably have disappeared from memory except for CCF leader M. J. Coldwell. Looking for a way to avenge an earlier *Citizen* editorial attacking his performance in Parliament, the Socialist leader sent a copy of the Bren gun editorial, with the concluding sentence underlined, to Justice Minister Ernest Lapointe. In the House, he demanded to know how Lapointe planned to deal with the *Citizen*: "Men have been prosecuted and interned for far less than this," Coldwell said.

The *Citizen* responded by publishing an explanation saying the editorial was meant to be metaphorical—that the returning soldiers would shoot with ballots, not bullets. But it wasn't enough for La-

April 4, 1935

Opposite: A full-page array of diagrams on April 22, 1935 showed how trapped Nova Scotia miners were being kept alive. Some journalists of the 1990s believed they had invented the "infographic," but they were at least six decades behind the leaders.

pointe. With King's blessing, the *Citizen* and Bowman were charged with subversion for publishing opinion "prejudicial to the safety of the state" and "likely to prejudice the recruiting, training, discipline or administration" of the military.

Publisher Harry Southam was outraged. And hurt. "For the government to hale the *Citizen*—with whose record of public service you have been personally acquainted for 40 years . . . is a matter of grave concern," he wrote to King while the case was pending. "But to have the minister of justice state the complained-of article was subversive—this is to say, pre-judge the case—is surely anything but fair."

Three months after the editorial was published, Magistrate Glen Strike agreed with the *Citizen*'s explanation and dismissed the charges. But the resentment lingered on both sides for many years. Bowman and King never renewed their close friendship. In fact, the *Citizen* continued to go after the Liberals for war supply patronage, and King never hesitated to criticize the paper in the House.

For his part, Southam resigned as chairman of the board of the National Gallery—he'd been appointed by King—and dropped his plan to donate his $250,000 art collection, including paintings by Matisse, Picasso, Van Gogh, Gauguin and Monet, to the gallery.

"I don't regret the chance to influence affairs," Bowman wrote of the affair in 1949, "but I do regret that we allowed it to cloud our journalistic duties from time to time."

April 29, 1935
SUNSHINE AND FRESH AIR.
(Excerpt from an editorial.)

Last Sunday in Ottawa, listeners to the Empire short-wave broadcast from London could hear the crowds cheering at Wembley Stadium in the annual battle between football gladiators for the English cup. During the interval, the martial strains of a military band came through while the crowds still cheered. It brought a vivid sound picture of the remarkable scene where 100,000 British football fans, mostly wearing caps—and sporting the partisan colors of either Sheffield or West Bromwich Albion—cast off the cares of the day to enjoy themselves.

British Premier Ramsay MacDonald, the supreme peacemonger, may be denouncing Chancellor Hitler's policy; Germany may be preparing a new submarine menace; Sir Stafford Cripps may be saying that war is inevitable within five years unless the nations become converted to Socialism—the whole world may seem to be out of joint, but the British people retain the good sense to get out into the fresh air whenever possible.

At Easter time, Britain takes a real holiday—extending from Thurs-

February 28, 1936

day night to the following Tuesday. The silver jubilee celebrations [for King George V] next month will be followed by Whitsuntide in June, another great religious holiday time in the British Isles. Canada could well take a leaf out of the British holiday book. In the desperate pursuit of business on this continent, Whitsuntide [seven weeks after Easter] has been almost completely forgotten. It is one of the most beautiful times of the year in this country. It should be made a great national occasion of excursions to the hills, lakes, woods and seashores. But Canadian workers are kept with noses to the grindstone, bowed in a state of worship before the sign of the dollar.

Canada could be just as prosperous without so much of this devoted adherence to the gospel of hard work. It is true that a day off is taken about once a month in summer, beginning with May 24, on to Labor Day. With the harnessing of hydro-electric power to do more of the heavy work, however, some of the benefits should be distributed to the Canadian people in the form of more opportunities to enjoy sunshine and fresh air. Doubtless it will come in another generation.

May 8, 1936

June 12, 1935
SURPRISED TO FIND NUDISM
IS NOT FLOURISHING IN OTTAWA.
Recent Arrival Queries About Location of Camp Nearest
to Ottawa, and Thinks He Is Being Spoofed When Told
There Is No Such Practice Indulged In These Parts.

WANTED, a nudist camp! A young fellow, recently arrived in Ottawa, has been making the rounds inquiring as to where the nearest nudist camp is situated. Speaking to a *Citizen* reporter he explained that his physician advised him to attend a nudist camp for his health.

He was informed that he would find no sun-tanned Adonises lurking behind the luxurious shrubbery of the Gatineau hillsides nor any alluring Venuses basking by placid pools in the cool depths of the forest.

Apparently much surprised that nudism does not flourish in Canada to the same extent as in Europe, the young newcomer appeared to think the reporter was evading the question when he was told that there were no known nudist forums in the Ottawa district.

Not daunted, however, he declared that he would pursue his investigations further. He expressed the thought that in this bright land of invigorating sunshine and fresh, lambent breezes he would surely find other disciples of the outdoor cult.

"There are just two reasons why nudism is not popular in this country," the reporter told him, "mosquitoes and black flies! You can take your pick."

It was also pointed out to the young gentleman that if he thought Canadians were just a bunch of "softies" he might be surprised to learn that we have residents who think nothing of chopping a hole through the ice and taking a dip in thirty degrees below zero weather.

Perhaps the answer to the young fellow's problem might be found in the old pioneer slogan: "Go west, young man!" Out around Nelson B.C., among the Doukhobors he will find many devotees of the mystic cult of the sunburnt epidermis and the blistered pelt.

October 22, 1936

October 27, 1936

July 16, 1936
CUMMINGS ON ITALY.
What Mussolini Really Is Like and Why He Dominates
All Italy Today by Force of Character. Some of His
Meannesses and His Compelling Audacity.
Italy's ambassador to Canada found A. C. Cummings' series of stories on life under Mussolini so one-sided, he visited publisher Harry Southam to complain. Southam told him that if he found freedom of the press such an annoyance, he might feel more comfortable in Italy. Here's an excerpt from the series' third instalment.

BY A. C. CUMMINGS
From The Evening Citizen's London Bureau.

ROME, July 7. (By mail).—A blacksmith's son, offspring of generations of poor peasants, a revolutionary Socialist in youth, a fighter in the Great War, founder of a party that has proclaimed new political ideals for 43,000,000 people and a new kind of state in which to embody them, a man who defied fifty-two nations and won a colonial war of aggression that in a few months created a new Roman empire—Benito Mussolini, aged 53, dictator of Italy and one of the most powerful men in Europe—what sort of man is he?

Physically, he is surprisingly short of stature—five feet six and bulky like Napoleon. He is partly bald, grey-haired with dark eyes that gleam when he is aroused, and a heavy bulldog jowl that comes out well in photographs, paintings and sculptures. He has a wide mouth, a huge voice, gesticulates with thick arms and broad shoulders when he is excited, and gives the impression at once of a man of athletic build and unbounded vitality. No ascetic Hitler here, though, like Hitler, he is a teetotaller and almost a vegetarian. At the first moment of meeting, he gives the impression of an urgent, driving personality, keen, alert and in all things the opposite of the easy-going, laughter-loving, subtle and emotionally-explosive Italian type.

The other day I saw him flash by in the street in a huge automobile on his way from the Villa Torlonia, a secluded aristocratic home in its own park in the northeast quarter of Rome, to the immense, reddish-brown Palazzo Venezia with its medieval battlements and square tower looking out on the Capitoline hill in the centre of the city and on the white, gigantic marble monument to King Victor Immanuel the Second that contains the tomb of Italy's "Unknown Soldier."

Here he works for sixteen or eighteen hours a day. From the single balcony of the building facing the square and marked by two huge fasci—the Fascist insignia—he speaks thunderously to crowds of religious Black Shirts who acclaim with a fervor that has to be seen to be believed their incomparable "Il Duce," or leader. . . .

"They go berserk here at times," an English colleague told me rather disgustedly. He had seen so many patriotic demonstrations arranged by Mussolini and the Fascist party to keep up the "revolutionary spirit and tempo," as they call it, that he, like Queen Victoria on a famous occasion, was "not amused" any longer.

Mussolini is a brilliant actor. He loves to make drums beat and flags wave and crowds yell at his every sentence. He is vain—and sensitive in his vanity. He is an incomparable spellbinder and knows the value of giving color and life and picturesqueness to the business of governing. Yet he is far too shrewd to be taken in either by his own theatricalism or that of others. He can talk to the elderly Fascist-controlled Senate in the language of a serious and responsible statesman; he can discuss with his friends, and sometimes with foreign journalists, the affairs of Europe, with a contemptuous and cynical realism that shocks them; and he can converse with the peasants of his own district in Romagna, in the plain, simple, not to say coarse language they best understand.

He is at once emotional and calculating, reserved and volcanic, immensely self-contained—no one, not even his veteran Fascist colleagues, takes liberties with Mussolini—and entirely self confident. "I make my own decisions," he proudly says, "and I alone nurture them."

Unlike Hitler, his fellow dictator of equally humble origin, Mussolini is widely read. He speaks French and German and can peruse an English newspaper. While a revolutionary Socialist writer in early life, he learned how to get to the heart of a subject. He assimilates facts quickly. He can choose when experts differ. It has been said that he is "Europe's best plagiarist." Certainly, he has borrowed most of his political ideas. Even the Fascist salute was not his suggestion but that of Gabriele D'Annunzio, the poet.

"Mussolini's outstanding quality," a diplomat with 35 years' continuous knowledge of Rome and of Italian politics told me, "is his uncanny capacity to estimate men. He has no high regard for the average man. He is cynical about human nature. He has no illusions about what people will do if their self-interest prompts them. But he knows in an extraordinary way what individual men will respond to, how they may be influenced or intimidated or fascinated. For the rank and file he has a glamour that is not all due to the fantastic propaganda that pervades all

REMAINS IN SMITHS FALLS

March 6, 1937

March 8, 1937

Italy about him. He can compel thousands of people to obey him. . . .

"He is no super-man, of course. I do not mean to convey that impression. Personally, I hate the ideas he represents. I detest his ruthlessness and his streak of cruelty. But his faults do not blind me to the man's remarkable personality."

Mussolini has many other faults besides those mentioned. He never forgives or forgets an insult or a defeat. The Lipari Islands, lonely little specks of land off the coast of Sicily, hold in prison-exile today hundreds of his political and personal enemies. Just lately he released from "confino" nearly a thousand persons—some of them Communists. This was not because he forgave them. . . .

He is, unlike Hitler, a good "family man." His wife, Donna Rachele, lives in seclusion at the Villa Torlonia. No newspaper man or woman has ever interviewed her though many have tried. She has borne five children. The eldest daughter, Edda, now the Countess Ciano, wife of the newly made foreign secretary (appointed at the age of 33), is believed to be her father's favorite and to inherit many of his abilities. The youngest daughter, Anna-Maria, became gravely ill a few days after I arrived in Rome and Mussolini spent hours at her bedside hidden away in the country—the Italian press was forbidden to say where.

"Mussolini is obviously not a neurotic like Hitler," I said to my diplomatic friend, "but like Roman emperors of the past, is equally greedy for dictatorial power. May he not, consequently, develop paranoic ideas, delusions of greatness and grandeur, as other autocrats in their day have done?"

"I do not believe it for a moment," said the man who knows Mussolini as well as most men know him. "He is essentially sane in spite of his occasional grandiloquent ideas and flamboyant oratory . . . . So I can say with every confidence that there is little if any possibility of him becoming the danger to European peace that Hitler is."

Immediately After The First Explosion

This picture shows the giant dirigible beginning her downward plunge almost immediately after the first explosion, and shows clearly how quickly the flames spread through the entire length of the craft.

GIANT DIRIGIBLE MEETS HER DOOM

Great clouds of smoke, shot through with burning wreckage, shoot toward a drizzling sky from the twisted, burning wreck of the great German dirigible, Hindenburg. A few moments before she was swinging proudly in to her mooring mast at Lakehurst, N.J., her passengers waving gaily from the windows. From this wreckage came the terrible screams of the victims who were trapped, and into this went the rescuers

May 8, 1937

September 26, 1936
HAPPY ENDINGS.

Nellie McClung is mostly remembered as a feminist leader, especially for her role in the 1929 court case that declared women are "persons." But she was also a playwright, novelist, essayist and, during the 1930s, a wistful newspaper columnist. Here's an excerpt from a series of personal reminiscences written for Southam newspapers.

BY NELLIE L. MCCLUNG
(Special to The Citizen.)

As people grow older, they become keenly alive to the appearance of age. Women have cried at the sight of the first grey hair. Lapses of memory, which in youth seem humorous, become tragic as we grow older. "The falling of the leaves of memory!" we say gaily, when we realize we have told our friend the same story yesterday, but we say it with a grim foreboding knowing the days are evil.

There is one quality of mind I hope I may retain, even after my hair falls out, and my eyes grow dim. I hope I can still believe in miracles; the fortunate, unbelievably happy coincidences of life. The things which just happen, and might not happen again in a thousand years.

Everyone could tell a story of how one time at least, luck was with us. I remember a day, when as a special reward for good behavior, I, the youngest of the three girls, was taken berry-picking to the Souris river. The way was long, and rough, but it was high adventure for me; and besides the joy of berries we were invited to supper at neighbors, who lived near the little country store at Millford where we did our trading.

I do not remember how the "take" of berries stood, but I do remember that just at the end of the day when by the sun we knew it was near supper time, I fell down a steep and treacherous bank and ripped one stocking from ankle to knee and skinned my leg.

Now a skinned leg will heal but a torn stocking is serious. I bore my affliction with fortitude until I realized that I could not go to the neighbor's with a bare leg, "passing the store and all." Then I lifted up my voice and wept, that one bare leg disbarred me. But I claimed the right to go with them as far as the woods sheltered me. I would wait for them in a clump of bushes—the last clump. The two girls agreed to this, and we set out, following a wagon road which led to the store.

We had gone but a short distance when I saw something gleaming on the road. I advanced cautiously not daring to hope—I had been fooled before by the tin disk off a plug of tobacco—but this gleam was real. An American quarter lay in my hand, and I raised a glad shout. Here was deliverance!

The girls went on to the store, bought a pair of green cashmere stockings which I put on, knowing nothing of microbes or infection, and went with them merrily to the feast. Green stockings evidently were poor sellers, and that's why these sold for a quarter. Later, when in Sunday school, we read of the ravens feeding Elijah by the brook Cherith—I found no difficulty believing it. I had seen a miracle too.

•

There was a verse written about a man who always believed the clouds would break—always thought tomorrow would be better than today, and I must say I like the type and would be glad to think I might be eligible for membership in the Believers' Club, though I have not quite the optimism of the man who spent his last quarter for an oyster-stew (though he knew his money would bring more real sustenance if he bought fish and chips) but there might be a pearl in the oyster stew!

May 10, 1937

I was at a meeting this week, where many old friends were gathered; people I had not seen for years, and I was shocked to see how old some of them looked. Time goes over us like a blight to be sure, and the years like great black oxen plough the world. But it was not the wrinkles, or the sunken eyes or trembling hands of these few which seemed the worst; it was the lack of interest in their faces. Men and women whom I remembered as people of thought and action had dulled down into boredom. They looked like people who expected the worst and did not care if it did come.

•

In contrast to these sunken ones, there was an old man of eighty-one who told me he did not like Victoria, there wasn't enough action there and he was going up the Peace River.

"There was too much sameness even in weather," he said. "Fine weather here, day after day, days as alike as two beans. I like a good rousing crackling thunderstorm—clears the air like nothing else and makes us all glad when it's over—I may come back here in a few years when I slow down. Nice place for old folks sure enough, but I can't put in my time throwing horseshoes. I like action—have left word with my boys that if I ever do die, I want them to trot horses at the funeral."

We discussed *As Strange as it Seems* [a radio adventure series] over the supper table, but we only got as far as the first story, told by a retired Hudson's Bay man. He said the Company had one time brought one of their old river boats for 400 miles down the Peace River and 100 miles down the Slave, to the post at Fort Fitzgerald, where it was landed on a beach and tied up. There were certain parts of it that might be useful, though the boat itself was condemned and would be left on the beach to rot. In the days when the boat operated it had often drawn a scow, which was old and abandoned, too, but it had not been brought down with the boat, being utterly useless.

A week after the boat was beached, the scow arrived and drew in beside its old friend. It had made the 500 mile trip on its own, and came to rest on the beach, as neatly as if directed by a skilled hand. It had been floated off its resting place by the high water, but just why it had not gone ashore and how it came in at the spot just beside the riverboat is not so easily explained. But the fact remains that it came....

The romantically minded may say there was an attraction between the boat and the scow after their long years together, which guided the scow on its last long trip to rejoin the friend it had followed so long. Anyway it is pleasant to think of the two old friendly craft, sitting side by side, slowly yielding to the sure disintegration of wind and weather.

June 4, 1938

June 4, 1938

November 19, 1936
I WAS A COMMUNIST AGITATOR.
By an Ex-Member of the Party.
A Frank and Startling Disclosure of the Inner Workings
of the Communist Party in Canada by Man Who Was
in Inner Council for Nearly a Decade.

An 11-part series written by an unnamed Communist who had
"seen the light"—to quote a Citizen *promotion—created a bit of a stir*
when it was published in Southam newspapers. MPs demanded
to know the author's identity so police interrogators could learn more
about Communist activities in Canada. His name was never given
because, as a Southam official said, the police "most certainly
know these things already." This is an excerpt from Part 4.

June 27, 1939

Following my graduation from the Communist college, I was transferred from the Young Communist League to the Communist party. I
was only about 19 years of age at the time and was hence eligible to belong to the Y.C.L. for another five years, but party leaders apparently
decided I would be of more value to them in the older organization.

The Communist party is organized on the same general lines as the
Y.C.L. Orders are received from Moscow. The business of bringing reports and having them rubber-stamped by the membership goes under
the high–sounding name of "Democratic-Centralism." Members of
other organizations who love to move, second and debate resolutions
and motions would break their hearts in the Communist party, for no
motions or resolutions are ever allowed on the edicts from Moscow.

In place of the expression of opinion on the merits of the Moscow
orders, the Communists have substituted a system of self-criticism.
Everything that is done by the party members must be self-criticized,
individually and collectively. The members, after they have staged a
relief strike or other disturbance, always foregather and question the
wisdom of their manner of handling their jobs.

Thus nothing is ever an unqualified success for there is always something that might have been done better, differently. The group itself
then assumes the faults of the members and its report is sent up
through all the various branch executives to Moscow and is supposed
to guide that august body in future decisions.

The Communist party is a great borrower of ideas. It took lessons
from the Christian church for its youth policy and it has aped the
American gangsters in its party organization, for it has both "front"
men and the mysterious movers behind the scenes—the brain trusters.

The front men are those whose names are well known to the public,
"the rabble-rousers." And candidates for public office. Tim Buck
[leader of Canada's Communist party] is a "front man" and so is Jacob

Penner, Winnipeg alderman and Jim Litterick, Winnipeg M.L.A. But they are far from being the brains of the Communist party. The Bennett government thought it had captured the No. 2 communist when it sent Tim Buck to the penitentiary. It did nothing of the sort.

•

Canada's outstanding Communist is none of the men named above—he is Stewart Smith, son of the Rev. A. E. Smith [an early Communist organizer in Canada], former M.L.A. for Brandon. Smith, certainly one of the most brilliant men in the Communist movement anywhere, is the brain of the Canadian party, as well as its Stalin.

Each district has its "brain" men as well as its front men. As an example, John Navizowsky, who ran as a candidate in the Selkirk constituency in the last federal election, is the "brain" of the Manitoba district. The brain men are being constantly switched around so that one seldom if ever gets to know them all, or even a majority of them. In the Communist party, you know only as much as it is imperative for you to know, no more.

As a Communist organizer and agitator, you encounter these brain-trusters in strange places. You will be sent into a relief camp to organize a strike or into a lumber camp or mine settlement. You are the absolute boss of that area; you give all the orders and assume the responsibility for seeing that headquarters' orders are carried out, even though they seem impossible. Then, when you have brought the broth to a boil one of the brain-trusters comes to town. He is never seen on the streets, takes no part in any activity in public, but he takes full charge of the situation and issues all the orders.

•

The Communist party differs from the Young Communist League in one respect—it is always prepared for the inevitable "Red hunt." Every officer of every Communist organization has a trained substitute who will step into the breach immediately anything happens to the leader. There are substitutes for Stewart Smith, Tim Buck and Jim Litterick, trained and waiting to assume full charge should any of these fellows land in jail. And the substitutes also have substitutes. While the authorities might conceivably arrest every leader of the party in the country today, the party would function just as efficiently tomorrow as if nothing had happened. . . .

July 7, 1937
LITTLE TROUBLE AT AYLMER
AS "SHORTS" BANNED UNDER BYLAW
PASSED BY COUNCIL.

While in the nearby summer cottage areas anything went in the line of dress (in some cases nearly everything!), the main streets of Aylmer

June 26, 1939

in comparison were sartorial models of propriety this morning.

As the lakeside municipality sweltered under a temperature of near-ly ninety degrees, female residents obeyed the new bylaw prohibiting persons from appearing on public streets in shorts or bathing suits. In striking contrast, residents of the various summer resorts, which are actually part of the town, disported themselves on the lawns about their cottages, on the streets of Wychwood, Lakeview, The Cedars and Alexandra Bay, and on the beaches, in the minimum of clothing.

On the Wychwood tennis courts a perspiring youth was playing, at-tired in bathing trunks only, while a young matron watched, wearing the scantiest of sport shorts.

A survey of the various cottage areas reveal that the popular form of dress was a bathing suit or shorts. Scores of bathers enjoyed them-selves on the beaches in the latest abbreviated swim suits.

Seeking relief from the heat as well as a modicum of comfort, many of the townspeople went as far as they dared. Only one woman who might have been classed as adult was seen walking on the street of Aylmer in shorts. This was a girl in her late teens, who was accompa-nied by her mother.

Two young ladies were seen at different parts of the town wearing slacks and sweaters. The *Citizen* asked one of these young ladies if she thought she was breaking the law. She replied that slacks were all right and that only shorts were taboo, and many were in evidence.

A rather humorous touch was given by three Ottawa women who, at-tired in very brief costumes, consisting of shorts, sweat shirts, slippers and sun-glasses, drove up in a large car and parked directly in front of the town hall and police station. They said they only came out to Aylmer a few times each summer and were not aware there was a by-law prohibiting such costumes. When told that according to the strict letter of the law they might be arrested they said in that event they would stay in the car.

When the bylaw first went into effect there was considerable protest both from residents of the town and from visitors over this so-called "Mrs. Grundy" piece of legislation. However, the edict is no longer a novelty and is being accepted as a matter of course....

Chief Delbert Dumoulin this morning stated that he had had no oc-casion to yet warn even one girl. At any rate, he declared, he did not in-tend to make any arrests unless some person openly and repeatedly flouted the provisions of the bylaw....

Hotel keepers said that they would not admit women to their premises unless they were properly attired. If the woman happened to be a guest of the hotel she would be politely "tipped off."

April 2, 1940

The charming chap threatening with the chair may be the near-est thing to a Neanderthal man, but to wrestling fans everywhere he is "The Angel" (Maurice Tillet). "The Angel" makes his second appearance at the Auditorium tomorrow night, and is expected to tame "Wild" Bill Longson in one of the main bouts. Frank Sexton and Frank Taylor meet in the other feature attraction, while Harry Kent and Jerry Monohan will tangle in the semi-final, and Walter Podolak and Pete Baltron in the preliminary.

Ten Thousand Men On Guard Duty In Canada

Waterways, Govt. Buildings, Industrial Plants And Other Points Now Watched by the Militia.

Men From Ottawa and Hull Units Included

War Planes Roar Over the Capital City On Way To Atlantic Coast.

The Department of National Defence moved swiftly during the week-end and instituted precautionary measures against possible sabotage and espionage. As war clouds hung over the world the local armories bristled with activity as a call was issued to commanding officers to furnish men for special guard duty at government buildings housing valuable military, naval and air force equipment and data.

10,000 Men on Duty.

The call for men to serve voluntarily at vulnerable coastal and inland points was issued Friday night by Defence Minister Mac-

August 28, 1939

July 8, 1938

SANCTUARY FOR PERSECUTED JEWS.

The conference on political refugees at Evian-les-Bains, initiated on the invitation of President Roosevelt to consider means for the sheltering and re-domiciling of those people no longer wanted in Germany, is one that will be widely welcomed. The political refugees with which the conference is primarily concerned are the Jews, although Nazi Germany is responsible for creating many other political refugees whose blood is indubitably Aryan.

The British Empire is naturally looked upon as the most hopeful source of refuge. The State Department of Washington has already made it known that it regards the British Dominions, together with the continent of South America, as the principal haven for homeless and unwanted Jews. Apart from a comparatively small influx, increased slightly in view of the special circumstances, it is obviously impossible to look for a solution of the refugee problem through assimilation or infiltration into the more populated nations or communities.

Another "national" home in some other part of the New World will be more likely what the conference will seek to provide. The new haven should, also, be one that will be complementary to the existing one in Palestine. Again, it should be capable of being tolerably self-supporting within Jewish national boundaries: the oranges and grapefruit, figs and dates of Palestine to be exchangeable for the lumber, paper, fish, minerals and manufacturers of the new home.

It will be recognized that these are the products specifically of Canada within the British Empire, and that there are empty spaces in this Dominion where thousands more than the unwanted Jews could be assured of asylum and the opportunity to make a new life for themselves. The conference, however, may be disposed to search for a more self-contained area for another national home.

Such an island site, Newfoundland, now under British commission rule in the interests of foreign bondholders, could perhaps be suggested as providing the resources necessary for this complementary exchange with Palestine. In area, it is capable of housing the dispossessed Jews of Germany and those so-called "surplus" Jews of other European countries. The journey could be conveniently made from Europe and the Mediterranean by water. The genius of the Jewish race is undoubtedly great enough for the financing of industry, trade and commerce between the sub-tropical and north temperate regions of the two parts of such a greater Jewish national home. Race rivalry in other export markets could thus be eliminated.

It must, of course, be recognized that there are already 190,000 Newfoundlanders, proud of their ancestry, still inhabiting the land of their fathers, even though they may be suffering unemployment, want and hardship. But it is not likely that a duplication of the Palestine minority problem would arise, although there would necessarily be many questions of adjustment.

Failing such a solution as that contained within the square miles of fertile, wooded Newfoundland, capable of so much further development, Canada may be invited seriously to consider the establishment within the Dominion of a Jewish enclave. Empty spaces there may be in South America, but it is more probably that the inter-governmental conference will be of the feeling that, as the Zionist home in Palestine is under British protection, the presently sought refuge shall also be under the Union Jack.

Hon. T. A. Crerar, minister of resources, has given assurance that the Dominion government is "very sympathetic" with the problem of the unwanted Jews. That sympathy, being general no doubt among those gathered in conference at Evian, should be able to bring about a workable solution with honor and respect for all concerned.

After nine days of high-minded speeches of sympathy for the plight of Germany's Jews, the Dominican Republic was the only one of 33 countries at Evian to offer sanctuary to large numbers of refugees. Needless to say, nothing came of the Citizen's *idea to create a haven for Jews in Newfoundland. Nor did much come from Thomas Crerar's assurances. Canada accepted fewer than one per cent of 811,000 Jewish refugees admitted into countries around the world over the next few years.*

May 22, 1939
THREE LUCKY WORKMEN TALK INFORMALLY WITH THE QUEEN.

To use a word from the era, the Citizen's *excitement over the visit of the king and queen was grandiloquent. For weeks, the paper prepared readers for their arrival with an endless string of stories on the history, role and daily lives of the monarchy. There were two supplements, a calendar, photographs, placards and flags to wave from the roadside. Here's a less conspicuous aspect of the coverage.*

BY REGINALD HARDY

"She's the loveliest gal I've ever seen.". . . "Her pictures don't do her justice.". . . "I was so nervous and excited I could hardly speak.". . . "She speaks beautiful French."

The air was filled with excitement. Everybody spoke at once, but none louder and with more reason that the three whose job it had been a few moments before to lower the mammoth 3-ton cornerstone of the Supreme Court building into place at the ceremony presided over Sat-

Britain Leaves War or Peace Up To Fuehrer

Sends Hitler Momentous Message Designed To Bring "Showdown" and Relieve Years of Tension

Parliament To Hear Prime Minister Today

Admiralty Warns Merchant Shipping To Stay Out Of The Mediterranean.

Canadian Press Cable.

LONDON, Aug. 28.—Fuehrer Hitler had his choice tonight—war with his grey-clad Reichswehr pitted against the combined military strength of Great Britain, France and Poland, or peaceful negotiations with the Poles in a spirit of conciliation and mutual confidence.

Showdown Sought.

The British government sent Hitler a momentous message designed, reliable quarters said, to promote a "showdown" in Europe and leave it up to him to decide whether the world is to be plunged into war or whether he is to pin his faith on diplomacy shorn of all threats of violence.

What Hitler's choice would be no one in London pretended to know, but the

August 29, 1939

urday morning by Her Majesty the Queen.

For they had chatted informally with the King and Queen after it was all over.

The proud individuals, representing workmen from Montreal, Ottawa and Toronto, were J. B. Gauthier, 1981 Masson street, Montreal, master stonemason; George M. Lyon, 479 Slater street, Ottawa, and George Reid, a ruddy Scotsman from Toronto.

Apparently it all started when His Excellency the Governor General remarked to the ever-smiling George Reid: "You're a fellow countryman of mine, aren't you?" To which the reply was a beaming "Yes."

Then came the big moment when Lord Tweedsmuir presented George to the Queen.

"You are a Scotsman, aren't you?" queried Her Majesty.

Again the "Yes" in an accent so thickly Scottish it could be cut with a knife.

"How long have you been in Canada?"

"About thirty years, Your Majesty," replied George, his bright face wreathed in a jovial smile.

"You don't seem to have lost your native accent."

George was too thrilled with the entire proceedings to do anything more than grin. And when the King spoke to him, too, he was too moved to utter a word.

Then Her Majesty walked over and shook hands with George Lyon, himself a Scotsman, with Prime Minister King acting as official introducer. Lyon was even more wrought up than Reid and could tell newspapermen nothing more than that he chatted informally with the gracious Queen. "She asked me if I was married and I told her I was. After that I just can't remember what I said." Lyon's young son, George Jr., and daughter, Marjory, looked on proudly as their father was honored.

Last to receive the rare honor was Jean Baptiste Gauthier, who scampered down from his lofty perch atop the giant stone as the moment for his turn approached.

Her Majesty, with her usual graciousness and thoughtfulness, spoke to Jean in his native tongue, French. "And she spoke with a beautiful accent," Jean said afterwards.

His Majesty was an interested onlooker as the Queen spoke with the men. He shook hands with each of them.

May 13, 1940

January 2, 1940
TODAY WE PRESENT THE WOMAN
OF THE NEW DECADE—1940. EVERY INCH A PERSON,
SHE WILL FACE PROBLEMS BRAVELY.
BY MARION YOUNG

She's easy on the head and heart as well as the eyes. She's the kind of woman you'd take to dinner-for-three with the boss or a class reunion dance as well as home to mother. She's every inch a person—a real individual with definite stands as well as standards, without being the slightest bit unfeminine.

Her name is Woman of the New Decade. And she nips in the bud any man's inclination to long for the good old days.

To the woman of the twirling nineteen-twenties, she would seem too serious, too mature, just no fun to have around.

To the woman of the depression-ridden nineteen-thirties, stunned and baffled by the passing of an old order and floundering to find a place in the new, she would seem clear-visioned beyond belief.

She'll be calmly courageous in times of war—here, as she is in Europe today. She'll be kindly and understanding but with a steadfast anchor in war's inevitable aftermath. She'll face what is to be faced, including problems of social significance, instead of ducking the issue in the mad manner of the 'twenties. Or allowing herself to become confused as she has in the 'thirties.

She'll throw off the dour cloak that is a patchwork of religious prejudice, snobbery in any form, a superficial attitude toward anything that really matters. She'll make it her business to see and understand the minute tributaries of the swift-flowing current of human frailties as well as big issues—social, political, economic. Having seen and understood, she'll have the courage to take a stand, to stick by it.

She'll come to have an old-fashioned reverence for truth and loyalty, for a treaty made in good faith, whether between individuals or nations. She has seen enough results of lying, double-crossing, the selfish attitude toward one's fellow man. Undisturbed by the hollow laughter of the cynics, she puts a premium on simple truths—trite though they may sound.

And yet her high standards don't allow her to be prudish. She's intelligent and well-informed, natural and good looking, which makes you like to look at her, dance, eat, swim, play golf or work with her.

For the first few months of the decade there may be a slight period influence on her dress. Later on, however, she'll get into the simple, handsome, well-bred kind of clothes which Paris designers are turning out right now. Her dresses may get shorter by the end of next year. Three years from now she may have them below mid-calf again. She may accept a trend toward lowered waistlines. Now and then throughout the decade her hats may be sillier, more incongruous than any she has worn yet. In some years, they may be more severely tailored than her husband's fedora.

At the moment she likes natural makeup—powder to match her skin, rouge and lipstick in shades which harmonize with her natural blood tones. Her hair is neither long nor ultra short. She prefers to be slender

April 12, 1941

but not thin.

But she may go back to orchid and fuchsia makeup, wear it for several seasons or possibly several years. Maybe the long, Hollywood bob will catch her fancy once more. She might even try unswept hairdos again.

However, don't let fads in fashion and cosmetics fool you into thinking that the Woman of the New Decade is a myth. That she continues to follow the latest fashion simply is further testimony to the fact that she has lost none of her femininity. Underneath, she's not the same.

YOU'LL LIKE HER BETTER, THIS NEW WOMAN.

July 1, 1940
Uncle Ray's Corner.
HITLER LIKED WAR IN BOYHOOD DAYS.
(An excerpt from a daily column for young readers.)

A small mustache may have had something to do with the history of the modern world. Adolf Hitler had the mustache, and it made many persons think of him as a clown, something like Charlie Chaplin in the movies.

That idea was in the minds of people who might have stopped him before it was too late. When they learned better he had gathered power, and the world was heading toward widespread war.

Hitler's life is an amazing story, and I am going to take it up step by step, today and in days to come. You will see how anger and blazing words helped him to gain his power.

Hitler was born at Braunau, in northern Austria, on April 20, 1889. His 52-year-old father had met with a little success in life, but not much. The father had borne the name of Alois Schicklgruber until the age of 40. Then he had changed the family name to Hitler.

When the boy was old enough, he was sent to a grade school. One of his teachers later reported finding him "stubborn and quarrelsome." He would not give time to certain subjects, but he seems to have made progress in history. Many pupils do not like history textbooks which are "filled with wars and battles." This young Austrian was different from those pupils. He took a keen interest in war.

One day he found in his home a two-volume history of the Franco-Prussian war. He read it from start to finish, and it made him suppose there was "glory" to be found in war.

German was spoken in his household, and he was pleased by the smashing blows the German-speaking Prussians had dealt to France 30 years before. The reading of the history did much to form the pattern of his life. In later years, when the Germans lost a war after invading France, he grew bitter in the extreme.

April 12, 1941

The elder Hitler had held a place in customs-office work, and wanted his son to follow the same career. The son, however, had another idea. He wanted to become an artist.

—UNCLE RAY
NEXT: Hitler's Vienna Years.

October 10, 1940
YOUNG RECRUITS EXCITED ABOUT MILITARY LIFE.
More Than 700 at Cornwall Camp Up Early,
Eat Heartily, Then Go On Route March.
"They Are Excellent," Says Lieut.-Col. Larose.
(*Excerpt from a feature story:*)

CORNWALL, Oct. 10.—(Staff)—Over 700 young recruits at Canadian Militia Training Camp No. 31, here, tumbled out of their spring beds this morning, enjoyed a cold shower, polished off a breakfast of cereal, bacon and eggs, coffee, toast and marmalade—and then expressed their satisfaction in no uncertain terms.

"Say, this is better than home!" . . . "Hey, this camp life is all right!". . . "Boy, they treat you like a prince here!" These and various other like comments were heard as the boys, a good many of them Ottawa lads, mustered on the parade ground in front of the camp, northeast of the town, to begin the first of 30 days of intensive military training.

Seven hundred and ten of them, to be exact—they had all been examined by the camp medical officer—had received their smart khaki uniforms, and were ready for whatever came next.

The first day in camp had meant "early rising" for a good many of them for exactly at six o'clock "Reveille" was sounded and the men rolled from their beds—not bunks—and made for the showers. Then came breakfast in the big dining rooms. Finally there they were on the parade ground, many of them wondering what a sergeant looked like and if he was as bad as he is sometimes painted.

After half an hour's rather intensive drilling they marched off in companies for a short route march during which halts would be made along the road and they would receive instruction from the officers on general duties and discipline. It was obvious from the first that the boys really had their hearts in the thing. Although many of them had received some previous military training, a good many others were entirely new to military life. But despite this all three companies presented a very smart and soldierly front.

"Well, what do you think of the boys?" The *Citizen* reporter asked Lieut. Col. Rodolphe Larose, E.W., officer commanding the camp.

Col. Larose smiled with satisfaction.

"They are excellent," he declared, "and they are going to make fine

soldiers. The percentage of recruits we have had to turn down on account of physical defects has been extraordinarily small, only about five and a half per cent. The rest of the boys are in fine physical shape—and more than that, they are really happy to be in camp and satisfied with their surroundings."

Col. Larose declared that the camp, in his opinion, was a model one. Sanitary arrangements were of the highest order. The camp kitchen was a modern one. He smiled as he described the sleeping facilities. "Real spring beds and mattresses," he said.

Although the first recruits arrived in camp only yesterday, the entire instructional staff of 177 officers and men—all members of the permanent force, have been on the ground for one week. As a result, when the recruits arrived, they found everything in smooth running order and no time was lost in examining the men, issuing clothing and getting them settled in their billets....

"The men had a wonderful time last night," explained Col. Larose. "You have no idea the amount of talent that we have here. Some of the boys arrived with mandolins, banjos, guitars and fiddles. It was not long before they were all having a regular hoe-down."

Col. Larose is not inspecting the men closely until they have been whipped into shape. But he is delighted at the fine appearance they already present.... And if the men were worthwhile watching as they started out on their short route march this morning they looked even finer upon their return. Something had happened to them. There was a military swing and spirit to their march as they trooped back into camp. The steady tramp of "boots, boots, movin' up an' down again" had worked into their ears and their hearts.

They felt and looked like soldiers!

May 13, 1941

October 13, 1941
JAZZ IS "SCRAMBLED EGG" MUSIC,
MINISTER DECLARES.

Jazz is "scrambled egg music" and life today in Canada is just as scrambled eggs, Rev. Dr. A. E. M. Thomson of McLeod United church told his congregation on Sunday evening in a sermon entitled "The Jazz Fool."

"Young men and young women seek new thrills—run the whole gamut of life and are satiated at 18. They become as the chaff that the wind driveth away," the minister said. "But he who lives a fast life, cometh to fast judgment.

Pictured in the minds of young moderns, the minister said, the present day marriage ceremony should run something like this:

"Boy: 'Kid will you marry me?'

"Girl: 'Yeah, man!'

"Boy: 'But do you love me?'

"Girl: 'I'll tell the world I do.'

"And then before the minister:

"Parson: 'Do you take this man to be your wedded husband?'

"Girl: 'I'll say I do, you said a mouthful preacher, step on the gas and let's go.'

The minister said this attitude, prevalent in Canada today, made more essential than ever the need for the home for discipline, the school for instruction, and the church for faith.

"The home is the safeguard and restraint for our holy traditions, standards and ideals. The school must be safeguarded so that our children are taught in the right direction. Straight thinking is necessary for straight living. And our church must teach the virtues which come from Godliness and can come from no other source in the world," the minister concluded.

January 9, 1941

December 3, 1941
GIRLS WHO DO A MAN'S WORK WANT MAN'S PAY, NOT PRAISE.
BY RUTH MILLETT

"They're wonderful"—they say of the women who step in and take over men's jobs in wartime. Everybody thinks they're wonderful—and everybody says so, including the men whose highest praise of a woman worker is, "She does the job as well as a man."

Yes, the men are willing to hand the women everything in the way of credit. But with all their admiration for the willingness of women to step into men's jobs and fill them skillfully, there's seldom even a whisper that since the women are doing men's jobs well, they ought to be paid equally with the men whose places they have taken.

And the women, pleased with the praise and the publicity, seldom raise a protest.

That is true in most countries. But it looks as though the women of Australia have decided that they would rather have equal pay with men than any amount of praise and publicity.

Twenty-eight trade unions in that country are asking for equal pay for the sexes. And one company, the Melbourne Tramways Board, has already recognized the principle of equal pay, giving women tram conductors the same wages as men.

What is happening in Australia may happen in other countries where women have been pushed into men's jobs by war or the demands of national defence.

It could happen here, if women would get wise to themselves and answer all the "aren't you wonderful to be holding down a man's job" flattery that is handed them with the common sense answer, "Well, if I'm doing a man's job as well as a man could do it, how about paying me what you would have to pay a man?"

Syndicated columnist Ruth Millett's work appeared on the Citizen's *women's pages throughout the 1940s and '50s.*

August 21, 1942
THRILLING TALES OF CANADIAN HEROISM.
Courage of Commandos In Hellfire of Dieppe
Is Vividly Described. Hardened Men, Battle-Tested Now,
Relate Stories Stamping Raid as Rivaling
Last War's Vimy in Point of Valor.
Among Canadian war correspondents, Ross Munro of The Canadian Press *was respected as hard working, fearless and a first-rate writer. Here's his account of the Canadian raid on Dieppe, which appeared on front pages around the world after it was picked up by The Associated Press. After the war, Munro worked for the* Citizen *as a political writer.*

BY ROSS MUNRO
Canadian Press War Correspondent.

SOMEWHERE IN ENGLAND, Aug. 21.—At Canadian Army camps in Britain today stories of the heroism and courage of Canadians in the hellfire that was Dieppe on Wednesday were recounted by hardened men who now have been battle-tested.

There were countless deeds done on the shores of France and in the streets of Dieppe that never will be told. Too many did not return for a complete picture of the Canadians' individual heroic performances ever to be assembled.

But at the bases of the Essex Scottish, South Saskatchewan Regiment, Royal Hamilton Light Infantry, Fusiliers Mont Royal, Toronto Scottish, Winnipeg Camerons, Royal Regiment and the Black Watch there were plenty of accounts from fighting men to stamp the action as something rivaling the last war's Vimy in point of valor.

And as an eyewitness to the manner in which these men faced withering fire from strong Nazi fortifications without a trace of fear— rather, in fact, with sheer enthusiasm at getting into action at last—I can testify there is no praise too high for the courage of the Canadians.

At this particular time, when the results of the war's biggest raid are still being studied by the chiefs of the Allied commands,and the benefits and losses are still being calculated and casualties enumerated, there is no opportunity immediately for giving many names.

They are still to come as the story unfolds from wherever these Canadian assault troops base among the Canadians in England or re-

The Neighbors   By George Clark

"You're not worrying about air raids. You've just found an excuse to sit down 'here alone all winter."

February 6, 1942

cover from their wounds in Canadian army hospitals.

At that, though, there are stories without number already.

They tell of a wounded regimental sergeant-major unable to walk who was carried waist-high into the sea and re-embarked by comrades who refused to leave him behind when the withdrawal was ordered.

His name was not immediately available on account of his being in the wounded category and casualties are still being tabulated, but he is married, 42, a typical western Canadian from Saskatoon.

He landed on the beach with units of his regiment in the early morning of Wednesday's assault. Shortly afterwards he received a shrapnel wound in the leg and as he could not walk he was carried by his battling comrades to a captured pillbox.

There the soldier lay while the fortunes of war swayed across the pebble-dappled beaches and through Dieppe's narrow streets. He stayed until mid-afternoon when, their job done, his men came back for him.

Willing hands lifted him and then ducking, scrambling and taking advantage of anything offering even the most meagre cover, the western Canadian was carried to the shoreline, out into the sea by wading men and placed aboard the landing craft despite heavy enemy fire.

Doctors told of a Canadian private arriving at a dressing station in a pair of army shorts with a blanket wrapped around him. It was all he had after being picked out of the sea but as they were fixing him up he stuck out his hand and said, "I've still got this anyway."

He clutched a sea-soaked but still intact snapshot of his wife.

..... *"so little time to do so much"*

March 5, 1942

May 5, 1944

FORMER CITIZEN REPORTER
IS 'DEPUTY MAYOR OF ORTONA'.
(Special to The Citizen.)

WITH THE CANADIAN CORPS IN ITALY, May 5.—The priests know him, the town doctor knows him, he gets stopped in the streets to engage in frequent chatter with the high and the low. To the Canadians who know him, Lieut. "Bill" Boss, army public relations officer and an Ottawa boy, has become known as "deputy mayor of Ortona."

He learned to speak Italian in the Sicily days and to correspondents delving into things Italian he has become an interpreter of high value. But it is in Ortona that he has reached his heights.

When Nicola Mosca, a former student at Rome University, was confirmed in the sacristy of the shattered Ortona cathedral Bill Boss sponsored the confirmation. The Moscas, the leading family in town, already had crammed 27 people into six rooms still fit to be used in their home but they made room for Bill and invited him up for a week-end.

For anyone doing a story on Ortona he is invaluable. He knows the mayor, the doctor, the town major, the bishop, the back alleys, the ruins and, as important as anything in Italy, all the town gossip.

Lt. "Bill" Boss, a former reporter on *The Evening Citizen*, is the son of Maj. and Mrs. W. Boss, 13 Ivy avenue. Educated at Lisgar Collegiate Institute where he was leader of the school orchestra, he took his M.A. degree at the University of Ottawa. For several years he led the Ottawa Concert Orchestra, which he organized. He joined the Lanark and Scottish Regiment in 1940, as second lieutenant, transferring to the 1st Corps Troops in Ottawa in 1941 and was appointed lieutenant with the public relations office of the 4th Armored Division, going overseas in the fall of 1942.

August 1, 1944
"THINGS LOOK OKAY NOW, BOYS,"
SAYS INJURED CONNIE SMYTHE.
BY ALAN RANDAL.

A CANADIAN ARMY HOSPITAL SOMEWHERE IN ENGLAND, July 31.—Connie Smythe, manager of the National Hockey League Toronto Maple Leafs, is lying in this hospital tonight with severe wounds which knocked him out of action on the Normandy front.

The 50-year-old major, who fought in France in the First Great War and didn't have to go this time, is seriously ill. A piece of shrapnel ripped into his back near the base of the spine when he ran to put out a fire in one of his ammunition trucks hit by a German flare.

German planes dropped flares and bombs around his ack-ack battery that night, and Smythe caught it when the shells in the truck began exploding and the Nazis machine-gunned the soldiers trying to fight the fire. It is not known whether he was hit by his own ammunition or by a German bullet.

The visitors allowed him are few. "You can stay for just a minute," said the doctor when we called today. "He is a very sick man."

The doctors won't allow Connie Smythe to talk much. But his tanned face broke into a smile as we walked in and he said "Hello there, Bill," to Col. William Abel, of Canadian military headquarters, an old friend. He was too ill to discuss that hot night action along the Orne river front, and we didn't ask him.

His memory was in good shape, though. When he saw this correspondent he said, "Say, there's the guy I saw chasing a doodlebug (robot bomb) story a few weeks ago." That was just before Connie, artilleryman and flier of the last war, when he won the M.C., led his "Sportsmen's Battery" of gunners over to the Normandy beachhead.

The minute was soon up and Connie waved a hand and smiled again as he said, "Things looks as though they're going to be okay now, boys."

Outside, the surgeon who placed Connie on the seriously-ill list said

May 1, 1944

June 6, 1944

he was getting every possible attention. They were taking no chances in ensuring his recovery and that was why visitors were few. Last night he had a visit from his son who is in the navy and that cheered him up a lot, the surgeon said.

"But he's a sick man and it's a tough spot for him," he added, explaining that Connie was a man who had led an active life and consequently didn't like lying around in bed, and that furthermore, was not as young as he used to be.

Smythe recovered and returned to help the Maple Leafs win
another five Stanley Cups before he retired in 1955.

July 15, 1944

September 16, 1944

5 O'Clock Edition

THE EVENING CITIZEN

FINAL

102nd Year, No. 274. OTTAWA, CANADA, MONDAY, MAY 7, 1945. 20 Pages. 3 Cents.

IT'S ALL OVER IN EUROPE!

NAZI SURRENDER COMPLETE

Sign At Eisenhower Headquarters In Reims Schoolhouse

Allied World Explodes With Joy And Relief At The News

Titanic Conflict Ends After Nearly Six Years Of Strife

Joy Tempered Only by Realization That War Against Japan Remains To Be Won.

LONDON, May 7.—(CP)—The greatest war in history ended today with the unconditional surrender of Germany.

The surrender of the Third Reich to the Western Allies and Russia was made at Gen. Eisenhower's headquarters at Reims, France, by Col.-Gen. Jodl, chief of staff for the German army.

This was announced officially after German broadcasts told the German people that Grand Admiral Karl Doenitz had ordered the capitulation of all fighting forces, and called off the U-boat war.

Japan Still to Go

Joy at the news was tempered only by the realization that the war against Japan remains to be resolved, with many casualties still ahead.

The end of the European warfare, greatest, bloodiest and costliest war in human history—it has claimed at least 40,000,000 casualties on both sides in killed, wounded and captured—came after five years, eight months and six days of strife that overspread the globe.

Arrogant German armies invaded Poland Sept. 1, 1939, beginning the agony that convulsed the world for 2,076 days.

Unconditional surrender of the beaten remnants of Hitler's legions first was announced by the Germans.

The historic news began breaking with a Danish broadcast that Norway had been surrendered unconditionally by its conquerors.

Gal 2—Titanic Conflict — — — mm

Then the new German foreign minister, Ludwig Schwerin von Krosigk, announced to the German people, shortly after 2 p.m. (8 a.m. EDT) that "after almost six years' struggle we have succumbed."

Ordered by Doenitz

Von Krosigk announced Grand Admiral Karl Doenitz had "ordered the unconditional surrender of all fighting German troops."

The world waited tensely. Then at 9.35 a.m. EDT came the Associated Press flash from Reims, France, telling of the signing at Gen. Eisenhower's headquarters of the unconditional surrender at 2.41 a.m. French time (8.41 a.m. EDT). Germany had given up to the Western Allies and to Russia.

London went wild at the news. Crowds jammed Piccadilly Circus. Smiling throngs poured out of subways and lined the streets.

Grand Admiral Karl Doenitz in an order broadcast today ordered all his Nazi U-boats to cease hostilities.

The Flensburg radio broadcast a three-day-old order of the day by Doenitz to his submarine crews telling them:

"Crushing superiority has compressed us into a very narrow area. Continuation of the struggle is impossible from bases that remain."

London Dresses Up.

Great Britain was clearly expecting a V-E Day announcement at any time. London began to dress up for the big occasion by draping flags on some downtown buildings.

The German-controlled radio in embattled Prague admitted new advances by the Russians. A broadcast from a German-held station at Prague said Soviet troops under Marshal Ivan Konev entered Bohemia from Saxony at a point probably 60 to 65 miles north of Prague.

US 3rd Army armored columns had thrust to within 50 miles south and southwest of Prague. The two armies were squeezing ever closer to that revolt-torn capital.

The Patriot radio in Prague said Lt.-Gen. Patton's tanks were only 15 miles away.

Citizen Features

	Page		Page
Amusements	15	Once Over	20
Bridge	14	Personal	3
Casualties	15	Puzzle	14
Editorial	20	Radio	15
Financial	19	Serial Story	14
Fun Page	14	Sewing	4
Gallup Poll	19	Sports	8
Home Page	4	Uncle Ray	4
Little Benny	20	Want Ads	18

Today's Events

City Council, 7.45 p.m.
National Gallery, open from 10 a.m. to 5 p.m.

See Page 19 for Late News and Closing Market Prices.

Goebbels' Body Found in Berlin

By Duncan Hooper.

MOSCOW, May 7.—(Reuters)—Unconfirmed reports reaching me today said that the bodies of Joseph Goebbels and his family had been found in an air raid shelter near the Reichstag in Berlin.

Nazi Minister Tells Germans To Accept Fate

LONDON, May 7—(CP)—A broadcast on the Flensburg wavelength today said Germany had capitulated unconditionally.

Admiral Karl Doenitz has "ordered the unconditional surrender of all fighting German troops," the broadcast said.

This statement attributed to German Foreign Minister Ludwig Schwerin von Krosigk was broadcast to the German people:

"German men and women: The high command of the armed force has today at the order of Grand Admiral Doenitz declared the unconditional surrender of all fighting German troops."

The broadcast was recorded by the British Ministry of Information.

"We Have Succumbed

"After almost six years struggle we have succumbed," the Krosigk broadcast said.

(Concluded on Page 2, Col. 4.)

All of Canada "Turns It On" In Celebration

The 11,000,000 Canadians who went solemnly to war against Germany in September, 1939, had their victory day today and they greeted it with an explosive enthusiasm that filled streets with paper and sound, hearts with thanksgiving and eyes with tears.

Reports that started flooding in from one end of the country to the other all bore the same stamp of feelings unloosed in an unbridled celebration without parallel since the armistice of the First Great War.

Even the successive surrenders of great hordes of German troops on scattered fronts in past days, even the obvious fact that German defeat had been inevitable for weeks failed to sap the thrill from the anti-climax that was the official announcement of German surrender.

(Concluded on Page 12, Col. 5)

Truman Praises Canadian Arms

SAN FRANCISCO, May 7.—(CP)—Prime Minister Mackenzie King today received the following message from President Truman:

With capitulation of the German armies in the Netherlands, Denmark and northern Germany, the battles of the Canadian Army in Europe have ended in final victory. Please accept my warmest concongratulations on the stirring achievements of Canadian arms and be assured that the American people share with the desire to pay tribute to the signal contributions which our Canadian comrades have made to the military defeat of Germany."

Churches Are Holding Services This Evening

Services of prayer and thanksgiving will be held this evening at 8 o'clock in all Anglican, Baptist, Presbyterian and United churches in Ottawa. The citizens of Ottawa are urged to attend these victory services.

This announcement has been made by Bishop Jefferson, Revs. Robert Good, John MacKay and M. L. Orchard on behalf of their respective churches. United church services will be held at 7.30.

On 30th Anniversary Of Lusitania Sinking

NEW YORK, May 7 — (AP) — Germany's unconditional surrender today came on the 30th anniversary of the U-boat sinking of the Lusitania—Britain's empress of the seas—which caused the death of 1,198 persons.

The big luxury liner was torpedoed May 7, 1915, 10 miles off Kinsale Head, Ireland. It sank in 20 minutes. Perhaps no other one act of the First Great War did more to alienate from Germany the sympathy of neutral nations.

Mid-Town New York Buried Under Paper

NEW YORK, May 7—(CP)—Reverence and ribaldry mingled in the streets of mid-town Manhattan today when New York's millions learned that Germany had surrendered unconditionally.

Less than a minute after the first Associated Press flash was received from Reims, France, scraps of paper started floating from the towers of Rockefeller Center as office workers dropped everything to launch the celebration.

The whole mid-town section soon was littered with torn-up telephone books, ticker and teletype tape, newspapers and ribbons. Two hours later the impromptu confetti still was floating down, and some streets were literally inches deep in it.

Square Jammed

Times Square was virtually impassable as thousands stood to watch notices being posted up outside newspaper buildings. New York remembered the "false armistice" of April 28, and some at first were skeptical of Edward Kennedy's world beat from Reims, but when a sign was posted up saying that the news had been officially announced in London, a hysterical shout of relief went up.

Special policemen diverted traffic to side-streets and those thoroughfares soon also were almost impossible to move through as cars, taxis and trucks hooted impotently but joyously.

A woman stopped on 42nd street and began to pray. Soon a little knot of passersby had joined her as she offered her thanks: "We praise thee, O God, who has said that wheresoever two or three are gathered together..."

SPARKS STREET SCENE—Thousands of Ottawa's young people lost no time in celebrating the defeat of Nazi Germany this morning. The above picture shows a group of celebrants, mostly young people, at Sparks and Metcalfe street, before noon today. By one o'clock, the crowds on Sparks street were so dense that traffic was halted. An indication of how the streets were littered with torn up paper is given in the above picture, which shows paper streamers flying from the buildings.—(Photo by Newton.)

Enemy Asks Mercy As Terms Signed

By Edward Kennedy

REIMS, France, May 7—(AP)—Germany surrendered unconditionally to the Western Allies and Russia at 2:41 a.m. French time today. (This was at 8:41 p.m. EDT Sunday.)

The surrender took place at a schoolhouse which is the headquarters of Gen. Eisenhower.

Signs For Germany

The surrender which brought the war in Europe to a formal end after five years, eight months and six days of bloodshed and destruction was signed for Germany by Col.-Gen. Gustav Jodl.

Jodl is the new chief of staff of the German army.

It was signed for the Allied Supreme Command by Lt.-Gen. Walter Bedell Smith, chief of staff for Gen. Eisenhower.

Russia and France Sign

It was also signed by General Ivan Susloparoff for Russia and by General Francois Sevez for France.

General Eisenhower was not present at the signing, but immediately after Jodl and his fellow delegate, General Admiral Hans Georg Friedeburg, were received by the supreme commander.

They were asked if they understood the surrender terms imposed upon Germany and if they would be carried out by Germany.

They answered yes.

Germany, which began the war with a ruthless attack upon Poland followed by successive aggressions and brutality in internment camps, surrendered with an appeal to the victors for mercy toward the German people and armed forces.

Jodl Speaks

After signing the full surrender, Jodl said he wanted to speak and was given leave to do so.

"With this signature," he said quietly in German, "the German people and armed forces are for better or worse delivered into the victors' hands.

"In this war which has lasted more than five years, both have achieved and suffered more than perhaps any people in the world."

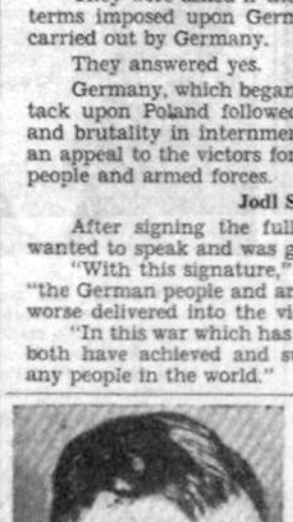

Lt. Gen. Walter Smith

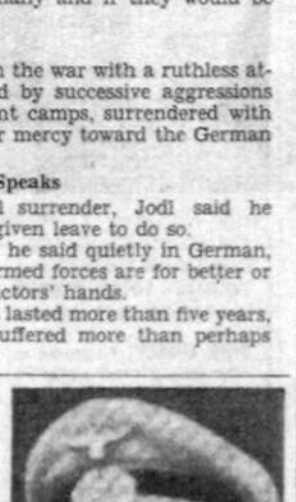

Col. Gen. Gustav Jodl

AT HISTORIC CEREMONY—Signing for the Allied supreme command at Reims was Lt. Gen. Walter Bedell Smith, chief of staff for Gen. Eisenhower. The surrender documents were signed for Germany by Col. Gen. Gustav Jodl. Russian and French officers also attached their signatures to the papers.

Ilsley States Tomorrow Is Public Holiday

Hon. J. L. Ilsley, acting Prime Minister, told the people of Canada in a broadcast address today that "there is every reason to believe that official word will be received by the early hours of tomorrow morning that Germany has surrendered unconditionally."

Speaking over a national network of the Canadian Broadcasting Corporation at 4 p.m., EDT, Mr. Ilsley announced the issuance of proclamations making tomorrow, May 8, a public holiday in Canada and authorizing the observance of next Sunday, May 13, as a "day of prayer and solemn thanksgiving."

At the end of his statement, Mr. Ilsley read over the air the two proclamations.

Motorists May Get More Gas

TORONTO, May 7—(CP)—An oil controller's announcement issued today said, "It is quite possible that a portion of certain of the petroleum products which have been going to Europe now may be made available for the motor public on this continent."

The announcement added, however, "that gasoline rationing cannot be dispensed with for some time.

"If, as and when relief comes it will be by way of an increase in the value of the coupon."

The announcement explained that "we still have our armies to move, most of them a long way from their bases. . . . In addition to the army requirements there are new demands arising out of the movement of food to liberated areas, all of which also has to be done by the motor driven vehicle."

Motorists were warned not to use up their coupons in anticipation of "immediate total relief."

The announcement said no definite word of relaxation of controls could be expected until all Allied countries could receive information from chiefs of staffs as to present and future requirements.

No Evening Papers on Tuesday, May 8th

Tuesday, May 8, having been declared a public holiday to celebrate Victory in Europe, The Evening Citizen will not be published.

The Morning Citizen will be issued as usual and will be delivered by carriers to homes of Evening Citizen subscribers in Ottawa and surrounding towns. It will also be available on news stands that are open on the holiday and from street vendors.

Death Notice.

CAMERON—On Monday, May 7, at a local hospital, Norman Allen Cameron, of White Lake, Ont., in his 54th year. Funeral from the residence at White Lake on Wednesday, May 9, at 2.30 pm. 731½

Wild Scenes As Ottawa Citizens Stage Celebration

Thousands Jam Uptown Streets When News of Defeat of Nazis Announced.

Through a blizzard of rainbow colored paper fragments and a streaming jungle of ticker tape, thousands upon thousands of Ottawans in uncounted numbers marched yelling and singing through downtown streets this morning in the greatest mass demonstration of relief and joy ever to be witnessed in Canada's Capital.

Slow to get started as the first lone Citizen bulletin announcing the official end to hostilities in Europe was posted on Sparks street, the news picked up and spread like wildfire throughout the city. And as it did, Ottawa citizens turned out to celebrate.

Tons of paper poured out of office windows on the heads of the crowds below. Torn up tax papers appeared to be the most popular form of ammunition, with confetti, bathroom tissue, letterheads and great long ribbons of adding machine paper added.

Led by thousands of youngsters on bicycles citizens joined in a giant impromptu parade that snaked its way through the center of the city tying traffic in knots.

Continuous Din

Cheers and yells burst from thousands of throats, automobile horns from long lines of cars that joined in the parade kept up a continuous din, and to this was added the cataphony of at least 10,000 tin horns, whistles, clackers, and almost every other form of noise-maker.

Windows were jammed with spectators who joined in the fun by hurling paper and streamers on the crowd below. Hundreds of flags appeared as if by magic from the tops of buildings, from awnings and from doorways and windows.

Hundreds of cameras were trained on the crowds. Motion picture equipment ground out hundreds of feet of film from the tops of motor cars. Street cars in long lines were halted by the mobs, and police were helpless as the throngs, completely disregarding traffic, streamed in the center of the city's busiest streets from curb to curb.

Buried Under Paper.

The downtown sections of the city were buried under tons of paper and the scene looking up Sparks street was reminiscent of Times Square during big celebrations.

A great silence fell over Victory Loan ceremony crowds on Confederation Square as the sun streamed down, and the blue coated massed bands of the RCAF broke out into the strains of "O Canada." As soon as the last note had died away there was an incomparable outburst of cheering from an enthusiastic crowd that just would not be silenced.

Old Lady Leads Band.

A little old lady with a Union Jack took over the leadership of the band for a few minutes using the flag as a baton.

Hundreds of citizens paused to look in the window of a Sparks street drug store where a copy of The Citizen announcing the Armistice in 1918 had been placed.

(Concluded on Page 12, Col. 6)

Surrender Violates Pact, Tokyo Protests

NEW YORK, May 7 — (AP) — The Tokyo radio, heard by the Federal Communications Commission, quoted Japanese Foreign Minister Shigenori Togo Sunday as saying that Heinrich Himmler's reported "unconditional surrender offers" violated the terms of the German-Japanese Italian tri-partite pact. He added that Japan "reserves the freedom to re-examine all her relations with the German Reich pending the qualifications of the situation in any way."

Both Churchill And The King Speak Tuesday

Tomorrow Will Be Treated as V-E Day.

LONDON, May 7—(CP)—The Ministry of Information announced that tomorrow will be treated as V-E Day.

Prime Minister Churchill will broadcast at 3 p.m. tomorrow (9 a.m. EDT), the King at 9 p.m. (3 p.m. EDT).

The ministry statement said that in accordance with arrangements between the three great powers, an official announcement will be broadcast by Mr. Churchill at 3 p.m. tomorrow.

(Both Mr. Churchill's and the King's addresses will be broadcast locally over CBO and CKCO.)

The announcement added that "His Majesty, the King, will broadcast to the peoples of the British Empire and the Commonwealth tomorrow at 9 p.m., British double summer time (3 p.m. EDT)."

"In view of this fact," the announcement said, "tomorrow will be a public holiday and the day after, Wednesday, will also be regarded as a holiday."

"Parliament will meet at the usual time tomorrow."

AP "Flash" First

This announcement came four hours after the Associated Press had flashed the surrender news from Reims, France, where the surrender pact was signed.

The Press Association attributed "the surprising delay in announcing V-E Day, in spite of the complete capitulation by the Germans," to the importance "attached to synchronizing the news in London, Washington and Moscow."

E. P. Stackpole, Press Association's correspondent in the parliament lobbies, said an hour before the ministry's announcement that the official word was not expected until tomorrow.

There were telephone calls all day between London, Washington and Moscow. The Press Association said there apparently were differing views on when the public should be informed, "but finally tomorrow was decided upon."

The Press Association said Gen. Eisenhower and Field Marshals Montgomery and Alexander were expected to speak tomorrow after the addresses by Mr. Churchill and the King.

Close-Down on AP After World Scoop

NEW YORK, May 7.—(AP)—The International News Service said today it had received the following dispatch from Supreme Allied Headquarters in Paris:

"Allied military authorities ordered suspension of the Associated Press' filing of news dispatches from everywhere in the European theater of operations as a result of publication of a dispatch saying Germany had surrendered unconditionally.

"This order was authorized for publication, but there was no textual announcement."

Similar word was received by the United Press.

After receipt of Edward Kennedy's dispatch from Reims telling of the German surrender only two minor dispatches had been received in New York from the AP bureau in Paris up to 12.30 p.m., EDT.

Weather Report on Page 12.

Newspaper Wars

The Eleventh Decade, 1945-1954

TREMENDOUS CHANGE came to Ottawa at the end of the Second World War. Fuelled by an explosion in civil service hiring—nearly 55,000 returning soldiers were added to the bureaucracy by 1949—the population of the capital region doubled to nearly 350,000 in 10 years. The aftershocks could be seen everywhere—in the suburbs spreading to the west and east of the city, in the rapid growth of the retail and service industries, in the jammed streets unsuited for the surge of traffic.

The boom also raised the stakes for Ottawa's two English-language dailies. When the war ended, the *Citizen* and *Journal* had been running neck and neck for about a decade, each selling roughly 51,000 copies a day in late 1945—and each looking for an edge in the tussle for new readers. At first, the *Citizen* looked to have the upper hand. In early 1946, Southam head office gave the go-ahead to increase news staff and offer attractive rates to advertisers who agreed to deal with the *Citizen* only.

Whatever advantage that provided was soon lost when the paper's compositors walked off the job in June 1946. For years, the *Citizen* and *Journal* had a joint contract with the unions representing pressmen, mailers and compositors. But after the Southam company shut unions out of some of its western papers, the compositors' union decided to retaliate by targeting the *Citizen*. Naively, the *Citizen* expected the *Journal* would lock out its compositors and cease publication in a show of solidarity. Instead, the *Journal* agreed to limit extra newspaper sales for two weeks and to deal with the *Citizen's* exclusive advertisers only if approached. Fearing a long strike would irrevocably hurt sales, the *Citizen* organized volunteer crews—women's editor Jean Logan went to work on a linotype machine—and engaged friendly print shops in the Ottawa Valley to help put out a makeshift paper. It wasn't much to

January 12 1945

Opposite: May 7, 1945, the news the world had been hoping for through six years of suffering.

291

look at—poor quality photos, wobbly headlines, lots of typographical errors—and it never grew bigger than 16 pages. Still, it was enough to bring the union back to the bargaining table.

In all, the strike lasted less than a month. But its effects were felt for years. In their short time on the picket line, the strikers had convinced many Ottawans the *Citizen* was a bit of a bully. And the *Journal* had lost little time filling the vacuum—by early July 1946, its circulation stood at 65,000 compared to the *Citizen's* 39,000. Indeed, it wasn't until 1950 that the *Citizen* again pulled even with the *Journal*, setting the stage for one of the liveliest, long-term newspaper rivalries in Canada.

The strike also had several unexpected effects. It ended the *Citizen's* 40-year prohibition on liquor advertising, a ban publisher Harry Southam lifted only with the greatest regret. "As a result of that walk-out and the reduction on our revenues . . . we pretty much had to accept copy from any advertiser willing to pay for it," he wrote in a memo to his brother, Wilson, in 1951. On the upside, the strike prompted the *Citizen* to lure to its newsroom a few big names—including the celebrated war correspondent Ross Munro—to win back readers.

In the early 1950s, with the paper back on its feet, the 78-year-old Southam decided it was time to retire. It had been 55 years since he'd arrived in Ottawa in 1898 to help his brother sell ads, and 33 years since he'd taken over as publisher. He turned the job over to his son, Robert, who had worked his way through the ranks since the 1930s. When the younger Southam left in 1977, the father-son team had spent 57 consecutive years in the publisher's chair.

January 12 1945

February 19, 1945

WAR BRIDES ARE WONDERFUL.

BY WINSTON MILLS, CITIZEN STAFF WRITER

Gladys Williams, comely, cheery and a nurse and fire watcher in Warlingham Hospital, Surrey, married gunner Isaac Guindon of snow-buried Maxville because an usher at the pictures thought she was with the Canadian solder when she began gassing about the moon.

Sheila Harbour, rather pensive, small and blonde, married Gunner Wesley Clarke of Ottawa some time after she was introduced to him by Pte. Jackie Robertson, also of Ottawa, at the Palais dance hall, Croydon, England. She was a charge hand at the Burnham Pen and Pencil Company in Croydon.

Jane Livingstone Ritchie, daughter of a Church of Scotland lay minister in Glasgow, petite, well educated and quick of understanding, met Pte. William R. Stephens of Ottawa at a dance and married him at the famous Pollok Church, Pollokshaw, Scotland. Their reception was in the Ca'Dora and they honeymooned romantically at lovely Loch

Lomond on Scotland's west coast.

Travelling the CNR from Montreal the other day with Gladys, Sheila and Jane convinced this reporter that Johnny Canuck from Ottawa makes no mistakes when he chooses an Old Country bride.

"My girl friend and I were gassing about the moon in a queue in front of the pictures," said Gladys, eyes shining with memory behind her prim spectacles. "Isaac was right behind us. We weren't paying any attention to him, but when we went into the pictures the usher thought we were together and so she put us together."

The other girls pressed their noses against the chill panes of the CNR coach when Gladys got off at Maxville last week. For Gladys was driven away from the snow-laden station in a cutter. A cutter with a fur robe over the seat, like a fairy princess.

"Oh, what fun," said Sheila, then, to a passing trainman, "Sing out when we come to Ottawa, won't you?" She was thinking, possibly, the same thing might happen to her.

January 12 1945

Sheila got up at seven every morning back at Croydon to be at work for 8 in the grim and sooty pen and pencil company—an ARP helmet atilt on her blonde curls. But she still had time in the evenings to go to the Palais and to meet Ottawa's Wesley Clarke and that's why she was aboard the train bound for Ottawa and her husband.

"Doodlebug Alley" was what they called much-bombed Croydon, she said. And one morning at 3 o'clock she and her brother heard the first faint whisper of an air raid siren and scrambled into the stuffy Anderson shelter in their back garden. Stella, her sister, more tardy, was blown from the front to the rear of the house when a "bug" landed on the road outside. She was unhurt, but the back wall of the house fell on the Anderson, burying Sheila and her brother for three hours.

Sheila Harbour she was, in those days, 22 and pretty. She's still pretty, but now of thoughtful demeanor. She likes what she has seen of Canada, its space, its freedom, its trains and its expanses of blue sky and white snow. "Here I hope to live my life," she said, as the CN train pounded into the outskirts of Canada's capital past the Hurdman switch tower.

And now we come to Jane. Prim and proper, Jane told this reporter nice girls didn't go into Scottish pubs. "I saw into one once from the top of a tram," she said. . . .

Jane is 25, very tiny and smart. Her father, a lay minister and missionary, tramped the misty Shetlands and the wild Orkneys with his small daughter on lay missions. "That's why I didn't mind the rough ocean crossing," said Jane, "it was nothing compared to those steamer rides in the North Sea to the islands."

She was watching a performance of *Madame Butterfly* in the Royal Theater, in Glasgow, when Hitler's first bombs struck. They fled to the street. Glasgow's air-raid arrows as hastily erected as the shelters they pointed to, directed them to a subterranean tunnel under a department store. Safe from the shrapnel which pinged on the streets outside, they prayed the building wouldn't collapse. . . .

Then, later, Ottawa's Pte. William Stephens arrived on leave. He danced well, and he sensed the innate fineness of this Scottish lass. Now, to her, "he's the best husband in the world," for whom she wishes an unpretentious job, a home and a little family, rooted firmly in the Canadian soil. . . .

After Jane got to know Bill, the family, at the peril of an outburst from the bride-to-be, had to remain silent when the Canadian news came on the wireless at 8.10 each evening. "When I heard one night that Ottawa was a girls' town," she said, "I thought I'd better get over here quick."

So Jane is here with all the others. And if these three are fair samples all Canada should rejoice in its good, new citizens.

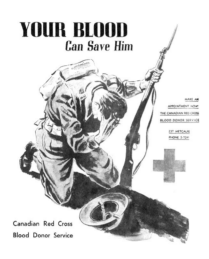

YOUR BLOOD
Can Save Him

MAKE AN
APPOINTMENT NOW!
THE CANADIAN RED CROSS
BLOOD DONOR SERVICE

237 METCALFE
PHONE 5-7241

Canadian Red Cross
Blood Donor Service

PUBLISHED IN THE INTEREST OF THE RED CROSS BY A. J. FREIMAN, LTD.

February 2, 1945

March 3, 1945
DIARY OF OUR OWN PEPYS.

From its start in the early 1930s, associate editor E. W. (Ernie) Harrold's weekly column, "Diary of Our Own Pepys," was among the Citizen's *best known features. The column was modelled on the brilliantly eccentric diaries of Samuel Pepys (pronounced "peeps"), a 17th-century British civil servant. At first, Harrold struggled to find his own voice—his early columns were stiff imitations of Pepys' old English style—but by the late 1930s, his writing had evolved into a splendid mix of news commentary and personal reflection. For a time, the column was syndicated to newspapers in Canada and the U.S., and in 1947 a collection was published as a book. This excerpt is from one of his later columns, written about six months before he died.*

SATURDAY, FEBRUARY 24.

Up, and downstairs to hear the 8 o'clock news, a ritual that nowadays I face each morning with high expectancy, for those ten seconds or so of silence before the broadcaster's voice is heard are full of suspense, I wondering whether the next words will be, "The German armies threw down their arms this morning as disorder swept the Reich," or, "Uprisings broke out in Germany today following the collapse of the eastern front," or "Organized resistance virtually ceased on the west front today." But they do not come, and sober reflection afterwards makes one feel foolish for hoping that they might. So to work, but not for long, making haste to go home to see what I could do about the water that hath "backed up" and through my roof staining the ceiling of my bedroom, and I succeeded in stemming the flow. So afoot to the city and home and within all evening....

MONDAY, FEBRUARY 26.

Wakened early, and to the office and all morning at matters of business and afterwards looked at *Time*'s photograph of Mr. Churchill's mystery hat, and I am now sure it was the sealskin headpiece given to him by the Press Gallery here four years ago, and then fell upon an article by R. J. Needham in the *Calgary Herald*, in which he wonders why 12,000,000 Canadians depend for their advice to the lovelorn upon American soothsayers like Geo. Antheil, Dorothy Dix and Mary Haworth, he being sure there are people here competent to dispense such advice, and he suggests it may be the Canadian character, "which is inclined to be serious, even morose," producing writing on politics, architecture and military strategy, "but not about the tender and passionate emotion of love." So I made some inquiries and learned that Mr. Antheil's daily counsel in *The Evening Citizen* draws from 20 to 60 letters a week, few of the writers suspecting that Mr. A. does not occupy an office in the *Citizen* building, and that many of them demanding immediate response are answered by a wise member of the staff who, I am sure, could conduct a department as well as Mr. A., and she tells me the correspondents range from their 'teens to their dotage, and that the responsibility of advising people on tragic personal affairs—which may mark a turning point in their lives—is not to be lightly undertaken. And it all minded me of the day some years ago that John McKinley, late judge of the Juvenile Court, asked me to join him in launching an advice column in Canada, but after I had got all the advance material ready, he decided not to go on with it.

TUESDAY, FEBRUARY 27.

Busy in the morning until near noon and then abroad and met Y. Karsh, who tells me he hath finished my picture, and that it will be unveiled to an impatient public this week-end, news that filled me with mixed feelings, and so to the Canadian Club to hear Dean Mackenzie, president of the National Research Council, discourse on "Science in War and Peace," and I was glad he called it re-search and not ree-search, and he told us some mighty interesting things, but, I mused ruefully, I hope Science will get around one day to a roofing system that will end the backed-up water trouble I have mentioned, as well as a storm window that will fit and is ayreproof and will not get out of joint in our Siberian winters. So at the office again and home, carried thither in [Mackenzie King adviser] L. W. Brockington's handsome coach, who tells me of meeting two nephews of B. K. Sandwell, one in Tasmania and the other in Italy....

FRIDAY, MARCH 2.

To the office and read the *This Happy Breed* letters, and nobody has yet pointed out that the title of the film is from Shakespeare's "This

Six-Year-Old Anne Heggtveit.—(Photo by C. F. Quick.)

Skiing Of Wee Ottawan Attracts Army Cameramen

Canadian soldiers overseas will shortly see 6-year-old Anne Heggtveit of Ottawa in action on ski slopes in a specially prepared winter sports movie taken last week at St. Sauveur des Monts in the Laurentian Mountains by a Canadian Army Film Unit directed by Lt. Charles Quick.

Anne, born on January 6, 1939, is a daughter of Mr. and Mrs. Halvor Heggtveit of 35 Charles street and was skiing on Hills 69 and 70 at St. Sauveur last week when Army photographers spotted her in action and observed the attention focused on her skiing.

Placing their movie cameras on Hill 69, a famous ski slope dedicated to the memory of the late Sir Arthur Currie, Commander-in-Chief of Canadian Overseas troops in the Great War of 1914-1918, the Army cameramen took shots as she slalomed the steep hill, doing right and left Christiania swings.

Center of Attraction.

Wherever enthusiasts gathered last week, from Shawbridge to Mont Tremblant, the wee Ottawan's ability was the chief topic of con-

versation. "Klister" Smith, a Norwegian skier, reported that 55 miles away at Mont Tremblant he had heard tales of her ski feats.

The way the Ottawa mite got up the steep hills was also something that gave the ski fraternity a surprise. Climbing up on her father's back 6-year-old Anne tightly clasped her arms around his neck while he grasped the tow rope and was pulled up the long and steep 40 degree slope. On one day alone of her ski holiday Anne made more than 100 trips up the tow on her father's back.

A member of the Ottawa Ski Club and a regular weekly visitor to Camp Fortune lodge she learned skiing from her father, a former Canadian Cross-Country Champion and member of Ottawa's well-known skiing family of Heggtveits.

Some 85 members of the RA Ski Club of Ottawa now on a ski holiday at St. Sauveur will also be included in the film. Lt. Charles Quick of the Canadian Army Film Unit is assisted by Lt. George Cooper of Ottawa and Ernest Ide of the National Film Board.

March 24, 1945

happy breed of men, this little world, this precious stone set in a silver sea;" lines which, as Winnie-the-Pooh would say, Explains a Lot, and so worked until evening and later heard Prime Minister King's greatly anticipated statement to the nation, which did not tell much that most of us didn't know, and the situation seems to me that Mr. King is quite right in theory and his proverbial luck makes that theory right for him.

—E. W. H.

May 7, 1945
LITTLE BENNY'S NOTEBOOK.
*Lee Pape's folksy humour column was also a regular feature
on the* Citizen's *editorial pages for many years.*

May 8, 1945

May 10, 1945

Pop was smoking and thinking and ma was just thinking, saying, I don't see why I should have a gold inlay put in a tooth as long as it has an old-fashioned filling that's still doing active duty. What's your opinion, William? she said.

My opinion is that sleeping lions should be left undisturbed, in other words I agree with you, pop said, and ma said, Naturally if the tooth was in the front of my mouth where it showed, it would be a different story for esthetic reasons, but the tooth happens to be way in the back where it's none of the public's business even at my widest smile, so why go to the bother and the expense?

Why indeed? pop said, and ma said, The dentist was very honest and straightforward about it. He told me that naturally an inlay is to be preferred to a filling when other things are equal, and yet this filling may have several useful years of service ahead of it. The point is, of course, the *House and Table Magazine* is sold only by subscription, and it's impossible to pick one up on the news stands, she said.

I'm afraid I must of dozed off and missed a vital link in your conversation, pop said, and ma said, I'm referring to a two-part article in *House and Table* called Chintzes for Every Room.

I read the first installment at Laura Hintchfield's tea and bridge the other afternoon, but I don't get to Laura's house more than twice a year, and the only other place I ever see *House and Table* is in the dentist's waiting room.

It costs 6 dollars a year now to subscribe to *House and Table*, and it wouldn't be very economical to subscribe for a year just for next month's number, so perhaps I'll compromise. I mean I won't have the inlay put in, but I think I'll go to see the dentist some time next month just for a general cleaning. Don't you think I'm wise, William? ma said.

I think you're Napoleonic, my dear, and in the meantime keep your chintz up, pop said. Being the end of the subject.

—LEE PAPE

August 8, 1945
THE JEW WANDERS ON.
(Excerpt from a column.)

BY HAROLD GARDNER, CITIZEN STAFF WRITER

The fires are burning out in Europe. Sympathy and material aid have been extended to all who suffered at the hands of the Nazi barbarians. All, that is, except the Jews who, despite the fact that they were the first to feel the heel of the New Order and who have been subjected to the most inhuman and uncivilized treatment conceivable, still have so very few champions to fight their cause.

Of the 7,000,000 Jews who lived in countries west of the Soviet Union before 1933, it is estimated that only 750,000, or slightly more than one-tenth, have survived the persecutions of the Germans and their satellites. According to recent shocking reports 5,000,000 were exterminated while 1,000,000 were given refuge in Russia and several thousand others found safety in other Allied countries . . . . History has yet to record a greater sacrifice made of any people. They died and as the echoes of their death-calls still sound hollowly in the caverns, a complacent world murmurs "too bad," and promptly forgets.

They may forgive but they should not forget. They should not forget the Buchenwalds, the Dachaus, the slaughtering of millions of men, women and children, by gas, by electricity, by shooting, by torture, and by every horrible means ever devised. They should not forget the report of General Georges P. Vanier, distinguished soldier and Canadian envoy to France, who found finger-marks gouged out of clay walls of dungeons where the Jews were incarcerated. These marks were made by the prisoners as they struggled to escape jets of live steam played on them by their fiendish captors.

The Jews are an ancient and honorable people with great pride and dignity. The majority of them are not content to sit back and ask sympathy. They have suffered a great blow these past twelve years and all they are asking is to be allowed to help themselves. Never in all time have the Jews been poorer in numbers or economically.

It seems strange that a democratic world can sit idly by and ignore what has happened to the Jews, not only since 1933 but for more than 1,000 years. Neither at San Francisco nor at Potsdam was one official voice raised to express regret or offer help to these people who have suffered so much for so long.

If only as a tribute to the Jews it is time to sit down, take stock and do away with the problem which too many shrug off as a hopeless snarl. Their courage which has brought them through from one dark age to another, should be rewarded. They are human, feel pain and insult, and deserve a place in a peaceful world. They have bought their security

"That you may look to the future confident, hopeful and above all free."

The Goodyear Tire & Rubber Co. of Canada, Limited   GOOD YEAR

May 8, 1945

with great suffering and loss of life.

A step in this direction would be the establishment of a National Homeland for the Jews. This would be a two-fold help. In the first place, the plan would allow refugees into Palestine. Many countries in Europe have expressed their welcome to a return of displaced Jews. However, those Jews who lived in Germany and escaped have no wish to return there. They will never forget. A home must be found for them and Palestine would be admirable.

On the other hand, the creation of a Homeland would help diminish anti-Semitism in other lands. For example, the Jews in Canada would be able to walk the streets with their heads held high because they had a home just as other people. A Homeland would serve as a backbone to the Jews and give the rest of the world a different concept of the race.

Of course, there is the Arabic claim to Palestine. The oil they can offer the Allies should be weighed most carefully against the blood shed by Jewish servicemen and their efforts for a democratic cause. Another fact which should be considered is that Palestine is far from being the land of milk and honey described in the Testament. It is a difficult land to farm and travelers have returned filled with praise for the progress made by the Jews on the land and in the cities . . . .

But there still remains the point that the Jews have shown they prize Palestine and will guard it carefully. They have earned a right to the land.

Claims Body Of Hitler Found In Berlin Ruins

By Ned Nordness.

WITH THE BRITISH 2ND ARMY, May 8.—(AP)—Col. Anotoly Pilugin, war correspondent of Tass, Soviet news agency, has said a Russian general had stated that the body of a man identified as Adolf Hitler had been found in the ruins of Berlin.

The Russian general was not named.

During a meeting two days ago between Field Marshal Montgomery and Marshal Konstantin Rokossovsky of the 2nd White Russian Army, Russian officers asked Pilugin, who is attached to the British 2nd Army as a war correspondent, whether Britons believed Hitler was dead or alive.

Pilugin said he replied there was a mixed opinion, but that the Russian general, whose identity he did not disclose, stated that the Russians had found in Berlin the bullet-torn and battered body of a man identified as Hitler.

All Holland Now In Hands Of Canadians

By William Boss.

UTRECHT, Holland, May 8 — (CP Cable)—All Holland is in the hands of the 1st Canadian Corps, commanded by Lt.-Gen. Charles Foulkes of Victoria, BC, and London, Ont.

Formal liberation was completed almost without incident and the liberators were greeted by tumultuous demonstrations.

May 9, 1945

November 3, 1945
THE DREAM-CITY OF MR. GREBER

News about French architect Jacques Greber's return to Ottawa to prepare a sweeping plan for the capital filled the city's newspapers for months in late 1945. After weeks of squabbling—some thought his plan too grand—the Citizen's *editorial writers finally weighed in with their view. Their editorial was published on Page 1, a sign of the importance the* Citizen *attached to Greber's ideas. Here's an excerpt:*

A dream-city, symbolic of Canada's greatness among the nations, may sound too extravagant a description of the project which Mr. Jacques Greber, world-famous architect, who lived under the Germans, has outlined for the planning and beautification of Ottawa. But Mr. Greber is a practical man, not given to dreams.

Since he was first here in 1938, the federal capital plan, as then projected, has undergone a significant change. Then it was a question of creating a beautiful modern capital for a Dominion. Today, as Mr. Greber has rightly stressed, it is a question of preparing for what will ultimately become a world-city, a great international centre, the Geneva, perhaps, of the New World, and certainly one of the world's outstanding capitals.

The implications of this forecast may not yet be as fully recognized by the people of Ottawa as by the outside world.

As the outcome of her extraordinary development during the war, Canada has become one of the "Middle Powers." She has a voice in world affairs greater than ever in her history. Ottawa has become a diplomatic centre with ambassadors from many countries residing here. The aeroplane has abolished distance from Europe. International gatherings and meetings of governments can be as readily arranged for Ottawa as they used to be arranged for Paris and Vienna. Canada, moreover, has today that curious quality, prestige, not only within the British Commonwealth but outside it everywhere.

No plan for Canada's capital, consequently, need be considered too grandiose, nor need it be looked upon as a necessarily distant achievement. Mr. Greber's brilliant architectural imagination clearly reveals to him the alluring opportunity Ottawa affords for his gifts. In his native France, as in Britain, the accumulations of centuries, the legacies of dead generations, have too often covered the land with huddled, smoke-befogged aggregations of human dwellings, with sprawling agglomerations of dingy industrial suburbs stretching their grimy tentacles into what should have been sun-lit greenbelts available for the citizens' enjoyment. Such unpleasing relapses into the unplanned and the ugly have been well described by a Belgian poet as "octopus cities."

Such cities must never be allowed to arise in Canada. It is, therefore, well to know that what is projected for Ottawa is an ultimate assurance against such horrors. Here, as Mr. Greber senses the capital of the not-so-distant future, there will be a plan and a topographical framework in no sense rigid but capable of expansion as needs require. There will be every facility for the expansion of commerce and industry in their proper environment. The transport system, as is proper in this era of rapid invention, will be modern, and, let us hope, as far as possible, free from noise and accident. Wide and good roads; easily accessible airports; social and community centres, including convention halls, for Ottawa must be host to visitors on the largest scale; well laid-out government buildings designed to give maximum service to the public; open spaces, greenbelts and forests to roam and find health in; exhibition grounds; stadiums and sports grounds for physical enjoyment—even winter sports, because Mr. Greber sees no reason why the climate here could not be capitalized for Ottawa as it has already been in such skiing centres as St. Moritz in Switzerland or Mégève in France.

Fortunately, over a great part of the Federal area, the work of the Canadian architects and planners will be untrammelled. They have no accumulations of age-old blunders to try to correct. Much of the region to which Mr. Greber and his technicians will apply their talents is

August 15, 1945

August 15, 1945

"free and virgin." Observed from the air, it discloses a topography which could be described as the planners' delight.

Mr. Greber's satisfaction with it is obvious. Here he has few, if any, of the frustrations he had inevitably to meet in replanning such cities as Lille and Marseilles. He can release his imaginative yet practical mind for what, in one sense, is a true work of art.

August 16, 1945

August 16, 1945

February 19, 1946
LADIES KEEP ORDER IN RUSH FOR NYLONS
Clerks Who Awaited In Fear and Trembling
For Stampede Had No Cause For Alarm

When the Citizen *first ran Bettie Cole's byline in 1941, it marked the integration of female writers—previously relegated to the women's pages—into the realm of "hard" news. Though her previous journalistic experience consisted only of filing social notes to the* Sherbrooke Record, *Cole's diligence and love of newspaper culture allowed her to become the self-described "first girl journalist on the men's general staff." The story excerpted here appeared on the business pages.*

BY BETTIE L. COLE
Evening Citizen Staff Writer.

Insofar as Ottawa is concerned, the Battle of the Nylons fizzled out. There was no battle. In fact the nylon shoppers were so quiet and orderly in their shopping that store managers and clerks alike were delighted and amazed.

In some places people stood for two hours in sub-zero weather, waiting patiently. As soon as they got their nylons they headed for coffee counters and warm food.

It had been expected that there might be near-riots as hundreds of women, and, yes, men, too, crowded through doors and raced for stocking counters. Clerks stood waiting with fear and trembling, dreading the moment when the battle would begin—but the battle failed to develop. Many women were heard to say, "If we don't get them now we will later. It is not a matter of life and death." The manager of one store declared that "within a few months we will be begging people to buy stockings they will be so plentiful."

In some places after the doors opened nylons were all gone in 15 minutes, while in other stores they lasted half an hour.

At one Sparks street store the line-up extended two blocks and some nylon-seekers in it waited from seven o'clock until nine. One of these, Miss Mary Christian of Laurentian Terrace, smiled happily as she emerged from the store just after it had opened with the first pair sold there. "They are the first pair I have ever owned," she said, "and it was worth the wait." Asked by *The Evening Citizen* if she was not nearly frozen after waiting two hours in the nine-below-zero weather, she replied: "No. I came dressed for it. I have waited a long time for this day." She was literally bulging with clothes.

The second customer to get a pair of the precious nylons was a man, James Harris of 509 Booth street. Grinning broadly he confessed they were for his girl-friend. "Boy, she will love you!" someone remarked. He also agreed that it was worth the two-hour wait to get them. . . .

An air force officer wandered into a large chain store just after nine o'clock and, seeing the long line-up, asked what was going on. "A nylon sale," a clerk told him. "What's that?" he asked innocently.

"What are nylons?" repeated the clerk incredulously. "The best silk stockings that can be bought!"

"You mean," he asked, "that if I get a pair everything will be hunkey-dorey with me and my gal?"

"Yes," said the clerk. "OK then, here goes!" he declared as he walked to the end of the long line and took his place.

Three clerks stood behind the counter of one large department store and waited. Cards had been sent out to regular customers. One lone woman approached and was served immediately. There was a long pause. Then another came. "This is a great system," the owner of the store told *The Evening Citizen*. "There is no rushing this way."

In a well-known glove and hosiery store clerks stood idly behind counters. Nylons were not on sale. Customers had been told that. "Let 'em rush at other stores if they wish," said one. "We feel smug. Let's go out for coffee." Three of them did.

BING AND OTTAWA GIRL—"Der Bingle" (Bing Crosby) knows a beautiful girl when he sees one and found Miss Terry Sasz of Billings Bridge one of the prettiest he had ever seen when they met at Jasper Park recently. Crosby is dressed in the costume he wears in "Emperor's Waltz", which was partially filmed in Jasper.

July 29, 1946

October 5, 1946
BROADCAST COMMENT.

By the mid-1930s, radio had become an important source of news and entertainment, but it would be another decade before most newspapers decided it warranted the kind of attention given to plays and movies. In large part, the reluctance stemmed from the view that radio was competition—an approach many papers would later apply to television.

BY CLAUDE C. HAMMERSTON.
Radio Editor, The Evening Citizen.

For a long time I have campaigned in this column for a good, lively Canadian comedy program. Well, we seem to have one. I am referring to the "Wayne and Shuster Show" on Thursday nights at 9:30 over CBO. These two Canadian lads, who had several fingers in the "Army Show" and wrote the scripts for last season's "Johnny Home" show, have been partners-in-writing since they were 14 years of age.

Wayne and Shuster have something that is as good as many of the American comedy programs, and can run circles around some of those broadcast across the border. Their gags are good. They are spicily put across, and the pace never slackens from start to finish. They could, however, use a little more of [CBC-BBC broadcaster] Bernie Braden's dialect talent. The singing of Georgia Dey is good and Samuel Hersenhoren's music excellent.

The only fault with the show—and the only item that spoils the whole proceeding—are the commercials. It is unfortunate that a sponsor can't put on a program without lousing it up with repetitious plugs for the product. One plug at the beginning and one at the close should be sufficient. The sponsor gives the impression that he doesn't give two hoots what goes on between the commercials.

Nazi Warlords Were "All In" On Treachery

NUERNBERG, July 27 —(AP)— British prosecutor Sir Hartley Shawcross today concluded his summation against 22 ranking Nazis on trial on war crimes charges with a plea for "retribution to these guilty men."

Winding up his eight-hour speech which began at yesterday's session of the international military tribunal, Sir Hartley named each defendant, from Hermann Goering to the absent Martin Bormann and then declared: "These are guilty men."

"On their fate, great issues must still depend. This trial must form a milestone in the history of civilization, not only bringing retribution to these guilty men . . . but also that the ordinary people of the world—and I make no distinction between friend and foe—are now determined that the individual must transcend the state."

Again and again the British prosecutor hammered home his thesis that a careful campaign of deception, treachery, intimidation, murder and blitzkrieg had been planned deliberately by the men in the dock.

All Knew Of Plans

"Everyone of these men knew of these plans at one stage or another," he asserted. "Everyone of them acquiesced in this technique, knowing full well what it must represent in terms of human life.

"How can any one of them now say he was not a party to common murder in its most ruthless forms?"

As he ticked off the defendants, one by one, he called the name of Julius Streicher, the Nazis' No. 1 Jew baiter, and demanded his execution.

"It is long since he has forfeited all right to live," Sir Hartley declared.

July 27, 1946

October 16, 1946
PROBE GOERINGS'S MYSTERIOUS FADE-OUT.
How Nazi Gangsters "Took It".
Streicher's Scream Scares Reporter.
(Excerpt from a news story.)

BY KINGSBURY SMITH
Representing The Combined American Press.

NUERNBERG, Oct. 16—(Special)—All 10 of the Nazi war criminals executed here this morning went to their deaths with stoicism.

I was one of the eight Allied correspondents who witnessed their deaths on the gibbet. They took place in the brightly-lighted gymnasium in the Nuernberg jail-yard, only 35 yards from the death cells where the condemned spent their last days.

Three black-painted wooden scaffolds stood inside the death chamber. Two of them were used alternately to hang the condemned men individually while the third was held in reserve. Ropes were suspended from a crossbeam supported on two posts.

Most of the executed men endeavoured to show their bravery. Some were bitterly defiant and some grimly resigned, while others called on the Almighty for mercy.

Julius Streicher, the Jew-baiter, shouted "Heil Hitler!" before he died. As in the case of all the condemned, a warning knock by a guard preceded Streicher's entry through a door in the middle of the death chamber . . . . He wore a threadbare suit, a well-worn bluish shirt and no tie. He was renowned for his flashy dress in the days of Nazi power.

Streicher was stopped immediately inside the door by two army sergeants who closed in on each side of him and held his arms, while another sergeant who had followed him in from behind removed manacles from his hands and replaced them with leather cord. It was originally planned to permit the condemned men to walk from their cells to the execution chamber with their hands free, but all were manacled in their cells immediately following discovery of Goering's suicide.

Streicher's scream of "Heil Hitler" sent a shiver down my back.

As its echo died away, another American colonel standing by the steps of the scaffold said sharply to an interpreter: "Ask the man his name." In response to the query, Streicher answered: "You know my name well." The interpreter repeated his request and the condemned man shouted: "Julius Streicher."

Guards then started moving Streicher up the steps. As he mounted to the platform, the beady-eyed Jew-baiter called out: "And now it goes to God." Streicher was swung around to face the audience in front of him. . . . With burning hatred in his eyes Streicher looked down at the witnesses and shouted: "Purim Fest, 1946." (Purim is a Jewish holiday celebrated in September).

An American officer near the scaffold then asked the man if he had any last words and Streicher snarled: "The Bolsheviks will hang you one day."

Just as the black hood was about to be placed upon his head, Streicher said: "I am with God." And as it was being adjusted Streicher's muffled voice could be heard to say: "Adele, my dear wife."

At that moment the trap was sprung with a loud bang. When the rope snapped taut and the body swung wildly, a groan could be heard distinctly from within the dark interior of the scaffold.

In order to get the executions over with quickly, security forces would bring in one man while the prisoner who preceded him still was dangling at the end of the rope. . . .

After the executions were completed and with the body of Seyss-Inquart still hanging awaiting pronouncement of his death, the gymnasium doors opened and guards entered carrying Goering's body on a stretcher. This was placed on the floor beneath the two scaffolds.

Generals representing the four-power Allied Council ordered the army blanket covering the body removed so that the world's press representatives could make note of the fact that Goering was dead.

The former Reichsmarshal, holder of more titles and possessor of more medals than can easily be listed, was clad in black pajamas with a blue shirt opened on his chest. His head was turned to one side and his hair was ruffled. There was an agonized expression on his face. . . .

July 6, 1946

July 31, 1946

May 10, 1949
JOSEPH SMALLWOOD
MOST CONTROVERSIAL CITIZEN
This is the second of a series of articles on Newfoundland
by Ross Munro, Evening Citizen Parliamentary Writer,

designed to indicate what the union with Canada
means, and what it will mean to the new province.

BY ROSS MUNRO

ST. JOHN'S, Newfoundland—The most controversial citizen in
Newfoundland today is the new premier of the tenth province—
Joseph Smallwood.

He's ardently admired on one hand and despised and ridiculed on
the other. I've never known a provincial premier who has been the
centre of such a stormy and personal dispute.

To the thousands of people who followed Smallwood's urgings and
voted for Confederation, this thin, dapper man is a political hero of giant stature. They are delighted by the way he's gone to bat as premier—and he really has—working eighteen hours a day running the
province.

The multitude of poorer people give their thanks to him for the baby
bonus. Letters from the outports pour in on him expressing gratitude
for this windfall. Some even come addressed to "Sir Joey Smallwood."

The poorer people are with him, too, because he represents to them
their strong arm against merchants of St. John's Water Street, and the
friend of what Smallwood now calls "the toiling masses."

Many of the premier's political enemies grudgingly admit he has
started off like a house afire but they contend his cabinet is atrocious
and they rake over Smallwood's past, which consists of a few reasonable successes as a newspaperman and broadcaster, but failure in business, including a piggery at Gander during the war.

Some of St. John's leading citizens can't keep from profanity in talking of the premier. They literally spit out their dislike for the man and
his indifferent past. They say Smallwood has no administrative or executive experience. They keep harking back to the argument that the
premier failed in business. "How can a man like this be a good provincial leader?" they ask....

The truth about Smallwood is somewhere between the two extremes—of almost lavish admiration and this violent hatred.

I would say that the best feature about Smallwood is his political genius. He also is a great showman and political propagandist. Besides,
he has learned to use radio probably more effectively than any political
figure in Canada. He is terrific on the air and radio is the only way to
reach the great bulk of Newfoundland people.

He revels in his new power, but I doubt if he will ever run wild and
ruin the province financially. There are bound to be some strong men
in the new cabinet who will balance out his flash enthusiasms. It is
doubtful whether he himself knows when to be cautious and when to
go flat out for something. That may be his Achilles heel.

Smallwood has no desire for money or worldly goods. He's always

Our Boarding House

October 11, 1948

October 25, 1948

just got along and it has never bothered him. He still wears his old blue striped suit and lives in the same very modest red house by the waterfront, even when he's premier. He puts on no airs. That is another phase of his political strength.

Politically, I would think the new premier is perhaps closer to being a socialist than a Liberal, although his party is at present called Liberal. Cynics say he is a Liberal because it was politically opportune for him to be at this time. It is not impossible that later on Smallwood may slide to the left completely and become a socialist leader, linking up with the C.C.F. and taking that part of the Liberal party of Newfoundland with him which would back him in such a move. . . .

Smallwood sits amiably at the head of a huge desk cluttered up with books, documents, Liberal propaganda and maps, and right in front of him is a litter of letters and telegrams eight inches high.

In the centre of it all is an electric razor—perhaps a bit of a stage prop, but a mute hint to people who stay too long that Joe Smallwood is so busy he has to shave in his office.

Beside his chair is a battery of three telephones and a radio, and you can't talk to him for five minutes without the telephone jangling, a couple of secretaries rushing in and out and a new visitor or two arriving.

Yet Joe Smallwood sits there in cocky confidence. Nothing fazes him. You'd think from his composure that he'd been running a vast corporation for years.

He hasn't missed a political trick since taking office. A while back there was starvation reported from a Labrador hamlet. Smallwood dramatized the plight of the people and sent aircraft and an ice-breaker to their rescue. His action brought another flood of letters of commendation. Then he ascertained that prices on soaps and some other commodities had risen abnormally in some areas and he immediately jumped in to slap on price ceilings on those articles.

"This is the first chance I've really had to show my supporters that I'm out to protect the interests of the little man," Smallwood told me the day I visited his office. . . .

Smallwood keeps a box score of the reaction of his public. The latest is 200 letters each day, which he reads, but finds trouble, naturally, answering very promptly; plus 50 telegrams and 200 telephone calls. One hundred citizens on an average call on him each day at his office, jamming the hallway of the Colonial building.

It is an operation unique in any Canadian capital.

October 11, 1948

July 21, 1950
A NIGHT OF DICE IN ROAD HOUSE NEAR AYLMER
Unlike the tense relationships that often exist between reporters and police today, things were a lot cozier in the 1950s when tips and

favours were commonly exchanged for mutual benefit. This story, co-written by legendary crime reporter Joe Finn, was published alongside a news item—by the same writers—about a police raid on the illegal gambling operation the two reporters visited a few nights before. The reporters told police where to find the craps game. In exchange, the police invited the reporters along on their raid.

Fan Fare

October 25, 1948

BY JOE FINN AND TED HANRATTY
Citizen Staff Writers

"Come on boys, get those bets down! Who's the next lucky shooter comin' up? Oh, it's Solly—the guy who made all those passes the last time! Yeh-h-h-h-h, he rolls a 10—'big Dick.' Who says he makes it the hard way?"

That was the general run of the "come on" we listened to a couple of nights ago when we broke the law and had ourselves a fling (all for the edification of our readers) at a craps game in nightly session a mile east of Aylmer.

The set-up, while not a "floating crap game" in the same sense as those which move each night to a different location in larger centers, might be termed a "semi-floater." Our investigations disclosed that it has operated at various times on the Mountain Road, the Chelsea Road—even in the Billings Bridge area on the Ottawa side at an earlier stage.

One of the many "features" of the enterprise was taxi service for patrons who were driven to and from the "club" free of charge, win-lose-draw. For more affluent cash customers who preferred driving out in their own cars, a spacious parking space—well guarded by a half-dozen "look-outs"—was available.

No beer or liquor was served on the premises. The player could, however, get his favorite brand of soft drink or a sandwich at a well-equipped little sandwich bar, and he could also buy cigarettes or cigars. Those items were not, however, "on the house."

Our brief "research" into the background of the resort has failed to unearth anyone who took any sizeable amount of folding money away with him. But on the "taken" side of the ledger it's a different story. The young son (just turned 21) of a prominent Aylmer man dropped $800 the same night.

Plenty of other patrons contributed $100, $200, and $300 to the "cause," and we will not deign to mention the "pikers" (such as ourselves) whose losses were as ridiculously low as $10, $20 or $25.

When we pulled up in style outside the small white cottage the other night we were given the once-over (and none too lightly) by five pairs of sharp eyes. The idea, apparently, was not "are these guys coppers?" but only, "could they be guys with the idea of sticking up the joint?"

Seemingly we passed the acid test, for we were admitted. Presently we were standing shoulder to shoulder with 15 or 20 other "guests," and beginning to "get our feet wet," so to speak.

The voices of the players were subdued despite the unmistakable air of gambling excitement, and the first recognizable commentary we heard was, "Who'll bet four the hard way? Who'll bet two fours—two sixes—two threes? Five's the point! Five'll win this time! Five's gotta win this time."

A little later when we had purchased $10 worth of chips, the long, thin, casual looking dealer remarked to no one in particular: "Don't you worry at all about losing, gentlemen. We pay the taxi fare back to town, win or lose."

A plump, dark-skinned shooter, his forehead bathed in sweat, prayed: "Get hot, dice! A feber and we leave 'em. Come on, dice! Three and two!"

We recognized a few of the players, but none of them paid any attention to us. One was a grocery store owner from Ottawa, and another was a small-time gambler who would bet on anything—and frequently does.

Still another member of the "cast" was a tavern waiter from Hull. He stood, tense and watchful, beside a young married man with a family of four. The look on the face of the latter said plainly: "I can't afford to lose this dough, but I'm losing it just the same."

And so it went. "Lay down your dough! Read 'em and weep!" Occasionally a player left the big, green topped table and sauntered out to the sandwich bar for a spot of refreshment, possibly with the forlorn hope that a cheese-on-rye might change his luck.

When we finally called it a night (our cash had gone the way of all good things), and were escorted to a waiting taxi words we heard were: "Don't roll the d— dice so hard! This ain't no barbotte game! This is a game of skill, not strength!"

Those priceless gems of philosophy were lost and swallowed in the cloud of dust kicked up by our taxi as it sped over the narrow little side road.

October 7, 1950
Austin Cross At The World Series.
CELEBRITIES ARE A DIME A DOZEN.
Joltin' Joe DiMaggio And Eddie Sawyer
Talk About Their Trips To Ottawa.
No Citizen *writer of the 1940s and early 1950s was better known—or more prolific—than Austin Cross, who was at home covering crime and fashion or economics and tragedy. But Cross's real strength was his knack for capturing the flavour of the city, which he did for 15*

July 24, 1950

years in his daily column, "'Cross Town." Even on his many out-of-town assignments, like the story from the World Series excerpted here, Cross always kept an eye open for the Ottawa angle.

BY AUSTIN F. CROSS
Evening Citizen Staff Writer

NEW YORK—Even if you never looked at the game, it's worth while to attend the World Series. Celebrities a dime a dozen, men with muscles and molls with mink, living ghosts of yesterday like 1915 Philadelphia hero Grover Cleveland Alexander—wrap all this up with a thousand other eye-popping items and you still only have caught a corner of what I saw at the Yankee Stadium Friday.

For the record, the fast-fading Phils lost a game they should have won, the score being 3-2. I expect there are a few words about this elsewhere in *The Evening Citizen*. But, absorbing as such championship play is bound to be, what goes on around the game is more enthralling. Among other things I had a brief interview with [Philadelphia manager] Eddie Sawyer, who recalled he had been in Ottawa.

"I was not very important then," he recalled, with a wry smile, "and I suppose nobody would recall me. But I managed the Amsterdam ball team in the same league Ottawa was in. I used to stay at the Chateau Laurier."

"Any vivid recollections of Ottawa?" he was asked, while he steadily signed autographs.

"Yes, a bad ball park and fine people." (Mr. Sawyer should see our park now!)

Then there was Joe DiMaggio. It is hard to get at him for long, because the press never leaves him alone. He is sought out ten times as much as any other player, or non-player, on the field.

"Yes, I was in Ottawa a while back," said Joltin' Joe. "I stayed with Dr. Charles Shapiro. You might give the Shapiros my regards. I had a good time in Ottawa. Then we went up to Lake Ste. Marie."

By that time, he was engulfed with photographers, interviewers and autograph requests, so a salute to Shapiro, and I let him go.

If you have the idea that going to a game means being there at 1 p.m when it starts and leaving about three, when it is over, think again. I got out there at 11:20, and there were easily 200 newspaper men and photographers on the field. You can see who you like, and photograph what you like, and within bounds do what you like, till 12:20 when the press are cleared off the field, and they all try to squeeze their way into the temporary press boxes. The fellow who does the best talking gets the best places; the other gets thumbed out. It is no place for the tongue tied.

My ticket said I was a roving reporter, not entitled to any specific

seat. I accordingly went and sat in a very fancy box, not far from Base-ball Commissioner Happy Chandler. This box was reserved perma-nently in the name of the Ryerson Oil Co. I sat there until well after the game started, when the oil men showed up. Then I moved along to an-other empty box, this one belonging to some Pittsburgh industrialists. When they turned up, after the third inning, I found a seat in the press box between Hi Goldberg of the *Newark News*, and a Mr. O'Donnell from the *Waterbury Republican*. The man beside him turned out to be a gate-crasher, but he lasted through the game without being ousted.

Not far from me was Red Smith, the sad-faced man who grinds out a funny column that appears in *The Evening Citizen* and many other fine publications. Near him was big Dan Parker, his huge hulk hovering over the flimsy portable like a black cloud over an outdoor piano. Park-er was whacking off some funny stuff about Casey Stengel changing his lucky batting order and defying the fates. Other famous bylines were chewing away at cigars and with their traditional light felt hats bashed in and askew, were hustling out smart, quick summaries against early deadlines....

In the fancy boxes, most of which are rented for the season, you saw enough mink to cover Lansdowne Park, nor was it any of your cheap brown stuff. This was silver mink, worth about $100 a square inch. Then there were the orchids. Apparently any lady who sits in a box feels she is not properly dressed without them and a visit to the Yankee Stadium today would have given Nero Wolfe, famous sleuth and or-chid fancier, quite a field day.

Not so far away from where I crash-landed in the oil tycoons' box was Ex-President Hoover. Close by was Gene Tunney, former world's heavyweight champion. Behind me sat Guy Lombardo, and Mrs. Lom-bardo. He had played earlier for the audience. After they called for a minute's silence, and when it came the time to play the "Star Spangled Banner," it was the Royal Canadians who played the Yankee music.

July 24, 1950

March 23, 1951
MAKING A DEBUT ON TELEVISION
(Excerpt from a prescient editorial:)

There is no evidence to show that the hockey players of the Toronto Maple Leafs and Montreal Canadiens played any harder the other night because the CBC's new television camera was trained on them. It was merely TV's warm-up in Canada, an omen of things to come.

Across the line, television has just grown out of the short pants of sports spectacles into the adolescence of political melodrama. The United States congressional committee investigating the relation of gambling to crime, headed by Senator Estes Kefauver, conducted hearings in several cities in the presence of TV cameras. The results have evidently been startling.

It may be an exaggeration to claim that 30,000,000 people watched the inquiry in its final hearings in New York. But there is no doubt that, in the United States at least, a new dimension has been added to politics. It may be that future Senate inquiries will be conducted as TV spectacles. Perhaps the politicians will see, behind the TV camera, the voter and play up to him. Does a TV camera infringe the individual's legal rights? . . . .

The difference between testifying in an open courtroom crowded with spectators and newspapermen and testifying with a television camera trained on the proceedings, seems to be only a matter of degree. Experience in St. Louis confirms the belief that, if something of crucial concern to the public is occurring in the courts or in a legislature, the public will rush to see it. The Kefauver committee's hearings in New Orleans were conducted at night, with TV coverage. The local movie theaters, it is reported, found business sharply off, as everyone stayed home to see the politicians tangle with the big-time gamblers.

February 8, 1952

November 16, 1951
BENNY GOODMAN THRILLS
BIG CROWD WITH MOZART

Lauretta Thistle was the Citizen's *first full-time arts reporter, paving the way for a long string of notable female critics including Audrey M. Ashley, Betty Swimmings, Evelyn Erskine, Janice Kennedy, Lois Moody, Barbara Crook and Lynn Saxberg.*

BY LAURETTA THISTLE
Citizen Music and Theatre Writer

Benny Goodman, clarinetist, was soloist at the first of the season's concerts by the Ottawa Philharmonic Orchestra in the Capitol theatre last evening, and the audience of 1,900 was treated to a superb performance of a Mozart concerto.

No explanations or apologies were needed for having the celebrated Mr. Goodman as the soloist—he has been accepted as a performer of serious music for years, though he made his name and his fortune through jazz.

Nevertheless, straddling both fields is no mean feat, and it was most interesting to see how well he could submerge his strong individual style and use his virtuoso technique purely in the service of Mozart.

It was beautiful playing that he gave us, characterized by fine tone and just enough flexibility of phrasing within a rhythmically exact framework. The long sweep of the phrasing in the adagio and the bright tone of the sunny rondo movement made exciting listening.

In such praise is implicit the assumption that the orchestra was also in good Mozart form. It was indeed. Conductor Eugene Kash had prepared his players well, and in tone, tempo and volume they were admirable partners for the distinguished soloist.

After intermission the orchestra and Mr. Goodman presented three contemporary "classics" from the jazz realm—"The Man I Love," by Gershwin; "I Only Have Eyes For You," by Warren and Dubin; and "Dizzy Fingers," by Confrey.

Feeling decidedly shaky about having to pass opinions on a subject so specialized and fast changing as contemporary jazz, this reviewer made sure of being accompanied by someone who is well abreast of the trends and preferences. We were assured, and hasten to pass on the information, that these symphonic arrangements were really "solid," and that not only was the performance on the "licorice stick" superb, but the orchestra was remarkably "hep."

Having no encore ready, Mr. Goodman offered to play "Dizzy Fingers" again, only faster. To the great delight of the audience he either found or pretended to find that Mr. Kash had taken his words too literally, and he soon pantomimed a plea for mercy and slower pace.

January 19, 1952
HOCKEY MANIA

Long before it became fashionable to write about hockey as a metaphor for Canada, Bruce Hutchison penned this eloquent essay on the game and its hold on the national psyche. Hutchison, once described as "Journalism's Sage," originally wrote this piece for the Victoria Daily Times, *where he was editor in the 1950s.*

BY BRUCE HUTCHISON

As a sheer work of art a Canadian hockey game is a wondrous and deep thing. It is, I suppose, the only authentic art form indigenous to this country, our first major contribution to the culture of the ages. It is also a basic political force in our national life.

We may be divided racially, geographically and economically but in hockey we all speak the same language, understand the same rules and feel the same passions. One might say, indeed, that a mere athletic contest exercises a stronger centripetal power in Canadian society than all the policies of statecraft, drawing a diverse people together in the common possession of a mystery.

For a mystery hockey assuredly is. Not, of course, in its outward manifestations—which are obvious enough, consisting only of certain physical acts hardly as skillful as playing the piano or writing the report of a hockey game on the sport pages—but in something else entirely.

February 8, 1952

The mystery lies not in the player but in the spectator. Having known many of the world's best hockey players intimately, I can testify that they are not mysterious fellows at all and some are quite simple-minded. The spectator, however, is quite another matter. He, too, may lack mystery and understanding as a private citizen. He may be little better than an idiot in the ordinary affairs of life. Place him in the hockey rink, assemble him with other worshippers in the temple of the mystery, and he is something else entirely, his subconscious takes control, he seems to become a ravening beast, screeching for blood, when in fact he has become a Canadian.

Thus from coast to coast, even in this evergreen land where nature grudges him natural ice, the soul of the Canadian is revealed, naked and unashamed, when the opening whistle blows and the priestcraft, wand in hand, begins to perform its curious ritual.

It is no wonder, though, that foreigners misunderstand us when they listen to the hoarse animal shouts of the worshippers. Even to a hardened Canadian like me, who visits the temple infrequently, the spectacle is a little shocking. It shakes me to the roots and sets me wondering about democracy.

For observe the outward manifestations of the mystery: Here are six young men on the ice who have come from some other part of the country, who have no interest in the city for which they propose to risk their necks, who apparently are doing a night's work for high pay and nothing else. Here are several thousand local residents who know the players only as public performers, as mercenaries hired from abroad, and yet greet them and cheer them and grumble at them as if they were their own native sons.

A group of hirelings, by donning a sweater of a certain hue, has become the pride of the community and receives far more affection, comprehension and understanding than the mayor or the member of Parliament. The crowd will cheer itself speechless in praise of these hired performers and the performers will break their bones if need be to satisfy a city in which they are strangers, from which they will depart with the first spring thaw.

Here the mystery and its unifying results begin. Despite distance, race and class, every community is united around its hockey team. The French Canadian player is at home in Victoria. The prairie boy is the hero of Toronto. And in the worship, in the jubilation of victory or the gloom of defeat, the humblest spectator is the equal of the richest man in the rink. All are gathered up together in the passion of worship and in the lifestuff of the nation.

I would be the last to disparage the genius of the politicians who make our laws, the writers who make our books, the artists who make our pictures, but in gauging the true culture of the nation and reckoning its tensile strength, let the student not neglect hockey.

Let him also observe by this Canadian phenomenon how thin the veneer of modern civilization really is. Some thousands of peaceable, law-abiding citizens enter a rink and instantly they are converted into a band of howling savages. They enjoy the fine points of the game, the work of the artists, but they love the fights better. At the least sign of violence they are a Roman mob clamoring for the head of the gladiator.

And even though the visiting team is composed of mercenaries, without interest in the city whose uniforms it wears, it becomes almost an invading army to be treated with hatred, derision and contempt. Its mistakes are jeered. If by accident a visitor collides with a local player he is condemned with a scream of rage which would chill the blood of Nero. If he fights with a local player he is regarded as hardly better than a common criminal.

A mob, any mob, is a terrifying sight. A mob at a hockey game, unless you understand the nature of the mystery, would instantly destroy your faith in the democratic process. For how can these assembled maniacs be trusted to leave the rink and cast their votes in an election? You might rather trust the government of the country to the inmates of the mental homes, who seem more sane, or even to the hockey players.

A young man interested in politics and aspiring to a public career sat beside me at a recent game, the first he had ever seen. He listened to the animal sounds, he watched the swaying bodies and observed the tortured faces and he decided that if this was the voting public he would never run for office. He entered the rink a Liberal and a reformer. He left a Tory and a reactionary.

Of course, he had misinterpreted the mystery. In time he will howl, squirm, suffer torture and ecstasy with the best of them and next morning will turn up as sane a citizen as you will find anywhere. Nay, saner. In the terrifying winter climate of Canada it is only hockey, I am convinced, which, by providing an outlet for our Polar tensions, a little warmth in our frigidity, preserves our national sanity.

Only a Canadian can understand that.

December 3, 1952
JET'S SONIC BLAST ROCKS CAPITAL.
Explosive Sound Spreads Fear
Of Sewer Eruption. Police, Fire Departments
Flooded With Scare Calls
(Excerpt from a Cold War news story:)

A jet plane, streaking through the sonic barrier directly over Ottawa for the first time, sent residents scurrying from their homes at 11:40 o'-clock this morning when the loud blast of sound shook buildings all

April 28, 1953

over Ottawa.

For a time it was believed that some serious accident had occurred, but Royal Canadian Air Force spokesmen confirmed the actual cause shortly after noon.

The loud, terrifying blast with accompanying concussion, came when a Sabre jet from the Uplands base broke through the sound barrier at the bottom of a 40,000-foot dive. The Sabres go through the sonic barrier purely as a part of the training course from time to time, the RCAF stressed. . . .

Within minutes people all over the city were out in the streets endeavoring to learn what had happened, and switchboards at city hall, the *Citizen*, and the various police stations were swamped with calls.

In at least one case actual damage was caused by the unusual occurrence. Ceilings and walls in the kitchen at the home of Mrs. Arthur Jessup, 508 Churchill Avenue, were cracked and bits of plaster fell about her as Mrs. Jessup was busy preparing lunch at her stove.

The blast was heaviest in the western and southern sections of Ottawa, although it was also plainly felt in various buildings in the downtown areas.

Air Force officials told *The Evening Citizen* at noon that each time planes exceed the speed of sound a blast occurs at the precise moment the sonic barrier is crossed. The phenomenon usually occurs thousands of feet above the earth, however, and is rarely heard for that reason.

The explosive sound scared city waterworks and engineering officials. "We were afraid a main had burst," a City Hall spokesman commented.

The engineering department was in a state of fear and trembling lest there had been a sewer-gas explosion. Such explosions have occurred in Ottawa in past years and caused heavy damage.

At the same time, numerous residents, especially children on their way home from school at lunch time, were badly frightened. . . .

Mrs. Jessup told *The Evening Citizen* that her entire house was shaken by the mysterious blast. "I was standing by the stove cooking," she said, "and suddenly small pieces of plaster fell and a big crack ran across the ceiling and down the corner of the kitchen wall. The stove seemed to move up and down. It scared me half to death and I ran out to call my husband who was working down the street."

Principal W. D. T. Atkinson, dictating a letter at the time, reported the blast shook Glebe Collegiate and brought Miss Marion Woodside, school nurse, running to inquire about where the explosion was. . . .

February 8, 1952

March 3, 1953
WILDERNESS NO DEADLINE HAZARD
FOR THIS CREW
Citizen Speeds Up News And Photo Coverage
With Mobile Phone Unit

Two men sat in the front seat of the big sedan, which raced along the highway toward the city. One of them, the passenger, held a telephone clamped to his ear. He spoke rapidly into the mouthpiece.

"Hello, city desk. We're about 20 miles out. We've got the pictures, and here comes the story. Give me rewrite."

At the other end of the telephone connection, in the city room of *The Evening Citizen*, a rewrite man went into action. He jammed a pair of headphones to his ears, slipped a sheet of copy paper into the type-writer and yelled "shoot" into the phone by his side.

He typed steadily for several minutes while far away, nearing the Capital but still many miles distant, the reporter in the automobile "talked" his story into the office.

This kind of thing has been going on at the *Citizen* for almost a month now, ever since we gave *Citizen* readers another "first" in Ottawa by installing a mobile telephone unit in a photo-car operated by *Evening Citizen* photographers Bill and Jean Newton....

Now, it doesn't mean a thing if a reporter finds himself with a hot story and no regular telephone to call his office. He grabs the telephone on the Newton dashboard and starts talking, saving precious minutes when deadline is near....

With the Newton mobile telephone, reporters can stay "on the scene" until the story is wrapped up. They don't have to leave the story to search out a phone, and they can call in the facts to the city desk even as their car races for the Newton darkroom with "pix" which will illustrate the news story.

The new equipment has already played a starring role in *The Evening Citizen*'s coverage of an accident at Cumberland when a truck went through the ice, the recent fire at Lac Ste. Marie and yesterday's multi-million dollar blaze at the Chats Falls powerhouse.

The receiving and sending set sits on the automobile dashboard just like the telephone on the table at home.

To call the office, the reporter or photographer has merely to lift the receiver and ask for the mobile operator. If the office wants to contact the car, the mobile operator makes the contact in a matter of seconds. A call to the car is announced by a bell and by a light, which flashes on the dashboard. If the driver is out of the car, a horn blows.

The car can make phone contact with any place in the world providing the unit is within range of a Bell Telephone Company transmission tower. It is a two-way radio communication between the car and the

April 28, 1953

tower, and from there on the thing is done by telephone wires. . . .

April 13, 1953
YOU'RE EITHER WHITE—OR BLACK
The Citizen's brilliant columnist Jack Scott has been
sent to South Africa to tell Canadian readers firsthand about the
bitter race struggle there. Today he makes his first report.
BY JACK SCOTT

JOHANNESBURG, South Africa—You make your choice, such as it is, at three o'clock in the morning.

You've arrived in Johannesburg at that ungodly hour, eight hours late because of a defect in a tail-heater of your Pan-American Clipper away back there somewhere over the North Atlantic. Was it two days ago or two months ago?

The form that the weary immigration official hands to you gives two choices. You are required to make a cross beside one of them.

You are either "European" or you are "non-European." From now on it matters little if you are Canadian or American or Eskimo. You are either black or you are white. It is that simple, and that tragic.

Having committed yourself to being a member of the master race, the formalities of inspection are brief and perfunctory. The customs official, unable to locate a serial number on your typewriter, grins and yawns and marks down the only numbers he can find—6,5,4,3,2, which are on all typewriters to adjust the pressure of the keys. You wonder what he would do if you did not have this privileged complexion.

You walk into the main lounge of the airport to await the bus that will take you into the city. It is a large lounge with cane chairs and low tables. A "non-European" steward (for you have already begun to think this way) brings you tea. Leading off the lounge is a small fly-specked room perhaps ten feet square. There is a sign over the door: "Nie Blanke Sitkamer." That is the lounge for non-Europeans.

It is the first of the ten thousand signs you will see with those words, "Nie Blanke"—Not-white.

From now on you will drink your tea and wash your hands and eat your food and use the toilets and drink the water and use the entrances that are there for you, the European. You are in South Africa.

•

In the morning you are awakened in your hotel room at seven and startled into springing erect by a motherly-looking woman who is pouring your tea. You will get to know this dear creature rather well, for when the colonial brings his tradition and his way of life to the far corners of the globe, he brings it with a vengeance.

The chambermaid will cart away your oxfords in the morning and return them honed to a gloss they never knew, bring you the newspa-

per (oblivious to the fact that you are sleeping in the raw), open the drapes across your window and draw them at night, find your pyjamas, which you thought were lost forever, in your bag, and lay them neatly on your bed with the covers impeccably folded back, bundle your dirty laundry and pop her head in every so often to see if there's anything she forgot.

In 12 hours you will wonder how you ever lived without her.

You go down to the dining room where the waiters are East Indian—that, of course, is "Nie Blanke"—and while you ponder the menu you listen to the two people at the adjoining table. There is a woman and a man. The woman is the wreckage of all that a once-proud Empire held dear, complete with lorgnette. She does the talking. The little man beside her studies his nails from under the hoods of his eyelids.

"The mawster will have tomawto juice," she tells the East Indian who smiles and nods. "And let me see—ah, yes, the mawster would like kippers..."

You sip your tepid tomato juice, for here there is even a greater scorn of refrigeration than in England, and you catch the East Indian staring discreetly but contemplatively at the mawster and his good lady.

•

You have an air mail letter to be sent off and, having finished your cold toast, you walk out to the Enquiry desk. The man behind the desk, as you can tell by his accent, is of Dutch descent. He would doubtless be more at home speaking Afrikaans, which is to the true Dutch tongue what French-Canadian is to pure French.

He wears an ornate, moss-colored uniform with gold epaulets and gold chevrons on the sleeves. He is extraordinarily obsequious and so it surprises you when his manner changes as he turns to a black man, also in moss-green but without epaulets or chevrons.

"Weigh this, Jim," he says curtly.

"Yes, sir," says Jim. He puts the letter upon the small postage scales. "Weighs less than half an ounce, sir," he says.

The white man wheels on him with such rage that it astonishes you. "Damn it, Jim," he says, "I've told you before there's no postage rate for anything under half an ounce. Why tell me it's UNDER half an ounce, man? How many times must I tell you that?"

"I should have remembered that," the black man says, with a slow shake of his head.

The white man sighs extravagantly and turns to you with a smile you are intended to share. "They can't seem to learn anything," he says.

You look at him coldly, bewildered by the non sequitur of his diatribe and embarrassed for the colored man.

"Traveller, are you, sir?" says the white man, all smiles and cordiality. "We certainly hope you will take to South Africa."

Carnival

"I don't suppose it has ever occurred to you what a waste of good grazing land this is!"

April 28, 1953

May 7, 1954
A NIGHT OF CELEBRATION
Band Plays Until 5 A.M. For Dream-Miler
BY PETER INGLIS
Citizen Special Correspondent

LONDON—Roger Bannister slept until lunch time today, all tuckered out from running the first four-minute mile in history yesterday and then celebrating the event in a night club until 5 a.m.

The six-foot medical student strolled quietly into St. Mary's Hospital here, where he is studying, just before lunch.

The telephone rang ceaselessly at his home this morning; lights flashed on the hospital switchboard; telegraph boys found themselves sadly out of training as they trotted up and down the Bannisters' garden path at the rate of about one a minute; newspaper reporters hunted him in perspiring packs.

When at last he appeared, he collected a pile of congratulatory telegrams from the hospital letter rack and was surprised to learn that an even bigger pile was waiting for him at home.

At 5 a.m. Roger had all the breath back that he lost during the run and was crooning, "Time On My Hands," into a microphone in a West End night club.

It had been a night of celebration with Chris Brasher and Chris Chataway, the two pacemakers who helped set the record time of three minutes, 59.4 seconds.

With three girlfriends they went to a night club, where Roger was recognized and greeted with a rousing cheer. He dragged Chataway and Brasher into the spotlight with him and smiling shyly, said: "I have got two better boys."

The band stopped playing at 3:30 a.m. and the night club officially closed. But the band leader and the drummer stayed on to play for the three athletes and their partners.

After the race in Oxford yesterday afternoon, Bannister had slipped away to one of the numerous quaint old world pubs in the university town and called for a shandy—a mixture of lemonade and beer which is a great favorite of England.

But back in London it was an occasion for champagne and the corks popped. The 25-year-old Bannister waived all rules. "A late night and champagne now and then does not hurt," he said.

So they celebrated until the light of another day broke over a misty London just stirring to the news that shouted from the front pages of the morning newspapers that Britain had produced the first man to conquer the incredible four-minute mile.

August 31, 1954

December 22, 1954
OTTAWA SENATORS AND OTHER VICTIMS

Mr. T. P. Gorman blames television for the demise of his Ottawa Senators, and up to a point he is undoubtedly right. Yet it has been found again and again that when an already shaky situation exists in the entertainment field, TV administers the coup de grace but is not necessarily the sole cause of ruination.

One factor is the quality of the entertainment offered. In the case of sport, this has come to mean, for the most part, a winning or at least a strong and highly colorful team. At one time, a team lacking these attributes might continue to draw enough patronage to survive until more fortunate days—as was Ottawa's own experience two decades ago after the capital left the National Hockey League. But the struggle becomes more intense when TV offers attractions right in the home.

Ottawans may still feel incredulous that they are now bereft, for the time being at any rate, of senior hockey. For Ottawa and the Valley have been described as the cradle of the national sport. Yet the malady is almost a universal one. Even the largest American cities are feeling its influence. There must be as much sentimental attachment to Connie Mack and the Philadelphia Athletics as to any sports aggregation on the continent, yet not even the efforts of Philadelphia business men this fall availed to save the club from migration. Had the Athletics been riding high in the first division of their league, it might and probably would have been different.

A few days ago, Mr. Frank Shaughnessy, president of the International League, pointed out that the major leagues are talking about enlarging from eight to ten clubs apiece. "This means," was his skeptical comment, "you're going to have four more losing clubs and, as everyone knows, losing clubs don't draw."

It may be, of course, that professional entertainment of any sort isn't worth saving, and that each community should concentrate on the amateur kind. If this course is followed, rather than a nice balance between the two as has been past practice, the results will be reflected in time on the television screens, where the professionals at the moment are enjoying their heyday. There won't be any more Rocket Richards, Stan Musials or perhaps even Jackie Gleasons, because the crops of talent will have dried up for want of nourishment at their roots.

August 31, 1954

THE OTTAWA CITIZEN

Seaway Edition   OTTAWA, CANADA, THURSDAY, APRIL 28, 1955   Page 1

THE
ST. LAWRENCE SEAWAY

Another Link In The Unity Of Two Great Nations

THE UNITED STATES   THE DOMINION
OF AMERICA   OF CANADA

Dwight D. Eisenhower, President Of The United States
—Portrait by Karsh

Louis St. Laurent, Prime Minister Of Canada
—Portrait by Karsh

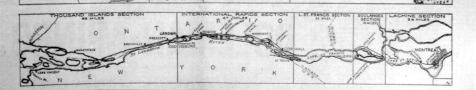

Liberal vs. Tory

The Twelfth Decade, 1955-1964

SOON AFTER HE became editor of the *Citizen* in 1961, Christopher Young took a drive through the Ottawa Valley. Although he'd been in the city for a few years as a Southam News Service parliamentary reporter, Young was unsure he had a feel for readers living on the farms and in small towns that lay beyond official Ottawa.

As he cruised farther from the city, out past Almonte and Middleville and Lanark, toward Perth and over to Smiths Falls, he noticed the frequency of *Citizen* boxes along the roadside began to fall off as *Journal* boxes became increasingly prevalent. Puzzled, Young pulled into a country store to investigate.

"Why, this is Tory country," he remembers being told. As a newspaperman from Ottawa, of course, he knew the *Citizen* was the paper of choice for Liberals and the *Journal* for Conservatives—just as he knew the Valley tilted toward the Tories and the city toward the Grits.

But he wasn't prepared to actually *see* the split in partisanship. "It came as a bit of a shock," Young said in the 1980s, recalling the experience as a graphic reminder that politics in the 1950s and '60s was still part of the fabric of daily life. Out in the Valley, whose store you shopped at, which church you went to, what newspaper you took, had a lot to do with your political stripe.

Back in Ottawa, Young devised a plan to appeal to rural readers—more coverage of farm issues, more feature stories—but swept up in the convulsions of Parliament in the early 1960s, the *Citizen* never really ly put the strategy into place. Indeed, for pure political excitement Young couldn't have picked a better time to take charge of the *Citizen's* news operations. By 1961, John Diefenbaker's once invincible Conservative majority had been seriously eroded by scandal and bad decision-making. In the 1962 election, the Tories were reduced to a minority.

Nobel Prize Winner—Hon. Lester B. Pearson, former secretary of state for external affairs, today was awarded the 1957 Nobel Peace Prize, the first Canadian ever to receive the world's highest award in the cause for peace. Mr. Pearson, whose weekly commentary on foreign affairs, appears each Saturday in The Ottawa Citizen, was "thunderstruck" when he heard about the announcement in a reporter's phone call to his home here. (Full story on Page 7).

October 14, 1957

Opposite: The new St. Lawrence Seaway dominated the Citizen's attention on April 28, 1955.

The next year, the Liberals returned to power, although again as a minority.

In both campaigns, the *Citizen* not only supported the Liberals, it lambasted the Conservatives, telling readers in one infamous 1963 editorial that the re-election of the Conservatives would "bring the country to ruin just as Nero invited destruction upon Rome."

Certainly, Young's personal views were passionately small-l liberal, but the Conservatives blamed the *Citizen's* new anti-Tory vehemence on the editor's relationship with Lester Pearson—he was the Liberal leader's nephew by marriage. In 1964, Tory MPs cited the family tie during an unsuccessful attempt to drag Young in front of a Commons committee for an editorial accusing a Conservative of bribery. In print, Young referred only once to his link to Pearson—to dismiss it as irrelevant. He preferred, he said, to show he could separate his personal and professional sentiments by going after the Liberals when he thought they deserved it, as in the Gerda Munsinger sex scandal. But such instances were infrequent, and the *Citizen*—and *Journal*—settled into the Liberal-Tory pattern they'd established back in the '40s.

Locally, the two papers also locked horns on several key issues—the *Citizen* favoured the Queensway, which went ahead in 1957, and it pushed for a children's hospital and an arts centre, as long as it wasn't built on a prime site by the Rideau Canal (it was, at last, in 1969). The papers also went head-to-head on the crime beat, working feverishly to get to stories first, the *Citizen* scoring big in 1960 with an exposé of corruption in suburban Eastview (later Vanier) that ended with the town treasurer in jail.

January 18, 1955, one of very few copies of the paper during the 1955-1968 period that survives in its original form, not microfilm. As a result, the illustrations in this and the next chapter come from just a handful of editions.

February 2, 1955
ATTRACTIVE OTTAWA GIRL
HOLDS DOWN MAN'S JOB

Behind glass at the Bell Telephone office sits an attractive girl in a yellow suit. She is Elizabeth (Betty) Quinn, first girl ever to hold down the man's job she now has. As unit manager, she enjoys one of the top ranking posts in the local phone company.

A native of Ottawa, she was born on Lisgar Street, daughter of the late Dr. Quinn, and today her office is not far from where she first saw the light of day.

Geographically, she never got very far, but in the business world, she has reached the top.

"She's the first girl ever to hold this job," declared J. E. Huchison, district manager. "And she's doing it well, too."

It is true that she is pretty, and it is true that she was wearing a striking yellow suit the day the *Citizen* went to see her. But appealing as both may be, it was neither of these things which impressed the mere male reporter most. It was her voice.

Miss Quinn has a sweet and low voice. Shakespeare said: "Her voice was ever soft, gentle, low, an excellent thing in a woman." This low key approach intrigued the writer who asked:

"Do you always keep your voice down there?"

She smiled and said she believed she did.

"Do you ever blow your top and go up an octave?" she was asked.

"If I blew my top you wouldn't know it," she smiled.

For years before she went to her new glass cage promotion, Miss Quinn recruited personnel and also was chief instructor in the gentle art of using the phone.

Last fall at the *Citizen*, after she had given a lecture on phone etiquette, one of the *Citizen* executives answered the phone, screamed into it, and banged it back on the cradle. La belle Quinn promptly bawled our man out—in a soft key, naturally.

Among the things she had enjoyed in her past had been recruiting new personnel. She liked it when she went to the collegiates and sought prospects. But she takes her recruits "when she finds them."

"Once," she remembered, "I got a recruit at a cocktail party!"

Asked if she could do the traditional telephone routine with enunciated numbers, she began: "You mean ni-yun, ni-yun, thurreee..."

Yes, she could do it but had not had to work on the operator's switchboard. She was the executive type, she felt.

Wondering if romance was not better than slugging over a desk, Miss Quinn was asked: "If you had life to live over again, would you still do this work?"

"Certainly, I love it," she said.

"How about men? Do you like men?"

"Men," she said, as her face brightened, "men are great fun. But getting married is another matter."

Then the reporter was downright unchivalrous:

"Ever been asked?"

A hurt look then: "Of course."

May 21, 1955
WHY NOT A BALLAD OF RATTLESNAKE PETE?
(Excerpt from an editorial.)

Why all the fuss about Davy Crockett of Tennessee? Hasn't Canada plenty of heroes to celebrate? Conscientiously patriotic parents are asking these questions as their offspring chant the ballad of the "King of the Wild Frontier" and sport the 'coonskin cap.

Crockett was a frontiersman who fought the Creek Indians, became a state legislator and a congressman and was killed by Mexicans at the

January 18, 1955

Alamo. Since he's become an idol of youth, it's just as well that the "racy" stories for which he was famous have been forgotten—or have they? Alert manufacturers cashed in on the popularity of the ballad about Davy, written by a member of Walt Disney's music staff....

Canada had few Injun fighters, thanks to the rule of the Mounties. Its traditions are less rambunctious than those of the Americans. Its split personality makes Quebec none too keen about Wolfe, while Ontario's admiration of the English-scourging D'Ibervilles is perhaps lukewarm. Too many outstanding figures, churchmen or aristocrats, are unsuitable for rousing balladry. But the memory of some notable Canadian women is kept sweet by certain candies, if not in song. Catchy names like Eric the Red and Lief the Lucky remain to be exploited. And what of the rascally Radisson, the heroic Dollard? Why not Paul Bunyan's jeans or Tecumseh's moccasins?

After all, what's so remarkable about a man from Tennessee? That's where Sam McGee came from, and he was a weakling. According to Robert W. Service's ballad, Sam's friend in the Yukon had to put him in an improvised crematorium and even then he was only comfortably warm. Rattlesnake Pete, who has just passed away in Calgary at the age of 94, was more picturesque than the self-taught Davy Crockett. He never did learn to read or write. He was an Indian scout, cowpuncher and prospector. As a secret agent of the Mounties, he dined with Jesse James, played billiards with Louis Riel and hob-nobbed with Sitting Bull. The Canadian who can catch the popular fancy with a ballad about Rattlesnake Pete may make a fortune and at the same time save the sagging prestige of his country.

January 18, 1955

June 2, 1955
10,000 AT REOPENING
Whether Man's World Or No, Mayor Whitton
Snips Ribbon To Open Joe Feller's Big Store

Mayor Charlotte Whitton has "felt like slamming the door shut on a man's world in the past couple of weeks," she said last night.

The Mayor made the statement in the course of officially reopening Joe Feller's "Doorway To A Man's World" on Rideau Street. She was one of more than 10,000 people to attend the ceremony.

Mayor Whitton snipped the ribbon before the crowd jamming the Rideau Street entrance shortly after 8 o'clock. At that, she apologized for being late for the function. She blamed "a couple of steers that broke loose" for tying up traffic.

"They weren't members of council," she added jocularly. "They were really from the abbatoir." (The steers the Mayor referred to escaped from the Isabella Street cattle pens. One was shot by police on Lisgar Street and the other 23 were recaptured).

When she got serious, Mayor Whitton praised Joe Feller and other Rideau Street merchants for making it "one of the finest shopping streets in Canada. You have faith in the city and this store is proof of that faith," she said. ...

She told her listeners the first time she remembered Joe Feller, he had come before council "and kicked up his heels."

"I didn't know then," she said, "how things are arranged outside Board of Control and council. But I soon learned."

Mayor Whitton then carefully snipped the fancy red ribbon near the end, ignoring the pleas of cameramen to "cut it in the middle, Your Worship."

"Mrs. Feller wants to use the ribbon again. How do you think I get my surpluses?" she said. ...

The Mayor later posed for pictures with little Donna Lee Feller, who received a big hug from the chief magistrate. In return, Mayor Whitton was given a kiss.

When asked by photographers to look at the camera, Mayor Whitton said: "Nothing doing. I keep an eye on anyone that's kissing me."

Long after the dignitaries had left, crowds continued to pour through the doors to examine both the store and the carefully placed merchandise. Bouquets of flowers from other merchants and friends of the store were liberally scattered about the ground floor.

A large number of "gifts" were handed out during the evening. Announcers would ask if anyone in the crowd was wearing a "Joe Feller tie" or other apparel. The lucky person would get the equivalent in merchandise. About 100 people received gifts of shirts, socks, ties, jackets and suits.

Women as well as men were noticed in large numbers in the store. On one occasion, Joe Feller overheard a pair of women say: "These gifts are only for men. It's too bad we can't wear ties."

Mr. Feller explained the store didn't carry apparel for women, but gave the women each a rose from a nearby bouquet.

January 18, 1955

November 11, 1955
TEMPORARY BANDSHELL GOOD
Philharmonic Opens Season With Glenn Gould, Top Solo Pianist
BY LAURETTA THISTLE
Citizen Entertainment Editor

The Ottawa Philharmonic Orchestra opened its season last night in the Capitol theatre with a concert that was intriguing to both eye and ear.

This first concert, performed in the presence of the Governor-General, introduced the new collapsible "shell" erected to give better acoustics, and also introduced the brilliant young Canadian pianist

Glenn Gould in the role of soloist with the orchestra.

The shell, a series of huge aluminum arches, covered with canvas, has an undeniably makeshift appearance, bound to set us all longing anew for a proper concert hall for Ottawa. For a ghastly few minutes during the second half of the concert one of the powerful spotlights trained on the shell was unshielded, so that we were threatened for a time with harsh lighting. The error was corrected, however, and the audience was able to concentrate on sound rather than light.

Any proper report on improvement of the sound from use of this shell would have to be made after listening from a dozen or so spots in the theatre. One who meekly kept her assigned seat all evening can only report that the improvement in sound, though not dramatic, is considerable and hope that (a) the fancy lighting effects will not be carried too far and that (b) we'll soon have a hall where such makeshift devices will be superfluous.

When the Philharmonic celebrates its hundredth birthday [in 1994], it will probably not have any finer solo performance to remember than 23-year-old Glenn Gould's performance of the Beethoven "Second Concerto." From the first entrance at the piano, when he had calculated the dynamics exactly, and when the phrasing spoke of pure joy in the music, he was utterly, completely, gloriously in the vein. He scaled his performance fairly small, as befitted a work that has more of the Mozartish Beethoven than the Beethoven of the "Eroica," but within that frame there was room for the most exquisite choice in phrasing, dynamics, and surges of feeling.

There's no use pretending that the orchestra was able to match Mr. Gould in phrasing, but there was reason to be proud of the various sections (particularly the woodwinds) for their gracious and sunny and accurate playing. One entrance (the one for the few short concluding notes after the long cadenza in the first movement) was, though perhaps metronomically correct, just inept enough to be annoying, but most of the time the orchestra gave us good Beethoven.

Thanks are due to Conductor Eugene Kash and to soloist Mr. Gould for sticking to the printed program and allowing no encores. It seems that this year our orchestra is growing up.

As a salute to the rebuilt Vienna State Opera House (and perhaps also to the new shell for his own orchestra) Mr. Kash began the program with Beethoven's "Consecration of the House Overture." The next salute was to Sibelius, who celebrates his ninetieth birthday on December 8. Mr. Kash chose the "Tapiola Suite," a powerful "mood" piece evoking the mystery of northern forests. It's full of demanding passages (though not quite as exacting for the brasses as some other Sibelius), and the Philharmonic surmounted most of the technical problems and conveyed a good deal of the atmosphere.

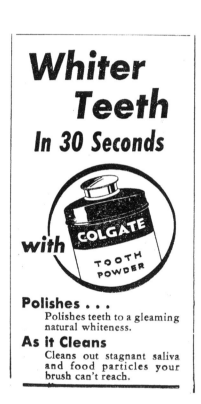

January 18, 1955

Finally presumably as a third salute (to Canadian composers) Mr. Kash conducted the first Ottawa performance of the "Miramichi Ballad," a work in three movements by Kelsey Jones, who formerly lived in Saint John, N.B., and is now in Montreal. The work is based on three lumbermen's folk songs, each dealt with separately. It would be a far better work if it were cut down to two movements. We suggest throwing out the first, (which has as unwinsome a tune as you could find, and an unimaginative treatment) and keeping the second and third. . . .

February 2, 1956

CANADA LOSES A HOCKEY GAME

It is always disconcerting when a country suffers defeat in a game it regards as its very own. The British, for example, were fearfully embarrassed when a group of colonials from the other side of the earth first beat them at cricket—on English turf, too. After a while the novelty of being beaten by the Australians wore off, and it was possible to be philosophical because there were still things the British seemed able to do better than anyone else. Then in quite recent times, came the shock of being beaten by Russians, Hungarians and other outlanders at soccer. But no matter; just about then some great runners began to smash world records and to help restore the national morale.

The trouble about Canada's loss of a hockey game to the Americans at the Winter Olympics is that there is practically nothing else this country excels at in an athletic way at the moment. There seems to be no Percy Williamses or Ethel Catherwoods on the horizon. Plenty of good athletes, yes, but no superstars.

This may help explain the heart-rending cries that have been rising into the frosty air since the news of that 4-1 reverse at the hands of the Americans was flashed from Cortina. Yet there are compensations, and Lucille Wheeler has helped dispel the moans by earning a bronze medal, the greatest success yet achieved by a Canadian skier.

Anyway, Canadian hockey and Canadian sport will survive, and perhaps be all the better for this week's experience, even should the Olympic title be lost as well. Canadians should really be gratified that other countries like their game so well that they work hard to break the monopoly of the originators. The same compliment, as noted, has already been paid to British cricket and soccer (and rugby, too), and also to the Scandinavian art of skiing. Next it may be the turn of the sacred American institution of baseball to bow to a foreign yoke; the Japanese as well as several Latin American nations have taken it to their hearts.

Russia won the gold medal, the U.S. took silver and Canada bronze. It was Canada's lowest-ever finish in Olympic hockey. Canada, the gold medallist in 1952, would not win again until 2002.

January 18, 1955

January 21, 1955

May 16, 1956
THERE WAS QUIET HEROISM
IN THE SUDDENNESS OF TRAGEDY

Fifteen people, including 11 nuns, were killed when a CF-100 military jet slammed into the Villa St. Louis, a rest home for nuns, 12 kilometres east of Ottawa in Orléans. Cause of the crash, the worst aviation disaster in Ottawa history, was never determined. Here's an excerpt from a Page 1 article recounting some of the survivors' stories.

Even in the suddenness of the catastrophe there was quiet heroism. In the face of flaming death many of the Grey Nuns at the Villa St. Louis last night risked personal safety in leading others from the pyre that was their rest home.

Under the circumstances, this orderly retreat of the religious sisters was the more remarkable.

Accustomed to a placid, simple life of strict adherence, this sudden upheaval found the nuns maintaining their composure, devoid of panic and hysteria. With the same quietness and clarity of mind those who survived described their harrowing experiences to *Citizen* reporters.

Typical of their religious calling, they showed no flair for the sensational, no avarice for self-glorification, no hunger for exaggeration.

"I was lying in bed awake when suddenly I heard an ear-shattering explosion. I opened my door and was met by a burst of flames. I only had time to grab my clothes, my cross and a statue of the Blessed Virgin Mary."

These were the words of Mother Louis-Marie, a member of the General Administration of the Grey Nuns of the Cross, minutes after she arrived at the nuns' Mother House on Bruyere Street. She was one of some 20 sisters who were taken there by auto about 11 p.m. from the flaming building.

Mother Louis-Marie stood stunned and dazed with six of the sisters who had been taken to the Mother House in one car. The worst fears of the group—all occupants of the second floor—had not yet been confirmed as the full details were not known.

Sister Joseph Edwidge, a resident of the rest home who is originally from Lowell, Mass., heard the "shattering noise" and then heard the sisters calling "sorte." She said that she assisted a sister who was trying vainly to get out through a window.

"I grabbed her and as we got near the exit we were helped by four or five men who had rushed to the scene. It was an unforgettable experience," she recalled later in a visibly shaken condition.

"It was as if someone had suddenly set a torch to our home," Rev. Sister Marie des Martyrs said. "The explosion struck like a thunder clap and the walls began to shake and showers of sparks fell at my bedroom window. Glass was shattering everywhere.

"It was frightening. The first explosion was engulfing us from everywhere. I jumped out of bed, donned my slippers, grabbed my robes over my arm and ran into the hall.

"Someone was calling from the exits, 'This way, this way.'

"I saw Sister Louise Auguste of Sudbury, her face was blackened with smoke. She was dragging something. Then I realized it was our poor sister Therese du Carmel. She had suffered a stroke and was paralyzed. Sister Louise Auguste got her out."

Once safely out in the yard, Sister Marie des Martyrs saw her companion Sister Jean Marie go to the top of one of the high, wide verandas at the front of the building.

"She didn't seem to know where to go. She sat down on the edge of the roof, her legs dangling over the side. We all called to her to jump.

"Just as she went over the side, I saw a young student priest from Holy Rosary Scholasticate rush under to try to catch her. But he didn't make it. I think Sister Jean Marie broke her legs."

"I had just prepared to go to bed when the crash came," Sister Louise Auguste. "It was about 10:15 p.m. The plane came over and then hit the middle of the roof and blew up.

"The whole building seemed to burst into flames at once. I think everyone on the top floor must have been burned. Many on the ground floor also were unable to get out.

" It happened so fast no one can really tell about it. It could have been only a few minutes after the first great crash when the roof fell in. I had just time to run out and help lift a few sisters who were disabled. Then the whole building seemed to go up like a torch."

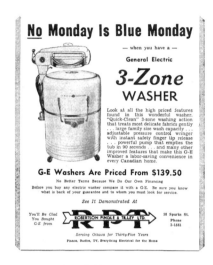

January 21, 1955

June 11, 1956
"UNDERGROUND" ELVIS FANS
FLUSHED OUT BY OTTAWA COP
Ottawa authorities, like "squares" everywhere, didn't know what to make of Elvis Presley when the rock 'n' roll idol soared to fame in the mid-'50s. His music was banned at school dances, his records were confiscated by teachers and Catholic students were prohibited from attending his 1957 Ottawa concerts. Little wonder some of his fans were forced into hiding to enjoy his records, as this excerpt shows. A story on Elvis's Ottawa visit follows.

BY BEN DWORKIN
Evening Citizen Staff Writer
A floating Elvis Presley fan club forced to go "underground" to thrill to the music of their favorite singer was flushed out by a policeman last night.

January 29, 1955

Saturday
CBOT
Channel 4

11.00—Children's Concert
3.30—Cowboy Corner
4.30—Mickey Rooney
5.00—Wild Bill Hickok
5.30—French Children's Show
6.00—14, Rue de Galais
6.30—Army Show
6.45—News and Weather
7.00—Bishop Sheen
7.30—Holiday Ranch
8.00—Jackie Gleason
9.00—On Camera
9.30—NHL Game
10.45—Re Fraynes
11.00—The News
11.10—Billy O'Connor Group
11.25—Wrestling ·

CBMT—Montreal
Channel 6

4.30—Mickey Rooney
5.00—Children's Corner
5.30—Disneyland
6.30—Army Show
6.45—The News
7.00—Bishop Sheen
7.30—Holiday Ranch
8.00—Jackie Gleason
9.00—On Camera
9.30—NHL Game
10.45—Re-Fraynes
11.00—News
11.10—Billy O'Connor Group
11.25—Wrestling

CBFT — Montreal
Channel 2

5.30—Tic, Tac, Toc
6.00—Music
7.15—The News
7.30—Colette et ses copains
8.00—Aux quatre coins du monde
8.30—Regards sur Canada
9.00—What's My Work
9.30—Hockey Game
10.30—Quiz
11.00—Dernieres nouvelles
11.02—Late Film

January 29, 1955

It was not the music that authorities objected to particularly. It was the choice of a music rendezvous that got the youngsters in wrong.

When Const. James Flahven went to investigate a disturbance at the Ottawa Public School Board property at 320 Gilmour Street (next door to the administration building) he thought his ears were playing tricks on him. The vacant two-storey brick building was locked and every window boarded up—just the same, music by Presley came wafting down from the second floor.

He checked more closely. On top of the fire-escape at the rear of the building he found a window board loose. There was an opening but not large enough for the policeman to wriggle through.

He tapped on the board with a flashlight. The response was immediate. One by one heads popped through the opening followed by young bodies—10 boys and 10 girls—aged 11 to 15 years. They told Const. Flahven that they were not allowed to play Presley at home, and so circumstances forced them to find a place to enjoy their favorite music.

The constable jotted down the names and addresses—just in case. He was about to leave when one shy little girl asked permission to go back.

"I left my record player and Presley records behind. Is it all right to get them?" she asked.

It was OK with the policeman. He even helped her back into the window. She soon reappeared records and all.

April 4, 1957
HONEST HE IS!
Elvis Every Bit A Pro
BY BOB BLACKBURN
Evening Citizen Entertainment Writer

They say Elvis Presley was singing at the Auditorium last night. You couldn't prove it by anyone who was there, though.

He appeared all right, wearing a $4,000 gold jacket and a black shirt with a plunging neckline and doing some sort of tribal dance resembling an African fertility ritual.

But whether the audience came to hear him or he came to hear the audience was a matter for debate. At both afternoon and evening shows an ear-splitting screech went up at his first appearance and didn't end until well after his departure.

It was impossible to tell what he sang, let alone how he sang it. His physical performance, however, vulgar or not, was solidly professional.

Presley's stage performance contained nothing new to anyone who has seen him on the TV or movie screen, but his backstage performance at two press conferences was something else. With his hair out of his eyes and the sulk wiped off his face, he undergoes a complete change of character.

In all honesty, no one could find anything to criticize about him backstage, except possibly to point out that anyone who can make a million dollars in a year should be able to afford underwear or else keep his windbreaker zipped up.

Presley handles a press conference like a veteran statesman (except, perhaps, that few statesmen jibe with reporters while perched cross-legged on a table). He answers readily and intelligently, doesn't try to weasel out of questions, doesn't get huffy, and remains honest even if it's to his disadvantage. And he tops it off with a sharp sense of humor and quick wit.

On the Notre Dame Convent school ban on him: "I'd like to invite whoever did this to come and see the show. If he still thinks it's harmful to kids after that, okay."

On rock and roll: "Music can't have anything to do with making a person bad."

On his movie, *Love Me Tender*: "Certainly it wasn't a great movie—just average. It would have done as well without me. I didn't do a top notch job. I was just glad of the chance to be in it."

On a recent smear in a scandal magazine: "I'm a boy. I do what other boys do." On the magazine's description of his wooing technique: "Sounds like fun."

On his professional future: "I'm just taking things as they come. I'll keep on until people get tired of me. It could happen, likely as not."

On the rigors of being a teenage idol: "Not having any privacy gets on your nerves, all right. But it's part of the business. That's what made me. I haven't got a beef."

His opinion of Ottawa: "I haven't had a chance to see it. I slept all day. The people are friendly, but it's a little cool outside."

It sure wasn't inside.

November 4, 1957
CHALLENGE OF SPUTNIK II
(<i>Excerpt from an editorial.</i>)</center>

Once again, the Russians have made a spectacular advance toward the conquest of outer space. Evidently proceeding on a careful schedule, they have sent their second satellite into an orbit that takes it around the earth at a maximum height of more than 1,000 miles.

Not only is *Sputnik II* better equipped with scientific instruments than *Sputnik I*, but it is also inhabited. If the dog within *Sputnik II* survives her trip unhurt, and manages to parachute safely to earth inside her air-conditioned container, it can be assumed a Russian satellite manned by one or more humans is not far off. It can also be assumed,

January 29, 1955

as Western scientists now say, that the Russians have reached the stage where they can send a rocket to the moon any time they wish.

In the past three weeks the world has become conditioned to the idea that, in certain fields at least, Russian science is equal to, and perhaps surpasses, the work of scientists elsewhere. *Sputnik I* provided the first evidence of this fact daily. In a world of international co-operation, where science would be used solely to improve mankind's lot, this would be a matter for rejoicing. But in the world as it is, Russia's progress has brought anxiety....

In the West, the main reaction has been to estimate the value of the satellites in relation to Russia's military power. And in Russia, Mr. Nikita Khrushchev, leader of the Soviet Communist Party, used *Sputnik I* as a propaganda weapon when he threatened Turkey with destruction in one day.

Although Russia for the moment has the lead, there can be little doubt that the West will catch up. Just as the West has no monopoly on brains, neither has Russia. It is a matter of organizing the available resources, and Western capacity for organization, given enough incentive, has been proved before. And it is equally certain that if the desire to build bigger and better rockets and earth-girdling satellites as weapons is a major goal in this race, then it will become possible to wipe out not only Turkey, but any country—and indeed the civilized world— in a single day.

This is indeed the point toward which the world has been travelling in recent years. There has been ample warning from political leaders that new weapons under development would be capable of wiping out human society. The Russians have proved beyond dispute that the weapons are here.

Unfortunately ... political rivalries, constantly threatening war, continue to bedevil humanity. It is in this field of politics, as much as in science, that progress must be made. For unless an accord is reached between Russia and the West which will result in a stable peace rather than the present uneasy truce, unless war is outlawed and the issues that lead to war are settled, *Sputnik II* may become a signpost on man's path toward self-destruction. To survive, mankind must become capable of conquering its inner, human conflicts as well as its physical environment. There, equally with the need to maintain scientific progress, lies the challenge to Western and Russian statesmanship.

WRITES POEM ON FLIGHT OF SPUTNIK

LANSING, Mich. (AP) — Michigan Governor G. Mennen Williams, turned to poetry Monday to express himself on earth satellites.

T h e Democratic governor came up with this:

"*Oh little Sputnik, flying high*
With made-in Moscow beep,
You tell the world it's Commie sky,
And Uncle Sam's asleep.
"*You say on fairway and on rough,*
The Kremlin knows it all.
We hope our golfer knows enough
To get us on the ball."

October 15, 1957

November 22, 1957
DOCTOR DOZES NUDE ON FROZEN TURF
BY JOHN E. BIRD
Special to the Evening Citizen
A 41-year-old Canadian biologist has proved it's possible for a white

man to sleep outside in the nude—without bedclothes—in below-freezing temperatures.

Dr. J. S. Hart, head of the animal physiology section of the division of applied biology of the National Research Council in Ottawa, performed the feat as a member of an international physiological expedition which visited remote central Australia last summer.

Members of the expedition spent July and August, winter in Australia, with the area's aborigines who are able to live without clothes throughout the year.

The object was to seek information on the range of climate adjustment of which the human species, particularly whites, is capable. The experiments were conducted in weather just below the freezing point.

Dr. Hart said in an interview that he and other members of the expedition found it possible to sleep outside in the nude without shivering at below-freezing temperatures provided they were sheltered by a wind-break and flanked by two small fires.

But Dr. Hart and his colleagues didn't relish their experience. They found they were exceedingly uncomfortable before falling asleep and even more uncomfortable after awakening. The aborigines did not experience discomfort and slept through the night like babies.

It was a different story when the fires were removed and each subject was given only a single blanket for covering.

"Under these conditions," Dr. Hart said, "we shivered and thrashed about all night. Sleep for us became impossible, while the natives slept as soundly as when they had their fires to keep them warm."

July 2, 1959
PHILIP AND ROCKET ON FIRST NAME BASIS
BY JACK KINSELLA
Citizen Sports Columnist

It was eight years or so ago since their last meeting, Maurice (Rocket) Richard was saying last night, but His Royal Highness Philip recalled the occasion in detail.

"I was very surprised, to tell you the truth," admitted the pride and joy of the Montreal Canadiens as he reflected on the events of the state dinner to which he was invited as a representative of sport last night at Rideau Hall.

"Do you know," he added, "that he even recalled what he said to me on that occasion?"

The occasion was a hockey game at the Montreal Forum several years ago when the Queen—she was then the Princess—and her husband visited Canada.

The Royal couple sat immediately behind the Canadiens' bench, and while they had met Captain Butch Bouchard formally, there had been

Reds See Moon Trips In 3 Years

The Russians are talking about expeditions to the moon about 1960-65.

And trips to Venus and Mars between 1962 and 1967.

Current issue of the Soviet News Bulletin, distributed in Ottawa by the Soviet Embassy, makes the forecasts.

The article is about the LVM (LVM are the initial letters of Moon, Venus and Mars in Russian) for flights to the moon, Venus and Mars by standard cosmic rockets, radio-guided from the earth by one set of apparatuses.

The plan has been put forward by a young Soviet scientist, Y. S. Khlebtsevich, at the Moscow Planetarium recently.

Launching of artificial satellites by Russia and the United States was the first, highly important practical step, he writes.

October 15, 1957

no introduction to the rest of the players on the team.

"But the Prince came down behind our bench," recalled the Rocket, "and he slapped me on the back. He said (and very few hockey players would likely have forgotten the exact words of such a greeting), 'Nice going, Rocket. I hope you have a good year'."

No sooner had the Prince and the Rocket begun to converse last night—in French, naturally, as Prince Philip speaks fluently in the language—but the latter brought up the subject of that first encounter.

"I remember that night we saw you play at the Forum eight years ago," the Prince told the Rocket. "It was quite a game, too."

According to Richard, Prince Philip said he greatly enjoyed the few hockey games he had seen on visits to Canada (once at the Forum, and again at Maple Leaf Gardens) but that he regretted to say he had never seen a game in England.

As men will, the Rocket unabashedly admitted to calling Prince Philip by his given name, and chuckled about it afterwards.

"I don't know," he said, "it just seemed natural at the time. I wasn't even thinking about it. He didn't seem to mind at all, and if I remember, called me Maurice or Rocket, I just forget which."

Did they talk about any other sports, say, cricket, or polo, or even soccer?

"No," replied Mr. Hockey, "we stayed on that subject, and I was glad. I wouldn't have known too much about cricket or those other sports."

Talking to the great Canadiens' star last night, I couldn't help but think that he looked ten years younger than his real age of 38. He appears as if he could play hockey for another decade, as indeed the Canadiens probably would wish.

"I'm in pretty good shape right now," he said, "but I'll be really starting to work at it in another month. I want to be in as perfect a shape as I can for the opening of practices."

As for his injured ankle, the Rocket said it never felt better. "I walked over 15 miles one day while on a fishing trip," he said, "and I walked over rough ground. It never even bothered me."

Not much doubt about it, the only conclusion is that the fabulous Mr. Richard has discovered, somewhere, the fountain of youth. He just goes on, and on, and on....

Swears and Wells
Furriers in Seven Reigns

1834-1957

WILLIAM IV
VICTORIA
EDWARD VII
GEORGE V
EDWARD VIII
GEORGE VI
ELIZABETH II

GOD SAVE THE QUEEN

October 11, 1957

May 16, 1961
PRESIDENT KENNEDY'S VISIT
(Excerpt from an editorial.)

President Kennedy's visit to Ottawa draws attention to the things that both unite the United States and Canada and the things that divide them. The goals are the same: these unite the two countries. Both want a world at peace, and living in freedom. But they are sometimes divided over tactics. Because that division at times gives the appearance of a sharp split between the two countries, some Americans and Canadians imagine the difference is about fundamentals. That is a point of confusion that should be cleared up.

Cuba is an example. Both countries want to keep Cuba out of the Russian orbit. If Canada has differed from the U.S. over Cuban policy, it is because Canada thinks the U.S. has pursued the wrong tactics in trying to keep Cuba out of the Communist bloc. By seeking to quarantine Cuba—as though a nation can indeed be "quarantined"—the U.S. has left that country with nowhere to go except into the Russian camp. Possibly Cuba would have found its way into the Soviet bloc in any case. But perhaps not. Certainly, the situation could not have been much worse if Washington had not pursued the policy it has during the past 18 months. In other words, Ottawa does not agree that Washington's tacticians are infallible. And that is where many of the differences between the two countries arise.

Apart from foreign policy, the disputes between the two nations on such questions as trade, U.S. investment in Canada, and food disposal programs are of a transient quality. There is nothing here that cannot be resolved through the kind of good will that has led the administration in Washington to resist increased tariffs during the post-war years, and that has been causing much soul-searching among American corporations in recent months....

Mr. Kennedy and his wife have won great personal regard in Canada, as in the U.S. and abroad. Some leaders win respect, and some win affection; not very many receive both. Mr. Kennedy is well on his way to earning that rare place in the hearts of the North American people. He is saddled with some of the errors to which the previous administration committed his country. But he is vigorously trying to shape a policy of his own, aimed at making his country a keystone of the free world without dominating it, and deeply conscious of the need for social reform if the free world's goals are to be attained.

This charming couple are welcome indeed—as allies and, more important, as friends.

October 14, 1957

April 16, 1962
1957-1962: YEARS OF FAILURE
*(Excerpt from a typically tough-worded editorial
castigating John Diefenbaker's Conservatives:)*

Four years ago the Canadian people decided to give John Diefenbaker and his new Conservative government a full chance to show what they could do. They had been in office only nine months and had not

October 14, 1957

October 15, 1957

been able to command a clear majority in Parliament.

The Liberal party, by contrast, had held power for 22 years before 1957. Stunned and disorganized by the defeat of that year, they were in no position to fight a vigorous campaign in 1958. They barely had time to elect a new leader before Mr. Diefenbaker sounded the call for another election. He won the largest majority in Canadian history.

Two months from today, we will be asked to pass judgement on the Conservative government and on the Liberal party that has developed over the past five years. This newspaper strongly believes the national interest will now be served by the election of a Liberal government.

The Conservatives have had their chance. If they were ever going to prove themselves as a competent, vigorous and inspiring government they would have done so in five years. They have failed. On every important issue that has faced the country since 1957, they have been unequal to the task: continental defence, including the terrible question of nuclear arms; economic policy, dominated by the pressing human problem of unemployment; international trade, dismissed in the last part of the Conservative term by the historic movement toward European economic unity.

Mr. Diefenbaker's government has failed to develop a coherent, effective policy to meet any one of these problems, let alone all of them. Every government makes mistakes. The last Liberal government made several serious ones. But it is doubtful that any two dozen Canadian politicians could have made so many mistakes in five years as have the members of the present cabinet. . . .

The years of the Diefenbaker government have been a clownish interlude which we could ill afford. It is time to choose a serious-minded government that will recruit the best possible brains for an acutely serious time. Lester Pearson and his advisers can provide such a government. Mr. Diefenbaker derides the able and experienced men and women who have come forward as Liberal candidates. If they were once in the civil service, he spits on them as "bureaucrats." If they had any important part in the great story of Canada's war effort, he brands them as "totalitarians."

Two months hence, the voters will make their decision. If they choose wisely, they will choose a government that puts achievement before propaganda, action before invective, and the future of Canada before political advantage. They will put Mr. Diefenbaker where he belongs: shaking his long finger in opposition. They will put Mr. Pearson where he belongs: in government.

April 17, 1962
A SOCIETY OF GOURMETS
BY AUDREY M. ASHLEY
Citizen Staff Writer

How would you like to spend four for five hours each month eating your way happily through a seven-course meal and generally pursuing the gastronomic arts in the company of other calorie-carefree, dedicated souls?

This is the aim of the newly-formed Gourmet Society of Ottawa, which held the first of its monthly dinner meetings last night. You must be prepared, however, to observe the gourmet's 31-point code of modern dining—and this may not be as easy as you think.

For instance, the true gourmet does not smoke much, if any, for an hour or two before a dinner, and not at all during dinner, at least until dessert and coffee. (This nearly proved the undoing of a few members last night; some of the men were observed sneaking out part-way through the proceedings. One unfortunate diner, his face a becoming shade of pink, left the table to the accompaniment of boos and hisses from his companions, and host Morris Berlin sternly challenged him to leave his cigarettes on the table.)

A gourmet does not like music with his meals; nor does he dance immediately before, after, or—perish the thought—during dinner. He does not engage in strong debate or other encounters which foster emotional strains which affect the digestion. And he never, but never, indulges in hors d'oeuvres with his aperitif lest they blunt his appetite.

Being a gourmet, in fact, is no picnic. But the rewards are great.

Consider the meal provided by the Town House's beaming young chef, Vincent. First of all; as an aperitif, a glass of Dubonnet, to be consumed at least 15 to 30 minutes before dinner; then Scampi à la Vincent, which caused considerable controversy at the table.

Many of the guests leaned towards the "shrimp" school of thought, but the gentleman on our right announced, with a convincing air of authority, that he had looked them up the night before and they were actually Dublin Bay prawns.

Next came Consomme Royale, delicately flavored, with small shapes of a fascinating substance floating in it. "Pasta," said some. "Egg," said others. "A kind of chicken jello," said Mr. Berlin, settling the matter.

Then Truite en Chemise (Trout-in-a-Shirt?), a whole trout (yes, head, eyes, tail, the works), sauteed in butter and wrapped in a tissue-thin crepe. With the fish was served a moderately dry white wine, Pouilly Fuisse 1959.

The entree was Coq de Bruyere Suvorov—rock Cornish game hens stuffed with wild rice and foie gras, accompanied by Pommes Parisiennes (tiny round, browned potatoes) and grilled tomatoes, followed

October 14, 1957

by Salade Mimosa, a tossed green salad with chopped egg sprinkled on top. A sparkling Anjou rose wine, Prince de Galles, 1959, was served with this course. (Note: By this time it was 9:45 p.m., and dinner had started sharp at 7 o'clock.)

Dessert was Peche Milady au Surprise, a new kind of Baked Alaska with peach halves and strawberry, chocolate and vanilla ice cream. At around 10:30, the slightly soporific guests wound up the evening with coffee and Grand Marnier liqueur.

In his after-dinner remarks, Mr. Berlin observed cheerfully that Item No. 1 of the Gourmet Code had evidently been violated already, since it specifies that a gourmet leaves the table moderately well satisfied but still feeling that he could eat more.

It is doubtful whether many of the 60 members—who constitute a wide cross-section of Ottawa society including doctors, diplomats, government officials, teachers, businessmen and radio and TV personalities—went away with this unsatiated feeling.

Peter Jennings was elected president of the Ottawa society at last night's meeting . . . . Members of the Ottawa society were informed they automatically have membership in the Gourmet Society of New York, and may attend meetings when visiting that city.

Anyway, we have stew for dinner at our house tonight.

April 15, 1963

TELEVIEWS: FROM THE HEARTH

BY BOB GARDINER

Citizen Television Columnist

In providing my views on television in this column, I've often found myself indulging in an excess that critics in other areas of entertainment would consider, quite rightly, a scandalous lack of detachment. I reveal not only my personal viewing habits, but, quite often, those of my family.

The drama, film, or music critic, for example, attends the performance he is to review. He then discusses the technique, the artistry, and the moral content of the performance. The reader is not subjected, normally anyway, to being told of the critic's struggle to see over the hat of the lady in the seat ahead or of his attack of stomach acidity during the second movement, or act.

But the art or entertainment form he is reviewing is not trying to be all things to all men the way television is. Further, once the performance is over and the review is written, the critic goes home to a life usually far removed from the concert hall or theatre.

But TV doesn't fit this sort of routine. The set is right in the home, usually in the living room or den, areas in which a great deal of domestic living takes place. Ever since the day that the easy chair was moved

October 15, 1957

to another corner to make room for this piece of furniture, the set has been as integral a part of the home as the mantel clock, the thermostat or the tri-light. More so, even.

So, in writing this column, I have felt justified in relating the medium to the domestic environment I am best acquainted with—my own. Consisting of two school-age youngsters who demand a tomb-like atmosphere when their own multi-decibel programs are on, and then pick the time-slot of your favorite show to vent their sibling rivalry, a month-old infant whose feeding schedule coincides perfectly with the above-mentioned show; and a couple of pets guaranteed to want (1) in (2) out (3) or both simultaneously (again, you know when), it is a family unit not, I feel, too unrepresentative of most viewing homes.

I don't think it would be a true reflection of a show's impact if it was treated without reference to its effect on such a menage. Which brings me to my point, at last.

The celebration of Easter in Christian homes is, I suppose, a varying and personal matter depending on such intangibles as conviction, faith, devotion, doctrine. But it is, nevertheless, the celebration which forms the core of the Christian religion.

Good Friday is a day of great meaning and, while no show is made of it, is treated with due accord in our house. So when I turned on the set that evening, I was apprehensive of how a big brassy medium like TV would fit into the mood of the day.

I wondered if television could beam into a home and, at the very least, leave unjarred any of those feelings (no matter how obscure) the day's observance gives rise to without simply resorting to the sort of sincere, but creatively uninspired, performances best exemplified by the stock, children's Christmas pageant.

I found it could. Paul Almond's CBC production of *The Dark Did Not Conquer* was a refreshing piece of film work. It could have become just another travelogue of the Holy Land, but Almond's creative impulse forbade this.

He used the contemporary backgrounds in such a way that, combined with Douglas Rain's acting talent, the tale of Christ's Agony was given an illuminating air of immediacy. It was not flawless. (Christ, his disciples and the Galileans were Jews; why did some have Cockney accents? At times the camera became wrongly the eye of Christ—as he descended from the city, to Gethsemane, for example.) But, overall, it succeeded in its aim.

More devotional in character, the repeat of the *Place of The Skull* was an example of how TV can be used to proper effect while avoiding the prime insult of being platitudinous. *Newsmagazine* on CBC then let Christian leaders talk, and their words proved to be in perfect harmony with the strong fare preceding.

October 15, 1957

The entire bloc of programming was unflinching in its demand that, if this was your religion, you involve yourself in the content. It offered integrity; it had the right to ask it.

8:30 (13) Dick Powell Theatre. "Epilogue," a story about a Marine who is overtrained, starring Lee Marvin and Ricardo Montalban.

8:30 (4) Garry Moore. Guests are Allen and Rossi, Eydie Gorme and Dorothy Loudon.

11 (13) Pierre Berton. Guests are "Crazy Otto," Richard Gehman and John Fisher.

October 15, 1957

February 15, 1964
PRO OR ANTI, YOU CAN'T IGNORE THOSE BEATLES
No matter what his subject, or where his assignment, Christopher Young could be relied upon to provide thoughtful, compassionate, well-crafted writing. A sample of his award-winning political analysis appears on page 369. Here is his view on the Beatles, a few days after their first appearance on The Ed Sullivan Show:

BY CHRISTOPHER YOUNG
Editor of the Citizen

There are some issues in these agitated times on which one may decide to have no opinion. But there are other questions on which every man and woman worth a pinch of coon fur must form a judgement. One simply cannot be neutral, for instance, about medicare, or prohibition, or Charlotte Whitton. Nor can one be neutral about the Beatles.

It is now about a week since the Beatles hit North America, and the old continent has been shaking all that time. Like everyone else, I have spent an appreciable amount of that week in reading and thinking about the Beatles and a few minutes in watching them on television.

Thus informed, I am ready to stand up and be counted on the question of the Beatles. I know of no better way to express my considered judgement than in Beatles talk, thus:

"Yeah, yeah, yeah."

This approval, I hasten to add, does not extend to the hysterical teen-aged girls who squeal during a Beatles performance so loudly that it is hard to hear the Beatles beat. Still less does it extend to the Washington diplomatic set who, in the words of our hard-pressing correspondent there, "grabbed, shoved, fondled, jostled and pulled" at the Beatles at an embassy party the other night.

(One diplomat's wife went to the party armed with a pair of scissors, with which she sheared a lock of hair from the head of one Mr. Ringo Starr.)

But leaving aside the idiots who over-appreciate the Beatles, I find the boys themselves refreshing. Perhaps their music is second-rate, but they are fine showmen. It's fun to watch them, and that is the test of showmanship. Frame the Beatles in your 17-inch screen and you forget everything else, and that is the test of pure entertainment.

The Beatles are not embarrassing, as I have found the rock idols of the recent past to be. They are natural, relaxed and spontaneous. They do not appear to be in permanent pain, as so many pop singers do. And they do not give an impression of conceit, which is a rare gift in show business.

I have it on the unimpeachable authority of the British Broadcasting Corporation that the Beatles owe this last quality to their upbringing in the streets of Liverpool. In that environment, says the BBC, "it is a cardinal sin among youngsters to be 'big-headed'," i.e., conceited.

The Beatles, I learn from the same reliable source, originally numbered five: John Lennon, who is still the leader, and Paul McCartney, these two being the composers of Beatles-sound; George Harrison, who is still a Beatle; Pete Best and Stuart Sutcliffe. Pete Best, no doubt to his everlasting regret, left to form his own group before the Beatles hit the big time. Stuart Sutcliffe died at the age of 21. Thus depleted, the Beatles recruited Ringo Starr, he who lost a lock of hair at the British embassy in Washington, to be their drummer.

Just as Ottawa long ignored Paul Anka, so Liverpool was not the first city to acclaim the Beatles. They played rock 'n' roll there for several years without making much impression. Then one day they were called to substitute for a group of entertainers who had cancelled an engagement in Hamburg. And it was there they developed that mysterious emission of noise now world-famous as "the Mersey sound."

A flow of inquiries from Hamburg led a British music store owner to make a Beatles record late in 1962. A year ago, he made a second record, called "Please Please Me." It pleased multitudes, apparently, for the Beatles have never looked back—even if they could look back through those shaggy curtains of hair.

British sociologists are grappling earnestly with the Beatles phenomenon. They are analyzing the significance of the Merseyside background in terms of a revolt of the provinces against London's cultural domination, and the significance of the Beatles' lower-class background in terms of a revolt against the Establishment.

In British terms, the Beatles are everything Sir Alex Douglas-Home is not. Accent, haircut, clothing, age and vitality combine to embody that other England that lives outside Eton, Oxford and Westminster.

But these weighty inquiries dwindle in importance now that the Beatles have won international success in Paris, New York and Smiths Falls (where the RCA Victor plant is making 30,000 Beatles records every day).

Maybe they are just four happy Liverpudlians who are making a lot

October 15, 1957

of money out of making a lot of people smile, laugh, jump, squeal and even, in a manner of speaking, dance and sing.

October 15, 1957

The Little Woman

"For the last time — come to dinner!"

October 14, 1957

April 18, 1964
OLD JAPAN—6 CENTURIES FROM TOKYO

In the early 1960s, the Citizen *created a weekly travel section—many Canadian papers had been doing it for years—as a way to increase advertising from travel agencies and airlines. This story, part of a series by Peter Desbarats, later a Global TV news anchor and journalism instructor, rose a few steps above the usual promotional-style material that filled the travel pages.*

BY PETER DESBARATS
Citizen special correspondent

They say: One month in Japan and you have good memories for the rest of your life. Three years and you can't wait to get out. Five years and you'll never leave.

After three weeks, Ed McNally and I left Japan in a hypnotic trance. Many of the memories were impossibly Lafcadio Hearn—five-tiered pagodas, temples, ornamental bridges and mountain landscapes copied from Hosshig prints.

But these things are as much a part of modern Japan as transistors and population control and green tea in plastic bottles, and they are what I am going to remember in this final article.

•

About two hours drive from a rock 'n' roll bar in downtown Tokyo, where hostesses in tight pedal-pushers and padded bras bump and grind beside every table, Naraya Inn nestles in a valley of the Hakone mountains. No one really knows how long it has been there.

Ed and I arrived late in the evening after a long train trip aboard "The Swallow" from Hiroshima and a hair-raising drive over the mountain passes from Atami. Here and there along the road, between patches of fog and drifting snow, the headlights picked out broken sections of steel guard rail. I prayed, Ed passed the Suntory [a malt beer].

The owner and maids of the Naraya Inn bowed low as we alighted from the car. Ed slipped out of his loafers and I took off my half-wellingtons—an affectation that in three weeks convinced hundreds of Japanese that all Canadians tromp around in big black boots.

The large slippers reserved for foreign guests were produced and we padded down a wide interior hallway to the room. At the entrance we removed the slippers and walked in stockinged feet across the straw tatami mats to the low table in the centre of the room.

As we sat down on cushions the maid, Tomoko Satomi, shuffled into the room carrying a tea tray. She handed us steaming towels and poured hot green tea into exquisite ceramic cups uncluttered by handles. With the tea came a dark spade-shaped sweet jelly. Every Japanese inn has a distinctive confection which is always the first food that a guest receives.

After tea and a smoke, Ed and I stripped and Tomoko helped us into our kimonos. There is no such word as shyness in the Japanese vocabulary—in that sense.

First came the yukata, the light under-kimono that also serves as pyjamas and as a summer kimono. Then the heavy outer kimono and the belt wrapped around the waist twice and knotted at the back. Cigarettes and matches in one of the sleeve-pockets. Every good Japanese inn provides yukatas and kimonos with distinctive patterns printed or woven into the cloth.

One memorable day in Beppu on the southern island of Kyushu, when Ed and I ventured through the town in our kimonos, everyone knew that we were staying at the Suginoi Hotel. The biggest tourist attraction in Beppu that day was not the hot springs or the wild monkeys or the chairlift to the top of the mountain but the six-foot kimonos strolling through the town on hush puppies and half-wellingtons.

Tomoko led us to the main bath at the Naraya. Incidentally—one for men, one for women. We took off our kimonos in the anteroom and walked down a few steps to the bath which was the size of a small swimming pool and about three feet deep.

First we squatted beside the bath, scooped up the scalding water in tin pans and doused ourselves. Then, into the bath for five minutes at a slow boil. Japanese don't merely bathe. They cook.

Then out of the bath, soap, rinse and a final soak until done. Dry with a damp towel, wrap in kimonos and place contentedly beside the low table in the room where Tomoko is preparing a sukiyaki dinner over a portable gas fire.

Soup, raw fish, Chinese pickle, beef-vegetable sukiyaki, unidentifiable but delectable relishes in small bowls, hot sake and tea. Burp, pat belly. Look satisfied. Wave aside numerous compliments on skill with chopsticks and try to conceal rice that has dropped on lap.

After dinner, massage. The bed mats were unrolled on the floor and Hideko Suzuki tied us into amastyle knots for an hour. I played "Squid-jiggling Ground," on the harmonica. Ed sang. Hideko howled.

Night. Last cigarette, lying on the floor wondering why western beds have legs. The mysterious West. Water running into the pool in the garden beneath the window. Snow.

The Japanese call it "a silver world" and snow is treated as an artistic achievement. We saw the great temples in Kyoto the morning after a small snowstorm and everyone, puddling around in soaking-wet shoes, congratulated us on our luck.

October 15, 1957

After breakfast—soup, fish, rice, seaweed and soy sauce, pickles, and tea—we were guided into the garden to admire the snow and feed the carp.

Oh yes—another bath before breakfast of course. Ancient Japanese gentlemen also in bath. We felt particularly hairy.

Apparently there is a saying in Japan that a man with hair on his chest is a good man. Good saying.

At mid-morning, Miyoko Aoki arrived to conduct a short urasenke-style tea ceremony. Ed and I knelt in our kimonos, bowed, drank, looked suitably peaceful and contemplative and tried to say appropriate poetic things about the bowl in which the frothy green tea was served.

After lunch, we left the Naraya Inn for Tokyo. The owner bowed. Tomoko bowed. Miyoko bowed. Hideko giggled.

Ed and I cleared our throats and said. "Domo arigato," and "Sayonara." Great gasps of admiration at the sudden disclosure that we are, as they say in Quebec, bilingue.

"How far is it to Tokyo?" asked Ed.

"About six and a half centuries," I replied.

May 15, 1964
GIRLS SENT HOME
Schools declare war on short skirts

Ottawa high schools have declared war on short skirts. Three girls were sent home at one school this morning when they turned up in skirts that were considered too pert.

Laurentian High School principal J. W. Fawcett said the girls were dispatched home to change into something more appropriate when they appeared in class wearing a slit-skirt-over-shorts ensemble.

At Bell High School, principal W. R. McGillivrey said that after a few pert skirts appeared there, the order went out that they were to be put on the banned list and they haven't been worn since.

"We have a ban on shorts and these pert skirts are nearly the same thing," he said. "Shorts and slacks have always been forbidden."

Both Laurentian and Bell have also banned the culottes-skirt pants.

But most other principals contacted say they have seen only a few pert skirts and culottes in their classrooms but have made no ruling on them.

"The ones I saw seemed quite in order," said one.

Others say they haven't been confronted with the problems of whether to ban or not to ban—yet.

October 13, 1964
THOUSANDS PROTEST TV STATEMENT
BY JACK GOLDING
Citizen staff writer

Thousands of Canadians watching CTV Sunday night—from Nova Scotia to British Columbia—blew a royal head of steam and studio switchboards blazed for a couple of hours.

The hour-long show, *The Queen Comes To Canada*, ended with commentator Ab Douglas saying:

"The question remains, was it worth it? For all that was accomplished—the opening of a building here and making a speech there—was it worth the strife, the harsh words, oppressive security measures? We believe it was not. Goodnight!"

The echo of Douglas' punch line had scarcely soaked into the sound-proofed studio when the switchboard at CJOH lit up completely. Within the next couple of hours about 700 people phoned, 95 per cent of whom were angry.

Calls were funnelled to the newsroom where news director Joe Gibson, vice-president and general manager Stuart Griffith and CTV network program director Michael Hind-Smith of Toronto tried to cope.

October 15, 1957

Toronto's CFTO had a similar experience but possibly not as many calls as the Ottawa station. The Kitchener affiliate, CKCO, also reported angry viewers.

Calls were continuing Monday night in Ottawa and the general consensus of the complaints was that the show indicated the royal tour should not have taken place.

Originally, the CTV network questioned the wisdom of the Queen coming to Canada at this time.

About eight people got in their cars and drove to CJOH to complain in person and one man wanted to punch someone in the nose, but he wasn't sure whom.

Another threatened to rip a plaque from a wall.

A woman kept shouting, "I'm for the Queen! I'm for the Queen!"

Don Cumming of Ottawa produced the show and wrote the script. He said the whole purpose of the effort was to show the viewing public what happened in Quebec and why the tense atmosphere made the tour "go sour."

He considered the pictorial story with a combination of news comment to be objective journalism. The spirit of the program was to point up the Queen's calmness and show just what she had to experience, he said.

"Often people hear part of a show, get a wrong meaning out of context and miss the overall thought."

The Citizen

Ottawa, Friday, May 17, 1974, Page 53

Refugees from watery hell

Ordeal at Maniwaki

By Mike McDermott
Citizen staff writer

Like refugees from some far-away war, more than 3,000 men women and children who live within sight of the Gatineau River have been driven from their homes as the relentless flood water creeps ever deeper into their communities.

Residents of riverside homes from Maniwaki to Gatineau Point began moving out Tuesday after the Hydro Quebec dam at the Baskatong Reservoir was opened to relieve a dangerously high water level. By last night the exodus had reached near panic proportions with every available boat pressed into service and authorities worrying about a massive breakdown in sanitation conditions.

While government officials in Ottawa and Quebec City studied their cries for help, people who have lived in peace with the river for years continued their struggle along its 130-mile length for the fourth straight day.

It was not a struggle to hold it back, for that was impossible. It was a struggle to get out of its way.

It happened before, in 1947, and many of the homeless remember the way it was.

And it was never as bad as this.

Mrs. Marie-Rose Talbot remembers how the water took the flowers from the front of her house and ruined her husband's new car. But she didn't pay much attention because she had the family to worry about.

Wednesday night the 67-year-old widow was alone in her small basement apartment when the river crept into her kitchen. She left with some clothing, her $43 in savings and an electric kettle.

"The kettle is a gift from my daughter in Montreal. I just couldn't leave it there so I brought it along when the men took me away in the boat."

"I'm using it to make tea for the workmen."

She was helping out at an emergency centre.

The water on Mrs. Talbot's street was six feet deep when Amos Lecompte pushed his cup over for a refill.

He runs a small service station on the main street or rather he did. It's under debris-clogged water now and there is little hope the river will leave anything behind.

The electricity was cut Wednesday as the water began bubbling out of the storm sewer in the garage bay. Within three hours it was knee deep and Amos and his helper were stacking oil cartons and car assessories on higher shelves.

It was a waste of time. Last night he toured the area by boat.

"The place was locked up tight but I guess the water just broke down the windows. There's nothing left inside.

"I was 16 when the first one came in 1947. I remember we didn't have any school for two weeks. It seemed like a lot of fun then but I guess that was because I was just young."

The young seemed to have the monopoly on good spirits this time too.

"It's the excitment," said one. "I guess it's pretty terrible, but people are doing a lot to help each other and that's a good thing."

Most people however, don't share the boy's enthusiasm for excitement.

"It's like something you'd see in a movie or the television news from some country overseas," said a weary provincial policeman "Down at the food centre in the warehouse there's a long line of people waiting to be fed. It's hard to believe it's happening here when three miles away, on higher ground, you'd never know anything was wrong."

— *Barry Gravelle, Citizen*

Sons of James Langevin sleep in makeshift room at the home of their uncle Marcel Moreau

Regional school at Maniwaki becomes an island

Giant lumber yard began floating away as water moved in

— *Citizen photos by Lynn Ball*

Boats replace cars in flood-stricken Maniwaki

To the Suburbs

The Thirteenth Decade, 1965-1974

WHEN WILLIAM HARRIS brought his fledgling weekly newspaper to Bytown in 1845, he set up shop in the Byward Market. It only made sense. The Market was the commercial heart of the settlement of 4,500—mostly a collection of rowhouses and businesses huddled within a few hundred metres of the Ottawa and Rideau rivers—and Harris knew a newspaper should be where the action is. So when the action moved to Upper Town in the 1860s to be closer to Parliament Hill (Harris was long gone by then), Ottawa's half dozen newspapers quickly followed, relocating to Queen, Metcalfe and Sparks streets.

Not much changed over the next century, apart from the names of the newspapers (the *Citizen* was the only one to survive from the 1860s). By 1960, however, the region's economic dynamics had started to alter dramatically. In Kanata and Nepean to the west, Alta Vista to the south and Gloucester and Orléans to the east, a burgeoning suburban population began to draw the economy outward. With this expansion came a sharp rise in circulation for the *Citizen*, which by 1971 was selling 85,000 papers a day, a jump of nearly 20,000 in a decade and nearly 6,000 more than the *Journal*. The paper was getting plumper, too, as advertising nearly doubled to 30 million lines a year between 1961 and '71. (It reached a peak of about 50 million lines in the mid-'80s, falling back to about 25 million by 2005.)

Still operating out of the Sparks Street building it had occupied since 1904, the *Citizen* was feeling cramped. Its press capacity was being severely tested, but the purchase of new equipment required extensive renovations. Over the years, the *Citizen* had expanded several times so that it now occupied a rambling L-shaped property with entrances on Sparks, Queen and O'Connor streets. Any further expansion would not only be expensive, it likely wouldn't serve the *Citizen*'s needs for

July 4, 1967

Opposite: The Citizen's new offset press told the story of Gatineau River flooding, May 17, 1974.

347

long, given the rate of growth. To make matters worse, the paper was creating havoc on O'Connor Street, a busy downtown artery that became snarled several times a day by trucks delivering newsprint or carting away papers for distribution across the region.

It was time to move. The *Citizen* considered several downtown properties, but for the same reasons thousands of its readers were heading to the suburbs—cheaper land, more space—the *Citizen* settled in late 1969 on a four-acre site 12 kilometres west along the Queensway (a distribution priority) near the Pinecrest-Greenbank exit. "We're going where the population is going," publisher Robert Southam said in announcing the move. "The suburbs are where we see the future."

The move also allowed the *Citizen* to take advantage of a revolution in newspaper technology. The paper ordered a custom-made photo-composition computer system, allowing it to replace the hot metal type technology used by newspapers for centuries with "cold" type produced on film. It ordered a pair of new offset presses to improve the quality of reproduction. And its journalists were set up with video display terminals, making the *Citizen* only the second paper in North America to use electronic screens for writing and editing stories.

Not everyone was happy about the move. Reporters complained they'd be too far from city hall, the police station and courthouse, not to mention Parliament Hill. Advertising staff worried east end businesses would feel cut off. Gazing over the vast meadow across from the new building, virtually everyone said they'd miss downtown at lunch time. But *Citizen* executives insisted that only a paper located in the suburbs could reflect the lives of its growing suburban readership.

To be sure, there were growing pains. Several false starts were required before all the technical glitches were fixed and the presses rolled for real on Nov. 3, 1973. Judging by letters to the paper, readers liked the new product, or at least the impressive full-colour photos. Photographer Yousuf Karsh was so pleased by the photo clarity he offered a series of his portraits for publication. And before long, newspaper executives from around the world were touring the plant for a first-hand look at the new technology. What they were seeing was to become a major weapon in the fight that ended seven years later with the demise of the *Citizen's* long-standing rival.

July 4, 1967

July 4, 1967

February 16, 1965
A FAINT CHEER FOR OUR FLAG
Along with Ross Munro and Matthew Halton, Charles Lynch was one of Canada's most accomplished Second World War correspondents. In the '60s, as the chief of Southam News Service, he carved out an equally famous career as a ground-breaking political columnist. His work appeared regularly in the Citizen *for 30 years.*

BY CHARLES LYNCH
Southam News Service

Canada's "moments in history" are usually well disguised, and we have managed to hold most of them in dimly-lighted rooms, with much scratching of pens and mumbling of speeches.

Our reputation for non-showmanship was well maintained Monday when the Maple Leaf flag was run up on the flagpoles of the nation's capital. Of course, this one was too emotional to be entirely concealed — you can't very well put up a flag indoors.

So, a compromise was reached by the officials who manage such affairs, and 90 per cent of the ceremony was held inside. The remaining 10 per cent, including the unveiling of the new flag itself, took place out in the open.

It seemed almost an accident that a cheer was raised during the latter part of these proceedings, and members of the crowd who indulged in this unseemly outburst appeared quite embarrassed about it.

Certainly, nobody was urging them on.

As is so often the case on our great occasions, the main object seems to be to avoid giving offence to anybody—in this case, to those who had fought so long against the new flag, and for the retention of the Red Ensign.

Compromise was the order of the day. And while compromise is thought to be our most valuable national asset, it doesn't do much for moments in history and great occasions that are supposed to stiffen the sinews and summon up the blood.

These things we leave to others—the British, who can muster a great sense of occasion when they deem it proper to do so, and the Americans, who aren't ashamed to wear their hearts on their sleeves and can work up a patriotic lather at the bang of a firecracker.

The players in Monday's pageant walked through their parts like so many sleepwalkers, and the new flag, which turns out to be quite a gay concoction when the wind gets at it, was far and away the brightest part of the ceremony.

The desire not to give offence was apparent in the speeches of Governor-General Vanier and Prime Minister Pearson, both of whom seemed to be walking on eggs. And glowering from the sidelines, as though watching for a slip that might have injected some life into the proceedings, was John Diefenbaker, who didn't speak at all.

New flag supporters defend the quiet approach by saying that, after all, the main thing is that the Maple Leaf flag is now official and that enthusiasm for it will build naturally through the years as memories of the old flag fade.

Meanwhile, the whispered "hurrah" is the order of the day, and citizens who feel like weeping, either through joy or sorrow, are requested to do it quietly, and if possible in both official languages.

Apparently, Canadians abroad have taken up the matter of the Maple Leaf flag with somewhat more zing than was displayed in the capital. Defence Minister Paul Hellyer returned from a tour of our military establishments in Europe with word that the flag was a great hit everywhere he went.

Mr. Hellyer is hardly an unbiased witness, but I am prepared to accept his version on this one. The idea of a distinctive Canadian symbol has always been attractive to Canadians abroad—and who among us, while abroad, has not sought recognition as a Canadian when mistaken for a Briton or an American?

Nowhere did the Red Ensign fly more proudly than in Europe, in war and in peace, and it flew over some of our greatest scenes of valor. But it was not unmistakably Canadian, as was apparent to all who attended the 20th anniversary of D-day observances in Normandy last year.

Everywhere, there were clumps of Tricolors, Union Jacks, Ensigns and Stars and Stripes. Inevitably, the ensign blended in with the jack and sometimes it was omitted altogether.

I can understand that the new flag will strengthen the sense of identity of Canadians abroad. It is while abroad that I myself feel the sense of a distinctive Canada most strongly. Perhaps that is because Canadians abroad are not caught up in the infighting, and their thoughts of home tend to be uncomplicated by the fetters that bound our orators back here.

The hope is that the flag will help to simplify the thinking of Canadians at home on matters of nationhood, and unity, and even patriotism. To judge by Monday's mood in the capital, with its heavy overlay of civil service homburgs and diplomatic toppers, the new flag is going to find it dull going for awhile.

Perhaps by next July 1 our people, instead of going around asking one another, "What do you think of the new flag?" will be able to work up some emotion that doesn't have a question mark on the end.

Like, hooray!

July 4, 1967

Dennis the Menace

"You oughta join the asternauts. You could sit like that for a WHOLE WEEK!"

July 4, 1967

May 1, 1965
DIANA: SHE'S STILL A FAN
BY JIM RAE
Citizen Staff Writer

Diana, the girl who inspired Paul Anka's most famous song, is still one of the singer's most ardent fans.

"I guess I was never really in love with Paul," she admits eight years after the song became a smash, "but we were always very good friends. You could not help but like him for his enthusiasm."

Diana's full name is Diana Ayoub. Today she is an attractive brunette of 27.

"Paul seemed so young in those days," Diana recalls, "that I never really thought of him romantically."

Paul and Diana attended the same church—St. Elijah's at Lyon and MacLaren streets—and it was through this association that their friendship developed.

"There's no use trying to hide the fact that Paul was a bit of a monster then," Diana confesses. "He was such a dynamo of energy that he bugged everybody he met. He could even appear very brattish at times."

She never dreamed that the song Paul wrote for her would eventually sell 9,000,000 recordings and rank second only to Crosby's "White Christmas." Yet Diana, who lives at 868 Bronson Ave., never doubted that Paul would succeed one way or another.

"You just know that anybody who tried so hard will make it," she says. "How could he miss?"

Incidents stick in her mind—like the time Paul, ever rambunctious, spilled several cups of hot coffee in her lap from a tray he was carrying. (She still has the scars to prove it.)

Or like the time the singer promised to come back after he was successful and take Diana for a ride in his car—to make up for the many rides he had had in hers. True to his word, Paul came back and the couple went for the promised drive.

Diana denies there was a wide difference in their ages when the song "Diana" was written. Two years at the most, she says. If Paul was 15, she would have been 17.

While the song's lyrics begin with, "I'm so young and you're so old," Diana insists the age-differential was really more imagined than real and made for better lyrics.

Paul was bashful then, she remembers, and at first would only pick out the melody on the piano. "I think he was too embarrassed to sing the lyrics in front of me," Diana says....

Diana says they have met several times since Paul went to New York and made his name and his fame. The most recent meeting occurred by strange coincidence in Puerto Rico where Diana was holidaying only a few weeks ago.

"I met his wife, then, too," she says. "They make a nice couple."

Has the singer changed much over the years?

His former sweetheart thinks he may have "lost a little bit of his bubbliness" and the songs he composes now are sadder than his first ones.

—UPI telephoto

A 'stump' speech

Meredith at Pickens, Miss.

Civil rights campaigner James Meredith, July 4, 1967, who was the first black student enrolled at the University of Mississippi.

July 4, 1967

May 8, 1965
A LITTLE GIRL WITH A LARGE TALENT

When six-year-old Angela Hewitt won the recorder solo class for under-14s at the Ottawa Music Festival Friday morning, quite possibly the only person she surprised was herself.

The recorder, after all, is not her strongest instrument. And it must compete for practice hours with the harpsichord, violin, organ and the piano.

Musically, Ottawa's little prodigy, who lives at 221 Wilshire Ave., was born with the golden spoon in her mouth.

Her father Godfrey is organist and choirmaster at Christ Church Cathedral, while her mother Marion taught piano at Glebe Collegiate prior to her marriage.

So it is hardly surprising that Angela and her brother John, 9, have a certain musical talent.

Angela took to her first musical instrument, a toy trumpet, at the age of two. By her third birthday, she could play recognizable tunes.

It was then that she began to learn the piano, her most successful instrument to date. She was soon playing Christmas carols, and was reading music at the age of four.

For three consecutive years she has gained first-class honors in her Conservatory examinations for the piano. Last year at Rimouski she won the Quebec provincial championship for pianists under 7, for which she was presented with a $100 scholarship.

Last Christmas she played for the Governor-General and Mrs. Vanier at a staff-party at Rideau Hall, and later received a personal note of congratulations from them.

But it was this week's music festival which brought Angela her greatest success to date. Entered for 12 classes on piano and recorder, she took home 8 firsts and 3 seconds.

No less important were the words of the adjudicator in the piano division, Daphne Sandercock of Montreal, who described Angela's performance as, "truly brilliant, both in style . . . and technical mastery."

Nor can Angela rest on her laurels, for brother John, a late starter on the piano at the age of five, himself won three firsts and a second. Together brother and sister took the honors in the under-12 piano duet.

A pupil at the McGregor-Easson school on Dynes Road, her tastes in music remain broad.

Her favorite composers include Bach, Haydn, Mozart and the moderns, but she will happily play a highland air on the violin for her Scottish grandfather.

But she can't stand the Beatles.

Of course, Angela Hewitt went on to have a stellar career as a concert pianist and recording artist, earning raves for her Bach interpretations from critics around the world. She eventually learned to like the Beatles. As for her brother, John, he pursued a career in information technology.

July 17, 1965
'AT LAST . . . A QUIET TENANT'
In March 1965, Mafia kingpin Lucien Rivard escaped from a Montreal jail amid efforts to extradite him to the U.S., where he was wanted on drug charges. Rivard had somehow received permission to water the jail's outdoor rink, even though the temperature was above freezing, and the ice had already melted. He used the hose to climb over a jail wall. Fallout from the case eventually reached into the federal cabinet, and led to the resignation of justice minister Guy Favreau.

BY DOUG MACRAE
Citizen Staff Writer

WOODLANDS, Que.—"I've always thought of it as my doll house, but now I suppose I'll have to start thinking of it as Rivard's Retreat."

So says the gracious, grey-haired dowager May Birch, who unwittingly rented a sumptuous cottage on her one-and-a-half-acre estate here to the most wanted criminal in the country's history.

Mrs. Birch, a lifetime resident of this picturesque community in the Laurentian Mountains, told the *Citizen* she leased the cottage Monday to an unidentified man accompanied by his "wife and child."

"I identified him later from—what do you call those—mug shots, but the man, when he rented the cottage was a real gentleman," she said after all the hubbub had subsided early this morning. "I thought to myself, 'At last I've found a quiet and happy tenant'."

Mrs. Birch, who lives with a grand-daughter in the nine-room main house, was entertaining three village ladies when police brandishing shotguns and machine guns surrounded the house and the cottage.

"I thought it was a surprise party or something . . . that was my first reaction," she said.

She saw a man, presumably Rivard, leave the grounds 30 minutes before the raid, in a jeep-type sedan. She said the man returned less than 10 minutes before the four-force commando raid was launched.

Mrs. Birch said police told her they had arrested three men in the raid, and were looking for a fourth.

House guest George Wegg said the raiding party came in about 15 cars and numbered more than 50 officers.

"They were all around this place and the cottage at the same time, and they were along the shore in front of the land with dogs, and everything," he said. "They drove right over the lawns, and when Mrs.

July 4, 1967

Birch's grand-daughter woke up she was staring into the muzzle of a shotgun. I guess they didn't trust anybody."

Mrs. Birch said she didn't remember ever seeing a light from the cottage at night. When she visited the cottage after the raid she found blinds on all the windows.

"They were never covered like that before . . . they (the tenants) must have brought in the blinds after they moved in," she said. "I have no idea when Mr. Rivard might have moved in, because after I rented the home I didn't see a soul around it anytime."

Rivard apparently spent the last five days of his freedom in relative luxury. The cottage rests in lush woods on the landscaped grounds of the estate, on the shore of Lake St. Louis.

"My goodness what will people think . . . perhaps that I have harbored a criminal," Mrs. Birch worried. "It's the most horrible thing that could have happened to us."

December 29, 1965
LITTLE'S GETTING RICHER
. . . ON OTHER PEOPLE'S VOICES

In the 1960s, Frank Penn, a quiet ad salesman-turned-columnist, emerged as the city's premier entertainment writer, turning out well-crafted, often amusing articles on night club acts, musicians, actors and radio and TV personalities. For several years, he wrote a daily TV column that became essential reading for industry insiders across the country. Here's an excerpt from a feature on Ottawa-born comedian Rich Little's return to his home town.

BY FRANK PENN
Citizen entertainment columnist

Anyone whose voice has been pinched off to a painful croak by a flu bug knows what a miserable nuisance it is.

But when a cold can cost you 125 voices, along with your livelihood, you make it a rule to stay out of draughts and keep your feet out of icy puddles. Unfortunately, neither precaution did Rich Little much good this week.

Returning to Ottawa for a two-week engagement at the Chateau Laurier Grill, the local boy who made it very good south of the border was made to feel right at home.

On hand to greet him at the airport was an enthusiastic bacterium of the type which is currently keeping most of Ottawa's population dismally sneezing and the sales of pocket tissues at record levels.

Feverishly munching an assortment of vari-colored pills Tuesday afternoon, Little touched his throat tenderly.

"These things had better work," he said, "or everything I do tonight

July 4, 1967

is going to come out sounding like Rochester."

They must have been good pills. The only time Little sounded like Rochester before a SRO Chateau Grill audience Tuesday night was when he was rasping out with, "Yeah-suh Mr. Benny."

And on through the balance of the evening's two (and very different) 45-minute acts, Little's larynx never failed to wrap itself around the precise inflection and timbre of the individual voices in Little's private army of stars.

For the sake of those who already have booked up the two weeks of the engagement almost solidly, actual lines from the act must be left untipped. Suffice to say that all of his material is fresh and visually bright. But excellent as the professionally prepared scripts are, it is the parts he prepared himself that are the real show stoppers.

This is only partly due to the fact that his inside knowledge of things local shows him where to hit Canadian (and especially Ottawa) audiences right where the hilarity is.

A lot of the extra effervescence of his personal pieces comes simply from the fact that he is as fast a man with a quip as any gag-writer, and when it comes to writing that's tailored to the Little style, well, who better than Little to write it?

Not that anyone in the audience was wrinkling their foreheads in clinical analysis of where the chuckles were coming from. What they were doing was laughing. When they weren't applauding, that is.

Little, who strives mightily to avoid any hint of moss in his routines, has lifted his act well out of the rut common to many other impersonators. He borrows the voices of the stars—and gratefully acknowledges their contribution—but it is essentially himself—his own personality—which stamps each show.

He has been successful in developing a flexible and pleasant singing voice (it sort of sprang out of a Bob Goulet routine) and his performances include a number of songs sung strictly *a la* Little. Now, along with the singing lessons he religiously attends, he plans to take instruction in dancing. ("How else am I going to do Fred Astaire?")

Unlike some local performers who have gone on to showbiz stardom, Rich Little has never had to prove to hometown audiences that he deserved his successes. He enjoys working in Canada and is delighted to be in Ottawa.

But although he discovered long ago that "the U.S. entertainment business is conducted no more and no less efficiently than it is in Canada," Rich Little plans to make his home in California. "A performer has to go where the work is most plentiful," he explains.

Work certainly has been plentiful for the 27-year-old entertainer since he made the major step into the big time through an appearance nearly two years ago on Judy Garland's TV show. He has won acclaim

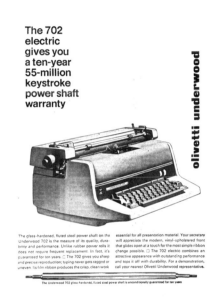

July 4, 1967

in a dozen major television programs, performed at every top-ranking North American supper club, made a brace of TV pilot films, lent his voices to the sound tracks of a score of films, as well as commercials for TV and radio....

From it all, one of his favorite stories concerns a recent commercial assignment in the United States. For it, he was asked to supply three "way-out" voices—two male, one female—for an animated cartoon.

"They didn't want any Hollywood stars, just distinctive voices to really make viewers sit up and take notice. I supplied the voices, the producer said, 'Great stuff,' and what an imagination I had to dream up these three real crazy voices right on the spot.

"I didn't explain to him. But anyone from Ottawa who happens to hear Charlotte Whitton, John Diefenbaker and Lester Pearson doing a sales pitch over a U.S. TV network will know what happened."

December 5, 1967
FUN AND GAMES IN GREY CUP-VILLE
It's unclear exactly why the Citizen *invited Canadian novelist Mordecai Richler from London to write about Grey Cup week in Ottawa. Whatever the reason, Richler didn't disappoint, filing a wonderfully irreverent account that portrayed Ottawa as a lifeless hicktown and, not surprisingly, offended more than a few local dignitaries. Here's an excerpt from his lengthy article:*

BY MORDECAI RICHLER

July 4, 1967

It was with considerable enthusiasm that I flew from England to Ottawa or—as Jack Kinsella's public release had it—Grey Cup-ville, where "the mild insanity launched inadvertently 58 years ago by Lord Grey (would) reach new heights of 'delirium puntens'" on the morning of November 27 when all nine Miss Grey Cup hopefuls would arrive at Ottawa's Uplands airport—a mass rendezvous that was contrived, Mr. Kinsella wrote, "at an altitude of 60 miles above Kazabazua Korners, an isolated hamlet in the heart of the Gatineau moonshine country."

Alas, on arrival in Ottawa on Monday, November 27, I found not mild insanity, but sour, disgruntled fans. The hometown Rough Riders had been eliminated 26-0 by Hamilton in the final Eastern Division game. Ottawa, contrary to expectations, would not be fielding its own team in the Grey Cup game. IT'S TIME TO CELEBRATE, ran the *Ottawa Journal* headline, but the joy is gone.

If spirits were sinking in Grey Cup-ville, duties were not neglected. At noon the intrepid boys and girls of the Fisher Park Junior School Band, shivering in their red capes, assembled in Confederation Square to welcome the nine Grey Cup girls and to watch Mayor Don Reid perform the official kickoff to the week.

Don Reid did not falter. He reared back and kicked mightily. Simultaneously, there was an exceedingly loud report in the skies. But Don Reid had not been resoundingly indiscreet. The loud report had been caused by a multi-gun salvo fired by the 30th Field Artillery.

Across the street, at the Chateau Laurier, I chatted briefly with a toothy matron as she sipped her Diet Pepsi. "We're all Miss Grey Cup chaperons," she said, "but we can't find the girls anywhere. Have you seen them?"

In one of the Chateau's many banquet halls, the girls were also being awaited at an official luncheon. Substantial-looking men drank patiently at the bar, wearing lapel badges that announced, "For a kickoff my name is . . . TUBBY." Finally, the girls, touchingly young, appeared in their miniskirted splendor. Gail and Bonnie, Marjorie Jean, Anne Louise, Leslie Jane, Su Lorraine, Julia and Lucie. Out of so much candy, I selected Miss Saskatchewan Roughrider for a word, consulting my form sheet first. Anne Louise Kennedy (age 19, 115 lbs. 35 1/2-25-35) liked tennis, badminton, volleyball, skating and skiing. She came from North Battleford, Sask., where she was the Boosters Club candidate for Miss Grey Cup. "What will you do if you win?" I asked.

"I am accompanied everywhere," Anne said, "by a chaperone and a guard."

"A guard," I said. "Whatever for?"

Anne wouldn't say, so I confronted a uniformed representative of the Capital Guard Service. "What are you guarding the girls against?"

His expression severe, he replied, "You will have to ask the men who hired us."

I did not stay for lunch, which began, ominously, with tinned fruit salad. . . .

•

In the evening, at the B'nai Brith Sportsman-of-the-Year dinner in honor of Jake Dunlap, a former Rough Rider star, I sat at a table with Ottawa and out-of-town sportswriters. My colleagues felt that so far Ottawa fandom had failed to show the proper Grey Cup zeal. [Citizen sports editor] Jack Koffman pushed his plate aside. "It's a crime," he said, "that we're not in the game this year."

This year, Centennial year, being the first time since 1940 that the game was to be played in Ottawa.

"The fans are cooling," Koffman said. "It's a shame."

Another sportswriter held up his hand, indicating a full mouth. We waited while he swallowed. He put down his knife. He put down his fork. He wiped his mouth. "It's human nature," he said.

Tuesday night the streets of our nation's capital continued to be muted. On Wednesday morning Mayor Don Reid, no party pooper,

—Citizen-UPI staff photo

Six above—at 18 below

January 9, 1968

"dropped a verbal bomb on city merchants." He denounced their lack of Grey Cup spirit. Ottawa responded smartly. The grizzled, middle-aged bellhops of the Chateau Laurier removed all the unanchored lobby furnishings, and barricades went up before the elevators. If I was still able to enter the parliamentary East Block, where our prime minister labored, without being stopped by anyone, it now became necessary to produce a pass before stepping into the elevator at the Chateau.

I made my way down icy, sober streets to the National Press Club, where the rival coaches, Ralph Sazio and Eagle Keys, were to reveal something of their battle plans. But Sazio, the Ti-Cat coach, was to be with us in spirit only. He would pronounce by long distance from Hamilton. "Now here are the ground rules," Jack Kinsella began. "You will ask questions in turn."

"But I've already written my column," one sportswriter protested.

Another asked, "Do we get a translator for Eagle Keys?"

Finally, Mr. Sazio came on the line. "Hello, Ralph," Kinsella shouted. Then, beaming at all 22 of us, he added, "There are 50 or 60 of the boys here to ask you questions."

Alas, no immediate questions sprang to mind. The boys were silent and hungover.

"Ha, ha, ha," Kinsella laughed, glaring at us. "The boys are a little reluctant this morning. Um, how's Joe Zuger's nose?"

A sportswriter asked, "Hey Ralph, would you like a frozen field on Saturday or a gooey one?"

Mr. Sazio did not hesitate or evade. "This is, um, a classic. The Grey Cup. We will go real good frozen or gooey, that is, um, even if the—ahm—weather rears its ugly head."

"You arrive at two o'clock from Hamilton, Ralph. What is your game plan for this afternoon?"

"Well, um, we won't practice. I feel it would be real good for the boys, um, to familiarize themselves with the feel, the electricity of the, um, Grey Cup spirit of Ottawa."

"They roll up the sidewalks here at nine-thirty, Ralph."

"We're going real good and we'll do a good job."

•

Following the conference, more confused than enlightened, I hurried to Wellington Street. This, after all, was Western Day in Ottawa, and a parade was promised. It turned out to be a paltry thing. Tatty. Forlorn. Paunchy men on horseback. Broad-bottomed girls wearing glasses with shell half-frames flinging their Stetsons into the air, crying yahhoo and yippee to no visible effect. They rode their charges into banks and bars. "Let's go that-a-way."

That night I joined 1,600 other pleasure-seekers at the Miss Grey Cup Pageant, sponsored by Ottawa Kiwanis. The pageant had a dis-

"Doesn't that look like Pierre Trudeau up ahead?"

January 9, 1968

THE TREBLE CLEF PRESENTS

Jimi Hendrix Experience

also

The Soft Machine

at the CAPITOL THEATRE
TUESDAY, March 19th at 8.30 p.m.
Tickets: 4.50, 4.00, 3.50, 3.00, 2.50
Box Office Now Open at Both Treble Clef Stores
177 SPARKS ST.   68 RIDEAU ST.
Mail Orders accepted with self-stamped
addressed envelope.

March 1, 1968

tinct 1940s band-show flavor, the Kiwanis ladies in their glittering fin-
ery and mountainous hairdos being sufficiently out of date to enhance
the illusion. A CBC orchestra, their violin bows seemingly Vaselined
smooth, played the old tunes, the nice tunes, and then a group called
the swingers bounced breathless on stage. "Grey Cup time is a rooting
time, a root-toot-toot-tooting time," they harmonized. Other wholesome, old-time acts followed, and finally there was Juliette, a dream in
candy floss pink, singing, "When you're smiling...."

Once the show was done, all nine Miss Grey Cup contestants came
onstage, cheeks glowing. A cynic in the row behind me said, "You can
bet your bottom dollar the winner is Miss Rough Rider."

Just so. The 1967 Miss Grey Cup was sweet, pretty Julia (Julie) May
Dixie. Julia, the form sheet said, was 19 years old, five foot one-and-a-
half inches, 100 lbs. and 34-24-34. She had blue-green eyes and blonde
hair. "Julie is a public school teacher for Nepean school board. She
plans to work toward her BA in education and wants to travel in Europe. Her hobbies are sewing, baking and being a majorette. On the
sports side she likes skiing, football, skating and swimming."

When the judge's decision was announced, Julie squealed with surprise. Her lovely eyes filled with tears. The other girls, good losers all,
gathered around to congratulate her. Gum chewing, sweaty photographers fell at her feet. Flashbulbs popped. Cameras churned. Micro-
phones were thrust toward Miss Grey Cup's slightly parted lips. Tomorrow, the world....

•

Later, at the Riverside Hotel (home of Upstairs at the Rib; home of
Downstairs at the Rib, with forty-five beautiful bunnies), I joined two
carousing young westerners at their table. Jim and Bob, who went to
the Grey Cup game every year, had left their wives at home in Regina.
"You've heard of a freakout," Bob roared. "Well, this is a week out."

Jim knew all the bunnies by their first names. "Hey there, Betty," he
hollered, "Hiya, Gail," as the harassed girls, their pinching bras discol-
ored by sweat, zipped from table to table.

"Yahoo! Go, Riders, go," the men at other tables shouted each to
each. Like Jim and Bob, they sat in pairs for the most part, without
women.

"Enjoying yourself?" I asked.

"Yahoo!"

But Jim shook his head. "Hell," he said feelingly, "if I were only a girl,
I could have such a good time here."

•

Friday evening I came for the 18th Annual Grey Cup Dinner, an event
whose tone had been definitely set by Chairman John Wilkinson's program poem:

—Citizen-UPI staff photo

Start of a new craze?

Typist Jo Ann Harper tries Ride-A-Rooing

New toy will add bounce to 1968

March 1, 1968

We hope you'll enjoy your visit with us,
And later—if you should roam,
You may not know when,
But—come back again,
And make yourself at home!

For an hour, maybe longer, the worthies at the head table awarded each other plaques and scrolls, paid handsome tributes to each other, and applauded themselves. Then there was an invocation by Chaplain Ernie Foote, who prayed to the Lord for good sportsmanship in tomorrow's contest, asking for integrity of play, not forgetting to add that all of us were involved in a bigger game, the game of life. . . .

When big Lorne Greene, born in Ottawa, was introduced, many people stood up and cheered.

"He's come back to us, all the way to Parliament Hill," MC Terry Kielty said, "from La Ponderosa."

Lorne Greene grinned at us. "I would have brought Hoss," he said, "but I couldn't get a plane big enough."

We laughed and slapped our knees.

Again and again men stood up to say how proud they were to be in Ottawa, and that the Grey Cup game was the greatest unifying force in the nation. Other, more brutalized nations were knit by civil wars or uprisings against tyrants, but Canada, our Canada, was held together by a pigskin. . . .

•

All the same, I did go to the game on Saturday. A punishing wind cut across the icy field, where the Roughriders were jumping up and down. One-two-three-four. Between exercises the imports from Florida and Texas blew on their reddening fingers and stamped their feet together. Wandering across the field, I stumbled across a milling group of pimply, bony girls in green-and-white tights, trembling with cold, teeth chattering, noses running. The Riderettes. Sex kittens out of Saskatchewan. A thoughtful bandmaster had provided them with woollies, sadly loose-fitting, to wear over their stockings. The 14-year-old girls, like the more warmly dressed men who would play in the game, kicked their feet together for warmth. Suddenly a TV camera came into play, the drums went boom, and the intrepid girls, after one last wipe of the nose with chapped hands, flashed radiant smiles and strutted away from me across the frozen field.

"Get 'em, get 'em," the Riderettes chanted. "Go, go, Riders." But the Riders were not going anywhere in 1967 [Hamilton won 24-1]. The dreary game was enlivened for me only once, when a youngster leaped onto the field, seized the ball, and, evading players and cops, threw it

March 8, 1968

into the stands.

"It's a weekend in the cooler for him," the man seated beside me said.

His companion was displeased.

"Now those . . . newspaper guys are going to make him . . . famous. If you ask me, they shouldn't even mention his . . . name."

Immediately after the game, a seemingly needless interruption of the Grey Cup week bacchanal, hotel-room parties were resumed. At the Skyline Hotel, the corridors spilled over with merrymakers. It would end in pushing and shoving, some tears, and a good deal of vomiting in corners. Meanwhile, everybody was overbearingly friendly. Lorne Greene, his white hair combed into a ducktail, his face tanned leather-wallet brown, emerged from a suite. A housewife squealed with delight. "It's Lorne Greene. Harry, go get Midge. Get Midge immediately or she'll never forgive me."

"Hey Lorne, where's Hoss?"

Greene smiled benignly.

At 1 a.m., I was jammed into an elevator with yet another group of celebrants, groping for each other between the eighth and ninth floors, not so much compelled by passion as driven by a need to hold each other upright. On the ninth floor, we were joined by an immense, magnificently built black man, a Hamilton lineman with a champagne bottle in his hand.

"You related to George Reed?" a drunk asked.

The black lineman looked down at the fat little fellow in the raccoon coat. "We're all related," he said.

January 2, 1968
20,000 COME OUT TO SAY GOODBYE
TO CENTENNIAL YEAR
Bobby Gimby, Centennial Pied Piper, leads
children in final Ca-na-da romp on the Hill

BY MIKE MCDERMOTT
Citizen staff writer

Critics said Centennial Year would go out with a whisper, but 20,000 Canadians proved them wrong.

Bundled against the cold, they crowded Parliament Hill, the old muffled in blanket overcoats and fur hats, the young in their celebration-colored winter trappings and the very young perched high on dad's shoulders to watch with awe this finale to Canada's birthday party.

It's Ottawa, Dec. 31, 1967 and Parliament Hill rumbles with the greatness of 20,000 voices, some loud, some faint, some good, some, well, not so good.

While dignitaries sipped cocktails and exchanged polite banter in the West Block cafeteria, television crews rolled up cables and dismantled camera scaffolds.

And Centennial Year is filed away in film cans to gather dust until the next big birthday. When Canada celebrates its second Centennial they will be a valued reminder of the first.

The familiar names were there, those now synonymous with Centennial Year—John Fisher, Bobby Gimby, Judy LaMarsh, Maurice Lamontagne, Governor-General Roland Michener.

And, of course, thousands of children.

Centennial commissioner Fisher recalled the lighting of the flame on Parliament Hill one year ago and said it lit "millions of symbolic flames in human hearts across Canada.

"A flame is warmth, and a common ingredient of the Centennial was warmth and happiness. Canadians were proud to stand up and say happy birthday, Canada, and I believe that they added in their hearts, happy birthday, dear Canada."

Governor-General Michener, arriving in a horse-drawn sleigh with Mrs. Michener, predicted that Canada would move on in 1968 to a "new and challenging" future. He paid special tribute to his predecessors, Georges Vanier, who died in March, and Vincent Massey, who died in a London hospital Saturday.

Maureen Forrester, Canadian contralto and newly-appointed Companion of the Order of Canada, sang "Praise Be To Thee." The CBC orchestra, directed by Eugene Kash, played Handel's "Royal Fireworks Music" as rockets streaked above the Peace Tower and showered the Hill with multi-colored explosions.

March 25, 1968

March 13, 1968
JONI MITCHELL PLEASES
AUDIENCE AT LE HIBOU

In hindsight, it's more than a little amusing to note that Bill Fox, later a grizzled political reporter and brass-knuckled press secretary for prime minister Brian Mulroney, began his career writing glowing accounts of delicate flower children.

BY BILL FOX
Citizen special correspondent

Picture the ideal female folk singer—long blond hair, beautiful, witty, a good guitarist, and a clear soprano voice—the kind you believed didn't exist any more—this is Joni Mitchell.

Performing at Le Hibou Coffee House for a two-week engagement, Joni has come a long way from her early days as a singer and song writer on the Prairies.

Her songs have been recorded by established stars like Judy Collins,

Buffy Ste. Marie and Ian and Sylvia. She has appeared on television programs such as *Let's Sing Out*, *Take 30* and *The Way It Is*.

Recently, she recorded an album of her own songs to be released in April on Frank Sinatra's Reprise label.

But most noticeably, to Canadian audiences, anyway, Joni wrote and sings the theme song for the CBC public affairs program, *The Way It Is*.

Appearing on stage in a rust-colored mini-dress, Joni opened the set with one of her more famous songs, "Urge for Goin'."

She sings in a clear soprano voice, a rarity in this day of electronic music, accompanying herself on an acoustic guitar. She easily switches from a ballad to a semi-rock protest song. Her voice is haunting at times, and at others, it is like a young girl singing in a small-town music festival.

The themes of her songs vary from love and the eternal triangle, to the sea, and to war.

She smiles easily, resulting in an immediate rapport with the audience. Between numbers, she tells the story behind some of her songs or relates an amusing incident connected with them.

But the best example of her polished stage presentation occurred as Joni was preparing for the last number of the set. As she was tuning her guitar for "And So Once Again," one of the strings broke.

Undaunted, Joni set the guitar against a stool and sang the number, the story of a young man and his girl who break up when he goes off to war, without accompaniment, something a lesser performer would never have attempted.

Joni Mitchell, perhaps Canada's foremost female folksinger, seems to be well on the way to the big time.

He's a war hero—at 13
Ta Thai Manh, aged 13, shows off his military bearing and a garland of flowers at a ceremony in Saigon when he was awarded a medal and made an honorary member of the South Vietnamese Rangers. Captured by the Viet Cong, he escaped and then led the Rangers back to seize his captors.

March 15, 1968

DESPITE THE ECONOMIC MIRACLE

GERMANS CAN'T ESCAPE THEIR BURDEN OF NAZI GUILT

Citizen associate editor Charles King spent the past
three weeks touring five European countries on both sides
of the now-rusty Iron Curtain. In the fourth in a series of articles,
he examines the troubled conscience of West Germany.

BY CHARLES KING

Associate Editor, The Citizen

March 26, 1968

Wherever you go in West Germany these days, you run up against that Conscience. Even kids who hardly drew breath in Hitler's days seem determined to prove that they are really not the people who bore responsibility for the atrocities, and the mass slaughter of Jews that took place under the Nazis.

World War Two is now a quarter of a century behind us. But the memories of the horrors it brought, and the overwhelming destruction it caused, are still tender and fresh.

Germany is a new land. It was almost totally rebuilt after the war, with German sweat and American cash. The results are spectacular.

Soaring, glass-fronted buildings and luxury limousines; streamlined passenger trains and sleek, brightly-painted tourist steamers; opulent theatres and concert halls all combine to suggest an elegant and so-phisticated civilization unsurpassed in the Western world.

The Germans have money, and they have good taste. They have a rich sense of history, and deep religious feeling.

You look around at the economic miracles of the past 20 years and ask yourself: Can this be the country that put its trust in Hitler and sowed the seeds of its own destruction?

The same question appears to haunt the Germans themselves. At least in the presence of foreigners, they never raise the subject of World War Two. But if you ask, they are ready with detailed dates and statistics of the catastrophe that befell them under Hitler's guidance.

The glorious old city of Cologne, whose giant twin-spired cathedral served as a landmark for Allied bombers, was 92 per cent destroyed in its central area, 70 per cent flattened in its suburbs.

Fifty thousand of its civilian population died in air raids. Thousands more fled into the country to avoid the rain of death. The city's popula-tion, 760,000 in 1939, had shrunk to a mere 40,000 by 1945.

Four of its five bridges across the Rhine, which bisects the city, were knocked out by bombs; the fifth was destroyed by retreating German forces. Today there are eight bridges across the river; the city's popula-tion is at an all-time high of 860,000; and not a scar remains of the grim history of wartime.

Dusseldorf's story is even more impressive.

More than 200,000 civilians died there in the war years; the central part of town was 80 per cent destroyed. Yet today the city of iron and steel is totally rebuilt, and ranks as one of Europe's most beautiful cities. Its strikingly modern Deutsche Oper am Rhein runs up an annu-al deficit of more than $2,000,000, but the cost is borne willingly by civic authorities.

The city's tourist office employs 50 people to publicize delights for visitors, and the promotion is paying off, as its well-stocked shops and restaurants and well-fed burghers attest.

But Dusseldorf, like Cologne, and Frankfurt, and all the Rhineland that knew such destruction less than a quarter century ago, still bears a terrible burden of guilt.

In Frankfurt I witnessed a students' demonstration on the steps of a downtown church. The leader carried a broken swastika, and on his head he wore a statesman's black silk hat.

Police moved in to break up the protest before it got out of hand, but

April 23, 1968

the message of the students was clear: They were showing their distaste for the alleged past Nazi associations of West Germany's President Heinrich Luebke.

The state president had appeared on television the night before to deny published charges that he approved blueprints for Nazi forced labor camps in World War Two.

Leaders of the two political parties which rule Germany in coalition, the Christian Democrats and the Social Democrats, backed up the president, terming him "blameless" and a "convinced democrat" who had been subject to harassment and arrest by the Nazis.

But Luebke's denials had a hollow ring in the ears of many Germans I met. And his main accuser, Henri Nannen, editor of the mass circulation weekly magazine, *Stern*, repeated the charges against him in a television interview after the president spoke.

As long as men old enough to have rubbed shoulders with the Nazis remain in positions of influence and power in Germany, the doubts and uncertainty will continue.

But so far as I could tell on brief inspection, the Germans' devotion to democracy and racial tolerance is real enough.

It's just that history weighs heavily on the national conscience. And considering what Hitler wrought, perhaps that is all to the good.

—Citizen-UPI staff photo

Wrapped up in Trudeau

Gloria Beattie of The Citizen's classified advertising department is going all out for Prime Minister Trudeau. The dress is part of the latest political fad to hit the city. She has to be careful though or the whole deal could go up in smoke. The dress is made of paper.

June 11, 1968

April 8, 1968
ON TO TRUDEAU'S 'JUST SOCIETY'

Although it would dampen its enthusiasm over the years, the Citizen *was an early booster of Pierre Trudeau, citing "his rare intelligence . . . and a force and style that are equal to the times" three years before he became prime minister in 1968. Here's an excerpt from an editorial marking his selection as Liberal leader:*

April 6, 1968, will stand in future times as one of the decisive dates in Canadian history.

Whether it will make the opening of a new chapter of constructive work, of achievement, of excellence—or of something contrary to those hopes—remains for the unfolding of the story. But there can be no doubt that when 1,203 out of 2,365 delegates to the Liberal convention cast their votes on the fourth ballot in favor of Pierre Elliott Trudeau, they made a decision to embark on an adventurous and challenging approach to the future of this nation. . . .

The *Citizen* believes the convention made the right choice. Like all great enterprises, this one has its dangers. But unless this country sets its goals high and broad, it will remain indefinitely a quiet backwater of mediocrity—or it will shiver into futile fragments.

Mr. Trudeau, now the prime minister-designate, crystallizes his goals for Canada in a phrase: "The Just Society." It is a worthy call to action. It implies not only justice for individuals and for collective groups of Canadians, both ethnic and regional, who have known something less than justice in the past—it implies also justice for other peoples whom Canadian action may affect: potential immigrants to Canada and the citizens of foreign countries in which Canadian foreign policy may have some impact.

Like the retiring prime minister, this new one tests his actions against high standards of moral and intellectual excellence. He can therefore expect to be judged against this kind of standard. His candidacy for the most powerful office in the land has been so unusual and so dramatic that it has bathed him in a shining moment of favorable publicity worthy of Camelot. He cannot expect this idyll to continue long.

Mr. Trudeau is a man of great personal courage and candor. He has a swift, abrasive tongue and a ruthless wit. He will never be an ambiguous force in public life, and the division between the desire for serenity and the urge for adventure that Saturday's vote revealed within his own party will not make it easy for him to weld the Liberal party into a cohesive instrument at the service of his admirable objectives.

Our wish for the new prime minister is that he will be able to achieve his Just Society, within the limits of the possible and the time framework of his own lifetime. Prophecy is risky, but those of us who have encouraged and supported Mr. Trudeau's candidacy are committed to risk in a good cause. Therefore we endorse the final words that Lester Pearson addressed to the Liberal convention on Saturday night as he congratulated the new leader: "He will lead a government that will do great things for Canada, our beloved country."

June 8, 1968

February 4, 1969
'IT'S FIGHT IN VIETNAM OR CANADA'
BY TRACY MOREY
Citizen staff writer

Peter Charlebois is a cute Canadian kid. In cowboy boots and bell-bottoms, he exudes that combination of shyness and self-assurance common to 18 year olds. He wears a peace insignia on a chain around his neck.

Next week, he returns to the rice paddies of DaNang, Vietnam, to kill a few more "Gooks," as he calls them.

A former Rideau High School student, Peter moved with his parents, Mr. and Mrs. Bill Charlebois, from Ottawa to California two years ago.

For a while, he did the "pink satin shirt and shoulder length hair" bit on Sunset Strip, he says. But he always liked the idea of the military. "It was just something I wanted to do . . . a change in my life. I was curious."

So he enlisted in the Marines—"You know, tough, like you see it in the movies. I just thought I'd try it."

Six months and a Purple Heart later, he cannot even think of questioning the U.S. presence in Vietnam, although the war he volunteered to fight is in "a sickening place that everyone wants out of."

"It's gotta be right what we're doing," Peter said nonchalantly this week during a short visit back to Ottawa to see old friends. "We're fighting over there rather than have them over here. Otherwise the Communists would be in the States and in Canada."

And, how can those hippies know anything about the war they are protesting? he asks. "You can't say anything about the war unless you've been there," he retaliates.

If the Americans do pull out, hundreds of thousands of marines, including some of his friends, will have wasted their lives, he says.

"If we stay, we'll get the job done," he affirms.

It seems to him that the Americans are making progress in Vietnam, although the South Vietnamese people themselves hardly seem to care. The common people in the jungle, he says, "just swing with whomever offers them the most."

"They really don't care. They live in grass huts where the smell is fantastic. They have no regard for human life."

Later, Peter explains that the first time he killed somebody he was scared. "But, what can you say. You just kill them. Somebody tells you what to do and you do it. You don't think twice about killing people."

You see a lot of killing, but after a while "it's just like a dream," he explains.

Peter was trained to be a mortar man. In this capacity he got the shrapnel shot in the elbow which won him the Purple Heart. The wound from a 79-mm. grenade was fixed up and he was fighting within two days.

He'll be on a machine gun when he returns, and though he laughs that "you'd have to be crazy to want to go back," pay increases and promotion possibilities will encourage him and some of his buddies to re-enlist when their term is up.

Made for each other

July 4, 1968

January 2, 1970

THE SOUNDS OF THE SIXTIES

Melodies, tribal rock, funny names—and Hey Jude

This time 10 years ago, local disc jockeys were feeding us the sweet, flowing melodies of the year's top tune—"Theme from a Summer Place" by Percy Faith.

Hardly a fitting beginning to a decade that was to reverberate to the deep tribal love rock sounds of *Hair*, and names like Creedence Clearwater Revival, Blood Sweat and Tears, Rhinoceros, Thunderclap Newman and, of course, the Beatles.

Certain well-aged and time-honored names survived the change, however.

In 1969 Henry Mancini, with "The Romeo and Juliet Theme," and Elvis Presley, with "In the Ghetto," were placed respectably in the Top 60.

It was a decade that gave us the Motown Sound and The Supremes. It also gave us the frug, the jerk, the mashed potato and . . . the list goes on and on, but it all started in 1962 with the great Chubby Checker hit, "Twist."

For a brief moment, the Sixties also gave us the Bossa Nova.

The decade closed with a Beatles' single at number three and their *Abbey Road* LP the number one album, though adoring fans feared they might never again know their idols as news of trips to the guru, marriages and John and Yoko's peace thing filtered across the Atlantic.

But the music scene now is stale, says disc jockey Al Pascal of CFRA, and "the '70s will need something big, a shot in the arm, like the Beatles."

It is evident that rock is here for a while, says Al, who says "Hey Jude" was the biggest seller of the decade in Ottawa.

The 1970s will see more and more album cuts being played on radio. This year, 20 to 35 per cent of singles at the top of the charts originally were on albums, where music is generally "better," he says.

Decade's biggest hits, year by year, on Ottawa radio:

1960—"Theme from A Summer Place," Percy Faith.
1961—"Exodus," Ferrante and Teicher.
1962—"Twist," Chubby Checker.
1963—"Limbo Rock," Chubby Checker.
1964—"I Want To Hold Your Hand," Beatles.
1965—"Back in My Arms Again," Supremes.
1966—"Ballad of the Green Berets," S/Sgt. Barry Sadler.
1967—"A Kind of Hush," Herman's Hermits.
1968—"Hey Jude," Beatles.
1969—"Crimson and Clover," Tommy James and The Shondells.

January 8, 1970
HOW TO PIN DOWN THE PM — SEND A GIRL
BY TIM CREERY
Southam News Services

PARIS—The French morning newspaper *Le Figaro* today reports Prime Minister Trudeau as saying that marijuana might be legalized in Canada if it is found to be no more harmful than tobacco.

AMERICAN
PRODUCTIONS INC.
present . . .
THE BEACH
BOYS

with Special Guest Stars
"THE BOX TOPS"
also featuring
"3's A CROWD"
FRIDAY, AUGUST 2nd
at 8.30 p.m.
NEW CIVIC CENTRE
LANSDOWNE PARK
Tickets: 4.50 - 4.00 - 3.50 - 2.50 - 1.50
Box Office Now Open at
Both Treble Clef Stores
177 SPARKS STREET
68 RIDEAU STREET

July 30, 1968

Le Figaro, evidently no slouch in journalistic strategy, sent a pretty female reporter on skis to track down the prime minister at Courchevel, the French ski resort. She reports on a luncheon interview with Mr. Trudeau. She quotes him as saying of marijuana:

"Thirty per cent of students smoke it. It's a question of knowing whether it's really dangerous or not. If studies show us that these cigarettes are no more harmful than tobacco I don't see why, after all, we wouldn't legalize sales. Psychologically, perhaps, this might not be a bad thing."

The correspondent, Huguette Debaisieux, found Mr. Trudeau spoke French with a slight English accent, could pass for 35 years old although he's 50, and poled himself down the slopes so fast she couldn't keep up.

"A fighter's physique," she sums up. "The secret agent type in American films."

"Waiter!"

May 13, 1970

Mr. Trudeau, she says, recounted to her the incident in which he socked a student demonstrator. She retells the story admiringly— though she has the incident in Montreal rather than Vancouver.

The prime minister also told her he planned to come to Courchevel last year but it was too difficult with Gen. de Gaulle still in power.

Of President Georges Pompidou, the prime minister said he'd had a long chat with him some years ago but "at present I don't know exactly what we could say to one another."

When asked to talk about Quebec, Mr. Trudeau said: "And Britanny in your country—no complications?"

Mr. Trudeau is reported to have set himself a rigorous schedule of eight hours skiing, eight hours work and eight hours sleep a day. But he admits he had already broken it to go dining and dancing.

Le Figaro's correspondent reports that the prime minister is under the protection of two agents—on skis—provided by the French ministry of the interior. They couldn't keep up with the PM on slopes, either, she says.

At the end of their luncheon, she reports, a young Canadian timidly approached the prime minister and gave him his toque.

"Be careful on skis, Mr. Trudeau," he is reported as saying, "We need you in Canada."

May 9, 1970
HOW THEY KILLED THE AMERICAN IDEAL
BY CHRISTOPHER YOUNG
Editor of The Citizen

So much that is deeply shocking has been happening in the United States and Southeast Asia that it is difficult to find a clear perspective from which to view the wreckage of policy and the destruction of hope.

The four children shot dead on an obscure campus in Ohio were not even leaders of dissent or believers in resistance. But the action would not be a shade more defensible if they had been.

The American troops plunging through the jungle villages of eastern Cambodia may or may not have razed an important guerrilla headquarters. But success cannot justify this willful escalation of the war, and failure will multiply the consequences.

In the White House, a president who had led his people and the world to believe he was trying to end the war has instead widened it—without consulting either his foreign allies or the leaders of his own Congress. He sits there today a baffled prisoner of his own folly, almost like Czar Nicholas in the Winter Palace, while soldiers and police hold back the angry people outside.

Yet something worse than all this has happened. The moral basis of American foreign policy has been destroyed—and of Western policy in general. We of the Western alliance have the right to speak in strong terms because we have accepted American leadership in what was seen as a defence of freedom against the threat of Communism.

The long, misguided war in Vietnam has so corrupted the purpose of that crusade that President Nixon can send an army into Cambodia to protect the right of General Lon Nol to shoot Vietnamese civilians and float their bodies down the Mekong River.

In undermining the moral basis of foreign policy, a work well begun by President Johnson, Nixon and the sinister clown he chose as his vice-president have broken faith with the historic ideals of America and shattered the confidence of everyone, American and foreign, who would keep that faith.

We hold these truths to be self evident, that all men are created equal, unless they are gooks, slopes, bums, snobs, hippies or paranoids. The system is not working. The American system, vaunted around the world as the answer to communism and dictatorship, as the key to peace and freedom, is not working.

In 1964 Lyndon Johnson won a smashing victory against Barry Goldwater. One of the important issues, one of the reasons for the landslide, was that Johnson took a cautious and moderate view of the Vietnam commitment, whereas Goldwater advocated all-out war. Johnson was elected on his moderate platform. Then he embraced Goldwater's policy, including the much-mocked idea of defoliating Vietnam's forests.

In 1968 Nixon was elected largely because of discontent over "Johnson's war." Though his campaign speeches were typically equivocal, it was clear that he encouraged the people to believe he would extricate the country from the quagmire in Vietnam with minimum damage to

New aid for apartments

This lobby phone was tested in Ottawa

Bell introduces intercom device

July 23, 1970

the national reputation.

Hubert Humphrey, who might well have been able to do this, was fatally handicapped by events at the Chicago nominating convention, when protests against the war produced an ugly overreaction from the authorities. Thus the American people have twice expressed themselves in presidential elections in favor at least of limiting the commitment in Southeast Asia. Each time the elected president has gone on to intensify the war.

Now we have Nixon stating formally, and with pride, that he will not be swayed by "political considerations" and does not care whether the people endorse his policy in 1972.

Knowing what we do of Nixon, this probably means that he expects his actions to be justified in the eyes of the voters by events between now and 1972. But the words themselves are chilling. They say that it does not matter what the people think—the war will go on because the president says so.

How does an American who disapproves of the policy react to this? Obviously, since his ballot is ineffective, by forms of protest outside the normal processes understood by tradition and the Constitution.

As of this week, the American who takes this other course is on notice that he is liable to be shot. Or in the cold words of his president, he "invites tragedy."

The president himself has invited tragedy, and he has it in full measure.

May 17, 1971

October 19, 1970

THE BELL TOLLS FOR ALL CANADA

The Citizen *supported Pierre Trudeau's use of the War Measures Act in the FLQ kidnapping crisis, but it did so with a condition: "Nothing less than the equivalent of an attack on the nation could justify such a break with our dearest traditions," an editorial said the day after the act was invoked. "When the crisis is past, the government will have to prove beyond doubt that such was the peril." This editorial was written two days later.*

The obscene murder of Pierre Laporte removes any doubt about the nature of the challenge to the Canadian society. It is not a political opinion we are faced with; it is a criminal conspiracy, prepared to commit any atrocity that will help destroy Canada.

Decent people throughout the country—and that is the vast majority—join in mourning a distinguished citizen. Pierre Laporte was a fighter. He fought for Quebec and for Canada. He fought for civil liberty in the days when it was not a very popular cause of his province, in the time of Maurice Duplessis. Where were these skulking killers of the FLQ then?

Laporte fought for reform bravely, openly and fairly. Both as a journalist and a politician, he took his stand on the firing line and accepted his victories and his defeats in the spirit of democracy.

He was seized by a pack of thugs carrying machine guns, and slain by deliberate calculation. No man's courage is protection against such barbarism.

The tragedy of Pierre Laporte reduces our doubts about the need for extreme measures to protect the Canadian society and its leaders. Throughout the land Canadians of every political persuasion and every kind of cultural and ethnic background are rallying behind the democratically elected authorities as they seek to hunt down the killers, the terrorists and those who like to play games with fire and bullets.

Canada will not again be a decent or secure society unless this cancer is destroyed. The bell that tolls for Pierre Laporte tolls for every one of us.

February 9, 1971

October 7, 1971
A LIVING LESSON (YAWN) IN POLITICS
BY MARSHA SADOWAY
Citizen staff writer

The metallic crash of locker doors flung shut echoes from the depths of Bell High School. The quake of students' stomping, shuffling feet competes for volume with the dull rumble of their voices.

In they amble, looking for their friends and seats in the auditorium. A man, red-faced and looking a bit sheepish, scurries around the door handing out Sid Handleman campaign-literature. He did the same thing at Confederation High School the day before, thrusting the Tory blue papers into hands.

The teachers stand around in clusters looking semi-serious. This is, after all, a serious occasion. For the first time, 18-year-olds will vote. And for the first time, a local school board—the Carleton Board of Education—has granted politicians the use of school time to campaign, in this case for election to the Ontario legislature.

The candidates march onto the stage single file, looking earnest and, above all, calm. Youth can tell if they're scared.

Everyone—about 350 students—settle down and the teacher-moderator says this is a solemn occasion and introduces the candidates.

The scramble for that still unknown quantity, the youth vote, is on.

Garth Stevenson is cool but aggressive. After all, the young are supposed to be the NDP's natural constituency. He talks about idealism, quality of life, desecration of our environment, poverty—the glossary of the young, the concerned, the politically committed.

He leaves out women's rights. Maybe he just forgot. On the other hand, when he mentioned it the day before at Confederation, it failed to bring out any politically-committed women's libbers.

Only one girl asked a question during the question and answer period and it wasn't of the "rights" variety. She liked studded tires and how did the parties stand on the matter?

Frank Marchington, the Liberal candidate, tries to be relevant. He talks about jobs for students. This was a major concern for the students at Confederation, so Mr. Marchington beats his opponents to the punch and has the answers ready.

Sid Handleman, the Conservative, is "telling it like it is." He understands how the purity and idealism of the NDP appeal to young people. But "hogwash," he says. One has to temper idealism with realism.

Some of the students are concerned and a few brave the scrutiny of their fellow students to walk up to the microphone and ask questions.

They ask about the route of Highway 416, public car insurance and American domination of Canada's economy.

Other young voters appear indifferent. The drift-out begins quietly but quickly. The first to leave try not to attract attention and hustle out on tiptoe.

While the candidates are outdoing each other, three girls discuss someone they all know and apparently dislike. Two others are huddled over an examination of their shoes. Several students are doing homework. Others slump with glazed-eye stares.

The drift turns into an exodus while the campaign blazes onstage. One student is reading *Time*. The one next to him studies a pencil balanced upright on his knee.

The first, sharp, shrill ring of the bell sends almost all of the young voters stomping and shuffling out. The second just about empties the auditorium. The hullabaloo in the hall drowns out the one on stage.

The class and the politicians are dismissed.

June 1, 1973

The Saturday Citizen

with
T̶...e, Color Comics, TV/Times

132nd Year, Number 174.   156 pages   Ottawa, Jan. 25, 1975   Home delivered 85¢ weekly.   35¢ per copy

Aid plans disappoint publishers

By Murray Campbell
Citizen staff writer

PETERBOROUGH — Representatives of Canada's book and magazine industry reacted with "profound disappointment" Friday to the federal government's program for assisting their ailing industry.

Reaction to the $15 million aid program outlined here by Secretary of State Hugh Faulkner was swift and highly critical.

Mr. Faulkner told about 250 people attending a two-day conference at Trent University on English language publishing in Canada that the Canada Council will begin handing out the money April 1.

He outlined a series of measures designed to help promote and distribute Canadian books but stopped short of trying to legislate change in the American-dominated industry.

Paul Audley, executive director of the 75-member Independent Publishers Association, said the government program offered no overall strategy for combatting control of the Canadian book market by foreign-owned publishers who account for all but 17 per cent of annual sales.

He said the program of government grants and loans will not be enough to help Canadian firms regain a sizeable chunk of the market. Canadian publishing firms had 38 per cent of national sales just three years ago, he said.

The aid program represents an "expression of faith by the government," Mr. Audley said, "but I can't see how it's going to stop the decline."

Graeme Gibson, novelist and chairman of the writers union — a group which wants to see restrictions on foreign publishers in Canada, said he was profoundly disappointed that Mr. Faulkner had not responded to publishers' requests for a chance to compete equally with foreign firms.

More on publications, Page 3

WEATHER

Snow changing to rain late in the day with a risk of freezing rain this afternoon. Mostly cloudy Sunday with occasional light snow. Total accumulation three to five inches. High today 35 (2 C). Low tonight 25 (-4 C) with temperatures lowering Sunday to 10 (-12 C) late in the day. (Details page 2).

Inside . . .

Heart attack claims former mayor

Charlotte Whitton dies

Charlotte Whitton, March 8, 1896-Jan. 25, 1975
Citizen photo

Leading civic figure more than 20 years

By Marsha Skuce
Citizen staff writer

Charlotte Whitton, a former mayor of Ottawa and one of Canada's most colorful politicians, is dead.

Dr. Whitton died at 3:30 a.m. today of congestive heart failure. She was 78.

She had been admitted to the Civic Hospital Jan. 5 after suffering a heart attack.

Funeral will be held Monday.

Fall ended long, colorful career

She spent the past two years in retirement at her Renfrew Avenue home after she fell and broke her hip. She was serving her sixth year as Capital ward alderman at the time and the accident ended her political career.

The tiny woman was a flamboyant, pugnacious figure at city hall for more than 20 years.

She once summed up her philosophy in her mother's words: "Children, you don't have to fight. But if someone wants a scrap, it's your Christian duty to meet them half-way."

After making a speech in 1951 about the lack of women in public office, she was challenged in a newspaper editorial to run for board of control. She did, campaigning under the symbol of a needle and a wisp of thread. And she won, topping the polls to become the first woman in Ottawa to hold civic office.

The death of the sitting mayor, just a few months after that election, moved her into the top position — and she became the first woman mayor of a Canadian city.

'Bigger job, bigger needle'

She then won election as mayor and served until 1956. (This time her symbol was a darning needle "because the job is bigger.")

In 1961 she ran again and served until 1964, when she ran and lost her last mayoralty campaign.

Undaunted, the next won election as alderman, only to be thrown out of office by the new city council. She was disqualified from remaining on council under a municipal act provision which prohibits a member of council from taking court action against the council.

Dr. Whitton opposed a bylaw and took action against the council in the Supreme Court of Ontario. She won.

Another election was called in 1967 to fill the vacancy. She ran and was returned in a record-breaking vote.

Her battles were legion and one of the most famous made headlines across the country.

Once, when she was mayor, she took exceptions to a controller's remark, which she interpreted as a double entendre and a slur at her unmarried status. She flew at him in a rage, punching and kicking, and had to be dragged off by a third person.

'I won the fight'

When she was asked later if she was embarrassed by the national publicity the incident created, she boomed in her loud voice. "Of course I don't mind the publicity. I won the fight."

On another celebrated occasion she threw the politicians and press into several theatrical, terror-filled moments. Angered by controllers' baiting of her, she whipped out a pistol and brandished it before their horrified faces — then pointed out it was only a toy.

Former mayor, now Judge, Kenneth Fogarty, said of her once: "She was never at a loss for words, usually the right words and very often the last."

One famous story she liked to tell concerned the time she, as mayor, met the Lord Mayor of London at a public function when both were wearing their ceremonial robes and chains of office.

"When the Lord Mayor of London leaned over to sniff a rose I was wearing on an evening gown he asked coyly 'If I smell your rose will you blush?' and I reached forward and replied 'If I pull your chain will you flush?'"

Tough, sometimes brutal foe

Quick-tempered and straightforward, Dr. Whitton was known as a tough, even brutal opponent. But she also had a reputation for being able to take as well as give.

She once had a confrontation with a former city traffic director, Thor Neilsen.

"Mr. Neilsen," she snapped, "It doesn't surprise me that you are Danish. And I would even say you are a great Dane. And a Great Dane, as everybody knows, is the biggest, dumbest dog on earth."

"Then in this case, Mayor Whitton," replied Mr. Neilsen, "I would say the city is better served by a dumb dog that a tired old grey mare."

She broke up in a bellow of laughter.

Career in pictures, Page 25

Change boosts butter 5 cents

By The Canadian Press

Agriculture Minister Eugene Whelan announced policy changes Friday that will boost butter prices immediately by five cents a pound.

He said in the Commons Friday that government-set minimums for industrial milk, butter and skim-milk powder are being increased. Fluid milk is not affected.

The change increases the target support price for industrial milk to $10.02 a hundredweight at the producer level from $9.41.

The increased revenue to producers will be achieved by increasing the minimum price of butter to 90 cents a pound from 85, an increase that will be borne fully by the consumer.

Producers also will see their skim-milk powder minimum boosted to 59 cents a pound from 54. But the government is increasing its subsidy to producers by the same amount, eliminating any need for a retail price increase.

The consumer subsidy will rise to 29 cents a pound from 24.

The changes are expected to carry the government through to April 1, the start of the 1975-76 dairy year, when major policy announcements are scheduled.

"There will be some increase," replied Mr. Whelan when asked about price prospects. "But it'll be very small."

Carleton pact reached

A tentative settlement was reached today in the deadlock between Carleton Separate School Board and its teachers.

Schools could reopen as early as Monday.

The tentative agreement was reached at 7 a.m. after a night of non-stop talks.

"There are still a few wrinkles to be worked out," said teacher spokesman Pat O'Neill. "But it looks pretty good."

Details of the agreement will not be released until both sides have ratified it.

Teachers and members of the board are apparently being contacted to arrange Sunday afternoon meetings.

Students under the Carleton Separate Board have been without teachers since the Christmas break.

Kissinger sees Nixon

SAN CLEMENTE, Calif. (AP) — State Secretary Henry Kissinger and former president Richard Nixon have met for the first time since Nixon left office in August.

They met at a dinner party at Nixon's seaside villa Friday following a speech by Kissinger in which he warned of the consequences of congressional involvement in foreign affairs.

Kissinger and his wife, Nancy, flew here by helicopter after the major foreign policy address to the World Affairs Council in Los Angeles.

Ronald Ziegler, Nixon's closest aide, told reporters as the guests arrived that "Mr. Kissinger will be here for several hours and there will be no comment."

Bomb kills four

Puerto Rican nationalist group claims 'credit' for pub blast

NEW YORK (AP) — The explosion of a powerful fragmentation bomb that set a Wall Street skyscraper quivering and damaged historic Fraunces Tavern killed four persons and injured at least 42.

A Puerto Rican nationalist group that has been linked with other terrorism here claimed responsibility for the blast that roared through the city's crowded financial district.

The bomb had been planted in the Anglers and Tarpon Club adjacent to the tavern. The dead, including one man who was decapitated, apparently were lunchtime patrons at the club.

Built in 1719, Fraunces Tavern was the scene on Dec. 4, 1783, of George Washington's tearful farewell to officers who served under him in the American Revolutionary War. It is about 400 yards from the New York Stock Exchange.

The blast sent glass fragments flying into the street. Diners in the 60th floor cafeteria of the nearby Chase Manhattan Bank building said the structure shook.

Fifteen minutes after the explosion, an unidentified telephone caller told The Associated Press it was the work of the FALN, a band of nationalist Puerto Rican terrorists.

FALN stands for Fuerzas Armadas de Liberacion Nacional Puertorriqueña (Armed Forces of the Puerto Rican Nation).

The group has claimed responsibility for other bomb explosions in the metropolitan area, but previous blasts caused no fatalities.

Later police recovered a note in which the FALN claimed the latest bombing was in retaliation for the "CIA (Central Intelligence Agency) ordered" murder of two young Puerto Ricans.

Doctors said nails and other pieces of metal were found in the bodies of those who died in Friday's blast as well as in some of the injured.

Mayor Abraham Beame rushed to explosion scene from nearby City Hall and denounced the bombing as "a senseless act of terror which defies all reason and decency."

SEX-FOR-LUNCH BUNCH THREATENS TO STRIKE

SUVA, Fiji (Reuter) — Gold miners are seeking a 30-minute mid-day sex break.

The miners say this is the best time for sex, their union secretary, Navita Raqona, said Friday.

The demand is one of a number of issues the 1,600-strong union is discussing with a mining company.

Raqona said a man has a sexual obligation to his wife, and if he goes home exhausted at 5 p.m. he cannot fulfil his duty.

The union wants the sex break added to the normal lunch break.

The union proposes to limit the sex break to married men.

"Alternative arrangements" would have to be made to compensate bachelors, said Raqona.

"We don't want to overdo this."

A Rival Goes Down

The Fourteenth Decade, 1975-1984

IT TOOK HIM A FEW YEARS to finally acknowledge what everyone already knew, but Art Wood's explanation for the *Ottawa Journal's* death on Aug. 27, 1980 was hard to beat for getting to the point: "We didn't go modern, and I guess we paid for it."

As the last publisher in the *Journal's* 95-year history, Wood took a lot of heat for not working hard enough to convince the paper's owner, Thomson Newspapers, to hang on a bit longer. It had barely been a year since the *Journal's* makeover as a morning paper brimming with bright new writers and daily features. Why not give it another year?

But the truth is that Wood had been assigned to Ottawa by Thomson, a newspaper company driven by bottom line interests, to stop the bleeding for good. If anything, the new-look *Journal* was losing even more money than before and the accountants at head office had run out of patience. They knew the score better than anyone: the *Citizen*, 142,000 papers a day, the *Journal*, 72,000; the *Citizen's* annual advertising lineage, 45 million, the *Journal's*, 22 million. And they knew it was at least a decade too late to catch up.

It's difficult to know, of course, how things might have turned out had the *Journal*, to use Wood's phrase, "gone modern" when it moved into new quarters on Kent Street in 1971. Perhaps it was already too late for the *Journal* to win the struggle with the *Citizen*. For years it had suffered under the bad management of the Sifton family of Winnipeg, while the *Citizen* prospered as part of the ever-expanding chain of Southam-owned papers.

What's certain is that as the two papers prepared to move into new buildings, the *Citizen* held a clear advantage. Its owners never considered equipping its new suburban site with anything but the latest in newspaper technology. The Siftons, unable to afford the plunge into

Paul Martin, Sr.,
January 4, 1975

Opposite: The Ottawa Citizen was in its second year at the new Baxter Road plant near the Queensway when the colourful former mayor and columnist, Charlotte Whitton, died. At this point the Citizen's new offset presses were printing better colour pictures than 90 per cent of North American dailies, but its file of black and white photographs still surpassed the colour files, including that of Whitton.

the computer era, decided on a blend of new and old processes for the *Journal* (the paper even dragged its ancient hot metal linecasting machines to the new building).

By 1975, the *Citizen* had widened the gap in daily circulation to nearly 20,000 from 6,000 four years earlier. But it wasn't just readers who were impressed by the *Citizen's* well-printed colour photographs and clean, modern design. Advertisers also liked the *Citizen's* sizzle, and they preferred its more urban readership. The two groups fed off each other: more readers brought more advertisers, which in turn attracted more readers. As if that wasn't enough, the *Journal's* typographers went on strike in 1976, an ugly confrontation that lasted two years and not only plunged the paper into debt, but hurt circulation and destroyed morale.

With its rival in disarray, the *Citizen* moved in for the kill. Russell Mills, the paper's young new editor, began to plunder the *Journal's* top staff, starting with legendary sports writer Eddie MacCabe before snapping up popular local columnist Dave Brown. Although the numbers are hard to prove, the *Citizen* claimed each defection brought 5,000 *Journal* readers into the fold.

In 1979, roughly $4 million in debt and on the verge of sinking, the *Journal* was purchased by Thomson Newspapers. In a final effort to keep it afloat, the paper was given more staff, a sleek new look and a fresh focus. But circulation didn't budge, the losses mounted and Thomson finally pulled the plug.

The story didn't end there, however. On the same day the *Journal* received its death notice, Southam closed its newspaper in Winnipeg, a simultaneous action that led to criminal charges of collusion against Thomson and Southam and a federal inquiry into the newspaper industry led by Tom Kent. The companies were eventually cleared of the combines charges, and Kent's major recommendations—including the creation of a Press Rights Panel with broad powers to prevent newspaper concentration and cross-media ownership—were mostly ignored.

Even so, it likely wouldn't have been enough to save the *Journal*. Its fate had already been written.

December 2, 1975

March 22, 1976
AT LAST, A SEX ORGY

Morton Shulman was a lot of things—politician, businessman, broadcaster, columnist and doctor—but he was best known for being outspoken. As Toronto's chief coroner in the 1960s, he crusaded for tougher car safety rules, a crackdown on drunk drivers, better fire codes and liberal abortion laws. After a career in Ontario politics, he turned his hand to the media as host of a muck-raking TV show and author of a syndicated newspaper column. This excerpt is from one of his more offbeat columns. Shulman died in 2000.

BY MORTON SHULMAN

Last week I went to my first sex orgy. Right off, let me admit the sexual revolution has been a great frustration to me. Half of my acquaintances are like George, living with his third beautiful wife, and the other half are like Stanley who goes about town accompanied by his 18-year-old mistress.

I must be deprived, for I have lived for 26 years in a fairly contented state with the same wife. And, as for 18-year-old girls, I do meet such creatures on brief occasions but I can never think of anything to say to them, nor do they show the slightest interest in me.

Two weeks ago my TV producer informed me that we were going to do a program on orgies—there's a trend, I'm told—and that in preparation I was to attend one so that I could ask intelligent questions.

She added, "You can participate or not, as you wish, and as admission is by couple I'll go with you as your date." I replied that I'd need my wife's permission.

Gloria's reaction was not at all what I had expected: "If you are going to an orgy, Morty, so am I," she said. "You tell your producer that I'll be your date." I dutifully reported back to the producer, who was not at all put out. "OK," she replied, "I'll take the station president. We can go as a foursome."

When I came home for lunch the next Wednesday, I was greeted by one very despondent wife. "I can't go to any orgy" she moaned. "How could I possibly take my clothes off in front of those beautiful 18-year-old girls with their flat tummies. You'll have to go with your producer."

The station president refused to be so easily disposed of, however, and the producer finally said, "In that case, I'll have to get you a date, and by the way, it's a dinner orgy—dinner first, then the orgy."

Came Saturday night and I bathed, brushed, shaved, left my apprehensive wife—whose parting shot was, "Don't you dare catch anything"—and went to pick up my date. I could not believe my good fortune—the lady was 34, unbelievably beautiful, intelligent and vibrant. A journalist.

We joined the producer and the president and went off to the orgy, which was to be held in a Toronto penthouse apartment.

I'm not sure exactly what I expected but this was not it. Perhaps those pictures of the glamorous people from the Playboy mansion had misled me—there were only two attractive women at the party and I'd brought them both. The sad fact is that the rest were terribly ordinary. They looked just like my neighbors.

And Gloria need not have worried about 18-year-old girls—the women were between 30 and 40 and the men were slightly older, some

of them balding and most of them paunchy. Far from being the wild sexual creatures of my imagination, they all turned out to be very nice people who were sitting about an apartment discussing the developing war situation in Rhodesia.

My second shock was the dinner: it was health food, all green and crunchy with none of those aphrodisiac lobsters or stimulating steaks.

After dinner, the 20 people in the living room gradually filtered down to about eight of us. I decided to explore the rest of the apartment to see where everyone had gone. You would not have believed what was happening in the rest of that apartment—twosomes, threesomes and one foursome.

I returned to tell my date what was taking place and to ascertain her wishes. Her reply was unexpected: "Morty, there is something I should have told you. My brother-in-law is . . ." (and she named a rich, powerful contractor whom I had once denounced in the Ontario legislature as an associate of bad company and who had responded to me with something less than affection). I had an instant vision of imminent mayhem and made the only possible courageous decision—I fetched the lady's coat and we exited as rapidly as I could get her out of there.

My wife was surprised that I arrived home from the orgy at 10 p.m. After I told her the sad story, she commiserated, "You're not really the type for that sort of thing—it's only for very sexy men."

May 3, 1976

August 6, 1977
STAR WARS: HYPE AND HYSTERIA
Freelance columnist Martin Knelman's views on the first Star Wars *movie went against the flow in 1977. But as more installments were released, they came to represent the opinion of many film critics.*

BY MARTIN KNELMAN
Special to the Citizen

Once upon a time, children wanted to grow up and become adults. But that was a long, long time ago, before psychologist Bruno Bettelheim had explained the psychoanalytic significance of fairy tales, before Marshall McLuhan had pronounced that education is what people have to unlearn in order to become truly tuned in, before Hollywood had discovered that with audiences desperate to get back to the innocent amusement of the past, there were huge profits to be made from creating fantastic spectacles for children of all ages.

Nowadays, adults yearn to reverse the growing-up process and get back to the magic kingdom of childhood. To make that trip, you smoke a little grass and go off to a movie that promises to restore the lost world.

Star Wars, the new movie by George Lucas, the man who made *American Graffiti*, had been acclaimed on the cover of *Time* magazine as "the year's best movie," and by the time I saw it the hype had reached hysterical levels. In *Newsweek*, critic Jack Kroll made up for being a week behind *Time* by gushing even more fulsomely: "I loved *Star Wars* and so will you, unless you're . . . oh well, I hope you're not. Lucas has made the rarest kind of movie—it's pure sweet fun all the way. He says it's a movie for children—what he means is that he wants to touch the child in all of us. Only the hardest of hearts won't let George do it."

Meet the hardest of hearts.

American Graffiti was an adolescent's view of the world, and the picture had a kind of manic energy about it.

The flaw of *American Graffiti* was in its refusal to admit that maybe the view of its high-school characters was a little limited. There wasn't any sense that we in the audience could feel something more than nostalgia—that we might take some satisfaction about having grown out of that phase.

Star Wars wants to take us back even further—to the joys of children's comic-book adventures like Flash Gordon and Superman—and to insist that this was the true, uncorrupted summit of our imaginative experience. But Lucas' childhood mythology has so little smartness that entering into its spirit is an act of deprivation.

You have to take it as an act of faith, or else get very, very stoned. Otherwise you may get bored and restless with the simple-minded story, thus revealing yourself as—horror of horrors—deficient in childish delight. *Star Wars* is a 70-mm trip for *Star Trek* freaks.

Set in the distant past, with intimations of a code of gallantry left over from King Arthur and his Knights of the Round Table, it's like *2001* played backwards.

The sense of action comes from the concept of characters zapping around in outer space, but though the film relies on special effects wizardry for its look and feel, the message is that we shouldn't trust computers and technology, we should put our faith in the old values of the heart. *Star Wars* is a sci-fi fable with a heart of mush.

Since the story is neither especially original nor especially complex, and the movie goes on for more than two hours, much of the interest shifts to gadgets and secondary characters—which in some cases are the same thing. The scene-stealers are supposed to be a sort of space-age, armour-suited Laurel and Hardy team—a good-hearted midget robot named Artoo-Detoo and a tall, thin creature with an effete British accent, by the name of See Threepio, with more than a faint resemblance to the tin woodsman from *The Wizard of Oz*. . . .

A head-movie wouldn't be complete without religion and *Star Wars*

June 1, 1976

pushes a vague, trendy sort of pop mysticism with evangelistic fervor. The keeper of the faith is an old bore named Ben, played with sanctimonious relish by Sir Alec Guinness. Ben is the young hero's spiritual guide—an outer-space fairy godfather. "The Force will be with you always," Ben advises.

In the midst of the showdown battle (a drawn-out, tedious affair that recycles all the clichés of wartime thrillers about fighter-pilots), the voice of Ben is heard advising "Let go of your conscious self. . . . Trust your feelings. The Force." The hero achieves victory when he turns off his targeting computer and goes by instinct.

At the door of the theatre, they're handing out snappy little buttons with the printed greeting: "May The Force be with you." This season, The Force is selling more tickets than anything else. And in Hollywood, that's enough to start a new religion.

November 28, 1978

MUPPETS BRIGHTEN TV SCENE

For several years while he was editor of Saturday Night *magazine, Robert Fulford wrote a weekly column for the* Citizen. *Given his usual forays into literature, film and politics, the column excerpted here was a bit of a departure.*

BY ROBERT FULFORD

The big TV stars around my house these days are creatures made out of felt, flannel, leather, and various plastic substances. They are all dummies, and they are all members of the cast of *The Muppet Show*, Jim Henson's elaborately brilliant parody of show business styles.

The Muppet Show is quite possibly the best thing on TV right now. Certainly it's the liveliest program I see. Compared to the Muppets, TV shows that use humans seem lifeless, unreal. And on *The Muppet Show* itself, the actual living persons who turn up—each program has one token human, someone like Judy Collins or Elton John—seem colorless and ill-defined. They fade into the woodwork.

They know it, too. And it makes them nervous. You can see them eyeing the Muppets with the edginess that afflicts stage actors when they work with children. Stars or not, the human beings know that the Muppets always upstage them. Even Rudolf Nureyev's magnetism is a pale thing when set beside a Muppet. Nearly naked in a sauna with Miss Piggy, singing "Baby, It's Cold Outside," Nureyev looked like a nobody. Miss Piggy controlled the screen.

The Muppet Show is a complete fantasy, but the marvelous thing about it—and this is often true of surrealism—is that it makes its own queer kind of internal sense. The Muppets themselves can be recognizable animals, or imitation humans, or creatures never before seen

WAGNER TORIES

RED TORIES

JOE WHO? JOE WHERE? JOE WHY?

BIG BLUE TORIES

DIEFENTORIES

HORNER TORIES

"The Tories can keep the country together"

February 7, 1977

on earth. But in their unreality they work together beautifully.

Perhaps this is simply because of the strength of Henson's imagination. But perhaps it's also because Henson decided that, since TV is at all times unreal anyway, he would make his show as unreal as possible. In any case, he's grasped one of the other main characteristics of TV—no matter how hard it tries to be original, it's always derivative.

Television essentially creates nothing of its own. There is no such thing as a great popular artist who has sprung from television—no one who could be compared with, say, Orson Welles or Duke Ellington or Alfred Hitchcock or Tennessee Williams. TV borrows most of its artists and nearly all its ideas from older forms. It twists them and builds on them, works variations on them, but it doesn't originate them. Most of TV is a distorted shadow of something else.

Henson has carried this to its logical extreme. He's taken as many show business conventions as possible and crammed them all into one half hour, turning each into a travesty of itself. He puts together a soap opera, a newscast, a cooking lesson (given by a cook, called the Swedish Chef, who can't be understood), a chorus line, a story of unrequited love. Then he binds them with the corniest show business convention of them all, the difficulty and terror of putting on a show.

September 1, 1977

Each week, the Muppets are involved in some sort of stage performance. We never learn where this is happening, but it seems to be a kind of opera house. There are two doddering old codgers, Waldorf and Statler, sitting in a plush box at the side, commenting on the action. The MC on stage is Kermit the Frog. Fozzie Bear is his apologetic assistant, constantly bringing news of fresh disasters—the musical numbers aren't ready, a cow is loose backstage, the owner of the theatre is threatening to close it down. Yet each week, just as in all those old Warner Brothers musicals, the show somehow goes on....

As the newscaster on *Sesame Street*, Kermit has been a favorite of mine for years. On *The Muppet Show*, his talents have taken on a new dimension. He's involved now in something that could never happen to him on *Sesame Street*: a potential romance. Miss Piggy is infatuated with Kermit. The idea of a pig in love with a frog may be bizarre but isn't funny in itself. Nevertheless, in Henson's hands—and with the help of the eloquently grotesque shriek that Frank Oz gives Miss Piggy for a voice—it seems endlessly comic. Kermit always resists Miss Piggy's attentions. She tries shyness, he doesn't notice her. She attempts to embrace him, he wriggles away. Her love turns to rage and she smacks him, he shrugs it off and goes back to work. Miss Piggy is interested in Kermit but Kermit is interested only in business.

Miss Piggy is a male chauvinist's outrageous comment on feminine wiles. With her huge snout, her thick eyebrows and her old-movie-star clothes, she's clearly a gross insult to that part of womanhood that finds itself irresistible. If she were human, she wouldn't be tolerated in our living rooms: as a puppet she's a permissible caricature.

Miss Piggy now has her own independent following. The current issue of *Film Comment*, the journal of the Film Society of Lincoln Centre, contains an article called "A Sow is Born," by Elliott Sirkin. It says: "She is, above all, a sister in that exclusive sorority that counts among its members Garland and Holiday, Magnani and Moreau, Bankhead and Bernhardt, and of course, Davis. . . . Piggy takes her audience on a journey to the farthest extremes of the heart. The end of the road may be despair and madness but art is the only religion she knows."

That may overstate the case, but you get the idea. In any case, Miss Piggy, despite what Sirkin says, is the despair of Sam the Eagle, who sees himself as the guardian of the show's artistic and moral standards. Sam represents High Culture. He's disturbed by the lowbrow material on the show, and he keeps trying to elevate the mood. Alas, he gets everything horribly wrong; when Nureyev is about to show up, Sam says he's an opera singer. But Sam, like Miss Piggy, never stops trying.

This fall, the TV schedules happened to be arranged so that there were certain weeks when you could see *The Muppet Show* three times. That always made for a good week.

August 17, 1979
DIEF'S LEGEND LIVES ON
(Excerpt from an editorial.)

There was no one like him in this or any other Parliament. He was one of a kind—a statesman on occasion, a gut politician with an unerring sense for the headlines, an unswerving royalist, a master of ridicule, a powerful opponent, a trusted friend, a lone wolf who distrusted his own followers, yet a champion of the underprivileged, and a man who passed up opportunities for wealth to serve what he regarded as the public welfare.

John Diefenbaker was all of those things, and more. And now he is gone. And an exciting, vengeful but colorful era of Canadian politics has gone with him.

Historians will devote volumes to debating his record as the nation's prime minister from June 21, 1957 to the day in April 1963 when his government collapsed in a welter of resignations and recriminations. It is sad that his own recollections of that period were not completed. As with Lester Pearson, his major political rival of the period, death took Dief before his memoirs were finished.

Perhaps his treatment by the Conservative party he led for a decade of victory and defeat was cruel. He alone was responsible for the party's unprecedented success in first turning the Liberals out of office in

July 4, 1978

1957, and going on to win the greatest majority in Canadian parliamentary history a few months later. But he was also made to bear the responsibility for the party's downfall and fragmentation in the years that followed, which is the fate of all political leaders in defeat. Despite his humiliation, he never bowed to his detractors, and fought on doggedly as a private member in the Commons he once dominated as prime minister.

How do we assess the Diefenbaker record? He led this country in a different time, when the realities of the Quebec "quiet revolution" had not become apparent. It was a time when the gesture of bilingual government cheques was enough to keep French-speaking Canadians content, and the promise of a distinctive national flag—eventually unfurled by his Liberal successor—served to satisfy the nationalist element. But there was more to the Diefenbaker story than promises.

No prime minister before had such a keen feeling for the nation's minorities, or such a popularity among the elderly and the poor. His government—unwisely, perhaps—sacrificed a balanced economy in the interest of better conditions for Canada's Indians, war veterans and pensioners. People always had a greater priority with John Diefenbaker than economics.

In his later years, full of the bitterness of a leader scorned by his party, he functioned in Parliament as a crusader, ignoring his own colleagues who failed to march to his banner. He showed his scorn, too, for the younger party leadership. He made life very difficult for Robert Stanfield and opposed Joe Clark at the convention called to succeed him in February 1976. It is a tribute to both Stanfield and Clark that they treated the Old Chief with unfailing courtesy and patience.

In Clark's case, that patience was rewarded, at last, by a comfortable acceptance on the part of Diefenbaker. There is satisfaction in the thought that when he died this morning Dief was at last at peace with the Tory party, within which he had warred so long and so savagely.

But no caviling about John Diefenbaker's methods will dim the record of his unique achievement. Parliament will not forget him and neither will Canada. His presence among us gave us pride and a keen sense of our nationhood. The country is poorer for his passing.

August 16, 1979

February 21, 1980
SOVIET GRAND MANTLE TORN
—AT LEAST A LITTLE

Eddie MacCabe was not only Ottawa's leading sports voice for three decades until the late 1980s, he was also a window to the city's past. His well-loved Christmas stories brought to life the street cars, the bars, the characters, the gangs, the boxing rings and hockey rinks of Ottawa when it was still a small town and life could be tough.

*As a sports writer, MacCabe was as comfortable covering
high school track meets as he was the NHL playoffs—and he did
plenty of both. Here's an excerpt from his spirited account of
Canada's Olympic hockey showdown with the Soviets at Lake Placid.*

BY EDDIE MACCABE
Citizen Sports Editor

LAKE PLACID, N.Y.—Canada's Olympic hockey team lost to the Russians last night, 6 to 4, and were eliminated from the Olympic medal round. That's the bulletin version of what happened.

Here's the rest of the story: They went down blazing, all guns smoking, and the little jammed-to-the-gunwales arena gave them a noisy and standing ovation for their efforts. Because the Canadian kids, average 21 years, played with so much heart and emotion they made a great contest out of what should have been an easy mismatch.

They could actually have won the game. That might have been a slight injustice, but the amazing possibility was there.

The Canadians didn't lose their shot at a medal last night against the Russians. They lost it earlier in the tournament with a shoddy effort against the Finns. And now the loss to Finland comes back as all the more heartbreaking because last night the Canadians showed what they can do. They demonstrated that if they had been able to wrangle their way into the medal round, they had a real chance at it. The gold.

The game against Russia demonstrated some other encouraging theories. The Canadians showed, even while losing, that the Russians are not invincible. They have dominated since 1972, but their great players are getting old.

Against these free-wheeling, devil-may-care kids, such Russian greats as Mikhailov, Maltsev and Kharlamov did not look as jet-propelled as they did against the NHL all-stars last year. And it might serve a purpose to remember, too, that in the last game of the Challenge Cup Series last year against the best in the National Hockey League, the Russians tramped on them 6 to 0.

Last night, goalie Vladislav Tretiak looked no better than mediocre and the tenacity of the Canadians unquestionably had the rest of the squad seriously frustrated. Boris Mikhailov, their veteran team captain, was upbraiding his mates and shouting at them on the ice and on the bench. The Russians got to swan-diving, trying to draw penalties and the Canadians read that as a sign that they were not driving on the net, that they were grasping at straws.

And it's all really so stupid, because they're so good they don't have to resort to underhanded methods, but they cheated. In all possibility, their little cheat made no difference at all, but they were using illegal sticks with too pronounced a curve in the blades.

— *CP photo*

Runs for cancer

PORT COQUITLAM, B.C. — Terry Fox, 21, a Simon Fraser University student who lost a leg to cancer, is training for a cross-country run to raise money for the Cancer Society. He has logged 4,800 kilometres training, and will start in St. John's, Newfoundland, April 19.

March 11, 1980

Late in the game, after Golikov scored a goal, Canada called for a measurement of a stick. Under the circumstances, referee Jim Neagles was allowed to refuse, and he did.

"We knew they were using illegal sticks," coach Lorne Davis said. "Before the game, we knew we could call for a measurement, and we had picked out Golikov. We called it and he went off the ice. . . . The referee said the man had to be on the ice. But he had been on the ice when we called it."

At any rate, it likely made no difference, but one is left to wonder, not about the referee but about the Russian need to cheat.

But the Canadians proved that a team properly prepared for the European-style game can do much better than a collection of superstars thrown together in a hurry. Canada's Ron Davidson, a Nepean lad, said: "There is no question in my mind that we (Canada) have the best hockey players. There isn't anyone out there can even touch Guy Lafleur. I know that."

But preparation, and playing European-system hockey, allowed a bunch of Canadian kids to get within hailing distance of a team generally acknowledged to be the best in the world. Though they were not beaten, the Soviet grand mantle of invincibility was at least torn. . . .

When the game was over, the Canadians lined up at centre ice and saluted the crowd with their sticks, and the appreciative multitude responded with a ringing ovation. Then the gallant kids trooped off, and there were many tear-spangled schnozzes in the building.

There were more tears in the Canada dressing room when Father David Bauer, the architect of this program, went in to thank the boys for all their effort.

"What a man he is," Davidson said. "We would have done anything for that guy. He taught me more about myself and life. And he taught us what it is to play for something besides money. I know it sounds mushy and old fashioned, but he gave us a different reason to play—for the game, and the people in the game."

So the Canadians didn't do it, but while it might sound contradictory, they proved that it can be done. And it was our brightest night in international hockey since Paul Henderson in 1972.

May 21, 1980

June 16, 1980
GAY LOVE: IT ISN'T WICKED OR UNIQUE
Few articles in Citizen *history generated the furious reaction of readers as a two-day series of stories on gays in Ottawa. Hundreds called to criticize the paper for "promoting" homosexuality on the front page. Many cancelled their subscriptions. Homosexuals accused the paper of reinforcing stereotypes and predicted an increase in gay bashing. Reporter Richard Labonté, who described*

*his life as a homosexual in one story, received more than
50 abusive calls, and was threatened outside his home. Here's
an excerpt from his story:*

BY RICHARD LABONTE
Citizen staff writer

At what age does a child learn to love? For me, the knowledge that I could and should came at 14.

And at what age is a child told that his love is wicked? At the same age—when the loved one is a childhood buddy named Jack.

We were inseparable at school, at play, while giggling after dark over mysterious pleasures. We were, in retrospect, in love.

But the disapproval of parents and peers was so searing that we retreated from each other—no surprise at that age—and from love: Jack, perhaps, forever—we never saw each other again; me, for nearly 10 years.

It took that decade to come to terms with homosexuality, to shrug off the attitudes and the values—and the irrational hatreds—of a culture determined to ignore, to condemn and to suppress my sexuality.

I was lucky, an inclination to challenge society's norms on several levels, including its oppression of lesbians and gay men, led to a decision, not too late and with little anguish, not to make mine a secret love.

Since then, it's been a lot of fun. And it certainly hasn't hurt anyone.

•

It can't really be said that I'm proud to be gay; that's just the way it is, and I'm quite happy this way.

And you'll never spot me on the street—unless you made the connection after seeing me hug a male friend hello or greet a male lover with a light touch of affection, just like any couple.

But not like many gay couples.

Many gay people are afraid to display that natural affection toward friends and lovers and each other, because the consequences are often tragic: jeers, physical attack, lost jobs.

Women have been thrown out of apartments in Ottawa for living with and loving other women; men—me, others—have been attacked with clubs and rocks in Ottawa for walking hand in hand with other men. It's not hard to understand why so many lesbians and gay men believe they must live furtive lives.

Everything in society—every movie, every billboard, everything done as second nature in public—reminds the gay person that he or she is considered unnatural and abnormal. No wonder that the usual defence takes the form of rationalizing secrecy, of living in a closet.

But every time we refrain from an act of public affection, every time

Merivale Gardens   —*Lynn Ball, Citizen*
Joan Millet hopes her neighbors will all quit smoking

October 2, 1980

we are unable to take a loved one to the office party, every time we cannot bring ourselves to challenge anti-gay comments, we die a little, a little every day.

There are nervous breakdowns, suicides, bouts of self-hatred, clandestine motel-room encounters which lead to another "homosexual slaying"—not because gays are involved, but because gays are not permitted to be gay.

•

How is a gay man—I will not speak for lesbians—gay?

There are the stereotypes: by swishing through life, by cruising the parks, by sweating in the steambaths, by prowling through public washrooms, by seducing every man he meets, by being obsessed with sex, by living lonely and alone.

There is truth to these stereotypes: some men, not realizing that they are only conforming to society's view of what they must be, swish and cruise and prowl and sweat, and are not happy, or do not believe that love is real unless it meets society's expectations of "manly," and so dress it up with macho leathers and denims.

Other men gladly embrace the stereotypes of promiscuity and anonymity and defiantly hurl them back at society, content to live completely at odds with the standards of monogamy and family unit.

But still others, most others, fathers of families and colleagues at work and neighbors next door and teenagers 14 years old—a wonderfully diverse bunch—fit none of the imagined homosexual styles.

They have accepted that they love other men, sometimes late in life, sometimes early; they are satisfied with a series of quick, sometimes anonymous, sexual encounters, or they live quietly in the company of a lover, for months or years at a time; they acknowledge and explore a gentle, pacific and non-competitive cast to their character; they develop a social circle of friends, gay and straight, with whom they are open and comfortable.

We are, as we have chanted, everywhere, and we are gay in many ways beyond but not excluding the bars, the baths, the toilets, the parks. The stereotypes don't apply. . . .

•

The end of shame for gay people, like the freedom of blacks from bigotry and the exorcism of sexism directed towards women, has depended on determined questioning of norms, has relied on radical enunciation of alternatives, and can only continue if society is pressed to move towards greater tolerance of its minorities.

But within the gay community, there is sometimes angry discussion over whether pressing for inclusion of sexual orientation in human rights codes—Quebec is the only province which promises lesbians and gay men freedom from discrimination—is the end of the struggle,

May 15, 1981

only the beginning, or even worth all the bother.

Laws don't change attitudes, some say: the struggle should take the form of a separatist culture, for example, or should include the abolition of all laws governing sexual behavior; others say gays should press hard on the political front by electing gays to political office—a movement under way in Toronto, where long-time gay activist George Hislop is a strong candidate for alderman.

It has taken a decade of anger and activism to make being openly gay even thinkable; it will take years more of battling myths, fear, ignorance and lies before being causally gay in Canada can be comfortable.

Why does this have to be? Gay people at the most extreme are only as much of a threat to the world of the majority as any other social movement—the feminist, the anti-nuclear, the socialist, the separatist—and surely are entitled to the freedoms any minority must be granted in a democratic majoritarian society.

That's the most extreme of us. The rest of us are a meek lot.

We want to live free of fear or physical threat; we want to assert our creativity and caress our companions and permit our fellow gays, young and old and men and women, to bypass the traumatic process of coming out—of convincing themselves that their style of love is not wicked, or worse, unique.

May 12, 1982

November 15, 1980
WHAT'S WRONG WITH THE RIDERS?
Owner Allan Waters evades
the tough questions, offers no solutions

Longtime football writer Tom Casey's perceptive article on Rough Riders owner Allan Waters presaged much that was to come for the football franchise over the next 15 years—losing teams, absentee ownership, mounting debts and the Riders' eventual collapse in 1996.

BY TOM CASEY
Citizen sports writer

TORONTO—Allan Waters is a self-made millionaire. He claims he got there by basing his business decisions on logic and hard work. And he claims he applies the same sound principles to his ownership of the Ottawa Rough Riders.

Given how the Riders have fared the past two seasons, Ottawa football fans might be right to ask if that's enough.

The team president has been criticized as an owner in absentia. Fans complain he hasn't done enough to make it appealing to go to Lansdowne Park. There is too much player turnover, they say, too much inconsistency on the field, and the halftime shows are lousy.

Some people say the team is not only an unprofessional organization, it's cheap. The Riders won't spend money to get quality players.

The fans are doing more than growl and complain. Some of them have stopped going to the park. For the second straight year, attendance has fallen. This season it dropped by about 19,000. The club also stands to lose about $100,000, the largest shortfall since Waters took over three years ago.

In an interview with the *Citizen* this week, Waters acknowledged many of these problems. He said he'll meet with head coach George Brancato, general manager Jake Dunlap and executive vice president Terry Kielty soon after the Grey Cup to tackle the team's pressing issues. But he refused to discuss solutions and left a strong impression that Ottawa fans shouldn't expect much in the way of change.

Last year the Riders had one of the lowest payrolls in the Canadian Football League and certainly the smallest in the Eastern Conference. Ottawa paid out about $1 million in salaries; Toronto, meanwhile, spent $2.2 million.

Waters admitted the gap is a source of concern to him, but he insisted he will remain within certain spending perameters.

"I've never spent thousands and thousands against my business competitors—if I did I would never have gotten ahead," said Waters, who owns controlling interest in the CHUM Limited radio empire.

"I've used a fair bit of ingenuity and creativity to get ahead. I think you can apply the same tactics to running a football team."

He strongly disagreed with the suggestion the Riders are a penny-pinching operation.

"I'm a man whose main concern is efficiency," he said. "I'm not one for frills. I spend what I need to spend. No more."

While many wealthy businessmen consider professional sports franchises their toys, Waters made it clear that's not his philosophy.

"Football is a business, let me assure you of that. When I purchased the club I didn't anticipate making huge profits nor did I anticipate taking big losses. So far neither has happened."

He also took exception to the suggestion the club is a convenient tax writeoff for his other business interests.

"Nothing of the kind," he countered. "People seem to think because I live in Toronto, I don't have a handle on the Ottawa situation—that's not true. I've been in business in Ottawa since 1967 when I bought CFRA. I'm in and out of Ottawa often enough to have a good reading of the Ottawa people and their demands as football fans. "

Waters is hopeful next year's full interlocking schedule will spark fan interest, and the club is plotting its own separate plan to tackle slipping attendance. However, he refused to say whether that includes increased benefits for season ticket holders. At the moment, the only advantage they get is first call on playoff tickets—when the team makes it

May 12, 1982

May 12, 1982

to the playoffs.

Waters also said plans are under way to revitalize the club after an indifferent 7-9 season. But just how, Waters wouldn't say except that the team will spend more money. How much more? Again, he wouldn't say. "That remains to be resolved," he replied.

Waters mentioned that next year, CFL teams will each receive another $300,000 in television revenue, increasing the total to more than $500,000 per club. But every team gets the increase, so there's no advantage to Ottawa.

Waters said he isn't interested in getting involved in bidding wars over players, anyway. Nor is he interested in buying a superstar.

"It has yet to be proven a big-name player can make a team," he said. "The answer in my view is to have a well-balanced team because the players will pull together more. When you get a superstar you often get the old story: 'Let the superstar do it.'"

How much is a reasonable income for a top player? Again, Waters was noncommittal. All he'll admit is that the pressure is on his organization to find talent.

"It means we have to beat the bushes and trade shrewdly — just like Ottawa used to before I bought the team. Even now I don't think we're that far off," he said.

Although last year's Grey Cup champions, the Edmonton Eskimos, don't have a superstar, they have a lot of well-paid players. Many of their players are in the $50,000-$60,000 range. Riders had only two players—Tony Gabriel and Condredge Holloway—who made more than $50,000 this season.

Edmonton also has two full-time recruiters and the club won't hesitate to spend $25,000 on a signing bonus. Riders consider $10,000 a large signing bonus....

"I know I'm repeating myself, but with good scouting, hard work and creativity, I think the Ottawa Rough Riders can pull it off."

Only time will tell.

November 14, 1983
SHE'S GOT A TICKET TO RIDE—DAILY
BY JENNIFER JACKSON
Citizen staff writer

For as long as anyone can remember, Georgette Pepin, 73, has travelled the bus daily from Montreal to Ottawa and back.

Some days, she says, she visits her cousin, Mary Pepin, 79. Some days she just sits in the Ottawa bus terminal and waits for the bus to take her home again.

Doesn't it ever get boring? "Oh, no, it keeps me healthy.

The doctor told me I shouldn't stay at home."

Georgette says she's been making the four-hour trip almost every day since 1928, eating breakfast at the Montreal station and lunch and dinner at the Ottawa station.

Has it really been 55 years?

Cafeteria manager Nicholas Phillias replies, "Does Georgette say she's been coming for that long? Then she probably has been."

Marjorie Brousseau, a waitress in the Ottawa Voyageur cafeteria on Catherine Street, says, "She's been coming here for as long as I can remember and I've been working here 18 years."

But why?

Georgette peers up, her brown eyes large through the thick lenses in her glasses: "I like it."

On Friday, Georgette said her cousin Mary was out of town. So she decided to just sit and wait for her bus back to Montreal.

"I don't think I'll go out today," she says waving a small, wrinkled hand at the freezing rain beyond the depot windows. "The weather isn't very good. I think I'll stay here."

Five hours later, she's still there, a tiny woman in an orange plastic chair, sitting quietly with her hands folded in her lap. She has no newspapers, no paperbacks, no knitting. Nor does she watch the tiny black television sets fixed to some of the chairs.

"They're too close to my eyes. I don't like them."

Instead, she watches people. They've changed over the years, she says. In the 1930s, they used to carry cardboard suitcases and their shoes were scuffed. Then suddenly, there were all these young boys in uniform. "I worked for the Red Cross, folding bandages."

Now, she says, things are different.

"I saw a young man the other day, his hair was like this . . . " She touches her fingertips together as if in prayer, indicating a punker's spiked hairstyle.

Every day is the same, she says. She wakes up in her Montreal boarding house and dresses, tucking her hair under her blue felt hat with the faded satin band and pulling on her brown coat and boots.

She walks to the Montreal bus depot, five minutes from her home near Dorchester Street and, by 5:30 a.m., she's in the cafeteria having her breakfast: toast, coffee, maybe some eggs, maybe cereal.

And then, at 7:45, she gets the Ottawa local, the bus that goes to all the small towns along the way.

At 11:45, she's in Ottawa and she heads for her usual table in the bus terminal cafeteria, a small table for two, just by the kitchen door. She sits with her back to the door, her coat draped over the opposite chair.

She orders different things, but she always orders a lot: "She has soup, juice, a big meal all the time," says Brousseau. "And don't you

November 3, 1982

make her wait because she'll let you know about it."

She pays her bill and calls her cousin, who may come to pick her up in her car. If not, Georgette may walk around a bit or just wait in the station.

Then she goes back in the cafeteria, has dinner and catches her bus in the early evening.

She walks back to her small room and goes to bed. The next day it all starts again.

But that's $17.55 a day for return bus fare and another $10 or so for meals. Doesn't it get expensive?

"Oh, I get by," She's vague about her income, but she does get the old-age pension, she says.

Georgette says she is one of 16 children, all raised in Montreal. She never married, and for a time worked as a hospital assistant until eczema forced her to quit, she says.

She doesn't come to Ottawa absolutely every day. For instance, last week she told Brousseau she wouldn't be making the trip today because she "had to help some people."

June 17, 1984
BLACK SATURDAY IN SHAWINIGAN
Before he became one of CBC's top television correspondents, Neil Macdonald's gritty, intelligent style and no-nonsense reporting earned him a reputation as one of the Citizen's *best young reporters. Here's an excerpt from one of his first political stories.*

BY NEIL MACDONALD
Citizen staff writer

SHAWINIGAN, Que.—As the preliminary whipping of Jean Chrétien came over the color TV in Taverne Chez Armand Saturday afternoon, Denis Savard had already lost interest.

Like most kids in Chrétien's home town 165 kilometres northeast of Montreal, 25-year-old Denis was brought up believing that the energy minister is just a bit this side of God.

But the future looked dim Saturday as Denis jammed a quarter into the pool table and viciously racked the balls:

"Turner, Who's he? Jean ate dirt just like me and the rest of this town. He knows what it's like to be *defavoris*. Shawinigan has no hope now."

To put a fine point on it, Saturday was a black day in Shawinigan. Brave-faced but black.

They were watching Jean the bonhomme, the guy who climbed out of the slogging factory trap, the guy who made Shawinigan his last name—they were watching him lose the leadership of the federal Liberal Party to an anglo from Ontario.

Friday night, a question on Chrétien's chances had brought an "Ah yes," with raised fists. By late Saturday afternoon, the question was met with shrugs, raised eyebrows, pursed lips and mournful whistles.

By the time Chrétien's defeat was finally announced, they could not have cared less. It's Jean or nothing. Shawinigan has no interest in the Liberal family or notions of unanimity.

There was real anger in the eyes of a laborer at Chez Armand as he glanced at the smiling face of John Turner on the TV screen.

"Ah, the hell with him," Albert Desrosiers muttered. "To hell with him. An Ontario guy. He's going to shake your hand and ask about you and care?"

Still, despite their disgust, Denis and Desrosiers both said they will vote Liberal in the next election.

"I wouldn't want to see any other party in power," said Denis. "Yes I would vote for Jean if it meant Turner became prime minister. You just have to live in Shawinigan to understand that."

In Baie Shawinigan, three kilometres away in the valley of the Saint Maurice River, Chrétien was still the hero he has always been.

Emmanuel Laberge, 63, watched Jean grow up in the brick house at 121 Rue Pie XII, beside his little billiard parlor.

The scrappy kid went from working in the Belgo pulp-and-paper plant to a lawyer's practice downtown to speeches in churches and a cabinet post. He even appeared with the Queen on TV.

Moreover, he held onto their values, marrying Aline from down the street and staying married.

Laberge didn't bother listening to the speeches Saturday night and couldn't care less about the convention coverage on television.

"Jean, he's a miracle. We are so proud. Petit gars, that doesn't mean he's a little guy. It means he's an ordinary guy. He's still among us."

Laberge gave up his billiard parlor—he says Jean played a pretty good game of pool—for the more profitable life of a depanneur.

In the store later, Rejean Rondeau lets out a snort when asked by Laberge whether Chrétien should be prime minister.

"Let us say there is no one like him. Everybody, everybody in this town loves the guy."

August 17, 1984

THE OTTAWA
Citizen

LOW 10, HIGH 17 /F1

THURSDAY, OCTOBER 3, 1991 FINAL • • •   50¢/$3 WEEKLY DELIVERED (GST included)

Law ends PS strike

◄ RCMP officer peers out from behind egg-splattered riot shield during Hill rally   Striker rises above sea of umbrellas by climbing post ▼

70,000 sent back on job at noon today

By David Pugliese

PUBLIC SERVICE ALLIANCE

The King lives — on Elvis Lane

By Carrie Buchanan

MISSION: POSSIBLE BUT PRICEY

Departments spend $550,000 describing jobs

By Louise Crosby

Talk's not so cheap

Some mission statements of federal departments are only a sentence or two and seem to state the obvious.

■ **Indian and Northern Affairs** is "working together to make Canada a better place for First Nations and northern peoples." The cost for outside work — $15,290

■ **Consumer and Corporate Affairs** aims to "promote the fair and efficient operation of the marketplace in Canada." Outside costs — $15,273

■ The **Canadian International Development Agency (CIDA)** supports "sustainable development in developing countries." That was prepared within the department.

STRIKE INFORMATION

For updates on the public service strike, just call 721-1990 on your touch tone phone, then enter 5000

TOUCHLINE

■ **PAY EQUITY:** Strike's forgotten issue/E1

Long-serving senator dies

Senator Hazen Argue died in Regina Wednesday at age 70. He was Canada's longest-serving parliamentarian, having served 18 years in the Commons and 25 in the Senate. His career spanned five decades and two political parties — the CCF, which he once led, and the Liberals. **Please see full story on page A4.**

Argue
5-decade career

INDEX

Citizen
PLEASE RECYCLE

Lottery
The winning numbers in Wednesday's 6/49 draw are 31, 36, 40, 43, 48, and 49. The bonus number is 33. The Encore number is 550674.

Action Line	G6	Editorials	A12
Astrology	F5	Fashion	D1
Births, deaths	G4, G8	Gordon	A13
Bridge	F6	Ibbitson	C3
Brown's Beat	C1	Letters	A12
Bureaucrats	A4	Living	D12
Business	B1	MacGregor	A2
Canada	A3	MacKinnon	A4
City-Region	C1	Nichols	A3
Classified	F1, G1	Scoreboard	H4
Comics	H11	Sports	H1
Courts	A5	Television	E6
Crossword	G3	Weather	D1
Dear Abby	D12	World	A6
Entertainment	E1	Young	A4

Main Citizen number	829-9100
Want ads	829-9321
Circulation	596-1950

MAIL: **The Ottawa Citizen**, 1101 Baxter Rd., Box 5020, Ottawa, Ont., K2C 3M4, is registered as second class mail No. 0279

Photos See **MISSION A2**

Canada joins OAS delegation to Haiti

By Norma Greenaway

WASHINGTON — Canada will join a nine-member delegation planning to fly to Haiti within the next day or so to demand that the military junta step down and that the country's first elected president be restored.

■ **NO COUP:** Military denies takeover A8

394

Goodbye Disco

The Fifteenth Decade, 1985-1994

TOM KENT'S SWEEPING IDEAS for reforming the newspaper industry never got much of a hearing on Parliament Hill. But a phrase that popped up several times during testimony at his inquiry resounded loudly at the *Citizen*: disco journalism. It was a clever jibe, but not entirely fair. Then, like now, the paper employed many first-rate reporters and editors. The *Citizen*'s local coverage was thorough and often creative, and generally cited as a factor in the *Journal*'s demise. During the early 1980s, the paper's parliamentary staff broke several important stories on the emerging constitutional crisis. In fact, Aileen McCabe changed the entire tone of the patriation talks when she revealed the contents of a memo outlining the Trudeau government's devious strategy to outfox the provinces.

But like most insults, the disco journalism crack carried more than a grain of truth. By 1980, soft stories (how to throw a toga party, where to buy the best doughnuts) and ill-advised contests were not only filling inside sections, they were beginning to creep onto the front page. After the launch of *tgif*, an especially frothy weekly entertainment and lifestyles section, humour columnist Charles Gordon quipped that the *Citizen* had become a newspaper for "people who move their hips when they read."

Stung by the criticism, and worried that Kent's inquiry could lead to unwanted government interference in newspaper decision-making, Southam's executives decided it was time for action. In 1982, they replaced publisher Bill Newbigging with Paddy Sherman, a diminutive hard-nosed newsman who had been running the Vancouver *Province*. "I was given a straightforward task: bring up the tone of the place," Sherman said later. "I thought I should get to work quickly."

And he did. On his first day, Sherman famously replaced a splash on

Regular Sunday publishing begins, September 28, 1988.

Opposite: By 1990, a new generation of computers brought about "desktop publishing," which allowed type to be produced in shapes, colours and configurations that were impossible by traditional means. These pieces of type were then pasted up with the text and headlines produced by the existing photo typesetters and prepared as four colour plates for the offset press.

ice cream taste-testing between editions with an analysis of Soviet politics. Within a month, he had refocused the paper's world, national and local coverage and launched the Observer, a Saturday section devoted to analysis, background and opinion. Sherman strengthened the staff by hiring several high-profile journalists, including columnists Roy MacGregor and Marjorie Nichols. And he set up the investigative reporting team—Stevie Cameron, Neil Macdonald, Dan Turner and Greg Weston—that later deposed Robert Coates as defence minister after disclosing details of his visit to a German strip club.

In 1985, Sherman surprised everyone by naming former official languages commissioner Keith Spicer as editor to replace Russell Mills, who moved up to become assistant publisher. Spicer's inexperience and quirky intellect resulted in some wild swerves, but they also led to upgraded arts and books pages and a lively insight section.

Over the next few years, the movement in top management became a game of musical chairs. Sherman moved to Southam head office and was replaced by Mills, who gave way to Clark Davey before Mills returned for a second go-'round. Spicer left to run the CRTC and was replaced by Gordon Fisher and then Jim Travers.

But throughout the comings and goings, the changes begun by Sherman started to pay dividends. From 1984 to '94, the *Citizen* scooped up a dozen National Newspaper Awards—it had won only one in the previous 35 years—as well as the prestigious Michener Award for Meritorious Journalism.

The improvements also left the *Citizen* in a strong position to respond to news that the Sun newspaper chain had bought the borderline upstart *Sunday Herald* and planned to launch a seven-day-a-week tabloid in Ottawa in September 1988. Within two weeks, the *Citizen* increased newsroom staff by two dozen and launched its own Sunday edition, getting it out 10 days before the *Sun*'s first Ottawa paper hit the streets. For *Citizen* staff it was a satisfying moment, but for reasons beyond the new Sunday paper—after eight years, competition had returned to Ottawa's English-language newspaper market. For journalists, there could hardly be better news.

September 12, 1987

January 7, 1985
TRIUMPHANT HOMECOMING FOR A RISING STAR
(Excerpt from a concert review.)

BY BILL PROVICK
Citizen music writer

It's not hard to flash back 10 years and picture Bryan Adams as a teenager living in Bells Corners, attending Colonel By High, putting his first bands together and heading down to the Civic Centre to check out the big names in rock.

Adams has confided that he used to imagine himself up on stage as the object of all the adulation and dream about it all happening to him. Saturday night the dream came true.

Though the fast-rising young rocker now living in Vancouver has performed here before as an opening act, this was his first time as headliner at the city's biggest indoor rock venue.

It couldn't have worked out better. The Civic Centre was packed to the rafters and the joint was rocking. Everyone—off-stage, on-stage and off-stage-climbing-on-stage—had an absolutely great time....

Adams isn't one of your pretty boy teen idols. In fact, with his jeans and white shirt over white T-shirt, his every-day, every-boy style nicely accentuates a youthful charm mixed with manly presence. Adams also has a voice that sounds as bruised at the concert's start as most rock wailers sound at the end of a particularly torturous performance.

No, Adams is no Prince and he's no Boss, but he is a real trouper—a hard-working, hard-rocking rocker who is fun to be with. His songs aren't the kind that will reshape rock, but they're strong and they're highly appealing.

For a good portion of Saturday's show, the ragged shrillness of the music down front almost undermined that appeal, but Adams was obviously pacing himself. And later, as he began to cut loose, moving more and interacting more with the excited crowd, the show got as good as expected—and as good as good rock shows get.

This all led to numerous encores, including a bunch of enthusiastically received songs from his new *Reckless* album. In fact, one got the feeling that Adams and company could have been there all night except the stage hands were obviously tiring from gently but efficiently pulling mobs of young women off the shoulders of the band.

Sometimes homecomings are triumphant because everyone wants them to be. Sometimes they are triumphant because they're earned. Such was the case with Adams. It may have seemed like a lot of grateful adulation to heap on one performer, but the kid worked hard and made his dream come true....

September 12, 1987

June 19, 1985
LITTLE THINGS CAN STILL MEAN A LOT TO A CANADIAN AT LARGE IN LONDON

For nearly three decades until his retirement in 2005, Charles Gordon was among the Citizen's *best-loved columnists. His droll wit and love of understatement belied an incisive intellect and a passion for social and political fairness, issues Gordon always approached with a firm, but light touch. His enthusiasm for jazz, books and baseball on the radio was well known to readers, as was the quiet patriotism that peeked out from behind his satires of Canadian life, as it does in this excerpt.*

BY CHARLES GORDON

LONDON—There is no reason for the Canadian, in London, in June, to feel the slightest bit homesick. All around him he hears accents like his own.

It's true that the accents belong to Americans, but a Canadian in London can't have everything.

Still, if he wants to keep up with the Expos, he can buy the *International Herald Tribune* or, for complete box scores, the international edition of *USA Today*. Even *The Daily Telegraph* prints scores—albeit occasionally and with somewhat less than full comprehension (a zero becomes a dash, as if the score were incomplete).

It is an unfortunate fact that no Canadian is now on display at Madame Tussaud's, but there is a bust of Sir John A. in the crypt at St. Paul's and a fine memorial to Gen. Wolfe—"who, after surmounting by ability and valour all obstacles of art and nature was slain in the moment of victory"—at Westminster Abbey.

A guide explains, a bit uncertainly, to an American tourist who Wolfe was. The American nods. "They beat the French," he tells the guide.

Canada's profile is not high, it must be said. A bus tour guide points out South Africa House, as the bus rolls through Trafalgar Square, and neglects to mention Canada House, which has been there longer than the oldest pigeon. Later, as the bus approaches Grosvenor Square, the guide identifies it as the site of the American Embassy—which it most assuredly is, judging by the size of the eagle sitting atop one of the city's ugliest buildings—and the Canadian Embassy, which it isn't, Canada having a High Commission, rather than an embassy.

The newspapers do not carry the best Canadian news—there is no mention of David Peterson or John Nunziata—but there are little items here and there. "Ottawa fails to end human rights rift" gets an inside page of *The Times*. A feature on James Bond's Miss Moneypenny in one of the weekend color supplements points out that she is played by Lois Maxwell, a Canadian.

And a certain amount of attention is paid to Conrad Black, who has just purchased what may turn out to be controlling interest in *The Daily Telegraph* (which may mean no more of those box score dashes).

The Guardian says that "the deal looks an extremely good one from the point of view of Mr. Black" and notes that "his mother's family was part of the syndicate that controlled the *Telegraph* in the last century."

The Sunday Times, in a profile headed, "The Canada dry who wants the Telegraph," says of Black that: "He detests journalists as a bunch of degenerate reprobates."

September 12, 1987

The Sunday Times then asks itself why Black never bothered with politics, "especially now his views are flavor of the month in Canada, the U.S. and the U.K. The answer, according to one old friend, was that Canada is too small to offer enough challenge. Fleet Street may just be the start of his U.K. ambitions."

On the financial pages of *The Observer* an advertisement for something called The Canadian Balanced Growth Fund of Waverley Asset Management says that "it is now becoming clear to the international investment community that since the new Canadian government was elected in September 1984 Canada has opened its investment doors for international business."

This has a reassuringly familiar ring to it. Meanwhile, Canada's aggressive export industry has managed to put Cooper baseball gloves into the sporting goods department at Harrods.

An even more exciting find is discovered in a Chelsea punk store specializing in second-hand American clothes, notable among them, if you can believe it, cast-off baseball uniform shirts dating from the pre-polyester era. One such, in grey trimmed with red, bears on the back the words Vanier Trucking Company.

Where it counts, Canada matters.

September 12, 1987

June 7, 1986

CHILDREN, MAYBE, BUT THEY FIGHT GROWNUP WARS
Before he became editor of the Citizen *in 1991, Jim Travers was an respected correspondent for Southam News, turning out insightful, hard-edged analysis from Africa, the Middle East and Parliament Hill. But as this excerpt shows, Travers' work also brimmed with compassion and a finely tuned sense of outrage.*

BY JAMES TRAVERS

RAMADI, Iraq—Dust puffs around their feet as the boys chase the patchwork ball, skittering and bouncing, over the stony, makeshift soccer pitch. It is a typical Middle East scene. On any given day, thousands of children in hundreds of cities and villages play pick-up soccer the way Canadians play street hockey.

But this is no ordinary town and these are not ordinary boys. This is a prison, and the players are Iranian children captured during the bloody and senseless Gulf war.

On this winter day when the sun already presages a blistering summer, 16-year-old Ahmad Taqi stands alone on the sidelines listlessly watching the game that will wax and wane all day. He is very slight, and the combination of his large brown eyes and loose-fitting fatigues make him seem terribly young, terribly vulnerable.

But Taqi is a veteran both of war and this showpiece camp built on the edge of the desert 115 kilometres west of Baghdad. Stirred by patriotic propaganda and recruited by the Revolutionary Guards, Taqi went to war for the Ayatollah Khomeini. And now, to please his captors, he wears on his green lapel a small plastic portrait of Iraqi President Saddam Hussein....

Taqi considers himself lucky. Three-and-a-half years ago, when he was 12, Taqi, his two brothers and many thousands of other Iranian children were given 15 days of rudimentary combat training and ordered into battle. Wearing plastic keys to paradise around their necks and with notes to Allah in their pockets, they became the vanguard of the "human wave" offensive that Iran thrust across the border into Iraq.

"You take the sweet drink they give and they say you will be unseen," Taqi says. The drink, or luck, worked for Taqi. But his brothers were cut down in what the Iraqis like to call their "killing zone."

Horror stories abound about the use of children in this war. Iraq claims teenage troops were used to clear minefields for tanks and as fodder for Hussein's modern cannons.

Iran, which has more than 1.2 million men in uniform, insists that no one younger than 16 serves in the Ayatollah's army. But the evidence, here and elsewhere, suggests otherwise, and no one buys the story.

The Gulf war has focused attention on Iran, but it is hardly alone in its recruitment of those that westerners automatically consider children. From here in the Gulf to southern Africa and most of the world's hot-spots, children are fighting grown-up wars. And more often than not, they are among the first and worst casualties.

In Libya, militarism has touched the lives of its 1.5 million students so deeply that, in the wacky lingo of Moammar Gadhafi's revolution, schools are called "barracks." Inside those barracks, army instructors show 14-year-olds how to use light automatic weapons. By the time Libyans, girls as well as boys, graduate from university, they are ready to fly a Soviet MiG 25 or operate a surface-to-surface missile.

The mix of youth and guns produces some of Libya's stranger sights and sounds. Girls can be seen with elaborate pantyhose peeking out below their uniforms and can be heard complaining that breaking down machine-guns chips nail polish.

But it also breeds a worrying brand of fanaticism. During the recent crisis with the U.S., a Libyan student wrote a note to a reporter claiming, "We could not wring the neck of a chicken but we could trample over the corpses of millions of American terrorists to bring peace to the world."

Across southern Africa, children have long been a part of the independence struggle. In South Africa, very young children are often at the front of stone-throwing crowds and just as often are injured or

September 12, 1987

killed by police whips and rubber bullets. So many children are anxious to fight the apartheid system that the African National Congress, the main opposition to white rule, has opened a school for them in rural Tanzania to keep them off the firing line.

In Zimbabwe, Mozambique and farther north in Uganda, children took to the bush to fight oppressive regimes; now, using the only skill they know, they rob and kill each other.

For many Third World children—nobody knows how many—war is an accepted part of life and death. In societies where almost all children work, where girls in their early teens marry and people die young, no one is surprised when boys go to war.

But there are other places, places on the fringes of the developed world, where child casualties are an enormous part of the national grief. Lebanon is one of those places.

"He just flew up into the air and exploded," is how a Shiite Moslem described the death of a five-year-old boy hit by a sniper's "mushroom" bullet. Lebanese doctors estimate that children make up to 30 per cent of the 100,000 war dead.

But it is the living that worry parents and sociologists. Recently a Beirut mother, Wafika Wairiy, gestured toward her youngest sons sleeping on a bed and said, "These children are different from those born before the war. For them there are too many guns."

Guns are almost everywhere in Beirut; where they are not, children invent them. Among the buildings and neighborhoods shattered by a decade of civil war, children play war games, eerily mimicking the staccato sounds of machine-gun fire and the terrifying whine of incoming shells. . . .

"With all this ugliness around them, one wonders what these children will be like when they grow up," says nursery school teacher Iman Khalife. "For them, life is ruined."

And so it is for the children of war everywhere.

September 12, 1987

September 25, 1988
GUILT: MOTHER TERESA'S COLD, PIOUS GAMBIT
*As a political reporter and columnist, Susan Riley developed a well-
earned reputation for swimming against the current. The column
excerpted here, written amid the otherwise glowing coverage
of Mother Teresa's visit to Ottawa, sparked a flood of angry letters
and calls from readers.*

BY SUSAN RILEY
Citizen national writer

The danger in attacking Mother Teresa is that we don't know for sure who might be on her side. What if there is a God? What if He has chosen the diminutive Albanian (as newsmagazines call her) to carry a warning to our sex-drenched, self-absorbed society?

What if—as she suggested in Ottawa on the weekend—abortion is Satan's work and Prime Minister Mulroney and the other prevaricating politicians are the devil's agents?

Maybe an awful punishment awaits those for whom abortion is not a "terrible, terrible evil" but an awkward tragedy.

These may seem fanciful, even paranoid notions—but not to anyone who was educated by The Nuns. Compared with The Nuns, the Jesuits were soft-hearted triflers.

On Parliament Hill (nearly swallowed by a shell-like stage), tiny Mother Teresa was the reincarnation of the small, intense zealots who taught so many Catholic children in the '50s and '60s to fear God and follow orders.

The Nuns were models of self-denial; the only thing they wouldn't share was virtue. Their faith, like a military drill, never deviated. They had a piety that precluded mercy. They talked a good deal about love—particularly love of God—but they traded in threats.

There was no room for ambivalence in their theology, nor is there in Mother Teresa's. That's what makes it so powerful, and so frightening. Over an echoing sound system, Mother Teresa repeated a familiar mantra: God loves us. We must love God. Every fetus is a gift from God. Then, to warm applause: "If you don't want the child, I want that child. Give it me."

It is, presumably, too literal-minded to wonder how a pregnant woman from rural Newfoundland, for example, would get herself or her newborn to Calcutta. Perhaps God will handle the travel details.

In other ways, Mother Teresa (like The Nuns) is chillingly practical. Women who have abortions and the doctors who help them should be imprisoned for murder, says the winner of the 1979 Nobel Peace Prize. It is as simple as a Grade 5 science lesson: "The child is God's creation. She is killing the child. The mother should be faced with that reality."

Then she unsheathed the most fearsome weapon in The Nuns' arsenal: guilt. A woman who has an abortion "will never forget that she, herself, has killed her own child." Not when Mother Teresa is around with her gentle reminders.

The Catholic Church didn't invent guilt, but The Nuns—particularly those who, like Mother Teresa, taught elementary school 20 years ago—perfected its use.

Sadly, Mother Teresa made no mention of the most humane, effective and inexpensive alternative to abortion: artificial birth control. But then blind faith tends to impair vision, and birth control—as The Nuns always said—can lead to sex.

Like the Pope, Mother Teresa is driven by conviction but handi-

selena
mienu

Business   Evening
Weekend Wear

101 Sparks Street
Ottawa 236-6738

September 25, 1988

capped by faith. It is a faith designed for a different culture and a different time. Her Catholicism is a human invention; God, if He really is omniscient, would never have been so narrow.

Mother Teresa doesn't seem to see that this society, disgustingly rich though it is, doesn't need discipline; it needs compassion. And not only for the unborn. It is easy to love a possibility; far harder to love an ordinary human being. The last thing a woman facing abortion needs is the harsh judgment of celibate clerics.

But it is impertinent to offer policy advice to a saint. After all, Mother Teresa and her sisters have saved thousands of the world's most wretched, and eased the dying of thousands of others. That good work gives her moral authority; the world's media and the anti-abortion movement have given her a political voice.

Despite her disclaimers, she has offered that voice to the Religious Right for whom abortion is only one front in a holy war against homosexuality, feminism, liberalism, and the metric system.

Around Parliament Hill last weekend, there were scarlet and gold ecclesiastical banners reading: Tradition. Family. Property.

Property? Since when has real estate become a cardinal virtue?

Like many recovering Catholics, I'm not afraid of The Nuns any more. Just of the company they keep.

Long Overdue

THE MOOS BROTHERS

September 25, 1988

January 2, 1989
SURVIVING SHORE'S SIBERIA

Lynn McAuley was not only a pioneer—she was the Citizen's *first female sports columnist and sports editor—her editing skills and genius for developing strong story ideas transformed the paper's "Weekly" magazine into the best insight section in Canada in the late 1990s.*

BY LYNN MCAULEY

On one of those sunny, crisp days just after Christmas, Brian Kilrea, who was within days of reaching his 500th career victory as a junior hockey coach, sat in his office talking about coaching.

This was natural enough, both things, Kilrea talking and Kilrea talking about coaching. He likes them both and he does both very well.

Eventually, inevitably perhaps, the conversation turned to those who had been his coaches, and out came the tale of Eddie Shore.

A lot has been said about Eddie Shore, most of it entrenched in the self-styled Shore legend in which he is fondly remembered as one of the toughest, meanest and most committed players ever to grace a National Hockey League rink. He is a product of the days when toughness and meanness were not called by their real names of violence and cruelty, and when commitment meant obsession, or blind loyalty.

He was a defenceman for the Boston Bruins in the so-called Golden Age of Sport, the mid-1920s and early '30s, the Depression Era when, we are told, heroes were more important than they are today.

Newspapers, in prose as purple and painful as a new bruise, provided the heroes. They stood as flawless, alabaster idols, larger-than-life, easily able to take their place alongside gladiators, doctors and ministers.

Shore's obsession and his violence basked in this rosy glow. Kilrea wore no such rose-colored glasses when he played under Shore in Springfield in the American League in the early 1960s.

When he retired as a player, Shore bought the Indians and ran the arena in Springfield. He was miserly beyond words, says Kilrea. He shovelled the parking lot himself, ran the concessions and cleared the ice. The thermometer never climbed much above freezing in Eddie Shore's arena, even in the dressing rooms.

Kilrea says his eye for strategy and technique was brilliant. But he also had odd notions and eccentric practices. For example, he didn't want his goalies going down to block shots, so he tied their heads to the cross bar so that they'd strangle themselves if they tried it.

Across the NHL, Springfield became known as Siberia, a gulag for players who had committed minor transgressions with other teams.

"He almost killed us," says Kilrea. "He had no hospital plan for the players, no proper medical attention. He looked on us as animals.

"'He wouldn't even give us proper equipment. We had to hold up our socks with old rubber bands. He didn't give a damn."

Once Kilrea broke his jaw in a game, a double fracture. While in the hospital, he got a call from Shore to get to the rink.

"'I thought he wanted to see me and ask me when I could be back. I get to the rink and he tells me to put on my equipment," says Kilrea, angry and incredulous still, after 25 years. "'Then he tells me to go to one end of the rink and (assistant coach) Pat Egan to go to the other . . . He wanted us to skate like hell into each other and butt heads. He wanted to see how much pain I could absorb so I could play in the game that night. Geeez."

In the end, there was a players' revolt, Kilrea appointed spokesman since he'd stood up to Shore in the past and survived. It was historic, too. Hockey was never to be the same.

"It was pretty bad. More than that, very bad. He threatened us all with fines for 'indifferent play.' And when we said we'd strike (then NHL president) Clarence Campbell phoned me and said that if we went on strike, that I'd never play hockey again. I even heard the Teamsters were ready to move in.

"We'd heard about Alan Eagleson (from another player) and we were pretty impressed. He flew to Springfield, and I don't think he believed what he saw.

June 23, 1990

June 24, 1990

"He forced Shore to sign a deal that made him sell the franchise. The next season, most of us went to the new L.A. franchise (in the NHL)."

Shortly after the so-called Springfield Indians crisis, Eagleson, his reputation earned, and a few members of the Boston Bruins met in a hotel room in Montreal and formed the NHL Players' Association.

"I didn't think much of it at the time," said Kilrea of his role in hockey history. "You never do, I guess. But I'll tell you, I can't believe anybody ever allowed that man to coach human beings. I still can't believe it, even now."

June 22, 1990
A MAN AND HIS FEATHER

Perhaps no Citizen *writer since Austin Cross in the 1940s and '50s was as versatile and prolific as Roy MacGregor. During a dozen years at the* Citizen *in the 1980s and '90s, MacGregor wrote columns and features about everything from the Constitution and life at the cottage to Alexandre Daigle and the fall of the T. Eaton Co. Here's an excerpt from an extended column about one of the defining moments of modern Canadian history.*

BY ROY MACGREGOR
Citizen national affairs columnist

December 7, 1990

WINNIPEG—It is, in the end, the story of one man and one feather. The man is there for history to measure. He has name, age and address: Elijah Harper, 41, of Red Sucker Lake, Northern Manitoba. He has a voice to speak for himself, a past that can be traced and on this day he intends to take action on a matter for which he will be forever judged.

At 12:30 p.m., his very soft "No" from the back row of the Manitoba Legislature is expected to bring an end to debate on the Meech Lake accord. Without unanimous consent, the legislature will adjourn for the weekend. It will sit empty all day Saturday, June 23, 1990, the final deadline for the constitutional amendment that has torn a country apart. On Monday it will be too late, and Elijah Harper knows he will be blamed and cheered for having done what no one else would dare.

The feather is not so easily explained.

To the vast, vast majority of Canadians it does not speak. No one knows where it came from. And what some say it has done here in the capital city of the country's central province would, for most Canadians, defy logic and ridicule belief.

The feather is from an eagle and it is held in Elijah Harper's right hand each time he gives that quick shake of the pony-tail that has said for more than a week now that the Manitoba legislature must stick to the rules of democracy. Every time Elijah Harper does this, the Meech Lake clock moves closer to doomsday in the eyes of his detractors, nearer to victory in the eyes of his supporters.

By day, the feather lies on his desk where he can reach out and touch it. By night it sleeps in a Bible, in the *Book of Isaiah*, and how it came to lie there may tell more of what happened in Winnipeg this week than anything else.

Elijah Harper may have been educated in the missionary residential schools, but he learned from those who followed the traditional ways, what the missionaries would call "heathen" ways.

He was born in the winter of 1949, born on the trapline, the second of what would eventually be the 13 children of Allen and Ethel Harper. He was raised by his grandparents, who clung to the old spiritual teachings. At eight, Elijah Harper was sent away to school where the battle to change young Indians into future whites was fought for eight unhappy years, until he came home again to take up trapping.

Like so many who came through this experience, he found he was straddling two worlds, with the footing unsteady in both. Like the others, he believed, wrongly as it would turn out, that he was alone. It is the mark of his generation....

Harper eventually made it to the University of Manitoba, where he soon linked up with another angry young native, Ovide Mercredi. They soon created an ever-widening circle that would include the likes of Phil Fontaine and Moses Okimaw, all of whom would play key roles in Winnipeg this last week.

They formed a native association and battled the university for their rights, and won. They forced the engineering students to apologize for a satirical newspaper that contained nothing but pictures of drunken Indians. They tried to impeach the president....

•

In 1987, the Meech Lake accord had been passed by 11 first ministers in secret without a single thought for aboriginals. The Manitobans fought alongside other aboriginals for three years, only to find that, on June 9, 1990, they were again left out, despite the promises of a parliamentary committee and the three Manitoba political leaders.

They were as outraged as they were by the engineers' racist attitudes back in the late '60s, but this time they were no longer angry students scrapping back. Mercredi was a lawyer and deputy chief of the Assembly of First Nations. Moses Okimaw was a lawyer. Phil Fontaine was the head chief of all the province. All powerful leaders.

But none of them in Elijah Harper's position.

Harper had gone home without his degree. He had worked and then become chief of his band. Then, in 1981, he became the first treaty Indian to be elected to the provincial legislature. He was elected again in 1982 and served in the NDP cabinet of Howard Pawley.

It was not an illustrious political career. He got in trouble instantly

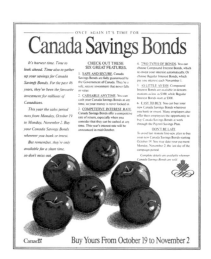

October 8, 1992

when, on election night, a man with no patience for Harper's noisy victory party tried to put his fist through the new member's nose. He got in financial trouble. He was arrested for failing to take a breathalyser test. His marriage faltered. His four children suffered.

But then, around the beginning of Meech Lake, Harper began to pull himself together. He quit drinking. And he started planning....

The moment Harper saw the Meech Lake deal, he called old friend Gordon Mackintosh, now a lawyer but once clerk of the legislature and a procedural expert. They soon discovered to their delight that the Manitoba government had incorrectly introduced the Meech motion.

Elijah Harper decided to run with it as far as he could take it. No one ever expected he would last until the end. Everyone thought he would buckle, at times even Elijah Harper himself.

It was said Harper was under the control of white anti-Meech lawyers. Not only was this patronizing and racist, it was wrong. The native lawyers outnumbered the whites five to two, and all ideas were first run past the 60-odd chiefs of the province. It was said he should have no expert advisers, yet no one questioned the prime minister dispatching a planeload of experts to argue the pro-Meech Lake side....

The meeting with the federal advisers was tough. Harper could not make the dealers from the Prime Minister's Office understand that he was not there to deal, just to listen out of politeness. They could not comprehend why he could not be bought when everyone else they had encountered was buyable. They did not seem to understand, Harper says, this was a stand for "morality," not a grandstand for some payoff.

October 8, 1992

•

But the PMO delegation did not know that, nearly 10 years ago, Elijah Harper had been one of the Canadian chiefs who had gone to London to ask the Queen to make sure aboriginals were as fairly treated in the Constitution as those who dared to call themselves the "founding" races of Canada. They did not know he had refused his invitation to attend the signing ceremony when the Queen came to Ottawa in 1982. They did not know that he has been waiting 10 years for this moment.

Still, they did wear him down, and Elijah Harper is convinced that if it weren't for the feather, he might not have lasted.

His older brother, Saul, a trapper and a dedicated follower of the traditional ways, felt that he was being told to walk to a clearing near Red Sucker Lake. He got there, and the eagle feather was lying in the middle of it. Saul gave it to Darryl Harper, a younger brother, who immediately brought it to Winnipeg, where he gave it to Elijah....

•

In the end, it was the other politicians who grew weary. As Elijah Harper gained strength, it was possible to sit in the Manitoba Legislative Assembly and visibly see the political will evaporate.

In mid-week, his band went out to the clearing at Red Sucker Lake to stand in a circle and ask for strength for him. Chief John Harper, a cousin, looked up into the sky and saw an eagle rising high overhead, slowly circling. Elijah Harper's people pointed and smiled and said the eagle was on Elijah's side and he was going to win.

By Thursday, Elijah Harper seemed as strong inside the legislature as he was outside, where thousands of aboriginals from across the country had gathered to cheer him on, buy $15 T-shirts with his face on the front, declaring "Elijah Harper for Prime Minister."

When Elijah Harper rose to speak against the accord, carefully holding the eagle feather, thunder struck outside, surprising the press who had gathered to talk on this golden summer's day. He spoke and then sat to a standing ovation, carefully placing the feather in his pocket. The feather, he decided, would go to the Mackintosh baby born in the midst of all this turmoil. It will be a reminder to the child that powerful forces were at work in Canada in the second last week of June 1990.

Forces that may, in time, be understood by historians making sense of what, for now, is beyond comprehension for ordinary Canadians.

The Far Side

Years later, Harold Zimmerman, the original "Hookhand" of campfire ghost stories, tells his grandchildren the Tale of the Two Evil Teen-agers.

October 8, 1992

June 1, 1991

OUR LAND: BEAUTIFUL BUT DISPIRITED

As a pure writer, probably no one in Citizen *history surpasses Ken MacQueen, whose elegant touch and eye for detail graced the newspaper's pages during two stints, as a reporter in the early 1980s and national affairs columnist in the '90s. Here's an excerpt from the first of seven essays he wrote on the state of the nation after the collapse of the Meech Lake constitutional accord.*

BY KEN MACQUEEN

ON BOARD THE CANADIAN—The last time I crossed the country, from east to west, was during the free-trade federal election of 1988. I thought: "I'll take the train because soon trains won't run across Canada." This spring, my work allowed me to explore the country again, from west to east. I thought: "I'll take the train because soon there won't be a Canada to cross."

How's that for progress? We are diminished. Poorer, sadder and more confused, all in less than three years. We are not just talking trains. But trains have a lot to say about where we are headed.

Since 1988, VIA Rail's "National Timetable" has dwindled to 46 pages from 62. The two transcontinental trains that left Vancouver daily have dwindled to one train leaving just three times a week. Before the latest round of federal cuts it was possible to buy a 30-day Canrailpass to go anywhere on VIA's route for a flat, cut-rate price. Today, Canrailpasses are sold only to Americans and Europeans—anyone, in fact, but Canadians, whose taxes have long subsidized the system.

Trains have a lot to say about where we are headed, which is nowhere fast. If VIA's "National Timetable" is emaciated, impractical, expensive and limited in scope and direction, surely it is only an accurate reflection of the other national timetable. That timetable is railroading us toward autumn 1992, and a probable referendum on the nation's future. Then, maybe, the end of the line.

A month spent travelling the country found many convinced that Canada's political leaders are, to belabor a point, asleep at the switch. They don't like the engineer much, either.

Perhaps the malaise eating at national will and institutions is the end product of free trade, just as opponents warned during the last election. More likely, though, we suffer passenger syndrome.

Free trade was not some trick sprung during the election campaign, it was a posted stop on the national timetable for years, had we chosen to deal with it. Meech Lake drifted by, too, with little substantial debate in coach class. Now, heading toward parts unknown, there is resigned grumbling, as though the only responsibility of passengers is to go along for the ride.

There is ample precedent for purchasing a rail ticket and riding it as a first-class metaphor to where you want to go. Jacques Parizeau, now leader of the Parti Québécois, once recounted a memorable journey from Montreal to Alberta: "When I left Windsor station, I was a federalist," he said. "When I arrived in Banff, I was a separatist." (If it's any consolation to federalists, Conservative cutbacks have since killed the VIA train to Banff.)

•

My trip offers no revelations of such magnitude. It is just a journey through a beautiful, if dispirited land. It begins in the cavernous Vancouver station, where this note is taped to a window of what once was the restaurant: "Opened 1930. Closed Permanently, Sept. 15, 1990." The newsstand is also empty.

It is a night train. Clouds soaked with the lights of distant Vancouver illuminate the Fraser River, its barges and moored log booms, and the stacks of fresh-sliced cedar shakes behind the sawmills. By morning, the window offers up the olive-drab hills of Kamloops. Three horses frolic in a field. An Aberdeen Angus licks her calf awake.

Inside the dining car, an older gent in a red shirt recalls the golden age of rail. "Ah, they used to pamper you. I loved the roast beef better than any restaurant."

Another morning, days later. The trip resumes, rolling toward Melville, Sask. A huge salvage yard flashes past, filled with neat rows of old combines, tractors and mowers, like the tombstones of dead farms. Ducks are exploring sloughs, geese are picking at the remnants of last

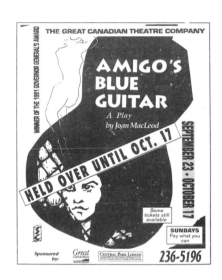

October 8, 1992

year's crop. Country station after country station drifts through the portable radio, bathing the empty fields with the offerings of Tanya and Tammy and Waylon. Songs that would normally trigger a gag reflex seem beautiful, even profound. The train is capable of that, jolting passengers with unexpected surges of intimacy.

Later, in Winnipeg, I read a story about Reform Party Leader Preston Manning, reminiscing about the days when his father, Ernest, one-time Alberta premier, rode the train east with other premiers to federal-provincial meetings. Manning allowed how three days on the train forced the premiers to get along. He is on to something here.

If there must be another first ministers' marathon, why not put them on a train? Fill the rest of the cars with normal folk, for balance, and shunt the train between the coasts until they reach an accord: the VIA National Timetable. If they can't feel anything looking out these windows, then there is nothing left to save.

Northern Ontario is in that leafless period between the snow and the flies. It is tattooed with old forest fires and sliced up with logging roads. Patches of skin are scraped down to rock. It looks hard, scarred and cruel, as though it just pulled bail the morning after a real chair-tosser at a Kenora hotel. . . .

Past Montreal now and, over roast beef in the dining car, a francophone businessman recounts a recent trip to Quebec City with a client from Edmonton. The Edmontonian complained about the "privileges" lavished on Quebeckers by the federal government. The Quebecker said that he is privileged to pay a hell of a lot more taxes than Albertans. "You know what really bothered him was that the sun rises in the east, that by the time Ontario votes, the election is over. So, I said, 'Maybe we should just have a referendum about the sun—let it rise in the west for a few years.'"

Later that night, as I am alone in my roomette, the train rolls slowly through downtown Sherbrooke. A silhouette in an apartment window watches back, his arms supporting himself against the waist-high sill in a wistful pose. He wants to be on the train, I think. And I want to be home. In Canada, we always want what the other guy's got. . . .

Disembarking at Halifax, I review a month of conversations, and the scenes from car windows, airplanes and along 4,467 kilometres of track. Here I can see the land is captured eloquently in the train stations of Vancouver, Winnipeg, Toronto, Montreal and Halifax, our monuments to lost optimism. They are impractical buildings, too big for us now with their high ceilings, grand halls and magnificent scale. Stations built by dreamers, filled only by echoes.

December 19, 1992
MEMORIES FROM A COLD WINDOW PANE

November 8, 1992

In four-plus decades as a columnist for the Journal *and the* Citizen,
Dave Brown became the undisputed voice of unofficial Ottawa,
crafting stories of daily life with humour and compassion and taking
up the causes of veterans, divorced fathers and others he perceived
as victims of injustice. But perhaps his most beloved columns were
the stories drawn from his own life, like this one for which Brown
won a National Newspaper Award.

BY DAVE BROWN

Sensing trouble and trusting his instincts, the boy froze in the
kitchen doorway. There wasn't the usual cheerful hello, so he assumed
there was nobody home. But there was. His grandmother was sitting at
the kitchen table, her back to the doorway, looking out the window of
the second-storey tenement they called home.

November 27, 1992

He was 16, with a zippered school binder tucked under his arm. Neither spoke. She had taught him to open his mind to his senses, so he
did. There was a flood of information.

The kitchen table still had lunch dishes on it, so she had been sitting
there all afternoon. Socks hung from a clothesline running across the
centre of the kitchen. There were rips in the oilcloth covering the un-
stable table. The view from the window was depressing. On a late winter day, dirty snow covered the flat roof of the building below. In better
days it had been a blacksmith shop, and now it was a rundown three-
table poolroom.

Beyond the low roof, in a vacant lot, junked cars rotted slowly. Beyond the rusting heaps, a collection of ramshackle buildings seemed to
be crying for an arsonist to end their misery.

She had shared so many memories with him that he sometimes felt
they could read each other's minds. He saw clearly that she had spent
the day contemplating her death. She had been playing mental memory tapes. She had played those same tapes to him as long as he could
remember. He saw them now.

She grew up on a farm and never stopped missing that life. She loved
the sounds and smells. Only a farmer knew what it was to be close to
nature, she often said. She married a man who took financial chances
and lived an up-and-down life. She had known great comfort and good
living. She stayed loyal as his fortunes changed.

The boy had learned that when she spoke of a "parlor" she was talking about a house she lived in during better times. Now she lived in an
apartment that had a "front room." He had known her through his
short life as a large, comfortable woman, a fountain of love and information.

Now, from the doorway, as if looking into her mind, he could see the
woman she had been. He remembered his grandfather frequently

boasting about his beautiful bride. "Flaming red hair to her waist, and a waist I could put my hands around, my thumbs and fingers meeting."

On warm autumn days they had escaped together to a hilltop overlooking a lake. Before opening their packed lunches they would pace off their dream home, arguing over the size of its many rooms. Then while they ate they would study the positioning of their fine house, to catch the most sun and the best view, but avoiding the north wind.

Now he saw her dreams reduced to a winter-streaked window, and could feel her pain as she accepted what would never be. He was embarrassed by it, and wanted to slip away quietly.

Before he could move she turned from the window. Their eyes met, and both knew instantly there was complete understanding. Nothing had to be said.

There were tear tracks down her cheeks, and she worked her rimless glasses loose from her ears, holding the boy's eye contact as if against his will. She began cleaning the glasses on her apron. She spoke the only words in their otherwise silent communion.

"Oh, Davey. You've got to do better than this."

•

Thirty-eight years later a man stepped up to take his turn on the 12th tee of a fine golf course.

It was a balmy autumn day and late afternoon sunshine was highlighting the beauty of the fairway. The course was in an area of large, expensive homes. One of them was his.

He inhaled the feeling of his good life, and turned to address the ball. He tried to tell himself he had come a long way. That he had reached a measure of success. That he had done better.

He paused. An odd choice of words, he thought. Better than what?

Better than a winter-streaked kitchen window. Oh, Davey.

Suddenly unable to see clearly, I picked up my ball and walked.

Now, a full season later, the memories are vivid. Loved ones long gone are with us still.

Her name was Anna Kaichen, and I was 25 when she died.

June 26, 1993
GOODBYE, MR. SISKIND
One of the toughest, most knowledgeable
critics of his time bows out
(Excerpt from a tribute:)

BY STEVEN MAZEY AND JAY STONE

Jacob Siskind retired this week after a career of more than 40 years as a critic of classical music. He was probably the best critic of classical music in the country. He was certainly the damnedest.

He was born in Montreal in 1928. He wrote music, theatre, film and dance criticism for four newspapers there, taught piano, studied music, psychology and English at McGill University and wrote pulp fiction under pseudonyms for U.S. magazines. He came to Ottawa in 1977 and wrote music and dance criticism for three newspapers here, two of which have since folded.

All this information comes from the *Encyclopedia of Music in Canada,* because Siskind refused to be interviewed for this story.

He laughed when he was asked, that long laugh filled with delight that was familiar in the *Citizen* entertainment department. He was laughing partly out of his strong sense of personal privacy, because he guards his personal life jealously and hates any public fuss.

(In a losing battle to avoid being recognized, he would insist that the photograph on his column be changed so that when he wore his beard in real life, the photo would show him clean-shaven, and vice-versa. For a photograph for a bus poster, part of a *Citizen* promotional campaign a few years ago, Siskind arrived with a false beard.)

He was also laughing partly at the very idea. It was a laugh we heard often. Sometimes it was when some musician or other—and he seemed to know them all—phoned to share the latest story of outrage in the Canadian arts scene. Sometimes it was at himself.

Once a composer put a word upside-down in a headline on one of Siskind's reviews. The word was "sound," but it came out in the paper as "punos." Siskind looked it up—it means a bleak, desolate area, which also described the music he was reviewing—and couldn't wait to show it to everyone. He was on the phone all morning, laughing.

It wasn't all fun and games, though, especially if you tampered with his copy. Someone once changed the phrase "all that glisters is not gold"—which is correct—to "all that glitters is not gold," and he wrote a blistering memo saying he didn't enjoy being made to look stupid.

Such things strike him as amateurish. He pronounces the word "amateur" in the distinctive British way, and he says it as if it was something he found on the bottom of his shoe. He often rebuked publicists for errors in their press releases, and he had an impressive collection of improperly addressed mail. He would throw away any letters addressed to Jacob Suskind.

His strictest standards applied to his work, and if you were a musician or a dancer who didn't meet them, he had a lot of critical tools at his disposal—the axe, the foil, and the garotte.

"The Haydn Symphony would not have sounded substantially different had it been played by a brass band in a Munich beer hall," he would write. "The slow movement was square and humorless and the Menuetto reeked of lederhosen and hiking shoes."

Sometimes you had to read his reviews with great care to see where

November 16, 1994

the knife had gone in: "Mannino was in fine form, opening with a verismo reading of the Beethoven *Fidelio Overture* that caught his audience and some of his players by surprise."

Sometimes Siskind would catch the news desk by surprise, too. Last week, Siskind wrote one of his classics, reviewing the Scottish Ballet's *A Midsummer Night's Dream* as if it was a dance parody and pronouncing it hilarious: "The dancers' costumes are another source of hilarity and, if that isn't enough, there's the dancing of the male principals."

The editors on the news desk treated all this straight, and headlined this review, "Modern Scottish Dream hits balletic funnybone." Siskind, of course, was delighted.

But if he was known as tough—he often savaged beginners, saying that it saved them the pain of a hopeless career—he was also respected as the most knowledgeable critic of his time. Siskind studied piano extensively, and while he could be devastating to a bad musician, he had a deep well of generosity toward anyone he felt had promise.

"I remember once in Montreal in the '60s," said Menahem Pressler, pianist with the Beaux Arts Trio. "There was a big snowstorm and only about 50 people turned up. Planes were cancelled and there was hardly any traffic, and there was Jacob in the audience.

"The next day he wrote the most glorious and loving and enthusiastic review. I remember the feeling of elation and excitement I had at the time. His review made me feel that I was on the right track."

Victor Borge, the musical humorist whom Siskind recognized was also a fine piano player, said, "I always looked forward to playing in Ottawa, not only because the audiences there have always been so nice, but because I would be playing for Jacob. I always knew that even if no one else noticed the little things I did in a performance, Jacob would."

Borge said he still has a clipping of a review Jacob wrote of a recording more than 20 years ago, in which Borge played in concert with some of the best-known serious pianists of the day and Siskind said he was pleasantly surprised by the tone quality of Borge's playing.

"Of course I have known since I was little that my *forté* was my tone, but it was so nice to see a serious critic appreciate it. . . . He caught in words what I was doing at the piano. He had my tone in his pen."

Angela Hewitt, the Ottawa pianist who won the 1985 Bach competition, remembers Siskind encouraging her when she was nine years old and won a concerto competition in Montreal.

"There are good reviews that say absolutely nothing, where you can tell the writer doesn't really know much about music, and I'd rather not have those. With Jacob, his knowledge is so obvious that he really makes you think about the things he says."

She's not alone. Franco Mannino, former NAC Orchestra conductor, calls Siskind "one of the best critics of the age." Siskind once shared a

November 16, 1994

letter from Mannino that thanked Siskind for suggestions he had made to improve a symphony Mannino had written. Siskind's ideas, Mannino wrote, much improved the piece.

But when he was critical toward professionals, he could make enemies. Irish flautist James Galway was in Ottawa to conduct the NAC Orchestra, and after reading Siskind's review, he told a fellow flute player he would never return here.

Mario Bernardi, conductor of the Calgary Philharmonic and the victim of many Siskind pans when he conducted the NACO, had this to say: "He was a nasty old bastard."...

Siskind learned to be thick-skinned about a lot of things, but he would never bend on matters of principle. He almost quit the *Citizen* several times.

One day about five years ago, the staff came in to find Siskind's desk cleaned out. He was at home. It turns out that someone on staff had written a letter to the editor taking issue with a Siskind review. The letter was printed in the paper, but Siskind's response was not. He took this as a sign of disrespect, and he was ready to resign over the matter.

It turned out that Siskind's letter was mislaid, and it was printed. But it took a high-level meeting with two editors and the publisher before Siskind was satisfied....

He came to Ottawa in 1977 as arts editor and music critic of the shortlived *Ottawa Today* newspaper from 1977 to '78, moving to the *Journal* and then the *Citizen* in 1980.

Here he was both music and dance critic, and he also wrote a weekly column on the arts and a column on classical recordings that was so influential that David Shore, owner of Counterpoint Classics on Murray Street, said Siskind's review of a Christmas album by Gino and Louis Quilico helped make it one of the biggest sellers of the year.

All this meant he was often at work seven days a week, his weekends and evenings filled with concerts he felt worthy of review. He wrote his reviews quickly and to the exact length needed....

His final arts column runs on Sunday, and after that, his voice will disappear from this newspaper.... He won't be missed by everyone.

When his impending retirement was announced, an Ottawa man wrote a letter to the editor bidding good riddance to "the self-appointed Prince of Pomp." It was a vitriolic letter, and it quoted a review from 1982 that had particularly outraged the writer.

This long memory so thrilled Siskind that he called the writer at work and introduced himself. "I loved your letter to the editor," Siskind said. The man hung up.

Siskind tells the story with wide-eyed delight. And then he laughs.

November 16, 1994

A BROADSHEET MAGAZINE • SUNDAY, JULY 14, 2002

THE CITIZEN'S WEEKLY

50 SEASONS
& all's well

Stratford's storybook milestone

CHRISTOPHER PLUMMER AS KING LEAR AT THIS SEASON'S STRATFORD FESTIVAL. PHOTO BY TONY VACCARO

INSIDE: Summer Reading by Toby Young ● Thumbs up for the thumb ● A big lie about fat? ● It's grim, it's macabre, it's Kathy Reichs ● Engine 40, Ladder 35 ● Imagination rules ● Taking on Tinky Winky ● How to choose a good mystery

416

Family Ties

The Sixteenth Decade, 1995-2005

IN EARLY 2003, almost 126 years to the day after William Southam paid $1,400 for a stake in his first daily newspaper, a rueful group of reporters and editors gathered in Ottawa to bid farewell to his family name. In reality, it had been years since the Southam family actually controlled the chain of newspapers that grew out of that purchase of the *Hamilton Spectator* in 1877. Conrad Black had acquired control of Southam's 14 dailies and 100-plus weeklies in 1996, dealing them for $3.2 billion four years later to the CanWest Global media empire owned by the Asper family of Winnipeg.

Through all the buying and selling, the Southam name somehow managed to survive until February 2003 when Southam News, the venerable news agency created in the 1920s to serve the chain's papers, was rechristened CanWest News Service. The journalists assembled to toast the old name's slip into history had long resigned themselves to the change. But they also knew what the Southams had meant to Canadian journalism. "Let's face it, the family had their share of kooks and misfits," said reporter Patrick Nagle, a Southam veteran in Vancouver, Montreal, Ottawa and Africa, "but they knew how to hold things together so we hacks could get out and do our work."

Nowhere had that been more evident than Ottawa, where the Southams rescued the *Citizen* from bankruptcy in 1897 and turned it into the city's largest circulation daily for most of the next 99 years. From the start, the family had seen the advantage of investing in staff and technology to outrun the competition. William Southam sprung for a new press in 1897, just as the Southam company did in 1993 when it approved a $31-million expansion to make way for a third press. "It amounts to a remarkable record of continuity and stability," says Carleton University historian John Taylor. "It's hard to imagine the paper

The Citizen's new owners brought in a new look and launched it with an explantory wrapper March 3, 1997.

Opposite: The Citizen's relaunch in March of 1997 changed not just the typefaces and page layout but added new sections, such as the Sunday broadsheet magazine, which made possible new ways of storytelling.

417

thriving so long and so well without the Southams."

By the mid-'90s, though, turbulence lay just around the corner. For several years, Conrad Black had been buying up Southam shares, grumbling from the sidelines about the company's economic performance and the quality of its newspapers. By the time he took control in summer 1996, major changes were inevitable—and quick in arriving.

Black, politically right-of-centre, said he was tired of the "overwhelming avalanche of soft, left, bland, envious pap which has poured like sludge" from the Southam papers. His message hit the *Citizen* like a freight train. Briefing himself on Black's thinking, publisher Russell Mills flew to New York to show his new boss an ambitious plan to remake the *Citizen* into a paper he would like—one with a more conservative approach. Black told him to get to work.

October 30, 1995

Back in Ottawa, editor Jim Travers, an admired former foreign correspondent, was offered another job. He declined and stepped down, saying that senior news managers should share their owner's views, which he did not. Travers was soon followed out the door by Peter Calamai, editor of the editorial pages and winner of four major journalism awards. Both ended up at the *Toronto Star*.

To guide the *Citizen*'s makeover as the flagship of his Canadian newspaper holdings, Black turned to Neil Reynolds, a shy eccentric whose reputation for going his own way and genius for winning National Newspaper Awards had earned him a sort of cult status during 14 years as editor of the *Kingston Whig-Standard*. The new editor's libertarian leanings meshed neatly with Black's conservative views, and with the owner's full backing, Reynolds began his overhaul.

October 31, 1995

Aided by a $2-million infusion, Reynolds brought in a small band of like-minded loyalists, he doubled the space for editorial material, added a new Sunday "magazine" section, gave photographs a sharper profile, and packaged it all in a crisp new format. To run the editorial pages, Reynolds hired William Watson, a conservative economist whose section soon displayed a new friendliness to Tory Mike Harris's Ontario government and a fresh flintiness toward Jean Chrétien's Liberals. Indeed, Watson's editorial urging Chrétien to consider resigning after just 3 1/2 years as prime minister created a furore when it appeared in the remade *Citizen*'s first edition on March 3, 1997.

Praise for the relaunched paper was not universal. There was criticism of Reynolds's penchant for putting too many pretty faces among the news copy—a variation of the "tits and analysis" formula perfected by Black's British paper, *The Daily Telegraph*—and for one-sided news coverage. But most of the experts and many readers seemed to like the changes, and sparked by the buzz, a decade-long slide in circulation began to reverse.

More change was in the air, however. The *National Post*, the Toronto-based newspaper Black created in 1998, was bleeding money. In 2000, with shareholders of Hollinger Inc., his media company, clamouring for better results, Black sold most of his Canadian newspaper assets to Winnipeg-based CanWest Global Communications. The sale made CanWest the country's largest media company, with holdings in TV, radio, newspapers and online services.

As the Asper family, CanWest's owners, adjusted to newspaper proprietorship, a freeze was put on hiring and, at the *Citizen* at least, Black's one-time commitment to significant space for news began to slip away. In the meantime, Reynolds left for the *Vancouver Sun*, another CanWest paper, and was replaced by managing editor Scott Anderson, one of the outgoing editor's trusted lieutenants and, at 36, among the youngest editors in the paper's history.

Anderson's mettle was soon put to the test. The paper's new owners had vastly different political views than Black. CanWest founder Israel Asper was a strong supporter of Chrétien, and when CanWest began to dictate editorial positions on some issues from Winnipeg, Anderson often found himself stickhandling the gap between the views of head office and those of his own editorial board. CanWest insisted the policy was in the best tradition of newspapers. As owner, it had the right to determine editorial positions on important issues. The papers were free to publish dissenting views, CanWest said, as long as they were the opinions of individuals. That was all very well in theory, critics said, but in practice the policy was likely to have a chilling effect on a paper's eagerness to present a variety of views.

The issue exploded onto the national stage in June 2002 when the Aspers fired Russell Mills over an editorial calling for Chrétien's resignation. CanWest president Leonard Asper described the editorial as the "final straw in a series of instances" in which the long-time *Citizen* publisher failed to get head office clearance for an editorial stance. Mills told a different story, and his dismissal sparked widespread protest from media analysts, unions representing journalists, and *Citizen* readers. It also created a rumpus in Parliament, where Chrétien denied applying pressure on the Aspers to get rid of Mills.

The Aspers soon replaced Mills with James Orban, a long-time *Citizen* business executive who became the first publisher in at least 50 years to assume the job without editorial experience. Some observers interpreted the appointment as another sign of CanWest's emphasis on the bottom line. But it is also possible to view it through a long lens, and see it as part of the symmetry of *Citizen* history.

When the paper began its seventh decade in 1905, it was owned by a family with deep media roots and its publisher was a businessman with an extensive network of local contacts. It entered its 17th decade 100 years later with family ownership at the helm and a publisher

August 31, 1996

whose business contacts in the community reach back to the 1970s. Whether they can carry the *Citizen* forward for as long and as vigorously as their predecessors is a question that will have to wait until the paper's next significant anniversary.

August 31, 1996

June 6, 1995
A MOTHER'S MOURNFUL SCREAM
Since her arrival at the Citizen *in 1990, Shelley Page has emerged as one of the country's top feature writers. In the mid-'90s, she wrote a hard-hitting local column that established her reputation as a reporter of great range, compassion and style. Among Page's most memorable work from this period are her columns on the death of Shayne Norris, killed in 1994 when his bicycle was struck by a car driven by an off-duty police officer. Here's an excerpt:*

BY SHELLEY PAGE

When Susan McNab was finally allowed to see her dead son, Shayne Norris, she was warned not to hug him in his coffin. Only touch his hands, she was told. When she clasped his long, slender fingers, she saw that his nails were destroyed.

"In his last breath, he must have known something terrible was happening and he must have gripped the handles of that bicycle so hard that he broke his nails."

She asked police how he had died, if he had suffered. Her questions were met with silence.

A month later, on the basis of a blood alcohol test that exceeded the legal limit, a driver was charged with impaired driving causing death, and leaving the scene of an accident. But it was five months after her son was buried that McNab learned the details of Shayne's death.

After she read them, she heard horrible mournful screaming. It came from her own mouth.

This week, Susan McNab stood in front of a class of Kanata high school students and told her son's story.

After months of silence, she has decided to tell people a bit about what was in that report, what was kept at first from Shayne's family. She wants to share with young people the impact and the horrors of drinking and driving. She plans to visit many such classes.

"I want to save lives," she said.

She spoke to a Grade 13 law class at Holy Trinity High School, a short distance from where 16-year-old Shayne was killed.

The students, a little older than Shayne, were thinking about their upcoming graduation. They expected a presentation from Mothers Against Drunk Driving, which McNab recently helped form in Ottawa. An OPP sergeant who runs a RIDE program came, too, armed with statistics about deaths caused by drinking and driving. Colorful posters were tacked to the blackboard....

When one girl saw the posters, the VCR set up to show footage of crash sites, she said, "This is cool."

They were not prepared for what Susan McNab said.

Last Aug. 22, Shayne Norris was travelling home on his bicycle on Robertson Road east of Kanata when he was struck and killed by a car. In the hours after the crash, a large field was cordoned off. Police kept Shayne's father, Russell Norris, away from the scene.

It was days later when Russ, Susan, and Shayne's sister Shannon, were finally permitted to see Shayne, who was laid out in his coffin.

Susan McNab described to the students in the classroom how she wanted to "give him a real big hug," but she was asked not to touch him. She explained her horror at seeing his broken nails.

After he was buried, she was tormented by his nails. She wanted to know if he had "lain in that field alive, waiting for someone to help him. I wanted to know how the police handled his dear body, hoping they had been loving and tender. But still, no one told me. I couldn't eat or sleep through all of this unknown."

Prescription drugs kept her from screaming out her agony. Ten days after Shayne's death, she was told that the coroner found no blood, which meant his heart had stopped instantly.

She felt a bit better, knowing he was taken immediately. Then there was a knock at the door last January. A Nepean police officer gave them the report on Shayne's death. McNab told the students what she learned in that report.

"Now I do know, now all I see is the smashed windshield with tufts of light brown hair implanted in the molding, I see Shayne's running shoes on the side of the road, I see his favorite ball cap a few yards away from the shoes. I take another few steps and find part of Shayne's skull, then an arm, a leg and then much further out in that field (half a football field length from the road), I find the face of my Shayne staring towards the Heavens above.

"Now I know how they handled my son's body—they picked it up piece by piece, their stomachs wrenching...."

After she finished, there was no gum-cracking among the students, no whispering of secrets in each others' ears. The girl who thought this was cool had mascara running down her face. A couple of crying students quietly left the classroom.

Propped on the board was a picture of Shayne with the words, "Grounded at 16." Beneath a coffin, it read, "no parties, no sports, no dancing, no fun, no friends, left for him."

Susan McNab ended her talk, "Please drive safe, drive sober."

Many students told her, "We will. We promise."

August 31, 1996

August 30, 1996

November 23, 1996

July 13, 1996
COURTING FROGS
Searching for green, slimy things that go 'gronk'
is a perfect summer pastime
(Excerpt from a feature:)

BY TOM SPEARS

"I don't see no p'ints about that frog that's better'n any other frog," says a lowlife character in Mark Twain's *The Celebrated Jumping Frog of Calaveras County*.

Obviously a non-connoisseur.

Frogs are slimy, grumpy-looking, and a lot of fun to chase around in the summer, the attraction lying chiefly in the stalking.

You move very slowly and get as close as you can before there's a splash and a green blur and the frog has disappeared so quickly you're not even sure which way it went. It's just gone.

We are drawn to frogs by their very human mix of moods—long periods when they seem perfectly unflappable followed by a sudden, panicky exit. Don't most of us lead lives like that?

And a drive to the nearest marsh or riverbank, taking your kids with you as an excuse, is a perfect way to waste a few hours in summer. Maybe not as exciting as a day at the Ex, but a lot cheaper and a lot more relaxing.

Watching these creatures is not a sport. More a matter of contemplation, really. The frog sits like a tiny green sumo wrestler, calm and unhurried, until you get too close and he's gone under a water lily or behind a few reeds.

Your typical frog-lover won't even know which species he or she is watching, probably because the typical frog-lover is still not 12 years old. You figure the loudest ones that keep saying something like, "Gronk," over and over from the middle of the pond are probably bullfrogs, especially if they keep you awake on a summer night.

But beyond that? Doesn't matter. We leave arguments over species to the birders. Frogs are there to enjoy, not to check off on a list of Species I Have Seen This Year.

Frogs appeal most to the very young. Kermit. The Frog Prince. We are born with an interest in all green, slimy things that wiggle and splash, but we lose it, perhaps when adolescence makes us crave sophistication, or perhaps under the discouraging gaze of our elders—Put that down right now! You don't know where it's been. . . .

Frogs were once everywhere in this area. Our cities grew up around three big rivers—the Ottawa, Rideau and Gatineau, as well as marshes like Dow's Great Swamp (now Dow's Lake). But development has drained and dried up much of our land. Before Centrepointe was built, you could walk through that area and hear frogs in all directions on a summer night . . . .

When you find a frog, take care of it. Their numbers are dwindling all over the world, prompting all kinds of research. A thinner ozone layer may be to blame, or a variety of pesticides that frogs absorb through their skin.

And in this region, hunting has done to bullfrogs what fishing did to the Atlantic cod. In the late 1970s, when commercial bullfrog hunting was permitted, the Ministry of Natural Resources estimated there were 800 bullfrogs in Mississippi Lake. In 1995, the count showed 360. In Tay Marsh off Big Rideau Lake, the count in 1978 was 300. In 1995, there were just 42. Because of a widespread decline on this scale, the ministry has banned all bullfrog hunting in Eastern Ontario.

So go. Grab a hat and some insect repellent and take a look at a form of life that hasn't really changed much since the time of the dinosaurs. In their own comical way, they command respect.

There, now you're an expert.

September 1, 1997

December 12, 1998
'THERE WAS NO OUTRUNNING THIS ONE'

For nearly four years, Diane Stuemer's lively weekly account of her family's round-the-world adventure aboard their sailboat Northern Magic *so captivated* Citizen *readers that thousands showed up for the Stuemers' homecoming in August 2001. This excerpt comes from a column written 15 months into the journey.*

BY DIANE STUEMER

Scarborough, Queensland, Australia

We were still two days away from Australia, on Day 10 of our final, stormy passage of the South Pacific, when we received our first inkling that more trouble lay in store. It came in the form of an Australian small craft warning. . . . about a developing low pressure system just 160 kilometres west, directly in our path to the Queensland coast.

The storm we had weathered during the first part of the voyage had already taken its toll on us, and we felt fragile and nervous. It had cost us three days of nausea and misery and had blown us badly off course. Afterward we had been forced to hand-steer for days while our motor carried us in a direction our sails would not. We were physically and mentally exhausted and desperately anxious for our ordeal to end. Yet now another tempest separated us from safety.

There was no hope of outrunning this one, or manoeuvering around it. It was also likely to bring us near the coast during darkness the following night. We never approach a strange harbour at night, and entering in darkness and during a storm was totally out of the question, so we decided to heave to, or stop the boat, so that we could time our arrival for early morning two days later. Although we wanted nothing more than to get to Queensland, instead we bobbed in place like a sitting duck, waiting, not knowing what misery the next day might bring. . . .

It wasn't 10 minutes [after breakfast] that the first squall hit. Our jib and small mizzen sail were both raised, and it was important that we not be knocked over by a blast of wind as we had before. As soon as I could feel the wind jump in force, I turned *Northern Magic* north, so that as the squall hit we were propelled along with it.

The sky around us had now turned into a witches' cauldron. "Bubble, bubble, toil and trouble" popped into my head, but Shakespeare himself never imagined a more sinister sky, nor evoked a greater sense of foreboding than I felt, looking helplessly at the maelstrom surrounding our small floating home, alone in a dark and violent sea. Low dark clouds with black borders swept from south to north. Solid grey sheets of rain reached down to the water. Huge thunderheads sprouted and towered ominously, looking like mushroom clouds from a nuclear bomb. Black cloud formations rose and reached out over us like giant hands ready to crush us. . . .

Now squall after squall came racing across the water. The wind had picked up to about 65 km/h, and each time a squall rampaged by, it increased to about 85 km/h, which is a shrieking, hard blast. I continued steering around and through the squalls as best I could, minimizing the strain on the boat and the sails. The squalls would come fiercely and last half an hour or so, during which time we would be pelted with slanting rain and the waves would rise to five metres or more. Once I really got into the rhythm of steering with them, I actually felt a sense of power and exhilaration and a keen sense of being truly alive. Everything depended upon my concentration. Often it took all my physical power to keep the boat on course, leaning my entire body onto the wheel. I stayed that way most of the day, and in this way we withstood perhaps 10 squalls.

Then, as we sailed through the dark curtain of the final squall, the sky turned blue. The rain stopped and the wind calmed. I was able to take my hands off the wheel for the first time in five hours. My right shoulder ached and I had no sensation in my right thumb, which had been gripping the wheel with all its might. I stepped into the navigation station below, where Herbert [Stuemer's husband] was resting on a bunk. Although exhausted, I felt proud and happy. I had brought us through the worst, and Australia was only 100 kilometres away.

Herbert, who for only the second time in his life—and on this trip— had been laid flat by seasickness, sat up looking flushed and feverish. His head was hot, yet his limbs were shivering under a thick blanket.

OTTAWA CITIZEN

ROAD CLOSED
CHEMIN FERMÉ

Locked in a power struggle
Communities band together to battle the elements

January 9, 1998

For half an hour I rested beside him.

Then I felt a strange change in the rhythm of the waves.

Outside, the pleasant blue sky had been swallowed by a hideous black and grey tumult of clouds. But what truly struck horror into my heart was the solid white wall that was travelling along the frothing surface of the water, galloping at an incredible pace not a mile away. It was heading directly for us. I scrambled back into the cockpit, disengaged the windvane, and prepared for the onslaught. I feared we had too much sail up, but it was too late to do anything about it.

When the squall hit, it was like nothing I have ever felt before. Even though I had a hood on, the wind blew my sunglasses right off my face. With us surfing at eight knots along with the wind, our wind indicator registered close to 50 knots, which meant we were experiencing almost 55 knots, or about 85 km/h. Within minutes, the waves were six metres high. Huge whitecaps roared on the tops of the waves, often crashing down all around us, onto our decks and into the cockpit. . . .

I steered with a steely gaze on the compass and forced myself not to look at the chaos around me. Sometimes out of the corner of my eye I could see some kind of muted electrical flash, lightning that was hidden behind the clouds or beyond the horizon. At first I was hoping this was simply another squall. But when it showed no signs of abating, I yelled for Herbert to come into the cockpit and take down our sails. I knew I really should have done this much sooner, but foolishly I had been trying to protect him from having to leave his sickbed. Herbert cast his sickness aside and furled in most of the jib. Then we sat in the cockpit taking turns steering. Hour after hour it went on, the dark day slowly giving way to an even darker night. . . .

In the dark, everything looked even more ominous. We could see very little in the black night other than the fluorescent brightness of the whitecaps. As we sailed through the deep trough between two waves, all we could see was a frothing mass of foam looming high over the boat, advancing threateningly, looking as if it would surely crash down right on top of us. The advancing, seething foam looked like a line of charging white stallions. Then, just as it looked as if we were going to be engulfed, the wave began to lift us up until the foam was no longer above us, but beside us, washing onto our decks or roaring into the cockpit. Now, instead of charging horses, it was as if the wave was a muscular titan, lifting us onto his huge shoulders until we mingled with his foamy white hair. For a moment we would perch there, until the giant rushed on past us, letting us slide down his back, his wild white mane flying away behind him. . . .

We decided our only option was to lie ahull, which means to take down all the sails, close up and simply let the boat take care of itself. Herbert wrestled down the remainder of the mizzen sail and furled in

the jib, we locked the wheel and then simply took our hands off it. After all our desperate and furious steering, it was nerve-wracking simply to give up control and let *Northern Magic* fend for herself.

For a few minutes, we braced ourselves in the cockpit, our hearts in our mouths, wondering what would happen. Although we had read about lying ahull, this was something we had never before had to do. But nothing happened, except we continued sliding up and down these monstrous waves, and in a few minutes we decided there was no reason to stay outside, exhausted and wet, any longer.

Once we settled down inside, we wondered why we hadn't done this many hours earlier. The sense of foreboding and desperation we had felt outside was much reduced inside the warm, homey cabin. We rested in turn while the other kept watch, sticking out a head every few minutes to make sure we weren't being run over by another vessel. The nearer we came to the coast, the greater were the chances of meeting another ship....

By 5 in the morning, the winds and waves were distinctly calmer, dropping consistently below 65 km/h for the first time in almost 24 hours. We were now less than 30 kilometres from land. At 6:30 we raised Brisbane on VHF radio and asked what the conditions were for entering the harbour. "No worries," answered the harbour master in his Queensland drawl, "It's a great day here."

Herbert and I were almost numb with exhaustion as Michael [one of their three sons] woke up from his makeshift bed in the salon and said brightly, "Well, that wasn't so bad." All we could do is look at him in stunned silence, then head back up to the cockpit to raise our sails and at last turn our battered boat for home.

August 16, 1999

September 8, 1999
A PAINFUL DEPARTURE FOR A PARENT
Over the years, Randall Denley's insightfully crabby columns on municipal affairs earned him the nickname 'Unofficial Mayor of Ottawa' and sparked a steady stream of letters to the editor. Still, none of his observations on politics ever brought a response equal to that generated by the personal column excerpted here.

BY RANDALL DENLEY

I said I wouldn't cry. It's unseemly. But then I decided, why not? It's not every day a son leaves home.

Like thousands of other parents, my wife and I spent Labour Day weekend taking our son out of town to start his university career. It ought to have been a joyous thing, logically. After all, he had the marks to get into the computer science program at Waterloo, he had worked hard to save most of the money he'll need and he has the maturity to live on his own. These are all things that we would have identified as goals a few years ago.

So then why does it feel so bad to lose him?

After more than 19 years, a son or daughter is so much a part of your being and everyday existence that when they leave, it's like losing a limb. Their departure marks the definitive end to the best part of your life. It's fine to look ahead to more personal freedom but it's scant compensation for the rewards of parenthood.

When a family is under the same roof, there is a level of casual, everyday contact that one takes for granted at the time. It's nothing dramatic, but you're all within easy reach of each other. Watching their development and hearing their observations about life is one of the pleasures of being a parent. Once someone moves away, all that's replaced by phone calls, e-mails and visits. It's a poor substitute.

It's not as if we didn't know it was coming and there is a gradual process of disentanglement that precedes the departure. Watching a child grow up is like a series of deaths. The three-year-old can only appear after the appealing two-year-old is gone. By the late teens, all the phases of childhood are history, some for the better no doubt.

So what you mourn losing is largely something that's already gone anyway. Still, that doesn't seem to make it feel any better.

The weekend itself was hectic. It's amazing how many goods have to be purchased to set one person up in housekeeping. At least now he has a full array of small appliances so there's no need to marry young. . . . Still, the activity was a welcome diversion from the cold fact that on Monday, we'd be driving home with the van conspicuously empty.

I couldn't help but dwell on the fact that all this was my fault, in a way. He'd pretty much made up his mind to attend Carleton when I helpfully suggested that he ought to at least consider what other universities had to offer. We made the campus tour of Waterloo last March, and he was hooked.

Who'd have thought he'd take my advice for once?

I can at least comfort myself with the knowledge that he's making the right decision. There is a time when striking out on one's own is the appropriate thing to do, as much as I hate to admit it.

The Kleenex box got a workout on the drive back, but we thought we had it under control until we got home. The first thing we saw coming through the door was the empty chair in front of the computer. This was the spot where we would almost invariably find him.

His room is full of reminders, too. The shelf-full of sports trophies, the discarded high school hockey sweater, years of *National Geographic*, strange memorabilia such as a baby shark preserved in a bottle (a souvenir of a trip to Florida). The essence of him is still there.

August 16, 1999

It's always easier for the person who moves away to attend university. They have an exciting phase of their lives ahead of them—new friends, new intellectual challenges, the freedom of adulthood at last.

When they return home for holidays, the group's complete again and things are as when they left them. For the old folks at home, however, it's not the same at all. It all happens so quickly. You think you're teaching them something, when the opportunities arise, sharing your accumulated "wisdom." Then, suddenly, it's all over. Class is out. Whatever they've learned has to be enough to carry them.

The parent has to learn to content himself with memories.

I keep telling myself he's only away, not gone, but I know it will never be the same again.

November 28, 2000

December 24, 2001

A CHRISTMAS TALE FROM PELICAN BAY

In 2002, Citizen *reporter Dan Gardner won a National Newspaper Award for his examination of the prison systems of four countries, and the lessons they hold for Canada. He met prisoner Tony Strong, featured in the column excerpted here, while researching that series.*

BY DAN GARDNER

Here is a tale for Christmas. There is no snow in this story, no presents and no jollity. But there is redemption, which, if I remember the story of Christ's birth, played some part.

My tale takes place in a maximum security prison called Pelican Bay. The name may not mean much to you, but prisoners in California hate and fear it the way an earlier generation of inmates did Alcatraz and San Quentin. Pelican Bay is a shiny new facility, a warehouse made of concrete and stainless steel that bristles with razor wire, video cameras and armed guards. It is the last stop in one of the toughest prison systems in the western world.

I visited Pelican Bay last summer and came across a man standing alone in the barren exercise yard. He was black, like so many of the prisoners, and had the paunch of a middle-aged man who spends a lot of time doing nothing. He said his name was "Tony Strong C60553."

My tape recorder hardly gave him pause. He was happy to talk. I asked questions about the prison but it was movies he really wanted to talk about. Or rather, one movie.

"*Shawshank Redemption,* I tell ya, that's the movie I like," he said. "Morgan Freeman. I like how he portrays the inmate's mentality and how you grow up in prison just like you grow up in life."

Strong has had lots of time to grow up. He was 19 years old, an inner-city tough, when he was sentenced to life in prison for first-degree murder. He has been inside for 22 years, 11 of them at Pelican Bay.

His attraction to "Red," the con played by Morgan Freeman in *Shaw-shank Redemption,* is understandable. Red isn't innocent. He did it. He killed a man.

But when we meet him, Red isn't the young thug who committed murder. He's a soft-spoken, middle-aged man trying to get from one day to the next. We watch him turn grey and lose hope as he's refused parole again and again. And finally, when he has given up, we watch him drop his mask and tell the parole board what he really feels: How he'd like to grab his younger self by the scruff of the neck and shake some sense into him, how he'd like to tell that kid what a fool he is, how it hurts the old man every day to know what the young man did.

And then, miraculously, he is given parole. Red is redeemed.

"I'm kind of like that guy," Strong says. "I'm not the same person who came to prison. I'm a totally different person. I'm the same body, but I changed a lot." True or not, Tony Strong won't get the sort of redemption Red received. In theory, he can be paroled but in reality, lifers are not released in California. Strong knows he's never going to leave.

I can't imagine the weight of that knowledge, or what it would do to me. But Strong says it hasn't broken him. "I appreciate life even more, even though I don't have my parents no more and I'm divorced and everything. I still have a lot to offer life. And if I have to do it in prison, I'm going to do it in prison, but I'm not going to give up."

It's religion that gives him hope, he says. He converted to Islam in prison. Now his conversation is peppered with thanks to Allah. "Islam changed my life," he says.

Many people roll their eyes at claims like that. There's nothing a prisoner can say or do to convince them he has changed. Some don't even care if prisoners do change. I'm not sure that there's anything that can be said to people who think this way. Those who do not allow for redemption may themselves be beyond it.

Still, whatever some may think, it is a fact that criminals can become better men and women. It happens every day. The redeemed don't appear in headlines, but they are out there. They are your neighbours, your colleagues. They have jobs and families. Very often, they do charity work and give of themselves more than others because they have had to think much harder about right and wrong than the rest of us. Some of the most decent men I've ever met were repentant murderers.

I can't be sure, but Tony Strong may be such a man.

He sent me a letter not long after we met. "Peace and blessings be upon you," it begins. "With over two decades of incarceration, I value life much more than the average, I only wish to help."

Why did he write? Is he trying to hoodwink a journalist, get him to write something nice to impress the parole board? Impossible. He knows he's never getting out.

December 30, 2000

What is possible is that even inside prison he has become a different man, a better man. He may have found redemption, as both Christ and Mohammed would wish.

Peace and blessings be upon you, Tony. Merry Christmas.

April 12, 2002

SHAKESPEARE ON THE HIGH ARCTIC

After 15 years as an arts commentator, humour columnist and movie critic, Jay Stone is probably the Citizen's *best known writer. It's a well-deserved popularity. Stone's movie reviews—insightful, biting, smart, funny—are the best in the country. Here's an excerpt from his four-star review of* Atanarjuat, *one of his Top 10 movies of 2002.*

BY JAY STONE

The remarkable *Atanarjuat: The Fast Runner* is a movie of such a vast landscape, of such exotic ritual, of such a broad canvas of ice and snow and hate and revenge, that it almost amounts to an entire movie genre of its own.

It is almost three hours long, it is told in Inuktitut, it stars native actors, it portrays life a thousand years ago in a forbidding place far above the Arctic Circle, and it has, at its centre, the most amazing chase sequence in movie history: a man runs stark naked—and I mean stark—across a wintery landscape, falling on the snow, splashing through puddles of icy water, running for his life.

In many ways, this is the play that Shakespeare never wrote, or perhaps the one he always wrote. To call *Atanarjuat: The Fast Runner* a kind of Othello of the High Arctic is unfair to both, but it gives you a sense of the myth, the scope, the ambition of its treacheries.

It was made by Zacharias Kunuk, an Inuit documentary-maker who brings a documentary eye and a love of oral history to a project that is entirely unlikely. Who would sit through it? Who has the patience for the slow accumulation of grievance leading to betrayal leading to violence leading to redemption? Who can stand three hours of tundra and cold, of people wrapped in animal skins and eating, in every other scene, something even more unappetizing: a raw bird, raw meat, chunks of caribou, cooked carcass of a seal taken off a dog sled frozen solid, a meaty teardrop turned to ice?

The slow accumulation is fascinating, however, and it comes in a story that is overwhelming in its meaning. *Atanarjuat* stands as both a document of a way of life seldom seen on film, and as a myth whose currents run under its specific territory—the forlorn coldness of desperate survival—and into the larger ocean of storytelling that has given us Greek epic poetry and Shakespearean epic tragedy. The fact that the movie was made the way it was, by a native filmmaker with a na-

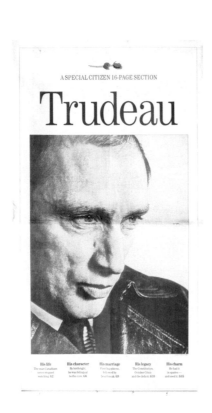

A SPECIAL CITIZEN 16-PAGE SECTION

Trudeau

September 29, 2000

tive cast in a place that can only be imagined (the idea of North, Glenn Gould called it) just makes it all the more amazing.

The film takes us into its world, and it is a while before we can get our bearings. The opening scene is a man pacing on the snow while his sled dogs bark: it seems empty, and we have to adjust to see its fullness. It is a world of such remote and difficult terrain that only a sense of community can hold people together: each character in *Atanarjuat* is like a small movie of his or her own, an island of needs.

Sauri is the leader of a small group of Inuit, an evil man (his name is reminiscent of a Lord of the Rings villain) who torments his rival Tulimaq, forcing him to eat the rear end of the seal, a typical bit of crude humour. The feud is passed on to the next generation. Tulimaq has two children: Amaqjuaq (Pakkak Innukshuk), who is strong, and Atanarjuat (Natar Ungalaaq), who is fast. Sauri has a son, Oki (Peter-Henry Arnatsiaq), who is dark, dangerous, and pushes the limits of what such hard communal life can allow.

Atanarjuat and Oki are both in love with Atuat (Sylvia Ivalu), who has been promised to Oki but loves Atanarjuat. The two men fight for her favours, in an ice house battle in which they hammer each other's temples with their fists until one of them goes into convulsions. Atanarjuat wins, and Oki vows revenge.

This blood feud is all the more compelling because of the knots that tie everyone together. They have to get along: a hunter who comes back empty-handed, who had bad luck at the seal hole, relies on his neighbours for a taste of that day's gristle or fat. Oki's sister, Puja (Lucy Tulugarjuk) is Atanarjuat's frustrated suitor and she functions as the Iago of this tale, if not its Lady Macbeth, but that doesn't stop her from living with his family, in the same tent.

This sort of proximity leads to a sexual betrayal that kicks off the plot. Sex, in fact, plays an important part in *Atanarjuat*: just because the nights are cold does not preclude an eroticism that is both playful and surprising. Under the caribou skins, these people are hungry for contact; the nights are long as well.

Atanarjuat gives us many such details of the day-to-day life of the Arctic, and they provide much of the movie's fascination: the arduous skinning of pelts, the use of bones as snow goggles that resemble modern sunglasses, the way dog teams are driven across the permafrost and then kicked for not going fast enough, the ingestion of yet another piece of fatty raw meat. The far horizon of the film is a sea of white, and yet there is a claustrophobic air as well: the open space closes in on you, and it acts as a counterpoint to the slowly dawning tensions of the narrative.

The people remain large, however: wrapped in thick skins, the characters maintain a deep humanity. There is a scene when Puja weeps

July 14, 2002

apologies for an act of treachery, and two women skinning pelts out on the ice exchange glances like suburban housewives watching a neighbour crying over her misbehaviour at last night's cocktail party.

Natar Ungalaaq is especially good as the title character. His naked run, a Northern Exposure of the truest kind, deserves some kind of award, if not medal for bravery. *Atanarjuat* is a long film that demands attention and patience, but it is a once-in-a-lifetime experience.

March 1, 2003
CARVED IN STONE
Eleanor Milne's art is embedded in Parliament Hill,
from the grand lobbies to the sidewalks.
(Excerpt from a newsfeature:)

September 12, 2001

BY PAUL GESSELL

Imagine for a moment the solemn, Gothic revival interior of the Parliament Buildings decorated with joyous, kaleidoscopic paintings that would run, like wild, laughing children, along the funereal hallways, up and down marble stairways and right into that bloody bearpit we call the Commons chamber.

Now imagine how such artworks might affect the tone of national politics. Imagine how they might inspire wonderfully creative, sunny solutions to all our most persistent problems. Imagine how Canada would be different if Eleanor Milne, the artist, and not Eleanor Milne, the dutiful public servant, had plumbed her soul, thrown caution to the wind and created the most daring Parliament Buildings in the world.

From 1962 to 1993, Eleanor Milne carried the lofty title of Dominion Sculptor. Now 77 and retired, but far from retiring, Milne designed and executed many of the stone carvings that bedeck the Centre Block. . . . She's been gone from the job 10 years, but the lanky Milne remains a force on the Hill. Milne's designs for carvings celebrating man's intellect have yet to be chiselled into the limestone. They remain a project for some future day, meaning that long after Milne retreats to that big sculptor's studio in the sky, her disciples will be carving her ideas, her artistry, onto the walls of Parliament.

•

Much of Milne's carving was done at night. From the scaffold where she stood with hammer and chisel, Milne became privy to some of Parliament's most scandalous secrets. MPs tended to ignore her, Pierre Trudeau being one of the few exceptions when he crawled right up onto her scaffolding one night to discuss her work.

From her perch, Milne soon discovered which MPs were having midnight trysts. And she soon learned who spent the night downing a bottle of scotch. Long before recycling became *de rigueur*, Milne and her crew of 10 used MPs' empty liquor bottles to carry onto the scaffolding small quantities of chemicals necessary for the cleaning and carving of the stone walls.

As it turned out, Milne carried her own secrets as she chiselled austere, heroic figures in a Romanesque style onto the pale grey walls of Parliament. She chose this restrained, classic style for the carvings because, as she says, she believed it matched the Canadian character: "We're not overly amazed at how large we are."

That is one side of Milne and her art—simple, direct and unsophisticated. There is another. Each morning at 6, after a long night of carving, when the sun rose and her shift ended, Milne returned home, relaxed, read and created extravagant semi-abstract paintings that remained bottled up inside her while on Parliament Hill.

At first, she just did drawings. Over the years, these blossomed into paintings, filled with mythological animals, humanoid figures and reckless swirls of brilliant colours. These paintings line the walls of Milne's home, a century-old brick mansion in the Glebe that has been in her family for almost a century. These are paintings filled with colour, joy, whimsy and a passion—viewing them is like discovering Michelangelo was a rock star between his shifts painting the Sistine Chapel for Pope Julius II.

Can these paintings really be done by the same person who did the staid carvings on the Hill?

•

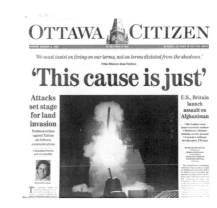

October 8, 2001

Milne is standing with a nosy journalist who has discovered her secret passion for boisterous canvases. She is told she's Parliament's answer to Dr. Jekyll and Mr. Hyde. She lights up like a Christmas tree. "Oh, yes," she says with a mischievous, amazingly girlish giggle. "Oh, yes." People who have seen her paintings, she says, sometimes think she was "stoned" or dabbling in "psychedelics." (For the record: No pharmaceuticals were abused in the creation of these paintings).

She laughs at the notion of decorating Parliament's walls with her lively paintings or, as she says, "burying the MPs in colour." But never fear, Mr. Speaker, Milne won't be splashing her true colours on the walls of Parliament. The sculptures she laboured over for 30 years were not meant to satisfy her vanity, but the enjoyment of a nation.

"When I work for myself, then I can say, 'This is what I like, this is what I'm going to do'," Milne explains. "When I was hired to work for the nation, I was hired to work for people who are educated, not educated, for the young and old, for people who are busy, who didn't have time to look at what we were doing—then I took on a different persona and thought of them as I was working."

From a shelf in a dining room in her rambling home, Milne picks up a stone sculpture obviously done by Mr. Hyde. It is small enough to fit into the palm of her hand. On one side of the stone a vaguely human figure has been carved. On the back is an abstract design. It is like some ancient, primitive idol, long buried in the barrens of the North.

This style of carving was not used on the Hill, Milne says, because most people would look and say, "What is that?" Instead, Milne wanted the public to view her carvings and exclaim knowingly: "Oh, I see."

Tourists who take tours of the Hill are often given only two minutes to view a particular set of Milne's carvings, to have the opportunity to exclaim, "Oh, I see." One set, a frieze that covers Canadian history from the arrival of the first aboriginal people from Asia thousands of years ago to the First World War in 1914, took eight years to create. That's two minutes to view a 40-metre-long frieze, 1.5 metres wide, five metres above the floor. That's like trying to read the Bible, from Creation to Judgment, in two minutes.

•

Milne won the job of Dominion Sculptor in a competition. Her rivals were 20 men ("I had the knowledge so they hired me"). There were 224 blank stones for her to carve—more than a lifetime of work. Thirty of these blocks in the House of Commons foyer were a priority. Captured in these stones was the history of Canada; Milne's task was to free the images. She immediately set to work to bone up on Canadian history, spending six months in the parliamentary library reading books, letters, journals and smoking like a steam engine. Yes, you could smoke in the stacks in those days.

Historians are a notoriously argumentative lot. Whose version did Milne accept? "Mine," she replies emphatically, with a flash of her sapphire eyes.

October 9, 2001

March 29, 2003

Sunday, June 22, 2003
'HE LEFT AN IMPACT ON YOU'

For years, sports columnist Wayne Scanlan seemed to be working in the shadow of big name writers like Earl McRae and Roy MacGregor. But Ottawa sports fans always knew they could count on Scanlan for smart analysis of the game, and for the human side of the story, whether he was dealing with a celebrity hockey player or an emerging high school gymnast. Here's an excerpt from his tribute to legendary hockey coach Roger Neilson.

BY WAYNE SCANLAN

To the end, his timing was impeccable. Roger Neilson always knew when to pitch the water bottle, when to raise a white towel in surrender to bad officiating, when to pat the back of his captain.

And so it fit that on the very day the brightest young players were being welcomed into the NHL at the entry draft in Nashville, a great light went out, hundreds of kilometres north, in Peterborough.

Neilson would have enjoyed the symbolism. A torch is passed. The next wave of kids is there to grab hold and use it to light the way along the path he walked so brilliantly for so long. A hockey legend bids adieu, knowing the game he loved like a spouse, lives on.

Yesterday afternoon at about 2 p.m., on the first day of summer, Neilson, Hall of Fame innovator and coach, member of the Order of Canada, lost his fierce and lengthy battle with two forms of cancer.

He was 69 and had no living relatives.

"You are never prepared for something like this," an emotional John Muckler, Senators' general manager, said in Nashville. "It's a sad day."

Not a person who met Neilson was unaffected by the meeting. At the draft tables in Tennessee, in homes throughout North America, hockey people felt a deep sadness at the news they hoped they wouldn't hear. Not yet. Not when there was still another season for Neilson to make his mark....

Senators head coach Jacques Martin is one of many in the game who can say Roger helped show him the way. A young Martin, just finding his way in the coaching profession, lived at Neilson's home in Peterborough while coaching the OHL Petes. Last month, when the Senators' great playoff run was over, when they'd come within a single goal of representing the east in the Stanley Cup final, Martin spoke about his team's defeat, but also his friend's great private battle.

"There was something very special about him as a person that left an impact on you," Martin said yesterday. Last spring, in a generous gesture to show his appreciation for Neilson's help, Martin stepped aside for two games to enable Roger to reach 1,000 games as a head coach.

To those who knew him, there was a simple explanation for Neilson's enormous popularity. To whatever extent he became famous, he remained utterly grounded, humble, deep of faith. Whether it was his appointment to the Order of Canada or to the Hockey Hall of Fame, both of which occurred during the past year, Neilson had a way of making it sound as though they had the wrong guy.

"You wonder why . . . when so many others seem to have done more," Neilson said of his Hall of Fame honour. You know he meant it.

Though Neilson never married, his longtime companion, Nancy Nicholds, understood Roger as well as anyone. They met in the 1970s when Neilson was coaching a minor-league team in Dallas.

"You certainly wouldn't call him normal," Nicholds once said. "He's consistently abnormal, but maybe that makes him more normal than the rest of us. He never pretends to be someone else. He is what he is, whether it's talking to an 11-year-old at a hockey camp, to an $8-million-a-year superstar or to the president of Israel. He's still Roger, barefoot and in his baseball cap."

July 30, 2003

Neilson could tell hockey stories with the best of the game's legends, but wasn't above poking fun at his notorious absentmindedness.

A creative genius who brought video analysis to hockey, who devised defensive schemes, who hired the NHL's first assistant coach, who used to send a defenceman out to defend a penalty shot by simply checking the shooter, Neilson could find his way out of nearly any hockey predicament. But couldn't always find his car in the Kanata Centrum parking lot.

Who among us could not relate to that? Or to a guy who knew how to save a buck. That's a partial explanation for Neilson's wild and crazy necktie collection.

When he was head coach of the New York Rangers in the early 1990s, Neilson was driven crazy by the $175 ties worn by then-general manager Neil Smith. As a form of protest, Neilson bought the worst looking ties he could find, then pretended he looked just as suave as Smith.

The ties became his trademark, and Neilson never had to buy another one. People would send them to him in bunches, along with all the heartfelt wishes, and cancer treatment suggestions. . . .

Yes, the game will carry on, pulled by the bright young men who tugged on their shiny NHL sweaters yesterday. But a piece of the game's heart has been cut out forever.

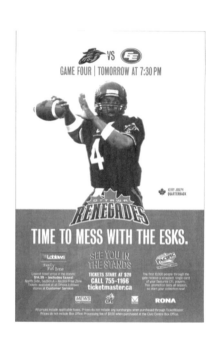

October 29, 2003
PEACE, BEAUTY AND A SCENE OF HORROR
Kelly Egan had been long recognized as one of the Citizen's *finest writers when he was asked to replace legendary local columnist Dave Brown in 2003. Here's an excerpt from one of his first columns, written a year after the murders of school teachers Bob and Bonnie Dagenais at their cottage in the Gatineau Hills.*

BY KELLY EGAN

Know it, especially know it today: they died in a beautiful place, a haven of their own choosing, and it speaks to us still about desire, about a shared longing.

Dodds Lake is shaped like a slightly curled finger, about two kilometres long, maybe 300 metres across and as deep as 45 metres, deep enough for lake trout to survive. It has sandy shallows in places and shores littered with fallen trees and boulders, some as large as cars.

It is almost exactly 80 kilometres from their home in the west end of Ottawa and lies near the village of Poltimore, north of Buckingham, far enough away to erase the effects of the city.

Coming up from Buckingham, you lose the asphalt on River Road at kilometre 72 and roll on a sandy mix the rest of the way, twisting and turning, at times nearly tossed into the little river called La Lievre. It is back country.

The terrain, finally, around the lake is hilly, to the point of comical, and the cottages on the high side are built right into the side of the mountain, just as they had to be.

The cottage owned by Bob and Bonnie Dagenais looks as though it grew right out of the hillside. It is painted dark brown and has a dark brown roof and is perched here, rather than anchored on a plain.

It is surrounded by broad decking: massive on the right side, with a mature, leafy tree sticking out some 20 metres, smaller around the front and medium-sized on the left. The side facing the water is constructed so that it is almost entirely made of glass, with two large patio doors in the centre, as though the lake provided the main theatre.

The building is set probably 20 or 25 metres above the lake level, high enough that there are 75 steps down to the shore. It has been nearly a year since the couple died and the steps, which wind down in stages, have acquired a veneer of moss, probably from a season of light use.

At lake level, an aluminum car-top boat is overturned, as is a green canoe, both sprinkled with brown pine needles, as though waiting for opportunity and a set of willing hands.

There is yet another large deck right on the water, tiered and wrapped around a big shoreline boulder. It is a feature of the place that the construction has worked with nature, not against it.

There are two empty chairs on the deck and it is easy to imagine the life here: the afternoons spent on the warm planks, the chilled drinks, the stack of magazines, the overturned book, the sunscreen, the water shoes, the rumpled towels, the cooler, the life jackets, the bathers dripping water; the tools of the cottage idler....

The sun came out briefly yesterday, and left golden swirls on the near sand, and lit up a dip in the hills across the lake. Fall's best colours seem past their peak, and the cast on the trees was muted; the yellows and reds and rusty mixes looking a little tired, drained of their best.

Some reedy maples stubbornly held onto their leaves, curled and dry and brittle, the colour of cooked pumpkin, awaiting a stiff breeze to deliver them into skeletal dormancy.

You can see the doorway where the insane circus began. You can try to imagine that, too, but you'll never get it quite right, which is just as well. The noise alone, sweet Jesus, the noise alone that must have exploded on that quiet night.

"Peaceful, eh?" asks Bill Pinkos, 60, a retired paper worker from Buckingham related to the new owner. "Real quiet." And so it is.

On and off, Mr. Pinkos is hauling cut wood into the back of a pickup truck, criss-crossing the property in his plaid jacket and blue ball cap.

And, without any coaxing, when I am almost out of earshot, chit-chatting with his wife, Thelma, he erupts briefly, with the kind of frus-

July 30, 2003

tration that attaches itself to senseless violence.

"No justice in our system, you know? Eye for an eye, just like the Bible says. That's what should happen. Shoot him with the same God-damn gun."

On the lakeside deck, at a large birdfeeder, chickadees are doing the swoop and perch, nuthatches are nimbly working their way down the bark of a pine and, overhead, the clouds are gathering again, in a grey, ragged mass.

There is beauty here yet. Some days, it is just hard to see, the light being weak and shadowed with anger.

February 26, 2005

January 23, 2004
'IT FELT LIKE A SLOW-MOTION ROBBERY'
Citizen reporter Juliet O'Neill made headlines around the world when the RCMP raided her home looking for clues to the identity of sources for her story on Maher Arar, an Ottawa software engineer suspected of having terrorist links to al Qaeda. Here's an excerpt from her personal account of the raid.

BY JULIET O'NEILL

My house is small, a downtown gem, close to cafés and the art gallery, my family and closest friend, a private sanctuary—until the doorbell began ringing over and over Wednesday morning.

There are six rooms in my little house. Before the day ended, there would be more than one RCMP officer per room to rifle through the intimate details of my life.

When the doorbell sounded, I peered out through my bedroom blinds, a tiny movement I would later discover was among the details recorded, in elegant handwriting, in Staff Sgt. Gary Legresley's notebook. He jotted it down when I looked out at 8:12 a.m. and again at 8:16. He was the officer in charge of the five-hour search of my home conducted by 10 RCMP investigators. My office at City Hall was being searched at the same time. I discovered this by phoning a colleague who had been locked out. The *Citizen's* office, it seemed, had been deemed a "crime scene."

Before answering the door, I decided to have a shower and get dressed. I had a wild hope that the men outside my house, and the people I could barely make out inside the unmarked police cars parked in my driveway, would be gone by the time I dried my hair. But when I got out of the shower, the doorbell was even more incessant, and now the phone was ringing, too. The normally cheerful sounds of my household seemed ominous. I tied back my wet hair, went downstairs and pulled up the front blind. Then I went to the door.

Staff Sgt. Legresley showed his ID through the window. I opened the door. Two others quickly entered with him. I didn't let them close the door behind them completely at first. Already it felt crowded, a little stifling. Seven other officers followed after I had been handed the search warrant, read my rights and given time to call a *Citizen* lawyer. I was told I could make the call in private, but an officer would have to be nearby.

Two of the RCMP were women, one a computer wizard who straight away accompanied me to my laptop computer, saying it was important to get me offline—in case I had alerted someone who could remove files from a remote location. I have a dialup connection to the Internet and I wasn't online. She told me that she, too, has a dialup connection at home, that since she spends all day in front of a computer at work, who needs a full-time connection at home?

The other RCMP woman will be remembered as "the underwear lady." It was no comfort that she, and others, wore white gloves as they went about their business, rummaging through my lingerie drawer, my socks and T-shirts, jewelry, cosmetics and hair mousse, handbags, clothes closets, pockets, shelves of sweaters, linens and towels. It was when I saw her pulling back the quilt on my bed that I felt shock. I realized I did not wish to express my emotions and held them in check. I went back downstairs to talk with Staff Sgt. Robert McMillan.

His card said he was a program manager from the "Truth Verification Section" of the RCMP's Behavioural Sciences Branch. He proposed that since the search would take several hours, he and I should just leave them to it and drive to his office where we could talk in a more serene setting about a leaked document and the source for it. I had reported the contents of the document in a Nov. 8 story about the Maher Arar case.

I told him I couldn't leave my home full of strangers.

I've never been robbed, but those who have talk about feeling violated that persons unknown have rifled through their things and taken the valuable bits away. That was how it felt: like a slow-motion robbery. Every once in a while, Staff Sgt. McMillan said it was going well. He was pleased with the pace and, when it was almost done, he sat down with lawyer Wendy Montgomery and me to say his piece again. "The most intrusive part is over," was how he started.

•

The press began gathering in my driveway soon after I alerted an editor and *Citizen* lawyer what was happening. Word spread quickly. As the press crowd grew, my emotional armour hardened. Each time I looked out, my distress eased. I felt protected by the sight of all the reporters and photographers from the *Citizen,* Global TV, CBC, CTV, the *Globe and Mail* and other news outlets. I felt sorry that they had to

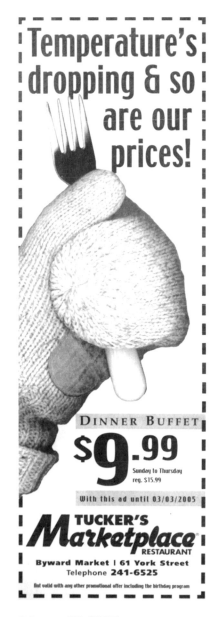
February 26, 2005

stand outside in the bitter cold and thought of an inside joke of the news business: "Hurry up and wait."

I was surprised when an RCMP officer offered to move the media mob, already restricted from coming close to the house, even farther away. "Those are my friends and colleagues," I told him. When one of the officers closed a blind against the long lens of a camera, I immediately reopened it. The officer didn't look me in the eye but he smiled and went back to taking my laptop apart on the dining room table. I realized that the RCMP group inside my home was fortified by two RCMP outside, one to keep the press at bay, the other a "media liaison officer" to appear on camera and answer questions.

Staff Sgt. McMillan explained the search was part of a "high level investigation." They were looking for a document and the person who leaked it to me. "My understanding is that you will be charged with an offence," he told me. The search warrant specified three offences under the Security of Information Act, which boil down to sending and receiving secret information and possessing a secret document. A lawyer later told me a guilty verdict could mean 14 years in prison.

"Ultimately it's going to be your decision where you want to go with this," Staff Sgt. McMillan said. He said he had been investigating the leak for two months. The document had passed through many hands in many departments and many people were under suspicion. "We want to put this to bed," he said. "I'm not pussyfooting around."

•

The major target—three of them went in together—appeared to be my home office: my laptop and Filofax, files, notebooks, cassette tapes, address books, contact lists, book shelves, photo albums, newspaper clippings, tax files and utility bills, bank and mortgage statements, letters, and my wooden box of treasured mementoes from anniversaries and other special occasions, and love letters from my great friend, James. I cringed when I saw them reading postcards and old letters from pals who now use e-mail. I'd left a pile of photos from an outdoor family birthday party on my desk. I wished they wouldn't look at them.

My office is cosy. I can see the steeples of the cathedral through the window when I'm writing at home. It was too cosy for them. The two experts in such things, the young woman and a young man, took my laptop down to the glass dining table and proceeded to take it apart with cute, miniature tools. When I caught a glimpse of what they were doing with the tools, their own laptops and a jungle of wires and imaging devices, I had to push away a surge of anger . . . .

When they arrived that morning, one of them videotaped the entire house. That was so that they could tape it again before they left and prove they had not ransacked the place, if it ever came to that. They did put things back in order, except my book shelves. . . .

July 29, 2005

When it was over, Staff Sgt. Legresley thanked me for co-operating. Not that I had a choice, I thought. I shook his outstretched hand and said: "I can't bring myself to thank you."

June 4, 2005
LAST MAN OUT

It was only with great reluctance—and a promise that he not be portrayed as a hero—that Ron DiFrancesco agreed to talk to Citizen *reporter Andrew Duffy about his harrowing escape from the Sept. 11, 2001 attack on the World Trade Center. Here's a excerpt from Duffy's powerful account.*

BY ANDREW DUFFY
Toronto

Almost four years later, Ron DiFrancesco still carries the South Tower with him—tiny fragments of glass and stucco that occasionally migrate to the surface of his skin.

Mr. DiFrancesco was the last man out of the South Tower before it collapsed at 9:59 a.m. on Sept. 11, 2001. He was, according to the official 9/11 Commission Report, one of only four people to make it out alive that day from above the central impact zone on the 81st floor.

The stories of some of those other survivors are well-known.

But the 41-year-old Mr. DiFrancesco, a soft-spoken father of four, has scrupulously avoided the media spotlight. He doesn't like talking about his escape; he believes it's disrespectful to the families of those who died to celebrate the decisions that allowed him to live.

Mr. DiFrancesco has rejected dozens of interview requests from journalists and filmmakers. He rarely discusses the day's events, even with his children. "They know it's still raw for me, even though I'd be more open to it now," he says. . . .

The years since the attacks have been difficult ones for Mr. DiFrancesco, who continues to undergo therapy for back and hip injuries. He has also sought the help of a psychiatrist to better understand what he describes as "agitation," and the guilt he feels about his survival on a day when 61 of his Euro Brokers colleagues died.

Mr. DiFrancesco sometimes suffers bouts of panic: when the lights flicker, for instance. Or, as was the case in August 2003, when he was caught on the subway as a massive blackout cut power across Toronto and much of the northeast.

At those times, it all comes flooding back. . . .

•

Mr. DiFrancesco was moving down a narrow hallway [to leave the building] when United Airlines Flight 175, which had been hijacked shortly after leaving Boston for Los Angeles, banked sharply into the

July 29, 2005

OTTAWA CITIZEN

All 309 aboard crashed jet 'miraculously' survive

Airbus skids off runway, bursts into flames at Toronto airport

Air France Airbus went down during fierce thunderstorm

Hundreds stranded as flights diverted here

Martin appoints close friend to Senate, despite his pledge to end cronyism

August 3, 2005

South Tower at 950 kilometres an hour. The Boeing 767 cut into the east side of the south face between floors 78 and 84, igniting an intense fire fed by 90,000 litres of jet fuel.

The higher wing cut into the offices of Euro Brokers while the fuselage destroyed the offices of Fuji Bank below.

Mr. DiFrancesco was thrown against the wall and showered with falling ceiling panels, cables and drywall chalk. There was a gaping hole in the office trading floor that he had just abandoned....

He thought there had been some kind of explosion below as he still couldn't conceive of a fully loaded passenger plane hitting the tower. There was chaos. He knew immediately that the situation was desperate. He knew that his life could depend on what happened in the next few minutes.

Picking himself up, Mr. DiFrancesco found that he was steps from Stairwell A. He followed six or seven people through a fire door and down the narrow passage. It was the beginning of a circuitous odyssey that would eventually take Mr. DiFrancesco out of the South Tower. The critically damaged building would stand for the next 56 minutes.

Mr. DiFrancesco would need every last one of them.

The South Tower had three emergency stairwells.... As it happened, only one of them—Stairwell A—had not been cut in two by the plane's impact. (Stairwell A was the farthest from the airplane's point of impact and protected by an elevator machine room.)

Mr. DiFrancesco and the others who started walking down that stairwell had no way of knowing that they'd lucked into the only possible escape route.

The stairwell was smoky and dark, lit dimly by a flashlight carried by Mr. Clark [co-worker Brian], who was leading the descent. The group made their way down three flights to the 81st floor, where they met a heavy-set woman and her male colleague. "You've got to go up. You can't go down," the woman said. "There's too much smoke and flames below."

A life-and-death discussion began. Was it better to go up and wait for firefighters to arrive? Possibly get to the rooftop for a helicopter rescue? Or was it better to risk a dash through the fire and smoke below—a dash that might only take them into the heart of the inferno? ...

Gasping for air, he decided to climb the stairs in an attempt to escape the smoke. He hoped to get onto a higher floor, possibly find some clearer air, and await rescue. He still didn't know what had caused the explosion....

Mr. DiFrancesco continued to climb, trying each fire door as he gained a new landing. He caught up with his colleagues from Euro Brokers. They met more people as they climbed. Some were going up, some down, all trying to find a way out of the stairwell. Cellphones didn't work. They were groping in the dark for the right answer.

All the while, the South Tower was rapidly losing its ability to stand over lower Manhattan. The tower had a unique design that distributed its weight between columns in its inner core and those along its exterior walls. The impact of the airplane had placed more pressure on the surviving steel columns, and the intense heat of the fuel-fed inferno was steadily robbing them of strength.

Mr. DiFrancesco believes he climbed as high as the 91st floor—he's not positive what floor it was when he stopped—in the 110-storey South Tower. All of the fire doors were locked. Panic rose in his chest. He was slightly claustrophobic. The higher he went, the more people crowded the stairwell. His mind filled with thoughts of his wife, Mary, and his children, all waiting for him.

Mr. DiFrancesco decided he couldn't wait any longer. Desperate to see them, he started down once more. Others followed his lead. But conditions this time were worse.

Mr. DiFrancesco worked his way down the stairs until the smoke thickened such that it was impossible to see more than a few feet ahead. He stopped at a stairwell landing in the middle of the impact zone where people were stretched on the floor. Everyone took to the ground beside them in an attempt to find a thin window of breathable air.

Mr. DiFrancesco and the others—he believes there were more than a dozen people—were face down on a strip of concrete, between two staircases. They were on the 79th or 80th floor. Some of those beside him began to slip into unconsciousness.

Then, Mr. DiFrancesco heard a voice.

"Someone told me to get up," he says. A devout Roman Catholic, Mr. DiFrancesco believes God told him to get off the floor of that South Tower stairwell. He doesn't know why; he's not one to proselytize. His faith, like much about him, is a private matter.

"I just have no other explanation for what happened."

Heeding the insistent whisper, Mr. DiFrancesco struggled to his feet and inched along the wall, his hands crawling ahead of him. He felt his way through the smoke and started down the stairs again. After several steps, he saw a pinhole of light through the blackness....

August 13, 2005

Acknowledgments

IN 1905, Edward Whipple Bancroft (Dinky) Morrison, the only *Citizen* editor ever to earn a knighthood, referred to his newsroom staff as a "devoted band of fellow-travellers." A century later, his words are a fitting way to describe the group of dedicated people who made this book—an enormous undertaking—come together so smoothly.

No one deserves our gratitude more than Mary Jane Starr, former director of the Centre for Newspapers and News at Library and Archives Canada. A librarian by vocation, she acted not only as a dogged researcher, but her advice helped us to keep our focus and her enthusiasm pushed us forward when the project seemed overwhelming. The polish of the later chapters is the result of her sharp eye for good writing, and the index is entirely due to her care and professionalism.

Others at Library and Archives who merit our thanks include newspaper specialist Sandra Burrows, who was always happy to dive into files or microfilm to find the answers to obscure questions, and newspaper collection custodian Susan Bourdeau, who, with her assistants, Carol Moher, Ellen Thompson, Kenneth Barr, and Harold Floyd, carefully pulled hundreds of old *Packets* and *Citizens* off the shelves to be photographed.

High praise is also owed to Carleton University history students Joel Legassie and Susan Joudrey for the months they spent squinting at microfilm as part of the exhaustive—and exhausting—search for material. Kathy Fischer also dug out early 20th-century material from the microfilm. The book is richer for their choices.

Other researchers who should be singled out for their efforts include *Citizen* librarian Liisa Tuominen, Algonquin College journalism student Gudrun Schultz, City of Ottawa archivist Serge Barbe, former *Citizen* reporter Marci Surkes and hockey historian Paul Kitchen.

For their help unfurling the life of *Citizen* founder William Harris, genealogists Alison Hare and Barbara Aitken as well as archivist Glenn Lockwood of the Anglican Diocese of Ottawa deserve recognition.

And for the thankless job of transcribing articles from microfilm to computer, we are indebted to Naomi Phillips, Andrea Cashman, Meagan Fitzpatrick, Stephanie Murphy, Ute Mikula, Colum Wood, Kelly Roesler, Kirstin Endemann, Bobbi LeBlanc, Drew Fischer and Jamie Sutherland.

Four books were of particular help in dealing with the history of the *Citizen* and the City of Ottawa: *News and the Southams,* by Charles Bruce (1968); *Ottawa Editor*, by Charles A. Bowman (1966); *The Private Capital,* by Sandra Gwyn (1984); and *A Victorian Authority: The Daily Press in Nineteenth Century Canada,* by Paul Rutherford (1982).

Linda Brown and Nancy Morrell of the 1860-era print shop at Upper Canada Village provided the typesetting that appears on the book's jacket, for which we are most grateful.

And finally, special thanks is owed to two *Citizen* staffers for their very different, but equally valuable contributions: assistant news editor Lynne Owen, whose meticulous proofreading gave the manuscript its final sheen; and newsroom manager Pat Hyndman, who always found the resources to get us through to the next stage.

Like any large undertaking, *Each Morning Bright* was both a journey of discovery and derailments. It was our good fortune to be accompanied by such a staunch band of fellow-travellers.

Selected index

447

Hind-Smith, Michael 345

History of Lower Town Ottawa 1826-1854 (Newton) xv

Hitler, Adolf 260-2, 263, 268, 270-2, 282-3, 293, 302-3, 363-5

hockey 63, 109, 136-7, 180-2, 182-4, 184, 264, 309, 311-3, 319, 333-4, 383-5, 399, 403-5, 434-6: American League 404; Boston Bruins 403-5; Canadian Olympic teams 327, 383-5; Capitals 147; Challenge Cup series 384; Cornwall hockey club 182-4, 184; Edmonton Eskimos 228-31; Federal league 183; Hall of Fame 435; Kenora Thistles 181; Montreal Canadiens 309, 333-4; Montreal Wanderers 181, 191; National Hockey League 229, 264, 288, 319, 384, 403-5, 434, 436; National Hockey League Players Association 405; New York Rangers 436; Olympic games 327, 383-5; Ottawa Hockey Club (Silver Seven) 109, 136-7, 180-2, 191; Ottawa Senators 229-31, 264, 319, 435; Ottawa Victorias 182-4; Pacific Coast League 229; Peterborough Petes 435; Quebec (team) 137; Shamrocks 147, 183; Soviet Olympic teams 327, 383-5; Springfield Indians 404-5; Stanley Cup 136-7, 176, 180-2, 229-31, 289, 435; Toronto Maple Leafs 288-9, 309; U.S. Olympic teams 327

Holland, George 58, 85

Hollinger Inc. 419

Holloway, Condredge 390

Holocaust 245

Holy Rosary Scholasticate 329

Holy Trinity High School 420

Homiletic Review, The 147

homosexuality 385-8, 403

Hook & Ladder Company 13

Hopewell, Magistrate 244

Horwood, Mrs. Allan 217

housing 210-1

Huchison, J. E. 322

Hughes, Katherine 178-80

Hull 51, 152-3, 176-8, 193-4, 243: Bridge street 194; Chaudiere river and mills 11, 27, 160, 169, 176-8; Desjardins street 244; Fairy Glen and Lake 208; Inkerman street 193; Iron Mountain 51; Perkins quarry 75

humour 91-92, 296

Huntley, Township of 15

Hussein, Saddam 400

Hutchinson, Bruce "Journalism's Sage" 311-3

hypnosis 184-6

Imperial Conference (1926) 237

Indians 15, 118, 164-5, 323-4, 383, 405-8

Inglis, Peter 318

International Herald Tribune, The 398

Inuit 430-2

Irishmen in Ottawa xi, xvi, 3, 15, 41, 89

Iron Curtain 363

Islam 429-30

Italy 270-2: Italians in Ottawa 115, 210; Ortona 287-8

'Jack Pine' (Thomson) 225

Jackasstown 74

Jackson, Jennifer 390-2

Japan 342-4

jazz. *See* music

Jennings, Peter 338

Jessup, Mrs. Arthur 314

jewelry store 186-7

Jews 278-9, 339, 363

Joe Feller's (men's clothing) 324-5

John Culbert and Son (insurance and real estate) 182

Johnson, Arthur S. 253

Johnson, James 117

Johnston, Dorothy 251

Johnston, James 14

Johnston, Lukin 260-2, 262-3, 263

Johnstown District xiv

Jones, Kelsey 327

Journal, The Ottawa 114, 143, 175, 206, 221, 291-2, 321-2, 347, 356, 375-6, 395, 411, 415

Journal of Commerce. See Chicago Journal of Commerce

Juliette 359

Junot, Henri 117

'Just Society' 365-6

Kaichen, Anna 412

Kanata, Ontario 347, 421, 436

Karsh, Yousuf 295, 348

Kash, Eugene 311, 326-7, 362

Kazabazua Korners, Quebec 356

Kemmler, Joseph 132-3

Kennedy, Janice 310

Kennedy, John Fitzgerald 334-5

Kent, Tom 376, 395

Khrushchev, Nikita 332

Kidd, George 166-7

Kielty, Terry 360, 389

Kilcoursie, Lord 136-7

453